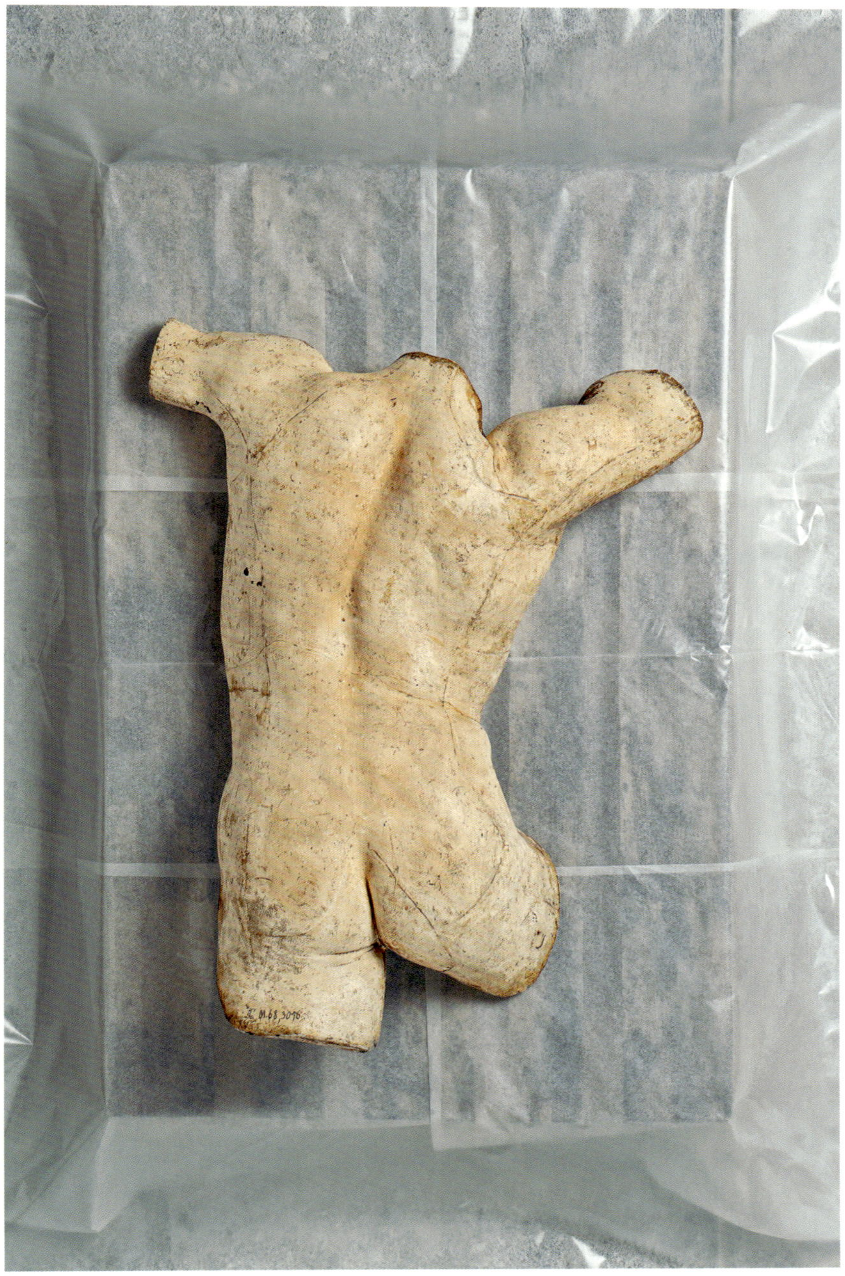

For the Gipsformerei, Staatliche Museen zu Berlin,
edited by Christina Haak, Miguel Helfrich and Veronika Tocha

Photography by Philip Radowitz

Veronika Tocha

Near

The Gipsformerei

200 Years of Casting Plaster

Life

Staatliche Museen zu Berlin
Preußischer Kulturbesitz

PRESTEL
Munich · London · New York

Contents

Preface

Christina Haak

'Be merry and take care the plaster casts are kept clean, that is the main thing!', Wilhelm von Humboldt is reputed to have said on his deathbed in 1835. This plea — be it based on fact or well-intended fiction — was more than an expression of the zeitgeist, which caused the popularity of plaster casts to climax in the nineteenth century, it has become more topical today than ever. Plaster casts have been undergoing a lively renaissance for several years now, as is attested by the impressive number of pertinent scholarly conferences. Casts command great interest both as historical objects and as forms for reproduction. They are repositories of information on the objects they replicate and they tell us a great deal about the history of collecting and exhibiting of art museums since their foundations. The revival in the appreciation of plaster casts assumes great responsibility for the scholarly appraisal and conservation of such collections. We must be prepared to shoulder this responsibility.

As an active manufactory, the Gipsformerei, Staatliche Museen zu Berlin is a special case among those collecting institutions of historical plaster casts that have made it into the twenty-first century. Alongside the Atelier de moulage, Musées royaux d'Art et d'Histoire in Brussels and the Atelier de moulage, Réunion des musées nationaux — Grand Palais in Paris, it boasts one of the few still operational casting workshops founded in the nineteenth century. Tucked away behind their mother institution, the workshops cultivates the seemingly anachronistic art and craft of artistic plaster casting, which, in days gone by, was a skilled occupation passed on by oral tradition. Today it is under threat. The great majority of the craftsmen and craftswomen in our workshop trained as stucco plasterers; after a three-year course of specialist training, they then qualified as artistic plasterers. Their hands-on expertise is of inestimable value, not least because they can assist in decoding the origins of historical plaster casts in a way that is tailored to each individual case. It is this (still) existing artistic practice that provides important answers to urgent questions of conserving and restoring moulds, models and plaster casts, and documenting this knowledge for future generations.

'"Come," said my friend, Professor Omnium, one clear morning, "let us take an excursion round the world!"' This 1882 quote from American writer and abolitionist

Moncure Daniel Conway is referring to the so-called Cast Courts of what was then the South Kensington Museum (today's Victoria and Albert Museum), but it is equally applicable to the Gipsformerei in Berlin. Anyone paying a visit to the premises of the Gipsformerei at their historic location in Berlin-Charlottenburg is likely to fall under its spell. It is a place with a unique atmosphere. Immediately, you feel like immersing yourself within the artisanal production processes and the wealth of historical objects. Wherever you look you can sense the potential that is stored in these rows upon rows of moulds and models waiting to be processed.

The holdings of the Gipsformerei are objects of practical use and of tools (rather than merely plaster casts as such). The collection is comprised of models and historical moulds based on more than seven thousand artistic and cultural objects from all eras and all geographical regions of the world, including large and small statuary, reliefs, coins, architectural elements, arts and crafts objects and cult items. For several years the academic research on the collection has steadily gained interest at the Staatliche Museen zu Berlin. The casts and moulds are seen as objects eminently suited for description and discourse, particularly the historiographic stocktaking of collections and institutions. As cultural artefacts in their own right they are at the centre of an ever-expanding field of object-related research.

The establishment of the Gipsformerei in 1819 was modelled on its Parisian sister institution, and since the opening of Karl Friedrich Schinkel's Altes Museum on the Museumsinsel in 1830, it has been part of the first museum in Berlin, making it the oldest institution in the Staatliche Museen zu Berlin museum cluster today. In 2019, the Gipsformerei looks back on a history spanning two centuries — an occasion to celebrate with an outstanding exhibition. *Near Life: The Gipsformerei — 200 Years of Casting Plaster* will however not be a jubilee exhibition in the traditional sense: the anniversary rather than claiming centre stage will mainly serve as a catalyst. The focus of the exhibition is on the collection objects themselves, which have been placed on display for what they are: models and moulds serving as tools and objects of use in a workshop still humming with activity.

The realisation of such an exhibition, which differs in many respects to what people have come to expect from the museum due to the unusual character of its exhibits, is the result of hard work by many people over a long time. First and foremost, I would like to thank curator Veronika Tocha, who has succeeded in opening up the collection of the Gipsformerei for this exhibition. Her innovative approach to the concept of the plaster cast has resulted in an exhibition that gives rise to many moments of surprise and delight. I would like to thank Andrea Müller for her impeccable project management. My heartfelt thanks to the commercial manager of the Gipsformerei, Miguel Helfrich, and workshop manager, Stefan Kramer, as well as all our colleagues at the Gipsformerei, who have accompanied this challenging project from the beginning. We are deeply grateful to all lenders who have complemented the Gipsformerei holdings with outstanding works from their own collections. I am also indebted to my colleagues at the other collections of the Staatliche Museen zu Berlin for loaning such fantastic works to *Near Life*. Finally, my thanks to all those who generously supported this major exhibition project, without support such an ambitious undertaking could not have been realised.

Preface

Miguel Helfrich

Powdery white plaster runs through the fingers of the artistic plasterer and slowly makes its way to the bottom of a vessel filled with clear water. Only when a small island of plaster appears above the water surface is the plaster gently stirred for the first time. This is the beginning of a long journey whose end point is marked by the finished plaster cast. At the Gipsformerei, Staatliche Museen zu Berlin this craftwork has been cultivated to perfection over two hundred years. Artistic plasterers and sculpture painters passionately strive for precision here as they create unique plaster casts from moulds and models.

That there is something special about this craftwork is announced by the fact that the 'tools' used are themselves valuable historic moulds: they are both production and collection items. These moulds taken more than a hundred years ago from works of art and living and dead creatures of all kinds are, in a manner of speaking, contemporary witnesses. Thanks to the elaborate and painstaking process to which they owe their existence, they succeed in placing before us an impressive copy of a moment long buried in the past — they are also entirely unique and cannot be replaced. In many cases, the originals perished long ago, but their memory survives in the negative mould and can be brought back to life by artistic plasterers. This process assumes great responsibility on behalf of the plasterers and demands meticulous care in the handling of the forms. Each plaster cast is an artisanal work and a unique specimen — the Gipsformerei is not interested in serial production. A long and complex process and a great deal of care and attention is required to produce these plaster casts of museum quality.

The archive of the Gipsformerei is made up of moulds and models, but that is not all. It also comprises the thinking hands and feeling heads of the artistic plasterers. Quite a number of traditional techniques required to achieve our standard of excellence are rarely practised outside the Gipsformerei these days. Here, exquisite artisanal and artistic knowledge and expertise is cultivated and handed on to future generations.

Taking casts from a variety of objects is an artistic technique applied since antiquity. Alongside the documentary aspect of casting, which aims to capture an object at a specific point in time, casts are also sources of artistic inspiration: casting realises a specific point of view and opens up new vistas in the act of replication. Different aspects of this method, both of historical and topical interest, are comprehensively addressed in the exhibition *Near Life: The Gipsformerei — 200 Years of Casting Plaster*.

How will this analogue craft tradition perform in an increasingly digitised world? Do stripe-light scanners and 3D printers constitute a threat for this time-hallowed craft? The historical forms stored at the Gipsformerei represent a unique body of physical data which would not be feasible to recreate digitally. Analogue information as encapsulated in the historic form is the foundation on which the Gipsformerei rests. It is therefore vital to ensure that these forms are preserved and taken optimum care of. However, even today, digital technology is already playing a substantive role in many aspects of the Gipsformerei and its activities. If originals are too sensitive for contact casts, scanning is the only option: for a cast of Nefertiti, for instance, no other option was available. The Gipsformerei and Berlin's Technische Universität have collaborated closely in this area since 2012. We have realised several projects involving both digital and conventional casting in conjunction with the TU. Another important aspect is the restoration and repair of old plaster moulds, which involves scanning and 3D print making. Digital technology complements traditional techniques and opens up new fields for the Gipsformerei to employ its expertise.

For the time being, traditional casts are far more accurate in the rendition of minute details than their digital alternatives. This is to do with the great number of steps required by the digital casting process. Firstly, the object is scanned; the resulting data provides the basis for the construction of a digital model. The next step is to print an initial analogue three-dimensional model. To achieve this, restrictions to the dimensions of the printing space must be taken into account: large objects, for example, cannot be printed in one piece, they need to be produced in several components. The resulting prototype is a raw model and needs to be reworked: fine but distinctly visible traces left by the printing process have to be dealt with. Only then can the printed object be used as the basis for the production of a model and pertinent form. There is no printing technology to date that leaves no traces. This may seem surprising, but what the developers of additive printing processes are aiming at, above all, is accurate measurements. In mechanical engineering, for example, printed objects need to fit precisely. The detailed rendition of a complex surface distinctly plays second place, even though this aspect is indispensable for the reproduction of museum quality replicas. What seems highly worthwhile asking is whether a combination of traditional and digital methods might lead to improved methods of digital casting.

Technological, scientific and artistic casting processes and the strategies for the replication of originals are bound to undergo great changes in the near future. We are at present in the preliminary phase of a development full of undreamt-of possibilities. The Gipsformerei, Staatliche Museen zu Berlin will not only be making significant contributions to this development, it will also make the interplay of traditional artistic craftwork and digital technology accessible to the public.

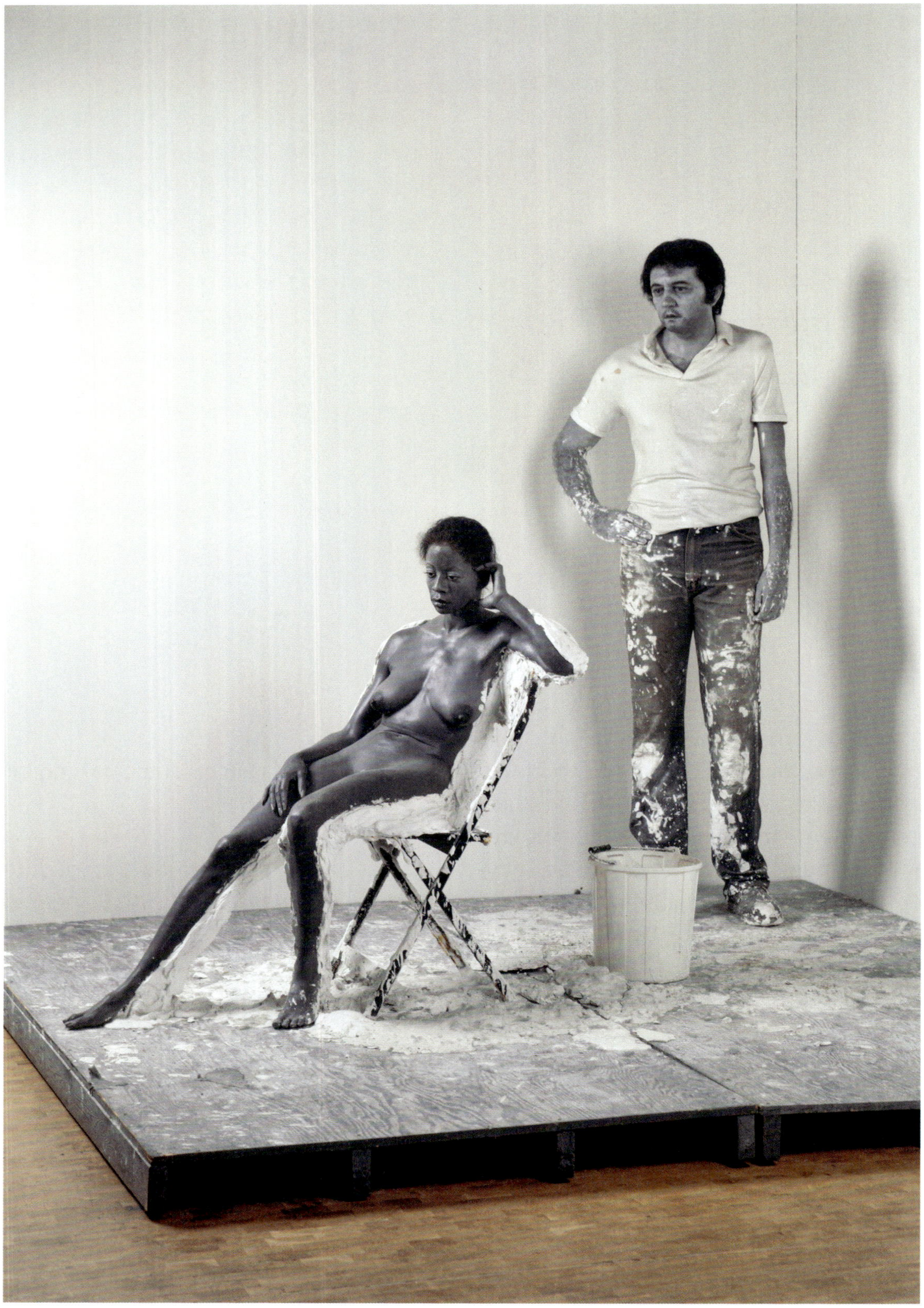

John De Andrea
Untitled / Studio Scene, 1977
Painted fibre glass, plaster, clothes, wooden chair, plastic bucket and wooden podium
Man: height 185 cm; woman: height 115 cm; podium: 12 × 243 × 444 cm
Museum Ludwig Cologne, ML 01285

Near Life: The Gipsformerei — 200 Years of Casting Plaster

Veronika Tocha

In 1977, American sculptor John De Andrea created a life-size duo of figures whose subject is an artistic lifecast. The sculptural group *Untitled* is both a studio scene and a self-portrait. We see a woman in the nude, seated on a chair in what looks to be a laid-back position; liquid plaster has been applied to her back and it seems to be in a state of curing. In his plaster-stained work clothes the artist is waiting behind his model. A bucket and surplus plaster on the floor emphasise the processuality of the workshop scene — a snapshot realised in the medium of sculpture. The work, however, not only depicts the making of a lifecast, it is itself the result of such a procedure. Both figures were cast in polyester resin, using moulds taken from the body. Thus, this double portrait reflectively points to its own production, making itself its own subject in the process.

Theme, medium, materiality and its self-reflexivity make De Andrea's *Untitled* an ideal beginning point for the subject of our exhibition, which is neatly summed up by its title, *Near Life: The Gipsformerei — 200 Years of Casting Plaster.* These figures aptly exemplify the concept and hypothesis of the exhibition and therefore also of this accompanying book. Out of all artistic techniques, casting comes literally closest to life.

Plaster casting is an archaic procedure. Its operating principle is indexical, which means it is characterised by a direct physical relationship, the contact made between plaster and human being, between signifier and signified. In De Andrea's scene, plaster is shown to be touching the woman's body, breathing down her neck as it were. The material of plaster is considered to be fine, adaptive and precise. If skin reacts to the application of the cold, wet plaster with goose pimples, if it breaks out into a sweat under the airtight plaster layer during the heat-releasing curing process, or if it is slightly deformed under the weight of this layer, these indicators of life are immediately documented in the surface of the mould. Given that plaster slightly expands in volume during the curing process, it is no wonder that it spreads to the most remote nook and cranny, to the smallest pores and most tender furrows. Skin is the organ that envelopes us as human beings and it is also the surface in which life leaves its traces and imprints. Plaster morphs into the envelope of an envelope, into the medium that secures these traces and makes them visible.

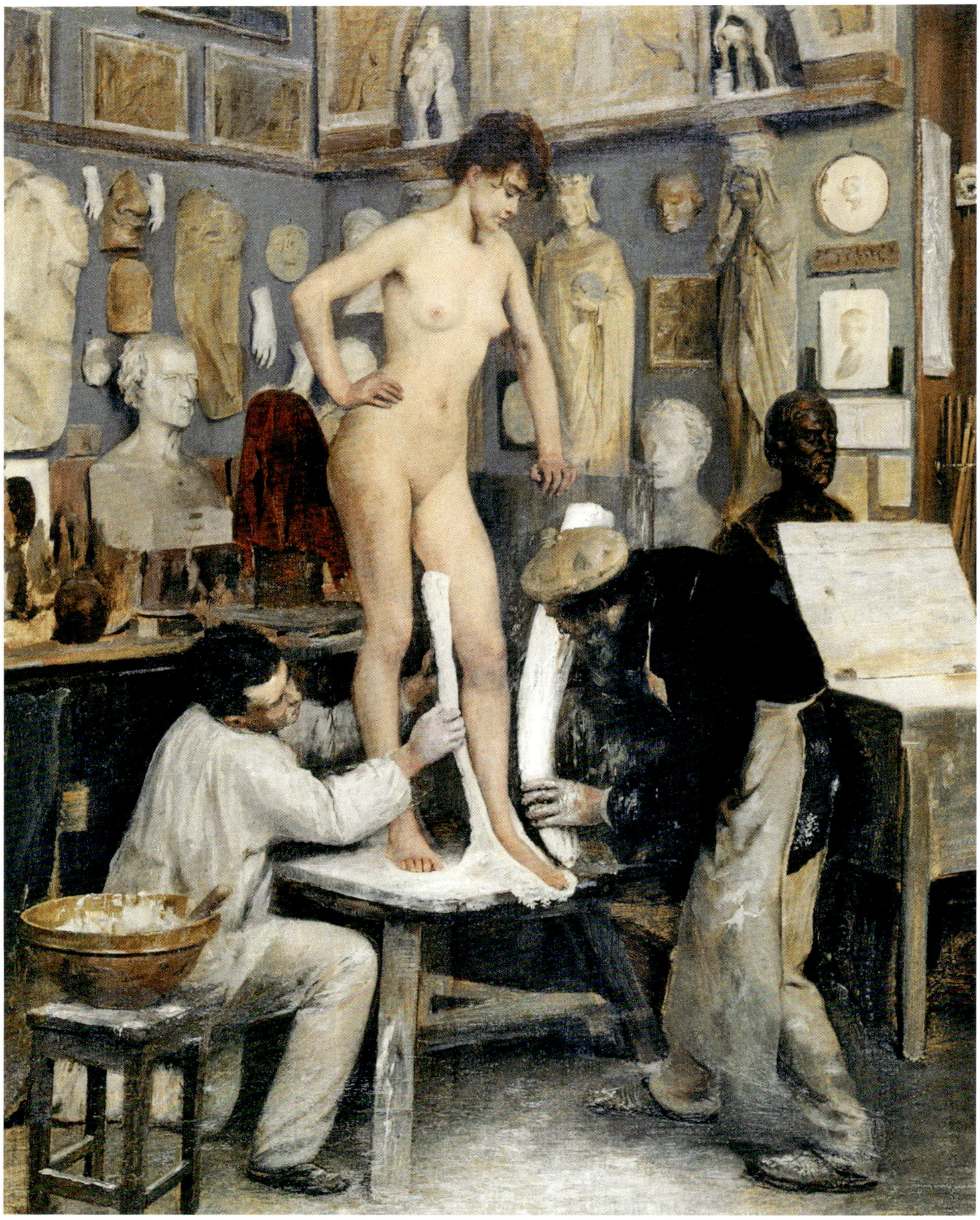

Édouard Joseph Dantan
Un moulage sur nature à l'atelier desculpture à Saint-Cloud, 1887
Oil on canvas, 80 × 65 cm
Private collection

Casting objects in plaster or some other comparable material or making an imprint is a cultural technique that belongs to humanity's oldest sculptural methods and has been practised over millennia, more or less unchanged. A liquid or malleable material is used to take a mould of a body or object, whose shape is then replicated as a negative mould or matrix. After hardening this becomes the basis for casting a positive. Once a durable mould has been formed, the process may be repeated as often as is desired. The surface of the moulded object is passed on to the matrix and from there to the cast; plaster casting as an imaging procedure based on direct contact gives an aura of authenticity, promising a brush with reality and a faithfulness to nature.

In the history of sculpture in Europe and North America from antiquity to the present, from the bronzes of the Classical Greek period to the synthetic resin casts of the American hyperrealists, the depiction of 'real' life has been an ongoing concern. Time and time again it has given rise to a great interest in realism. This is coupled by the fact that the processes of moulding and casting have been relatively accessible and therefore widely used as artistic procedures since time immemorial. They may form part of the process of visual invention, or be integrated into a work of art, both as conceptual and material elements. It may be the case that in the first stages of an artwork, casts are brought into play as models, or the cast of say a leg may serve as a means to achieve an approximation of a perfect form. The sculptures are legion when cast and freely modelled parts are joined together so well that in the finished product they can no longer be told apart.

Even though casts and castings were commonplace, in fact they were omnipresent in artists' studios, sculptures that owed their existence to casting were traditionally belittled, often to the point where they were denied the title of 'art' altogether. Casting was considered a dubious practice with which artists tried to secure an unfair advantage over their struggle to imitate nature: far from being the result of a free creative act, the lifelike sculptures they produced with this technique were said to be 'mere' mechanical copies, restricted to replicating the surface instead of giving bodily form to the soul of a portrait. From the beginnings of modern art history, the aptitude of casting to mimic nature was interpreted as a weakness, despite the fact that the sculptors who integrated this technique into their works — Verrocchio, Donatello, Canova, or Rodin — are regarded as particularly progressive, experimental, and therefore 'modern'. The omnipresence of casts in studio practice, on the one hand, and the negative opinions of art criticism towards casting techniques, on the other, have brought about a twofold consequence: casts both enable and limit sculpture, marking both a beginning and an end. Just as artists have relied for centuries on casting techniques in the initial stages of their work, the suspicion of having entered into too close an alliance with the cast may very quickly pull the rug from underneath the artwork in question, and, indeed, from underneath a career.

In *Near Life*, casting is viewed as such a twofold catalyst and determinant of the three-dimensional artwork. The exhibition's roughly two hundred objects document the crucial role casting has played in the history of sculpture, the reception the cast has met as well as the emancipation of casts to the status of works of art in modern art. The five chapters of the exhibition offer platforms to view *Near Life* from different perspectives: *Still Lifes and Nature morte* describes nature as the origin and telos (in the Aristotle sense) of art's attempt at mimesis. It brings together a large array of artistic and artisanal casts of inhabitants of the worlds of animals and plants, dating from the sixteenth to the twenty-first century, and demonstrates how artists have immobilised, fixated and transformed anything creepy-crawly, greening and blossoming in the world around us into three-dimensional works of art. The chapter *Too near to Life* shows that casts were not only relevant for art: the aura of authenticity and the quasi-scientific objectivity they extend held a special allure in the nineteenth century for those seeking to apply positivist methods of research in the natural sciences and the humanities. This attitude can be seen at work in the practice of anthropological lifecasting, of the kind produced by European explorers in Oceania, Asia, Africa, and in the ethnological exhibitions held in Europe in colonial times. The products of these practices are stored today in our collections as documents of a racist, inhuman branch of science. Continuing the focus on facial casts, the chapter *Ultimate Life* concentrates on the subject of death and the use of plaster casts to document that last expression on the face of the deceased as well the artistic interventions that render a respectful image. The correlation between plaster and the dead body, in that both stiffen, is exposed here as is the *likeness* of death, which marks the lifecast in general. In addition to the aura of stillness common to casts, it is the closed eyes – necessitated by the moulding procedure — which further enhances the impression of death. The chapters *In the Artist's Studio* and *The Case against Casts* explicitly focus, once again, on the use of casts in the studio practice of the sculptor, from antiquity to the present day, and on the controversy surrounding the entitlement of casts to be called works of art — a historical debate which dissolved into thin air, or was even completely reversed with the broadening of the concepts of art and sculpture in the twentieth century. An epilogue-like parade of five famous sculptures, each of which brilliantly testifies to a successful approximation of life, brings the narrative of both the exhibition and this accompanying book to its end.

Near Life is linked to a special occasion and thereby to a special collection that calls for celebration in 2019. On 8 December 2019, the Gipsformerei, Staatliche Museen zu Berlin celebrates its two hundredth anniversary: it is this festive occasion that the exhibition was conceived for. Two hundred years ago, a royal cabinet directive issued by Friedrich Wilhelm III provided for the foundation of the *Abguss-Anstalt*, as the Gipsformerei was then called. In the summer of that same year, the plaster caster Domenico Bianconi, recruited for the purpose in Carrara, had arrived in Berlin. Under the aegis of the first head of the Gipsformerei, Christian Daniel Rauch, he instructed craftsmen and apprentices in the art of plaster casting, an art in which Italy had long played a pioneering role. Like other great plaster casting workshops, such as those in Paris (founded in 1794) and in Brussels (founded in 1870), the Gipsformerei was part of the plans for the first museum in Berlin. When Karl Friedrich Schinkel's museum, today's Altes Museum, was opened on the Museum Island, the Gipsformerei joined the Königliche, then later the Staatliche Museen zu Berlin. It is therefore the oldest institution of the museum group.

The collection of the Gipsformerei is today comprised of almost seventeen thousand casting moulds and models based on more than seven thousand works from the history of art and culture, ranging from prehistory to the early twentieth century. In the two hundred years since its foundation, its collection areas have multiplied and undergone substantial diversification. Whilst the collection in its first decades concentrated on casts of ancient and classicist works, the foundation of museums and new building projects of the Königliche Museen as well as the establishment of exchange relationships with other institutions brought a steadily increasing stream of objects into the collection, based on originals from the Byzantine to the baroque of Europe's art history, anthropology and prehistory as well as early history objects from Egypt and the Middle East. Visitors to the Gipsformerei find themselves confronted with casts of all kinds, from all eras and all parts of the world. They will also note that the collection is by no means confined to works of art, even though the reproduction of mostly famous works in the history of sculpture continues to be the mainstay of the Gipsformerei.

As far as media are concerned, there are three types of objects in the collection of the Gipsformerei, including: approximately four thousand historical plaster piece and gelatine moulds and an additional three thousand more recent silicone moulds; secondly, roughly seven thousand (master) models, that is, those positive counterparts of the moulds which remain in the collection as file copies and include a great number of so-called original models (the first casts from the moulds taken directly from the original); and, thirdly, about three thousand painting models, which serve as templates for sculpture painters and have done so since the late nineteenth century when they first came into use. These models give the painters an exact idea of the original object's colouring and material appearance. Compared to other cast collections of the academy or the museum, where the 'products' of plaster casting workshops such as the Gipsformerei find a lasting home, the holdings of this collection are unusual. It is designed for use. Its objects serve a strictly practical purpose, namely the creation of casts in the manner prescribed by traditional craftsmanship. They disclose their identity as tools by the fact that the models often consist of several parts, that they are coated in shellac of different colours, that inventory numbers are inscribed on them in large lettering and that they come with visible reinforcements, keys, locks or splints. Over the years, however, as the history of the institution and its objects is foregrounded, the primary aspect of usability recedes into the background: the manufactory is now increasingly seen as a museum and this applies all the more so to its collection. As such, the Gipsformerei preserves two types of cultural assets. Firstly, the largely orally transmitted craftsmanship, which is in drastic decline — the expert knowledge of casting and moulding techniques can only be acquired and passed on within the handful of traditional workshops that are still operational in the world. Secondly, the collection of historical moulds and models is not only distinguished by its historical and aesthetic value, but that it is capable of lending a new lease of life to lost original works of art or objects; their long-term preservation and protection need to be reconciled with the demands of production.

The points of departure for *Near Life* are the special characteristics or even peculiarities contained within the collection of the Gipsformerei, which as an institution is incomparable; the wealth of objects it stores, making it a small yet universal museum in its own right; as well as the capability of plaster to mould any conceivable object. The history of plaster casting as we know it is usually oriented towards its product, the cast. What *Near Life* places centre stage for the first time are not the plaster casts, but the moulds and models; not the product of the workshop process, but the workshop process itself and its closeness to artistic work. *Near Life* is the first large-scale presentation of the Gipsformerei and its collection. In light of the exhibition's thematic focus on the casting of natural objects as a technique practised since antiquity by artists seeking to imitate life as closely as possible, the collection is made accessible in cross sections as well as representative selections, combined with works on loan from other collections. Until now almost completely unknown casts after nature from the collection of the Gipsformerei and master models of works of art (reputedly) based on casts are shown together with works of art from the recent history of art that owe their existence to moulds, or have elevated this sculptural tool to the status of an artistic means.

Any attempt at gaining an overview of the exhibited objects invariably raises the question of what all these casts and their different origins and use have in common, and how they differ from one another. It is quite obvious, for example, that facial casts may be made to play vastly different roles and serve different purposes, either as death masks, anthropological masks, anatomical teaching aids or works of art. The process of their production, however, is subject to a technological constant. For *Near Life*, the objects have been selected with this constant firmly in view, so to be able to differentiate between the great number of variants and applications of casting techniques and to raise awareness of this practice.

Art and craftsmanship, original and copy, positive and negative, active and passive, form and content, contact and distance, life and death, presence and absence, 'high' and 'low' are some of the binaries between which the history of casting unfolds, and the same may be said of the theme of *Near Life*. The exhibition's narrative was inspired by several formative projects. *La Ressemblance par contact: Archéologie, anachronisme at modernité de l'empreinte* (1997) by Georges Didi-Huberman is tantamount to a cultural history of casting. It throws light on how the technique was brought into disrepute by classical art historians and launches a successful attempt at rehabilitating the form. The exhibition *À fleur de peau: Le moulage sur nature au XIXe siècle* at Musée d'Orsay, Paris in 2001–02, and in a revised form at Hamburger Kunsthalle, *Hautnah: Die Abformung des Lebens im 19. Jahrhundert*, in 2002, provided a point of departure for further research. Additionally, more recent, large-scale, cross-disciplinary projects, spanning several epochs and based on the theme of the proximity to life, have been influential: for instance, *Ebenbilder: Kopien von Körpern — Modelle des Menschen* at Ruhrlandmuseum Essen in 2002, and *Like Life: Sculpture, Color, and the Body* at The Met Breuer, New York in 2018. With regard to the Gipsformerei more specifically, art historian Sibylle Einholz's work has been highly valuable in the preparation of the exhibition. She is to be given full credit for initiating the scholarly investigation of the collection as early as the 1990s and for drawing attention to the merits of casts and moulds 'taken from nature'. A list of further reading on this and other topics relevant to the exhibition can be found at the back of this book.

For the objects of the Gipsformerei collection to be presented in a way that transcends their relationship to an original and reveals their historical significance and inherent aesthetic qualities has required a large team and a great number of co-workers. As Deputy Director General and Scientific Director of the Gipsformerei, Christina Haak initiated the project of this jubilee exhibition and has been highly supportive of developing an exhibition concept that deliberately eschews the beaten track. Andrea Müller, in charge of project management, has contributed significantly to both the planning phase and the realisation of the exhibition for more than two years. The staff of the Gipsformerei, with its commercial manager Miguel Helfrich and workshop manager Stefan Kramer, have been involved with the project since its inception and have enriched it with their expertise. Aurelia Badde restored all the moulds and models shown in the exhibition in close collaboration with the Gipsformerei, and mastered the challenge of creating their presentability without impairing their functionality. Justine Tutmann has shown great commitment to the final stages of the exhibition, providing assistance on all sorts of curatorial matters. Nicolas Rauch, Janna Schaar and Mira Schröder of Schroeder Rauch have developed a felicitous exhibition scenography that combines heavy-load racks with museum-like display plinths, thus underlining the hybrid character of the objects. And Christian Boros, Helen Dengler and Ingo Maak from BOROS have developed a strong communication concept to reach our audiences.

Like the exhibition, this companion book, which will remain when the exhibition itself has become a thing of the past, is owed to a small group of fantastic people. Philip Radowitz has translated the objects of the Gispformerei and the spatial situation on-site into engaging imagery; his photographs form the centrepiece of this book. Barbara Krimm and Melanie Achilles from StudioKrimm have provided a state-of-the-art book design, which succeeds both in bringing order to its heterogeneous material and in highlighting its diversity. Julia Stoff has been in charge of the entire editing process and publication management and has shepherded this book into print with a sure hand. German copy-editing was realised by Rea Triyandafilidis and Otmar Binder's translation of the book into English was copy-edited by Laura Preston — all three contributed with diligence and endurance.

Alongside the lenders and authors, my colleagues in the areas of exhibitions, publications, education and outreach, communication, construction, technology and security and the relevant collections of the Staatliche Museen zu Berlin and the Hauptverwaltung Preußischer Kulturbesitz have turned *Near Life* into a polyphonic project.

To all these people, plus those named at the end of this book, I extend my heartfelt gratitude on behalf of the entire team.

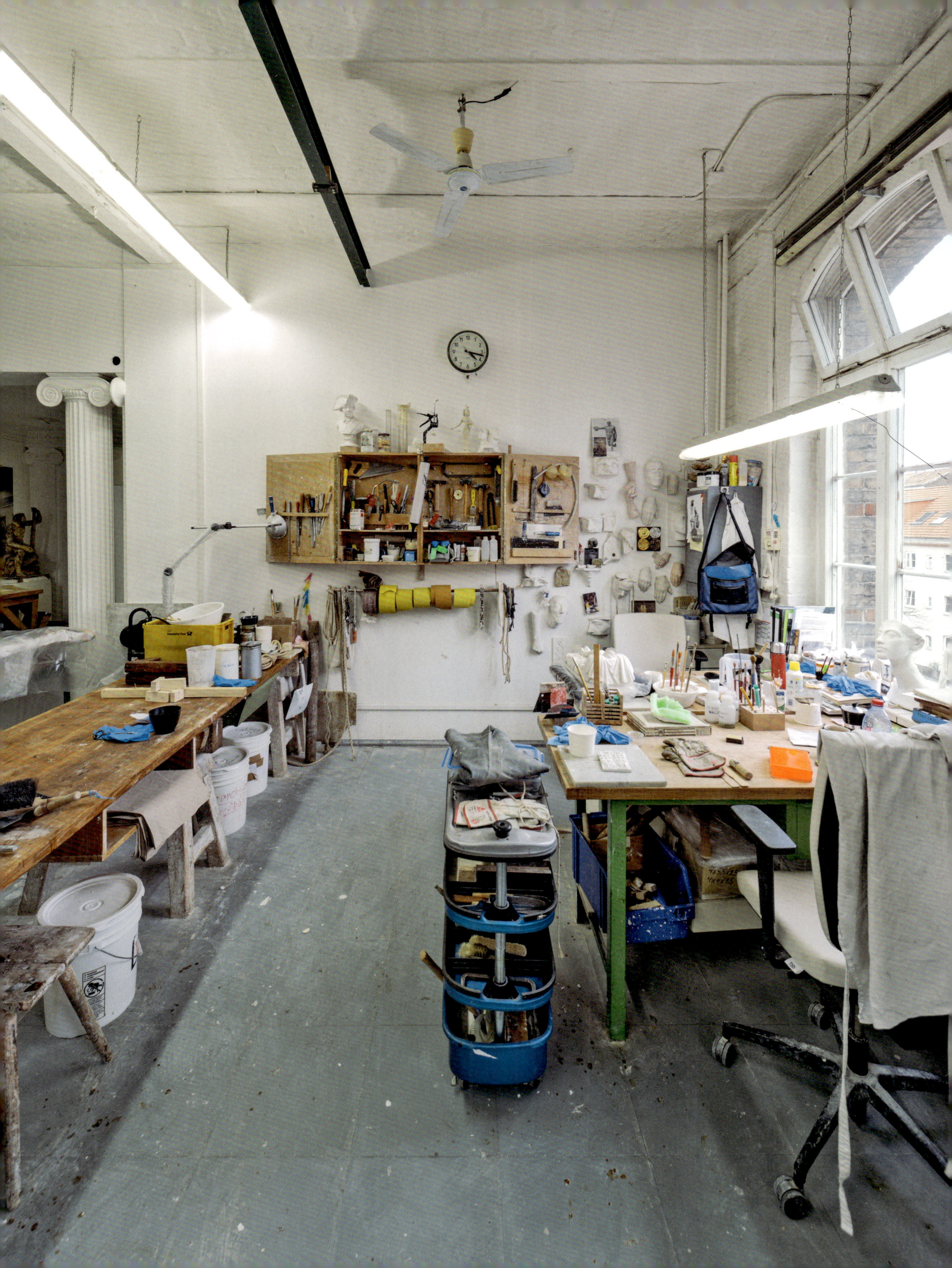

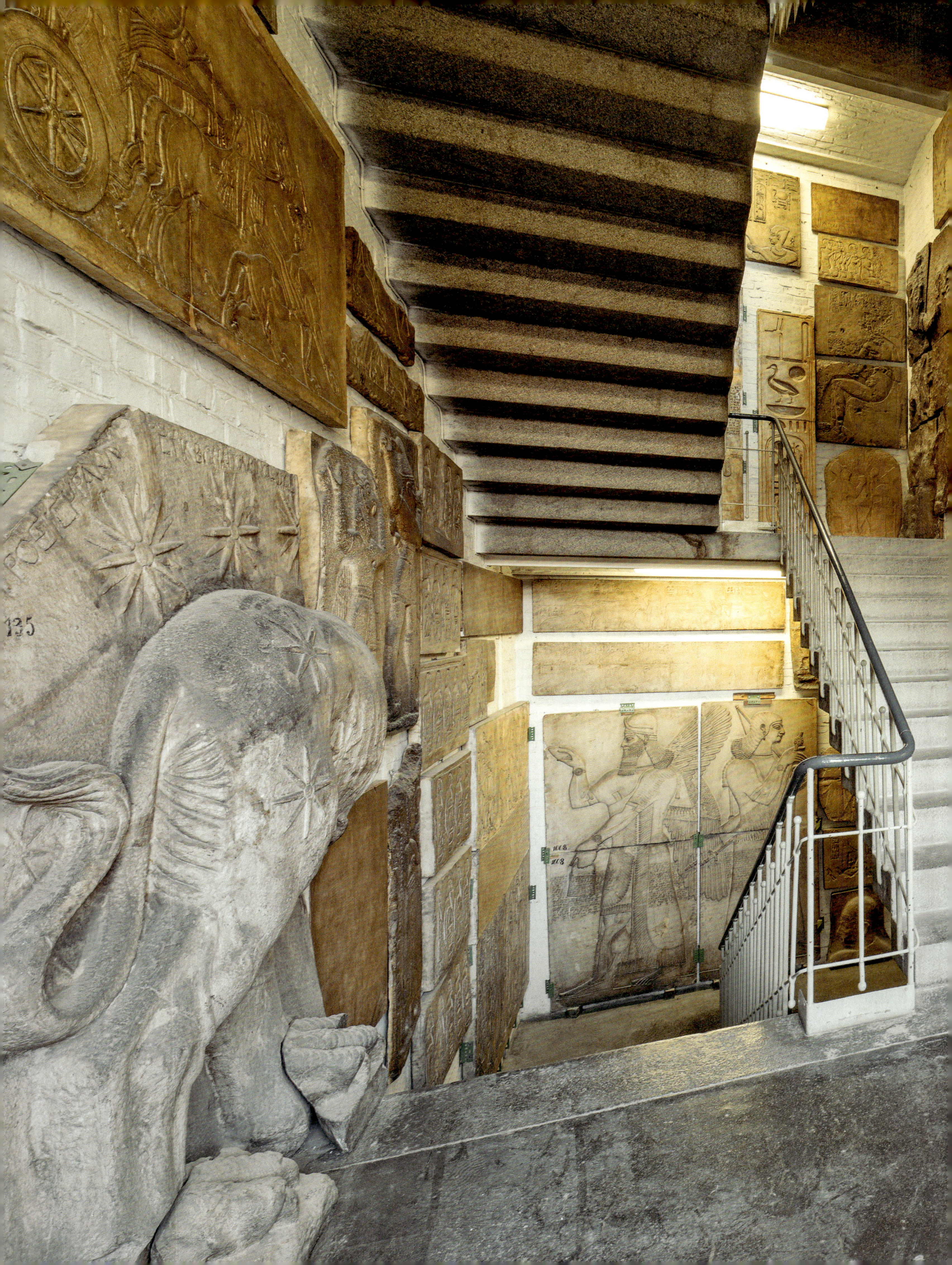
135

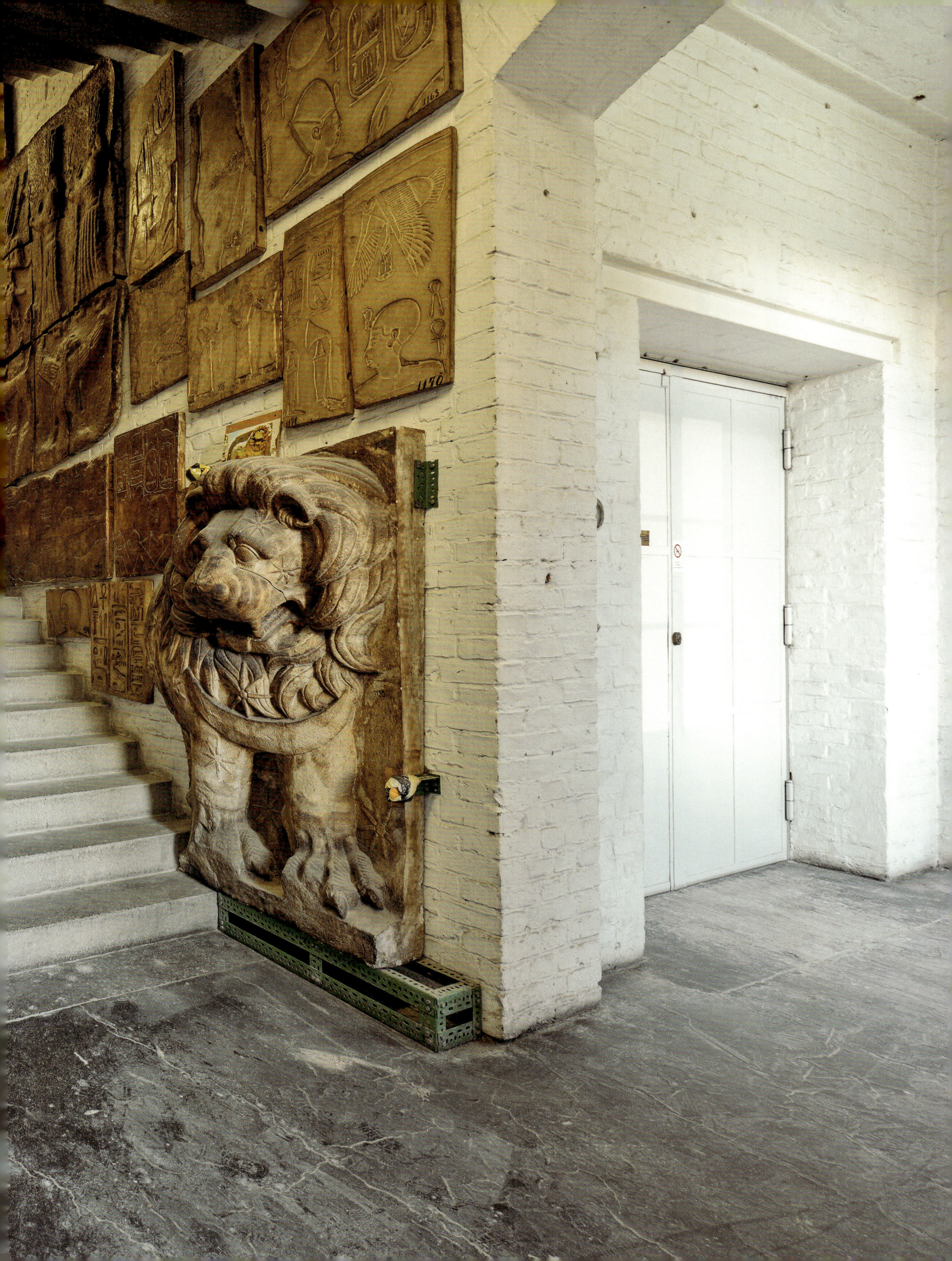

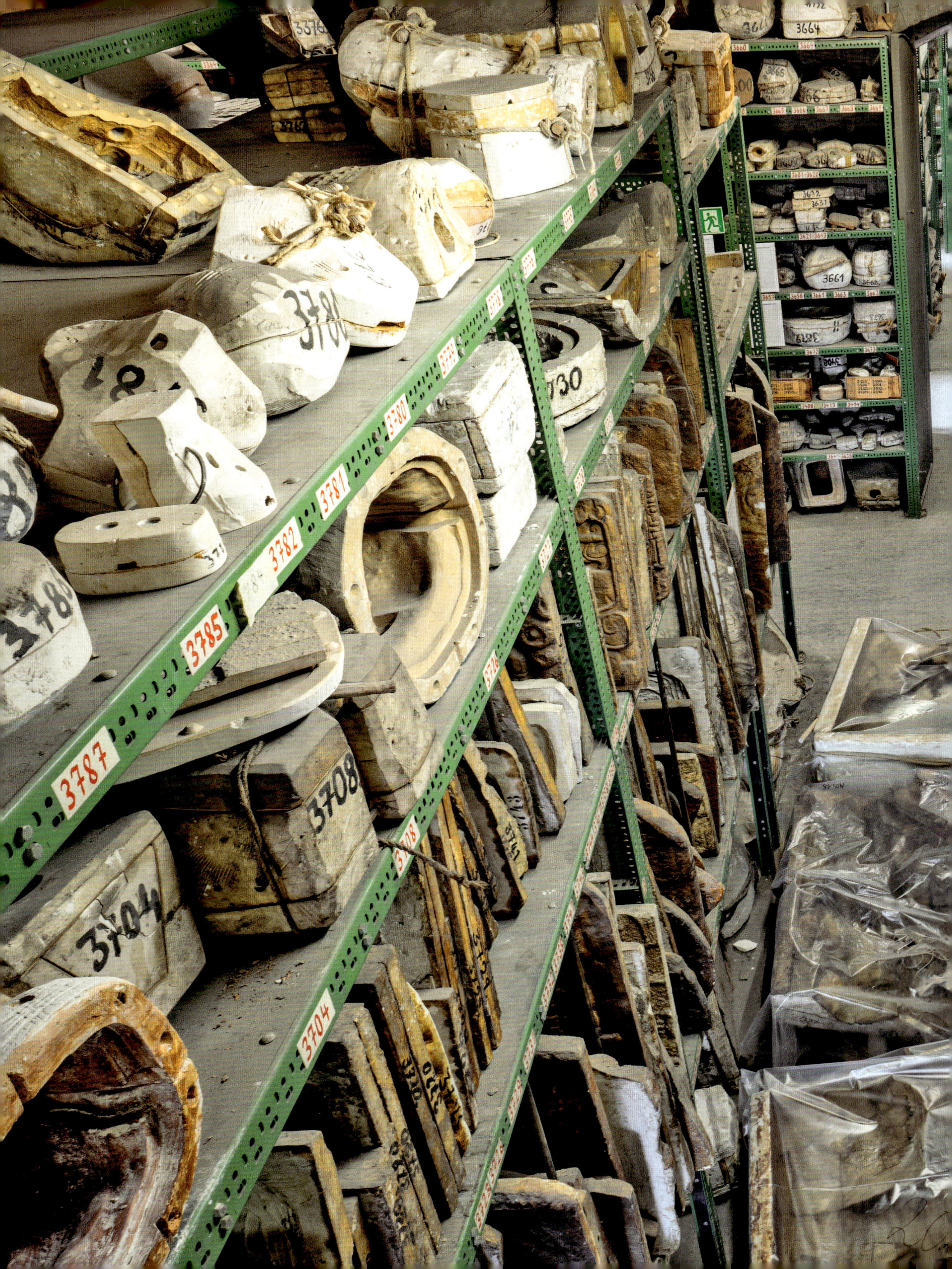

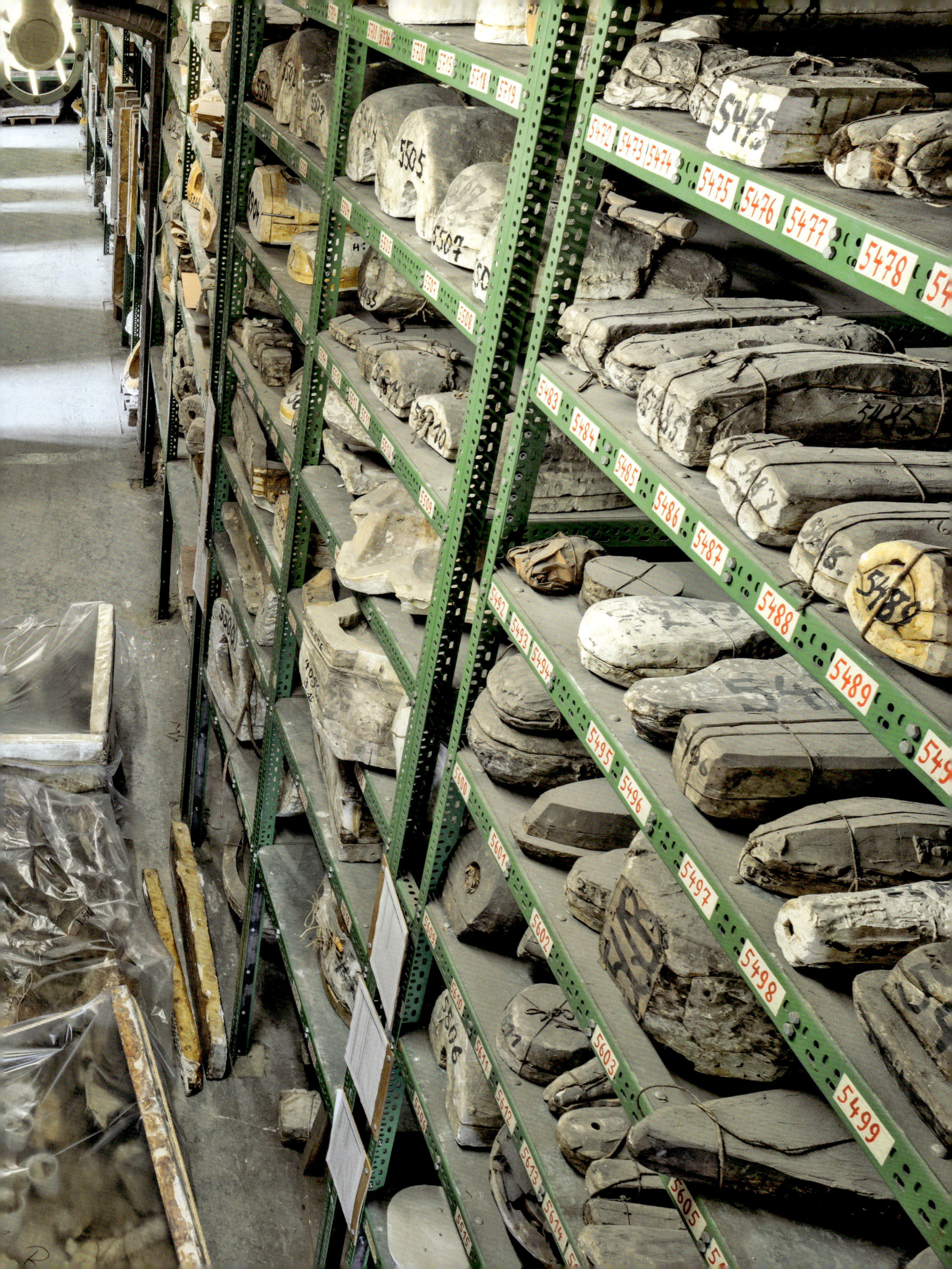
5475
5476
5477
5478
5483
5484
5485
5486
5487
5488
5489
5495
5496
5497
5498
5499
5603
5605

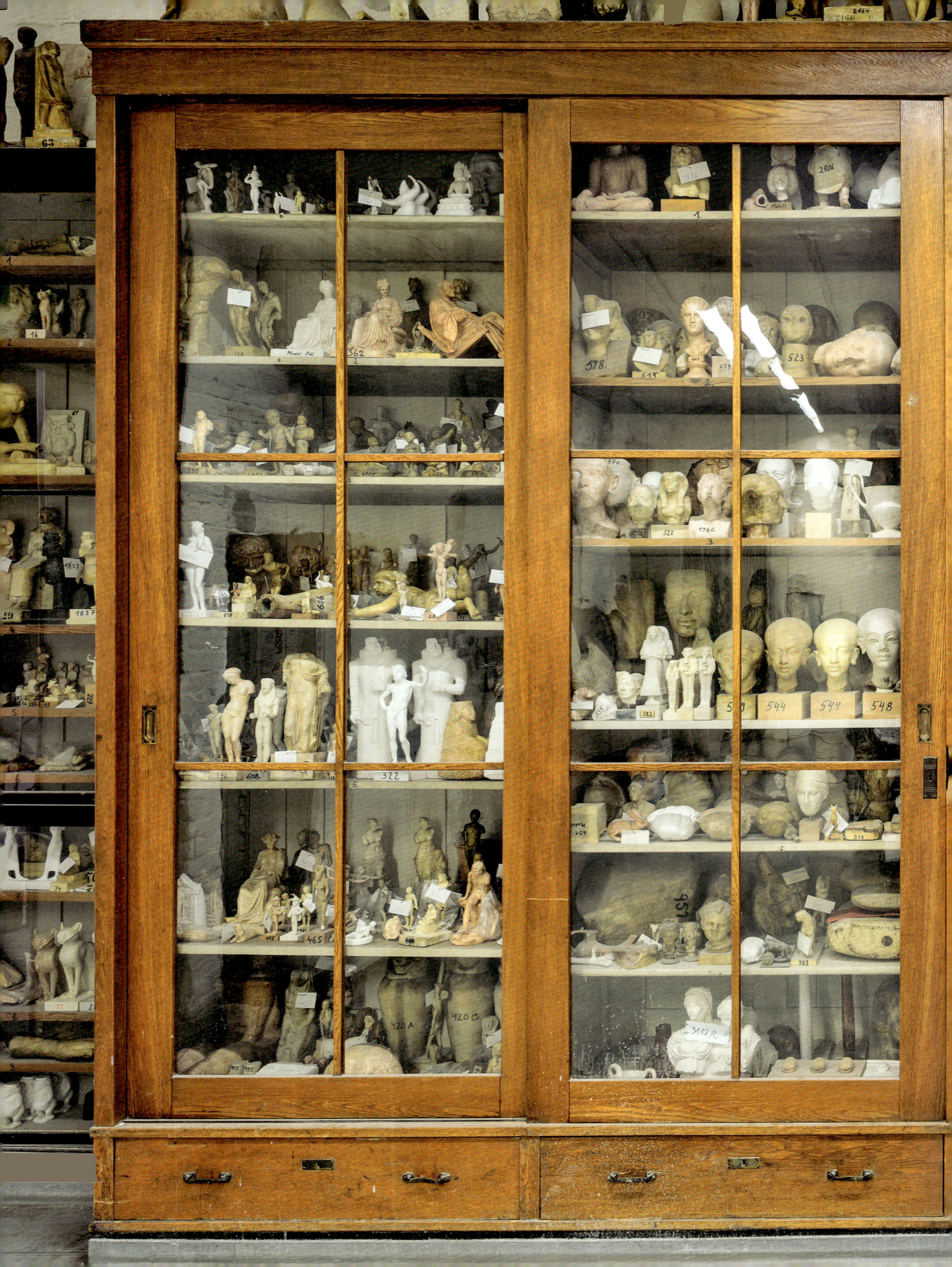
578
523
544
544
548
322
420 A
420 B

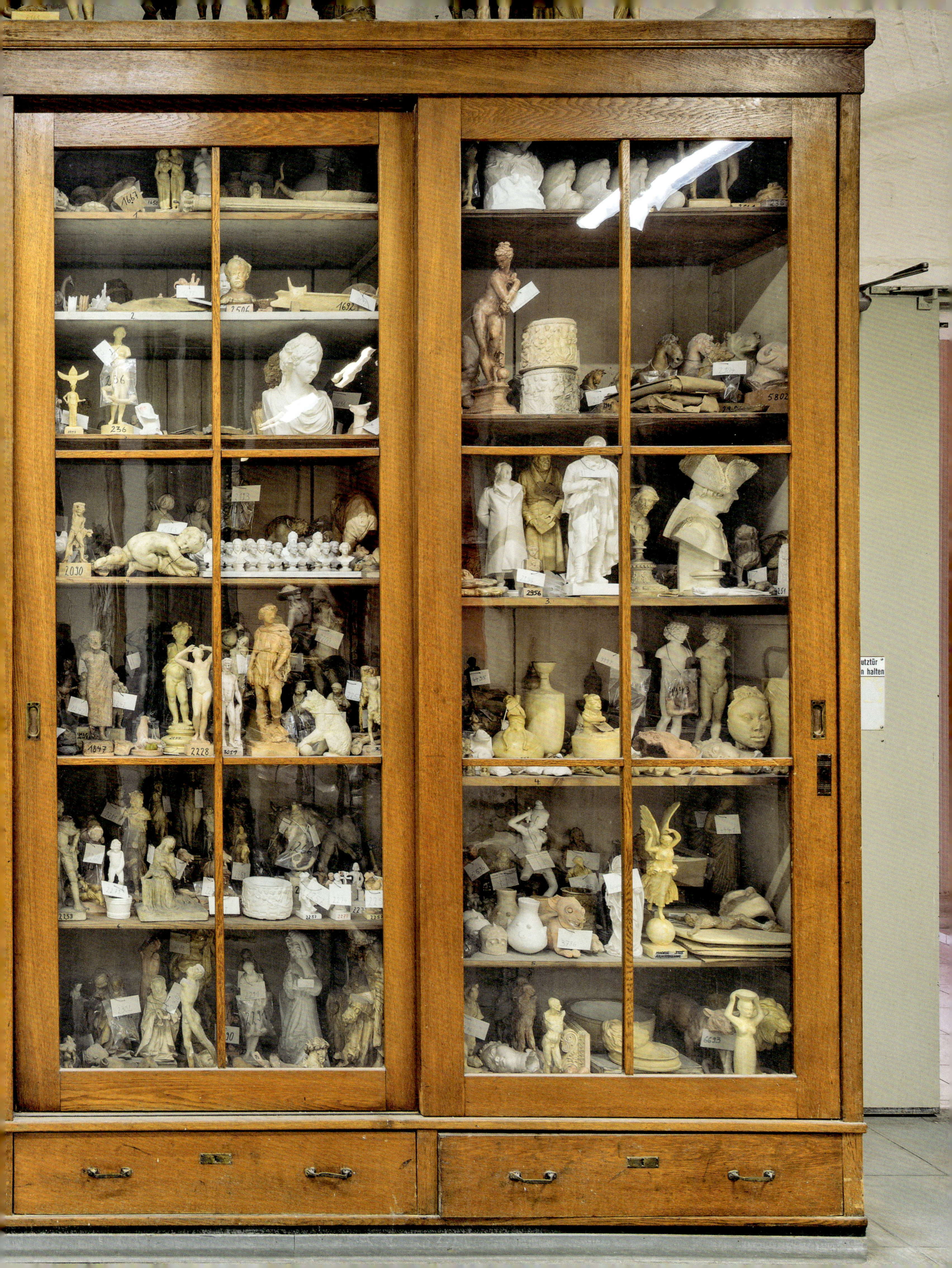
2030
1847
2228
236
2956
5802

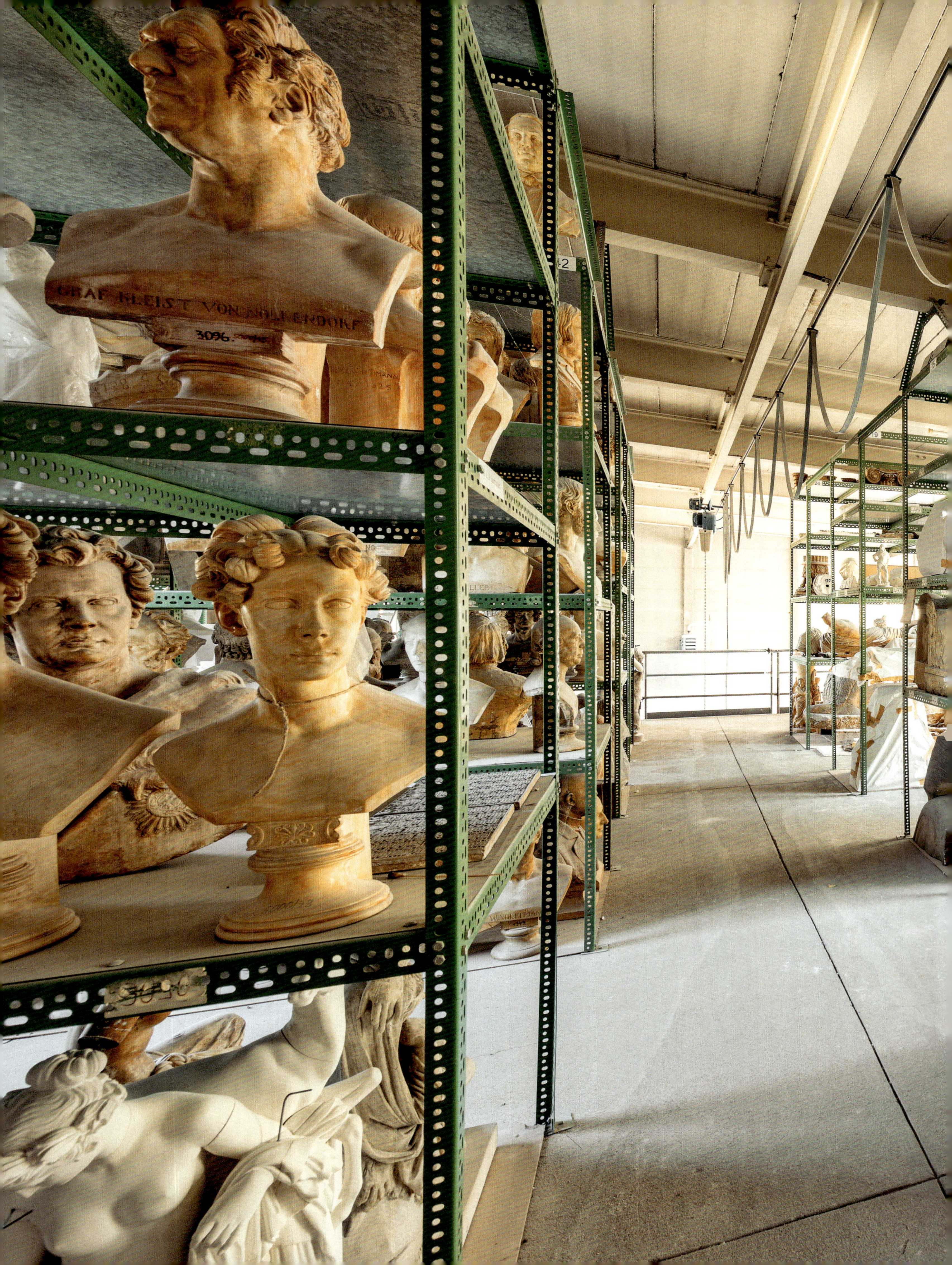
GRAF KLEIST VON
3096

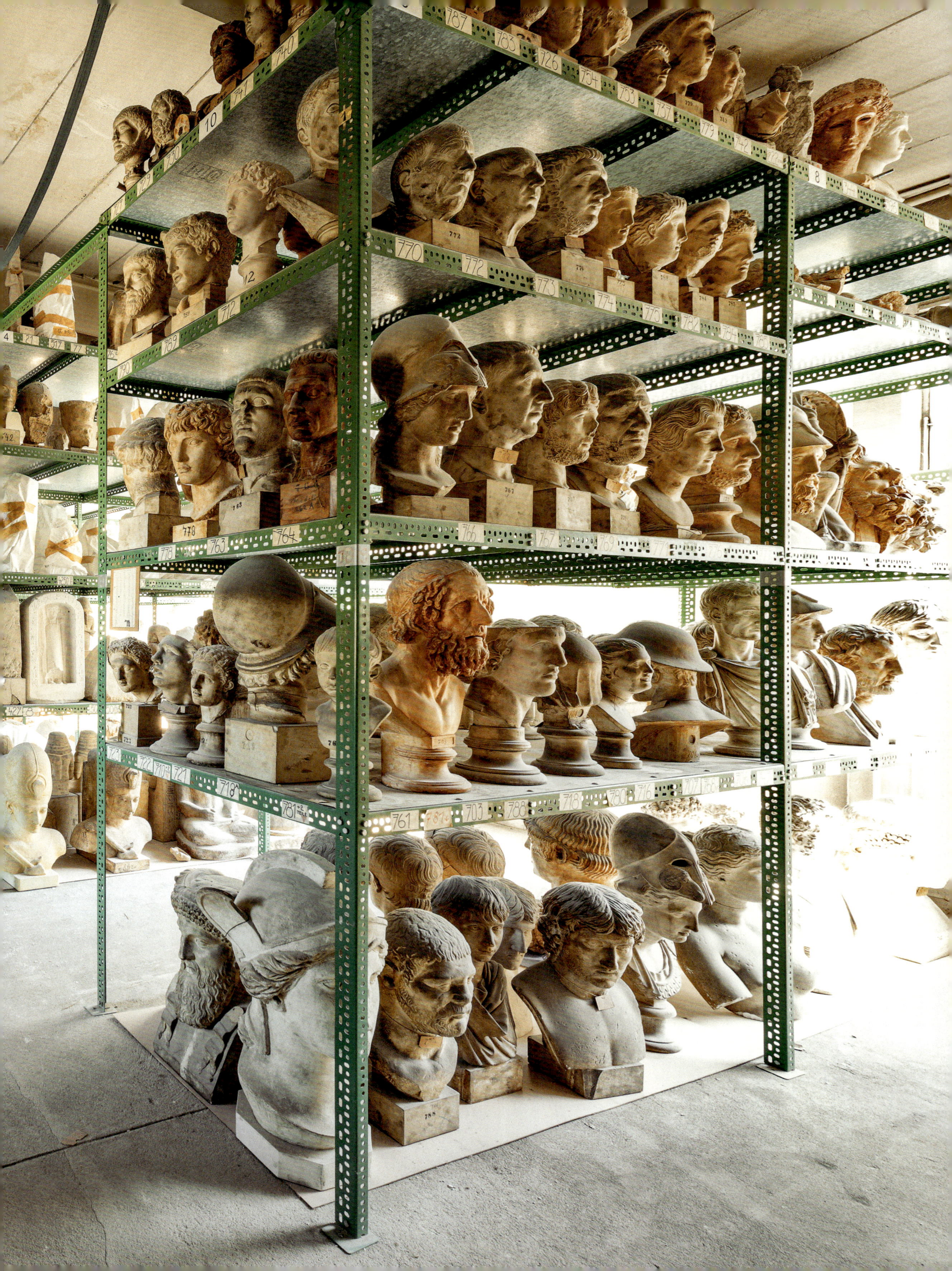

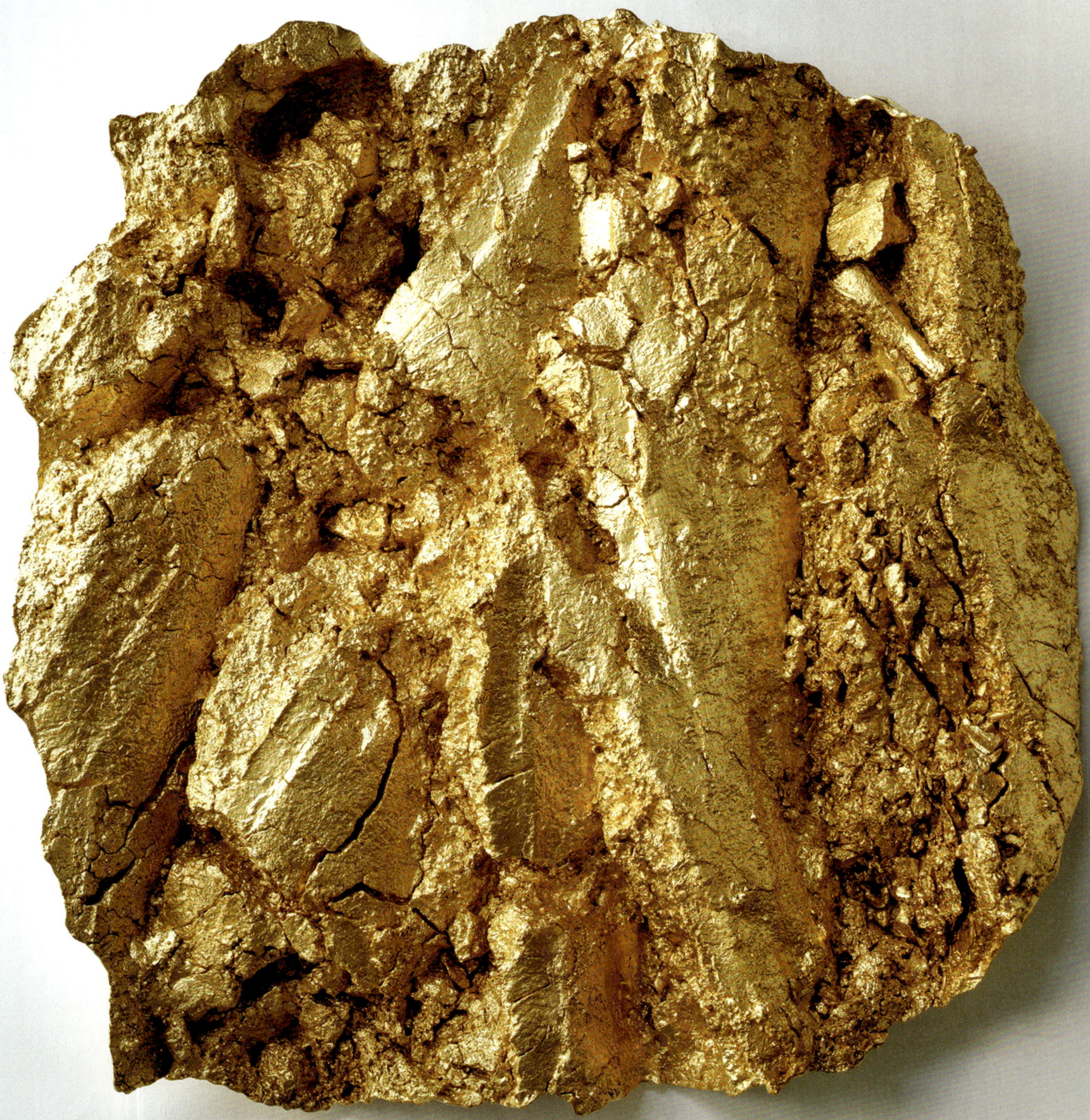

Still Lifes and Nature morte

Nature is both the origin and the goal of art's striving for likeness. In the history of sculpture in Europe and North America, which for centuries has been oriented towards antiquity's principles of mimesis and the imitation of nature, artists have always been inclined to produce casts after nature: they allow artists to capture life directly. At the same time the process of casting is restricted by its need to use immobile (ideally lifeless) forms of nature. Closeness to life and liveliness, mimetic realism and the semblance of death are therefore at odds with one another. Indeed, how close to life are casts in actual fact? And is an impression taken from nature an authentic evidence of reality?

This chapter deals with casts from the world of animals and plants, taken across different centuries and wide-ranging in origin and use. The focus is on the casts of animals from the Gipsformerei which were once used as models in art education of the late nineteenth century. As plaster proxies for live animals, they allowed students to study nature in interior conditions, and especially avoided the difficulties inherent to moving and perishable forms. Another focus of this chapter is on the metal casts of small animals from artists' workshops of the fifteenth and sixteenth centuries. They are proof that the Aristotelian premise of art's imitation of nature (*Ars imitatur naturam*) was given a technological update in the Renaissance. Following the example set by the Italians, casts after nature were not only used as study objects, but were integrated into sculptural works to create composite forms. The tradition of casting after nature is by no means a thing of the past, a point underlined by contemporary art such as the work of Asta Gröting, for instance, her gilded *Acker* (Soil, 2012). It pointedly showcases the empowerment of casts as works of art in their own right, a breakthrough in perspective that was achieved in the early twentieth century.

Crocodile
Master model, 1892
Staatliche Museen zu Berlin, Gipsformerei

The plaster cast of a crocodile cast after nature is part of the former collection of teaching aids of the Königliche Kunstgewerbemuseum (Royal Arts and Crafts Museum) in Berlin, which amalgamated with the collection of the Gipsformerei around 1900. In addition to the plaster casts of architectural elements, arts and craft, and select icons from the history of sculpture, this unusual subsection of the Gipsformerei collection comprises roughly one hundred casts of human body parts and animals. The teaching aids were designed for use at the Unterrichtsanstalt des Kunstgewerbemuseums (Teaching Institute of the Arts and Crafts Museum) in Berlin. Drawing from plaster casts served as a preparation for drawing from live models. These teaching aids were also made to be sold to other teaching institutions. As one of the objects 'especially suited for teaching purposes', the crocodile was included in the *Verzeichnis der in der Formerei der Königlichen Museen käuflichen Gipsabgüsse* (Catalogue of Plaster Casts for Sale at the Gipsformerei); its price was set at fifty Marks.

>> This approximately three-metre-long crocodile is more than a hundred years old and was presumably moulded at the zoo or natural history museum. There are indications that the procedure was carried out in great haste, for instance, the obvious lack of precision in several places and the blisters on the surface. The eyes have receded deep into their sockets, a sign that the cast was made after the animal had been dead for some time. In order to be able to render the mouth in its open state, something must have been stuffed inside to prop it open; there are telltale signs of this towards the back of the throat. Though, fortunately, the structure has come out rather well and the object is very effective. The crocodile has not been given a coating of shellac; it is an original cast, whose corresponding mould is no longer in existence. It had been left in storage for many years. The first thing we had to do was to free the model from a thick accumulation of dust. Comprised of eight parts, those that had broken off were reinforced with iron and stuck together again. Putting the feet back on proved difficult as they had been glued previously. The snout and other aspects of the animal had taken on a yellowish hue over time. Plaster of this age can become sulphurous, but we use diluted citric acid to remove any unwelcome discolourations.

Robin Schulz, artistic plasterer

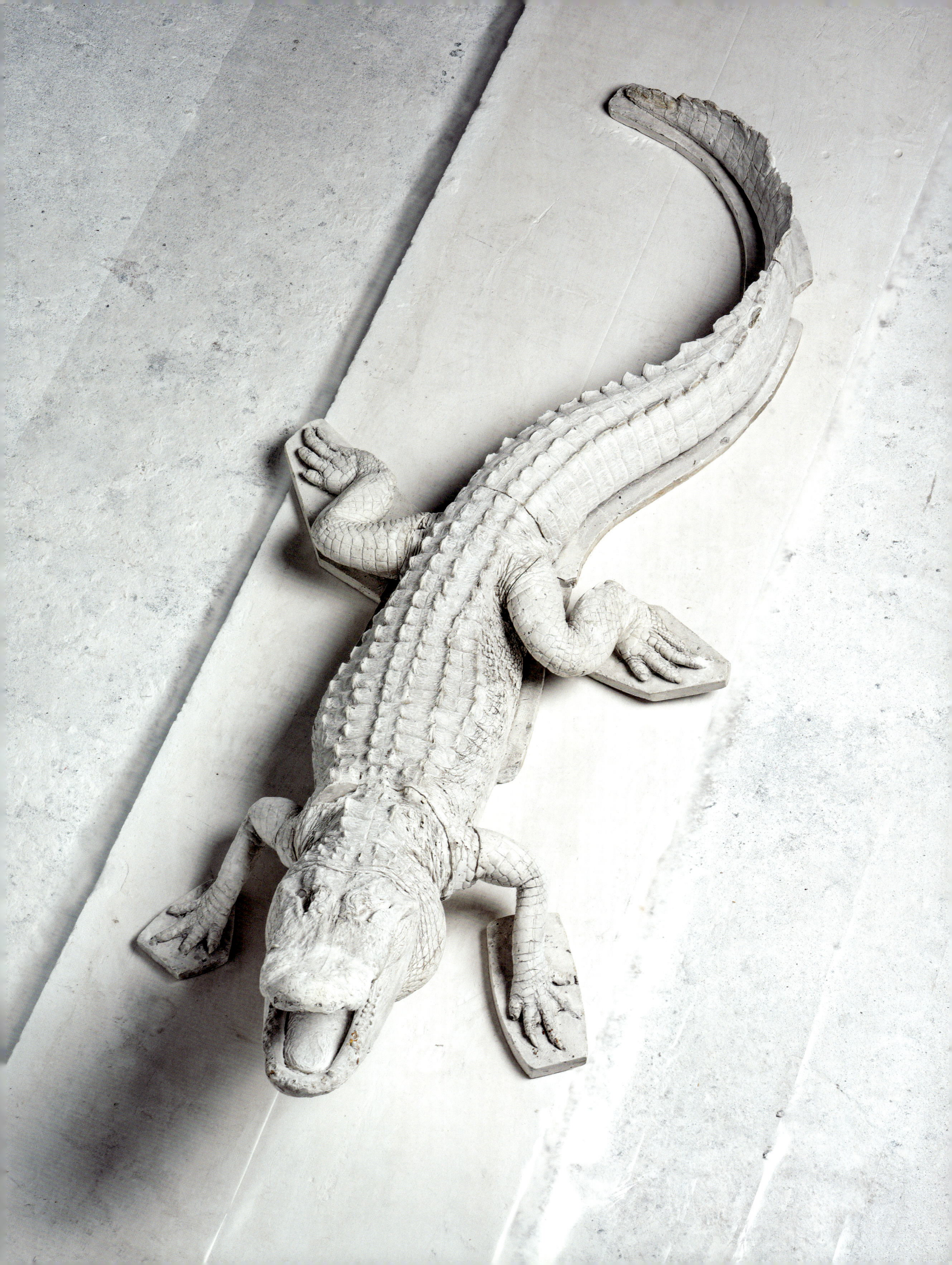

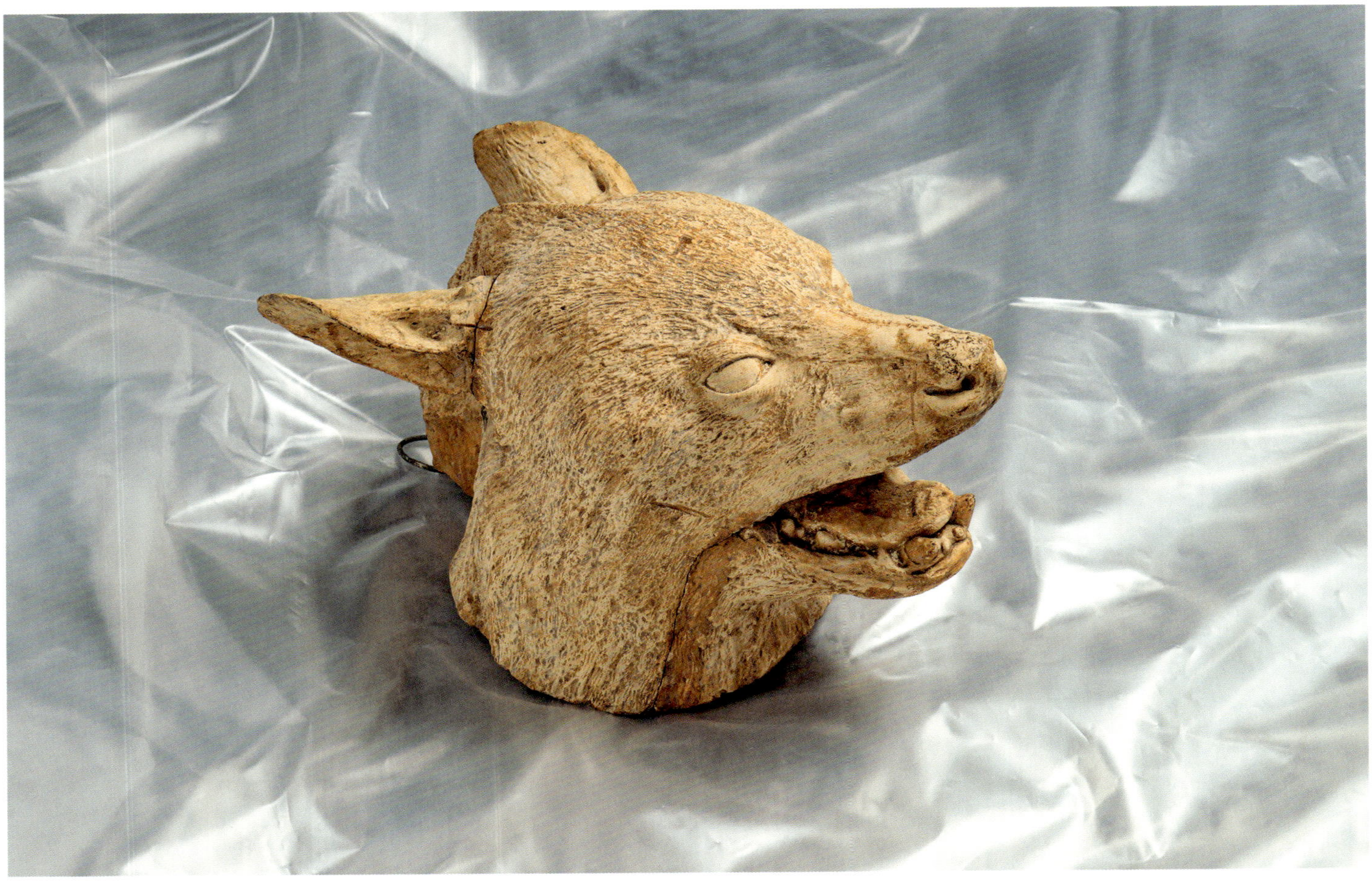

No more than five casts of animal heads taken from nature are to be found in the collection of the Gipsformerei: two goats, a panther, a wild boar and a wolf. They are dated between 1870 and 1892, and, like the crocodile, they form part of the Kunstgewerbemuseum's collection of teaching aids. While we lack any specifics as to how the cast of the croc came into being, it may be assumed that a practice like that of sculptor Josef Pallenberg (1882–1946) was involved, particularly in regard to the more exotic animals. Pallenberg took moulds from animal carcasses he had procured from zoos, and made a name for himself with the animal sculptures he provided for Hagenbeck's zoo in Hamburg. What a challenge it is to make a plaster cast of fur or hair is clearly seen in the texture of the cast surfaces. To remove the initial plaster matrix intact, a great deal of vaseline (or comparable substance) needs to be applied to the furry or hairy surfaces. Interestingly, the reproduction of surface details still proves difficult even with today's cutting-edge contactless technologies — not even 3D scanning and subsequent 3D printing managed to render in sufficient detail the coat of polar bear Knut (the star attraction of Zoo Berlin from 2006–11; see pp. 40–41). Since the computer scan is dependent on a certain surface density, Knut's coat could only be scanned in a wet state, which led to his fur looking stringy and rough.

Head of a Wolf
Master model, 1892
Staatliche Museen zu Berlin, Gipsformerei

Head of a Goat with Short Horns
Master model, 1870
Staatliche Museen zu Berlin, Gipsformerei

Head of a Panther
Master model, 1892
Staatliche Museen zu Berlin, Gipsformerei

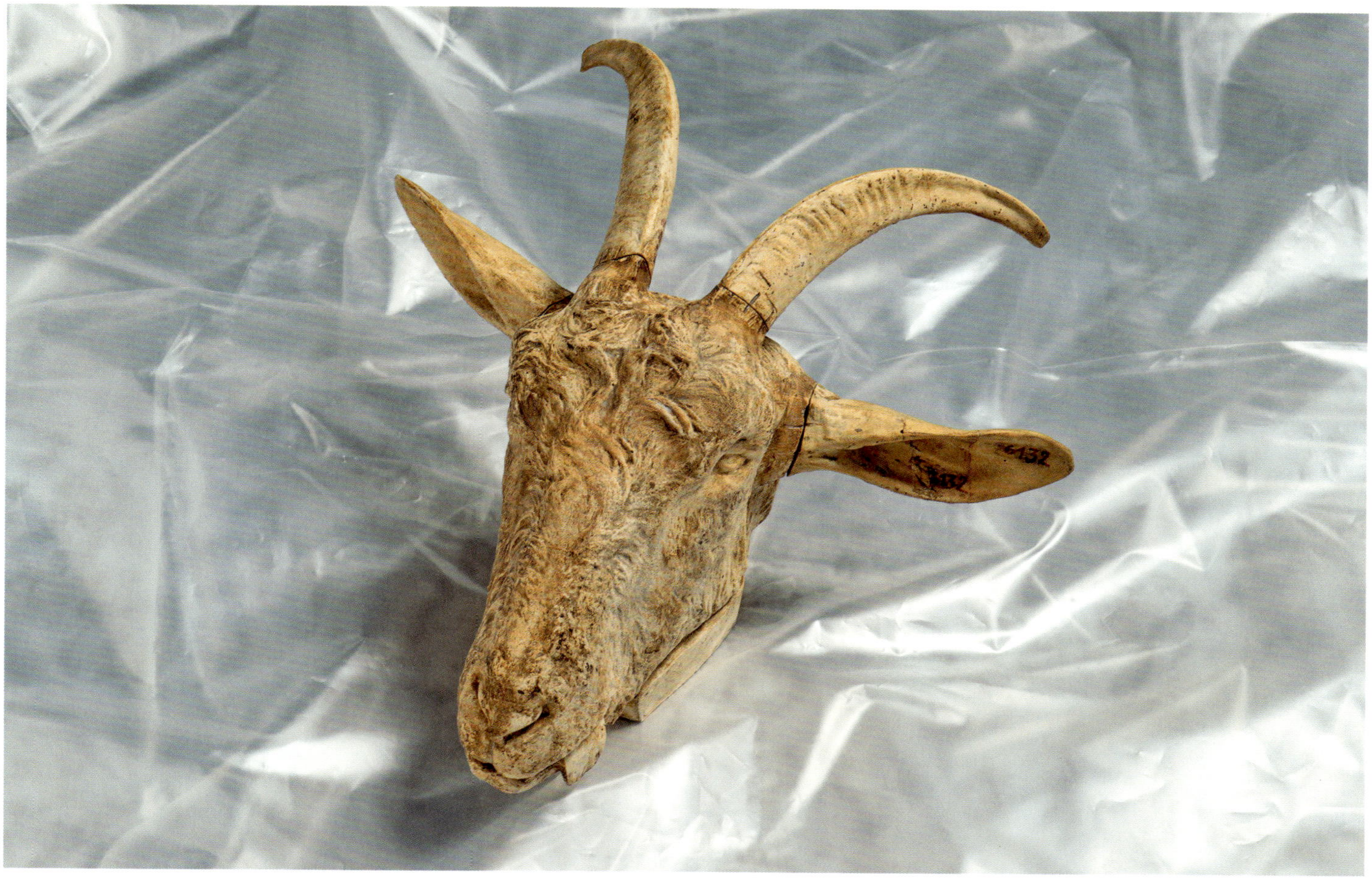
6132

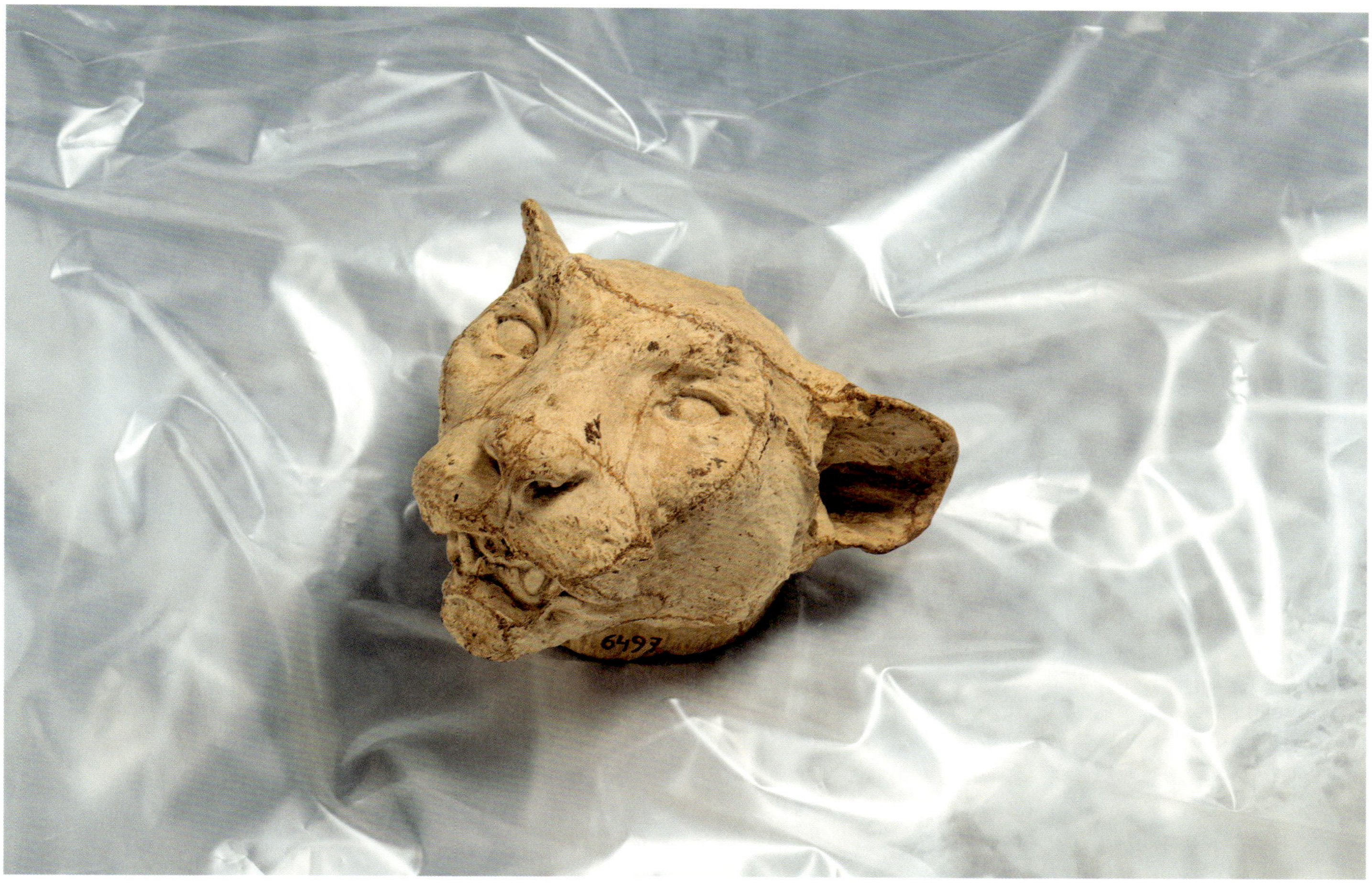
6493

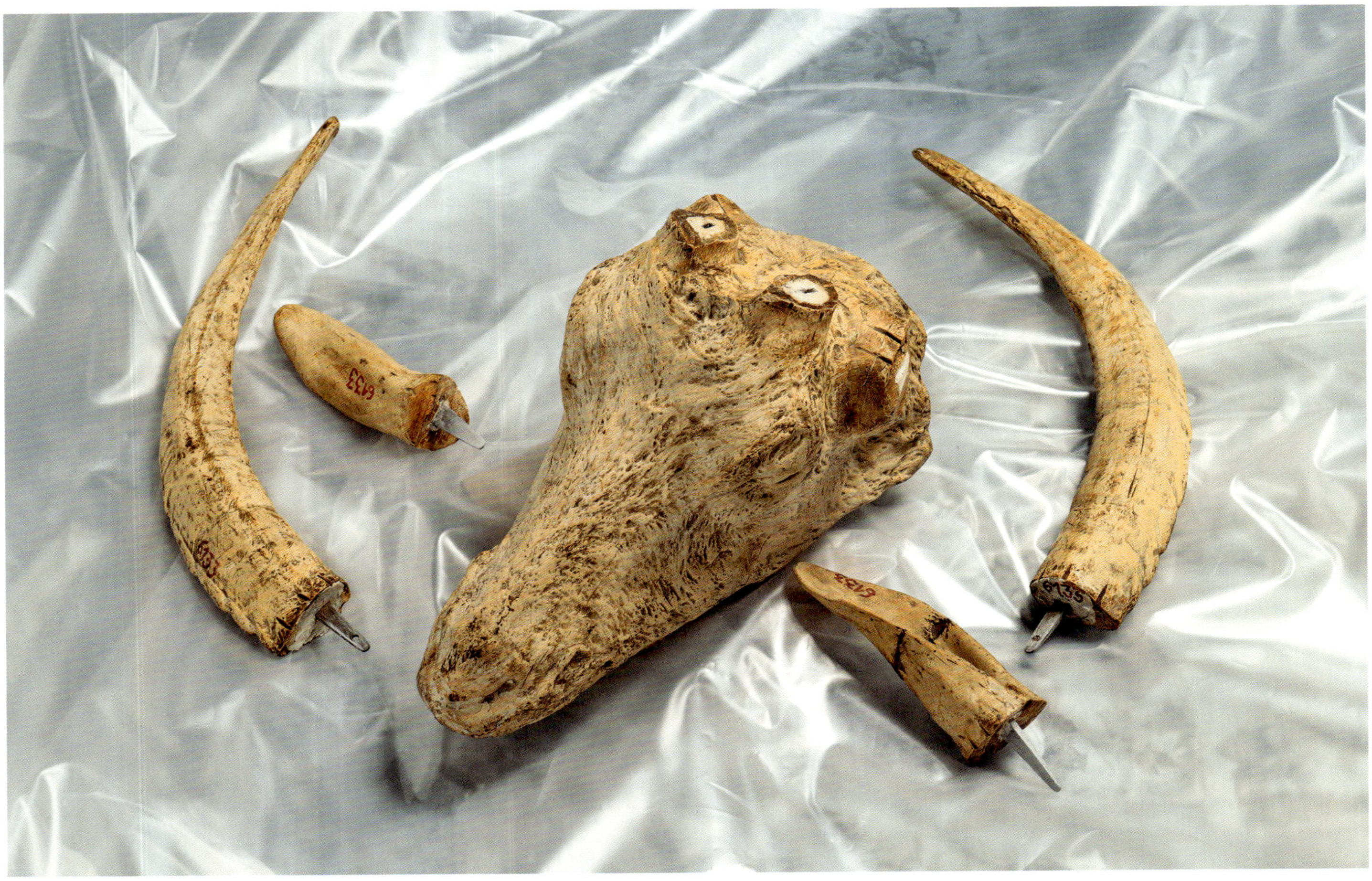

Head of a Goat with Long Horns
Master model, 1870
Staatliche Museen zu Berlin,
Gipsformerei

Head of a Boar
Master model, 1886
Staatliche Museen zu Berlin,
Gipsformerei

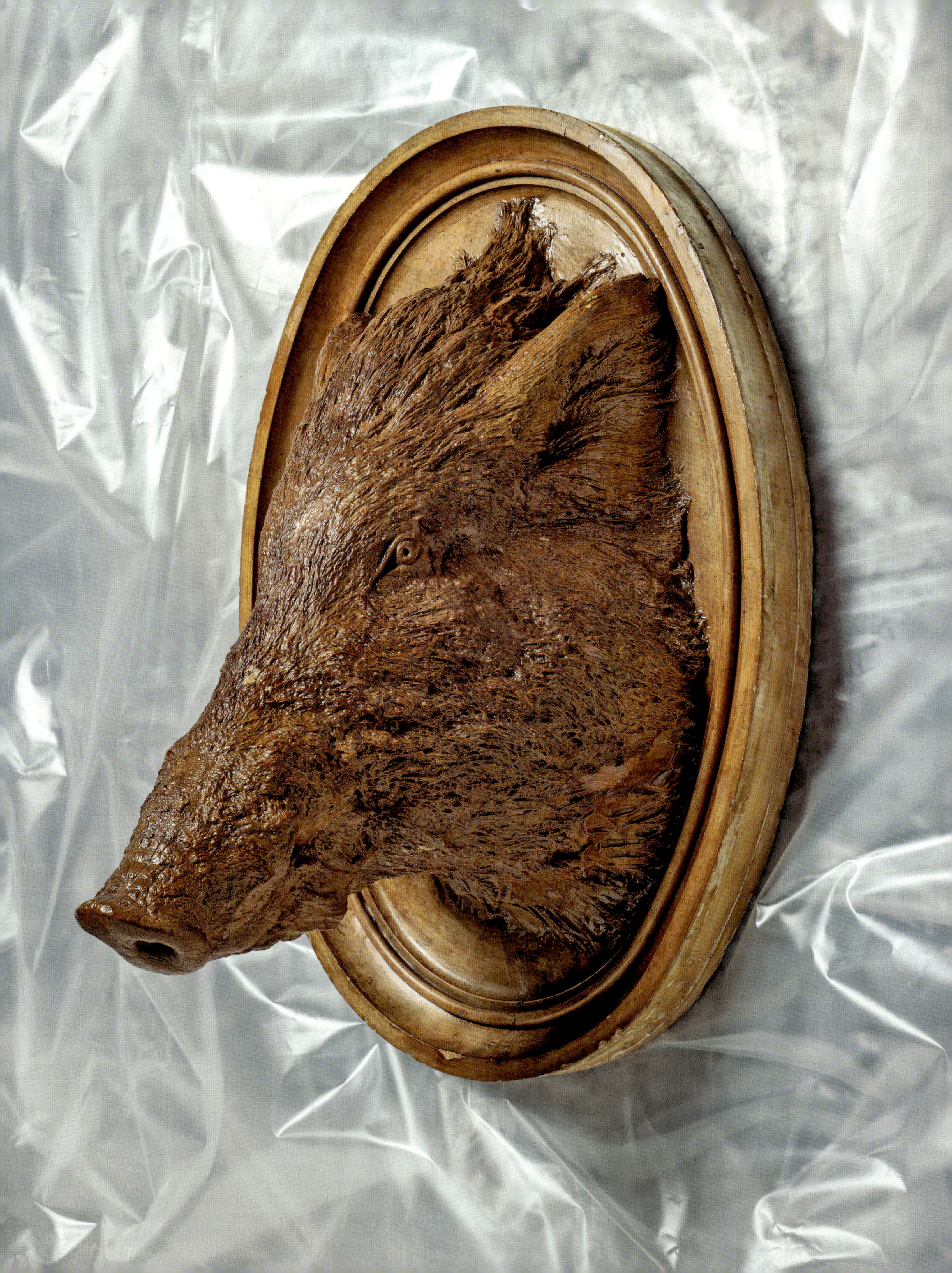

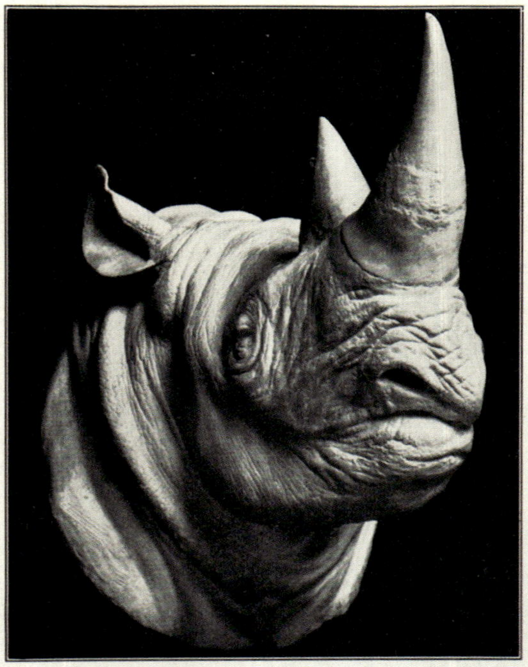

Nashornbulle (Cerathorinus aff. cucullatus Wagn.)
Naturabguß aus der Serengetisteppe

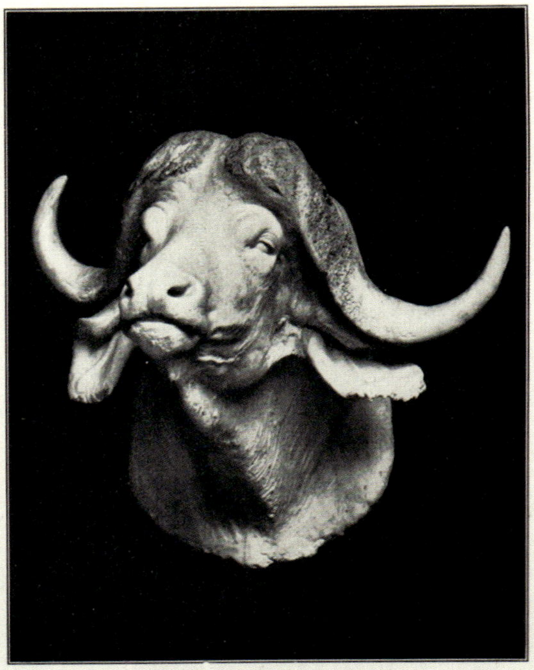

Büffel (Buffelus suahelicus)
Naturabguß aus Umbugwe

>> While I believe that for the study of particulars the zoological garden is not only welcome but even indispensable, direct experience — all things considered — of animals in their native habitat, where you can observe all kinds in great numbers, free and on a daily basis, and to absorb these impressions so to speak automatically, will show an entirely different picture. My intention, in addition to hunting and observing, was to make plaster casts of the quarry. It was presumably the first time anyone tried to gather 'records of nature' in this way. [...] For this purpose I had twenty cart loads of plaster with me, which, when circumstances were propitious (that is, when water was at hand and there were helping hands around and I had the time), frequently allowed me to take facial masks and casts of other body parts from all kinds of animals immediately after the kill. I packed the negatives inside empty food crates, carefully padding them with grass, and surprisingly: not a single piece was lost; for many months, the blacks [sic] carried the crates with this incomprehensible 'medicine' inside until we reached the coast — and in all likelihood they secretly made fun of the crazy 'mzungu' who insisted on covering his meat with this weird sauce before eating it. However, as far as I am concerned, this 'medicine' later cured many a mistake in the studio!

Fritz Behn, 1917

Excerpt from Fritz Behn, *'Haizuru ...': Ein Bildhauer in Afrika*, Munich 1917, pp. 233–35.

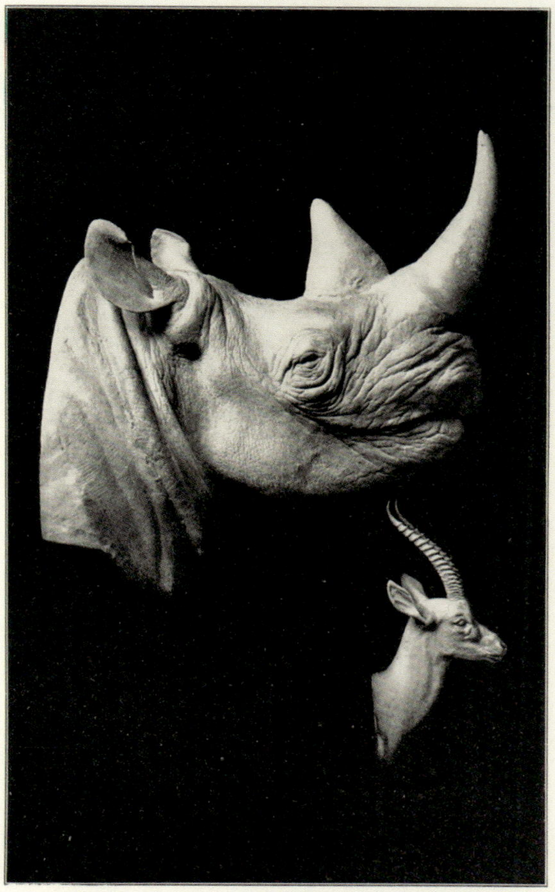

Nashornbulle und männliche Thomsongazelle (Gazella thomsoni Gthr.)
Im richtigen Maßstab zueinander. Naturabgüsse aus der Serengeti

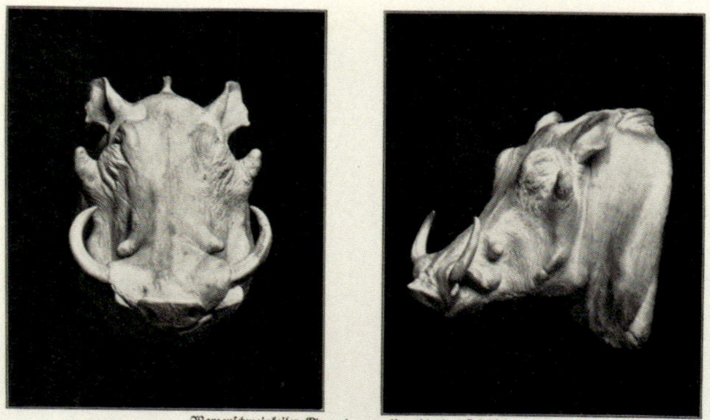

Warzenschweinkeiler (Phacochoerus aff. aethiopicus Schreb.)
Naturabguß aus der Ndassekerasteppe

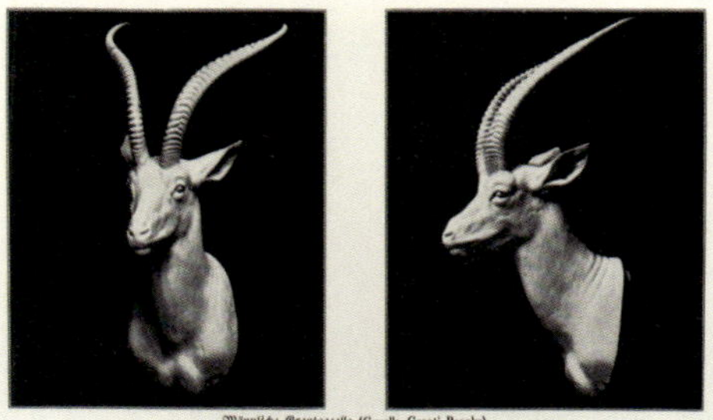

Männliche Grantgazelle (Gazella Granti Brooks)
Naturabguß aus der Serengetisteppe

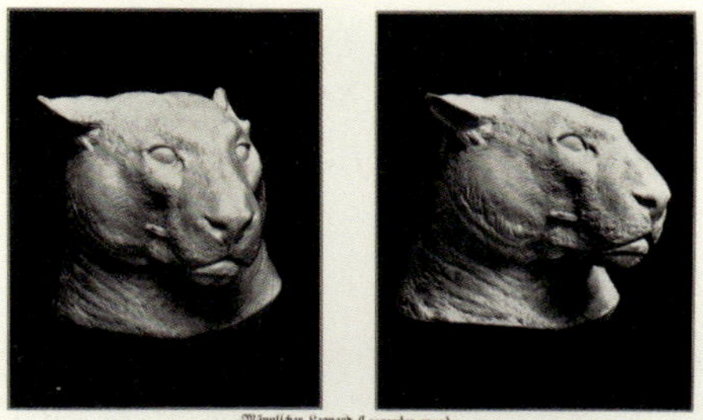

Männlicher Leopard (Leopardus spec.)
Naturabguß aus der Serengetisteppe

Photographs of plaster casts
moulded in Africa between
1907 and 1910 on killed wild game
by sculptor Fritz Behn.
In: *'Haizuru …': Ein Bildhauer in Afrika*,
1917, appendix
Staatliche Museen zu Berlin,
Ethnologisches Museum

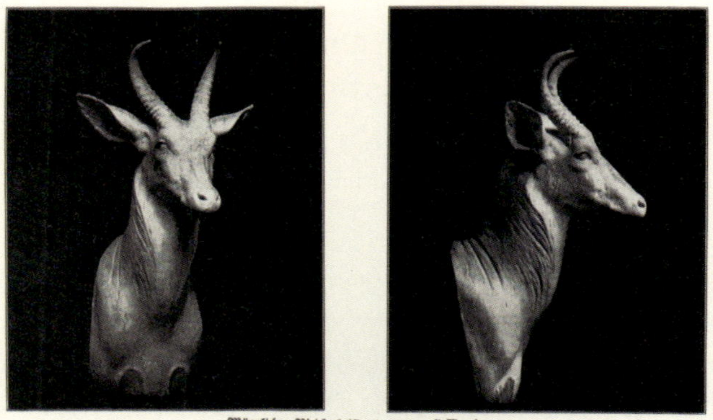

Männlicher Riedbock (Cervicapra wardi Thos.)
Naturabguß aus der Serengetisteppe

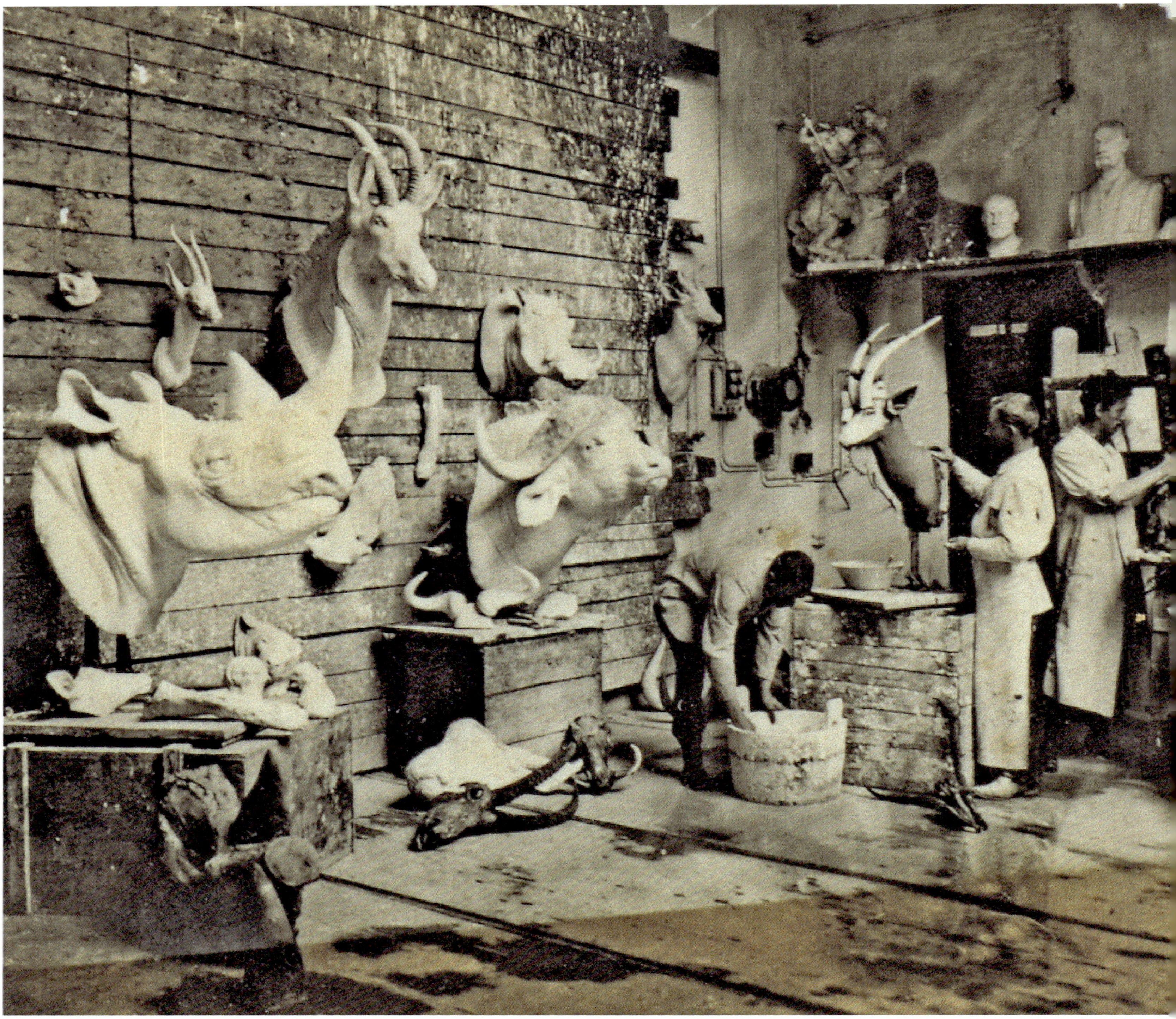

German sculptor Fritz Behn (1878–1970) belonged to those Europeans who visited the colonial countries around the turn of the century with the intention of making plaster casts of the local lifeworld. Between 1907 and 1910 he undertook expeditions lasting several months to today's Tanzania, then part of German East Africa. There, he hunted wild animals and cast them in plaster. For the sculptor aiming at technical perfection, the cast of an animal was tantamount to reality. It was this 'perception of nature' that provided Behn with the basis he needed for his sculptures of lions, antelopes and panthers, which made him one of the foremost animal sculptors of his time. His romanticising enthusiasm for Africa, however, was linked to a colonialist ideology of superiority. Later in his life this morphed into an anti-democratic, national socialist attitude, seriously discrediting his artistic achievements in the process.

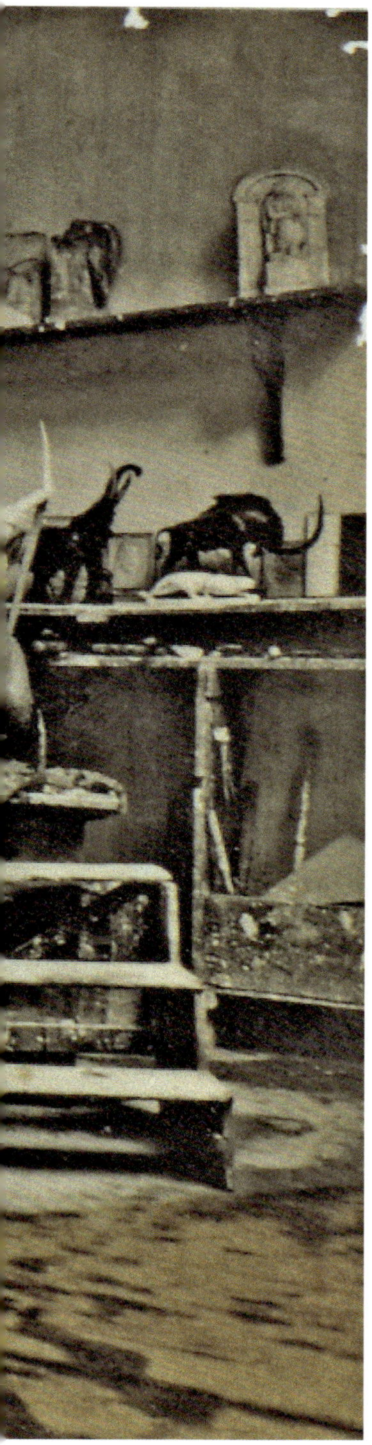

Unknown photographer
Studio of the Sculptor Fritz Behn in Munich, ca. 1910
Nuremberg, Germanisches Nationalmuseum, Deutsches Kunstarchiv

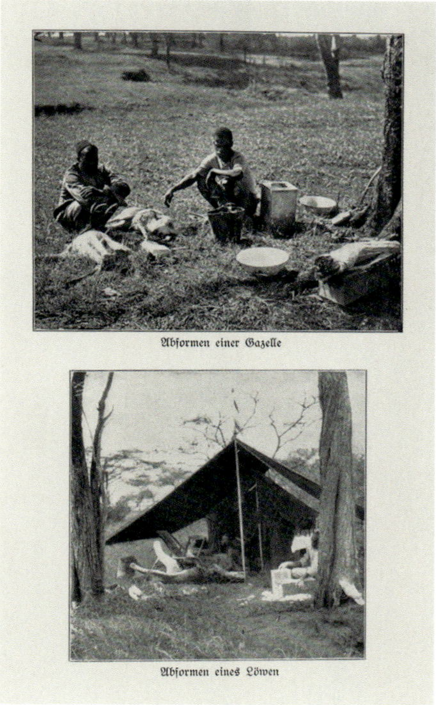

Fritz Behn
'Haizuru …': Ein Bildhauer in Afrika, 1917,
appendix and frontispiece
Staatliche Museen zu Berlin, Ethnologisches Museum

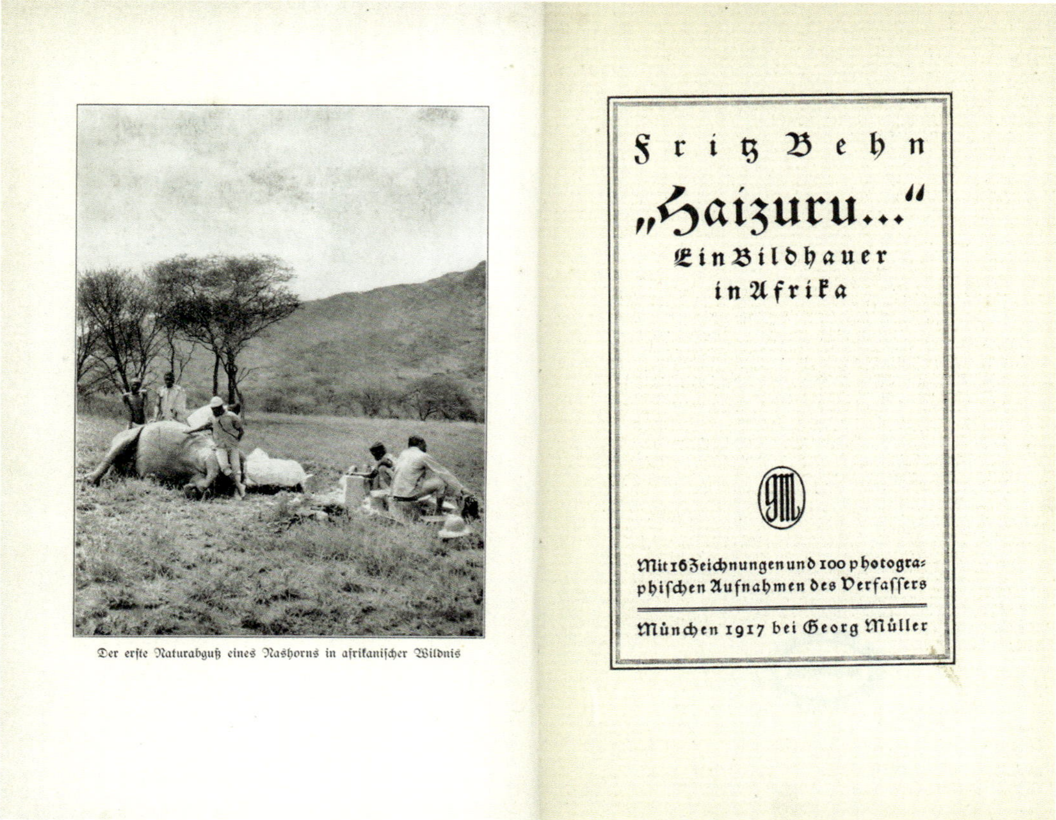

The casts of the braincases of eight mammals (two elephants, a gorilla, an orangutan, a badger, a dog, a gibbon and a seal) have been sold by the Gipsformerei since 1906 and were listed in the sales catalogue of that same year under the section title 'Anthropologisches Material'. In addition to the sales prices from four to twenty Marks depending on size, the catalogue lists the provenance of the braincases under 'Standort des Originals' (Location of the Original) as Anthropological Teaching Aid Collection of the Natural History Museum, Berlin. Cast no. 4075, the braincase of a human being from Central Europe, was part of the series on offer. It also provides insight into the context for creating these objects: physical anthropology, a branch of science that studied the biology of the human being in light of Charles Darwin's teachings, comparing humankind with other animals according to the theory of evolution.

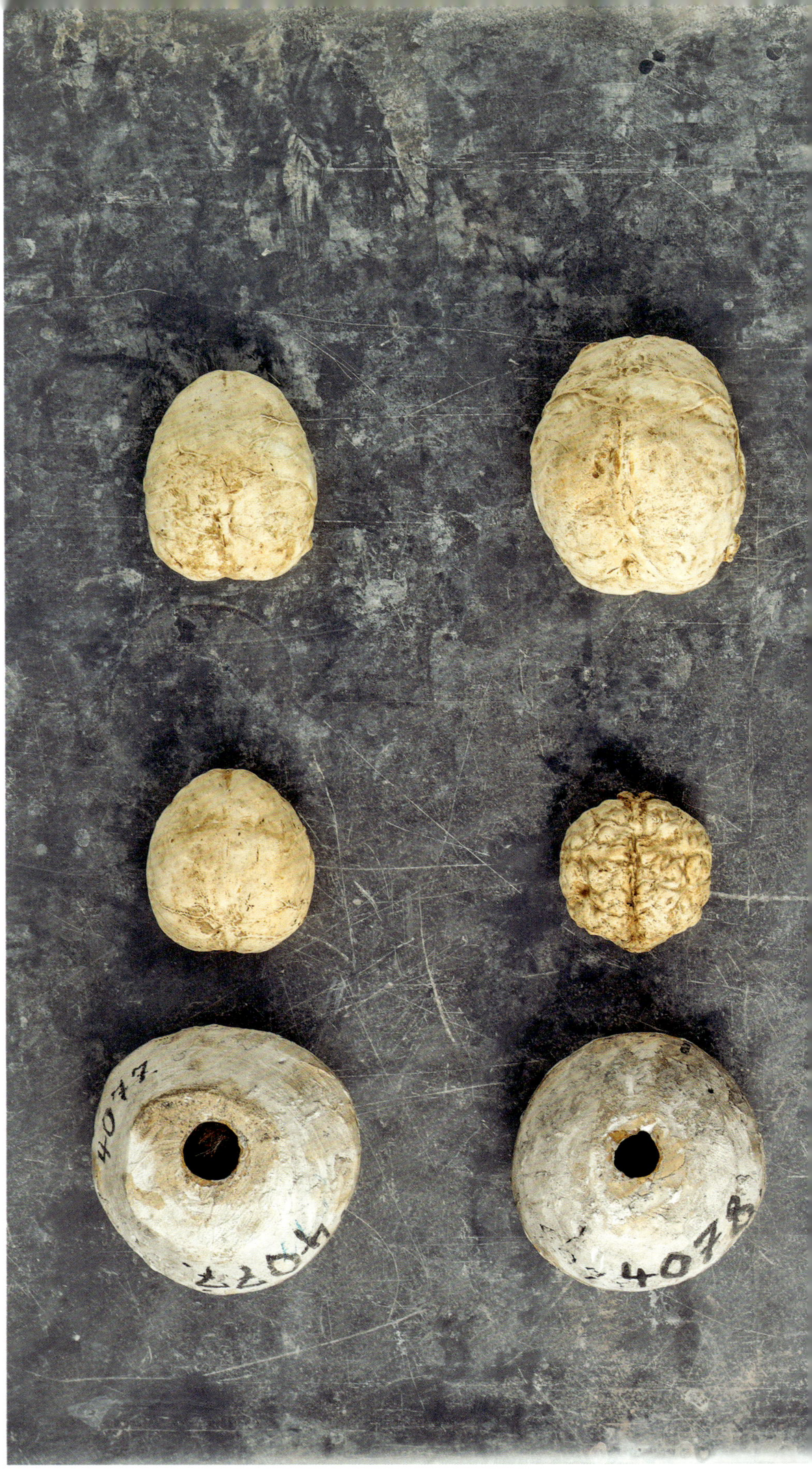

Braincase of a Gorilla

Braincase of a Human ('"Alpine" Race')

Braincase of an Elephant ('Young')

Braincase of an Elephant ('Old')

Braincase of an Orangutan

Braincase of a Seal

Braincase of a Dog

Braincase of a White-Handed Gibbon

Braincase of a Badger

Master models, 1897 and 1906
Staatliche Museen zu Berlin,
Gipsformerei

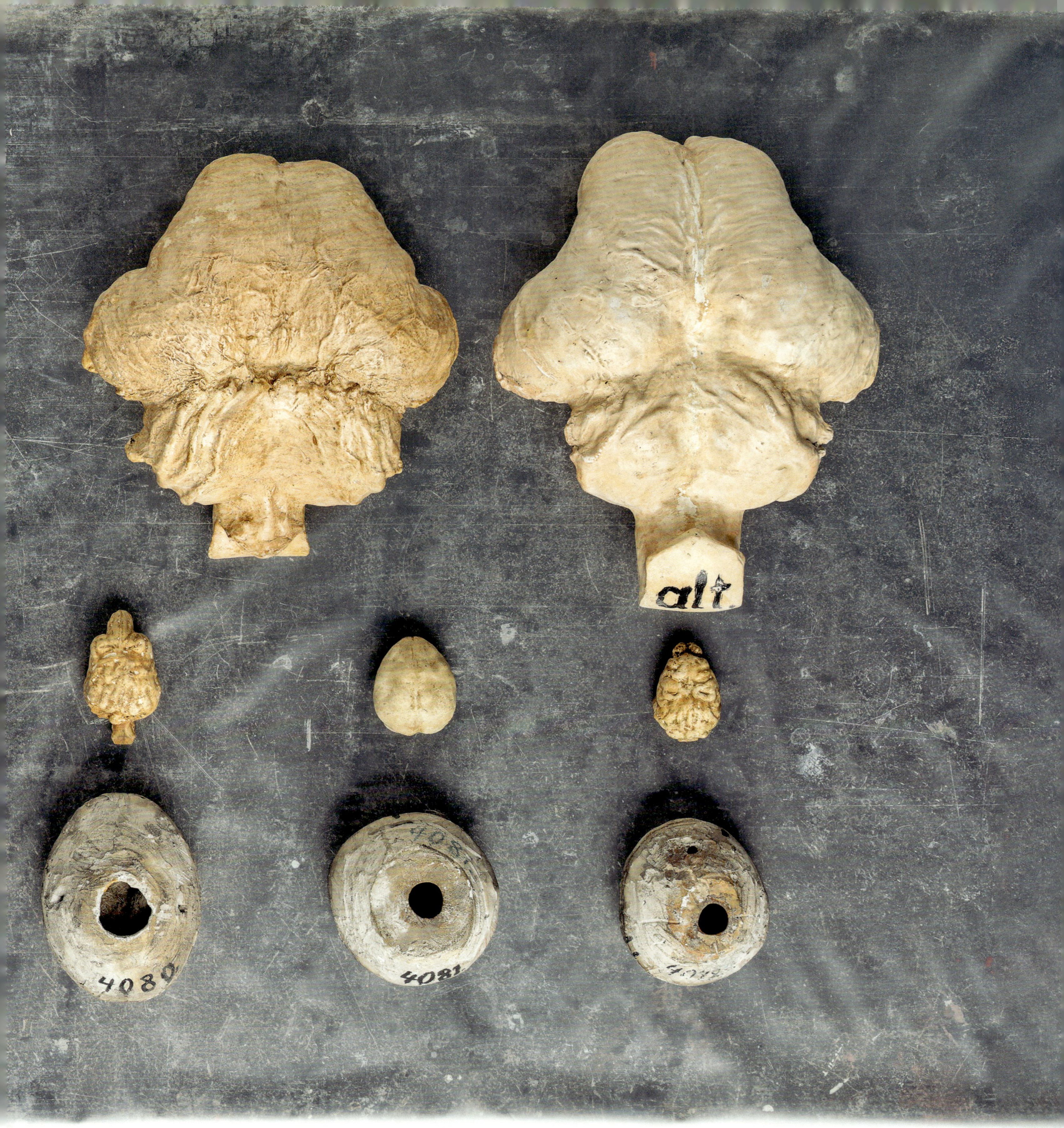
alt
4080
4081

Polar Bear.STL

Samuel Jerichow and Joachim Weinhold

After the untimely death of polar bear Knut in 2011, the main attraction of Zoo Berlin at the time, models of the creature's head and especially of its skull were urgently needed for a press conference. Due to extreme media interest the conference was held at short notice to present provisional findings of the investigations. The creation of a dermoplastic model of the kind on display at the Museum für Naturkunde in Berlin is a relatively time-consuming undertaking and was not possible to achieve until long after the press conference, when further research had yielded final results. A sculpture made with a mould — a routine procedure at the Gipsformerei, Staatliche Museen zu Berlin — would in principle have been possible had there not been such time and technical constraints. This is why the 3D Lab at the Institute of Mathematics at TU Berlin was commissioned with creating a 3D print based on a CT scan. Such production techniques are sometimes referred to as 'rapid prototyping' to emphasise the speed which gives them that extra edge over other manufacturing processes; the term is used less these days since the technologies involved are increasingly heading towards 'rapid manufacturing'.

For a 3D print, specific data sets are needed. They are either constructed by CAD programmes or generated by three-dimensional scanning techniques based on real objects, such as structured light scanning or computed tomography. This type of 'moulding' almost completely dispenses with the need to physically touch the object, which is important for museum exhibits or archaeological finds. While solid lifeless objects are ideal for this process, it becomes more difficult with soft objects — the skin and fur of the polar bear would likely yield to touch and affect the naturalistic rendering. However, a computer tomogram generated for research purposes at the Leibniz Institute for Zoo and Wildlife Research in Berlin provided a basis for the polar bear's 3D print, which could then be realised at short notice and had the added advantage of showing the polar bear's skull as well.

The link between 3D scanning and 3D printing goes beyond the benefit of saving time. Once an object has been digitised, it is available as a file and so can be used in many different ways. Prior to making the print, the object can be scaled up or down easily. This proves especially useful where the size of the object makes direct observation impossible, as in the case of plant seeds or astronomical objects. Digital objects are also easily mirrored, which can be helpful in the reconstruction of some damaged objects (for instance, designing the missing twin of a pair of rear-view mirrors on a vintage car). Digital objects are capable of being distorted, disassembled or fused with others to create new objects. They are also applicable for analysis, such as defining an object's exact centre of gravity or the quality of its surface. A range of measurements can be represented by the digital object, either numerically or as colour diagrams. And in addition to the diversity of scientific applications, there are a great number of applications available for rendering the objects: computers give access to tools that are simply non-existent physically; artistic skills in this procedure are an advantage but not crucial.

The digital object is a 'STL file'. A computer programme dedicated to the purpose of producing this file slices the object into images, which are then processed one by one. An example of such 3D printing technology is plaster printing, which in actual fact is nothing more than 2D inkjet printing realised with layerwise applied polymer plaster powder. The 'ink' in this case is a special binder that glues the plaster particles together. This printing method was used to render the sculptures of the polar bear's skull and head.

Splitting the object up into slice images, a necessary prerequisite for 3D printing, results in visible outcomes, which have advantages and disadvantages that need to be weighed against those of other technologies. The layers are usually 0.1 mm thick and become visible on the surface of the object as fine lines. In the field of art and design these lines are sometimes felt to be a distraction, if they cannot be meaningfully integrated into the design. In most cases they only make themselves felt in small volume objects. Sometimes it makes sense to regrind surfaces because of the roughness of the polymer plaster material; this may result however in the loss of minor details. In any case, the fragility of the polymer plaster requires a final coating with cyanoacrylate or epoxy resin.

The surface properties of plaster casts from the Gipsformerei are in an entirely different league to that of the polymer plaster 3D print. Yet it would have been impossible to make a physical impression of the polar bear without this method. The collaboration of the 3D Lab with the Gipsformerei over many years has made it clear again and again that traditional and modern replication techniques are not mutually exclusive, nor are they in competition with one another. They supplement each other in a way that is profitable for both.

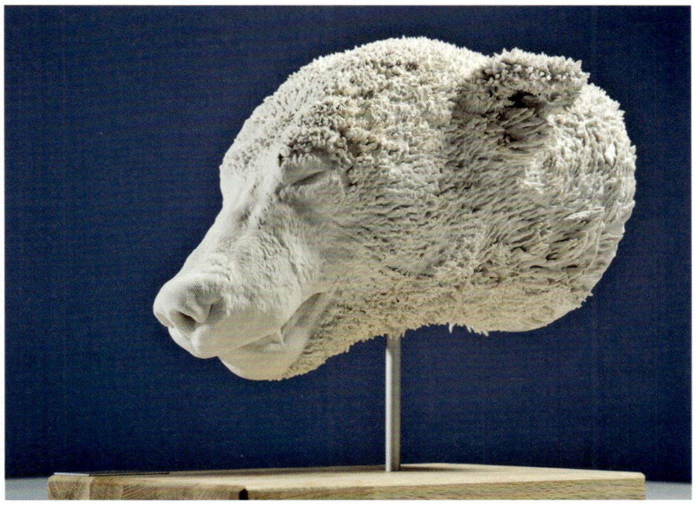

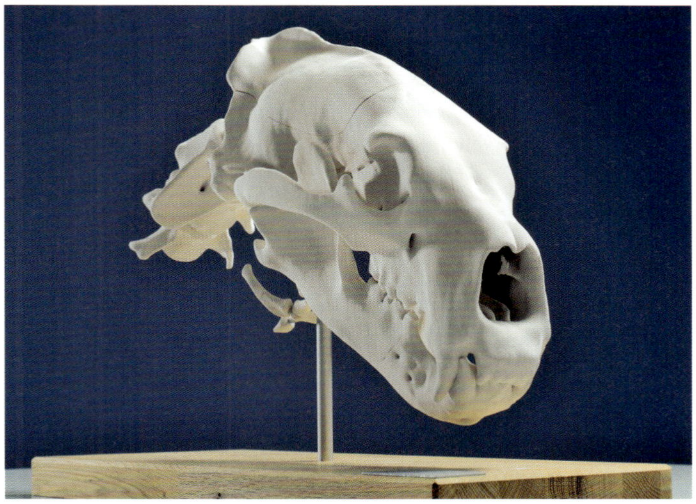

Head and Skull of Polar Bear Knut
3D prints on the basis of a computer tomography, 2011
3D Labor am Institut für Mathematik
Leibniz-Institut für Zoo- und Wildtierforschung, Berlin

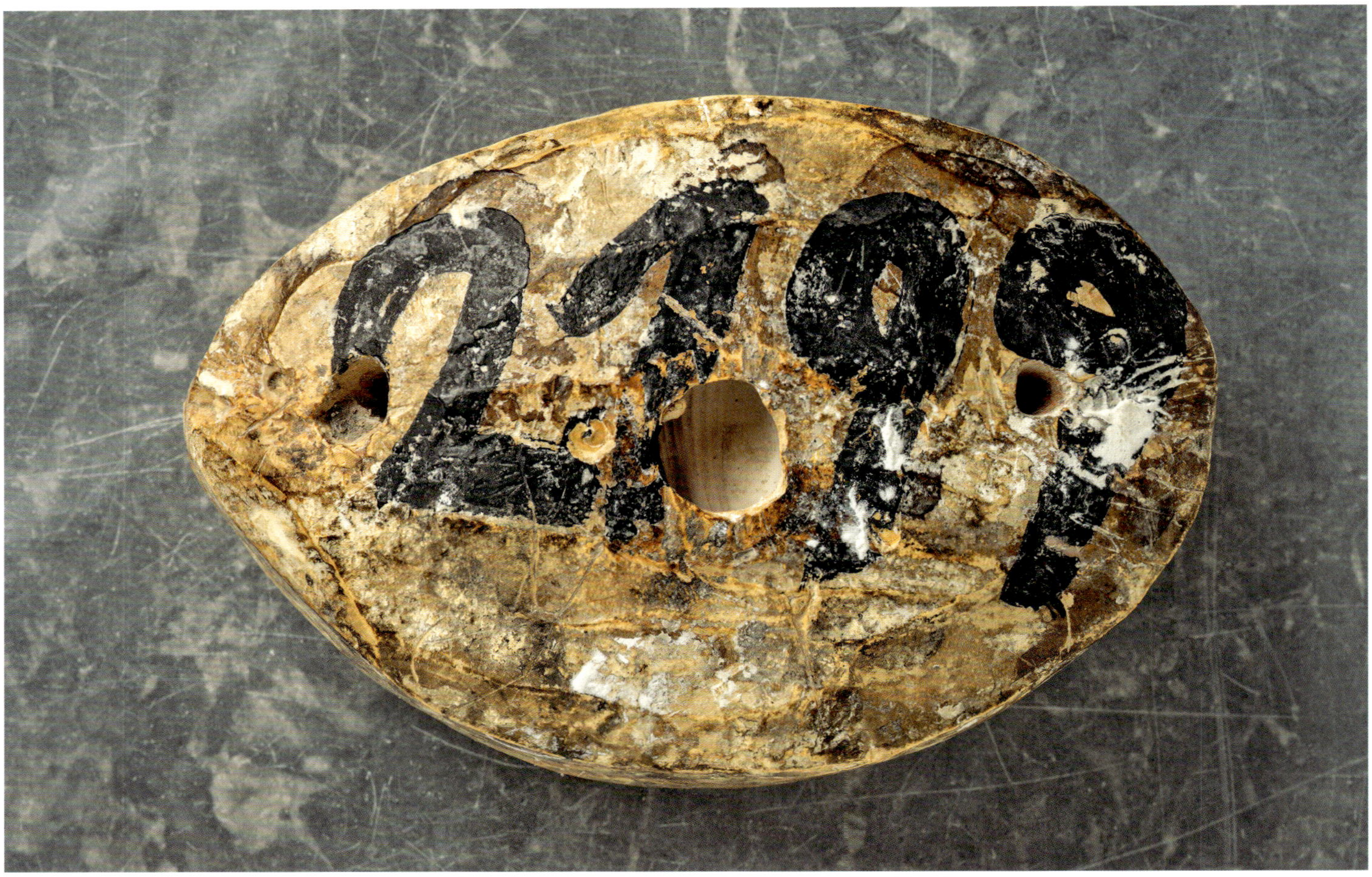
2199

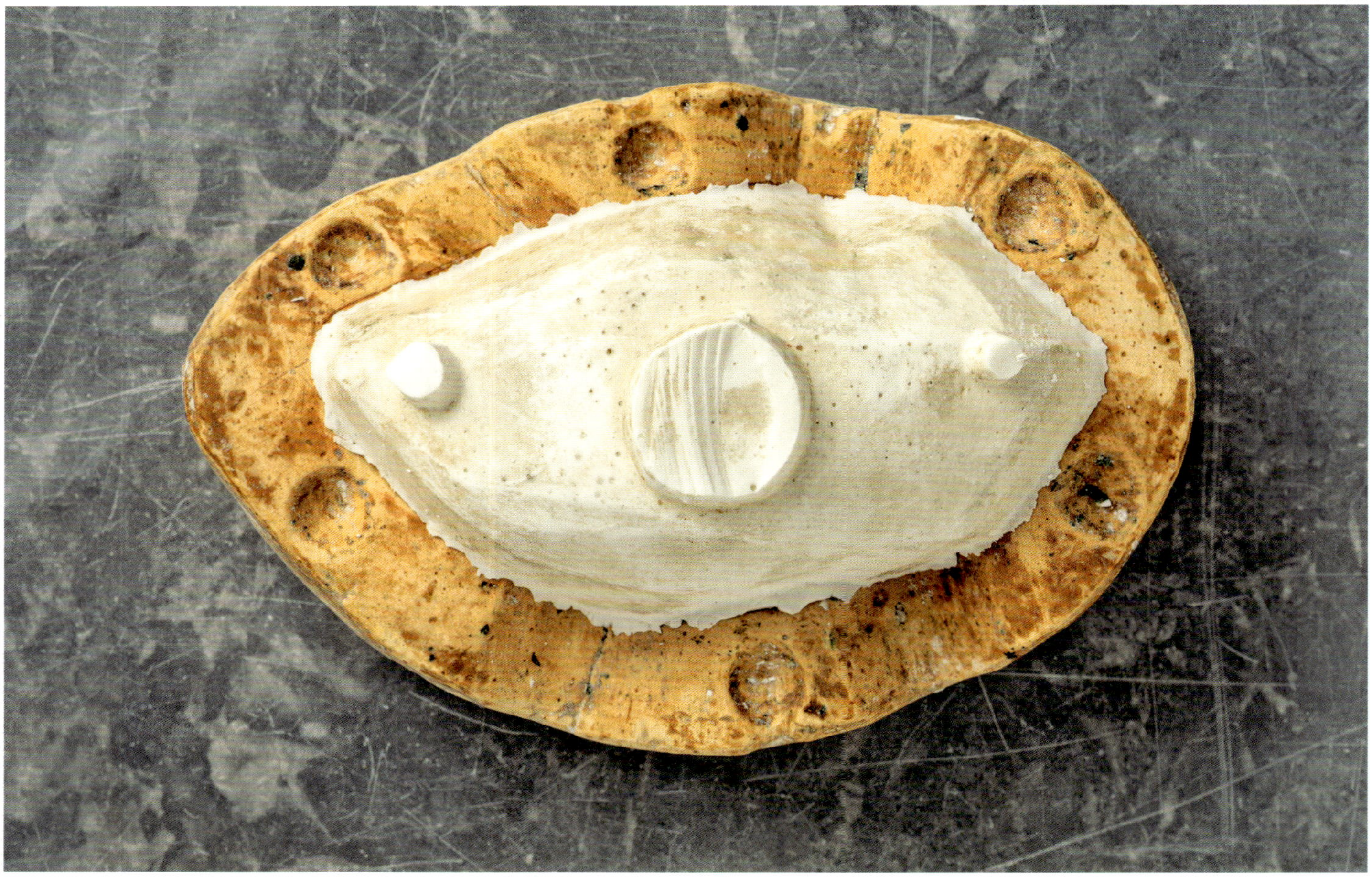

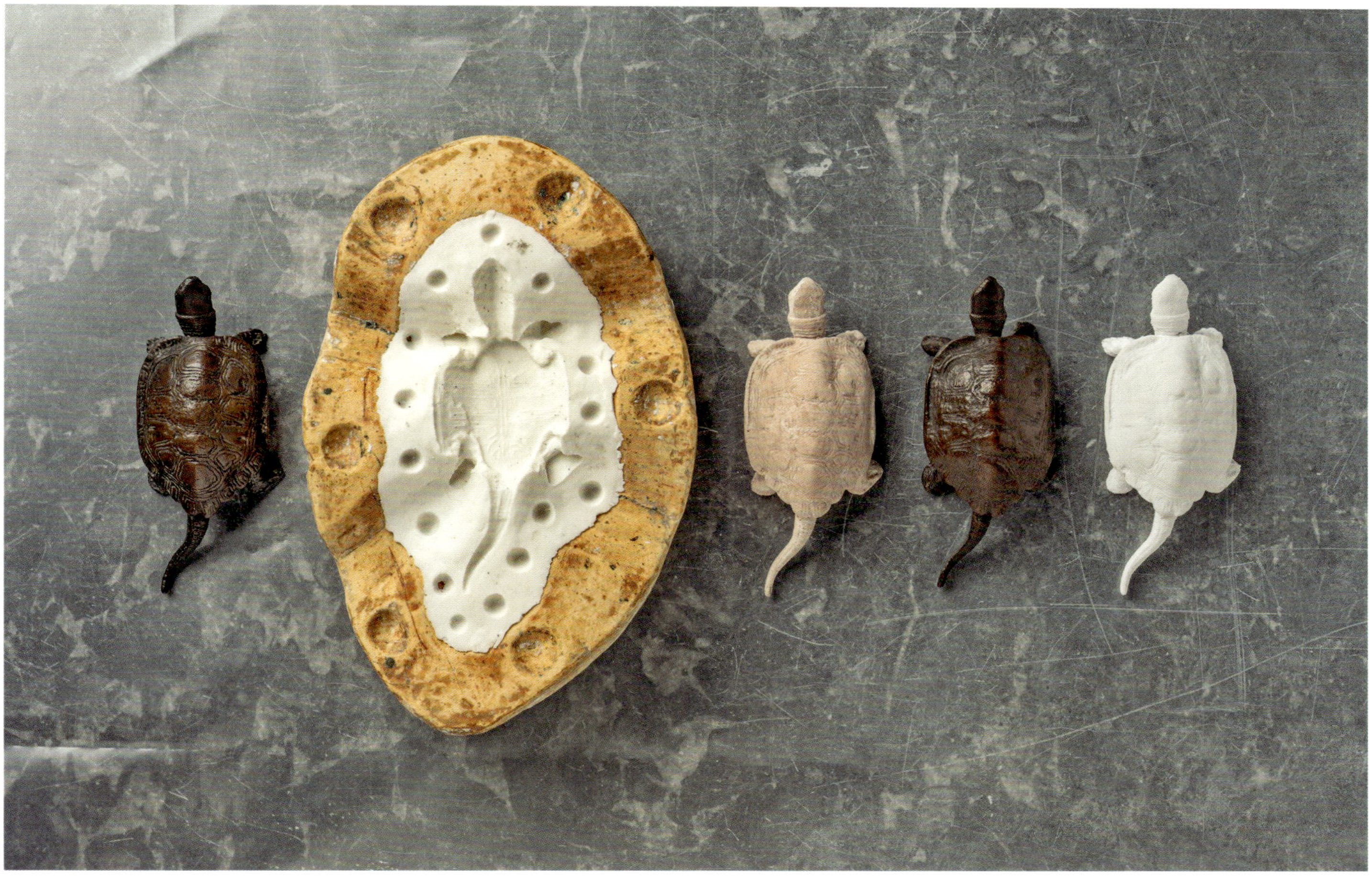

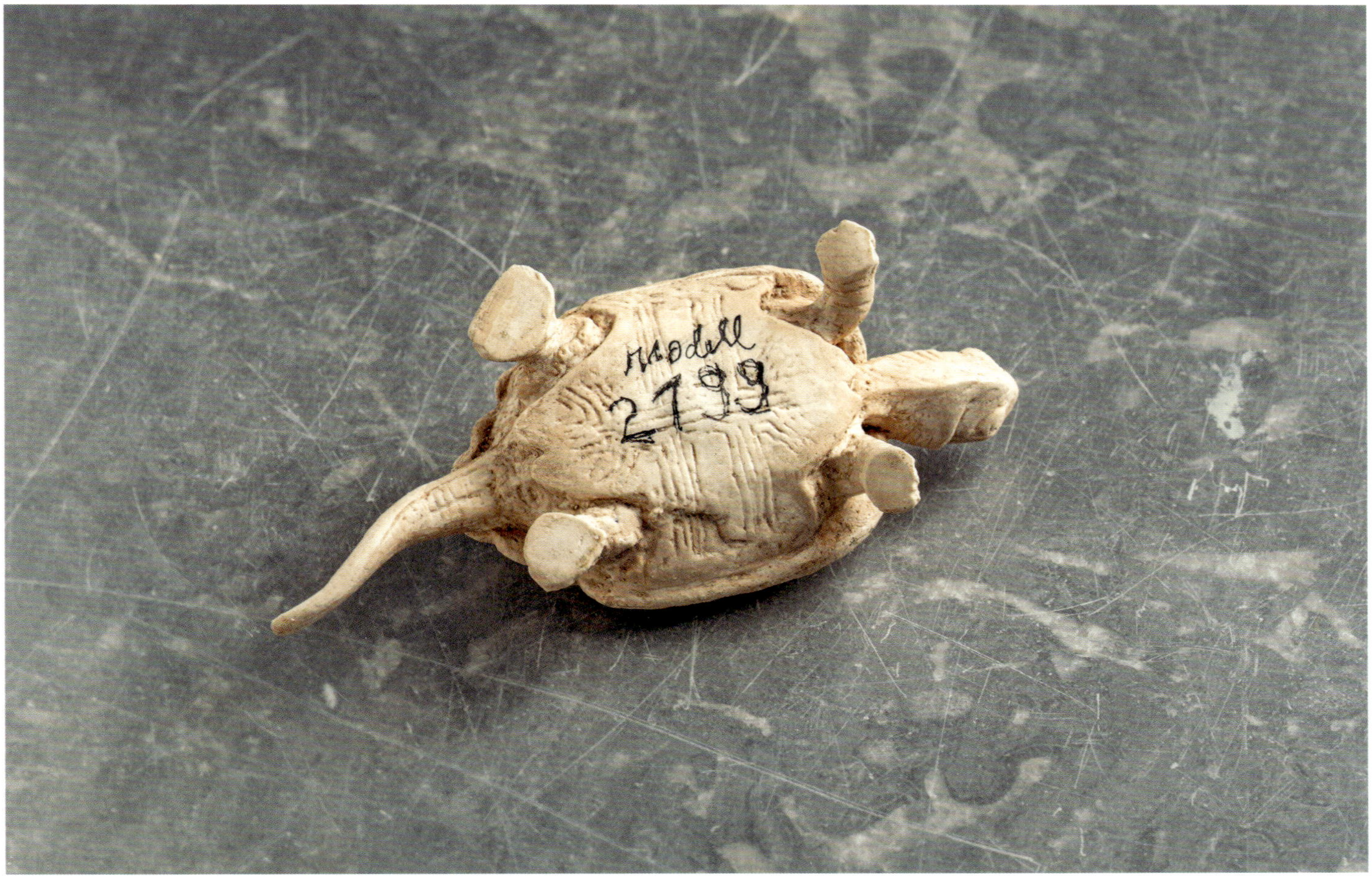
Modell
2799

Previous page

From the 'Original' to the 'Copy'
Bronze cast by Andrea Briosco (Il Riccio), with silicone form in mother mould, master model, painting model and raw casting
Staatliche Museen zu Berlin, Skulpturensammlung und Museum für Byzantinische Kunst, Gipsformerei

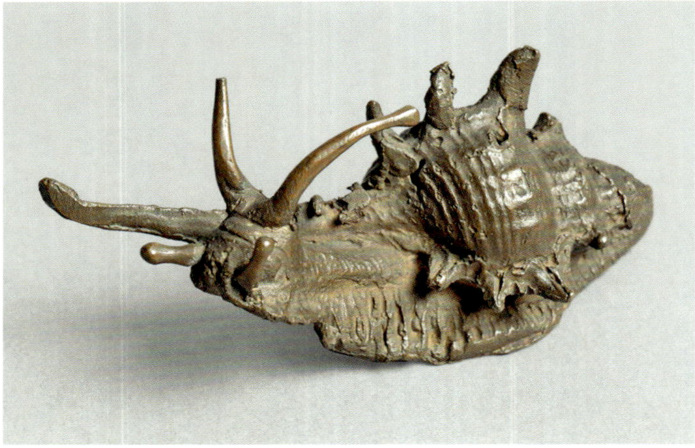

Unknown artist
Sea Snail, Padua,
early 16th century
Kunsthistorisches Museum Wien, Kunstkammer

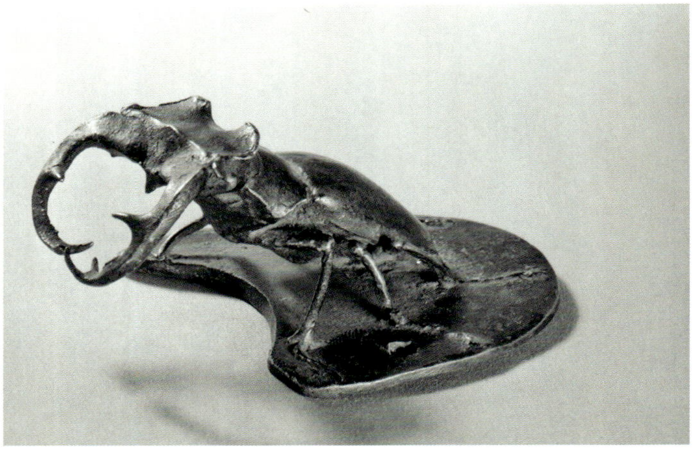

Andrea Briosco (Il Riccio)
Stag Beetle, Padua,
early 16th century
Staatliche Museen zu Berlin, Skulpturensammlung und Museum für Byzantinische Kunst

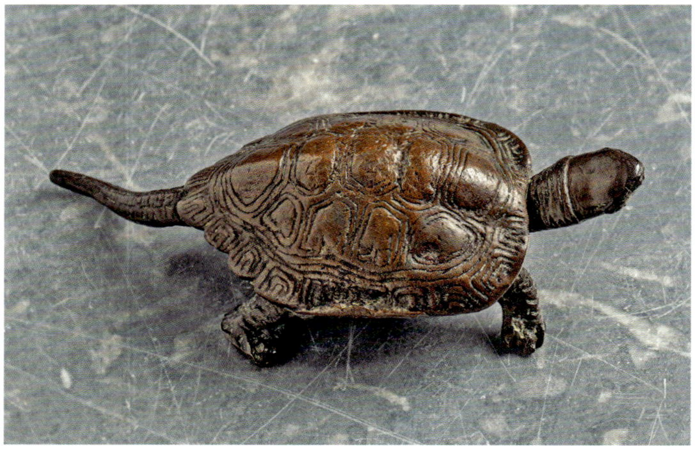

Andrea Briosco (Il Riccio)
Tortoise, Padua,
early 16th century
Staatliche Museen zu Berlin, Skulpturensammlung und Museum für Byzantinische Kunst

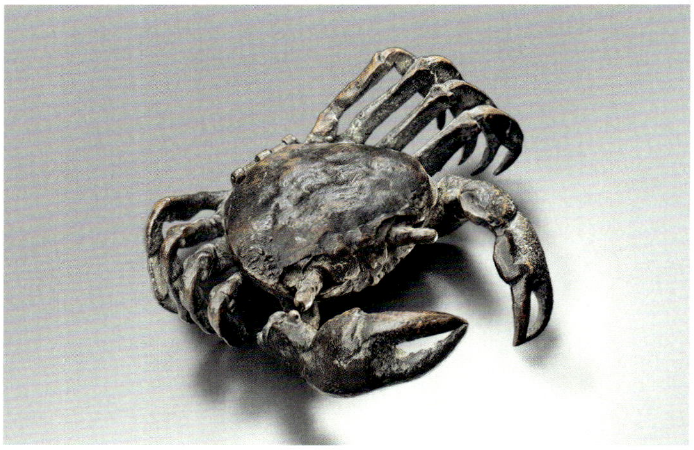

Andrea Briosco (Il Riccio)
Brown Crab, Padua,
early 16th century
Staatliche Museen zu Berlin, Skulpturensammlung und Museum für Byzantinische Kunst

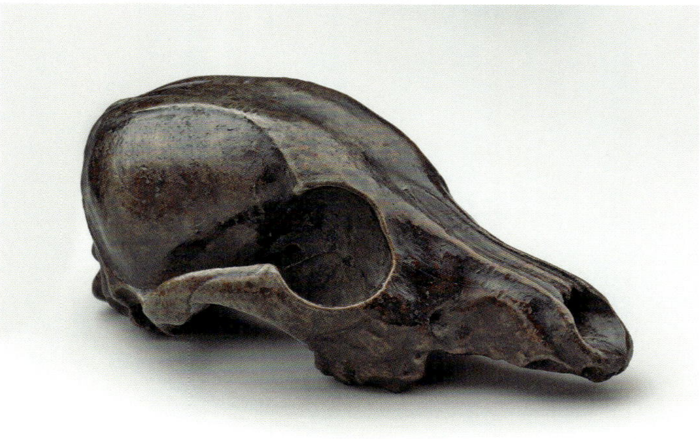

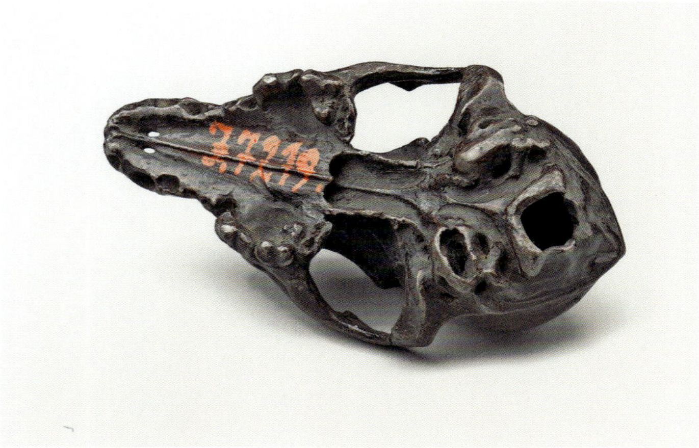

Unknown artist
Skull of a Foxhound,
Padua or Venice, 16th century
Staatliche Museen zu Berlin,
Skulpturensammlung und Museum
für Byzantinische Kunst

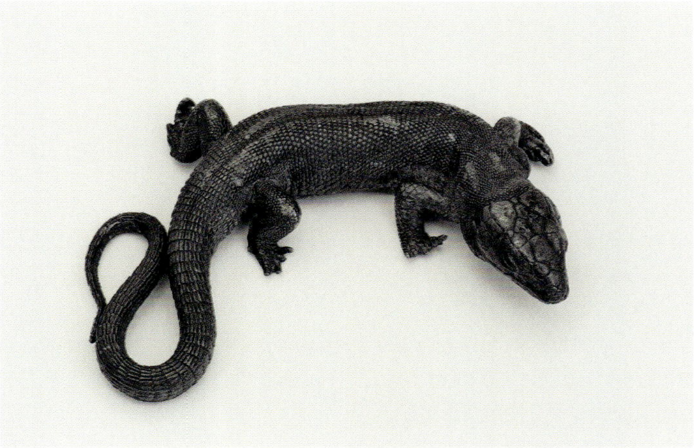

Wenzel Jamnitzer
Lizard, Nuremberg,
mid-16th century
Staatliche Museen zu Berlin,
Kunstgewerbemuseum

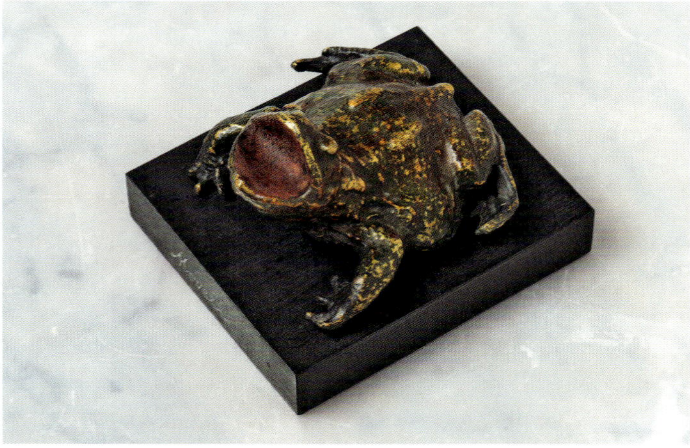

After Andrea Briosco (Il Riccio)
Toad, Padua, early 16th century
Painting model, 1933
Staatliche Museen zu Berlin,
Gipsformerei

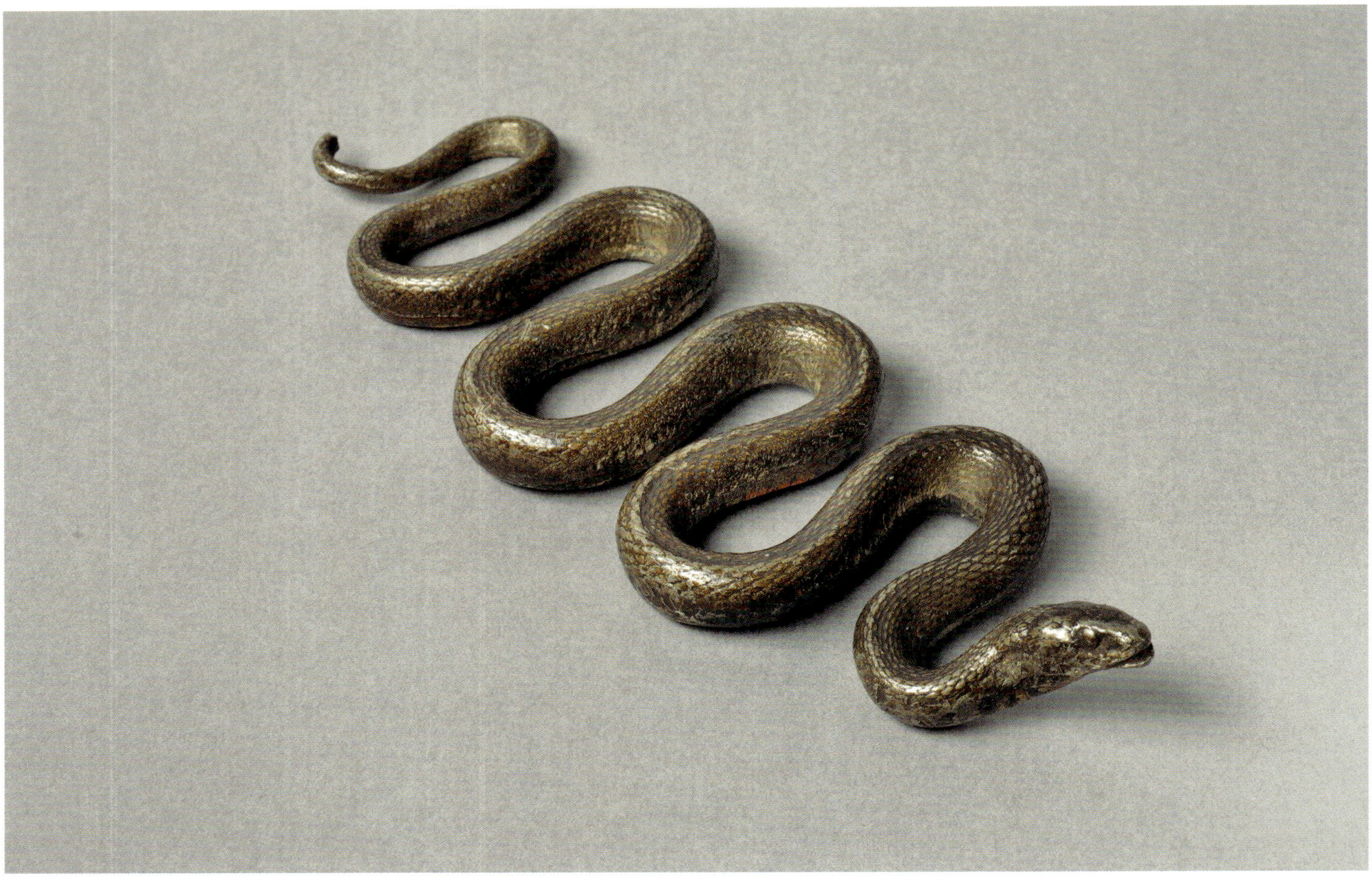

Unknown artist
Snake, Padua,
early 16th century
Kunsthistorisches Museum
Wien, Kunstkammer

Around 1400 the sculptor Cennino Cennini (ca. 1370–1440) elaborates on how to take casts of ‘a bird, a beast, or any kind of animal or fish’ in his *Il Libro dell’Arte* (A Treatise on Painting, see pp. 56–59). Halfway between a medieval workshop manual and an early modern treatise on art, this book, presumably written in Padua, invokes antiquity and advances the claim that art’s highest calling is the imitation of nature. Paduan sculptor Andrea Briosco (1470–1532, also known as ‘Il Riccio’), must have been acquainted with the book; his work comprises numerous bronze casts of snakes, lizards, toads and crabs. Such casts of animals attest to a new kind of scientific interest and to a progressive concept of art relative to the conventions of the quattrocento. They appear in Northern Italy and later north of the Alps as either simple workshop models, functional forms (made into inkwells, for instance) or elaborate handcrafted objects (such as oil lamps and goblets). An artist from German lands who immediately comes to mind is the Nuremberg goldsmith Wenzel Jamnitzer (1508–1585), who transformed small animals and plants into artworks with masterly refinement. The bronze, silver and lead animal casts on display in the exhibition are like three-dimensional snapshots of nature. On closer inspection, however, it is clear that it would have taken both considerable effort and artistic input to place and stage the lifeless animals, to cast the fragile scales of a lizard or the finely articulated extremities of a stag beetle. Accordingly, casts after nature are by no means purely scientific or objective replications of reality. They are the result of subjective, interpretative acts carried out by creative individuals.

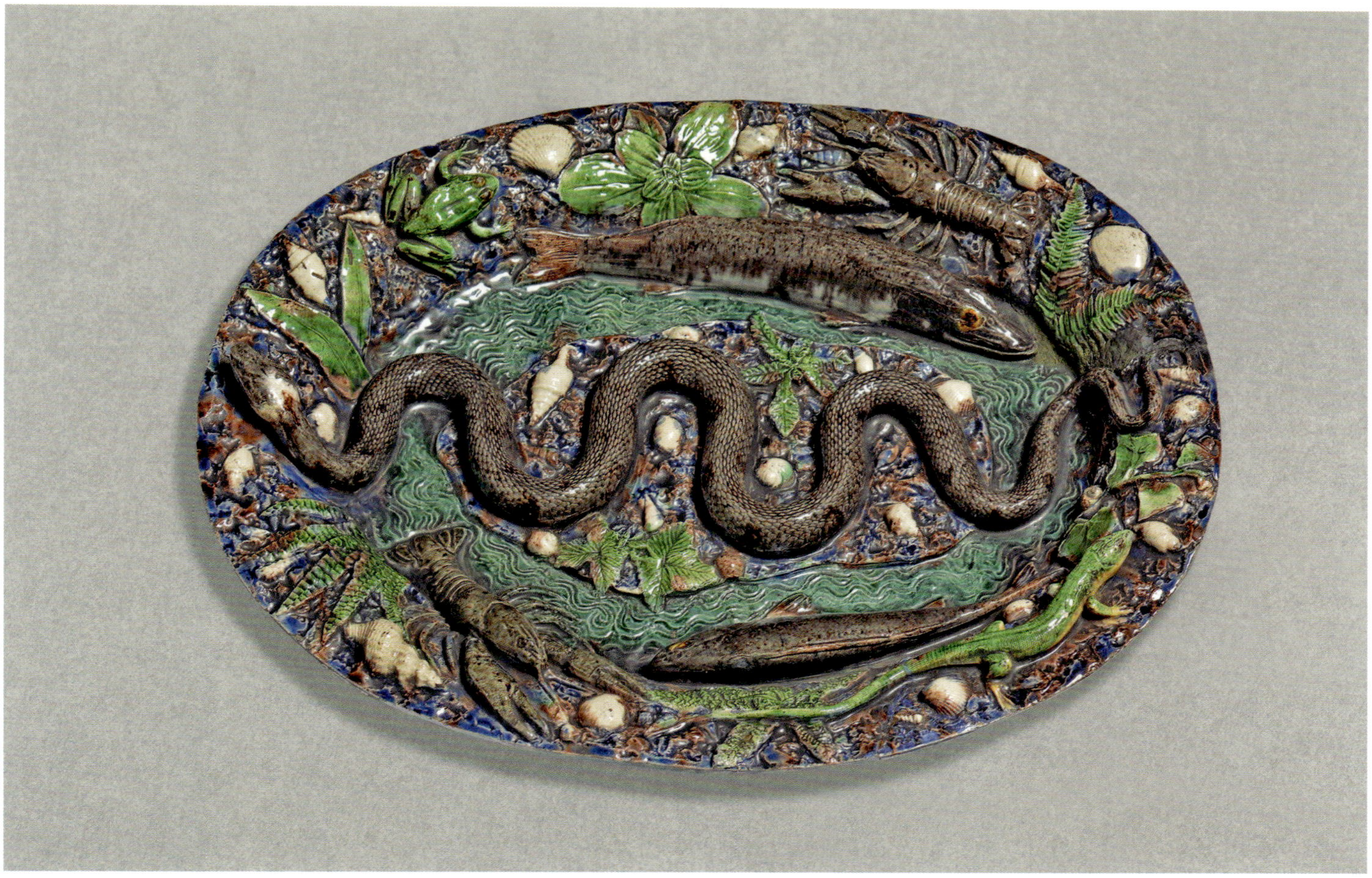

Bernard Palissy
Bowl, late 16th century
Museum für Kunst
und Gewerbe Hamburg

France, in addition to Italy and Germany, was another centre for the modern production of exquisite casts after nature. Ceramicist Bernard Palissy (1510–1589) is commonly credited with inventing what is known as *rustiques figulines*: ceramic casts of snakes, lizards, frogs, fishes and plants integrated into painstakingly designed ornamental tableware. According to hearsay, Palissy killed these small animals in a mixture of vinegar and urine. He then fixed them into a desired posture — usually in mid-movement — with needles, brushed them over with olive oil and applied the plaster. The resulting negative was filled with liquid clay. The casts were mounted on separately produced footed bowls, platters or jugs; a mould was then made of this arrangement and used as the basis for a ceramic cast. Palissy is most famous for his coloured lead glazings, the production details of which he kept a jealously guarded secret. The result rendered still lifes so close to nature that they gave the impression of the actual animal having been glazed. Palissy's production technique is often mentioned in the same breath as that of the della Robbias, a family of sculptors operating an early industrial workshop in Florence during the fifteenth and sixteenth centuries. However, the glazed terracottas mass-produced by the della Robbias do not come anywhere close to Palissy's finely articulated ceramics. The *rustiques figulines* attracted imitators and copyists right up until the twentieth century and engendered committed Palissy revivals during the Arts and Crafts Movement of the nineteenth century.

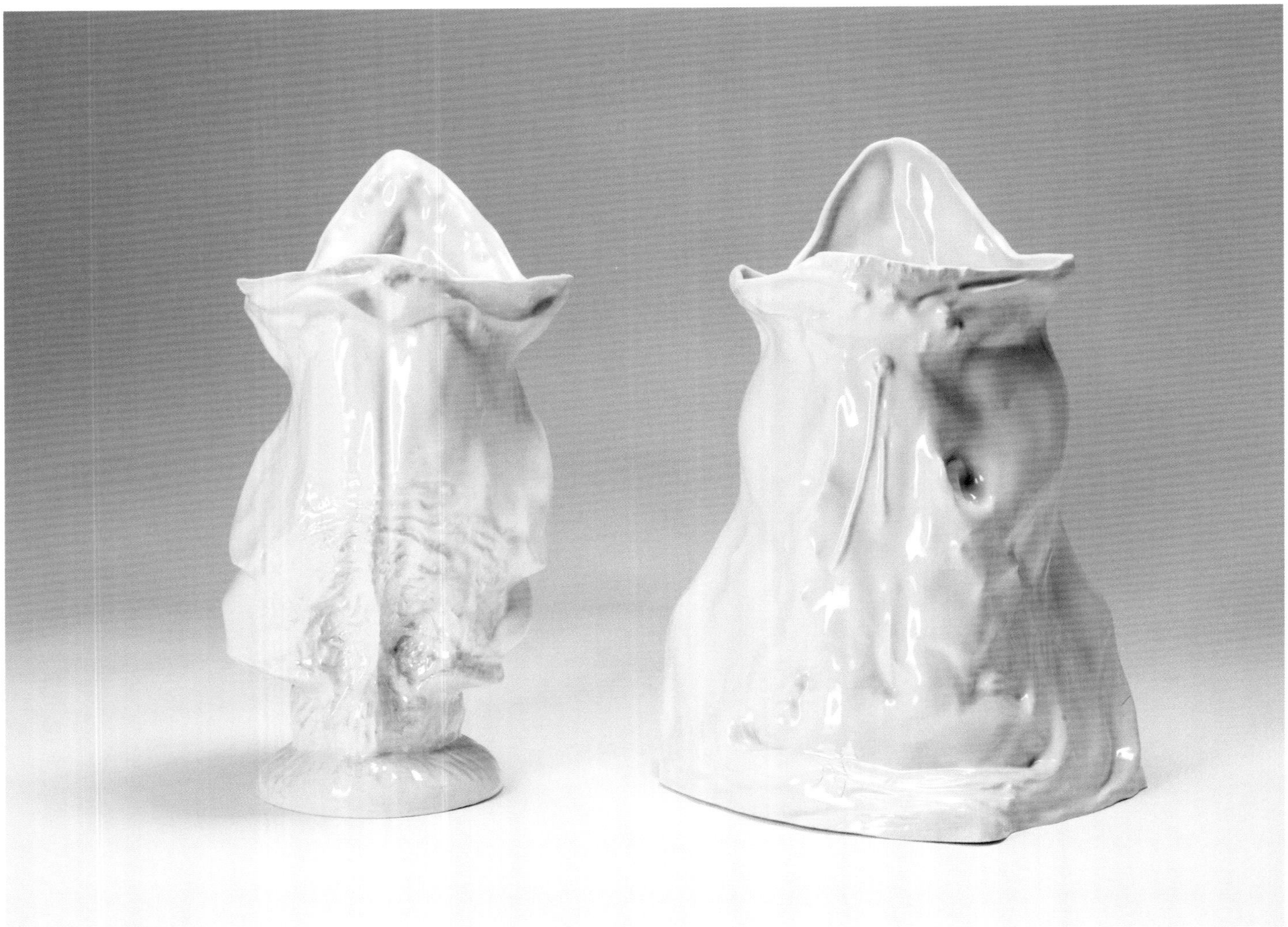

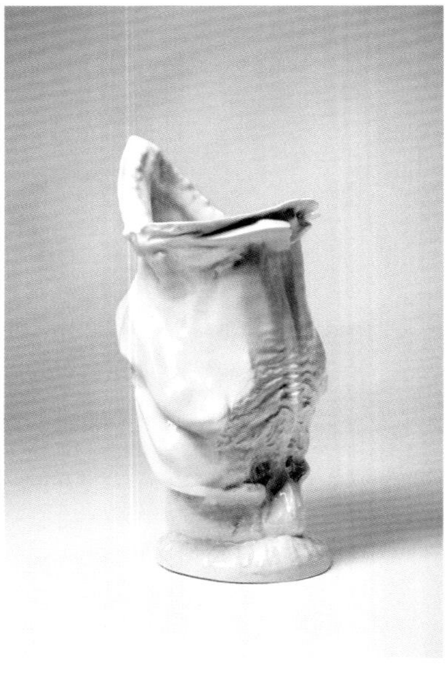

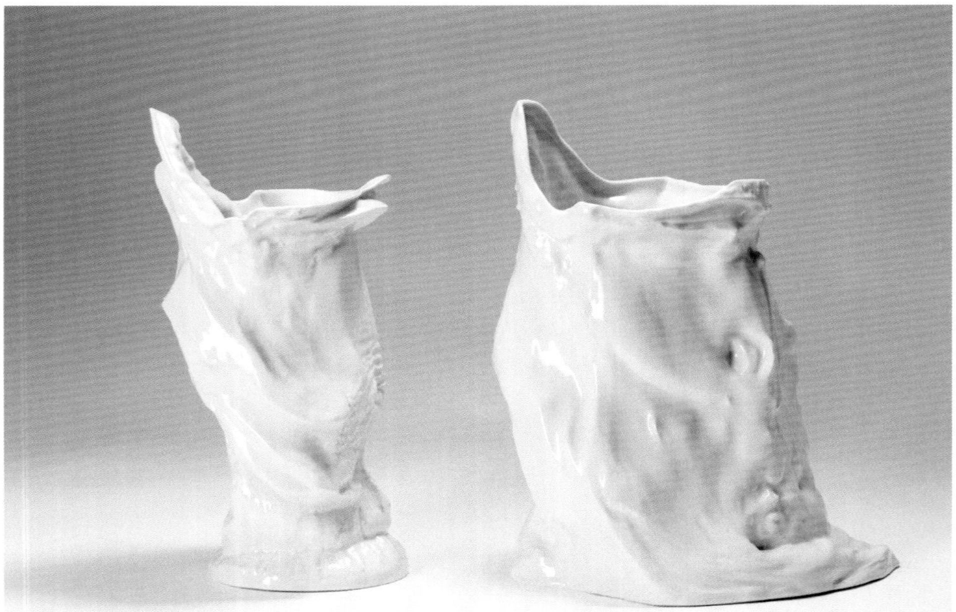

Maria Volokhova
Pearlescence IN and
Pearlescence OUT, 2016
Courtesy of the artist

Pearlescence consists of two vase bodies based on the double casting of the head of a monkfish. Despite its reputation as the epitome of ugliness, the monkfish is a delicacy. Its tail — tiny compared to its head — is an expensive delicacy, whereas the head almost comes for free. Having come across this extraordinary maritime creature at the fish counter of Kaufhaus des Westens in Berlin, I bought the head and took it back to my workshop. As I examined the creature more closely, I became fascinated with the inner life that its open throat revealed. Peering into the fish's mouth, a hollow space surrounded by beautiful, soft structures appeared. As one can not grasp all this beauty just by looking at it, I came up with the idea of taking moulds of the fish, from both inside and out. What interests me most is the aesthetic of ugliness, symbolised in this case by the monstrosity of the monkfish, as well as turning inside out the inner appearances and processes of things. I am fascinated by structures and the beauty of certain phenomena to be found in nature, even though they may not commonly be considered aesthetically valuable. Porcelain is an exquisite material steeped in tradition, which contrasts form and content in fascinating ways. In this project, I tried to avoid both artistic exaggerations and simplifications and to rather show nature's creations as I find them. Since I would never be able to model natural structures with the same degree of precision as nature has made them, I consider myself fortunate for being able to resort to the technique of casting.

Maria Volokhova, artist

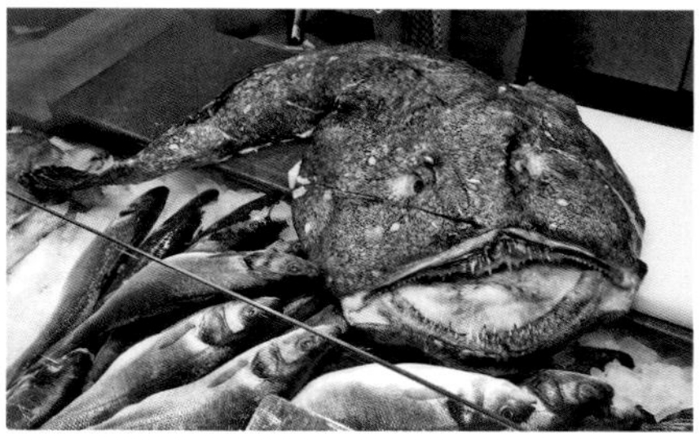
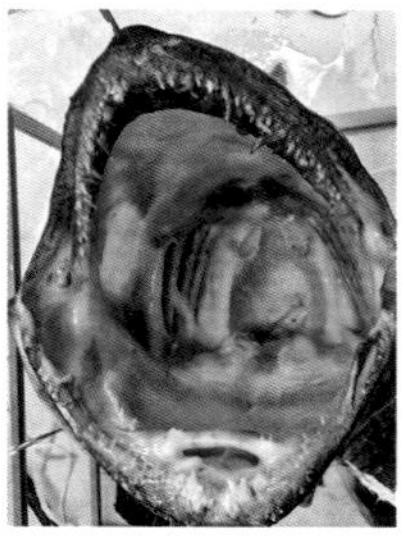
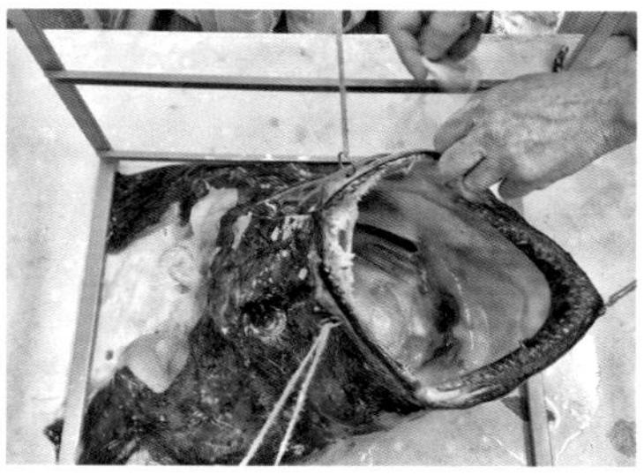
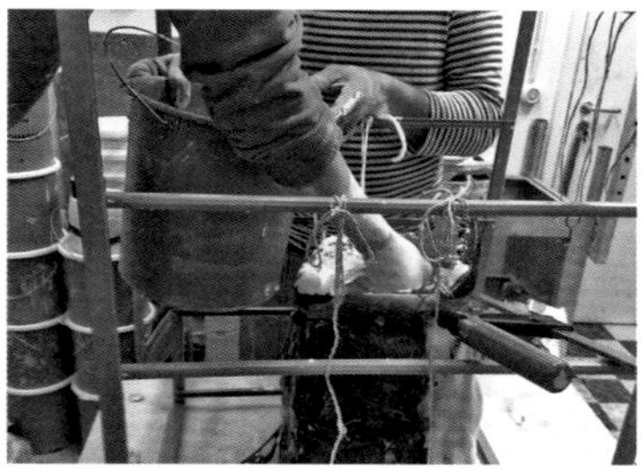
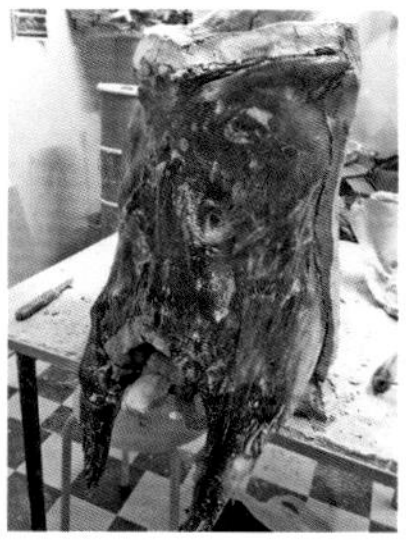
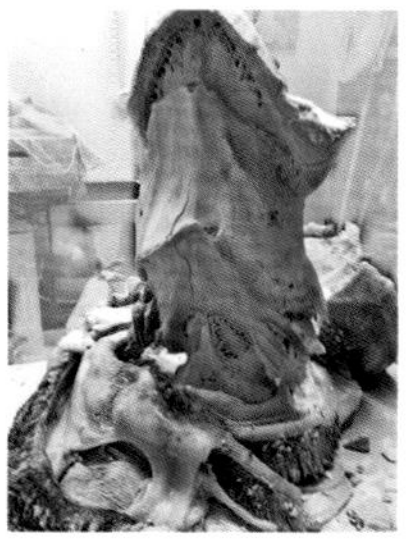
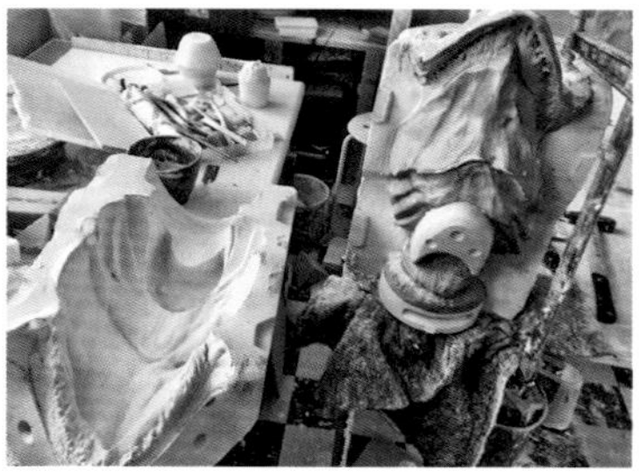
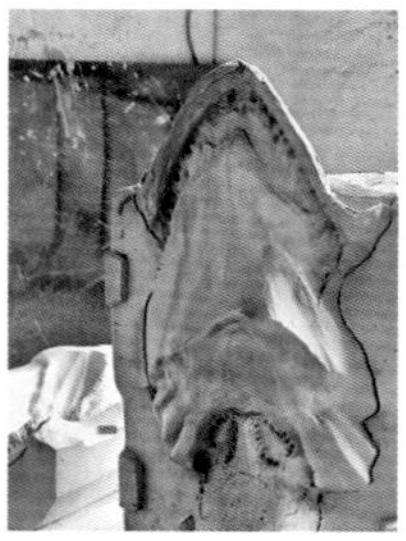
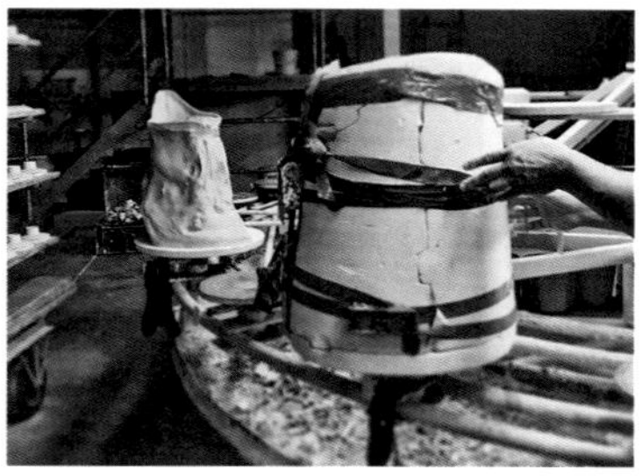

After Nature, Near Nature? The Plant Casts from Moritz Meurer's Collection of Teaching Aids

Angela Nikolai

The supplement of the November/December 1891 edition of the *Verkündigungsblatt des Verbandes deutscher Kunstgewerbevereine* features the review of a special exhibition in the atrium of the Königliches Kunstgewerbemuseum Berlin, which at the time was housed — and had been since 1881 — in the Martin-Gropius-Bau alongside its teaching institute, the so-called *Unterrichtsanstalt*. The exhibition presented samples of works made by students and two- and three-dimensional teaching aids. On the three-dimensional models, the reviewer Ferdinand Moser (1859–1930) had this to say: 'The vexed issue regarding the availability of models which merciless winter used to confront us with in classes devoted to drawing from nature seems to have ceased to be a direct existential question: what was on display in Berlin, over and above a great number of pressed and preserved natural forms, was a collection of splendid bronze casts and highly perfected metallised forms of plants and animals.'[1]

Even though this is just a short quote, it remains intriguing for several reasons. First, the focus is on bronze casts of leaves, buds and plant stems — a small number of which has survived in the archive of the Universität der Künste Berlin; some of them are on display in this exhibition.[2] Moser briefly touches on the context of their origins, too: the study of plant life in drawing class, a highly desirable complement to arts and crafts education which was called for with increasing urgency in the late nineteenth century. This must be seen against the backdrop of efforts to reform training in the applied arts[3] to improve standards in tuition, with the ultimate goal of raising the overall aesthetic quality of manufactured items. The study of nature was supposed to facilitate this development. What the focus on plant forms was hoping to achieve was an up-to-date, organic idiom of style, an autonomy of design and an end to the dominant practice of copying as a design strategy.

The objects on display were meant to ensure that the study of nature — a somewhat ambitious undertaking — had a place in the curriculum. Galvanised sculpted objects taken from nature and the plant casts as described by Moser constituted, together with graphics and dry and wet specimens, the bulk of the collection of teaching aids which arts and crafts teacher Moritz Meurer (1839–1916) had been commissioned by the government of Prussia to supply for the *Unterrichtsanstalt*. Between 1891 and 1896 Meurer and his six assistants produced the required visual aids in his studio in Rome. A corpus comprising one hundred ninety casts and sixty-three bronzes of plant sections modelled at an enlarged scale was complemented by plaster casts, partly realised as reliefs, partly as three-dimensional models, of inflorescences, buds, offshoots and leaves (ill. right). Wall charts featuring drawings and graphics were supplemented by plant photographs, like some of the bronze plants the work of one of Meurer's assistants, Karl Blossfeldt (1865–1932). A series of two-hundred and fifty large-format wall charts was added to this collection in 1909.[4] In terms of media Meurer availed himself of the traditional training aids of artists. Two-dimensional models, such as drawings, lithographs and photographs, were part of the inventory at academies and applied arts schools, and this was even more true of plaster reliefs and sculptures in the round replicating models taken from nature or antiquity. The casts executed in bronze and brass, though, are a different matter,[5] in that they stand out from the common teaching media due to their materiality. They are reminiscent of Renaissance goldsmithing and the stunningly naturalistic casts of plants and animals made by Wenzel Jamnitzer (ill. p. 45).[6]

This association leads back to Moser's review and his claim that the casts of plants can serve as substitutes for living matter. This seemingly addresses faithfulness to nature — a requirement for casts used in teaching. It also relates to Meurer's teaching concept and the goals he pursued with it.[7] Following traditional anatomy teaching practice, Meurer proposed an approach where drawing and modelling plant structures would acquaint students with the principles of morphology. Guided by the focus on 'lineament, silhouette and the entire three-dimensional appearance of plants',[8] budding artisans were taught to appreciate the general order of types, proportional relations and growth characteristics in the world of plants. The goal was to deduce the natural laws governing the genesis of forms. In individual creative work, these laws were then to be transformed into artistic design principles. Basically, what Meurer wanted students of the ornamental arts to acquire was neither naturalism as a style nor botanical expertise as a basis for arts and crafts design.

It appears from what has been said that, in Meurer's view, the casts of plants were not to teach students taxonomic skills[9] nor encourage naturalism as a design norm. The (alleged) lack of style in mechanical image generation, as is the case with casts, was grist to Meurer's mill. The mimetic reproduction process met the practical need of producing durable substitutes for perishable plants. For Meurer, the main task and core competence of the bronze plants was the conservation of the three-dimensional appearance of the original plant, an achievement best seen in the specimens mounted on turned wooden legs (ill. below).

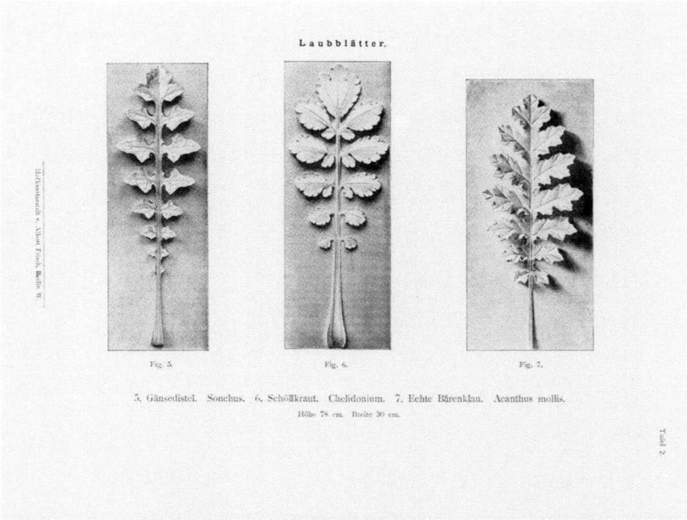

Laubblätter
In: Moritz Meurer, *Catalog der plastischen Pflanzenformen*, Dresden n.d. [1896], plate 2, Photographic reproduction of plaster bas-reliefs, collotype
Museum-Naturalienkabinett Waldenburg

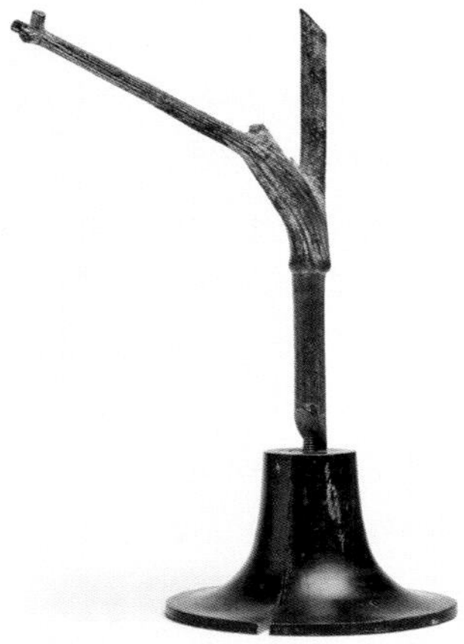

Giovanni Nisini
Meadow rue, inflorescence, 1893–96
Bronze cast, patinated, wood
20 × 11.7 × 24.5 cm
Universität der Künste Berlin, Universitätsarchiv, 321-153

If one bears in mind Meurer's study objectives — the functionality of the teaching aids and the specific characteristics of casts taken from nature — one aspect becomes quite clear: The mimetic replication qualities characteristic of the casts as well as the common goal of both teaching concept and teaching aids did *not* aim at a naturalistic appropriation of the plants and their parts. The intention was rather to initiate an abstract analysis and, later, an aesthetic production by the students — the translation of natural appearances into artistic forms. How and to what extent this contrast made itself felt in the use of the teaching aids and their reception is not known. Neither teachers nor students of the plant drawing classes left any testimonies nor did Meurer himself go on record about the use of the casts and how they performed in everyday teaching.

This then leaves us with the casts themselves: While expert craftsmanship at the Nisini Foundry in Rome ensured that the plant fragments closely resembled nature, this was somewhat contradicted by the unusual way the casts were mounted, presumably with a view to facilitating handling. In some cases the cast of a leaf seems to hover above its board and sometimes it gives the impression of simply having been dropped there; at other times metal plant stems extend from the board as if of their own volition (ill. right); sometimes several fragments are joined together almost like a pictorial composition (ill. p. 55 top left) or the board is shaped to match the outline of the plants (ill. p. 54 top right). The patination in all sorts of shades of green and the natural colour of brass do not always give a natural appearance, in fact, quite on the contrary.[10] Fine traces of leaf veins are removed along with the impression of surface movement, the result being a distinct sense of artificiality — the exact opposite to what had been intended. Quite at odds with faithfulness to nature, these interventions suggest that Meurer's casts should not be interpreted in scientific nor in documentary terms. Furthermore, they make the casts oscillate between closeness to nature and artificiality, marking, on the media-aesthetic level, a breakdown in the status of representation. In the last analysis, this Janus-headedness is at odds with Meurer's conviction regarding the unequivocal status of the teaching aids and reveals a blind spot in his understanding of the objects, the potential divergence between the facticity of the casts and their functionality.

Moser's 'vexed issue regarding the availability of models'[11] for the study of nature only found a partial solution in these casts. To no small extent that issue was made to arise again in the light of these visibly medialised lifecasts and their own aesthetic value.

1 Ferdinand Moser, 'Meurer's Ausstellung von Naturformenstudien', in: *Verkündigungsblatt des Verbandes Deutscher Kunstgewerbe-Vereine, supplement of the Zeitschrift des Bayerischen Kunst-Gewerbe-Vereins*, 12, 1891, pp. 80–81, here p. 81. Of the once-existent casts referred to here of a snake, the head of a snake, a frog and a toad, all listed in an inventory of bronzes at the Archiv der Universität der Künste Berlin, not one has survived or, to be more precise, not one has as yet been identified. See Bestand Inventare, Archiv der Universität der Künste Berlin, 18, pp. 111–18; 19, pp. 12–16. Unless otherwise stated, all translations by Otmar Binder.
2 For an account on the so-called Meurer Bronzes held today at the Archiv der Universität der Künste Berlin see Rajka Knipper, *Die Sammlung Karl Blossfeldt in der Universität der Künste Berlin: Lehrmittel für den kunstgewerblichen Unterricht*, SK Stiftung Kultur. Die Photographische Sammlung 2009 (ed.), online https://www.photographie-sk-kultur.de/fileadmin/user_upload/download/Knipper_20090312.pdf, accessed: 11.03.2019.
3 See Angelika Thiekötter and Eckhard Siepmann (eds.), *Packeis und Pressglas. Von der Kunstgewerbe-Bewegung zum Deutschen Werkbund*, exh. cat. Martin-Gropius-Bau Berlin May–November 1987, Gießen 1987.
4 See Moritz Meurer, *Vergleichende Formenlehre des Ornamentes und der Pflanze: Mit besonderer Berücksichtigung der Entwicklungsgeschichte der architektonischen Kunstformen*, Dresden 1909.
5 The reference to bronze casts is, strictly speaking, somewhat imprecise, as first investigations into the small group handed to Dresden's Kunstgewerbemuseum by Meurer's widow have shown. Sample testing that might lead to conclusions as to the alloys used for the casts is yet to be done. See Klára Němečková and Angela Nikolai, 'Die Pflanzenwelt von Moritz Meurer und der Dresdener Disput um das Naturstudium', in: *Dresdener Kunstblätter*, Staatlichen Kunstsammlungen Dresden quarterly, *Im Reich der Flora* 62, no. 2 (2018), pp. 46–55, here pp. 47, 54–55.
6 See Robert Felfe, *Naturform und bildnerische Prozesse: Elemente einer Wissensgeschichte in der Kunst des 16. und 17. Jahrhunderts*, Berlin and Boston 2015, pp. 19–40.
7 See Moritz Meurer, *Das Studium der Naturformen an kunstgewerblichen Schulen: Vorschläge zur Einführung eines vergleichenden Unterrichts*, Berlin 1889.
8 Moritz Meurer, *Pflanzenformen: Vorbildliche Beispiele zur Einführung in das ornamentale Studium der Pflanze; Zum Gebrauche für Kunstgewerbe- und Bauschulen, Technische Hochschulen und höhere Unterrichtsanstalten sowie für Architekten und Kunsthandwerker*, Dresden 1895, p. 44.
9 See Ulrike Meyer Stump, 'Modelle einer verborgenen Geometrie der Natur: Karl Blossfeldts "Meurer-Bronzen"', in: Philip Ursprung (ed.), *Herzog & De Meuron: Naturgeschichte*, exh. cat., CCA Canadian Centre for Architecture Montréal, 23 October 2002–6 April 2003, Baden 2002, pp. 312–19, here p. 316.
10 Felfe 2015, p. 35.
11 Moser 1891, p. 81.

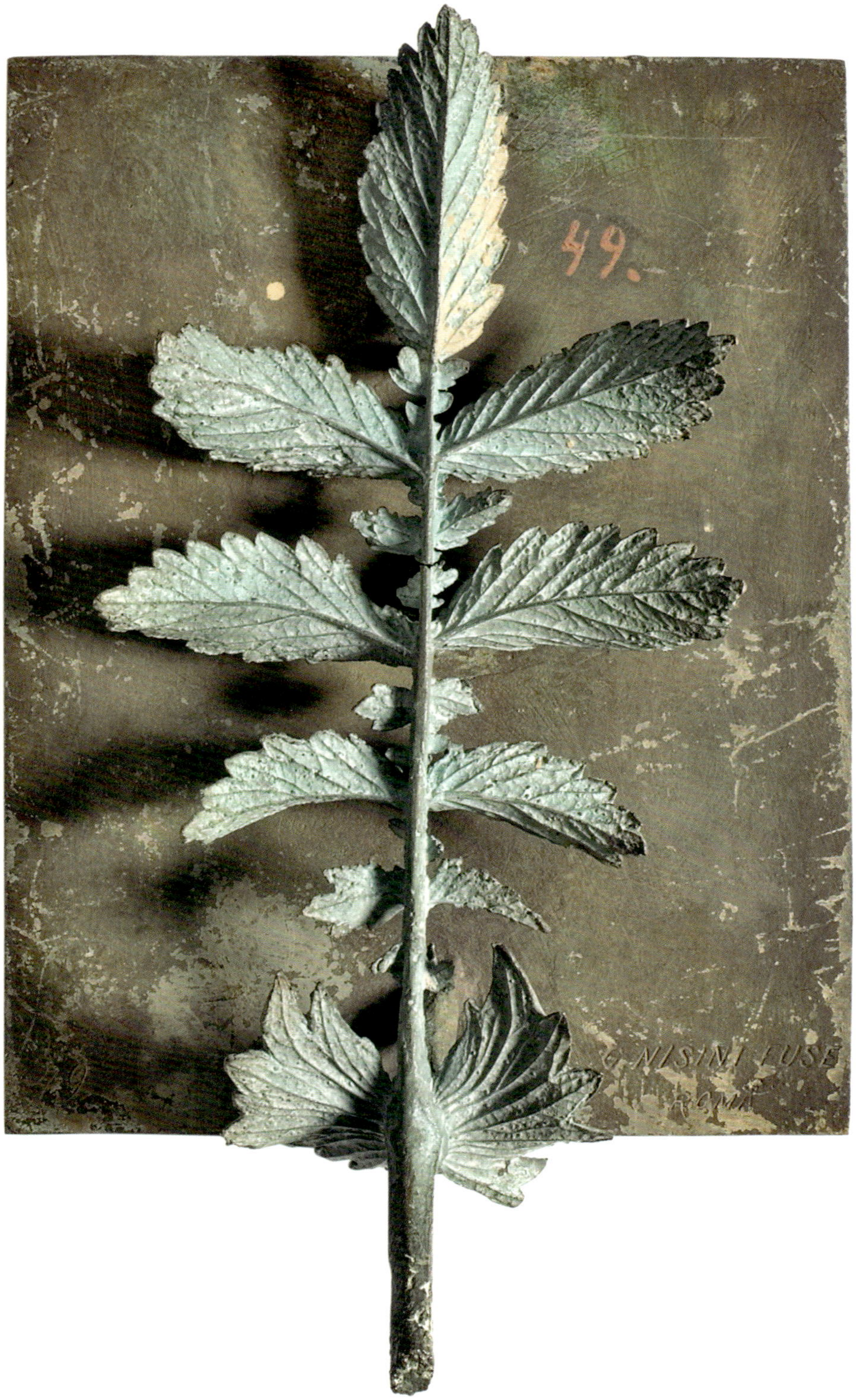

Giovanni Nisini
for Moritz Meurer

Agrimony, Leaf, 1891–92

Next pages

Giovanni Nisini
for Moritz Meurer

Squirting Cucumber, Leaf, 1891–92

Thistle, Leaf, 1893–96

Unspecified Plant, Shoot with Young Leaves, 1891–92

Meadow Rue, Leaf, 1891–92

Ailanthus, Leaf, 1891–92

Unspecified Plant, Leaf, 1891–92

Thistle, Terminal Bud, 1891–92

Sow Thistle, Leaf, 1891–92

Universität der Künste Berlin,
Universitätsarchiv

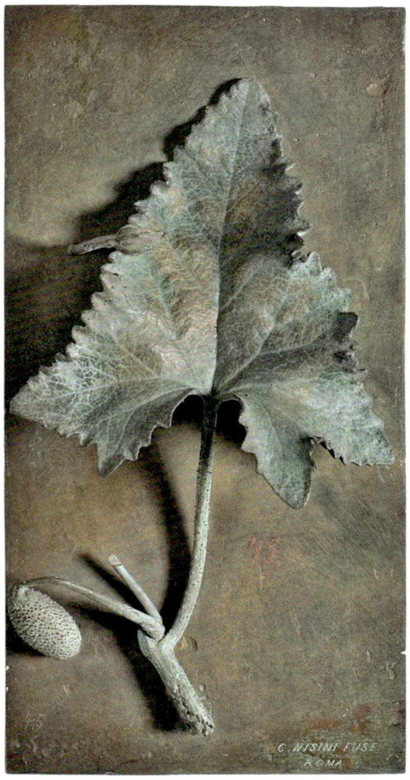
C. NISINI FUSE
ROMA

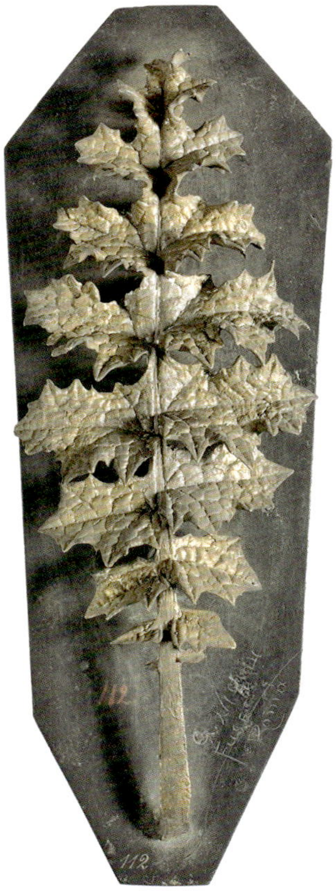
112

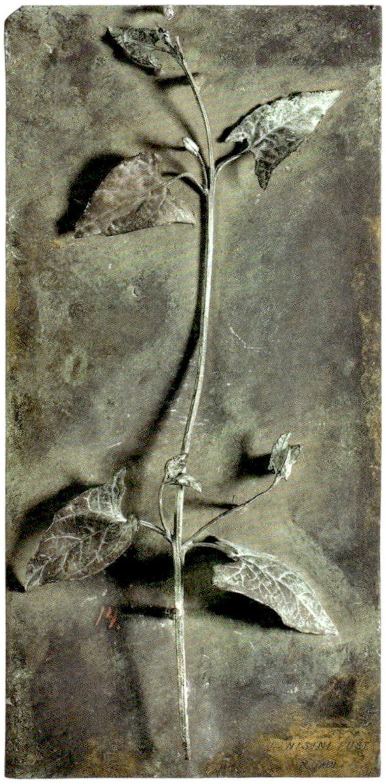
14.

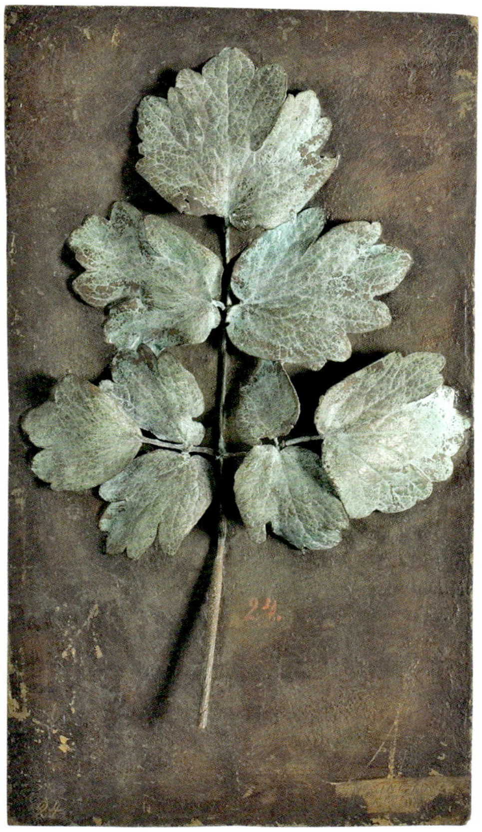
24.

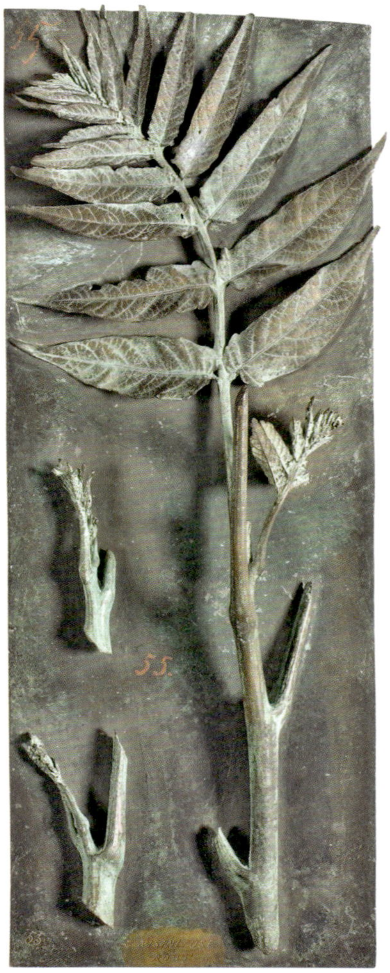

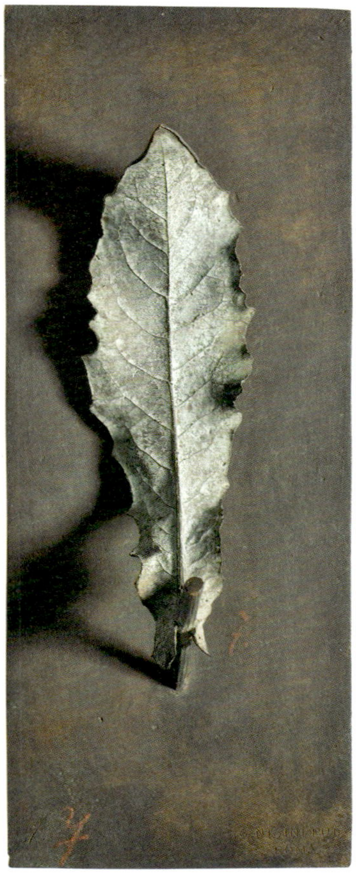

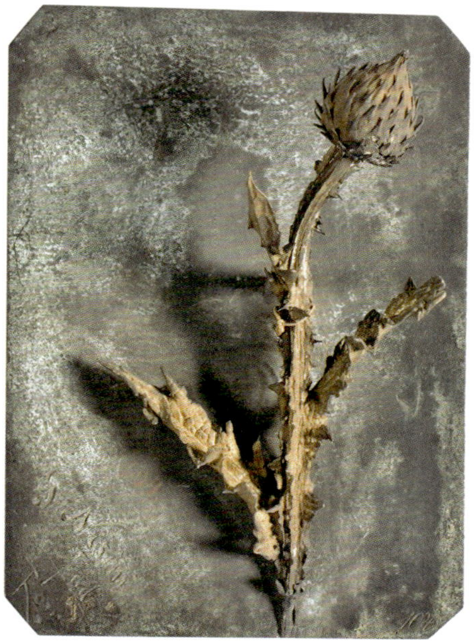

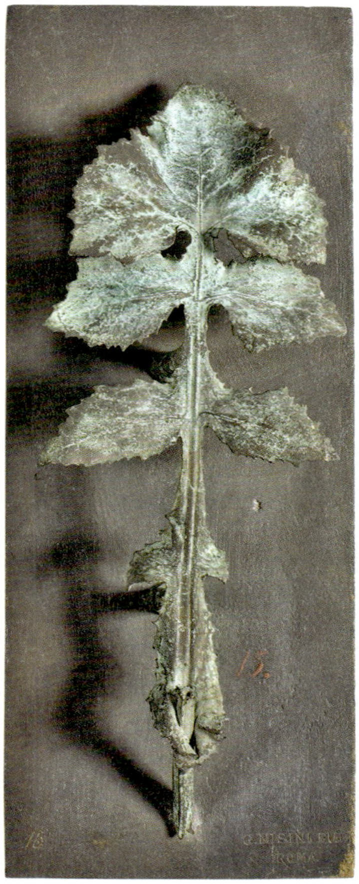

Cennino Cennini
Il Libro dell'Arte — A Treatise on Painting, ca. 1400

Chap. 163
Shewing how useful it is to take casts from the life.

I think I have said enough on colouring of all kinds. I will now touch upon another subject, which is very useful in drawing from nature, and similar things (and which contributes greatly to design); this is called taking casts (*improntare*).

Chap. 164
How to take a cast of the face of a man or woman.

Would you take a cast of the face of a man or woman, and in any position? Then adopt this mode. Let a young man, or woman, or an old man, come to you, and let the beard be shaved; for the hair and beard are difficult to do. Then with a large minever pencil anoint the face with some oil of roses, or other odoriferous oil, put on the capo, berretta, or cappuccio, and provide a band, about a span wide and as long as from one shoulder to the other, surrounding the top of the berretta; and sew the edge of it round the berretta from one ear to the other. Put into the holes of each ear a piece of cotton, and draw over them one end of the band, which you are to sew to the beginning of the collar; and give half a turn to the middle of the shoulder, and return to the buttons in front. Do the same to the other shoulder, then unite the ends of the band. Having done this, place the man or woman flat on a carpet, a desk, or a panel. Provide a hoop of iron, of the width of one or two fingers, with some teeth on the inside, like a saw. Put this hoop, which is to be two or three fingers longer than the face, round the face of the person; let it be held by your associate, suspended from the face, that it may not touch the face of the person. Take the band, and turn it round and round, putting the end of it, which had not been sewn, into the teeth of the hoop; and then confine it between the flesh and the hoop, so that the hoop shall be beyond the band, and leave about the width of two fingers or less between the band and the flesh, according to the distance you wish the paste to extend. You will now have to make the cast.

Chap. 165
How to enable a person from whose face a cast is being taken to breathe.

You must get a goldsmith to make two small tubes of brass or silver, which are to be round above and more open at one end than at the other, like a trumpet, each about a span long, and as large round as a finger, made as light as possible. The other end must be made the same shape as the nostril; but just so much smaller as to enter the nostrils without leaving any vacant space between them. Let a small hole be pierced through the middle of each, and bind them together.

Chap. 166
How to take a cast of the living face in plaster (gesso); how to remove and preserve it, and to take a cast from it in metal.

Having done this, and the man or woman still lying down, put these tubes into the nostrils, and let the person hold them himself with the hand. Have ready some gesso bolognese, or volterrano, fresh burnt and sifted. Have some cold water near you in a basin, and put some of it quickly upon the plaster. Make haste, for it soon sets, and let it be neither too thick nor too thin; with a drinking-glass put some of this composition over the face. When you have covered it equally, except the eyes, which you are to cover last, let the mouth and eyes be closed, but not forcibly (for which there is no necessity), but as if in sleep. When you have filled the whole space about a finger's depth, let it rest a short time until it be set; and remember, that when you are taking a cast of a person of high rank, such as a lord, a king, a pope, an emperor, you should stir in to the plaster rose-water as well as cold water; but for other persons it is sufficient to use cold water, from fountains, rivers, or wells, only. Your composition being set and dry, detach it gently with a palette knife, penknife, or scissors, from the band which you sewed round it; draw the tubes gently from the nose; let the person rise, and either sit or stand, while you hold the composition which is still on the face with your hands, and gently remove the mask from the face. Put it away, and preserve it carefully.

This process being completed, procure a child's girdle, and put it round the cast, in such a manner that the girdle shall project about the width of two fingers beyond the edge of it. With a large minever pencil oil the inside of the cast with any oil you please, and with all possible diligence, lest any accident should happen to it. Wet the plaster as before, and, if you like to add a little pounded brick to it, it will be an improvement to it; and then, with a glass or porringer, put some of it into the cast, which should be placed upon a bench, so that while you are filling it with the plaster, you may strike with the other hand upon the bench, in order that the plaster may enter equally every part of the cast, as the wax does into a seal, and be free from bubbles.

When the cast is full, let it rest for half a day, or one day at most. Then with a hammer proceed cautiously to break the outside cast, that is, the first form you made, in such a way as not to break the nose or any other part; and that you may do this the more easily, before you fill it, saw it nearly through in several places on the outside, but do not let your saw pass through it. When you have filled it, you can easily break it with a slight blow from the hammer. In this manner you may obtain the effigy, physiognomy, or cast of any person of rank. And you should know, that when you have made the first form, you may make a cast of it in copper, brass, bronze, gold, silver, lead, and generally of any metal you please; nevertheless, you should study under masters who understand the melting and casting of metals.

Chap. 167
How to take a cast of the whole figure of a man or woman, or an animal, and to make a cast from a model in metal.

You must know that the above-mentioned mode is that adopted by the first masters. I must also inform you that you may take a cast of the whole figure, like the naked antique figures, of which so many remain. You must select some naked man or woman, and let the person stand upright in a sort of box or case, which will reach as high as a man's chin, and let the case be joined together at the sides lengthways. Let a very thin copper plate be placed against the shoulders, beginning at the ear, and reaching to the bottom of the case, and bind it with a cord to the naked person, so as not to injure or press into the flesh. Then let the copper plate be fixed above the edge, where the case is joined. Cut four copper plates like this, and join them together, like the edges of the case. Then grease the naked person, put him directly into the case, mix a large quantity of plaster with cold water, and take care to have an assistant with you; and while you pour the plaster into the case in front of the man, let the assistant fill the back part at the same time, so that it may be filled to his throat:

with regard to the face, you may do that at another time, as I have told you before. Let the plaster rest until it be quite set and dry; then open the case where it is joined, separate the edges of the case from the copper plates with chisels, and open it as you would a nut, holding on all sides the pieces of the case and of the cast you have made. Withdraw the naked person very gently from it, wash him quickly with clean water, for his flesh will be as red as a rose. In this manner, when you have filled the surface of the mould, you may make a cast of any metal you please; but I recommend you to make it of wax, for this reason, that the paste may be broken without injury to the figure, for you may remove it at any time, and make any repairs that you find necessary. You may then join the head to it, and the whole being joined together, you may make a cast of the whole person or of any particular member. You may, for instance, take a cast of an arm, a hand, a foot, a leg, a bird, a beast, or any kind of animal or fish. But the animals must be dead, because they have neither sense nor firmness to stand still.

Chap. 168
How to model from the life, and then take casts in metal.

You may also make a model of a person in this manner: take a quantity either of paste or wax, well stirred and clean, of the consistence of ointment, and very soft; spread it on a large table, a dinner-table for instance. Set it on the ground; spread the paste on it to the height of half a braccio. Throw yourself upon it in any attitude you please, either forward or backward, or on one side. And if this paste take the impression well, you must extricate yourself from it dexterously, so as not to disturb it. Then let the mould dry. When dry, you may fill it with lead. Do the other side of your person (the opposite side to that which you have done) in the same manner. Then join them together, and fill them both with lead or other metal.

Excerpt from Cennino Cennini da Colle di Valdelsa, *A Treatise on Painting* (1437), translated by Mrs Merrifield, with an introductory preface, copious notes, and illustrations in outline from celebrated pictures, London 1844, pp. 100–05.

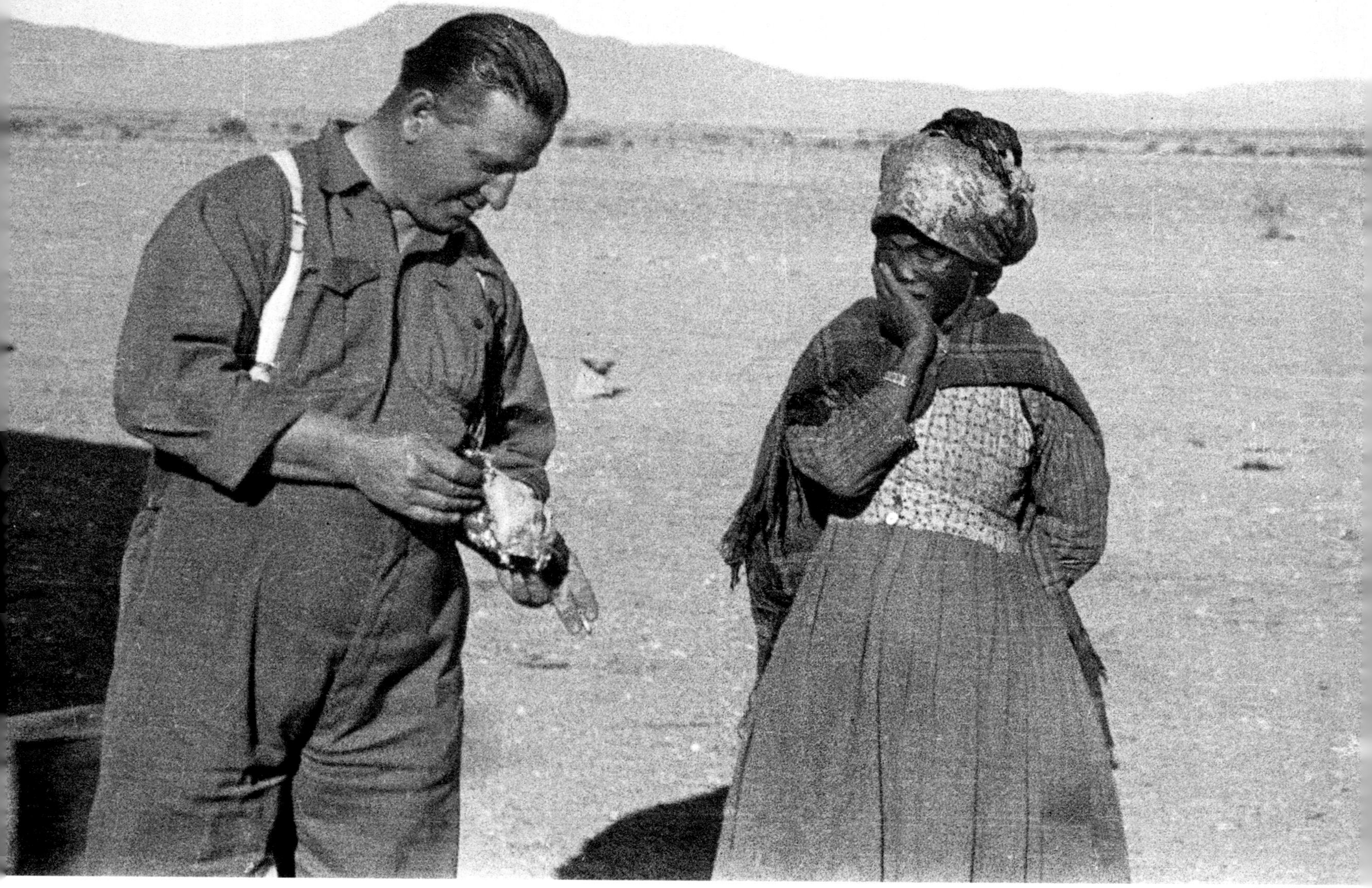

Hans Lichtenecker
Showing the Face Mask of a Woman
to a Woman called Lena
South West Africa
(today's Namibia), 1931
Photograph from the
Archive of Hans Lichtenecker
Private collection Wolfgang Wiggers

Too near to Life

The collection of the Gipsformerei comprises moulds of almost three hundred lifecasts, made by anthropologists on research trips to European colonies and at ethnological expositions in Berlin at the turn of the twentieth century. Facial and body casts were part of the methodological inventory of physical anthropology, which at the time concerned itself largely with reducing humanity to morphological and phenotypical characteristics that then formed the basis for the construction of typologies and a 'racial' nomenclature. This area of the Gipsformerei's collection is extremely sensitive on several accounts, including the origins of the moulds and their use, the potentially problematic issue of the significance human likeness has in certain Indigenous societies and the close relationship between lifecasts and the field of human remains.

'Don't they speak to us in a living language when we recognise the structure of the skin on them, don't they breathe life in their three-dimensionality, even if we have to think of them as being under the spell of peaceful slumber?' This is how anthropologist Alfred Maaß gushed about face masks from Sumatra in 1908. The perspective of those who were cast could not have been more radically different. 'I did not hear anything, my eyes were blocked and what was being played I do not know, but I could not breathe with my mouth and my ears were sore, sore, sore, that is how I was treated and I sweated, wet, wet from my sweat … and when it was lifted from my face I was able to get my breath back.' This is an excerpt from a sound recording documenting the voice of Petrus Goliath (transcribed by Levi Namaseb and translated by Memory Biwa), whose face was cast in 1931 by the artist and self-professed anthropologist Hans Lichtenecker in Namibia. In the narrative of this exhibition, the sensitive holdings in the collection of the Gipsformerei demonstrate that casts after nature can also get 'too' close to life. They show how thin the line is that separates ethically justifiable from ethically dubious mouldings, between dignified and undignified portraits of human beings.

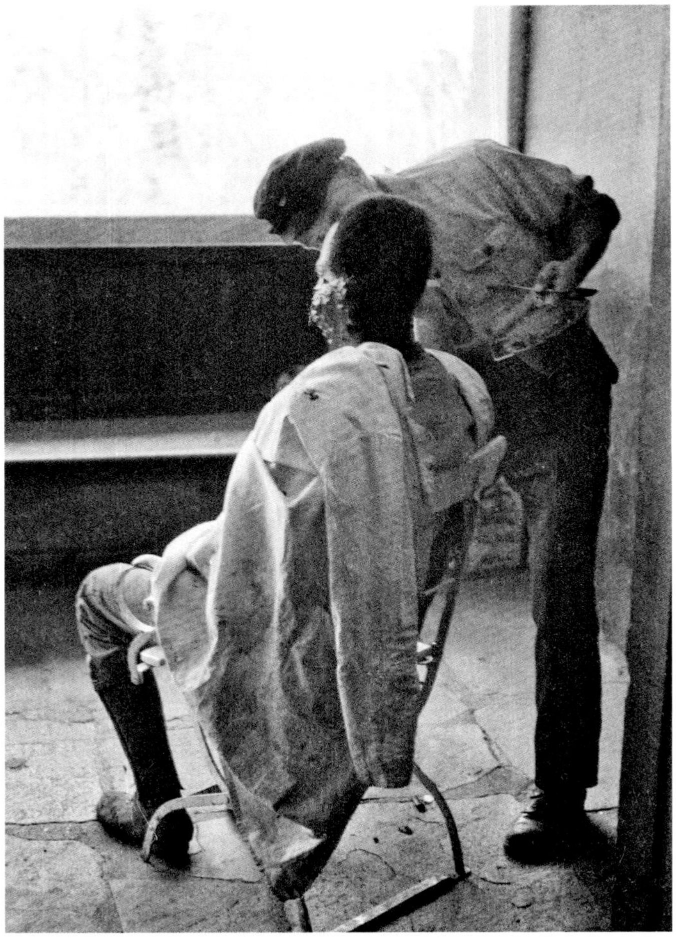

Left

Casting Wilfred Tjiueza

Right

Casting an Unidentified Man

Casting Wilfred Tjiueza

Hans Lichtenecker with His Collection of Masks

One of Hans Lichtenecker's Collaborators Showing a Face Mask to an Unidentified Man

South West Africa
(today's Namibia), 1931
Photographs from the
Archive of Hans Lichtenecker
Private collection Wolfgang Wiggers

» We are put back into abuse again. We are put back in the can. And I won't speak in there, and I am put back in it again, and I was told to speak. Now I don't know the things I am supposed to say. Now I am just screaming like a dog put on a metal trap. I don't know the person who will use these things later, who may know them. The people now having wrapped clay on their heads. It is said they should be wrapped with clay, they will be taken to another country. That they will be looked at by king's children. Now what will be done to these after this? And who will do these things? We Muniosona's fathers are left here.

Kana Je, 1931

From the recordings of Kana Je, translation from Otjiherero by Rhyn Tjituka, cited in: Anette Hoffmann, Britta Lange and Regina Sarreiter (eds.), *What We See: Reconsidering an Anthropometrical Collection from Southern Africa; Images, Voices, Versioning*, Basel 2009, p. 134–35.

In 1931, German artist Hans Lichtenecker (1891–1988) collected anthropometrical data, photographs, casts and sound recordings of people in what was then South West Africa (today's Namibia). The majority of the facial masks he made are now kept at the National Museum of Namibia in Windhoek. These were cast at the police station in Keetmanshoop; others were made on Farm Lichtenstein near Windhoek. Instead of plaster, Lichtenecker used Negocell, a hydrocolloid moulding material invented in 1926 by the Austrian physician Alfons Poller. Its elasticity makes it particularly suitable for undercutting areas of the face, such as the ears. Political pressure as well as the promise of fees and other rewards were used to persuade Namibians, male and female, to present themselves at the police station. Once there, they were used for making anthropometrical measurements, taken by Lichtenecker and his collaborators. The sound recordings were made with an Edison phonograph for the Phonogramm-Archiv of the Museum für Völkerkunde in Berlin. They comprise of songs, narratives and stories, some of which recall the colonial war, others convey personal suffering; there are also messages to the German people and reports on the casting procedure, which is vividly described as violent, humiliating and thoroughly unpleasant. We owe the privilege of being able to listen to these voices today to Anette Hoffmann. In 2006, she initiated the digitisation of these wax cylinder recordings and had them transcribed and translated from the local languages.

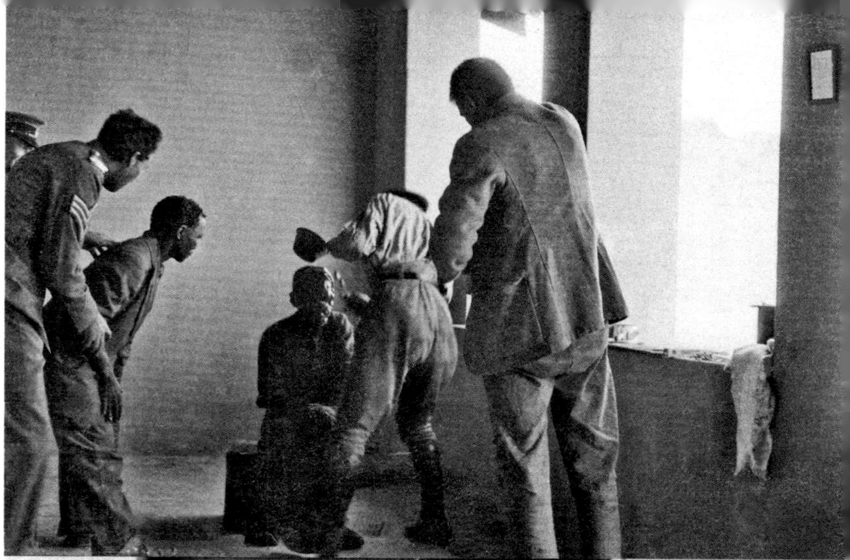

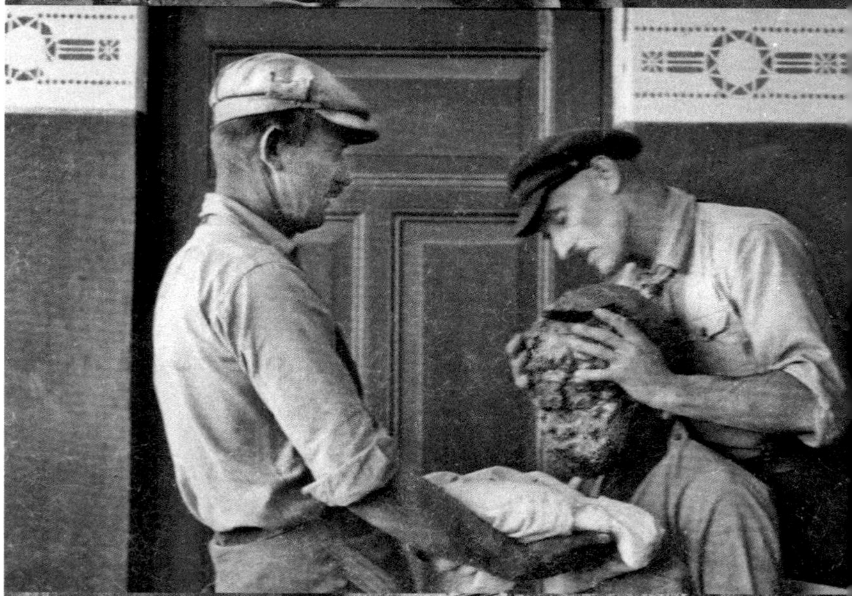

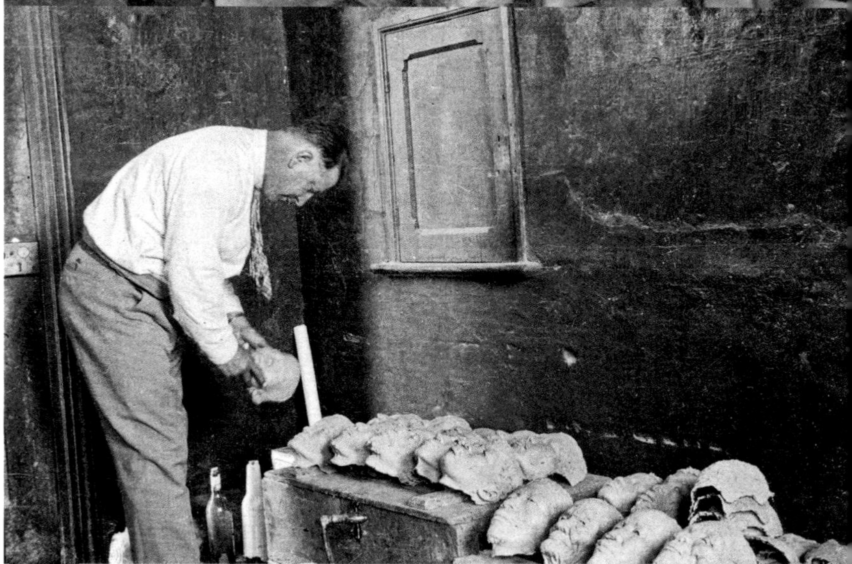

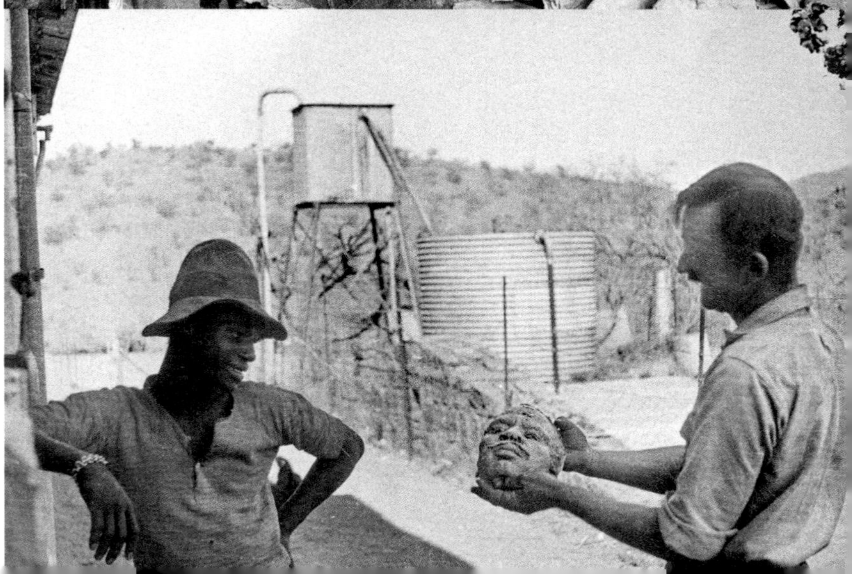

Anthropological Casts in the Collection of the Gipsformerei: A Stocktaking

Veronika Tocha

'The figures created by anthropologists in colonial contexts have forced people to bequeath to us their bodily shapes. Today, they challenge us to confront this history and to reexamine our handling of them.'[1]

The stock of anthropological casts at the Gipsformerei is a subject of discussion for the first time in its entirety in the exhibition *Near Life*. Aspects of the origins and the use of human lifecasts are addressed here in exemplary manner, and the question of how to deal adequately with such sensitive collection items is raised as a matter of principle.[2] This first stocktaking is designed to serve as a prelude to a more broadly based discussion in the future. Its point of departure and frame of reference is the *Verzeichnis der in der Formerei der Königlichen Museen käuflichen Gipsabgüsse (Prähistorische, ethnologische und anthropologische Gegenstände)* (Catalogue of Plaster Casts on Sale at the Gipsformerei of the Königlichen Museen [Prehistoric, Ethnological and Anthropological Objects]) from 1911,[3] which over fourteen pages in its part three lists 289 objects under the heading 'Anthropologisches Material'. The collection has remained practically unchanged to this day. In addition to a handful of full-body casts and the casts of body parts and busts, it features face masks primarily; roughly two thirds of which were taken of persons from Oceania and Australia, and roughly a third of persons from South East Asia and Africa respectively. The catalogue section is reprinted to serve as a guideline for the examination of individual objects and groups of objects, both in this chapter and in the exhibition. The approach to the biographies of the objects, which unfolds in keeping with the exhibition narrative, and the question concerning the closeness to life of the casts, focuses on the work process rather than on the finished product. It aims at making visible the individuals hidden behind the objects, who were both objectified and anonymised in the colonial production of knowledge. The Gipsformerei played an active part in this process by literally 'reproducing' it. Exemplarily, extant (first) names of the moulded individuals have been reinstated. Anthropological photographs are also taken into consideration, even though their origins are admittedly no less problematic than that of the face masks and just as likely to have been the result of discriminatory staging. They are nevertheless useful in helping to sketch a picture of the person in question and to link a nameless object to a face, an individual, a life. To highlight the problematic status both of the photographs themselves and our habitual reception of them, the black-and-white of the image has been inverted and the photographs placed on display in a portrait format.

The entire approach to the collection of the Gipsformerei is inspired, guided and supplemented by the research of cultural scholar Britta Lange and cultural scholar and africanist Anette Hoffmann, whose work has been seminal in the German-speaking field in this regard.[4] By means of the interdisciplinary, collaborative project *Verlorene Formen* (Lost Moulds, pp. 90–95) on the one side and documents from Hans Lichtenecker's collection produced in today's Namibia in 1931 on the other (ill. pp. 62–63), both positions have found their way into this exhibition. *Lost Moulds* is particularly concerned with the object biography of

What is the history of the object?

the lifecast taken from N'Kurui, a man from Southern Africa; the cast is part of the Gipsformerei collection but not included in the sales catalogue due to restrictions on reproduction rights. Lichtenecker's archive, which was opened up by Hoffmann, includes the usual measurement and profile data, drawings and photographs, casts and fingerprints, but also voice recordings. In relation to other 'mute' collections and narratives of explorers marked by limited perspectives, this archive is considered to be unique. The voice recordings now stored in the Phonogramm-Archiv of the Ethnologisches Mueum in Berlin preserve commentaries by African women and men on the moulding process: the moulded individuals are given a voice. Even though Lichtenecker's collection is only indirectly linked to the Gipsformerei, these recordings and photographs speak of things that are equally valid for the collection items of the Gipsformerei. As a primary source they tell of the ruthlessness, violence and transgression typically associated with anthropometry, the practice of measuring human bodies. Confronted with face masks and full-body casts, which bear witness to a forceful casting practice and so here are displayed as negatives (or, to be more precise, as closed or only partially viewable moulds), we can begin to form an idea of the debasing potential of this practice, which truly marks a low point in the cultural history of casting after nature.

If casts are generally difficult to categorise in terms of their mediality, the difficulty is compounded even further when they originate from colonial contexts. Lifecasts are neither illicitly trafficked cultural property nor 'human remains' in the strict sense of the term, but they are associated with the issues and problems of both fields. Lifecasts are artefacts. They were made using the principles of artisanal craftwork, sometimes even those of art, and they were produced for Europeans by Europeans in order to be taken to their native countries. Their production was frequently grounded in violence, coercion and inequality. What makes these lifecasts so problematic as products is the fact that they carry the appearance of an individual. In only a few cases have the original moulds been preserved which were in direct contact with the person being cast and so therefore may contain human material, such as skin particles and facial or body hair. What we are dealing with in the majority of cases are in fact remodelled casting moulds or positive (painted) plaster casts, whose material content has undergone multiple acts of mediatisation, transmission and translation. The more often an object is reproduced, the more distant it is from its original.

While lifecasts are not human remains, as long as the focus is on the object's materiality, in a metaphysical sense they must be seen as such in terms of their cultural significance to certain communities of origin. This is illustrated in Lichtenecker's report — utterly devoid, by the way, of any sign of understanding on his part — about a woman called Lena (ill. p. 60), who openly articulated her protest against the moulding procedure, showing herself convinced that '"faces" must remain in the same place where a human being lives [to which they belong] and must not [...] be carried around and put on display for the whole world'.[5] The status of each cast therefore must be determined on a case-by-case basis to ensure respectful treatment.

Their characater as artefacts links anthropological lifecasts to art, to the cultural history of casting and three-dimensionally measuring the world, one of the consequences of the positivist theory of knowledge characteristic of the nineteenth century. Moulding a human being during an anthropological expedition in the German colonies was on a par with the (possibly simultaneous) plaster casting of finds at an archaeological dig in Greece. When (between, say, 1880 and 1930) anthropologists or laymen such as Lichtenecker sought to create salvage-anthropological archives of 'races threatened with extinction', they were pursuing an objective that paralleled the salvaging of cultural property: 'In view of the frequently rapid disappearance of all originals', the idea was 'to save [what was still there] before it was too late.'[6] The alleged authenticity of casts provided a vicarious reality that could be shipped back to the home countries. Unlike the way archaeologists came by their finds, however, physical anthropologists had to create the objects of their research themselves through the use of anthropometrical procedures. Field research and the practice of craftwork were integral parts of both archaeology and anthropology, and quite a few anthropologists published detailed instructions on how to make plaster casts. These instructions describe the methods and techniques handed down throughout the histories of art and culture almost unchanged since antiquity.

In the sales catalogues of the Gipsformerei, these developments are reflected in the exponential growth of the relevant collection holdings at the turn of the twentieth century: between 1893 and 1911 the anthropological holdings grew from zero to almost three hundred objects, a rise in collection activities that is only paralleled by the field of ethnology. The 1911 sales catalogue, however, marks the climax in this collection area: a fervour of activity which had seemingly been 'plucked out of the air' within just a few years and then subsequently wound down again at the beginning of the twentieth century due to a shift in the scientific paradigm. In this context, an observation that holds true for collections in general is especially valid for the Gipsformerei as a (re-)producing manufactory: once an object becomes part of a collection, updated chapters have to be added to its biography.

1 Margit Berner, 'Zwei Spurensuchen: Objekte, Archive, Geschichte', in: Margit Berner, Anette Hoffmann and Britta Lange, *Sensible Sammlungen: Aus dem anthropologischen Depot*, Hamburg 2011, pp. 185–203, here p. 203.
2 The classification of moulds as sensitive collection items is indebted to the seminal plea advanced by Margit Berner, Anette Hoffmann and Britta Lange, see ibid. See also the newly edited guidelines for museums, Deutscher Museumsbund e. V. (ed.), *Leitfaden zum Umgang mit Sammlungsgut aus kolonialen Kontexten*, Berlin 2018.
3 Cp. Berner, Hoffmann, Lange 2011; Britta Lange, *Echt. Unecht. Lebensecht. Menschenbilder im Umlauf*, Berlin 2006; Anette Hoffmann, *What We See; Reconsidering an Anthropological Collaction from Southern Africa; Images, Voices and Versioning*, Basel 2009.
4 Anthropological casts were first offered for sale by the Gipsformerei in the supplement to the 1893 sales catalogue, which was published in 1900. The first list dedicated to 'prehistoric, ethnological and anthropological objects' was published in 1906; it comprised 207 items. No further lists of this kind were published after 1911.
5 Hans Lichtenecker, personal diary, Namibian Scientific Society, Windhoek, p. 40, cited in: Anette Hoffmann, Britta Lange and Regina Sarreiter, *Was wir sehen: Bilder, Stimmen, Rauschen: Zur Kritik anthropometrischen Sammelns*, Basel 2012, p. 37.
6 Otto Finsch, 'Anthropologische Ergebnisse einer Reise in der Südsee und dem malayischen Archipel in den Jahren 1879–1882: Beschreibender Catalog der auf dieser Reise gesammelten Gesichtsmasken von Völkertypen, mit 60 Körpermessungen', preliminary report, in: *Zeitschrift für Ethnologie* 15 (1883), pp. ix–xi, here p. ix.

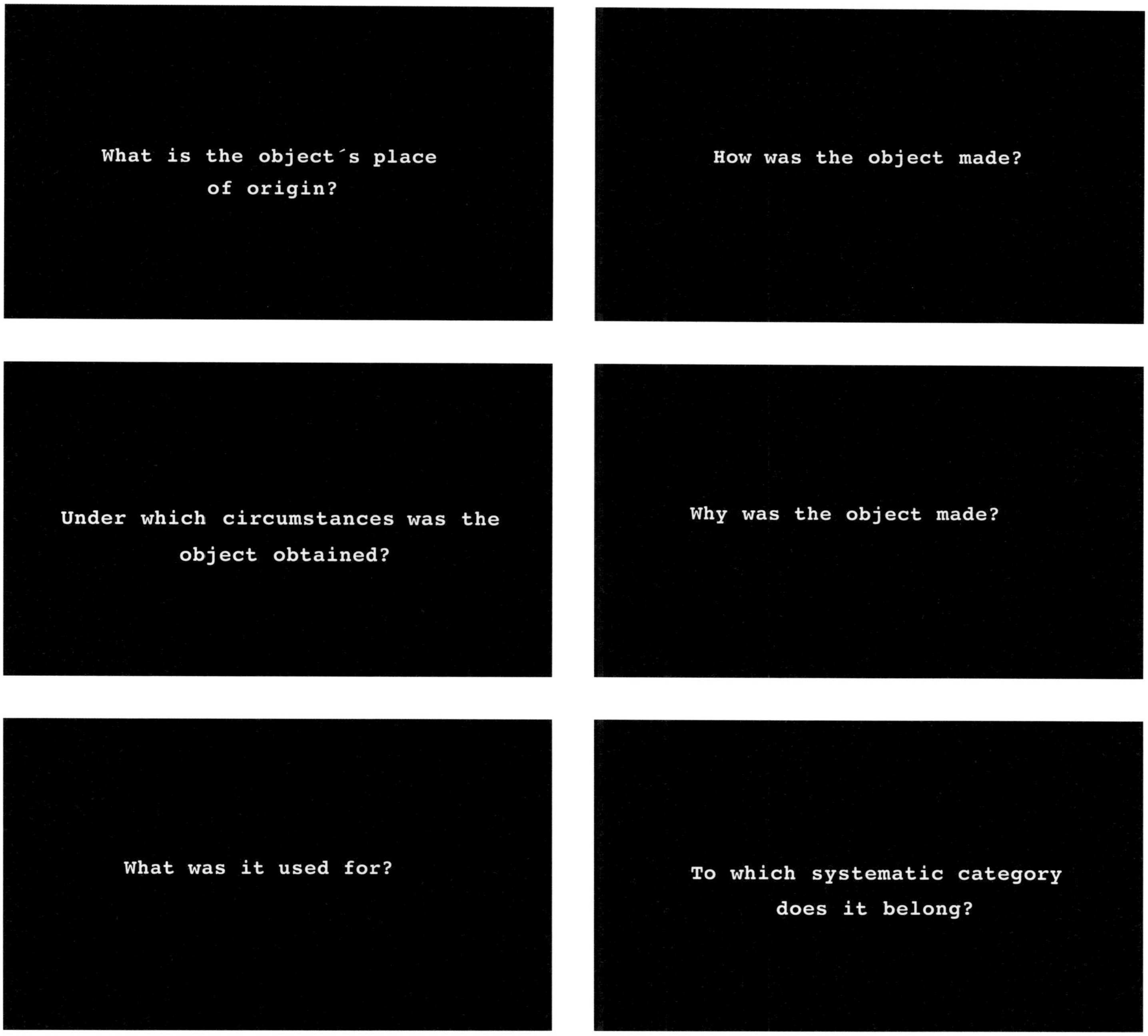

Pauline M'barek
Object ID, 2012
Courtesy of the artist and
Galerie Thomas Rehbein, Cologne

The Full-Body Cast of a Man Called Adjak

Inventory Number 4097

Adjak

— 50 —

DRITTE ABTEILUNG:

Anthropologisches Material.

Laufende No.	No. der Formerei	Gegenstand	Material des Originals	Standort des Originals	Höhe (in cm)	Breite (in cm)	Preis M.	Preis Pf.
768	4065	Ganze männliche Figur, angeblich „Süd-Australien"	—	—	170	—	100	—
769	4066	Ganze Figur einer Frau mit einem Kinde, angeblich „Nord-Australien"	—	—	160	—	130	—
770	4098	Dschagga-Büste	—	—	60	—	20	—
771	4097	Lebensgroße Figur eines Dinka	—	—	192	—	100	—
772	4082 a—d	*)Gesichtsmasken von vier Wayao (1, 6, 12, 29). Je 6,—M.	—	—	verschieden		24	—
773	4083 a—c	Desgl. von drei Wassukuma (28, 30, 31). Je 6,— M.	—	—	desgl.		18	—
774	4084 a b	Desgl. von zwei Wanyamwesi (8, 36). Je 6,— M.	—	—	desgl.		12	—
775	4085 a b	Desgl. von zwei Waganda (9, 20). Je 6,— M.	—	—	desgl.		12	—
776	4086 a b	Desgl. von zwei Männern von Groß-Comoro (10, 11). Je 6,—M.	—	—	desgl.		12	—
777	4087 a—c	Desgl. von drei Schilluk (23, 24, 37). Je 6,— M.	—	—	desgl.		18	—
778	4088 a b	Desgl. von zwei Wakussu (34, 35). Je 6,— M.	—	—	desgl.		12	—
779	4089 a—c	Desgl. von drei Wangoni-Männern (36, 39, 40). Je 6,— M.	—	—	desgl.		18	—
780	4090	Gesichtsmaske eines Mbisa (2)	—	—	27	16	6	—
781	4091	Desgl. eines Mfipa (3)	—	—	28	16	6	—
782	4092	Desgl. eines Msaramo (7)	—	—	29	24	6	—
783	4093	Desgl. eines Mkami (21)	—	—	27	22	6	—
784	4094	Desgl. eines Diggani (22)	—	—	26	26	6	—
785	4095	Desgl. eines Nuba (25)	—	—	25	24	6	—
786	4096	Gesichtsmasken von drei Wadschagga (54, 55, 56). Je 6,—M.	—	—	verschieden		18	—
787	5230	**)Gesichtsmaske eines Pygmäen aus dem Ituri-Walde (Gebiet des Häuptlings Salambongo)	—	—	25	—	6	—
788	5231	Desgl. wie vor.	—	—	24	—	6	—

*) Die Stücke 4082—4096 sind nach Originalformen gegossen, die Dr. F. Stuhlmann zu verdanken sind.

**) Die Stücke 5230 bis 5241 sind nach Originalformen gegossen, die Dr. I. Czekanowski auf der Reise durch Ruanda und Congo (Zentral-Afrikanische Expedition Sr. Hoheit des Herzogs Adolf Friedrich zu Mecklenburg) hergestellt hat.

Königliche Museen zu Berlin, General-Verwaltung (ed.)
Verzeichnis der in der Formerei der Königlichen Museen käuflichen Gipsabgüsse: (Prähistorische, ethnologische und anthropologische Gegenstände), Berlin 1911
Staatliche Museen zu Berlin, Kunstbibliothek

— 51 —

Laufende No.	No. der Formerei	Gegenstand	Material des Originals	Standort des Originals	Höhe (in cm)	Breite (in cm)	Preis M.	Preis Pf.
789	5232	Gesichtsmaske eines Pygmäen aus dem Ituri-Walde (Gebiet des Häuptlings Salambongo) . .	—	—	22	—	6	—
790	5233	Desgl. wie vor.	—	—	20	—	6	—
791	5234	Büste des Mutwa namens „Sebuleze", Ruanda, Landschaft Bugoye	—	—	30	—	20	—
792	5235	Gesichtsmaske des Mutwa Sebuleze	—	—	22	—	8	—
793	5236	Abguß der Kopfkalotte des Mutwa Sebuleze	—	—	20	—	4	—
794	5237	Gesichtsmaske eines Mutwa aus Bugoye in Ruanda	—	—	22	—	6	—
795	5238	Desgl., ebendaher.	—	—	22	—	6	—
796	5239	Desgl., ebendaher.	—	—	20	—	6	—
797	5240	Desgl., eines Bantu-Negers (Munya Ruanda) aus Mulera mit Mutwa-Typus	—	—	22	—	6	—
798	5241	Desgl. eines Munya Ruanda aus Mulera in Ruanda	—	—	20	—	6	—
799	5242	Desgl. eines etwa 25 jährigen Chamorro-Mannes	—	—	25	—	6	—
800	5243	*) Gesichtsmaske eines Mannes von 34 Jahren aus Padang Lawas, Sumatra	—	—	20	—	6	—
801	5244	Desgl. eines Mannes von 21 Jahren aus Kg. Dalam, Sumatra	—	—	21	—	6	—
802	5245	Desgl. eines Händlers von 55 Jahren, Sidjoengdjoeng, Mittel-Sumatra	—	—	24	—	6	—
803	5246	Desgl. desgl. von ± 35 Jahren aus Batoe Sangkar, Sumatra. .	—	—	23	—	6	—
804	5247	Desgl. eines Mannes von ± 35 Jahren aus Moeasa, Mittel-Sumatra, ...	—	—	22,5	—	6	—
805	5248	Desgl. eines Mannes aus Sumatra	—	—	21,5	—	6	—
806	5249	Desgl. eines Mannes von 20 Jahren aus Boekit Tinggi, Sumatra . .	—	—	19	—	6	—
807	5250	Desgl. eines Schneiders von 23 Jahren aus Tandjoeng Agam, Fort de Kock, Sumatra.	—	—	21	—	6	—
808	5251	Desgl. eines Mannes von 25 Jahren aus Boekit Tinggi, Sumatra	—	—	20	—	6	—
809	5252	Desgl. Kota Toedjoe, Sumatra .	—	—	20	—	6	—
810	5253	Desgl. Menangkaban, Sumatra .	—	—	22	—	6	—
811	5254	Desgl. eines Zimmermanns von 40 Jahren aus Padang Lawas, Sumatra.	—	—	24	—	6	—

*) Die Masken 5243 bis 5299 sind nach Originalformen gegossen, die Dr. J. P. Kleiweg de Zwaan, Leiden, auf einer mit Herrn Alfred Maass unternommenen Forschungsreise in Mittel-Sumatra hergestellt hat.

4*

Continued on page 72

The entry 'Lebensgroße Figur eines Dinka' (Life-size Figure of a Dinka), inventory no. 4097, is matched to a complete plaster piece mould in the Gipsformerei collection. Archive data in the Ethnologisches Museum links the mould to a first name, 'Adjak' or possibly 'Atjak', and the record of a plaster cast made in 1895. The name in turn leads to an anthropological photograph published in the Proceedings of the Extraordinary Meeting of the Berlin Society for Anthropology on 26 January 1895. This name and its related photograph are the few clues we have that point to a person, a man who had come from South Sudan to Berlin at the end of the nineteenth century. He was given the degrading role as 'show object' for the benefit of a German public hungry for spectacle. These scant documents give a vestigial identity and a face to Adjak. To date, no further information about his later life, the duration of his stay in Germany or the date and circumstances of his possible return to his native country has come to light. In European colonies, indigenous communities were solicited with (false) promises or a fee for their presentation in human zoos. When in 1895 impresario Willy Möller 'presented' a group of forty-five Dinka (an ethnic group native of South Sudan) in Castan's Panoptikum in Berlin, the physician and anthropologist Rudolf Virchow (1821–1902) chose Adjak as a model for a plaster cast destined for the Königliches Museum für Völkerkunde. Adjak was being treated like a commodity. 'The leader of the group, Herr Göring, cannot give permission for the Dinka to be moulded in my studio. He says these people are prone to catch a cold the moment they leave the house', writes sculptor Ernst Bernardien (1864–1944) in a letter of 4 February 1895 to the museum's founding director Adolf Bastian (ill. p. 70). Adjak therefore had to 'pose' at the Panoptikum. Bernardien refers to the procedure as 'modelling', at other times he mentions 'casting in the colour of gypsum' with plaster from the 'Formerei' of the 'Königliche Museen'. The letter contains information on the negotiations concerning Bernardien's fee and his royalties. According to the order book of the Gipsformerei, twelve casts were sold between 1902 and 1919. Their whereabouts, however, remain unknown and require further research. The lifecast made for the Königliches Museum für Völkerkunde remains part of the collection of the Ethnologisches Museum in Berlin.

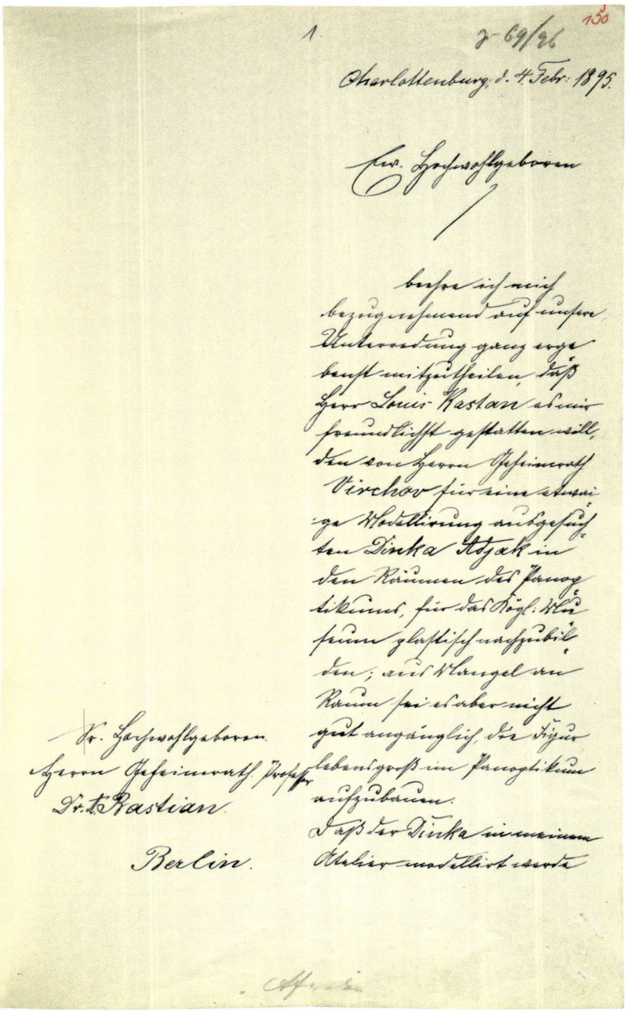

Charlottenburg, d. 4. Febr. 1895

Ew. Hochwohlgeboren

beehre ich mich bezugnehmend auf unsere Unterredung ganz ergebenst mitzutheilen, daß Herr Louis Castan es nur freundlichst gestatten will, den von Herrn Geheimrath Virchow für eine etwaige Modellirung ausgesuchten Dinka Adjak in den Räumen des Panoptikums, für das Kgl. Museum plastisch nachzubilden; aus Mangel an Raum sei es aber nicht gut angänglich, die Figur lebensgroß im Panoptikum aufzubauen.
Daß der Dinka in meinem Atelier modellirt werde

Sr. Hochwohlgeboren
Herrn Geheimrath Prof. Dr. A. Bastian
Berlin.

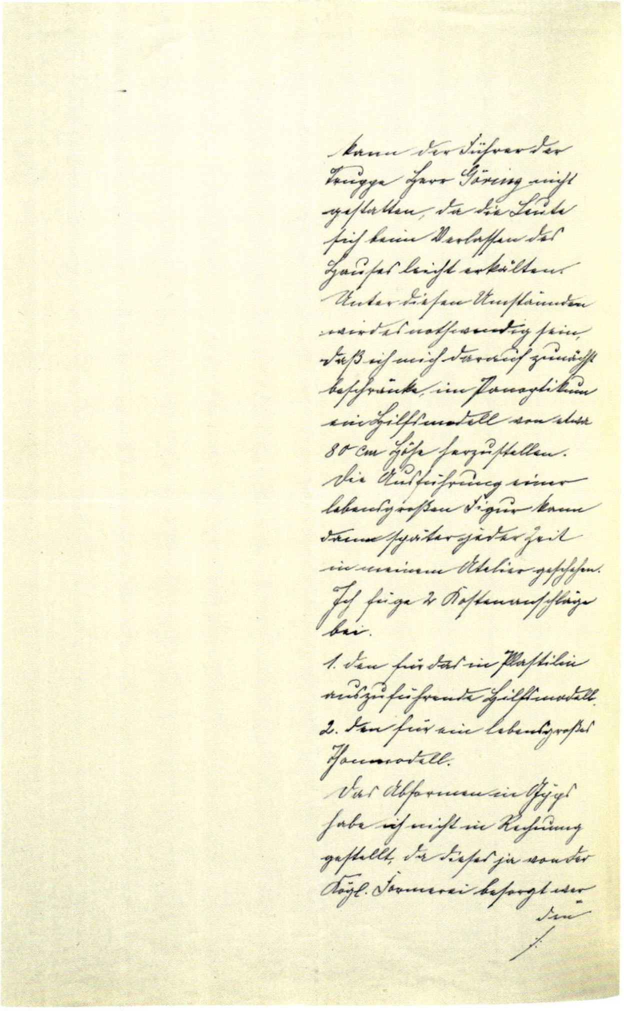

kann der Führer der Truppe Herr Göring nicht gestatten, da die Leute sich beim Verlassen des Hauses leicht erkälten.
Unter diesen Umständen würde es nothwendig sein, daß ich mich darauf zunächst beschränke, im Panoptikum ein Hilfsmodell von etwa 80 cm Höhe herzustellen.
Die Ausführung einer lebensgroßen Figur kann dann später jederzeit in meinem Atelier geschehen.
Ich füge 2 Kostenanschläge bei.
1. den für das in Plastilin auszuführende Hilfsmodell.
2. den für ein lebensgroßes Thonmodell.
Das Abformen in Gyps habe ich nicht in Rechnung gestellt, da dieses ja von der Kgl. Formerei besorgt werden

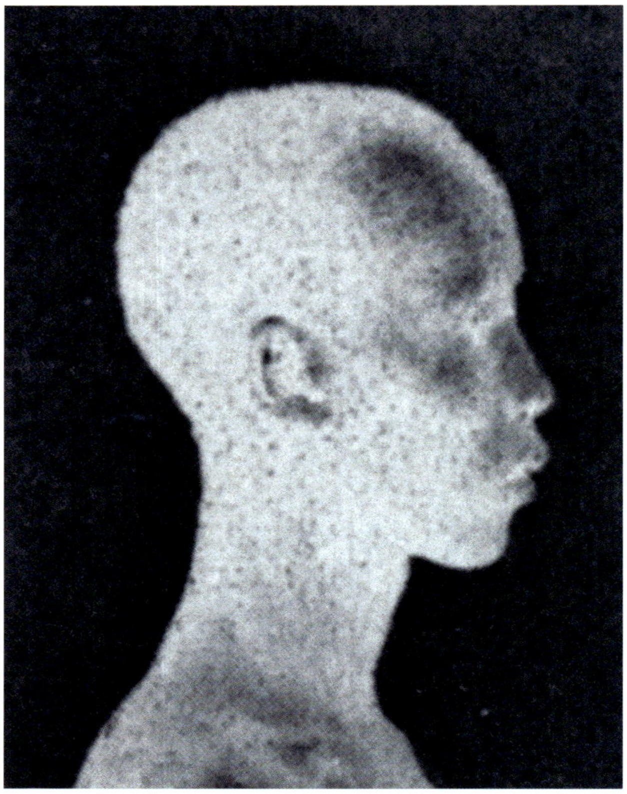

Handwritten letter from Ernst Bernardien to Adolf Bastian, 4 February 1895
Staatliche Museen zu Berlin, Ethnologisches Museum

Anthropological photograph of Adjak (inverted)
'Hr. Rud. Virchow bespricht die zur Zeit in Castan's Panopticum befindlichen Dinka (= Ausserordentliche Sitzung vom 26. Januar 1895)' (Herr Rudolf Virchow discusses the Dinka at present on view at Castan's Panopticum [= Extraordinary meeting on 26 January 1895])
In: *Zeitschrift für Ethnologie* 27 (1895), p. 161.
Staatliche Museen zu Berlin, Kunstbibliothek

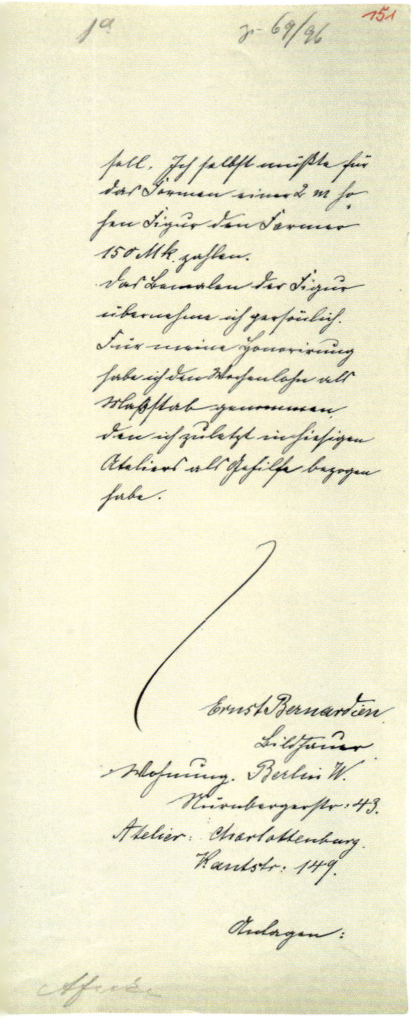

1a J-69/96 151

soll. Ich selbst müßte für das Formen einer 2 m hohen Figur dem Former 150 Mk. zahlen.
Das Bemalen der Figur übernehme ich persönlich.
Für meine Honorirung habe ich den Wochenlohn als Maßstab genommen den ich zuletzt im hiesigen Atelier als Gehilfe bezogen habe.

Ernst Bernardien
Bildhauer
Wohnung. Berlin W.
Nürnbergerstr. 43.
Atelier: Charlottenburg
Kantstr. 149.

Anlagen:

Afrika

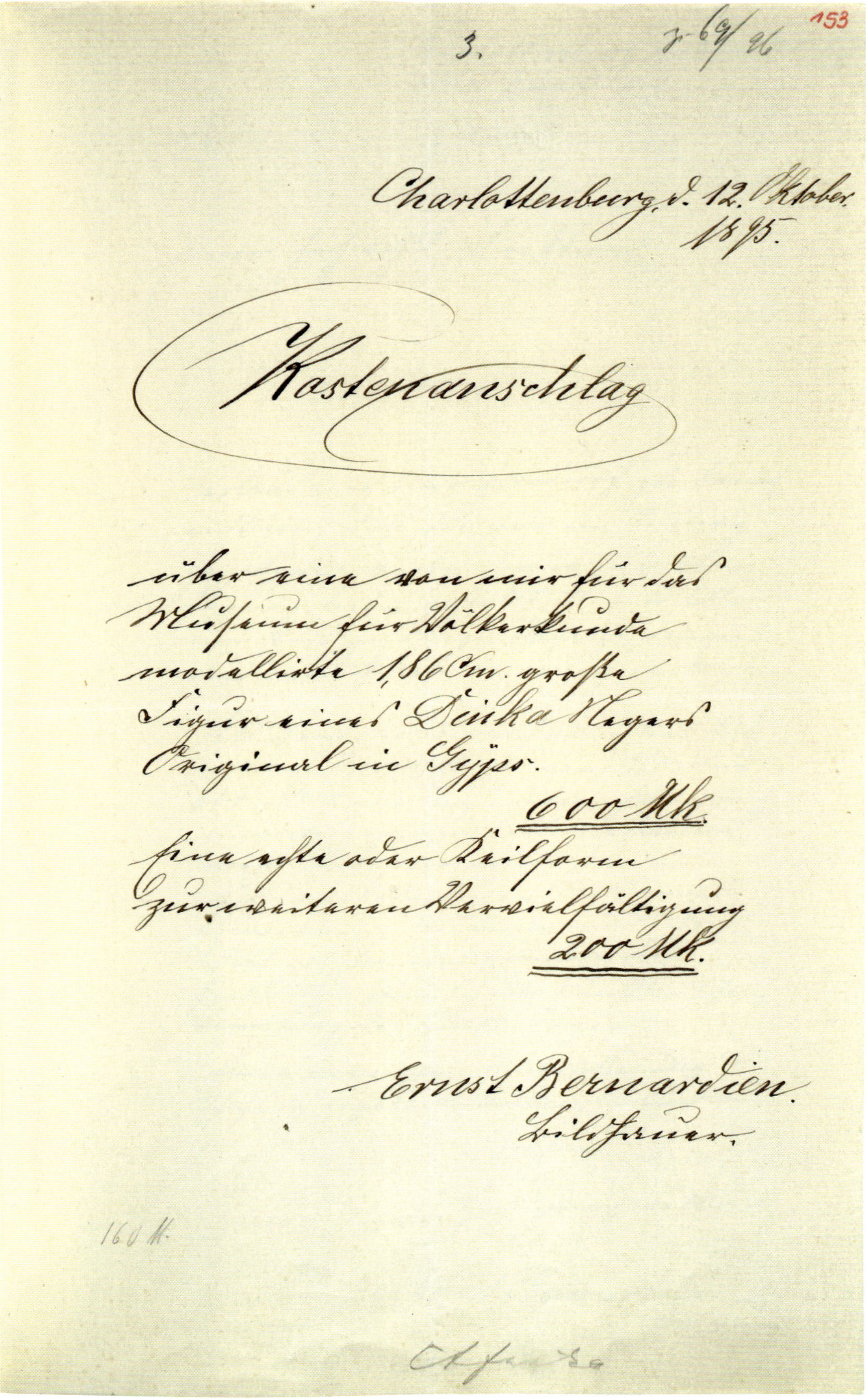

3. J-69/96 153

Charlottenburg d. 12. Oktober 1895.

Kostenanschlag

über eine von mir für das Museum für Völkerkunde modellirte 1,86 Cm. große Figur eines Dinka Negers Original in Gyps.

600 Mk.

Eine echte oder Theilform zur weiteren Vervielfältigung

200 Mk.

Ernst Bernardien
Bildhauer.

160 M.

Afrika

Handwritten estimate of Ernst Bernardien for casting the figure of Adjak in plaster, 12 October 1895
Staatliche Museen zu Berlin, Ethnologisches Museum

The Face Masks from the Collection of Johannes Pieter Kleiweg de Zwaan

Inventory Numbers 5243–5299

The collection of face masks derived from originals made by Dutch anthropologist Johannes Pieter Kleiweg de Zwaan (1875–1971) comprises fifty-seven objects, which makes it the second largest group of such objects in the Gipsformerei collection. Kleiweg created the masks in 1907 during a trip to Central Sumatra, which he undertook in the company of his Berlin colleague Alfred Maaß. Kleiweg travelled to Berlin prior to his voyage to be instructed by Felix von Luschan in the art of making face masks. It was Luschan who also insisted on having the forms cast at the Gipsformerei immediately after his return. Later voyages took Kleiweg to the Indonesian island Nias and to other islands of the Malay Archipelago. On these trips, another 131 masks were produced. These have not been included in the collection of the Gipsformerei. Handling groups of moulds of this magnitude with a view of sourcing the identities of the persons involved is a challenge that has not yet been adequately dealt with. Whereas the moulded persons from Nias are known by their (first) names, the face masks from Minangkabau are denied names in Maaß's book *Durch Zentral-Sumatra* (1909, ill. p. 74). What becomes quite clear from Kleiweg's detailed research report is how stressful the procedure was for the person being moulded and how inhuman the attitude of the European explorers. In *Die Insel Nias bei Sumatra* (1913), Kleiweg describes how, on one occasion, 'through the fault of the native', plaster had made its way to behind his ears, which meant that Kleiweg had to break up the mask with hammer and nail: 'a long drawn-out and rather dangerous manipulation'. He also describes that in removing the mask he had to pull hard 'evenly, taking hold of the rim of the mask with both hands', while his assistant 'held [the] head tight'. 'After what has been said', Kleiweg concluded, 'it is hardly surprising that it often takes a great deal of effort to persuade natives to have a mask taken of their face'.

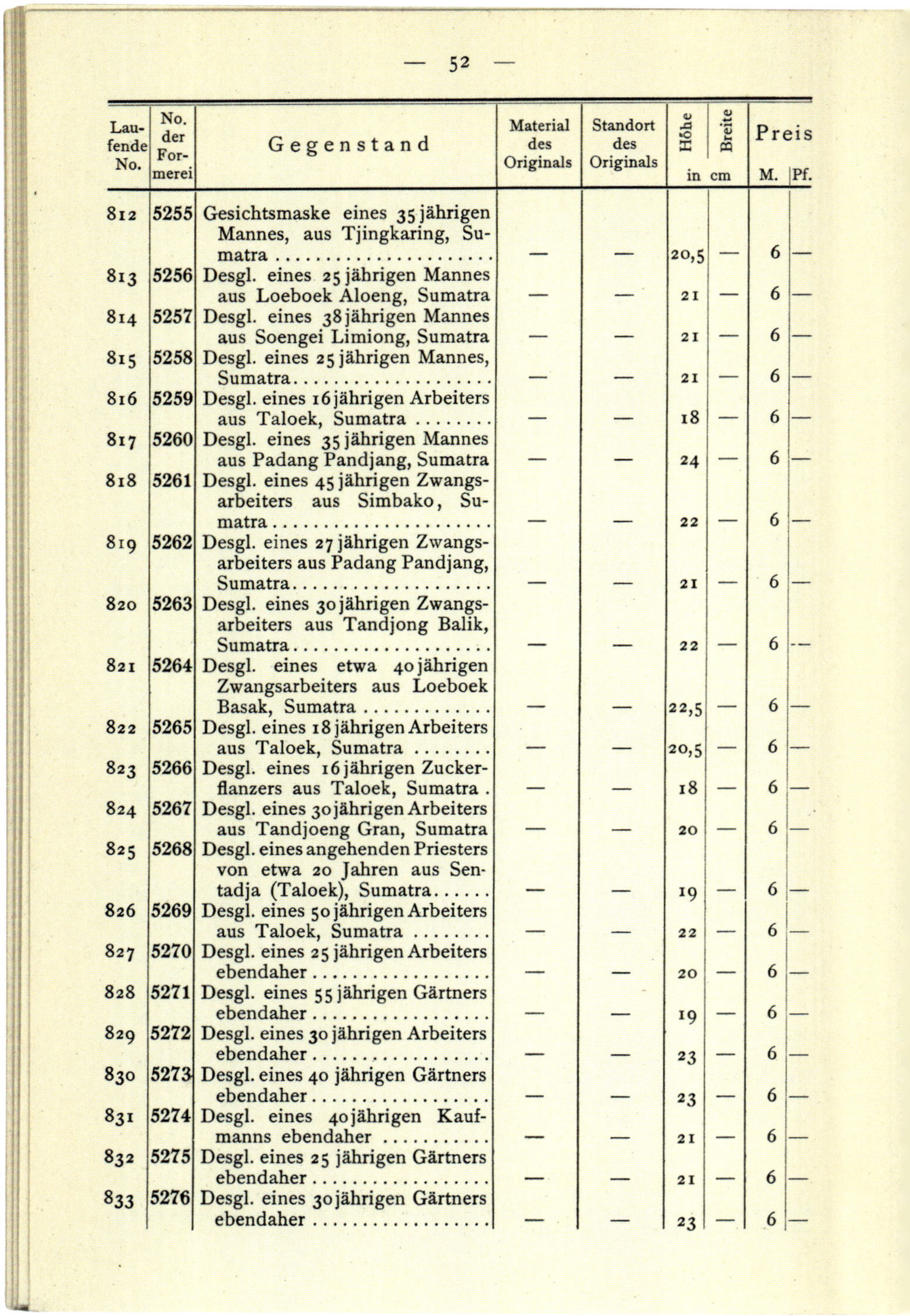

— 52 —

Laufende No.	No. der Formerei	Gegenstand	Material des Originals	Standort des Originals	Höhe (in cm)	Breite (in cm)	Preis M.	Pf.
812	5255	Gesichtsmaske eines 35jährigen Mannes, aus Tjingkaring, Sumatra	—	—	20,5	—	6	—
813	5256	Desgl. eines 25jährigen Mannes aus Loeboek Aloeng, Sumatra	—	—	21	—	6	—
814	5257	Desgl. eines 38jährigen Mannes aus Soengei Limiong, Sumatra	—	—	21	—	6	—
815	5258	Desgl. eines 25jährigen Mannes, Sumatra	—	—	21	—	6	—
816	5259	Desgl. eines 16jährigen Arbeiters aus Taloek, Sumatra	—	—	18	—	6	—
817	5260	Desgl. eines 35jährigen Mannes aus Padang Pandjang, Sumatra	—	—	24	—	6	—
818	5261	Desgl. eines 45jährigen Zwangsarbeiters aus Simbako, Sumatra	—	—	22	—	6	—
819	5262	Desgl. eines 27jährigen Zwangsarbeiters aus Padang Pandjang, Sumatra	—	—	21	—	6	—
820	5263	Desgl. eines 30jährigen Zwangsarbeiters aus Tandjong Balik, Sumatra	—	—	22	—	6	—
821	5264	Desgl. eines etwa 40jährigen Zwangsarbeiters aus Loeboek Basak, Sumatra	—	—	22,5	—	6	—
822	5265	Desgl. eines 18jährigen Arbeiters aus Taloek, Sumatra	—	—	20,5	—	6	—
823	5266	Desgl. eines 16jährigen Zuckerflanzers aus Taloek, Sumatra	—	—	18	—	6	—
824	5267	Desgl. eines 30jährigen Arbeiters aus Tandjoeng Gran, Sumatra	—	—	20	—	6	—
825	5268	Desgl. eines angehenden Priesters von etwa 20 Jahren aus Sentadja (Taloek), Sumatra	—	—	19	—	6	—
826	5269	Desgl. eines 50jährigen Arbeiters aus Taloek, Sumatra	—	—	22	—	6	—
827	5270	Desgl. eines 25jährigen Arbeiters ebendaher	—	—	20	—	6	—
828	5271	Desgl. eines 55jährigen Gärtners ebendaher	—	—	19	—	6	—
829	5272	Desgl. eines 30jährigen Arbeiters ebendaher	—	—	23	—	6	—
830	5273	Desgl. eines 40 jährigen Gärtners ebendaher	—	—	23	—	6	—
831	5274	Desgl. eines 40jährigen Kaufmanns ebendaher	—	—	21	—	6	—
832	5275	Desgl. eines 25 jährigen Gärtners ebendaher	—	—	21	—	6	—
833	5276	Desgl. eines 30jährigen Gärtners ebendaher	—	—	23	—	6	—

Laufende No.	No. der Formerei	Gegenstand	Material des Originals	Standort des Originals	Höhe (in cm)	Breite (in cm)	Preis M.	Pf.
834	5277	Gesichtsmaske eines 35jährigen Händlers aus Sentadja (Taloek), Sumatra	—	—	21	—	6	—
835	5278	Desgl. eines 30jährigen Hausarbeiters, ebendaher	—	—	22	—	6	—
836	5279	Desgl. eines 20jährigen Gärtners, ebendaher	—	—	22	—	6	—
837	5280	Desgl. eines 22jährigen Gärtners, ebendaher	—	—	22	—	6	—
838	5281	Desgl. eines 20jährigen Gärtners, ebendaher	—	—	21,5	—	6	—
839	5282	Desgl., ebendaher	—	—	22	—	6	—
840	5283	Desgl. eines etwa 30jährigen Gartenarbeiters, ebendaher . . .	—	—	22	—	6	—
841	5284	Desgl. eines 20jährigen Gartenarbeiters aus Kari, Sumatra	—	—	22	—	6	—
842	5285	Desgl. eines 20jährigen Mannes aus Sentadja, Sumatra	—	—	21,5	—	6	—
843	5286	Desgl. Sumatra	—	—	23	—	6	—
844	5287	Desgl. eines 20jährigen Mannes aus Tjerinti, Sumatra	—	—	20	—	6	—
845	5288	Desgl. wie vor, ebendaher	—	—	22,5	—	6	—
846	5289	Desgl. eines 30jährigen Mannes aus Padang, Sumatra	—	—	22,5	—	6	—
847	5290	Desgl. eines Mannes aus Taloek, Sumatra	—	—	22,5	—	6	—
848	5291	Desgl. eines 20jährigen Mannes, ebendaher	—	—	21	—	6	—
849	5292	Desgl. eines 35jährigen Mannes aus Padang, Sumatra	—	—	22	—	6	—
850	5293	Desgl. eines 30jährigen Mannes, ebendaher	—	—	21,5	—	6	—
851	5294	Desgl. eines 35jährigen Mannes, ebendaher	—	—	21	—	6	—
852	5295	Desgl. eines 30jährigen Mannes, ebendaher	—	—	22	—	6	—
853	5296	Desgl. eines 20jährigen Mannes, Sumatra	—	—	21	—	6	—
854	5297	Desgl. eines 24jährigen Mannes aus Moeara Lemboe, Sumatra	—	—	21	—	6	—
855	5298	Desgl. eines 30jährigen Mannes, ebendaher	—	—	21,5	—	6	—
856	5299	Desgl. eines 35jährigen Mannes aus Goenoeng Silihan, Sumatra	—	—	21	—	6	—
857	5300	*) Gesichtsmasken von zwei jungen Männern von ca. 18 Jahren von Agaña, Insel Guam (Marianen) (94, 95) je 6,— M.	—	—	19,2 resp. 18,8	—	12	—

*) Die Stücke 5300—5462 sind nach Formen gegossen, die Dr. O. Finsch nach der Natur geformt und dem Königlichen Museum für Völkerkunde als Geschenk überwiesen

Inventory Numbers 5297–5299, ill. p. 75

Mariano Deljado

Manuele Tanoi

Continued on page 76

Einige Bemerkungen zu den Gesichtsmasken.

Dazu Tafel II—VIII.

Von Alfred Maaß.

Nur der Reisende, welcher sich der Mühe unterzogen hat, auf seiner Reise Gesichtsmasken in Gips von dem Lebenden zu nehmen, kann die Schwierigkeiten dieser Aufgabe ganz würdigen. Neben manueller Geschicklichkeit gehört eine große Geduld und Überredungskunst dazu, die Eingeborenen für diese Aufgabe des Reisenden zu gewinnen.

Bedauerlich ist es deshalb, in manchen Sammlungen zu sehen, wie gering Mühe und Arbeit des Reisenden geschätzt werden, wie die Resultate seines Fleißes und Interesses für die Wissenschaft, in diesem Falle die Gesichtsmasken, verstaubt, beschmutzt, angestoßen daliegen oder aufgestellt sind, als wären sie etwas Nebensächliches, während sie doch dem Beschauer und Anthropologen die Form des Gesichtsfeldes ganz anders vor Augen führen als es eine Photographie vermag. Sprechen sie nicht eine lebendige Sprache, wenn wir auf ihnen die Strukturen der Haut erkennen, atmen sie nicht in gewissem Sinne durch ihre Plastik Leben wieder, wenn wir sie uns auch alle im Banne eines friedlichen Schlummers zu denken haben?

Ich erachte es nicht nur als eine Pflicht der Dankbarkeit gegen meinen Begleiter, Herrn Dr. Kleiweg de Zwaan, sondern auch als eine absolute Notwendigkeit, daß dieser Gesichtsmasken, die zu seiner voraufgehenden, mit so viel Fleiß und Liebe verfaßten Arbeit über die Anthropologie der Minangkabauer gehören, an dieser Stelle in Wort und Bild gedacht wird.

Um den Lesern die von Herrn Dr. Kleiweg de Zwaan mit Fleiß und großer Mühe angefertigten 57 Gipsmasken veranschaulichen zu können, habe ich sie auf sieben Lichtdrucktafeln (Tafel II—VIII) zur Darstellung gebracht. Um den Masken die Härte ihrer weißen Farbe zu nehmen, wurden sie auf den Tafeln etwas in Sepia abgetönt, damit die weichen Züge der Malaien mehr hervortreten.

128 Das Leutematerial für die Gesichtsmasken.

Das Material (die Leute, welche sich für dieses Arbeitsgebiet unserer Reise dienstbar machten und ihr Antlitz in Gips verewigen ließen) setzte sich aus 57 männlichen Minangkabauer Malaien zusammen. Ihrem Geburtsorte nach stammten sie aus den Padanger Hochländern und dem übrigen Zentral-Sumatra. Ihrem Alter nach waren es Leute von 16—55 Jahren, denen das Gesicht abgeformt wurde. Nach Beruf oder Lebenslage waren es Kaufleute, Kleidermacher, Zuckerrohrpflanzer, Gärtner und Tagelöhner sowie einer, der sich für den Beruf eines ḥadji (Mekkapilgers) vorbereitete; den Rest bilden Zwangsarbeiter (Strafgefangene). Ich lasse nun eine Liste zu den Tafeln II—VIII folgen, welche in hintereinanderfolgender Zahlenreihe die Nummern zu den Gesichtsmasken der Leute und gleichzeitig Geburtsort, Geburtsland, Beruf oder Lebenslage sowie das Lebensalter angibt.

Von den 57 Leuten befanden sich 14 Personen in einem Alter von 16—20 Jahren, 19 Personen in einem Alter von 21—30 Jahren. Abermals 14 Personen waren in einem Alter von 31—40 Jahren, 2 Personen in einem Alter von 45 und 50 Jahren, dann nochmals 2 Personen in einem Alter von 55 Jahren. Bei 6 Personen konnte das Alter nicht einwandfrei ermittelt werden.

Nr.	Geburtsort	Geburtsland	Beruf bzw. Lebenslage	Lebens-alter
Tafel II.				Jahre
1	Padang Lawas	Zentral-Sumatra	Zwangsarbeiter	34
2	Kampong Dalam	„	„	21
3	?	„	Kaufmann	55
4	Batu Sangkar	„	„	ca. 35
5	Muarå	„	Arbeiter	ca. 35
6	?	?	?	?
7	Bukit Tinggi	Padanger Hochlande	Arbeiter	20
8	Tandjung Agam	„	Kleidermacher	23
9	Bukit Tinggi	„	Arbeiter	25
Tafel III.				
10	?	?	?	?
11	?	?	?	?
12	Padang Lawas	Padanger Hochlande	Zimmermann	40
13	Tjingkaring	Zentral-Sumatra	Zwangsarbeiter	35
14	Lubuk Alung	„	„	25
15	Sungai Limiong (?)	„	„	38
16	?	„	?	?
17	Taluk	„	Arbeiter	16
18	Padang Pandjang	Padanger Hochlande	Zwangsarbeiter	35

Erklärungen zu den Tafeln der Gesichtsmasken. 129

Nr.	Geburtsort	Geburtsland	Beruf bzw. Lebenslage	Lebens-alter
Tafel IV.				Jahre
19	Simbakå	Padanger Hochlande	Zwangsarbeiter	45
20	Padang Pandjang	„	„	27
21	Tandjung Balit	„	„	30
22	Lubuk Kasap	„	„	38—40
23	Taluk	Zentral-Sumatra	Arbeiter	18
24	„	„	Zuckerrohrpflanzer	16
25	Tandjung Gran (?)	„	Tagelöhner	30
26	Sintadjå (Taluk)	„	Ḥadjischüler	18—20
27	Taluk	„	Arbeiter	50
Tafel V.				
28	Taluk	Zentral-Sumatra	Arbeiter	25
29	„	„	Gärtner	55
30	„	„	Arbeiter	30
31	„	„	Gärtner	40
32	„	„	Kaufmann	40
33	„	„	Gärtner	25
34	„	„	„	30
35	„	„	Kaufmann	35
36	„	„	Tagelöhner	30
Tafel VI.				
37	Taluk	Zentral-Sumatra	Gärtner	29
38	„	„	„	22
39	„	„	„	20
40	„	„	„	20
41	„	„	„	28—30
42	Karit	„	„	20
43	Sintadjå	„	?	ca. 20
44	?	?	?	?
45	Tjaranti	Zentral-Sumatra	?	ca. 20
Tafel VII.				
46	Tjaranti	Zentral-Sumatra	?	ca. 20
47	Padang	„	?	ca. 30
48	Taluk	„	?	?
49	„	„	?	ca. 20
50	Padang	„	?	ca. 35
51	„	„	?	ca. 30
52	„	„	?	ca. 35
53	„	„	?	ca. 30
54	„	„	?	ca. 20
Tafel VIII.				
55	Muarå Lĕmbu	Zentral-Sumatra	?	ca. 24
56	„	„	?	ca. 30
57	Gunung Sahilan	„	?	ca. 35

9

Maaß, Alfred. »Durch Zentral-Sumatra.« Band II.

TAFEL VIII
(zu Seite 127 u. 129)

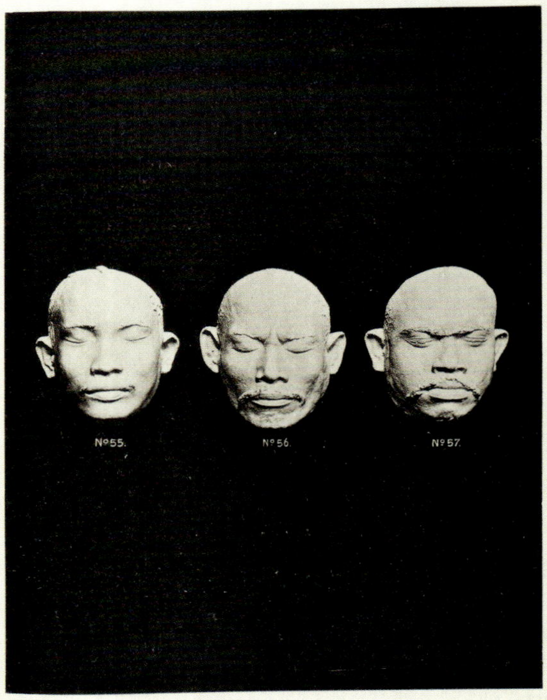

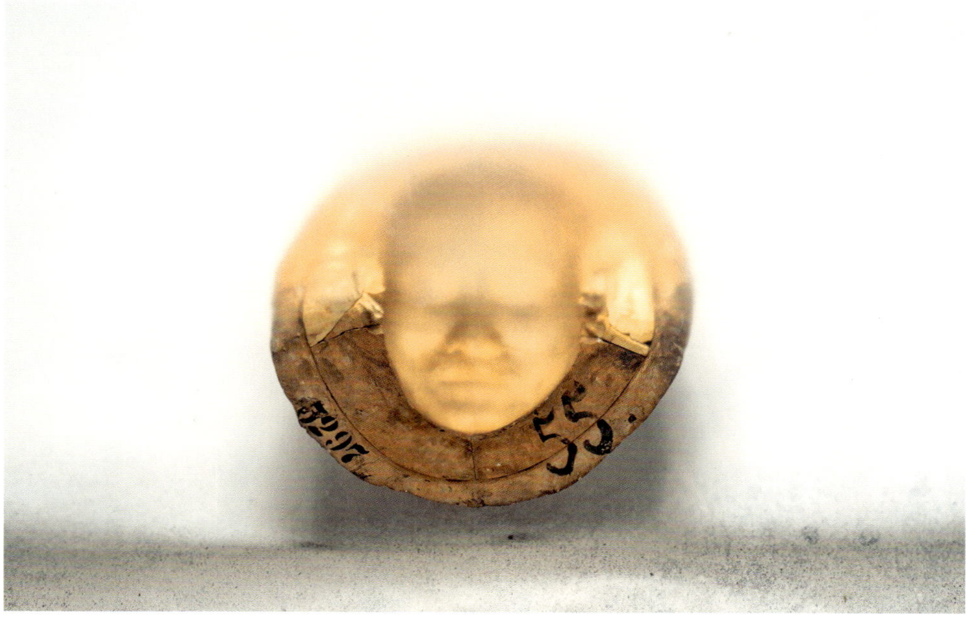

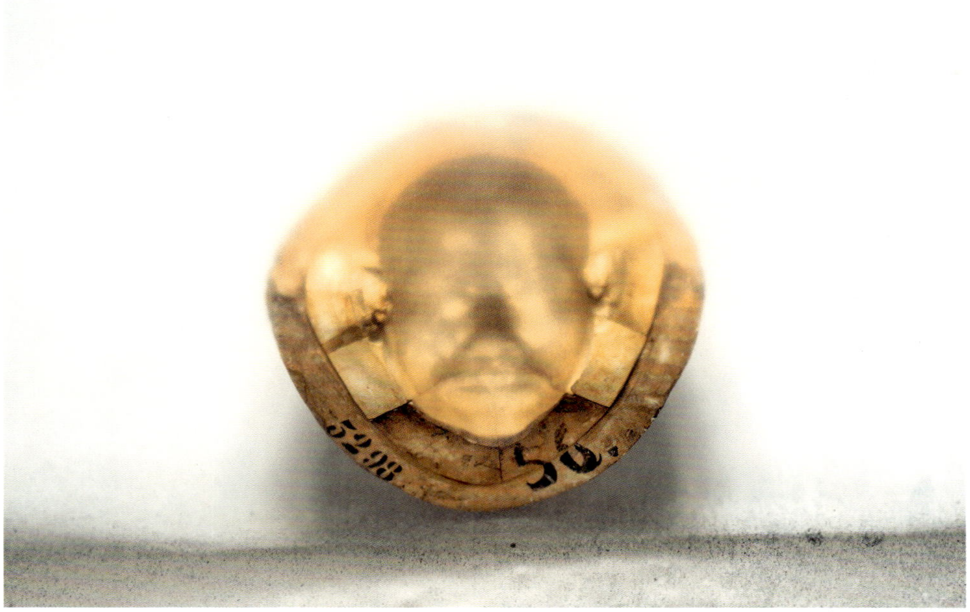

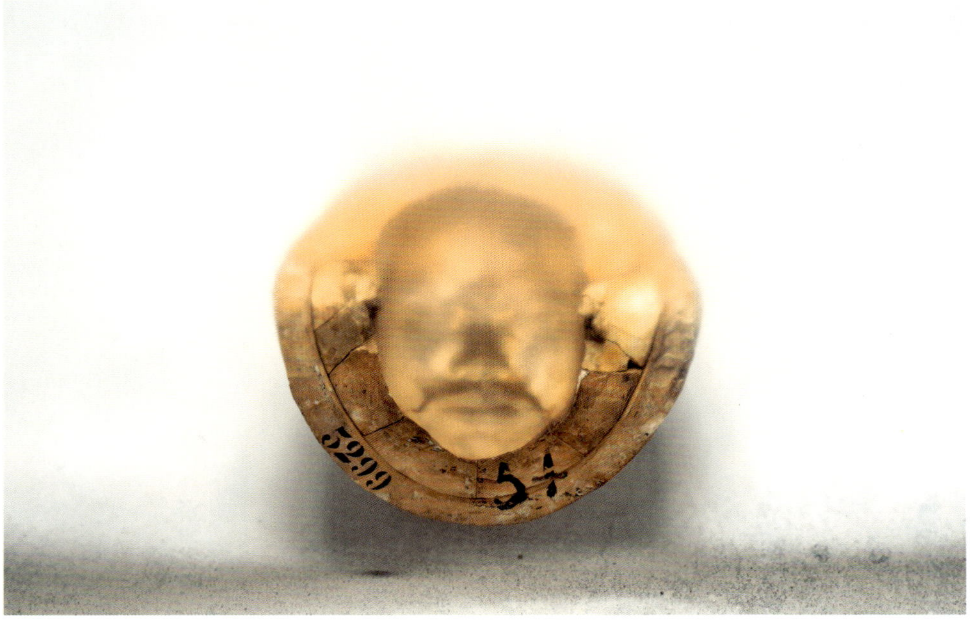

Alfred Maaß
Durch Zentral-Sumatra, vol. 2,
1912, pp. 127–29, plate VIII
Staatliche Museen zu Berlin,
Ethnologisches Museum

Plaster Piece Moulds for Face Masks of Three Not Yet Identified Men (behind foil):
('[Face Mask] of a Twenty-Four-Year-Old Man from Moeara Lemboe, Sumatra'; '[Face Mask] of a Thirty-Year-Old Man from the Same Place'; 'Face Mask of a Thirty-Five-Year-Old Man from Goenoeng Silihan, Sumatra')
Moulded by Johannes Pieter Kleiweg de Zwaan, 1907
Staatliche Museen zu Berlin,
Gipsformerei, 5297, 5298, 5299

The Face Masks from the Collection of Otto Finsch

Inventory Numbers 5300–5462

Ling
Eddewai
Iningemiss
Hiram
Robbin
Nanoa
Liaunitsch
Lijäman
Arriët
Li Kiaksa
Telän
Gloverkän
Warna
Kabua
Lailing
Lagadschimi

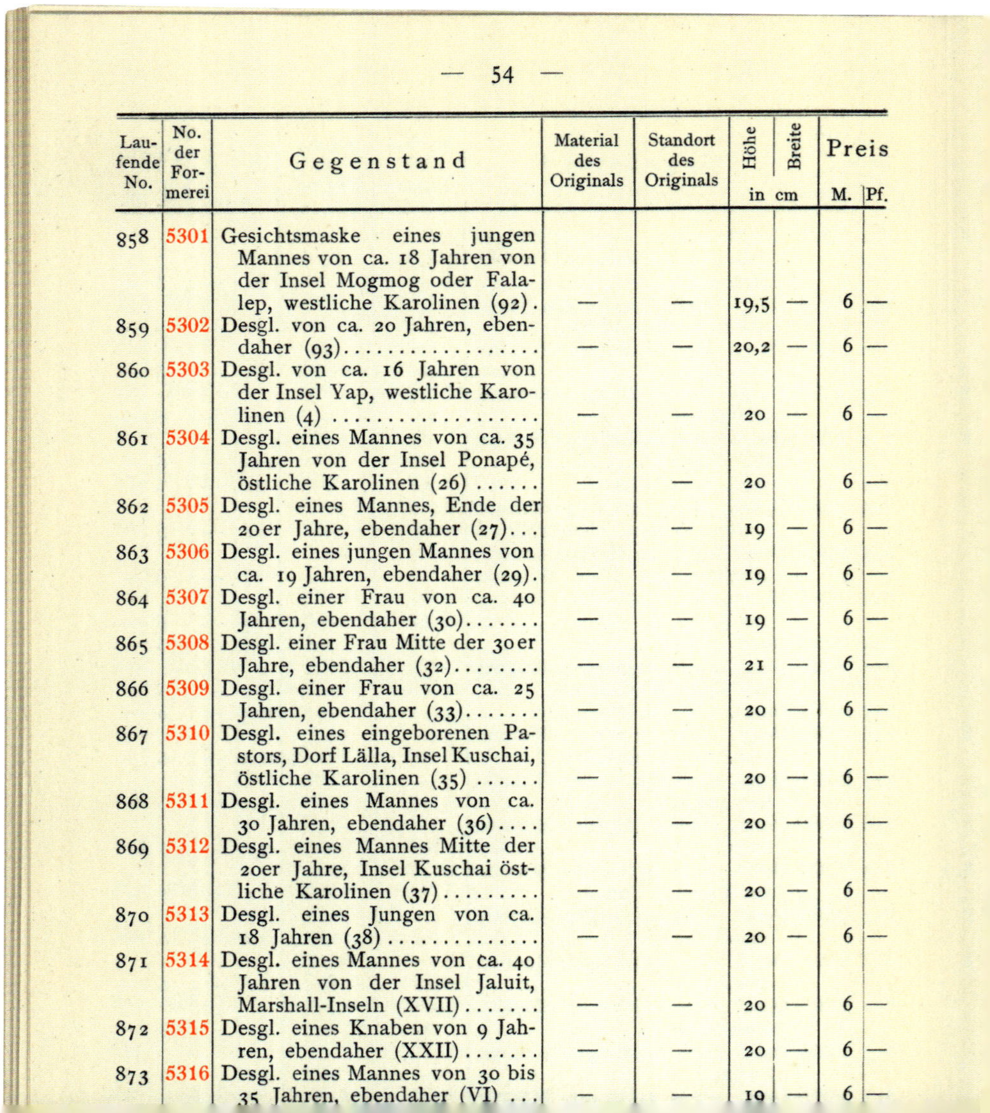

— 54 —

Laufende No.	No. der Formerei	Gegenstand	Material des Originals	Standort des Originals	Höhe (in cm)	Breite (in cm)	Preis M.	Preis Pf.
858	5301	Gesichtsmaske eines jungen Mannes von ca. 18 Jahren von der Insel Mogmog oder Falalep, westliche Karolinen (92)	—	—	19,5	—	6	—
859	5302	Desgl. von ca. 20 Jahren, ebendaher (93)	—	—	20,2	—	6	—
860	5303	Desgl. von ca. 16 Jahren von der Insel Yap, westliche Karolinen (4)	—	—	20	—	6	—
861	5304	Desgl. eines Mannes von ca. 35 Jahren von der Insel Ponapé, östliche Karolinen (26)	—	—	20		6	—
862	5305	Desgl. eines Mannes, Ende der 20er Jahre, ebendaher (27)	—	—	19	—	6	—
863	5306	Desgl. eines jungen Mannes von ca. 19 Jahren, ebendaher (29)	—	—	19	—	6	—
864	5307	Desgl. einer Frau von ca. 40 Jahren, ebendaher (30)	—	—	19	—	6	—
865	5308	Desgl. einer Frau Mitte der 30er Jahre, ebendaher (32)	—	—	21	—	6	—
866	5309	Desgl. einer Frau von ca. 25 Jahren, ebendaher (33)	—	—	20	—	6	—
867	5310	Desgl. eines eingeborenen Pastors, Dorf Lälla, Insel Kuschai, östliche Karolinen (35)	—	—	20	—	6	—
868	5311	Desgl. eines Mannes von ca. 30 Jahren, ebendaher (36)	—	—	20	—	6	—
869	5312	Desgl. eines Mannes Mitte der 20er Jahre, Insel Kuschai östliche Karolinen (37)	—	—	20	—	6	—
870	5313	Desgl. eines Jungen von ca. 18 Jahren (38)	—	—	20	—	6	—
871	5314	Desgl. eines Mannes von ca. 40 Jahren von der Insel Jaluit, Marshall-Inseln (XVII)	—	—	20	—	6	—
872	5315	Desgl. eines Knaben von 9 Jahren, ebendaher (XXII)	—	—	20	—	6	—
873	5316	Desgl. eines Mannes von 30 bis 35 Jahren, ebendaher (VI)	—	—	19	—	6	—

Numbering roughly 160 objects, the largest group of anthropological lifecasts in the Gipsformerei is based on moulds made by Friedrich Hermann Otto Finsch (1839–1917). Finsch had been commissioned by the Alexander von Humboldt-Stiftung für Naturforschung und Reisen in Berlin to visit various islands in the Pacific between 1879 and 1882. For Finsch the face masks he collected — two hundred by the time he returned — were the most important result of his expedition. His request in a letter to Rudolf Virchow of 20 June 1880 that the 'moulds are handed for casting to an able and skilful plaster caster and that the reproduction rights, apart from the originals, are reserved to me', was realised right away: casting forms were made by the Berlin sculptor and panopticum operator Louis Castan at Finsch's own expense and coloured plaster casts were placed on display, reproduced and sold in Castan's Panoptikum. In her research, historian Angela Friederici has shown that the complete collection of Finsch's face masks were sold to Paris, Florence, St Petersburg, Sydney and, in 1887, to the Königliches Museum für Völkerkunde in Berlin. She also writes of how incomplete series and small groups of these masks were handed to museums in Dresden, Leiden, Salford, Liverpool and London. Finsch gave the forms made by Castan to the Gipsformerei in 1900; subsequent sales of the casts were limited to small batches and individual masks. The last order was placed in 1926. A comparison of Finsch's travelogue *Anthropologische Ergebnisse einer Reise in der Südsee und dem malayischen Archipel in den Jahren 1879–1882* (ill. p. 81) with the sales catalogue of the Gipsformerei reveals that when these masks were integrated into the collection, the first names of the persons moulded, as recorded by Finsch, were removed: human beings were reduced to inventory numbers, to objects, to commodities. The re-attribution of names initiated by Britta Lange in 2013 has been extended to the entire collection records of Finsch's masks and added to the sales catalogue reprinted in this book. The aim here is to at least partially free the human beings behind these objects from anonymity.

— 55 —

Laufende No.	No. der Formerei	Gegenstand	Material des Originals	Standort des Originals	Höhe (in cm)	Breite (in cm)	Preis M.	Pf.	
877	5320	Gesichtsmaske eines Mädchens von 8 bis 9 Jahren von der Insel Jaluit, Marshall-Inseln (XXIV).	—	—	17,5	—	6	—	Nemar
878	5321	Desgl. einer Frau von ca. 22 Jahren, ebendaher (XX)	—	—	18,4	—	6	—	Nedschadschok (Nedjadjok)
879	5322	Desgl. eines Mädchens von 17 bis 20 Jahren, ebendaher (XXI)	—	—	18	—	6	—	Lanebal
880	5323	Desgl. eines Mädchens von ca. 17 Jahren, ebendaher (XIX)..	—	—	18,4	—	6	—	Libudschin
881	5324	Desgl. einer Frau von 17 bis 20 Jahren von der Insel Milli, Marshall-Inseln (39)	—	—	17,5	—	6	—	Limigal
882	5325	Desgl. eines Mannes von ca. 30 Jahren von der Insel Makin, Gilbert-Inseln (42)..........	—	—	20,6	—	6	—	Ankumari
883	5326	Desgl. einer Frau von 25 bis 30 Jahren, ebendaher (46) ...	—	—	18,4	—	6	—	Ideragünta
884	5327	Desgl. eines Mädchens von 16 bis 19 Jahren, ebendaher (47)	—	—	18,7	—	6	—	Ingama
885	5328	Desgl. eines Mannes von 40 bis 45 Jahren von der Insel Butaritari, Gilbert-Inseln (40).....	—	—	18,9	—	6	—	Detarrakap
886	5329	Desgl. einer Frau von 18 bis 20 Jahren, ebendaher (48)....	—	—	18,2	—	6	—	Ibobon
887	5330	Desgl. eines Mannes von ca. 30 Jahren von der Insel Maraki, Gilbert-Inseln (XII)..........	—	—	19,1	—	6	—	Tinnidigé
888	5331	Desgl. eines Mannes von ca. 20 Jahren von der Insel Apaiang, Gilbert-Inseln (43)..........	—	—	19	—	6	—	Tekarreó
889	5332	Desgl. eines Mannes von ca. 30 Jahren von der Insel Tarowa, Gilbert-Inseln (3)............	—	—	19	—	6	—	Tibbea
890	5333	Desgl. eines Mannes von ca. 40 Jahren von der Insel Maiana, Gilbert-Inseln (XVI).........	—	—	18,5	—	6	—	Nabuki
891	5334	Desgl. eines Mannes von ca. 25 bis 28 Jahren, ebendaher (2) .	—	—	19	—	6	—	Dingkaredea

	Laufende No.	No. der Formerei	Gegenstand	Material des Originals	Standort des Originals	Höhe (in cm)	Breite (in cm)	Preis M.	Preis Pf.
	873	5316	Desgl. eines Mannes von 30 bis 35 Jahren, ebendaher (VI) ...	—	—	19	—	6	—
Legeri	874	5317	Desgl. eines Mannes von 30 bis 35 Jahren, ebendaher (XVIII)	—	—	20	—	6	—
Dabelaibo	875	5318	Desgl. eines Jungen von ca 16 Jahren, ebendaher (5)........	—	—	20	—	6	—
Dschedschadschu (Djedjadju)	876	5319	Desgl. einer Frau von 26 bis 30 Jahren, ebendaher (XXIII)	—	—	18,1	—	6	—

hat. Vgl. Dr. O. Finsch: Anthropologische Ergebnisse einer Reise in der Südsee und dem malayischen Archipel in den Jahren 1879—1882. Beschreibender Katalog der auf dieser Reise gesammelten Gesichtsmasken von Völkertypen. Berlin, Asher & Co. 1884. Mit 6 Tafeln.

— 56 —

	Laufende No.	No. der Formerei	Gegenstand	Material des Originals	Standort des Originals	Höhe (in cm)	Breite (in cm)	Preis M.	Preis Pf.
Sari	898	5343	Gesichtsmaske eines Mannes von ca. 22 Jahren von der Insel Peru, Gilbert-Inseln (49)	—	—	18,8	—	6	—
Dschinturo	899	5344	Desgl. eines Mannes von ca. 20 Jahren, von Banaba (34)	—	—	18,5	—	6	—
Inginana	900	5345	Desgl. eines Jungen von ca. 16 Jahren, ebendaher (XI)	—	—	17,4	—	6	—
Emagto	901	5346	Desgl. einer Frau von ca. 30 Jahren, ebendaher (X)	—	—	17	—	6	—
Gai-inga	902	5347	Desgl. eines Mannes von ca. 20 Jahren, von Ontong, Java (60)........................	—	—	19,4	—	6	—
Dachoi	903	5348	Desgl. eines Mannes von ca. 30 Jahren, von den Hermit-Inseln (57)........................	—	—	19,3	—	6	—
Charly Tett	904	5349	Desgl. eines Mannes von ca. 50 Jahren, von Hawaii (187)..	—	—	19,4	—	6	—
Tautoa	905	5350	Desgl. eines Mannes von ca. 25 Jahren, von den Ellice-Inseln (50)........................	—	—	19,4	—	6	—
Worrontiro	906	5351	Desgl. eines Mannes von ca. 20 Jahren, von Rotumah (51).	—	—	19	—	6	—
Iporitu	907	5352	Desgl. eines Mannes von ca. 26 Jahren, von Matafele bei Apia (Samoa) (192)	—	—	20,2	—	6	—
Leoni	908	5353	Desgl. eines Mannes von ca. 30 Jahren, von der Insel Tutuila (Samoa) (190)..........	—	—	19,5	—	6	—
Tscham	909	5354	Desgl. eines Mannes von ca. 25 Jahren, von der Vavau-Gruppe (52)	—	—	18,3	—	6	—
Ssiua	910	5355	Desgl. eines Mannes von ca. 20 Jahren, von Niuë (53).....	—	—	18,3	—	6	—
Louis	911	5356	Desgl. eines Mannes von ca. 27 Jahren, ebendaher (55)....	—	—	17,9	—	6	—
Ngapaki Puni	912	5357	Desgl. eines Mannes von ca. 65 Jahren, von Neu-Seeland (128)........................	—	—	19,5	—	6	—
Honianate Puni	913	5358	Desgl. eines Jungen von ca. 17 Jahren, ebendaher (130)...	—	—	19,7	—	6	—
Wiremu Nera te Kanaë	914	5359	Desgl. eines Mannes von ca. 34 Jahren, ebendaher (125)...	—	—	20,8	—	6	—
Oriwia te Atiraukawa	915	5360	Desgl. einer Frau von ca. 50 Jahren, ebendaher (127)	—	—	18,8	—	6	—
Makit Muara Ením	916	5361	Desgl. eines Mannes von ca. 20 Jahren, von Palembang (Sumatra) (201)	—	—	18	—	6	—
Sablat	917	5362	Desgl. eines Mannes von ca. 35 Jahren, von Bengkulen (Sumatra) (202)	—	—	18,6	—	6	—

— 58 —

	Laufende No.	No. der Formerei	Gegenstand	Material des Originals	Standort des Originals	Höhe (in cm)	Breite (in cm)	Preis M.	Preis Pf.
To nomnom, To tarawiè	938	5384	Gesichtsmaske eines Mannes von 18 bis 20 Jahren, von Matupi (Neu-Britannien) (72, 67)	—	—	18,5	—	6	—
To kopíake	939	5386	Desgl. eines Jungen von ca. 18 Jahren, ebendaher (73)....	—	—	18,2	—	6	—
	940	5387	Desgl. eines Jungen von ca.						

		bis 28 Jahren, ebendaher (2) .	—	—	19	—	6	—	
892	5335	Desgl. einer Frau von 24 bis 26 Jahren, ebendaher (XIV)	—	—	18,4	—	6	—	Ideabegge
893	5336	Brust der vorhergehenden (122)	—	—	27,5	23	6	—	
894	5337	Büste desgleichen (122a)	—	—	47	40	20	—	
895	5338	Gesichtsmaske eines Mädchens von ca. 16 Jahren (XV)	—	—	18	—	3	—	Eddenigiau
896	5340	Hand eines Mädchens von ca. 8 bis 9 Jahren (1)	—	—	17,5	7	4	—	Ø
897	5341	Gesichtsmaske eines Mannes von ca. 30 Jahren von der Insel Apamama, Gilbert-Inseln (IX)	—	—	19,1	—	6	—	Diknëi

— 57 —

Laufende No.	No. der Formerei	Gegenstand	Material des Originals	Standort des Originals	Höhe (in cm)	Breite (in cm)	Preis M.	Pf.	
918	5363	Gesichtsmaske eines Mannes von ca. 23 Jahren, von Banjermassing (Borneo) (199)	—	—	18,5	—	6	—	Hadji Achmet
919	5364	Desgl. eines Mannes von ca. 28 Jahren, von Segli (Atjeh) (200)	—	—	19,2	—	6	—	Sisam
920	5365	Desgl. eines Mannes von ca. 25 Jahren, von Bonogiri (Java) (196)	—	—	18,6	—	6	—	Gromosmito
921	5366	Desgl. eines Mannes von ca. 35 Jahren, aus dem Kampong Batung (Java) (198)	—	—	17,5	—	6	—	Pa Kasimín
922	5368	Desgl. eines Mannes von ca. 27 Jahren, von Sumanap, Ost-Madura (195)	—	—	18,6	—	6	—	Liman — Inventory Numbers 5365–5371, ill. p. 81
923	5369	Desgl. eines Mannes von ca. 35 Jahren, aus dem Kampong Beleling (Insel Bali) (204)	—	—	17,7	—	6	—	Tútur
924	5370	Desgl. eines Mannes von ca. 30 Jahren, von Atapupu, Insel Timor (194)	—	—	17,6	—	6	—	Mauk
925	5371	Desgl. eines Mannes von ca. 25 Jahren, von der Insel Saleyer (203)	—	—	18,6	—	6	—	Bakálang
926	5372	Desgl. eines Mannes von ca. 25 Jahren, von Santa Maria, Insel Luçon (7)	—	—	18,5	—	6	—	Pedro
927	5373	Desgl. eines Mannes von ca. 25 Jahren, von Amoy, Süd-China (205)	—	—	18,2	—	6	—	Ling Yeng Kee Ohmée
928	5374	Desgl. eines Mannes von ca. 29 Jahren, von Nagasaki (8) .	—	—	19,1	—	6	—	Madakitschi
929	5375	Desgl. eines Mannes von ca. 33 Jahren, von Matupi (Neu-Britannien) (69)	—	—	20	—	6	—	Totem
930	5376	Desgl. eines Mannes von ca. 22 Jahren, ebendaher (71)	—	—	19,3	—	6	—	Ta mono
931	5377	Desgl. eines Mannes Ende der 40 er, ebendaher (64)	—	—	19,4	—	6	—	To makiale
932	5378	Desgl. eines Mannes von ca. 35 Jahren, ebendaher (77)	—	—	19	—	6	—	To worrap
933	5379	Desgl. eines Mannes von 28 bis 30 Jahren, ebendaher (68)	—	—	19	—	6	—	Tat taur
934	5380	Desgl. eines Mannes von 25 bis 28 Jahren, ebendaher (75)	—	—	18,7	—	6	—	Treisink
935	5381	Desgl. eines Mannes von 26 bis 28 Jahren, ebendaher (76)	—	—	18,9	—	6	—	To puang
936	5382	Desgl. eines Mannes von 22 bis 25 Jahren, ebendaher (70)	—	—	18,5	—	6	—	Turlom
937	5383	Desgl. eines Mannes von 20 bis 22 Jahren, ebendaher (74)	—	—	18,6	—	6	—	To wordok

— 59 —

Laufende No.	No. der Formerei	Gegenstand	Material des Originals	Standort des Originals	Höhe (in cm)	Breite (in cm)	Preis M.	Pf.	
959	5406	Brust eines Mädchens von ca. 15 bis 16 Jahren, von Matupi (Neu-Britannien) (99)	—	—	28	22	7	—	Jauratib
960	5408	Linker Oberschenkel einer Frau von ca. 20—25 Jahren mit Zierfarben, ebendaher (98)	—	—	51	—	10	—	Jegerámit

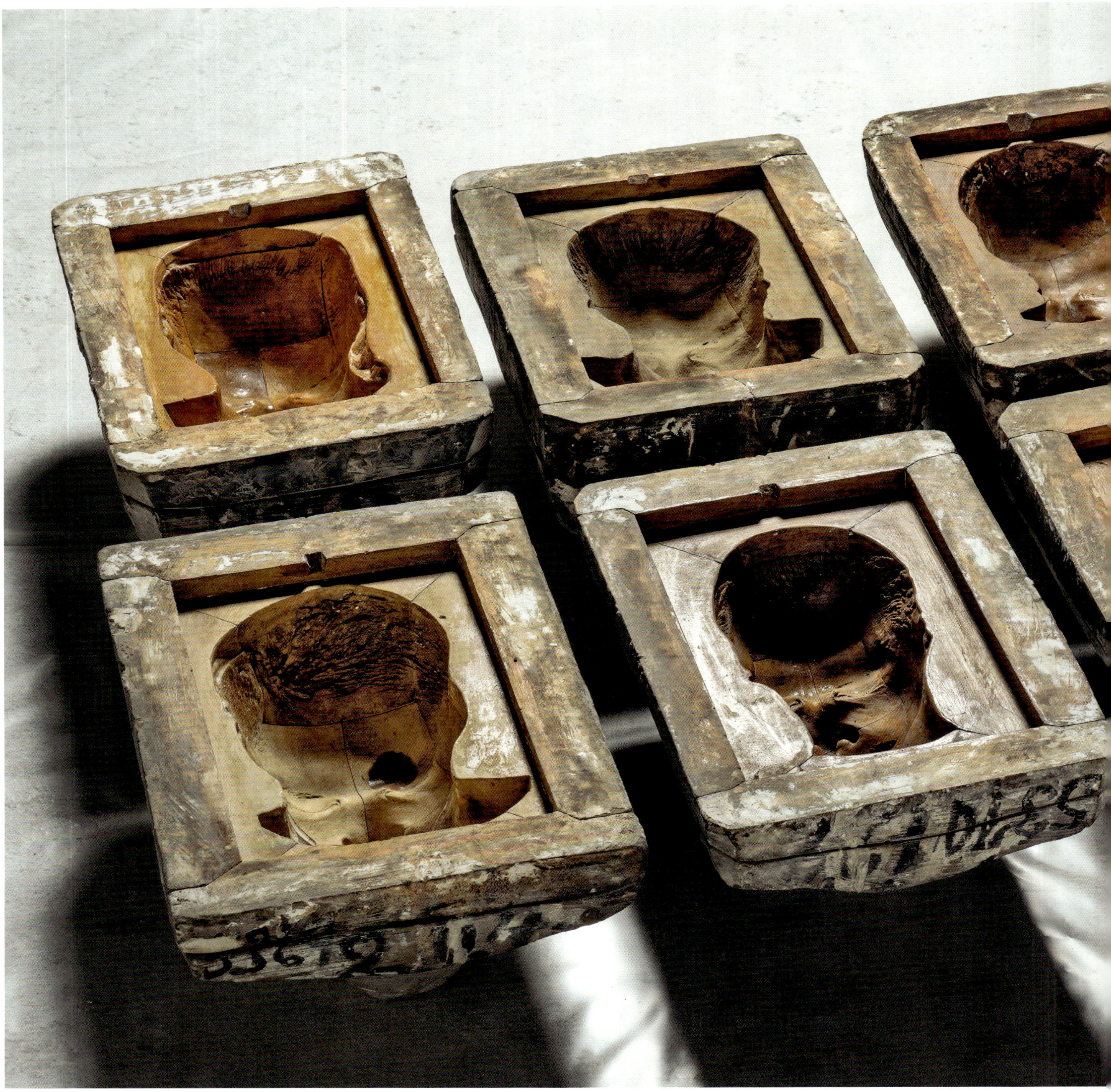

Plaster Piece Moulds for Face Masks of Six Men called Gromosmito, Pa Kasimín, Liman, Tútur, Mauk and Bakálang, moulded by Otto Finsch, remoulded by Louis and Gustave Castan, ca. 1883/87
Staatliche Museen zu Berlin, Gipsformerei, 5365, 5366, 5368, 5369, 5370, 5371

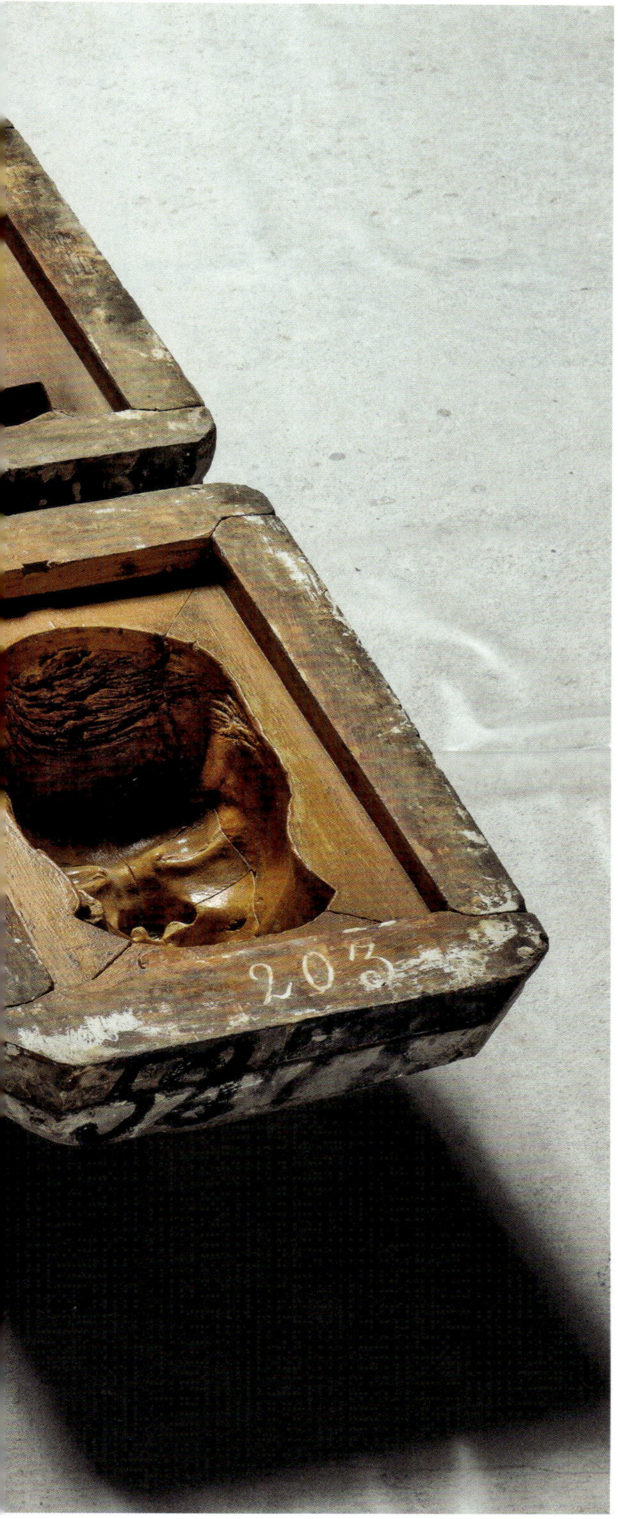

Otto Finsch
Anthropologische Ergebnisse einer Reise in der Südsee und dem malayischen Archipel in den Jahren 1879–1882: Beschreibender Catalog der auf dieser Reise gesammelten Gesichtsmasken von Völkertypen, mit 60 Körpermessungen, Zeitschrift für Ethnologie, vol. 15, 1883, supplement
Staatliche Museen zu Berlin, Kunstbibliothek

30

b) Javanesen.

Nach den Mittheilungen Dr. Vorderman's wird die grosse Insel Java (mit über 19 Millionen Einwohnern) von drei, auch sprachlich verschiedenen Stämmen: Javanesen, Sundanesen und Maduresen bewohnt, von denen ich durch seine Güte reine Typen zum Abgiessen erhielt.

No. 196. Gromosmito, von Bonogiri, Surakarta, Kaiserthum Solo.

Kräftiger, junger Mann von ca. 25 Jahren. — Höhe 1,66 *m*, Brustumfang 90 *cm*, Längsaxe des Schädels 186 *mm*. — Hautfärbung zwischen No. 32 und 33, aber schmutziger. Nase breit, etwas flach gedrückt; Nasenlöcher klein, nach unten geöffnet; Backenknochen stark vorspringend. Augen gross, etwas geschlitzt. Der innere obere Augenrand nicht herabgezogen; Wimpern lang, Augenbrauen stark, schwarz. Mund proportionirt; Unterlippe etwas voll, ansehnlich dicker als die obere. Haare lang, schlicht, schwarz; spärlicher Schnurrbart.

No. 198. Pa Kasimín, aus dem Campong Batúng, Passaruan, Java.

Kräftiger Mann, ca. 35 Jahr alt. Höhe 1,63 *m*, Brustumfang 81 *cm*, Längsaxe des Schädels 175 *mm*. Hautfärbung zwischen No. 29 und 30, fast zu No. 29 hinneigend.

Nase in gerader Linie verlaufend, breit, Kuppe stumpf gerundet; Nasenlöcher nach unten geöffnet. Backenknochen stark vorspringend. Mund gross, mit sehr vollen Lippen, sowohl die obere als die untere. Augen gross, voll, nicht geschlitzt; innere Augenwinkelwand nicht herabgezogen. Kein Haar im Gesicht, weil ausgerissen; sehr wenig über der Herzgrube; Stirn breit, gewölbt vortretend.

Gesichtsausdruck sehr weibisch, hauptsächlich in Folge des langen, ganz nach Weiberart in einen Knoten geschlagenen Haupthaares.

c) Sundanesen.

No. 197. Sati, von Banjuwaru bei Buitenzorge. Hübsches, gut gebautes Mädchen, ca. 16 Jahr alt.

Höhe 1,57 *m*, Brustumfang 84 *cm*, Längsaxe des Schädels 175 *mm*. Häutfärbung zwischen No. 32 und 33; im Gesicht heller, fast 33.

Nase eingebogen, breit, Kuppe sehr stumpf gerundet, mit stark aufgeworfenen Rändern; Nasenlöcher ziemlich gross, länglich-rund, nach vorn geöffnet. Backenknochen stark vorspringend. Mund proportionirt, Lippen schön, etwas voll, etwas roth durchscheinend (schmutzig, dunkelfleischroth), Kinn gerundet. Auge gross, voll, dunkelbraun; der innere obere Augenlidrand nicht herabgezogen. Haar schlicht, schwarz. Brüste sehr wohlgeformt, fest.

31

d) Maduresen.

No. 195. Liman. von Sumanap, Ost-Madura. Kräftiger Mann, ca. 27 Jahr alt.

Höhe 1,63 *m*, Brustumfang 79 *cm*. Längsaxe des Kopfes 186 *mm*. Hautfärbung zwischen No. 29 und 30, mehr zu No. 29 hinneigend. Stirn breit, hoch, gewölbt, Nase eingebogen, breit; Kuppe und Seitenflügel in einander verfliessend; Nasenlöcher etwas nach vorn geöffnet, gross, länglich, oval. Backenknochen stark vorspringend. Auge gross, etwas geschlitzt, der innere obere Augenrand merklich herabgezogen, wie bei Malayen; Augenbrauen stark, schwarz. Mund proportionirt, mit vollen Lippen, roth durchscheinend. Haar schlicht, schwarz. Spärlicher Schnurrbart, hauptsächlich über den Mundwinkeln; Backenbart ebenfalls spärlich, schwarz.

e) Balinesen.

No. 204. Tútur, aus dem Campong Beleling, Insel Bali.

Kräftiger Mann von ca. 35 Jahren. Höhe 1,60 *m*, Brustumfang 87 *cm*, Längsaxe des Kopfes 177 *mm*. — Hautfärbung zwischen 29 und 30, mehr zu 30 hinneigend.

Nase gerade, mit schwach gebogenem Rücken; Nasenspitze merklich vorragend, Kuppe gerundet; Nasenflügel nicht sehr hervortretend, daher Nase nicht so breit; Nasenlöcher nach unten geöffnet. Auge gross, etwas geschlitzt; obere, innere Augenlidrand herabgezogen; Backenknochen stark vorspringend: Mund breit, mit sehr vollen Lippen, dieselben dunkel, etwas roth durchscheinend. Haar schlicht, schwarz. Spärlicher Bartwuchs an Kinn und Oberlippe.

f) Timoresen.

No. 194. Mauk von Atapupu, Timor.

Schmächtiger Mann von ca. 30 Jahren. Höhe 1,67 *m*, Brustumfang 82 *cm*, Längsaxe des Schädels 176 *mm*. —

Hautfärbung etwa wie No. 30, aber schmutziger, bräunlich getrübt. Augen schwarzbraun; Haar schlicht, schwarz.

g) Buginesen (Celebes).

No. 203. Bakálang, von der Insel Saleyer, Süd-Celebes.

Kräftiger Mann, ca. 25 Jahr alt. Höhe 1,56 *m*, Brustumfang 84 *cm*, Längsaxe des Kopfes 186 *mm*.

Hautfärbung zwischen No. 29 und 30, dunkler als 30 und schmutziger;

	Laufende No.	No. der Formerei	Gegenstand	Material des Originals	Standort des Originals	Höhe in cm	Breite in cm	Preis M.	Pf.
			18 Jahren, ebendaher (73)....						
Tombadale	940	5387	Desgl. eines Jungen von ca. 18 Jahren, ebendaher (58)....	—	—	19,1	—	6	—
Tóllema	941	5388	Desgl. eines Jungen von ca. 15 bis 16 Jahren, ebendaher (63)........................	—	—	18,9	—	6	—
Triman	942	5389	Desgl. eines Jungen von ca. 15 bis 16 Jahren, ebendaher (65)........................	—	—	18,1	—	6	—
To kolemán	943	5390	Desgl. eines Knaben von ca. 9 bis 10 Jahren, ebendaher (61)........................	—	—	17,8	—	6	—
To panje	944	5391	Desgl. eines Knaben von ca. 8 Jahren, ebendaher (66)....	—	—	19	—	6	—
To matavu	945	5392	Desgl. eines Knaben von ca. 8 Jahren, ebendaher (62).....	—	—	18	—	6	—
Tongille	946	5393	Brust eines Mannes mit Ziernarben, ebendaher (89)......	—	—	27	18	6	—
Tewarden	947	5394	Brust mit Ziernarben in Radform, ebendaher (97)..............	—	—	28,5	17,5	6	—
Je girr	948	5395	Gesichtsmaske einer Frau von 30 bis 35 Jahren, ebendaher (81)........................	—	—	18,7	—	6	—
Je walil	949	5396	Desgl. einer Frau von ca. 30 Jahren, ebendaher (85).........	—	—	18,5	—	6	—
Je wangange	950	5397	Desgl. einer Frau von ca. 30 Jahren, ebendaher (86).........	—	—	18,6	—	6	—
Je tegoll	951	5398	Desgl. einer Frau von ca. 25 bis 27 Jahren, ebendaher (78)....	—	—	19	—	6	—
Injigok	952	5399	Desgl. eines Mädchens von ca. 18 bis 20 Jahren, ebendaher (82)........................	—	—	17,7	—	6	—
Je kabarra	953	5400	Desgl. eines Mädchens von ca. 18 Jahren, ebendaher (83)....	—	—	18,3	—	6	—
Je kupau	954	5401	Desgl. eines Mädchens von ca. 15 bis 16 Jahren, ebendaher (80)........................	—	—	18	—	6	—
Kiacki	955	5402	Desgl. eines Mädchens von 12 bis 13 Jahren, ebendaher (84)	—	—	17,5	—	6	—
Je wurma	956	5403	Desgl. eines Kindes von 10 Jahren, ebendaher (79)..........	—	—	18,4	—	6	—
Ø	957	5404	Desgl. eines Mädchens von ca. 8 bis 9 Jahren, ebendaher (87)........................	—	—	17,5	—	6	—
Jembitt	958	5405	Desgl. eines Mädchens von ca. 6 bis 7 Jahren, ebendaher (90)	—	—	17,6	—	6	—

— 60 —

	Laufende No.	No. der Formerei	Gegenstand	Material des Originals	Standort des Originals	Höhe in cm	Breite in cm	Preis M.	Pf.
Beiles	977	5425	Gesichtsmaske eines Mannes von ca. 25 Jahren, von der Insel Tumor (Shortland-Inseln) (103)	—	—	19,1	—	6	—
Tacho	978	5426	Desgl. eines Mannes von ca. 25 Jahren, von Buka (104)...	—	—	19,1	—	6	—
Tarongneu	979	5427	Desgl. eines Mannes von ca. 20 Jahren, von Wissale, Insel Guadalcanar (121)..........	—	—	18,7	—	6	—
Doduri	980	5428	Desgl. eines Mannes von ca. 30 Jahren, ebendaher (120)...	—	—	19	—	6	—
Numilote	981	5429	Desgl. eines Mannes von 30 bis 35 Jahren, von Viti-Levu, Fidschi-Inseln (101)...........	—	—	19,7	—	6	—
Vatisoni	982	5430	Desgl. eines Mannes von ca. 45 Jahren, ebendaher (116)...	—	—	19	—	6	—
Beni Launia	983	5431	Desgl. eines Mannes von ca. 30 Jahren, von der Insel Kandávu (Fidschi-Inseln) (96)....	—	—	19,7	—	6	—
Walu	984	5432	Desgl. eines Mannes von ca. 30 Jahren, von der Insel Maré, Loyalitäts-Inseln (191).......	—	—	19,7	—	6	—
Judschini (Harry)	985	5433	Desgl. eines Mannes von ca. 30 bis 35 Jahren, ebendaher (186)	—	—	19	—	6	—
Wedschi (Peter)	986	5434	Desgl. eines Mannes von ca. 27 Jahren, von der Insel Lifu (Loyalitäts-Inseln) (151)......	—	—	19,1	—	6	—
Alisse	987	5435	Desgl. eines Mannes von ca. 28 bis 30 Jahren, von der Insel Saibai (Britisch Neu-Guinea) (188)................	—	—	19,7	—	6	—
Waara	988	5436	Desgl. eines Mannes von ca. 30 Jahren, von Kerräma (ebenda) (160)...................	—	—	18,7	—	6	—
Aihi	989	5437	Desgl. eines Mannes von ca. 24 Jahren, von Maiva (ebenda) (183)	—	—	18,7	—	6	—
Irna	990	5438	Desgl. eines Mannes von ca. 30 Jahren, von Anuapata (eben-						

[illegible]	[illegible]	[illegible] von ca. 20—25 Jahren mit Ziernarben, ebendaher (98) ...	—	—	51	—	10	—	
961	5409	Gesichtsmaske eines Jungen von ca. 16 bis 18 Jahren, von der Insel Makada (59)	—	—	19,2	—	6	—	Ta Lulumboì
962	5410	Desgl. eines Mannes von ca. 20 bis 22 Jahren, von der Insel Kapaterong (Neu-Irland) (117)	—	—	19,7	—	6	—	Balla
963	5411	Desgl. eines Mannes von 18 bis 20 Jahren, ebendaher (118) ...	—	—	18,6	—	6	—	Baleigub
964	5412	Desgl. eines Jungen von ca. 18 Jahren, ebendaher (119) ..	—	—	18,3	—	6	—	Matawut
965	5413	Desgl. eines Mannes von ca. 20 bis 21 Jahren aus Lagunebange (Neu-Irland) (113)	—	—	19,2	—	6	—	Tomatap
966	5414	Desgl., ca. gleiches Alter, ebendaher (114)	—	—	18,8	—	6	—	Bullemazis
967	5415	Desgl. eines Knaben von ca. 13 bis 14 Jahren, ebendaher (115)	—	—	18,6	—	6	—	Najamuid
968	5416	Desgl. eines Mannes von ca. 24 bis 26 Jahren, aus Butbut (Neu-Irland) (107)	—	—	19,2	—	6	—	Tanget
969	5417	Desgl. eines Mannes von ca. 25 Jahren, von der Insel Nusa (108)	—	—	18,8	—	6	—	Tomaituk
970	5418	Desgl. eines Jungen von ca. 16 Jahren, ebendaher (110) ..	—	—	18,3	—	6	—	Wagelon
971	5419	Desgl. eines Jungen von ca. 15 Jahren, ebendaher (111) ...	—	—	18,2	—	6	—	Adutman
972	5420	Desgl. eines Mannes von ca. 20 Jahren, aus Kablemang (Neu-Irland) (109)	—	—	18,3	—	6	—	Wassangule
973	5421	Desgl. eines Knaben von ca. 10 Jahren, ebendaher (112) ...	—	—	17,5	—	6	—	Banjeru
974	5422	Desgl. einer Frau von ca. 20 Jahren, aus Butbut (Neu-Irland) (106)	—	—	17,4	—	6	—	Laramit
975	5423	Desgl. eines Mädchens von ca. 13 bis 14 Jahren, aus Albian (Neu-Irland) (105)	—	—	17,9	—	6	—	Pilage
976	5424	Desgl. eines Mannes von ca. 30 Jahren, von der Insel Tumor (Shortland - Inseln) (102)	—	—	18,5	—	6	—	Weling

Laufende No.	No. der Formerei	Gegenstand	Material des Originals	Standort des Originals	Höhe in cm	Breite in cm	Preis M.	Preis Pf.	
997	5445	Gesichtsmaske eines Mädchens von ca. 13 bis 14 Jahren, aus Anuapata (168)	—	—	18,9	—	6	—	Boni
998	5446	Desgl. eines Mädchens von ca. 16 Jahren, ebendaher (169) ...	—	—	18,5	—	6	—	Kabadi
999	5447	Desgl. eines Mannes von ca. 30 Jahren, ebendaher (163) ...	—	—	19	—	6	—	Luboko
1000	5448	Desgl. eines Mannes von ca. 26 bis 28 Jahren, ebendaher (159)	—	—	18	—	6	—	Gaawa
1001	5449	Desgl. eines albinotischen Mannes von ca. 30 Jahren, aus Hula (171)	—	—	18,2	—	6	—	Kwarinam
1002	5450	Desgl. eines Mannes von ca. 50 Jahren, aus Maupa (Britisch Neu-Guinea) (179)	—	—	19,5	—	6	—	Goápäna
1003	5451	Desgl. einer Frau von ca. 35 Jahren, ebendaher (181)	—	—	18	—	6	—	Wagiowoa
1004	5452	Desgl. eines Jungen von ca. 16 Jahren, ebendaher (180) ...	—	—	18,5	—	6	—	Rabu
1005	5453	Desgl. eines Mannes von ca. 35 Jahren, ebendaher (182) ..	—	—	19,5	—	6	—	Kairobui
1006	5454	Desgl. eines Mannes von ca. 40 Jahren, aus Mokanu, Astrolabe-Gebirge (175)	—	—	17,6	—	6	—	Wuikoroko
1007	5455	Desgl. eines Mannes von ca. 30 Jahren, ebendaher (173) ...	—	—	19	—	6	—	Akoigupa
1008	5456	Desgl. eines Mannes von ca. 20 Jahren, ebendaher (174) ...	—	—	18	—	6	—	Kiokiköoma
1009	5457	Desgl. eines Mannes von ca. 25 Jahren, aus Aguberi, Astrolabe-Gebirge (178)	—	—	18	—	6	—	Tawarumaraga
1010	5458	Desgl. eines Jungen von ca. 16 Jahren, aus Rona, Astrolabe-Gebirge (154)	—	—	18	—	6	—	Jaggat
1011	5459	Desgl. eines Knaben von ca. 9 bis 10 Jahren, von der Insel [illegible]							Boy

	Laufende No.	No. der Formerei	Gegenstand	Material des Originals	Standort des Originals	Höhe in cm	Breite in cm	Preis M.	Pf.
			30 Jahren, von Anuapata (ebenda) (157)	—	—	19,4	—	6	—
Häni	991	5439	Desgl. eines Mannes von ca. 28 Jahren, ebendaher (156)...	—	—	19,5	—	6	—
Wawuia	992	5440	Desgl. eines Mannes von ca. 25 Jahren, ebendaher (162)...	—	—	18,4	—	6	—
Wagi I	993	5441	Desgl. eines Jungen von ca. 18 Jahren, ebendaher (155)...	—	—	18,3	—	6	—
Möa	994	5442	Desgl. eines Knaben von ca. 9 bis 10 Jahren, ebendaher (158)	—	—	18	—	6	—
Maia	995	5443	Desgl. einer Frau von ca. 50 Jahren, ebendaher (164)	—	—	18,5	—	6	—
Gari	996	5444	Desgl. eines Mädchens von ca. 15 bis 16 Jahren, aus Anuapata (161)	—	—	18	—	6	—

Laufende No.	No. der Formerei	Gegenstand	Material des Originals	Standort des Originals	Höhe in cm	Breite in cm	Preis M.	Pf.
1015	5502	Gesichtsmaske eines Kai-Pygmäen, Gelang, vom Sattelberg, 1.48 m hoch. Deutsch Neu-Guinea......	—	—	22	—	6	—
1016	5503	Desgl. eines Kai-Mannes, Nemasaki, vom Sattelberg. Deutsch Neu-Guinea	—	—	25	—	6	—
1017	5504	Desgl. eines Kai-Pygmäen, Iqualeng, vom Sattelberg, 1.40 m hoch. Deutsch Neu-Guinea....................	—	—	24	—	6	—
1018	5505	Desgl. eines Kai-Mannes, Bangeng, vom Sattelberg, 1.54 m hoch. Deutsch Neu-Guinea..	—	—	25	—	6	—
1019	5506	Desgl. eines Kai-Pygmäen, Mede, vom Sattelberg, 1.45 m hoch. Deutsch Neu-Guinea.........	—	—	26	—	6	—
1020	5507	Linker Fuß eines Bukaua-Mannes vom Huvn-Golf, Deutsch Neu Guinea	—	—	27	12	5	—
1021	5508	Rechter Fuß desselben Mannes	—	—	28	11	5	—
1022	5509	Linker Fuß des Pygmäen Eisa, vgl. die Maske 5501........	—	—	21	10	5	—
1023	5510	Linke Hand eines Kai-Mannes, Fume, vom Sattelberg. Deutsch Neu-Guinea	—	—	16	7	5	—
1024	5511	Linke Hand des Pygmäen Eisa, vgl. die Maske 5501........	—	—	15	7	4	—
1025	4073 4074	Schädeldächer von Spy I und Spy II. Je 4,— M.	Nach Gipsabgüssen geformt	—	—	—	8	—
1026	4099	Schädeldach des Pithecanthropus von Trinil..................		—	—	—	2	—
1027	5200	Kopf eines Mannes aus einem Relief vom Burgtor in Sendschirli. Vgl. Hauptverzeichnis Form.-No. 1188	Dolerit	Königl. Museen Berlin	46	31	6	—
1028	5201	Desgleichen. Vgl. Hauptverz. Form.-No. 1191	desgl.	desgl.	36	31	5	—
1029	5202	Desgleichen. Vgl. Hauptverz. Form.-No. 1197	desgl.	desgl.	46	31	6	—
1030	5203	Kopf einer Frau, ebendaher. Vgl. Hauptverz. Form.-No. 1198......................	desgl.	desgl.	36	31	5	—
1031	4067	Ausguß der Hirnkapsel eines Elefanten I	—	Museum f. Naturk. Berlin	18	29	20	—
1032	4068	Desgl. wie vor II............	—	Anthropol. Lehrmittel-Sammlung Berlin	19	27	20	—
1033	4075	Ausguß einer kleinen sehr kurzen und hohen Hirnkapsel der „alpinen" Rasse............	—		12	12	4	—

Laufende No.	No. der Formerei	Gegenstand	Material des Originals	Standort des Originals	Höhe in cm	Breite in cm	Preis M.	Pf.
		9 bis 10 Jahren, von der Insel Salawatti (193)	—	—	17,9	—	6	—
1012	5460	Desgl. eines Mannes von ca. 50 Jahren, aus St. George d'Elmina, Goldküste (206)	—	—	18,8	—	6	—
1013	5461 5462	Zwei Gesichtsmasken von Männern aus Tasmanien. Je 6,— M.	—	Museum in Hobart	19,5 und 18,9	— —	12	—
1014	5501	*) Gesichtsmaske eines Kai-Pygmäen, Eisa, vom Sattelberg, 1.355 m hoch. Deutsch Neu-Guinea	—	—	21	—	6	—

*) Die Stücke 5501 bis 5511 sind von Prof. Neuhauss nach dem Leben geformt.

Tanté

Ø
Ø

Laufende No.	No. der Formerei	Gegenstand	Material des Originals	Standort des Originals	Höhe in cm	Breite in cm	Preis M.	Pf.
1034	4076	Ausguß der Hirnkapsel eines ♂ Gorilla	—	Anthropol. Lehrmittel-Sammlung Berlin	9	9	4	—
1035	4077	Desgl. eines ♂ Orang	—	desgl.	9	9	4	—
1036	4079	Desgl. eines Dachses	—	desgl.	4	5	4	—
1037	4080	Desgl. eines Hundes	—	desgl.	5	6	4	—
1038	4081	Desgl. eines Hylobates lar	—	desgl.	5	6	4	—
1039	4078	Desgl. einer Phoca	—	desgl.	6	9	4	—
1040	5204	Desgl. des Schädeldaches aus dem Neandertale	—	—	8	17	3	—
1041	5205	Kopf eines jungen Mannes von Guadalcanar	—	—	28	20	20	—
1042	5206	Kopf eines Melanesiers unbekannter Herkunft	—	—	32	20	20	—
1043	5207	Kopf eines Maori, mit Benutzung der hier unter No. 5357 verzeichneten Maske aus der Sammlung von Dr. O. Finsch	—	—	32	20	20	—
1044	5208	Kopf eines Mannes von Hawaii mit Benutzung der hier unter No. 5349 verzeichneten Maske aus der Sammlung von Dr. Finsch	—	—	31	21	20	—
1045	4069	Büste eines Mannes von der Goldküste nach der Natur modelliert	—	—	59	—	20	—
1046	4070	Dieselbe ohne Haare	—	—	57	—	16	—
1047	5209	Gesichtsmaske eines Yao	—	—	30	—	6	—
1048	5210	Desgl. eines Sioux	—	—	27	17	6	—
1049	5211	Desgl. eines Lappen, No. 5	—	—	24	17	6	—
1050	5212	Desgl. eines Lappen, No. 8	—	—	24	17	6	—
1051	5213	Desgl. eines Duala-Mädchens	—	—	21	14	3	—
1052	5214	Dieselbe mit nachträglich geöffneten Augen	—	—	21	14	3	—
1053	5215	Sechs Platten mit Profil-Porträts von Leuten aus Hawaii nach der Natur modelliert. à 6 M.	—	Cambridge Mass.	36 bis 41	26 bis 30	36	—
1054	5216	Büste eines Kalmücken	—	—	54	—	15	—
1055	5217	Dieselbe ohne Kopfhaare	—	—	52	—	12	—
1056	5218	Büste eines Eskimoweibes	—	—	34	42	10	—
1057	5219	Büste eines Eskimo aus dem Smith-Sound	—	—	32	—	20	—

The (Aborted) Body Cast of a Man Called Mhonera

No inventory number

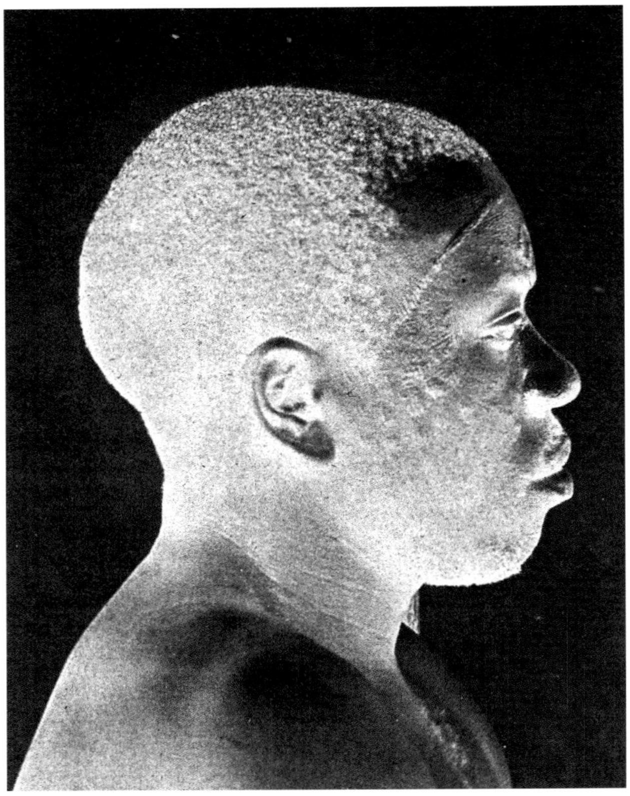

The case of Mhonera is a story of how lifecasting a human being for anthropometric purposes failed in positive terms — it is something of a favourable lacuna in the sales catalogue of the Gipsformerei, a symbol of resistance against the discriminatory treatment and degradation to the status of 'human material' as experienced at the hands of German scholars. Like Adjak, Mhonera was part of an ethnological exhibition in Germany. He was one of 106 individuals from East Africa, Togo, Cameroon and New Guinea involved in the *Erste Deutsche Kolonial-Ausstellung* (First German Colonial Exhibition), staged in Berlin in the summer of 1896. These people were accommodated in supposedly authentic 'villages' on the exhibition grounds of Treptower Park and were presented day in, day out to a curious mass audience. When Felix von Luschan (1854–1924) — who at one stage was assistant to the director of the Königliches Museum für Völkerkunde — was alerted to Mhonera's tattoos, he insisted on them being moulded by the Gipsformerei. Mhonera, however, refused to submit to this abuse of his body and by doing so motivated an even greater protest by the Swahili against the inhumane treatment they had experienced. This event has left a paper trail in the archives: from Luschan's bid to have the project approved by the general admission of the Königliche Museen Berlin and the Working Committee of the Colonial Exposition, the idea to recruit an expert (a certain Herr Greeff) to supervise the moulding to the request for free entry to the exhibition grounds for the plaster casters involved in the project. The records also show — from Luschan's point of view — the highly unsatisfactory result: 'The moulding of the scar tattoo has unfortunately come to nothing; the man absolutely wouldn't hear of it and there was no possibility of forcing him.' Interestingly, Luschan was reprimanded by the Working Committee (ill. p. 87). Mhonera appears as a nameless 'Konde' in the files of the Ethnologisches Museum, even though his first name, 'Nionêra (or Lionêra)', and other personal data are preserved in Luschan's 1897 *Deutschland und seine Kolonien im Jahre 1896*. According to Luschan, Mhonera was around thirty years old and an agricultural labourer from the region south of the Tanzanian coastal city Lindi. In the exhibition *ZurückGESCHAUT* at the Bezirksmuseum Berlin-Treptow (open since October 2017), Jan Dammel and Mnyaka Sururu put forward the appropriate spelling of Mhonera's name; this spelling is used here. Their research revealed that Mhonera received monthly wages of eight rupees and that at the end of a voyage lasting several weeks, which took him from Dar es Salaam to Hamburg, he arrived in Berlin on 9 March 1896. He returned to Lindi following the same route on 13 October of that same year.

Anthropological photograph of Mhonera (inverted)
In: *Deutschland und seine Kolonien: Amtlicher Bericht über die Erste Deutsche Kolonial-Ausstellung*, ed. Hans Hermann Graf von Schweinitz, et al., 1897, p. XII
Staatliche Museen zu Berlin, Ethnologisches Museum

Typewritten letter of the Working Committee of the Deutsche Kolonial-Ausstellung to Felix von Luschan, 17 August 1896
Staatliche Museen zu Berlin, Ethnologisches Museum

3. Zu E. No 927/96. 47

DEUTSCHE KOLONIAL-AUSSTELLUNG
GRUPPE XXIII
DER BERLINER GEWERBE-AUSSTELLUNG 1896.

Fernsprecher: Amt I. No. 75.

BERLIN, den 17. August 1896.
~~Schützenstr. 82~~

Sr. Hochwohlgeboren

Herrn Dr. von L u s c h a n

H i e r. 7.9.96

Zu den Akten
1.9.
Grünwedel

Zu den Acten der Gipsabformung des Konde-Mannes; einer Antwort scheint dieses alberne Entschuldigungsschreiben nicht zu bedürfen. v. Luschan
Mittelstadt.
1.9.96.

Ew. Hochwohlgeboren

erlauben wir uns auf das gefällige Schreiben vom 10. cr. ganz ergebenst mitzuteilen, dass die Veranlassung zu unserem Schreiben vom 6. cr. eine Beschwerde der Suaheli gegeben hatte, welche wir nach einer eingegangenen dienstlichen Meldung als begründet erachten müssen.

Das einzige Ergebnis aller Bemühungen war schliesslich die Abformung des Gesichtes eines Cameruner Mannes mit der typischen Taetowirung der Backengegend.
Das Stück ist inventarisirt.

I. 166.96
S. 390.
v L

Einem Suaheli sollte die Tätowierung abgeformt werden, und hierbei kam es, da verschiedene Stammesgenossen gegen die Procedur des Gypsens protestierten- wie wir beifügen wollen- teils aus religiösen Bedenken, teils wohl auch in Folge des kurz vorhergegangenen Todesfalles aus Aberglauben, zu einem für das Ansehen der Europäer unliebsamen Auftritte, der besser vermieden worden wäre.

Die sämmtlichen Suahelis haben diesen Vorfall benutzt, um bei uns Beschwerde zu führen und sich für die Zukunft vor Aehnlichem zu sichern.

Wir haben geglaubt, dass Sie Ihre Thätigkeit am besten würden ausführen können, wenn wir- die Arbeitgeber der Eingeborenen- keinen direkten Einfluss auf dieselben ausüben und uns

daher

4 zu 927/96 48

daher jeder Einmischung enthalten. Nachdem aber eine direkte Beschwerde bei uns eingegangen, konnten wir uns unserer Pflicht für die bei uns weilenden Leute, für deren Wohl und Wehe wir verantwortlich sind, einzutreten, nicht entziehen, namentlich aber auch um die Missstimmung herabzustimmen, die seit jenem Vorfalle unter den Leuten Platz gegriffen, und die sich nunmehr gegen alle Untersuchungen- auch gegen die ärztlichen- richtet.

Indem wir voraussetzen, dass Ew. Hochwohlgeboren im Interesse der Wissenschaft die wünschenswerten Forschungen innerhalb der durch die Eigenart der Leute und durch ihre Stellung gebotenen Grenzen fortführen werden, zeichnen wir

hochachtungsvollst und ergebenst

Der Arbeits-Ausschuss
der
Deutschen Kolonial-Ausstellung.

The Full-Body Cast of a Man Called N'Kurui

Inventory Number 4307

Plaster Piece Mould of the Lifecast of a Man called N'Kurui ('Luschan's Bushman'), 1906
Staatliche Museen zu Berlin, Gipsformerei

Typewritten letter of Felix von Luschan to A. von Dessauer, 23 November 1906
Staatliche Museen zu Berlin, Ethnologisches Museum

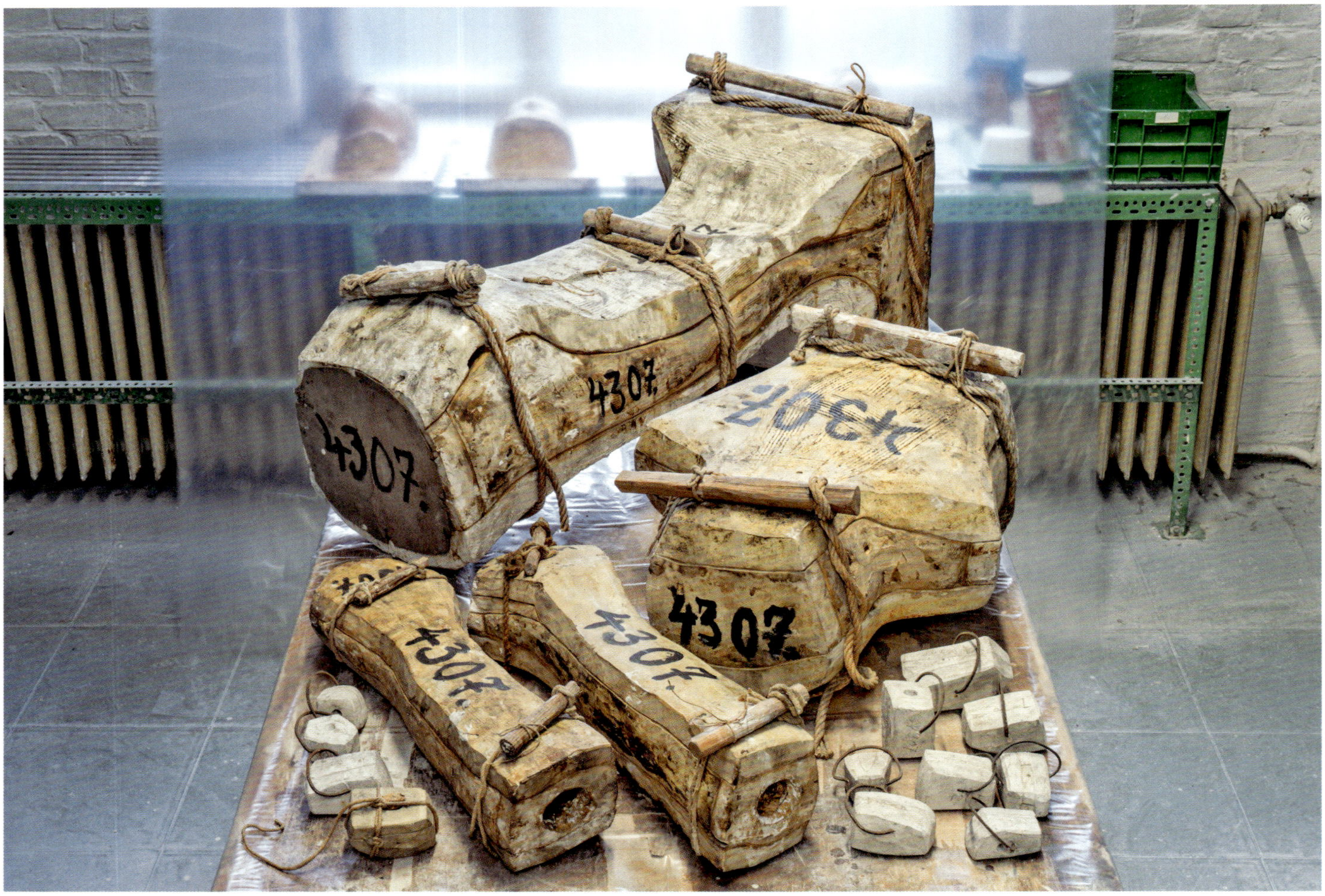

23/11.06.

40

Zu E. 252 / 06

E. 23. abges. 24.11.06 B.

B., den 23.11.06.

Herrn A. von Dessauer

Johannesburg Transvaal
P.O. Box 2083

Hochgeehrter Herr!

Mit grosser Freude kann ich Ihnen heute mitteilen, dass die für das Museum in Johannesburg bestimmte Buschmannfigur gleichzeitig zur Absendung gelangt. Die Fertigstellung stiess hier auf nicht unbedeutende Schwierigkeiten, da einzelne Formstücke nicht gut zu einander passten und ich doch jeden künstlichen oder künstlerischen Eingriff durchaus und um jeden Preis vermeiden wollte. Es lag mir daran, ein absolut authentisches und völlig einwandfreies Modell zu schaffen und das ist nun erst nach vieler Mühe möglich geworden.

Auch auf die Bemalung ist sehr grosse Sorgfalt verwandt worden. So hielt ich es besonders auch für richtig, neben der physiologischen Hautfarbe auch den Schmutz des Individuums zum Ausdruck zu bringen, wie man ja auch in Wirklichkeit, wenn man die ~~wirkliche~~ wahre Farbe eines lebenden Buschmannes studieren will, ihn erst künstlich und chemisch reinigen muss.

Wenn Sie die Figur näher ansehen, werden Sie unschwer die Stellen erkennen, die als gereinigt gedacht sind. Ich hatte erst einen Versuch gemacht, unseren eigenen Abguss so zu bemalen, wie ein chemisch gereinigter Buschmann in Wirklichkeit aussehen würde, aber der Versuch fiel nicht befriedigend aus und ich glaube, Sie werden mir beipflichten, dass es besser war, sich an die faktischen Verhältnisse zu halten. Ausserdem habe ich Sorge getragen, dass die Schmutzschichte als oberflächliche Lasur aufliegt und mit Seife entfernt werden kann, wenn man dort die ursprüngliche Farbe vorziehen sollte.

Die Figur ist hier noch nicht öffentlich ausgestellt, aber wer sie bisher gesehen hat, ist voll Bewunderung für sie. Jedenfalls haben wir da mit vereinten Kräften ein Werk geschaffen, für das uns noch kommende Generationen dankbar sein werden.

Auf die Verpackung wurde hier die denkbar grösste Sorgfalt verwendet und ich hoffe, dass Sie mir bald den richtigen Eingang werden anzeigen können. Wir schicken die Sendung frachtfrei ebenso wie uns s. Zt. die Formen zugegangen waren. Wenn es Ihnen möglich sein würde, uns die Kiste selbst mit ethnographischen Gegenständen und mit Schädeln und Skeletten [oder mit den Gypsabg. Formen einer Buschmann-Frau] gefüllt wieder zurückzusenden, würde uns das ganz besonders freuen.

I. a. H.

ges.

S. D.

v. Luschan

Lost Moulds

Margit Berner, Britta Lange,
Thomas Schelper and Kerstin Stoll

Thomas Schelper (artistic plasterer), Margit Berner (anthropologist), Britta Lange (cultural scientist) and Kerstin Stoll (artist) — we first met in 2012. What brought us together was a research project on the full-body cast of a male person from colonised South Africa, which was made more than one hundred years ago by a German scholar. Our joint search for information in the archives and on the casting procedure left us with many questions unanswered. In the attempt to find an alternative approach, we made a full-body cast ourselves in 2013. What we were aiming at was neither a re-enactment of reversed roles between colonial subjects nor the empathetic staging of long past transgressive behaviour. We wanted to find out what complex technological and artisanal, social and artistic aspects are involved in such a process which spans several days.

Among the historical models at the Gipsformerei, Staatliche Museen zu Berlin is the life-size full-body cast of an approximately 1.4 m tall male individual from South Africa. Moulded in Johannesburg in 1905 and cast in Berlin in 1906, the figure stands upright with his arms spread open from his body at approximately 45 degrees. Clearly visible on the cast's 'skin' are not only pores, but also the goosebumps which you would expect to form when a living human being comes into contact with cold liquid plaster — incontrovertible proof that this is a lifecast.

To make it easier to detach the mould from the body, a fatty substance such as butter or pomade was presumably applied to the hairy body parts. Separating threads were anchored in the liquid plaster. These were then pulled out halfway through the curing process and before the plaster had completely set. They divide the mould into several pieces and make subsequent handling considerably easier. Body moulds of this size are always made in discrete parts. The overlapping negative moulds, which can only be used once — this is why they are sometimes referred to as 'lost moulds' — were sealed with shellac and treated with a release agent before casting the body in plaster.

By carefully detaching the eleven body mould segments and repeatedly testing them to ensure a perfect fit, they were then assembled as a whole, probably with photographs and the man's body measurements recorded in writing to serve as guidelines. The pedestal, which is joined to the figure's feet, is the twelfth element of the mould. The plaster-covered seams were then painstakingly smoothed over in order not to disturb the appearance of the skin. Nevertheless, they remain visible, and today help us to understand the sculpture's origins. Iron rods coated with shellac to prevent corrosion were integrated into the figure as reinforcements.

Designed to be displayed as it is, the model comes in four parts to facilitate further moulding: the lower part of the body, the pedestal, the torso with the head, and the two arms. The arms are attached to the body via metal bushings, and a mother mould makes it possible to remove the torso. From these four model parts, durable plaster piece moulds have been made: these second-generation negatives were last used for a cast in 1937. Once the casting mould was made, the parts were then toggled together, soaked in wax for conservation reasons and their large openings closed with cardboard to prevent dust from entering. Today, they are kept in good condition in the mould depot on the upper floor of the Gipsformerei and could still be used for casting (ill. p. 88).

In the 2000s, the original cast of the 'Bushman' (as the man was once called) was repeatedly shown in exhibitions, including: *Theatrum naturae et artis*, Martin-Gropius-Bau, Berlin, 2000–01; *Ebenbilder: Kopien von Körpern — Modelle des Menschen*, Ruhrlandmuseum, Essen, 2002; *Wilde Welten: Aneignung des Fremden in der Moderne*, Georg-Kolbe-Museum, Berlin, 2010; and *WeltWissen*, Martin-Gropius-Bau, Berlin, 2010–11.[1] On all these occasions the cast was exhibited in its nakedness, illustrating the ideological orientation and iconography of early anthropology and ethnography — yet the 'Bushman' had always been presented fully clothed in the past. Its function was also to serve as evidence of the European 'ethnogenic' perspective on the 'Other' in science and cultural studies. Today, the 'Bushman' cast is no longer available for loan from the Gipsformerei as priority is given to researching its history.

For its first anthropological exhibition in 1930, Vienna's Naturhistorisches Museum acquired, among other artefacts, a coloured full-body cast representing a Transvaal Bushman 'according to Luschan' from the Gipsformerei in Berlin. Listed in the museum's inventory under 'No. 21,406', the figure is today stored in the collection depot of casts. In 2010, I decided to carry out research on its history.[2] The trail led to Felix von Luschan, who from 1900 was an associate professor and from 1909 a full professor of anthropology and ethnography at Berlin's Charité, and from 1904 to 1910 head of the departments of Africa and Oceania at the Königliches Museum für Völkerkunde (today's Ethnologisches Museum) in Berlin. Lifecasts constituted for him a crucial aspect of anthropological research. He taught the technique required for their production and commented on it extensively in his contribution to the 1906 edition of *Anleitung zu wissenschaftlichen Beobachtungen auf Reisen*.[3] In 1905, Luschan took part in the first meeting of the British Association for the Advancement of Science in South Africa's Johannesburg. He made use of his visit by taking anthropological measurements of 'natives' and making lifecasts of 'Bushmen', as he recorded in his published travelogue essay.[4] The only full-body cast of an individual Luschan rendered at the Pass Office near Johannesburg was made possible by the assistance of his wife, Emma. It is highly unlikely that the persons he studied at what was in effect a colonial institution set up to control civil society were in the position to refuse having their bodies measured and moulded.

During my research at the Staatsbibliothek zu Berlin, I found a folder containing a photograph of the 'Bushman' in a box labelled 'Südafrika' as part of Luschan's papers. Another box contains an envelope with the handwritten note 'Körpermessungen Südafrika' (Body measurements South Africa) and a list of names under the heading 'Visit of the British Association: Collection of Kafir Tribes at Native Pass Office, Corner of Market and Bezuidenhout Streets, Johannesburg'. Four of the extant data sheets list Johannesburg as the place where the anthropological data was registered; the date given is 28 August 1905. A registry states the 'Stammesname' (Name of tribe), contains the word 'Buschmann', and the box 'Eigenname' (Proper name) displays the word 'N'Kurui'; 'Alter' (Age) states 'etwa 64 Jahre' (roughly 64 years).[5] The fields for further personal data were left blank.

There are also references to the lifecast in Luschan's correspondence filed at the archive of the Ethnologisches Museum in Berlin, including the handwritten note 'N'Kurui etw. 60 J: 1371 mm hoch, Transvaal' (N'Kurui, approx. 60 yrs: 1371 mm tall, Transvaal).[6] The name — whether correctly rendered or not — points to a subject, to an actual person.

My contact with the Gipsformerei revealed that they store a copy of the cast. It appears from other files at the Ethnologisches Museum that the South African Museum in Cape Town and a museum in Johannesburg received a free copy of the cast in 1906 — a quid pro quo for the assistance Luschan had received in Johannesburg. While other museums, for instance, in Vienna, have displayed the figure with eyes opened thanks to a sculptural intervention, the eyes of the original cast at the Gipsformerei are squinched shut, attesting to the moulding procedure. Not only did

Luschan colour the cast at the Museum für Völkerkunde in Berlin, he had dirt marks applied to the 'skin',[7] illustrating his intention to present N'Kurui from the perspective of salvage anthropology as a specimen of a race soon to become extinct'. Cast in plaster, he 'was to be preserved as an outstanding representative of his race for future generations, when there would be no more living Bushmen'.[8] The man's figure in turn serves as a physical illustration of Luschan's anthropological research.

According to the sales list of the Gipsformerei, four reproductions were sold in the 1930s, which means that together with the four casts made in 1906[9] and the one purchased in 1930 by the museum in Vienna, at least nine copies were made. However, the object biographies of the casts require further research. The production and the biographies of the objects are yet to be explored. Were they put on display? Have they been destroyed in the meantime? In what media, in what contexts, do they — or did they — figure?

Moulding in plaster is a living anachronism. It is possible today to make a full-length, 3D body scan in a very short time: plaster moulding is an archaic procedure by comparison. For our moulding experiment we needed a lot of time, two whole days — as the model this gave me a chance to rest a little.

During the initial casting phase I kept thinking that I was being turned into stone. A part of my body, my left arm, no longer seemed to belong to me somehow. I continuously felt the change to the material covering me. At first it was wet and cold, but then dried quite quickly. My skin, now covered by plaster, started to twitch a bit. The plaster began to feel warm and then things happened in quick succession.

The sense of being at the mercy of outside forces I felt most strongly during the moulding of my head. My face and all my senses were somehow blocked: breathing and hearing, but only the most indistinct sounds, were still just possible. All I could smell was moist gypsum. Everything seemed to have moved to the periphery, only breathing assured me that I was still alive. Even though I felt I had actually left the scene, I remained present because three people moved around my body at all times, talking amongst themselves. It was strange to feel the surface of my body. I was given a second skin, made of something liquid, viscous — the slurry quickly turning into a hard shell. The meeting of incompatible materials seemed odd to me: stone on flesh, plaster on skin, a liquid material that hardened while embracing a breathing body. Basically, these things do not belong together. The situation is different when a statue is moulded with material that is turning into stone.

What I was totally unprepared for was the wedge that was put to my head to later split the mould. A powerful echo was produced in that resonance chamber, my head, and there was no way for me to escape. A film screened inside the plaster shell: I tried to imagine how people must have felt having their mould taken under force or threat, people who had been disenfranchised by colonialism. This activity would have been yet another turn for the worse, with people in those situations being deprived of all rights. Moulding in plaster, it occurred to me, made people paralysed with fear and not only in a societal sense, but actually, physically.

When the casting moulds of my body lay side by side on the grass in the garden, I wondered whether it would be possible to make a copy of myself. We tend to think that such a snapshot — a photograph or a cast — renders a body as it 'normally' or 'really' is. This is not so. And for the simple reason that the body has to be prepared for such purpose, in this case chemically, with vaseline or pomade, and it has to be made immobile. The body is anything but 'normal'. Instead, it is oriented towards a particular medium and what that medium supposedly makes visible. I experienced the plaster cast as utterly denuding. In its unsparingly brilliant white, it reveals every wrinkle, every pore, every what have you.

The negatives themselves, the lost moulds, seemed very beautiful to me for as long as they were there. Because their insides showed the impressions made, for example, by goosebumps, and because their outside was far from smooth as it displayed how the plaster had been applied. Illustrating the practical side of the procedure, they showed where the plaster had

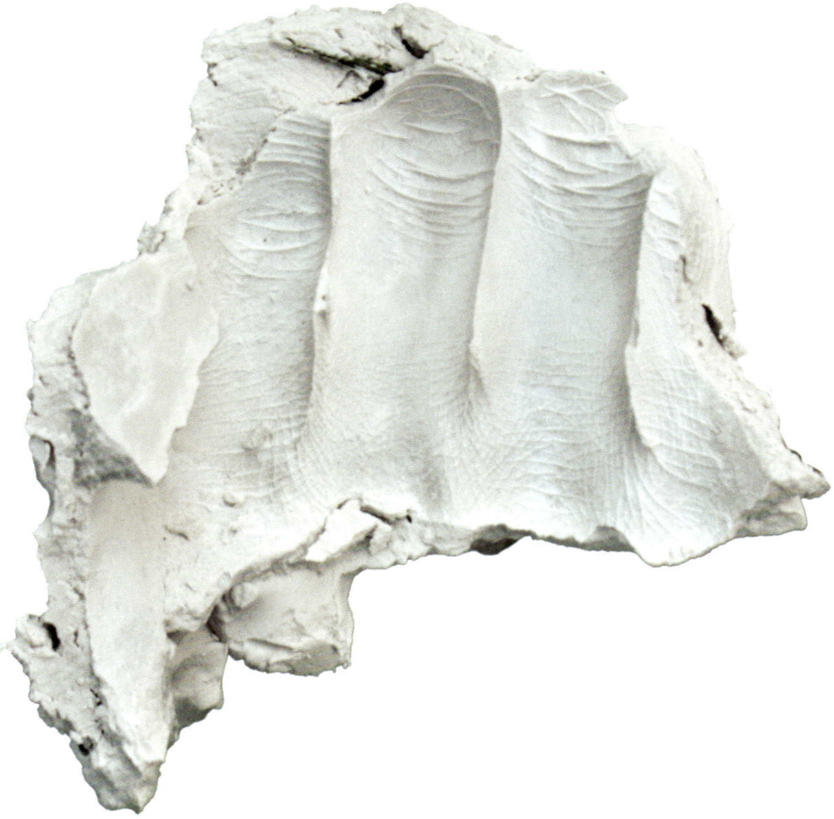

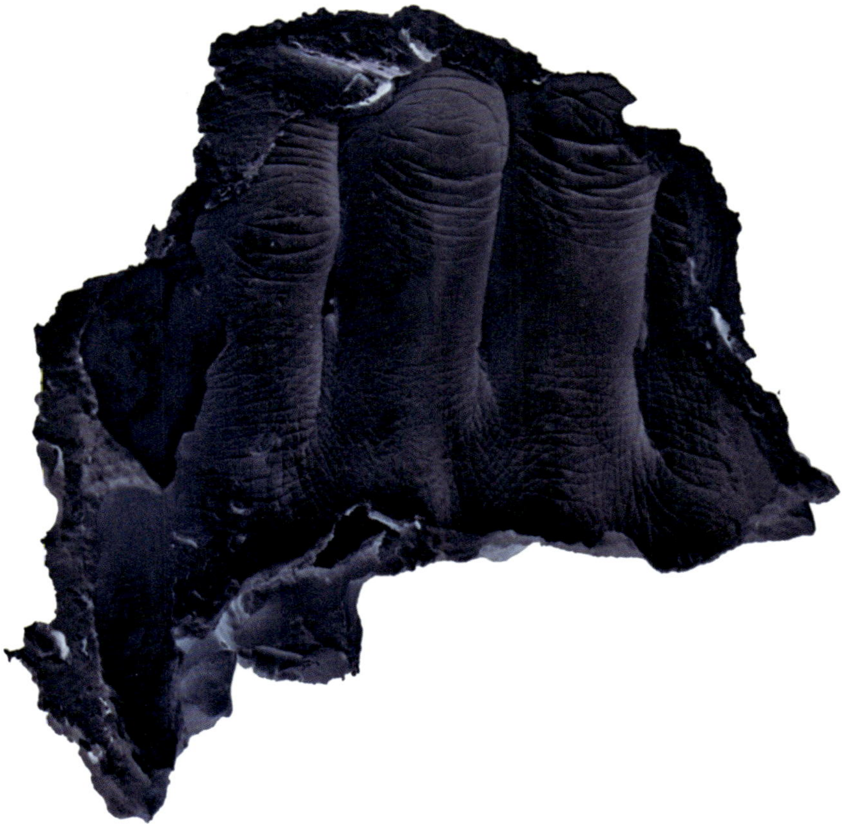

been added in blobs and where it had been poured. These moulds are now gone, but are documented in photographs and on film.

Before the actual model was made, I tried to envision what an encounter with it was going to be like. I imagined this as an alienating impossibility. After all, you cannot physically encounter your own body? It seemed weird that I would be able to touch my body as an independent entity. The strangeness and irrationality of this, however, lies in 'myself' and 'me'. Neither the matrices nor the potential positive are me. They are impressions or copies of my body taken in a special, prolonged moment.[10]

'Lost moulds', those negative forms of a body that provide the basis for casting the first positive are no more than part of an interim stage. They display the body as a negative impression, but the longer you look at them and the better the photographs you make of them, the more suggestive is the positive that seems to arise from them. It is there one moment and gone the next, almost like a fleeting image — a constant back and forth between concave and convex, between high relief and low relief, black and white, depending on one's perspective. From the negative imprints they have left, fingermarks seem to project outward, an effect that is best seen when converting the photographic positive into its negative. This is reminiscent of the images generated by a pseudoscope, a type of binoculars perfected in the nineteenth century which reverses depth perception, rendering visible something that cannot otherwise be seen. By uncrossing the perspectives of the right and the left eye, the interior of the negative seems to project outward — *INSIDE OUT*. It creates the positive of a negative and vice versa. Another type of instrument that generates images of what usually remains hidden are CT scanners, often used today in plaster casting. Such scanners use X-ray measurements to produce a great number of virtual 'slices' of the scanned object. From this data a digital 3D model is created — the inside is projected outward.

The first moulded negatives are referred to as 'lost moulds', as they have to be destroyed to retrieve the positive. They are a transitional product indispensable to the creation of lasting negatives from the first positive. It is the second-generation negative moulds that then document the past for the future. They are the basis from which an unlimited number of positives are produced and presented to the world.[11] It is therefore only the lost mould that was once in direct contact with the moulded body and displays the traces of this process. The contact lasts for about twenty minutes: the time plaster takes to cure and change from cold, wet and heavy to warm, dry and light. The body that is being moulded reacts to this change, and the process leaves its traces on the first casting moulds.

N'Kurui's 'lost mould' has indeed been lost and what has disappeared with it are the more tangible traces of his body and the stages of the casting process. They are accessible to our imagination, though, through the material object. Considering how time-consuming the casting process is, it must have created a complex social situation, involving researchers as colonisers and the colonised 'object' of research; two sides of a multifaceted communication process. Traces of the contact N'Kurui's body left on the original cast are still discernible in some places on the second-generation negative moulds, but most of them have been touched up to create a smooth appearance. They seem like a metaphor for obscuring the identity of N'Kurui, leaving us with questions to be addressed to the lost moulds: Who was he and where did he come from? Was he alone, did he have his family with him? How did he communicate with the colonials in power? Was he persuaded by the Luschans to consent to having his cast made, did he consent? Was he told what aim the scholars were pursuing? How did that affect him? What did it mean to him to have his moulding taken?

The full-body cast we made in our experiment in 2013 showed us that it is impossible to avoid creating seams in the cast where elements of the mould overlap, and how difficult it is for the moulding elements to fit absolutely flush. The situation also posed a problem for Luschan: 'Completion on-site was met with considerable difficulties, as the individual elements of the mould did not interlock sufficiently tight. I was nevertheless determined to avoid any artificial or artistic intervention at all costs. What I was aiming for was an absolutely authentic and completely flawless model, which was achieved only with a great deal of effort.'[12] Our creation of a full-body cast in 2013, too, required sawing, mounting, adapting, gluing and sanding on the positives. The ideas and ideals of what a body is supposed to look like mattered. Fiction too was at stake.

1 See Horst Bredekamp, Thomas Bruns and Jochen Brüning (eds.), *Theatrum naturae et artis / Theater der Natur und Kunst: Wunderkammern des Wissens*, exh. cat., Martin-Gropius-Bau, Berlin, 10 December 2000–4 March 2001, Berlin 2001; Jan Gerchow (ed.), *Ebenbilder: Kopien von Körpern — Modelle des Menschen*, exh. cat., Ruhrlandmuseum Essen, 26 March–30 June 2002, Ostfildern-Ruit 2002; Ursel Berger and Christiane Wanken (eds.), *Wilde Welten: Aneignung des Fremden in der Moderne*, exh. cat., Georg-Kolbe-Museum, Berlin, 24 January–5 April 2010, Leipzig 2010; and Jochen Hennig and Udo Andraschke (eds.), *WeltWissen: 300 Jahre Wissenschaften in Berlin*, exh. cat., Martin-Gropius-Bau, Berlin, 24 September 2010–9 January 2011, Munich 2010. In the *WeltWissen* catalogue, however, the figure was wrongly labelled and attributed to Otto Finsch.
2 Margit Berner, 'Zwei Spurensuchen: Objekte, Archive, Geschichte', in: *Sensible Sammlungen: Aus dem anthropologischen Depot*, ed. Margit Berner, Anette Hoffmann and Britta Lange, Hamburg 2011, pp. 185–203.
3 Felix von Luschan, 'Anthropologie, Ethnographie und Urgeschichte', in: *Anleitung zu wissenschaftlichen Beobachtungen auf Reisen*, vol. 2, ed. Georg Balthasar von Neumayer, Hannover 1906, pp. 1–123.
4 Felix von Luschan,'Bericht über eine Reise in Südafrika', in: *Zeitschrift für Ethnologie* 38, 1906, pp. 863–95.
5 Handwritten papers in Box 9, 'Südafrikareise', in the archive of Felix von Luschan, Staatsbibliothek zu Berlin — Preußischer Kulturbesitz.
6 Felix von Luschan, letter to the Generalverwaltung des Königlichen Museums, 11 March 1906, in the archives of Staatliche Museen zu Berlin, Ethnologisches Museum. ID. no. E 252/1906; ref. no. I B 36, Afrika.
7 Felix von Luschan, letter to Anton Heinrich von Dessauer, 22 November 1906, ibid.
8 Felix von Luschan cited in 'Diskussion über Pygmäen und Buschmänner', *Zeitschrift für Ethnologie* 46, 1914, pp. 154–76, here p. 173.
9 Delivery note (Gipsformerei order no. 297) in the archives of the Staatliche Museen zu Berlin, Ethnologisches Museum. ID. no. E 252/1906; ref. no. I B 36, Afrika.
10 These thoughts are based on an interview recorded immediately after the lifecast in September 2013.
11 Margit Berner, Britta Lange, Kerstin Stoll and Thomas Schelper, 'Verlorene Form: Eine künstlerisch-wissenschaftliche Auseinandersetzung mit sensiblen Sammlungsbeständen', in: *Casting: Ein analoger Weg ins Zeitalter der Digitalisierung?; Ein Symposium zur Gipsformerei der Staatlichen Museen zu Berlin*, ed. Christina Haak and Miguel Helfrich, Heidelberg 2016, pp. 174–85.
12 Felix von Luschan, letter to Anton Heinrich von Dessauer, 23 November 1906, with reference to the cast prepared for Johannesburg.

Previous page

Kerstin Stoll
INSIDE OUT, 2013
Two photographs of a plaster fragment to match the lost mould of a full-body cast
40 × 30 cm each
Private collection

In 1900, the London plaster casting workshop of D. Brucciani & Co. was commissioned by the British Museum (Natural History) to take a full-body cast of Eugen Sandow (1867–1925), the Prussian strongman who is considered to have 'invented' body building. For the museum this lifecast combined two educational incentives: it was to serve as a model of a burgeoning body culture and to provide the exemplar European — to be followed by casts of people of other origins. For Sandow, given his claim to have modeled his own body on Greco-Roman statuary, it was only logical to be photographed in the poses of sculptural masterpieces from antiquity. To have his body moulded while he tensed his muscles was an inevitable, if highly demanding process. 'The operation is painful [...] — one feels as if one were being suffocated, especially when the mould of the face is being taken', Sandow reported, and he noted not without pride that only one man in a hundred would have the stamina to endure this procedure. The casting process is the topic of an article in the magazine *The Strand*, which is reprinted here in full on the following pages. We can see that even though he was trapped in a plaster corset, the European strongman Sandow was in control of the process throughout. This fact is in stark contrast — several parallels notwithstanding, including the measurements taken of both body and cast — to the degrading treatment of the people in anthropological mouldings.

Sandow in Plaster of Paris.

A UNIQUE CAST.

Illustrations from Photographs by Arthur Weston, 16 and 17, Poultry, E.C. The copyright of Sandow's Grip Dumb-bell Co.

MY friend the Superior Person had been visiting the South Kensington branch of the British Museum, and he came back in high dudgeon. When I met him, indeed, he was literally spluttering with wrath. Evidently his very superior susceptibilities had suffered cruel outrage. "Great Scot!" he ejaculated, in replying to my look of inquiry, "what will the Museum be coming to next? A penny show with marionettes and performing dogs, I suppose. They've actually got a cast of Sandow the Strong Man—music-hall people in the British Museum, faugh!" And the S.P., having delivered himself of this outburst, turned on his heel and tempestuously took himself off.

Now, although I am very far from sharing his opinions on most subjects, his remarks certainly excited my curiosity. That there should be a cast of Eugen Sandow in the Museum did not surprise me very much—on the contrary, it seemed to me that the authorities would have been remiss in not seizing the opportunity of handing down to future generations a permanent record of the most perfect specimen of physical culture of our days—perhaps of any age. Still, I know what popular prejudice is—even in these enlightened days individuals still exist who regard the cultivation of the body as a thing to be frowned upon, who are perfectly willing to hold up to our admiration the beautiful human forms of classical times, but regard any attempt to emulate these worthies as pernicious in the extreme. So after examining the cast (about which I shall have a good deal more to say in a moment) it occurred to me that it would be a good idea to see Professor Ray Lankester and ascertain how the new departure of having the cast of a living man on view had come about.

Professor Lankester was good enough to devote a few minutes of his valuable time to me, and gave me a very clear idea of his object in advising the Trustees to have the cast made. It serves a twofold purpose, and is interesting to anthropologists for two reasons. Firstly, it presents a perfect type of a European man (and in course of time Professor Lankester hopes to have types of all the races), and, secondly, it furnishes a striking demonstration of what can be done in the way of perfecting the muscles by simple means. A good many people, he remarked, are fond of insisting that the mighty men of muscle which were portrayed in marble by the sculptors of the classical age were simply products of the sculptors' imagination: fancy presentments of men as they might be, rather than of any who actually existed.

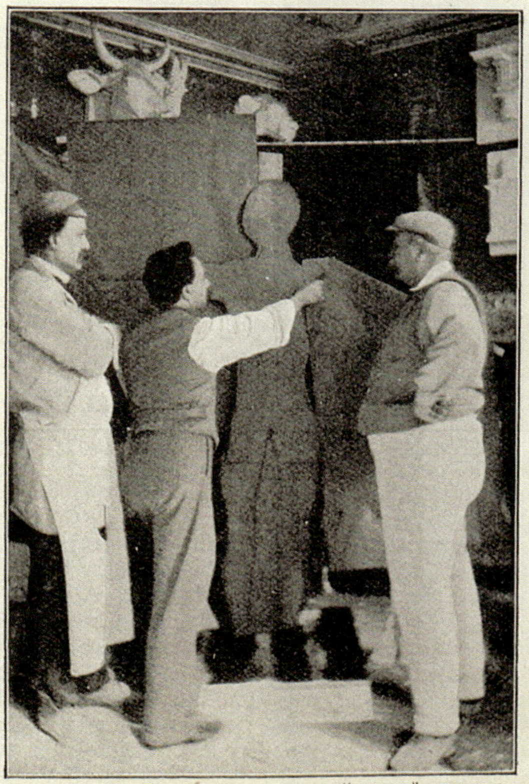

ROUGH PAPER OUTLINE FROM WHICH THE "SHELLS" ARE MADE.

But here we have a cast of a man who lives and breathes at this very moment which comes favourably out of a comparison with any of them. A cast, mind you, as Professor Lankester was careful to bid me remember—a model would have been of small value; but here we have the actual mould of the living figure, which must be correct in every detail. In the times to come this will show the world that such men as the great sculptors portrayed have most indubitably existed in the flesh. I am glad to say that Professor Lankester demurs very strongly from the notion entertained by a good many people that Sandow's wonderful development entitles him to be regarded as a "monstrosity" rather than as a physically perfect human being. As he so logically put it to me, who is to say what are the limits of muscular development—where the line is to be drawn where healthy development leaves off and monstrosity begins?

The ordinary athlete regards himself with his fairly well-cultivated muscles as superior physically to the man who spends all his time sitting at a desk or engaged in indoor occupation. Why should he be loth to admit that Sandow is as much ahead of him in this respect as he is of the ordinary individual? Certainly the judgment of the Curator of the Natural History Department of the National Museum is one that ought to carry weight, and I think enough has been said to show that he is fully alive to the educational value that the cast may prove to the public. He is probably the last man in the world who would be moved by considerations of what is likely merely to amuse and to gratify the idle curiosity of a certain section of the public.

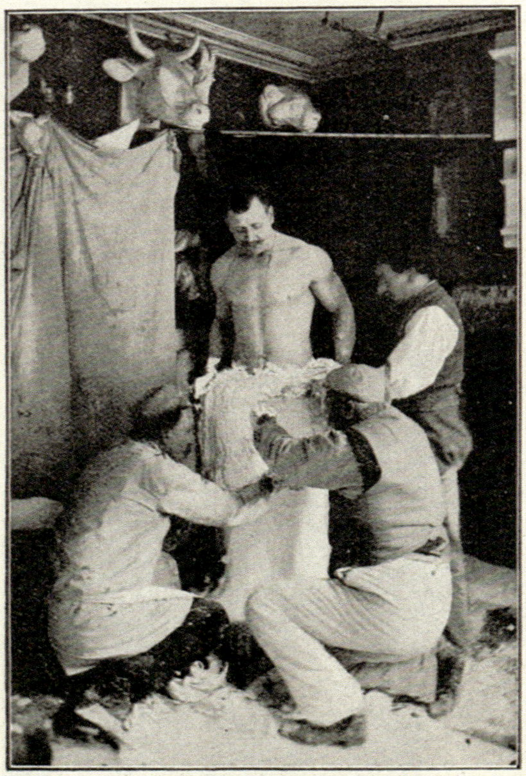

MOULDING OF FIGURE FROM FEET TO HIPS (FRONT).

But, as he also pointed out to me, the cast is interesting for another and entirely different reason from those already enunciated. It is practically unique of its kind; probably no such cast has ever been attempted, not to say satisfactorily completed. Of course, casts of hands, and feet, and faces are common enough, and now and again a cast of the whole living body in a recumbent, relaxed position has been taken; but this cast is entirely different, being no less than of the complete figure, posed, and with the muscles in a tense condition. The latter fact renders it doubly valuable from an anatomical point of view, as the muscles are shown standing out with great clearness, and of course this would not have been the case had the cast been taken from the figure in a condition of relaxation. Naturally this added very greatly to the difficulty of carrying out the work—not the least part of it falling upon the subject. Indeed, Messrs. Brucciani, the famous cast-makers, who undertook and carried out the work, told me that at the beginning they were exceedingly doubtful whether the attempt would be a success. The process was a long one and a tedious one—indeed, from first to last it occupied over a month. As it is highly probable that the majority of the readers of THE STRAND are ignorant of the process of cast-making a brief description of the work as kindly explained and shown to me by Messrs. Brucciani will give them a clearer idea of the exceptional difficulties which have just been tackled with such excellent results.

The ordinary process is a comparatively simple one. A mould roughly corresponding in shape but somewhat larger than the object of which the cast is to be taken is made. This is placed round the object and the intervening space filled in with plaster of Paris in a semi-fluid condition, and this, of course, moulds itself to the exact shape of the object it covers. The latter has prior

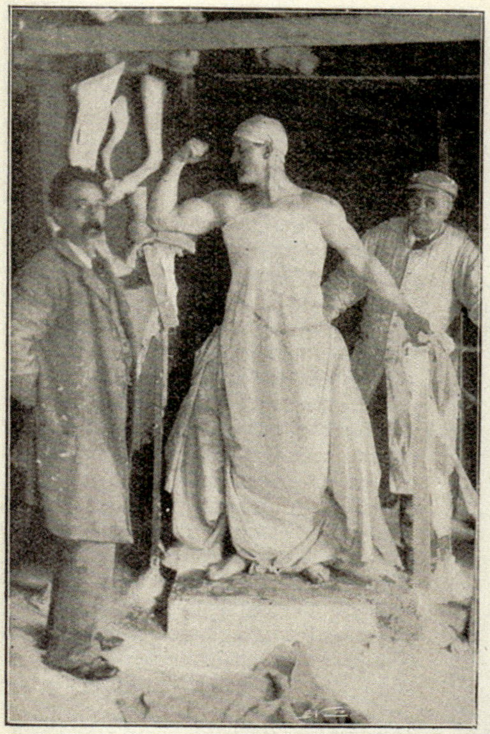

POSING FIGURE—THE SUPPORT FOR RIGHT ARM WILL BE NOTICED.

to the commencement of operations been oiled in order to prevent the plaster from sticking. When the plaster sets it is carefully removed in sections, and these, when placed together, form a perfect mould. Into this plaster is again poured; when this hardens the mould is broken off and the cast itself remains.

Now, all this seems simple enough, and so it is when an inanimate object is concerned or a portion of the human frame in repose. For in order to insure success while the mould is being made it is absolutely necessary that the subject should be practically still. That is so obvious that it is perhaps scarcely doing justice to the intelligence of the ordinary reader to lay stress upon it; the smallest movement tends to disturb the hardening plaster and mars the perfection of the mould. Is it surprising, therefore, that, as it takes from ten to fifteen minutes to complete each one of the separate pieces of which the complete mould is made up, Messrs. Brucciani were rather dubious as to the result? However, they got to work, and slowly, piece by piece, not without occasional disappointments and failures, the thing got itself completed. They are quite sure that no one but Sandow could possibly have "sat" for such a work of art. Fancy, you young men who are fond of baring your right arm and displaying that little lump of biceps you refer to as your "muscle"; fancy setting your teeth and keeping that muscle "up" for a quarter of an hour! And without moving it more than the proverbial hair's breadth! This is what had to be done, and, mind you, whether it was the arm, or the neck and shoulders, or the legs that were being operated upon, the whole pose had to be struck, all the muscles contracted, as otherwise the pieces would never have fitted properly when they came to be joined.

Certain mechanical devices had, of course, to be adopted to insure that the pose should be exactly the same on each occasion. The strain of holding the muscles tense was so great that only about a couple of moulds could be taken at one "sitting," and so Sandow had to submit himself to the ordeal day by day for nearly a month. The photographs which we publish give a very fair idea of the whole process. They were, of course, taken at the time, and the whole series

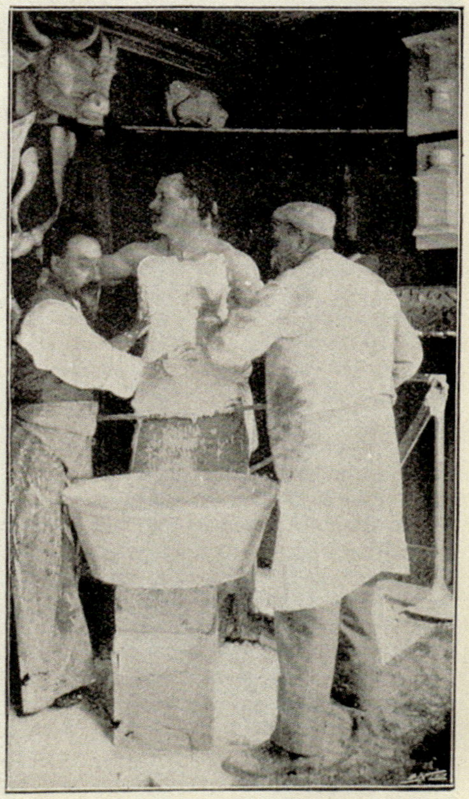

MOULDING CHEST AND ABDOMINAL MUSCLES.

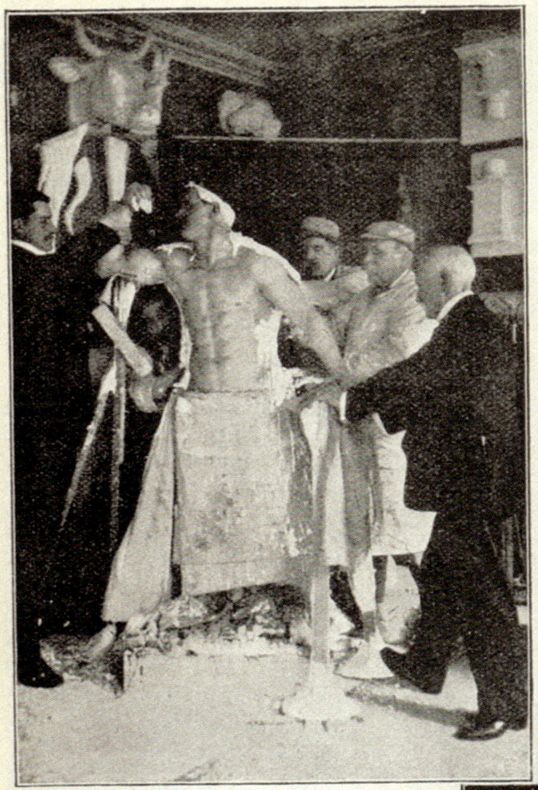

TAKING MOULD OF BACK AND SHOULDERS — THE SLIGHTEST MOVEMENT OF ARM WOULD DISTURB THE "DELTOID" AND "LATISSIMUS DORSI" MUSCLES.

(of which we give the most striking) show how the work was conducted from beginning to end. In the first instance, an outline in paper, roughly to measurement, of the figure in the pose proposed to be taken up was made; this was simply to serve as a guide for the making of the "shells" for supporting the plaster forming the moulds.

The mechanical arrangements for securing the same pose each time to which I have alluded were very simple. The position of the feet on the floor was marked out, there was a support for the right elbow, and also for the fingers of the right hand—this insured that the right arm should be in the proper position as regards the body and also flexed always at the same angle. The position of the other hand was also marked, and that of the top of the head. These were helps in taking up the pose, but, of course, practically none at all in keeping it so far as the muscles were concerned —they had to be kept contracted purely by an effort of will. It may be noticed that in the hands are clasped the grip dumb-bells; this was in order to facilitate the keeping the muscles tense and rigid.

The dumb-bell in question is made in two parts, with springs between them which have to be compressed before the two halves can be brought together—by bringing them together and then keeping them there the muscles were kept in the proper tense and immovable condition necessary for the successful execution of the cast.

After the shells were made it was necessary to mark out the figure into sections, each of which was moulded separately. A certain amount of margin was allowed in each piece, this being taken off afterwards according to the most absolutely correct measurements before the numerous sections were fitted together. Of course, by comparison, the work entailed over some of the sections was easy; thus, the filling in of the shell round the legs was in a manner plain

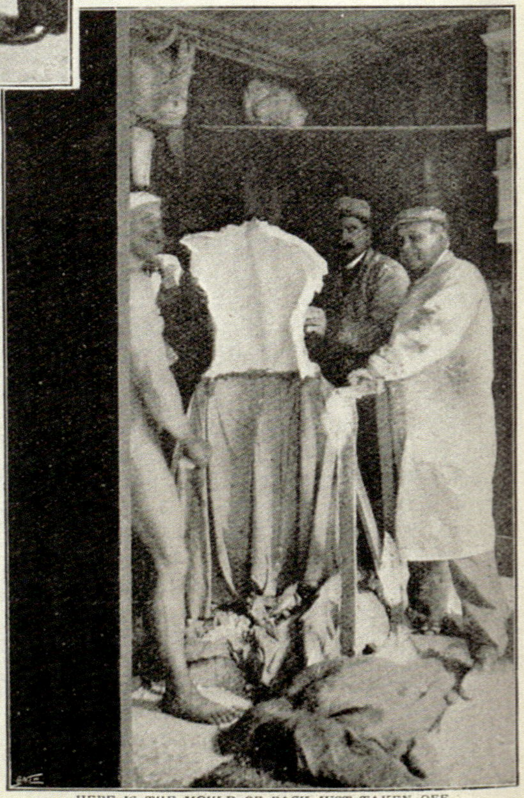

HERE IS THE MOULD OF BACK JUST TAKEN OFF.

sailing by contrast with the difficulty and anxiety entailed over other portions of the figure which it was so much harder to keep perfectly still. Possibly most trouble had to be taken over the front of the figure from the waist upwards—it will be noticed that the abdominal muscles are set, and that some of the chest muscles are brought out also. To "set" one's chest or abdomen long enough to be measured is simple enough, and is usually managed by holding the breath. Obviously this was out of the question in this instance; even Sandow could hardly be expected to refrain from breathing for the space of a quarter of an hour! How he managed it will be told in a minute in his own words.

In spite of almost complete immobility on the part of the subject it is more than probable—indeed, a careful survey of the completed cast as it stands in the Museum convinces me of the fact—that the cast in some respects does not, and cannot, do perfect justice to the living subject. Even an almost imperceptible movement affects the plaster, and slight

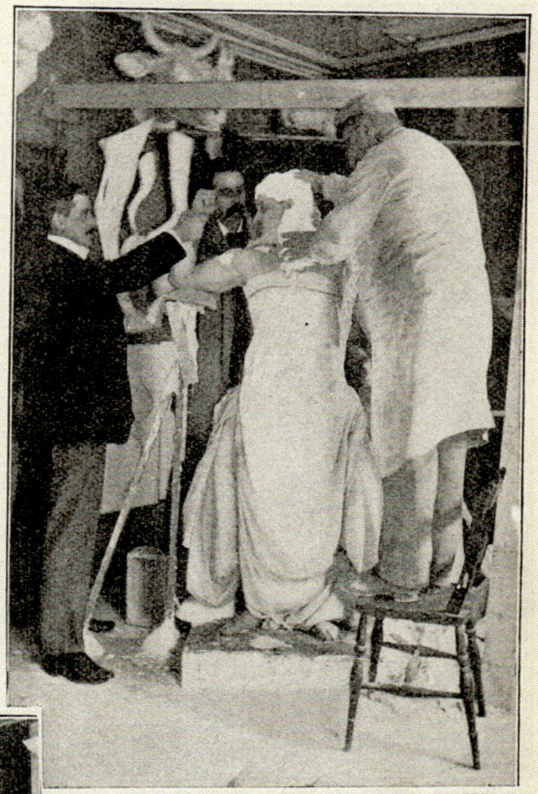

TAKING HEAD AND NECK — THE HAIR IS COVERED WITH A CLOTH.

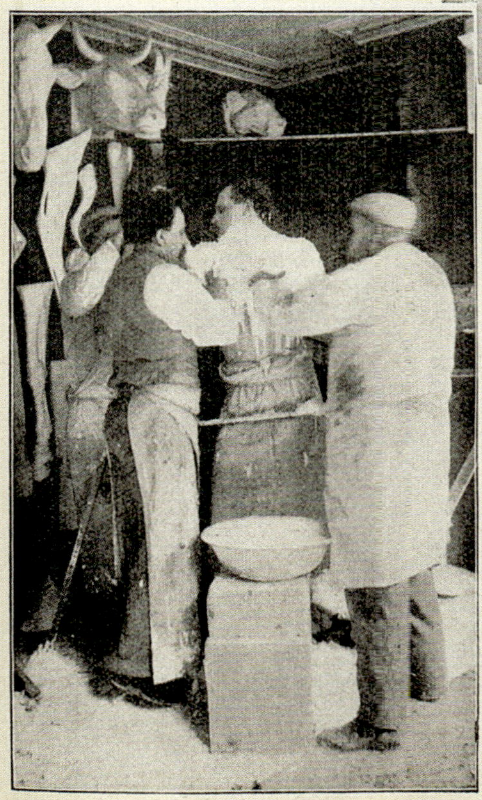

MOULDING UPPER PORTION OF BACK AND NECK.

movement there must have been, with the natural result that a few of the very finest lines may have been lost. This, to a close observer, especially if he be endowed with some knowledge of anatomy, is specially to be noticed in the muscles of the chest and the lower portion of the throat—very fine, indeed, are they in the cast, but here and there the effect of what a painter would call very minute *nuances* seems to be lost—at all events, that is the impression made upon those of us who have had numerous opportunities of inspecting the original.

Thus the cast is certainly not flattering; on the contrary, if it falls short at all it is that, while it represents very finely the development and the general contours of Sandow, it here and there is deficient in those fine lines, those little shades of muscle which soften the massiveness of the build and cause even his herculean figure to look shapely and graceful. Not that I mean to imply for a moment that the cast in any way gives an impression of unwieldy strength and coarseness of development — one has only to look at many of the classical statues in Great Russell Street to see that it does

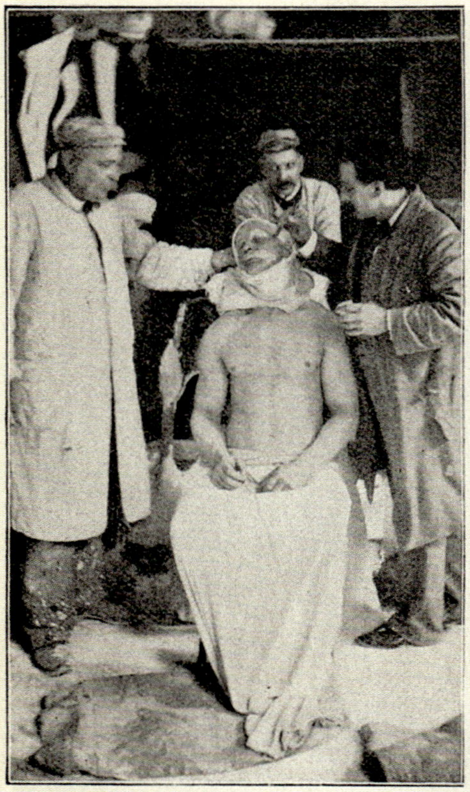

MAKING READY TO TAKE FACE—HAIR, NECK, AND MOUSTACHE COVERED WITH CLOTHS.

not suffer by the comparison; all I mean is that, beautiful piece of workmanship as it is, the dead plaster does not and cannot represent in its full perfection a form the charm of which to no small extent depends upon the fine gradations and mobile finish of its development.

Again, there are certain minor points of difference which the captious critic will no doubt seize upon with unholy glee. Do a few hairs in the moustache take a turn unseen in that of the original? Is the hair of the head a trifle too regular in its curliness? Well, let it at once be explained that there are limits even to the cast-maker's craft—that the taking of a mould of the separate hairs of a man's head is out of the question. The general contour of both hair and moustache were cast, but they were covered over with a piece of linen for the purpose, otherwise the consequences would have been very disastrous to the victim. He would have emerged from the ordeal, in fact, balder than the new-born babe; as it was, in spite of the body and limbs being well oiled before the plaster was put on, the removal of the latter caused him a good deal of trouble. So the hair and moustache, having been roughly cast as described, were modelled afterwards from photographs specially taken for the purpose. These and the eyes (the cast of the face, of course, being taken with the eyelids closed) were finished by skilled craftsmen, and are the only parts of the figure in which there is any possibility of any error having been made. Personally I have seen Sandow standing by the cast, and have carefully compared the two heads; I don't think that there is much to choose between them. Always excepting the fact that the cast is lacking in the fresh colouring and blue eyes of the original.

Here is another point which will probably interest both the earnest student as well as the curious layman. What are the dimensions of the cast? Here they are as taken by Messrs. Brucciani, with mathematical exactness:—

ACTUAL DIMENSIONS OF CAST.

	in.		in.
Chest	49	Thigh	25
Waist	36	Calf..	17¾
Biceps............	18	Ankle.....	9
Forearm	15½	Neck	17
Wrist	7¾	Height	69

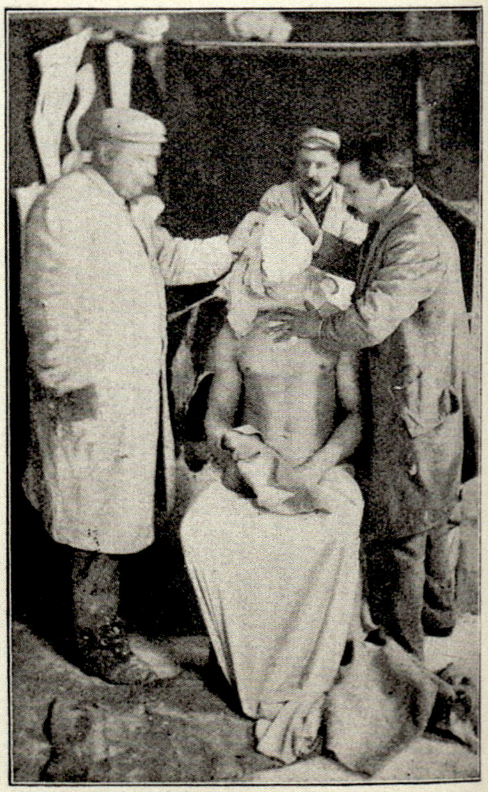

A VERY TRYING TEN MINUTES.

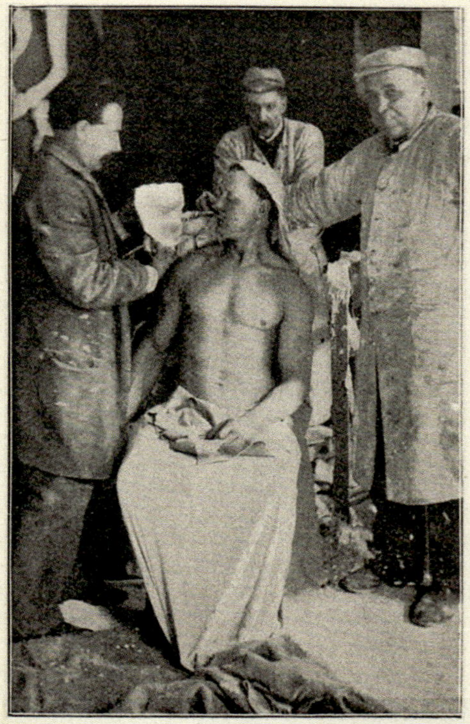

A SIGH OF RELIEF—THE MASK IS FINISHED.

Now, the probability is that a question will at once arise in the minds of a good many people, and especially of those who have read Sandow's book: How do these measurements taken from the cast compare with those given by Sandow himself? Do they exactly agree, and if they differ, are they larger or smaller? And, if so, why? These are quite fair questions, and as a preliminary to answering them I give the dimensions as they appear in the book. Here they are:—

DIMENSIONS AS GIVEN IN BOOK.

	in.		in.
Chest	48	Thigh	26
Waist	30	Calf...............	18
Biceps	19½	Ankle............	8½
Forearm	16½	Neck	18
Wrist	7½	Height	69¼

It will be noted that the figures are not identical—that in most cases those given in the book are bigger than those of the cast, whereas in one or two instances the reverse is the case. This is capable of a very simple—I might say obvious—explanation. The measurements given in the book are those of each limb taken separately, in the position which gives the greatest measurement and with the muscles contracted to their maximum extent. In the pose for the cast the conditions were far otherwise. To begin with, in no one case is any particular limb placed so as to bring the muscles out to their fullest extent. Again, as so many groups of muscles are contracted at once, it is apparent that the amount of nervous energy which in the other case would be concentrated upon the muscles of one limb is spread over a much wider space; and, lastly, it would have been quite impossible to keep up for a quarter of an hour or even ten minutes a tension which it was a strain to retain for a few seconds for measuring purposes. Had it been attempted the result would have been dire failure—after a minute or two the tension would have relaxed and the mould been spoiled.

On the other hand, in the cast the chest is 49in. as compared with 48in. (normal) of the book; the waist is 36in. compared with 30in.; but the height is only 5ft. 9in. as compared with a quarter of an inch more. Regarding the latter—the figure in the cast is not perfectly upright; the contraction necessary to show the development of the abdominal muscles takes a shade off the height. The forcing out, again, of the muscles makes the waist measurement much greater than it would be were the chest fully expanded and the former drawn in, while the extra inch round the chest is due to the slight increase from the normal which the pose entails.

And what does Sandow himself think about it all? Naturally he is pleased and

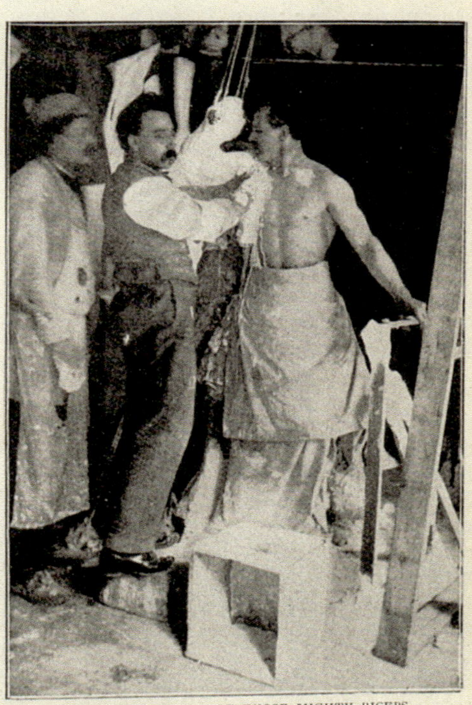

TAKING THE MOULD OF THOSE MIGHTY BICEPS.

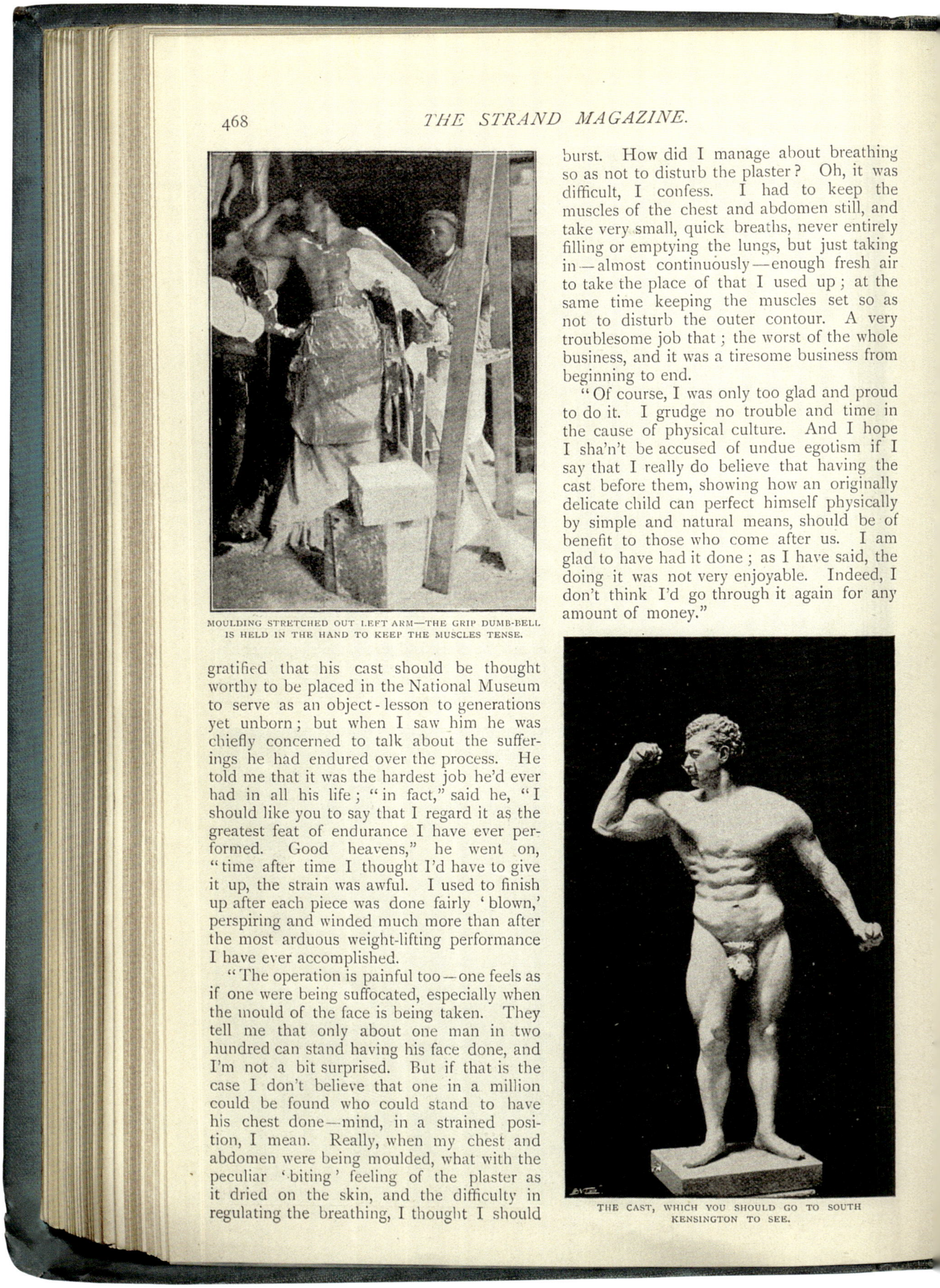

468 THE STRAND MAGAZINE.

MOULDING STRETCHED OUT LEFT ARM—THE GRIP DUMB-BELL IS HELD IN THE HAND TO KEEP THE MUSCLES TENSE.

gratified that his cast should be thought worthy to be placed in the National Museum to serve as an object-lesson to generations yet unborn; but when I saw him he was chiefly concerned to talk about the sufferings he had endured over the process. He told me that it was the hardest job he'd ever had in all his life; "in fact," said he, "I should like you to say that I regard it as the greatest feat of endurance I have ever performed. Good heavens," he went on, "time after time I thought I'd have to give it up, the strain was awful. I used to finish up after each piece was done fairly 'blown,' perspiring and winded much more than after the most arduous weight-lifting performance I have ever accomplished.

"The operation is painful too—one feels as if one were being suffocated, especially when the mould of the face is being taken. They tell me that only about one man in two hundred can stand having his face done, and I'm not a bit surprised. But if that is the case I don't believe that one in a million could be found who could stand to have his chest done—mind, in a strained position, I mean. Really, when my chest and abdomen were being moulded, what with the peculiar 'biting' feeling of the plaster as it dried on the skin, and the difficulty in regulating the breathing, I thought I should burst. How did I manage about breathing so as not to disturb the plaster? Oh, it was difficult, I confess. I had to keep the muscles of the chest and abdomen still, and take very small, quick breaths, never entirely filling or emptying the lungs, but just taking in—almost continuously—enough fresh air to take the place of that I used up; at the same time keeping the muscles set so as not to disturb the outer contour. A very troublesome job that; the worst of the whole business, and it was a tiresome business from beginning to end.

"Of course, I was only too glad and proud to do it. I grudge no trouble and time in the cause of physical culture. And I hope I sha'n't be accused of undue egotism if I say that I really do believe that having the cast before them, showing how an originally delicate child can perfect himself physically by simple and natural means, should be of benefit to those who come after us. I am glad to have had it done; as I have said, the doing it was not very enjoyable. Indeed, I don't think I'd go through it again for any amount of money."

THE CAST, WHICH YOU SHOULD GO TO SOUTH KENSINGTON TO SEE.

'Sandow in Plaster of Paris:
A Unique Cast'
In: *The Strand Magazine* 22,
no. 130 (October 1901),
pp. 461–68
Technische Universität,
Universitätbibliothek

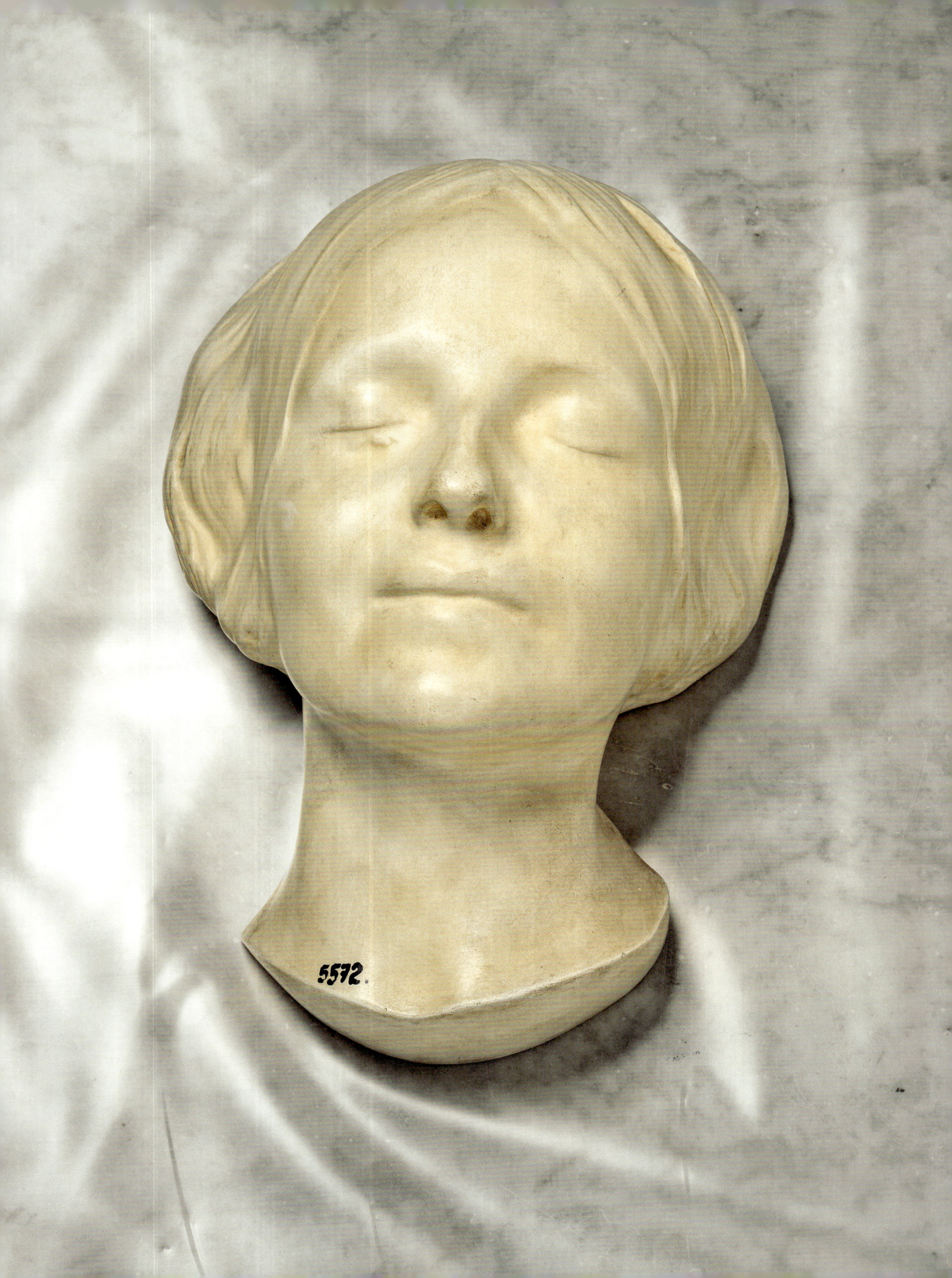
5572.

Ultimate Life

Plaster can directly capture life and is equally capable of documenting the end of life, that brief moment when life morphs into death. No artefact comes as close to achieving this as the death mask. From the physical contact with the face of a person who was alive only a moment ago it distils an allegedly authentic cast that confronts death with 'ultimate life', something utterly beyond its reach. Death masks are underpinned by a millennia-old tradition, ranging from the wax effigies of Roman antiquity (*imagines maiorum*) to the controversial death masks of the RAF terrorists Baader, Ensslin, and Raspe, which were made in the Stammheim Prison in Stuttgart in 1977. Perhaps the most widely known death mask is *L'Inconnue de la Seine* (The Unknown Woman of the Seine) from around 1900, on view here as a painting model from 1955. The peaceful portrait of a young woman, presumably a suicide pulled from the River Seine, has not only served as a source of inspiration for countless writers and artists, it has also been copied to produce Rescue Anne, the mannequin most commonly used for the teaching of cardiopulmonary resuscitation (CPR), which was first put on the market in 1960. It has become the prototypical symbol of life.

This chapter focuses on casts as remnants and relics, as after-images of lives once lived, as models for art and as unembellished expressions of death itself. The contact with the body of the dead person, the transfer of skin particles and facial hair from the negative mould to the positive cast, and the fact that posthumously moulded persons are no longer able to claim a right to the use and dissemination of their last image puts historical death masks at the centre of a number of ethical questions today. This is all the more valid for the famous plaster casts of the Pompeii dead and for contemporary works by artists such as Teresa Margolles.

After a development phase of two years, the first-aid mannequin Rescue Anne was put on the market in Norway in 1960. Shortly before, it had become clear that cardiopulmonary resuscitation (CPR) had great potential as a life-saving technique. Physician Peter Safar and toy manufacturer Asmund Lærdal joined forces to create a training model suitable for general use, which would allow people to familiarise themselves with the new technique. The mannequin was to resemble an unconscious human being; care had to be taken, however, to avoid anything that might frighten people. The search for a suitable model for the mannequin's features led to the death mask of *L'Inconnue de la Seine*. Rescue Anne became a huge success story. To this day the CPR life-saving technique is applied worldwide and is taught in first-aid courses as well as professional study programmes dealing with emergency situations — usually with assistance from Anne, whose face is still the same. The Lærdal company advertises its series of Anne simulator models with the slogan, 'The mask of death has become the face of life'.

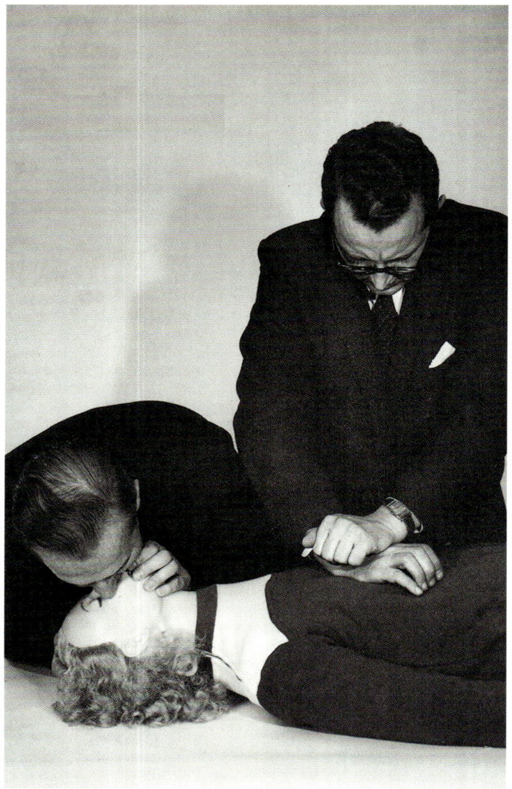

Asmund S. Lærdal and Han H. Dahll with *Resusci Anne*, 1960
In: Nina Tjomsland, *From Stavanger with Care: Lærdals First 50 Years*, Stavanger 1990, p. 31

Asmund S. Lærdal with Resusci Anne, 1961
In: *A-magasinet*, 11 January 2013, p. 49

From the death mask to the First-Aid mannequin: *The death mask of L'Inconnue de la Seine with two historical model heads*
In: *A-magasinet*, 11 January 2013, p. 48

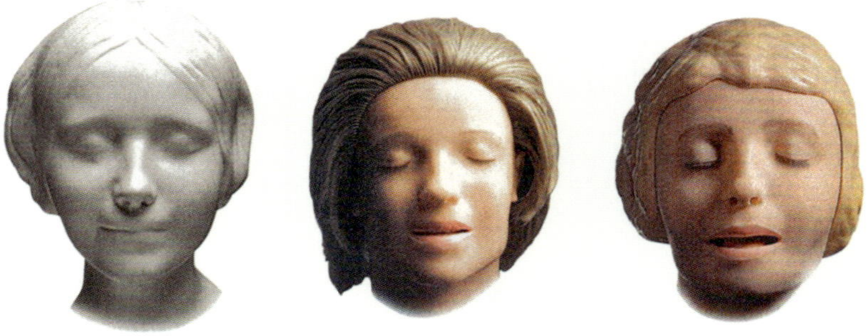

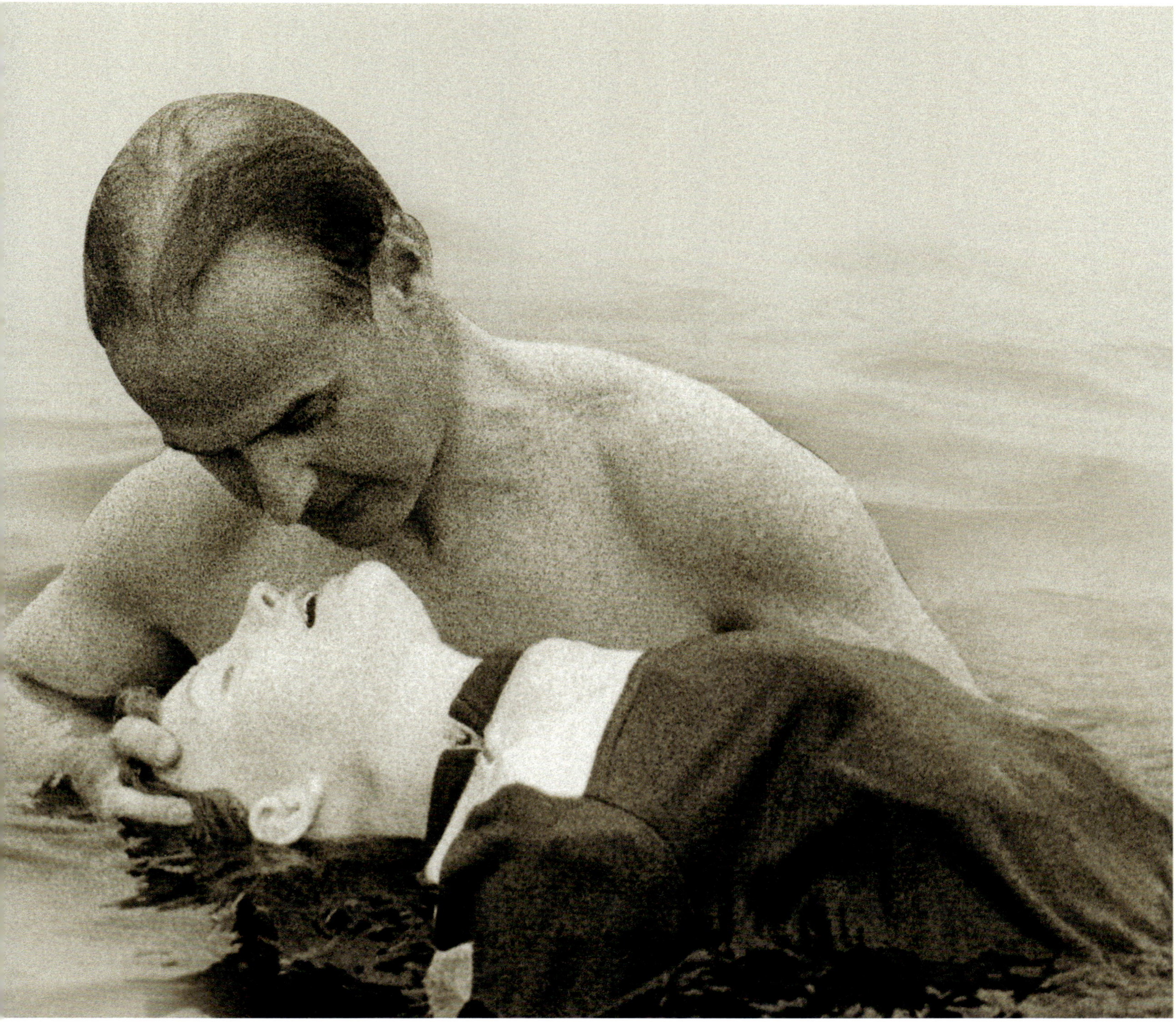

Death Mask Karl Maria von Weber (1780–1826)
Master model, before 1950
Staatliche Museen zu Berlin, Gipsformerei

» Usually the call for having a death mask taken goes out too late, and all one gets is a distorted image of life, where it would have been possible only hours earlier to capture the moment of the most glorious fulfilment. It is strange how widespread the erroneous idea is that one must wait for *rigor mortis* to set in, when in fact the artistic plaster caster should be the first to step up to the body of the deceased person. Only too often did I hear someone say how beautiful had been the face of the dead only moments before and how ugly it had become since — Come quickly, said the brother of a man who had just died, he is so beautiful. When I arrived on the scene less than an hour later, he no longer considered it possible to take a mask because the face appeared so ugly to him. In this case, however, all was not lost. All one has to do is give the dead the right treatment!

Georg Kolbe, 1927

Excerpt from Georg Kolbe, 'Das Abnehmen von Totenmasken', preface, in: Ernst Benkard, *Das ewige Antlitz: Eine Sammlung von Totenmasken*, Berlin 1927, pp. xli–xliii, here p. xli.

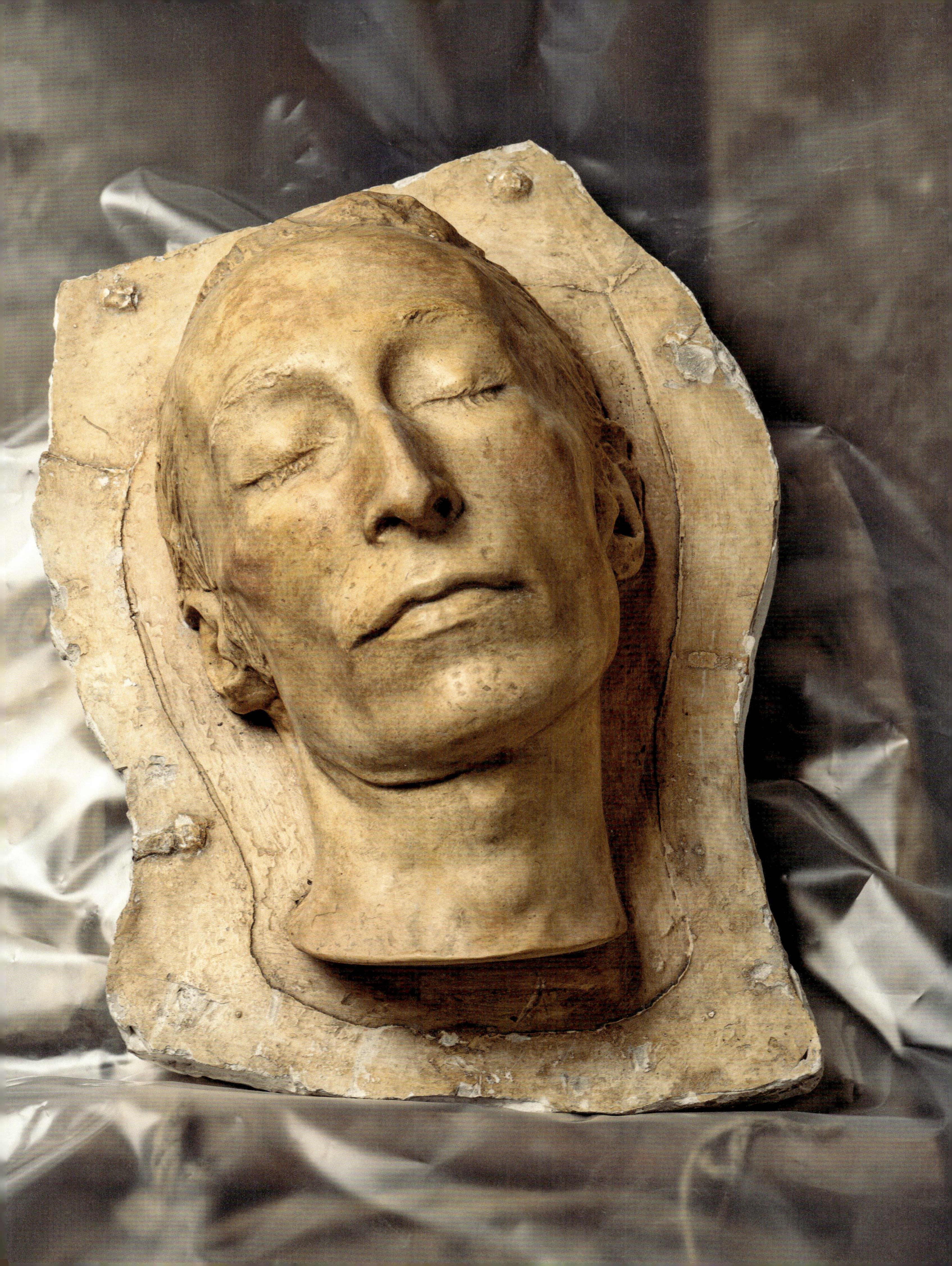

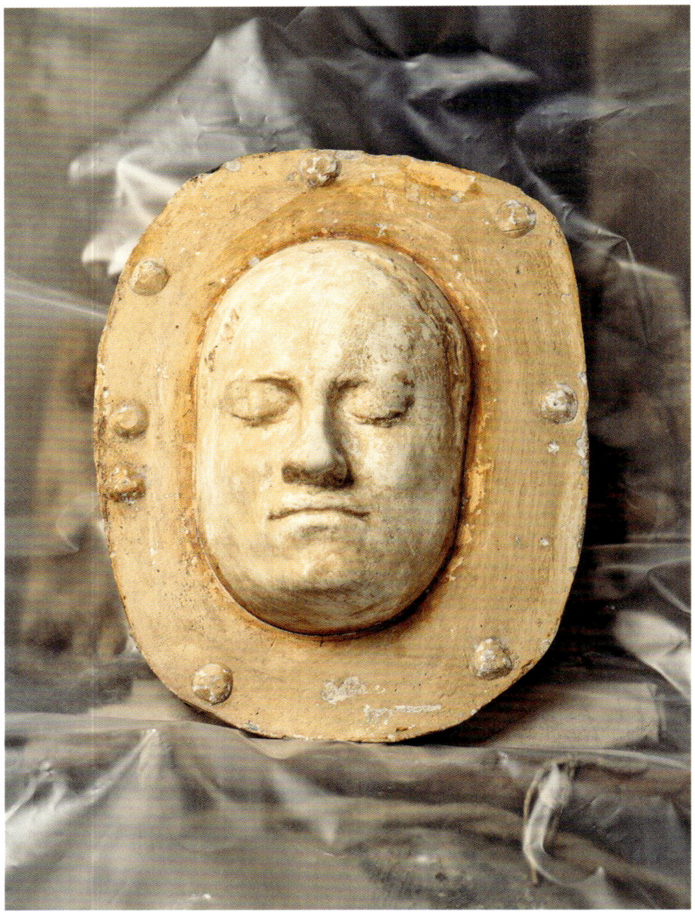

Death Mask of Charles XII, King of Sweden (1697–1718)
Master model, before 1950
Staatliche Museen zu Berlin, Gipsformerei

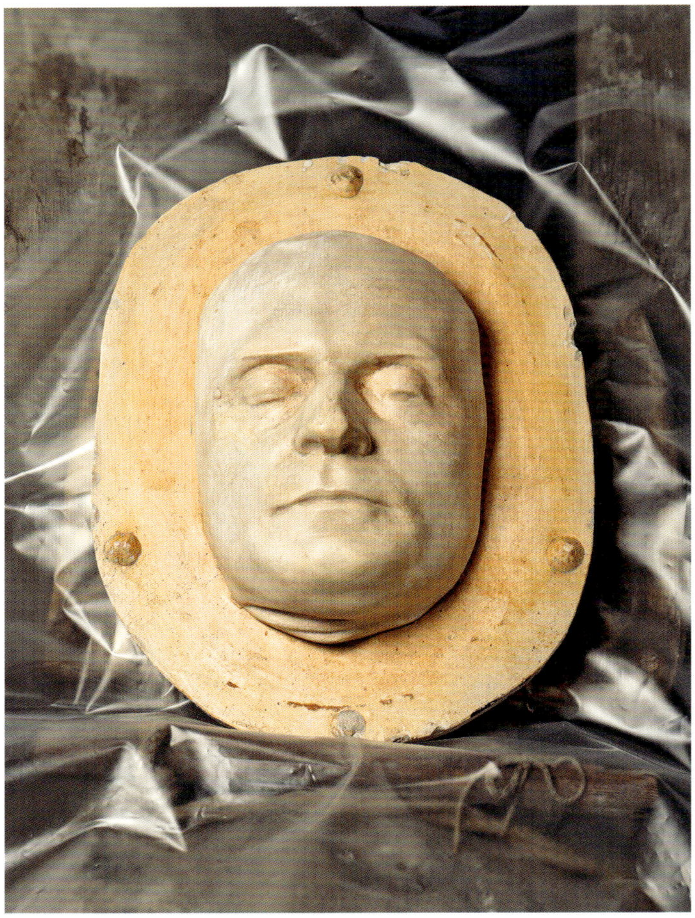

Death Mask of Gotthold Ephraim Lessing (1729–1781)
Master model, before 1950
Staatliche Museen zu Berlin, Gipsformerei

The death mask of Gotthold Ephraim Lessing was taken in 1781 by the sculptor and medallist Christian Friedrich Krull (1748–1787) at the instigation of the great writer's poet friend Johann Wilhelm Ludwig Gleim. Commonly regarded as the first middle-class death mask, it is also the first mask to function exclusively as a memorial object. It was not conceived as being in any way linked to a burial ceremony or the creation of a portrait bust: its sole purpose resides in itself. Lessing's mask marks the beginning of a European death mask obsession in the nineteenth century, focused on public figures and luminaries of all kinds. Disconcerting as this practice seems today, it was then omnipresent. If someone was about to die, the plaster caster already had his foot at the door, at least metaphorically speaking, in order not to miss that brief moment when life, when the soul, had not yet taken leave of the body.

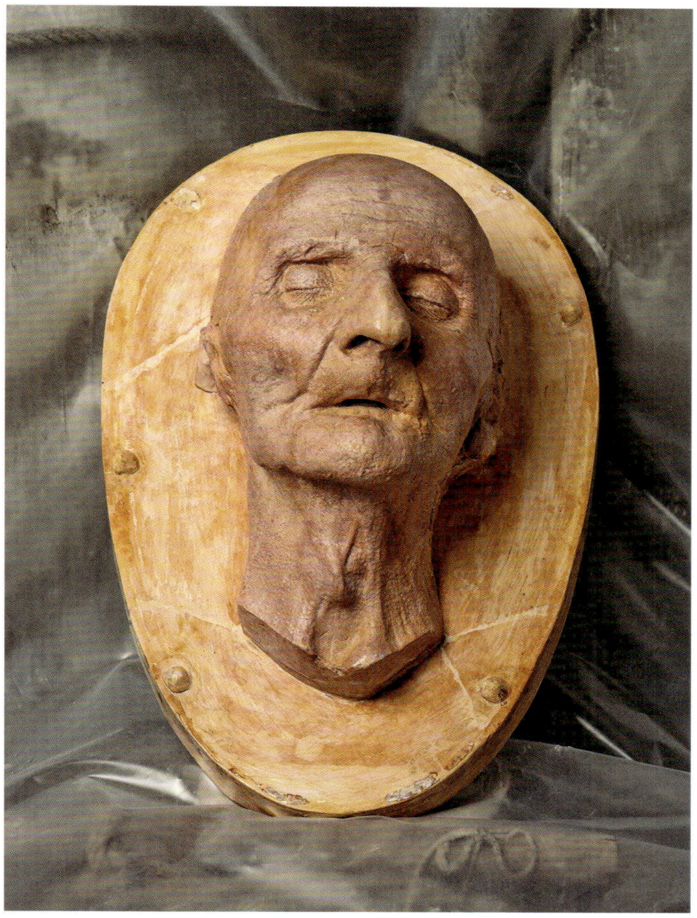

Death Mask of Anton Bruckner (1824–1896)
Master model, before 1950
Staatliche Museen zu Berlin, Gipsformerei

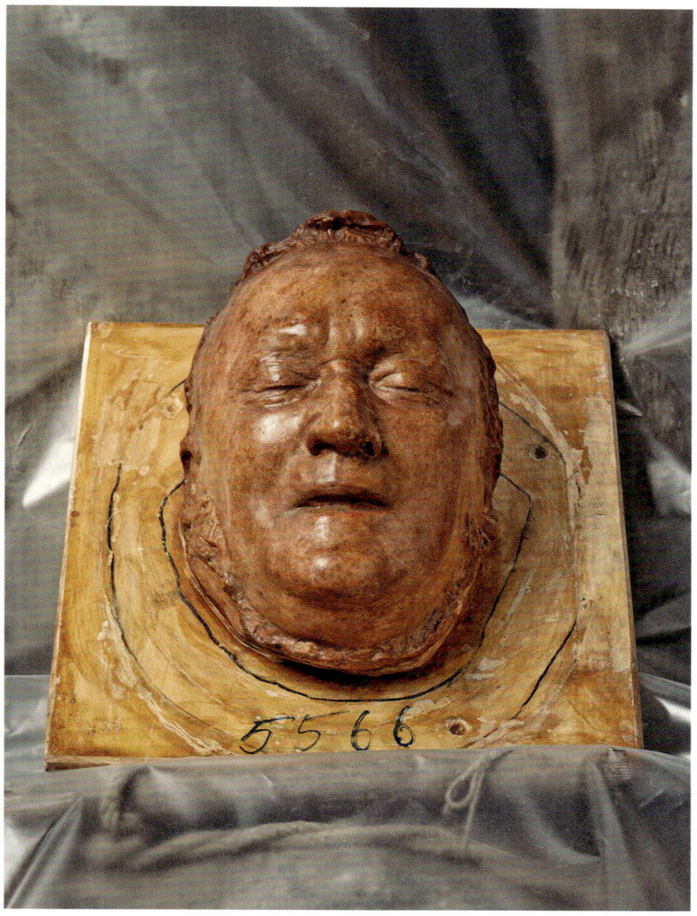

Death Mask of Richard Wagner (1813–1883)
Master model, before 1950
Staatliche Museen zu Berlin, Gipsformerei

'Death masks are works of art straight out of Nature's workshop', stated Ernst Benkard in his treatise *Das ewige Antlitz* (1927), which is considered to be the first art-historical analysis of this field of visual culture. This claim, which was also applied to photography, echoes an idea commonly regarded as outdated today: a death mask is made by Nature herself and represents an objective human effigy untainted by artistic agency. As artisanal products, death masks were often produced and sold in batches of varying sizes by plaster casters, modellers or even taxidermists. On closer inspection, however, each one is seen to bear the imprint of a human hand. They were supplemented, altered, interpreted, or made to conform to an artistic ideal. Sometimes they even bear the signature of their creator.

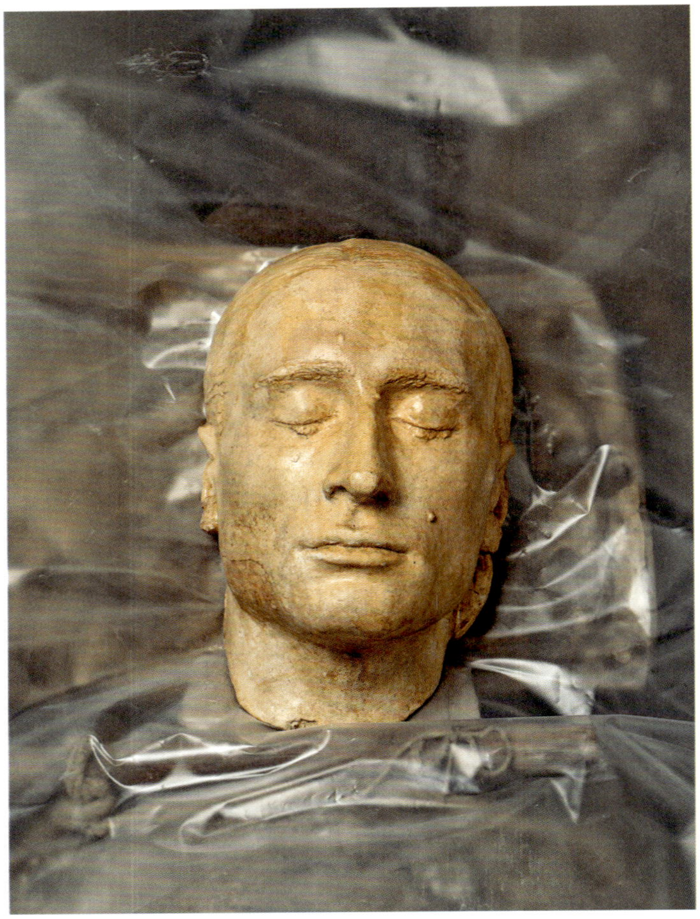

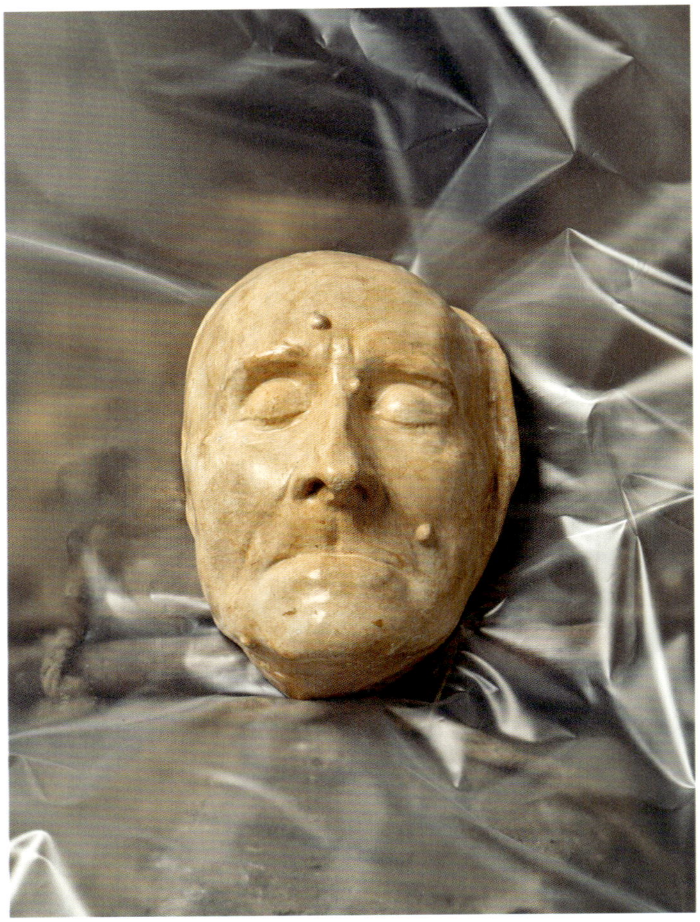

» In my forty-one years at the Gipsformerei, there was occasionally the request for taking a death mask. Moulding the face of a dead person is no easy task. The first step is placing a cardboard template round the face so that the plaster does not cover the entire head. Vaseline is then applied to the skin. The next step is brushing the face with liquid plaster. A separating thread is attached to the face lengthwise, depending on how undercut the face is at the chin and the ears. Only a very thin layer of plaster is applied to ensure its weight does not distort the features. With the help of the separating thread the mask is cut in two and removed from the face. The two-part negative mould is then joined together again. The casting form is degreased and coated in shellac. Grease is then applied once again so that the plaster will later come away more easily. As soon as the plaster has been poured and set, a hammer is taken to the form. This requires great care and must be done slowly so that the cast's structure is not damaged in any way. The features of the deceased person gradually emerge from the lost mould.

Peter John-Schoubye, artistic plasterer

Life Mask Franz Liszt (1811–1886)
Master model, before 1950
Staatliche Museen zu Berlin,
Gipsformerei

Death Mask Franz Liszt (1811–1886)
Master model, before 1950
Staatliche Museen zu Berlin,
Gipsformerei

Death Mask Johann Gottfried Schadow (1764–1850), 1850
Staatliche Museen zu Berlin,
Alte Nationalgalerie

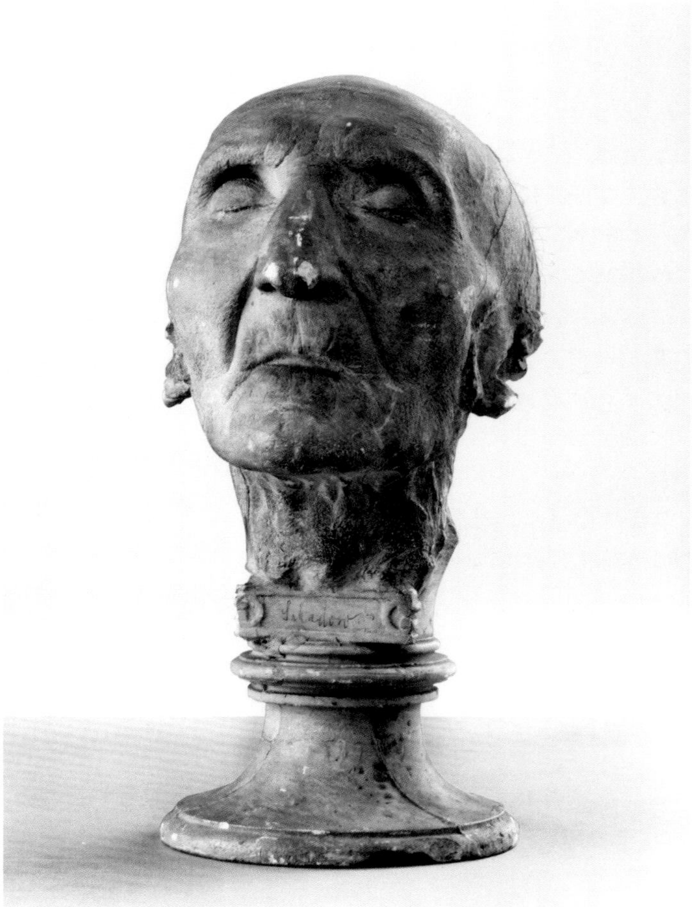

Death masks are no exception from the general rule governing casts, in that they, too, are based on primary models: 'originals' derived from the first negative mould taken directly from the face, the so-called 'lost mould' which has to be destroyed to obtain the first positive. Such an original is the death mask of Johann Gottfried Schadow on loan from the Alte Nationalgalerie and made by an anonymous plaster caster. In addition to the richly detailed rendering of the skin, with its multitude of pores, wrinkles and irregularities, the mask has retained traces of human matter. The plaster appropriated the whiskers and eyelashes and transferred them from the lost mould to the cast. Such characteristics were considered to be criteria of quality, both in death masks and in casts after nature more generally, since they guaranteed the object's authenticity. That death masks were still displayed as relics and memorial objects on living-room walls — and consequently the object of quick sales at plaster casting workshops — until only a few decades ago points to a shift in the significance we attribute to death. There was a time when death was seen as essential to life because it was inevitable. It was therefore made highly visible in daily life. Today, death is largely considered a taboo at least in the West. In many death masks, the faces are distorted by illness and/or death throes; they give an impression of lifelessness and may appear utterly macabre. Some masks display the immediate consequences of death: pointed noses, sunken cheeks, collapsed flesh. Some attest to the cause of death, such as the death mask of King Charles XII of Sweden, which displays an injury to the right of the forehead consistent with the headshot that killed the King (ill. p. 112). Others show a peaceful, relaxed expression reminiscent of someone asleep. The collection of the Gipsformerei comprises around fifty death masks that covers the entire range, from graceful idealisations to unsparing documents. If one adds the gelatine models that go with the cast masks, the aesthetic variation is even further expanded by the different shellac coatings.

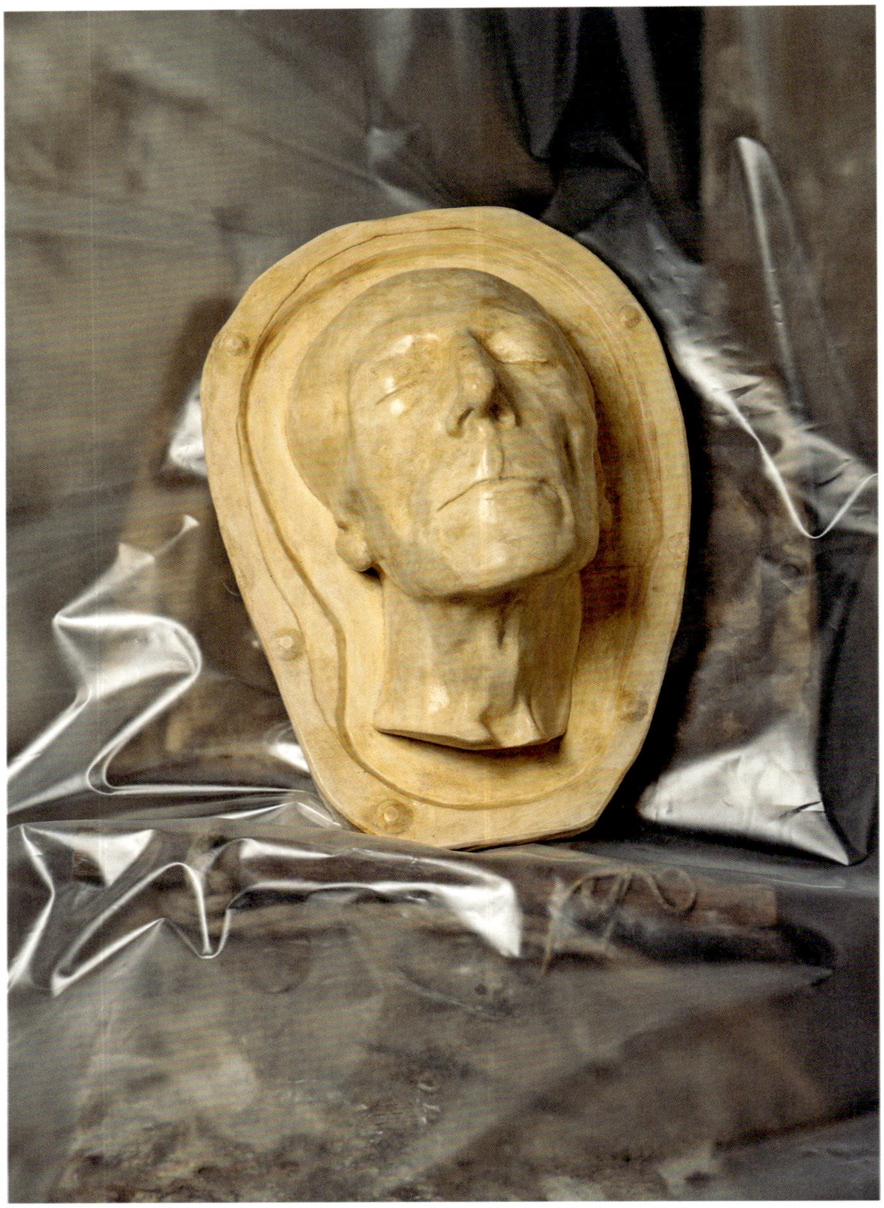

Death Mask of Frederick II of Prussia (1712–1786)
Master model, 1935
Staatliche Museen zu Berlin, Gipsformerei

The death mask of King Frederick II, who died on 17 August 1786 in Schloss Sanssouci in Potsdam, was made by sculptor Johann Eckstein (1735–1817). We hear of the difficulties that arose from Eckstein moulding the face 'as far as behind the ears' and with 'half the neck' from his colleague Johann Gottfried Schadow in a letter to the Crown Prince of Bavaria in 1812: 'Now he had problems prising the plaster mould open and so therefore tapped the skull with a wooden mallet, which made the chamber hussars present angry. If Eckstein had not had the good fortune of the plaster finally coming away, he would have been in for a drubbing.' Eckstein developed a bust from the death mask, which was realised in two wax positives. The bust, however, was judged to be insufficiently lifelike and lacking in expressivity. Schadow, for one, concurred with that assessment: 'Eckstein opened up the eyes and introduced changes and improvements in parts, which resulted in spoiling everything.' The death mask of the 'Old Fritz', which has been on sale at the Gispformerei since 1914, is presumably based on the Alte Nationalgalerie cast that includes the back of the head completed by the artist; this version was presumably based on Eckstein's now lost wax cast in the collection of the former Hohenzollern Museum at Schloss Monbijou in Berlin.

» The version of the death mask of Frederick II in the Alte Nationalgalerie collection was cast in several solid plaster pieces. It seems that the piece mould was not perfectly aligned during the casting process as there are signs of misalignment in several places. Other parts were glued on with resin at a later stage. Seams and gaps that had formed during the casting were not treated; they were left as they were, apparently to document the authenticity of the form. The entire bust was given a coating that today appears somewhat brownish and transparent. The coating is probably shellac and was arguably added to facilitate the moulding. The face exhibits the authentic features of the deceased King. The eyes are closed, the cheeks and mouth have shrunk. The skin appears dry, prominently so at the nose and cheeks. The back of the head and the bust's plinth are sculptural additions. The plinth still features the original wooden reinforcement, which provides a clue to the early date of this cast. The lifelikeness of the ears particularly raises doubts as to their authenticity: moulding them was obviously a technical challenge for the sculptor; he may well have resorted to interpretative additions.

Alexandra Czarnecki, Sculpture Conservator

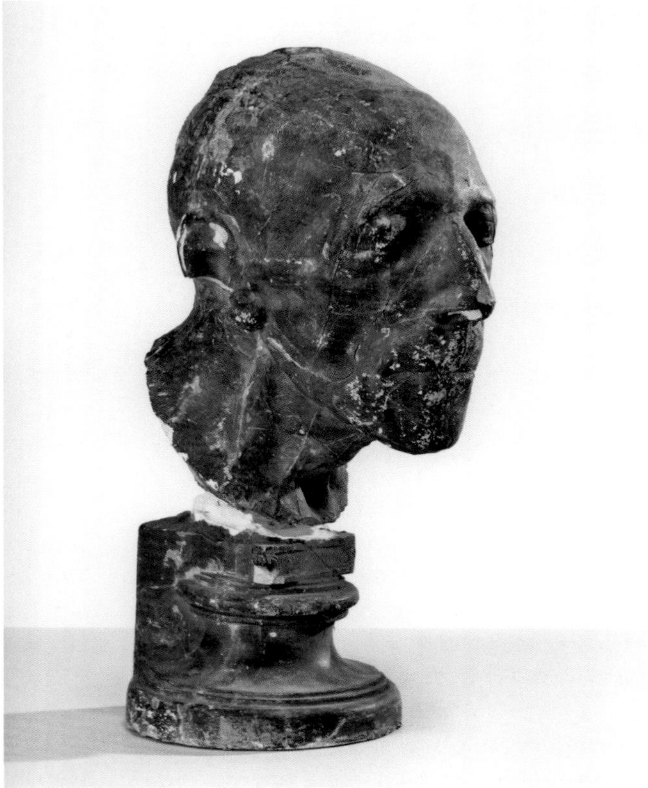

After Johannes Eckstein
Death Mask of Frederick II of Prussia
Cast, 1786
Staatliche Museen zu Berlin,
Alte Nationalgalerie

Admired for her beauty and grace during her lifetime and thereafter, Queen Louise of Prussia died in the summer of 1810, when she was only thirty-four. Her wax death mask was taken by the stucco plasterer and sculptor Christian Philipp Wolff (1772–1820). Today, it is part of the collection of the Stiftung Preußische Schlösser und Gärten Berlin-Brandenburg. The cast, an example of a mass-produced death mask, contributed significantly to the mythologisation around the Queen after her death. The bust of Louise was made in the context of a life-size recumbent figure by Christian Daniel Rauch that Frederick Wilhelm III commissioned as her funerary monument, is also based on this death mask. The monument was installed in the mausoleum of Schlosspark Charlottenburg in 1815.

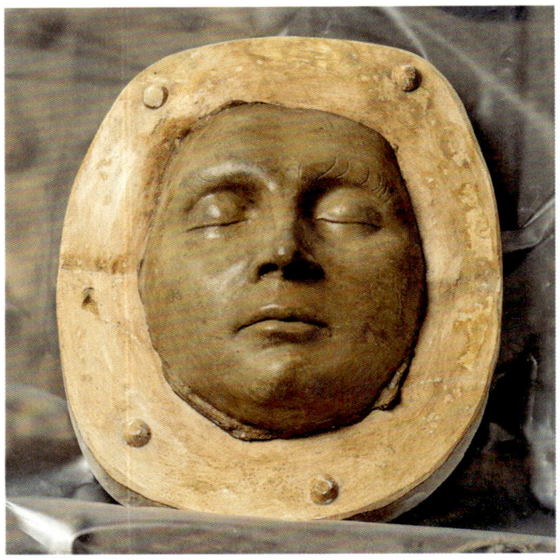

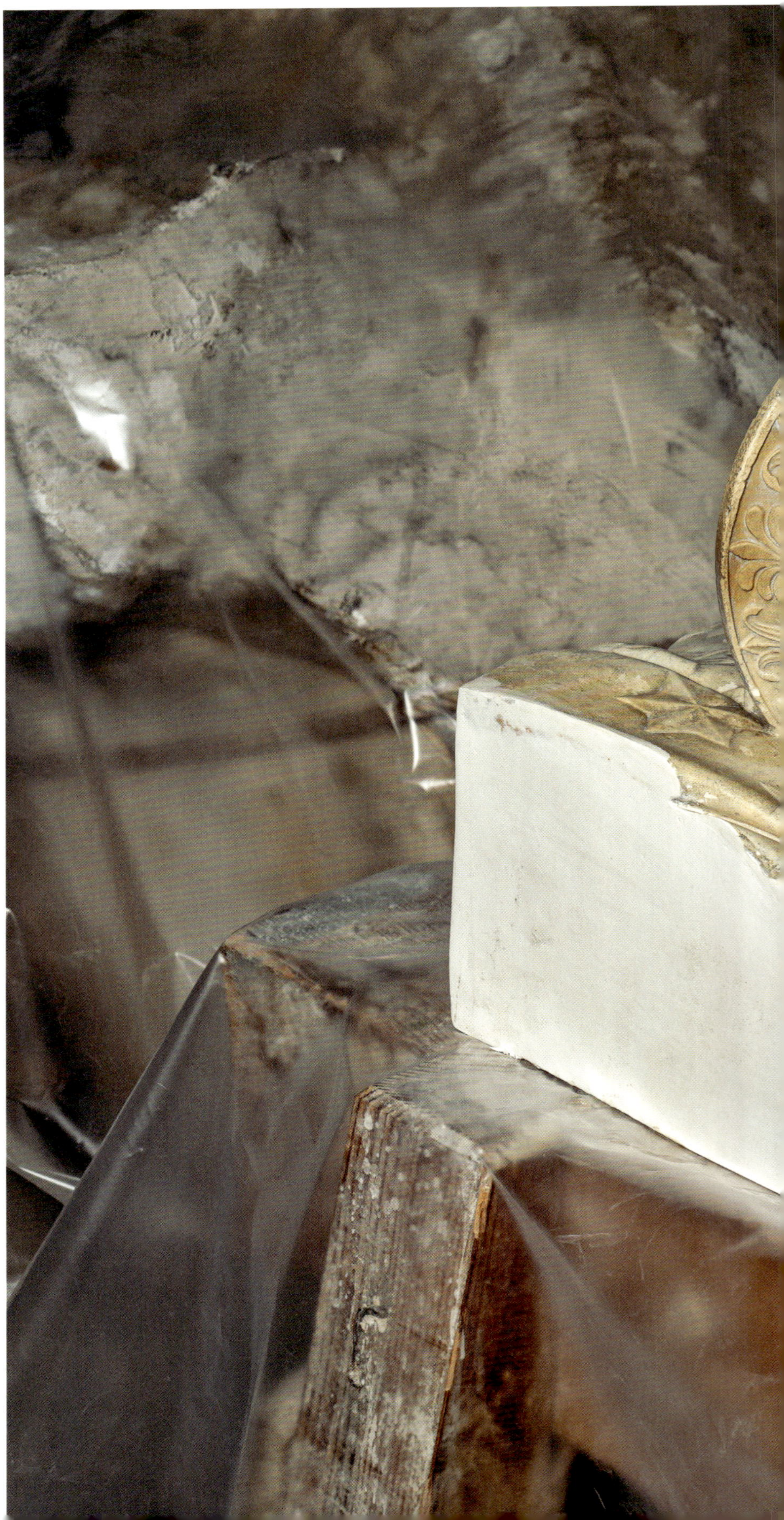

Death Mask of Luise Queen of Prussia (1776–1810)
Master model, before 1965
Staatliche Museen zu Berlin, Gipsformerei

After Christian Daniel Rauch
Recumbent Bust of Louise Queen of Prussia
Master model, before 1965
Staatliche Museen zu Berlin, Gipsformerei

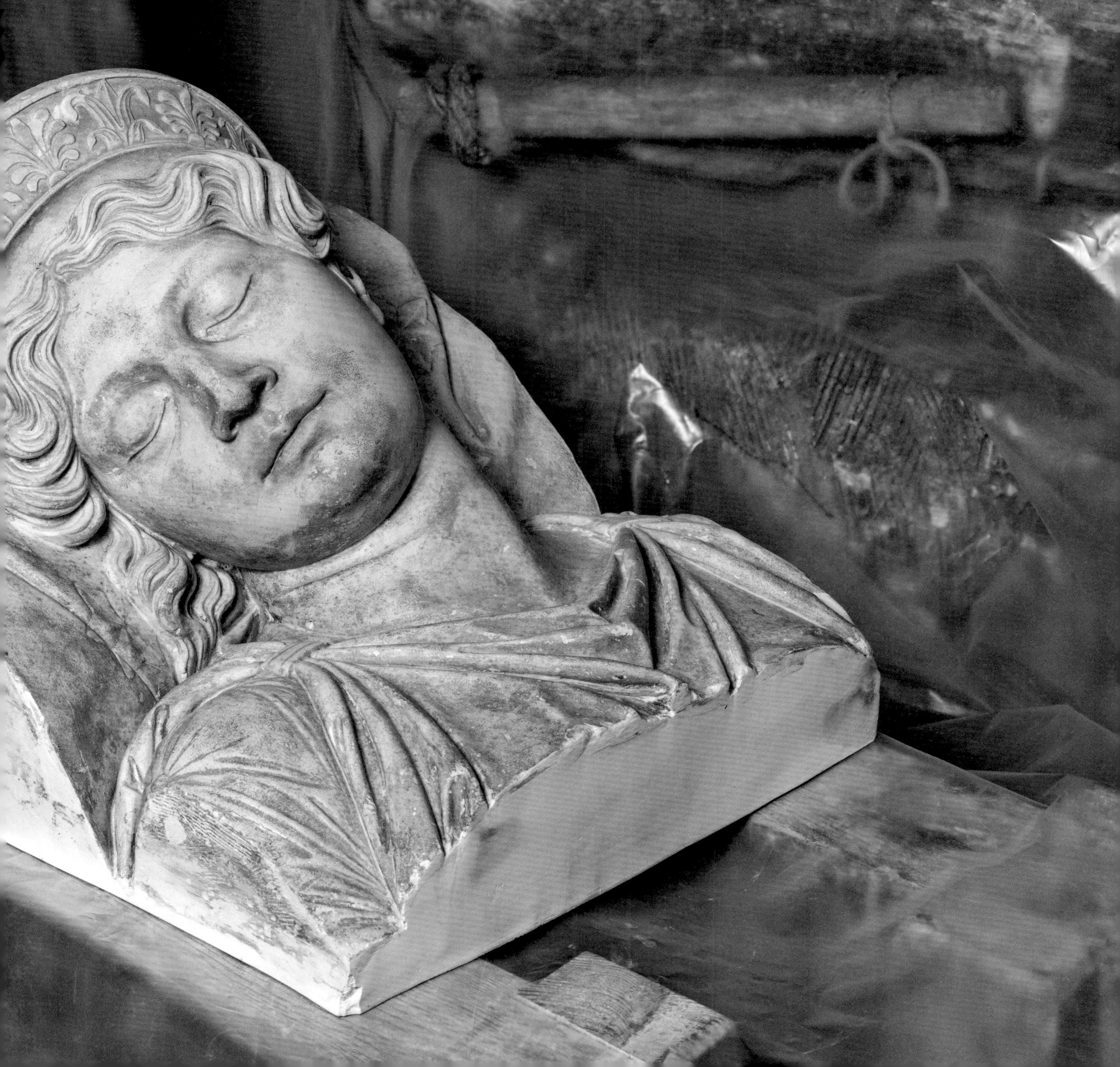

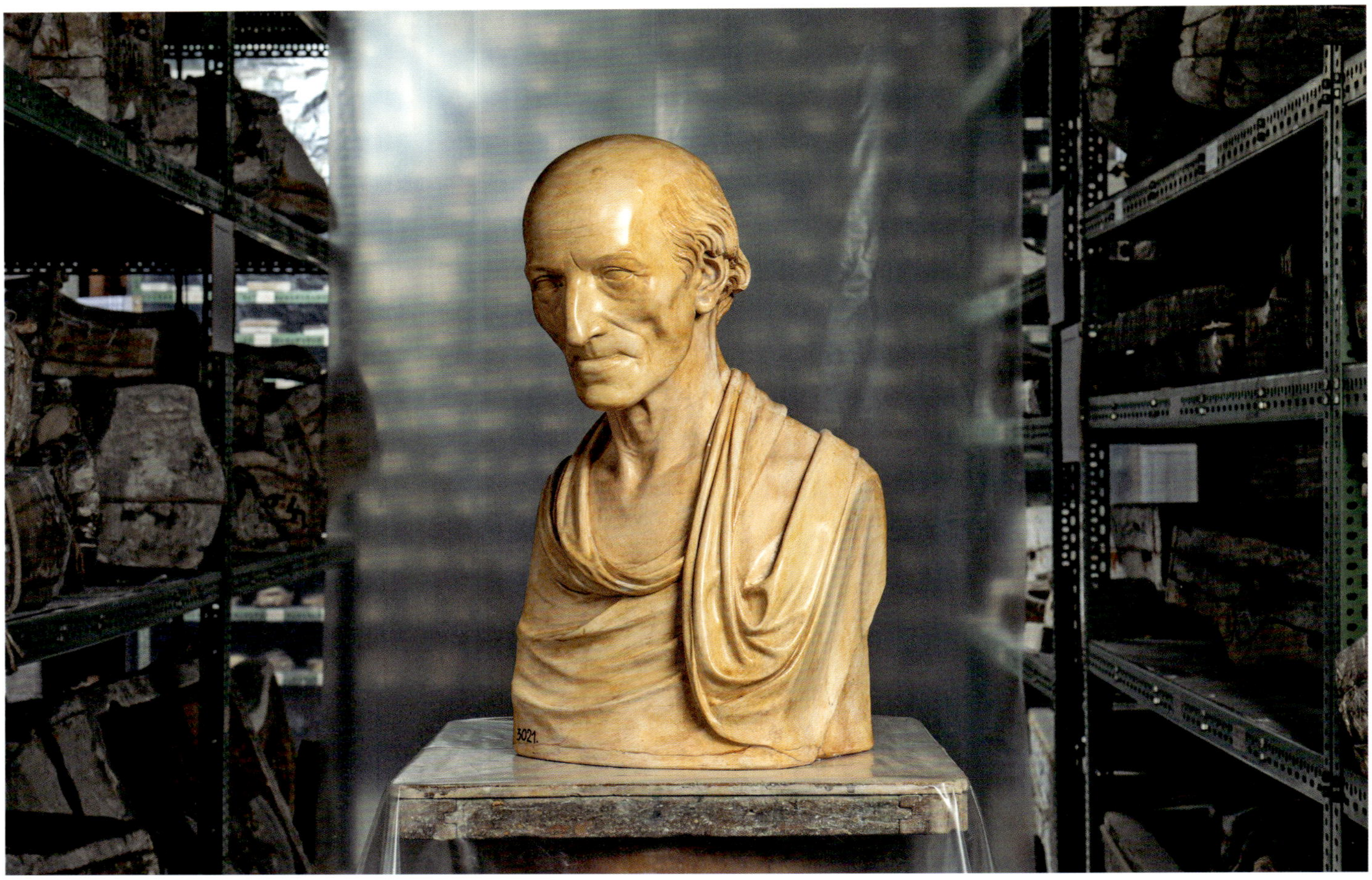
3021.

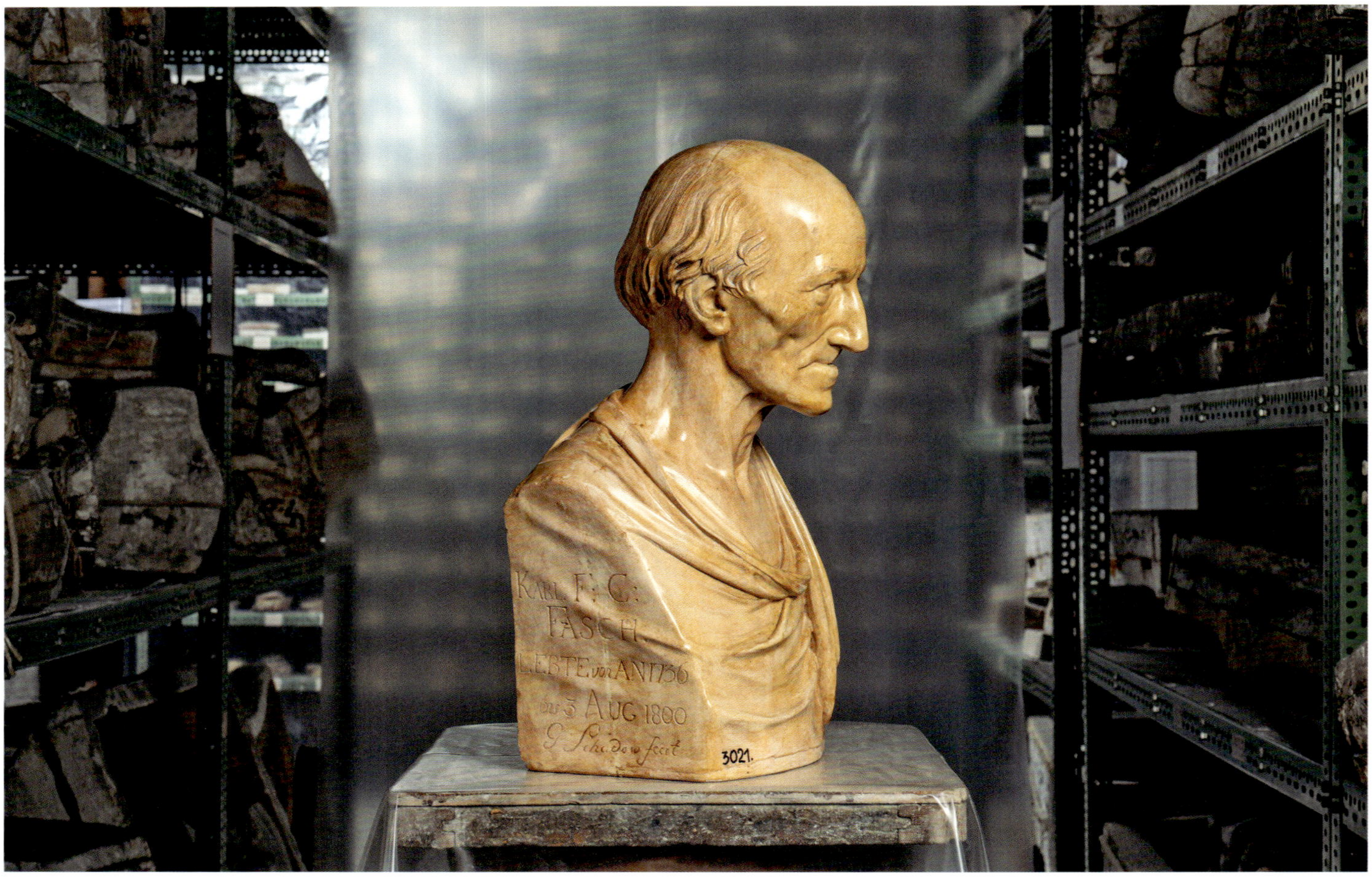
KARL F: C:
FASCH
AUG 1800
3021.

After Johann Gottfried Schadow
Carl Friedrich Christian Fasch, 1800
Master model, 1986
Staatliche Museen zu Berlin,
Gipsformerei

» It so happens quite often that I am commissioned to make a bust after the death of the person in question. I am expected to carry off the most difficult thing as if it was no great matter. This is hard enough to grasp even [when you work] from the liveliest of life. To reward myself for this and to relax again, what I do is I make a bust to my own liking, whether I have been given a commission or not; the model for which I see before me with my own eyes. Sometimes, however, even death has something that commends it for replication. After Carl Fasch had died, a decision was made to have his bust realised in marble. I had taken his death mask and had known him quite well in life. I was given his portrait, painted by Graff, which depicts him with a genial smile — a detail not helpful for sculpture, especially in an old man — as I was supposed to portray him as he was in life. However, I discovered in the cast of the mask such a serene, solemn, transfigured being; I was anxious that this quality was not lost, so all I did in marble was to replicate this.

Johann Gottfried Schadow, 1802

Excerpt from Johann Gottfried Schadow, 'Die Werkstätte des Bildhauers' (1802) in: *Gottfried Schadow: Aufsätze und Briefe, nebst einem Verzeichnis seiner Werke*, ed. Julius Friedlaender, Düsseldorf 1864, pp. 51–64, here p. 60.

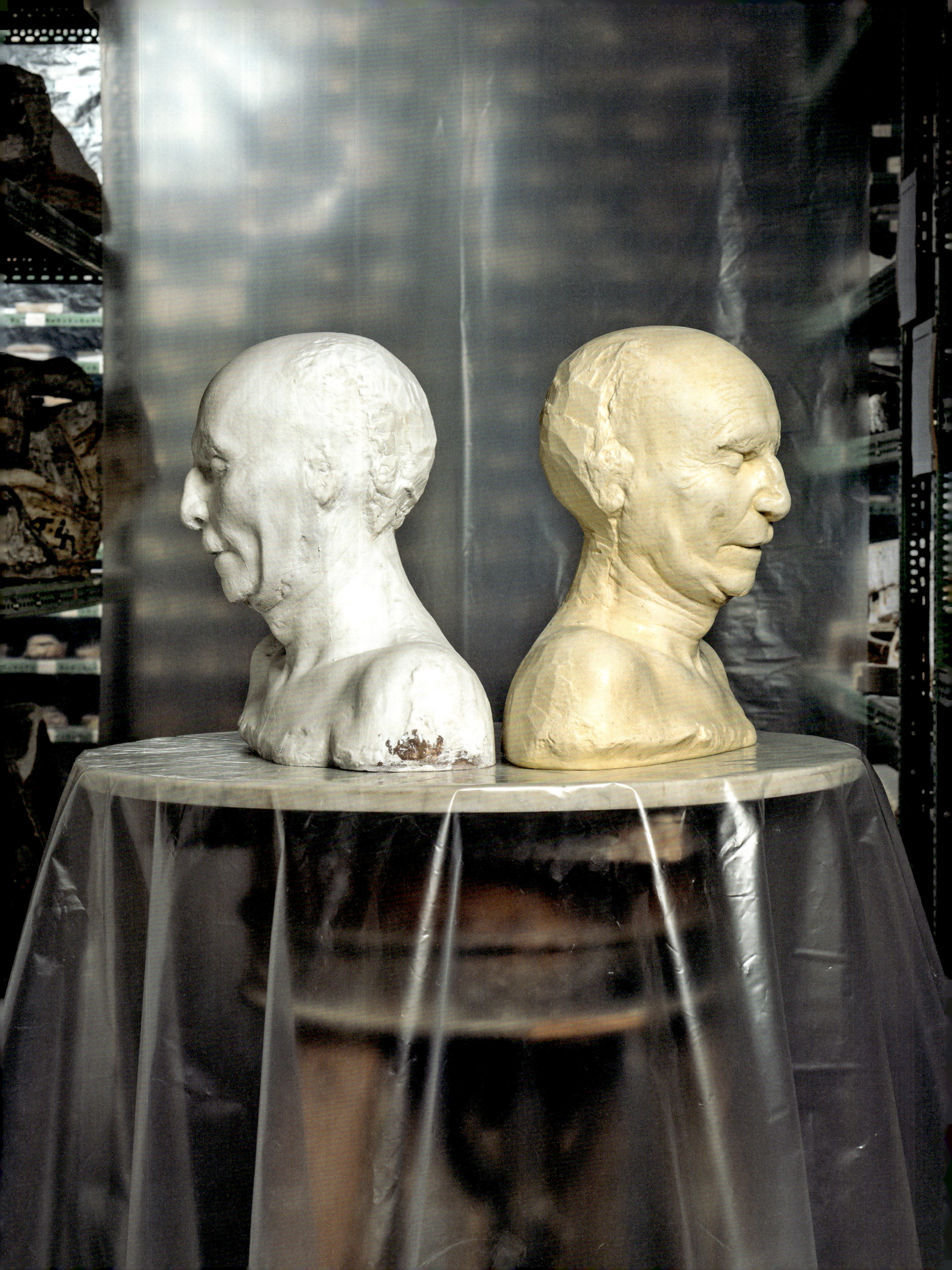

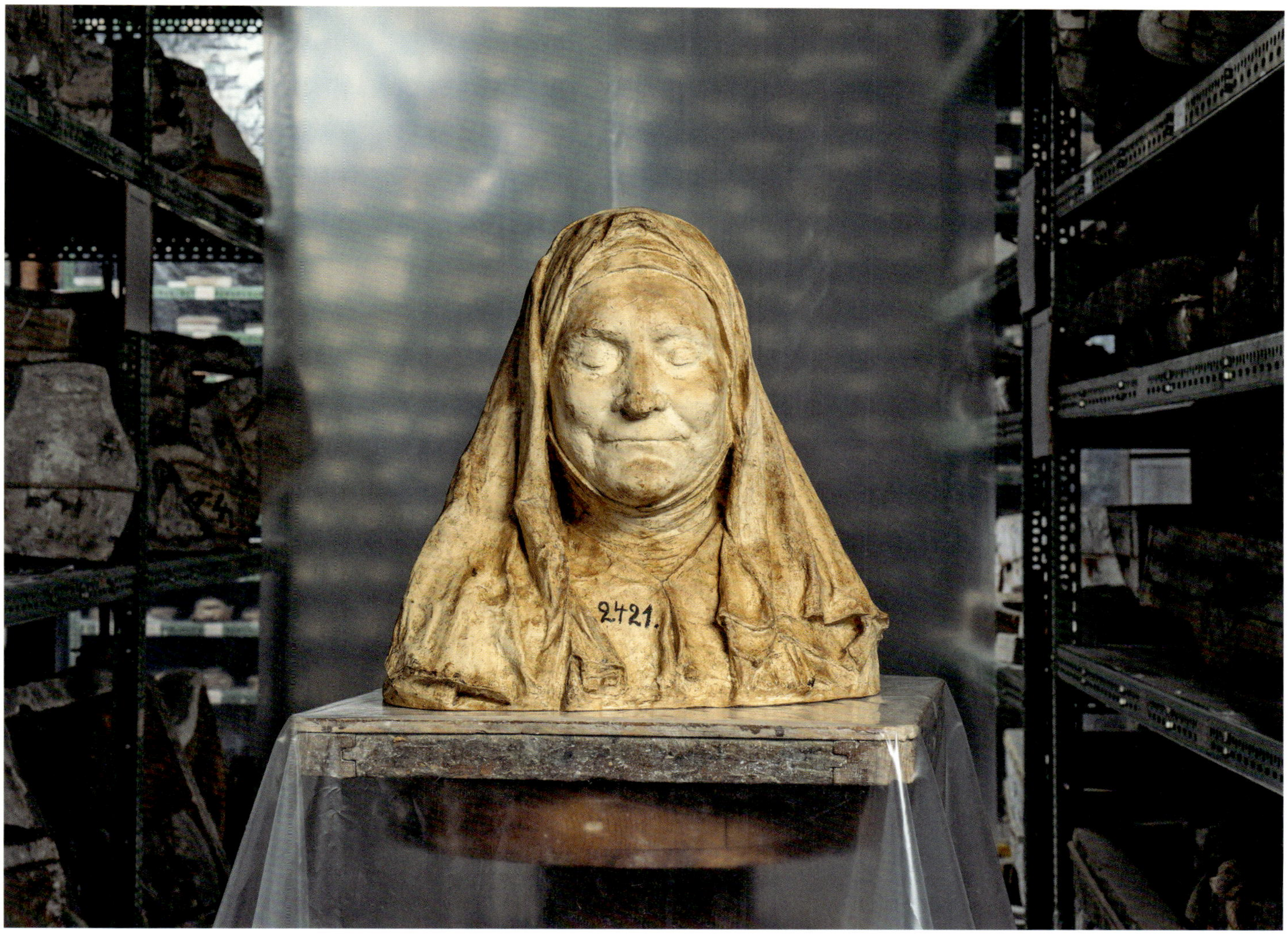

After an unknown artist
Death Mask of Filippo Brunelleschi Realised as a Bust
Master model, 1882 and cast, ca. 2000
Staatliche Museen zu Berlin, Gipsformerei

After an unknown artist
Death Mask of an Unknown Woman Realised as a Bust
Master model, 1882
Staatliche Museen zu Berlin, Gipsformerei

According to Giorgio Vasari, the Florentine sculptor Andrea del Verrocchio (1435–1488) was the first in early modern times to reintroduce the ancient practice of taking moulds from nature. That this practice in fact predates Verrocchio is proven by a number of extant objects, such as the death mask of Filippo Brunelleschi († 1446) (ill. left) and the death mask of a lady with a veil moulded in the round, likewise dating from the earlier part of the fifteenth century (ill. above). Even though these objects are at odds with Vasari's claim, the famous biographer was right in attesting to a boom of casting after nature in the quattrocento. It was a hallmark of the Florentine Renaissance to make use of death masks and body casts in the artistic work on portrait busts, funerary statuary and monuments — a practice that was to spread to Germany later, as is documented in our exhibition with works such as Johann Gottfried Schadow's bust of Carl Friedrich Christian Fasch (ill. p. 120) and the bust of Queen Louise (ill. p. 118–19).

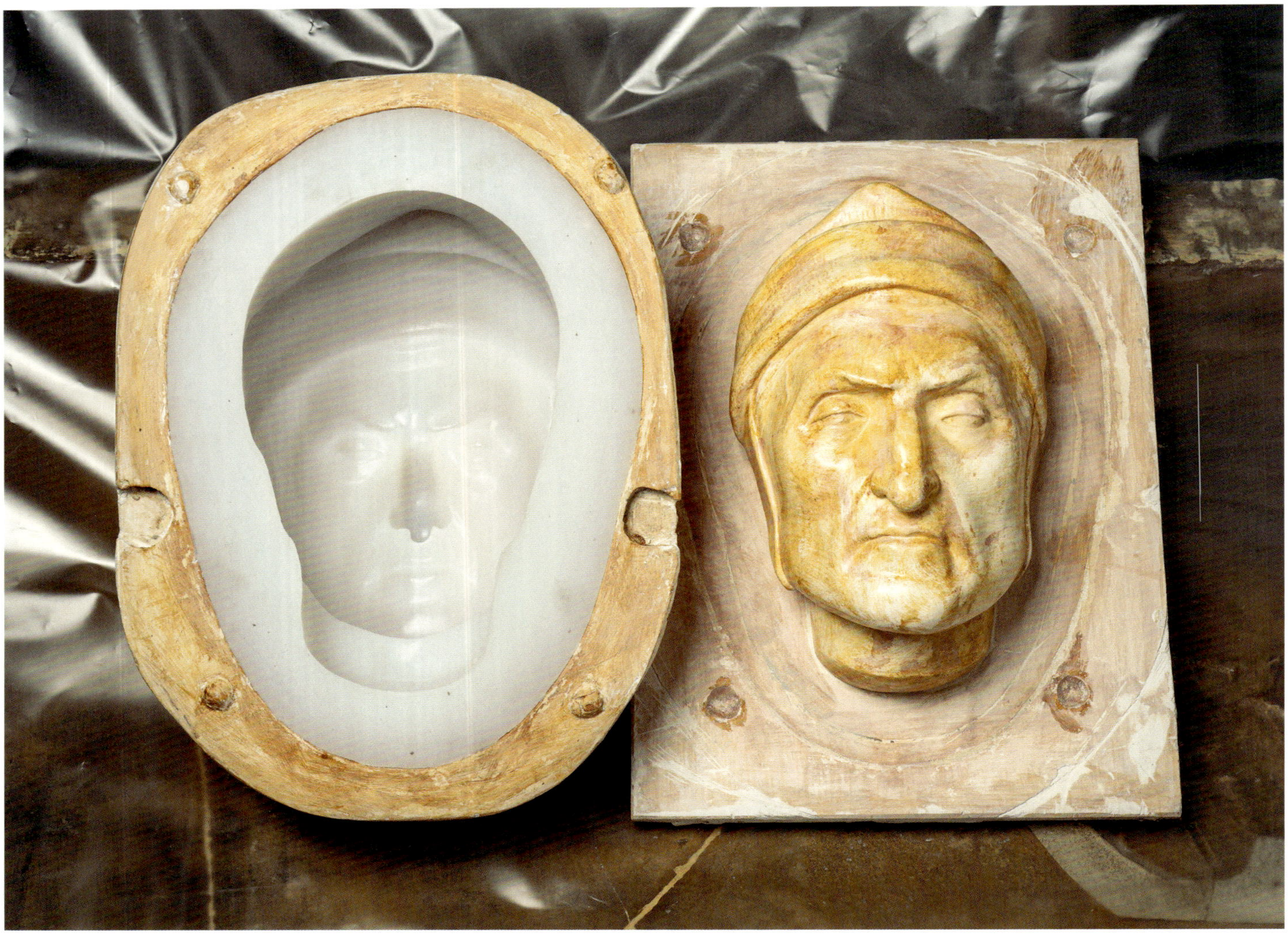

After an unknown artist
So-called Death Mask of Dante Alighieri (1265–1321)
Silicone mould and master model, 1824
Staatliche Museen zu Berlin, Gipsformerei

After an unknown artist
Death Mask of Dante Alighieri Realised as a Bust
Master model, 1995
Staatliche Museen zu Berlin, Gipsformerei

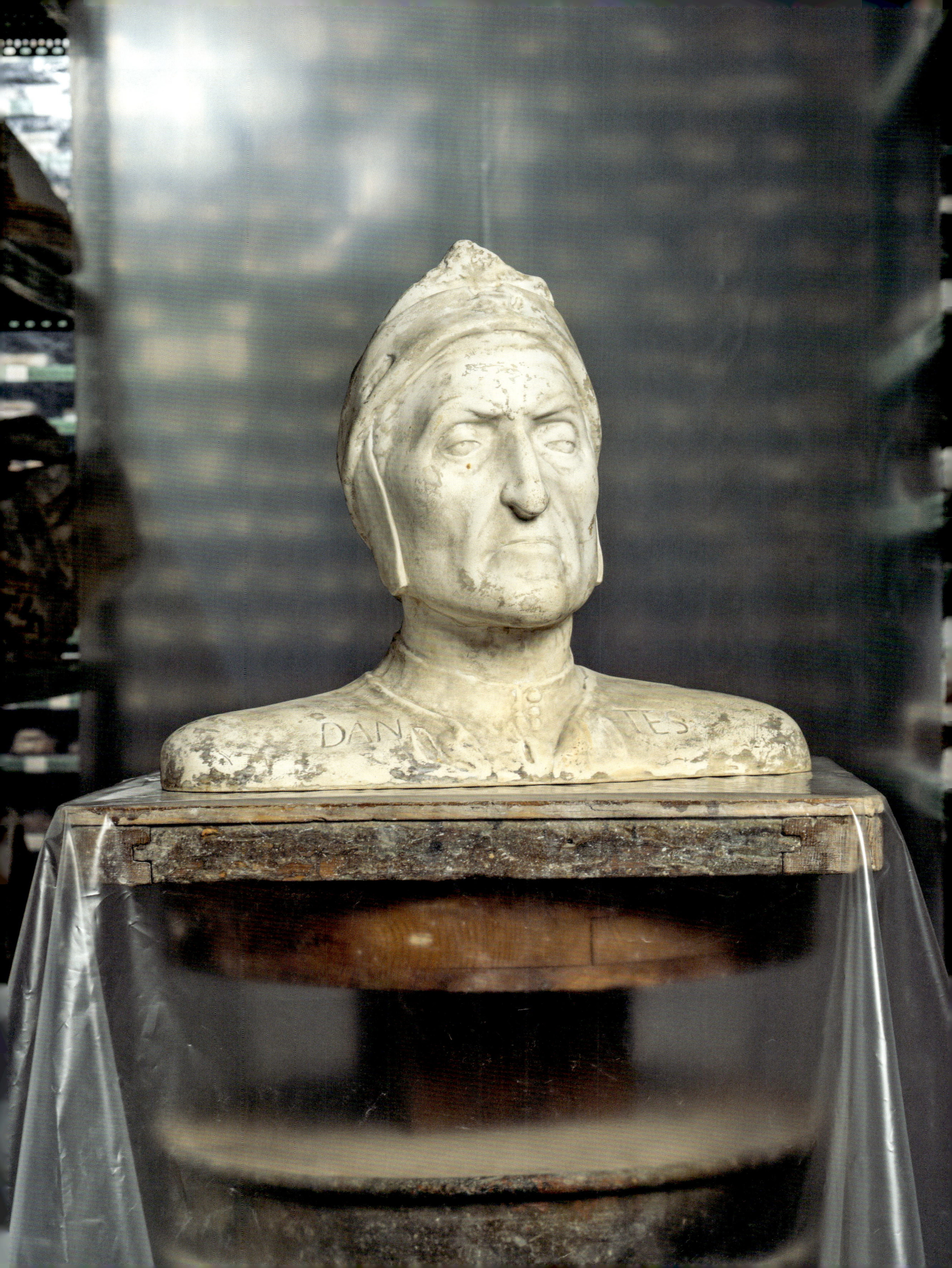
DAN
TES

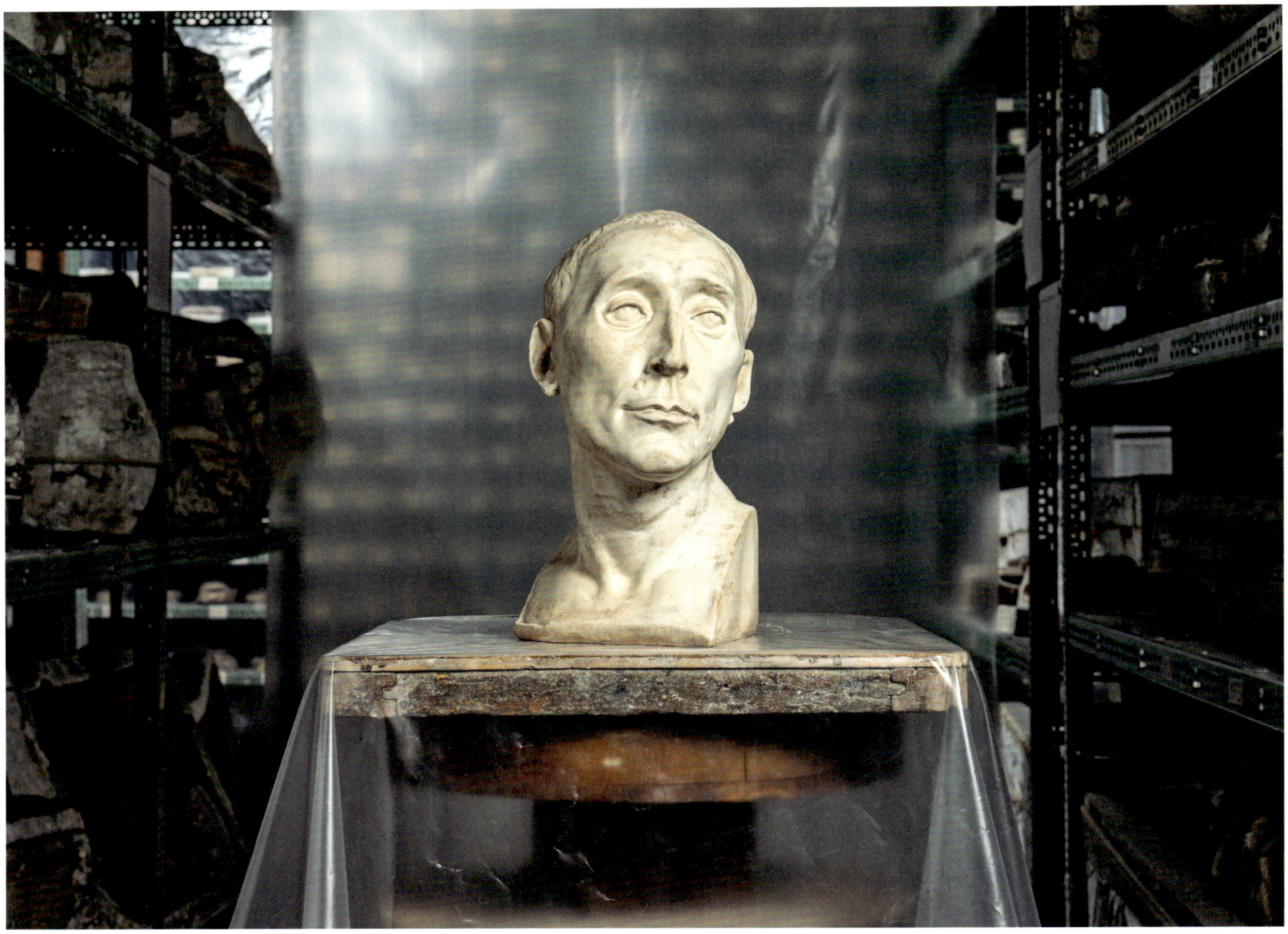

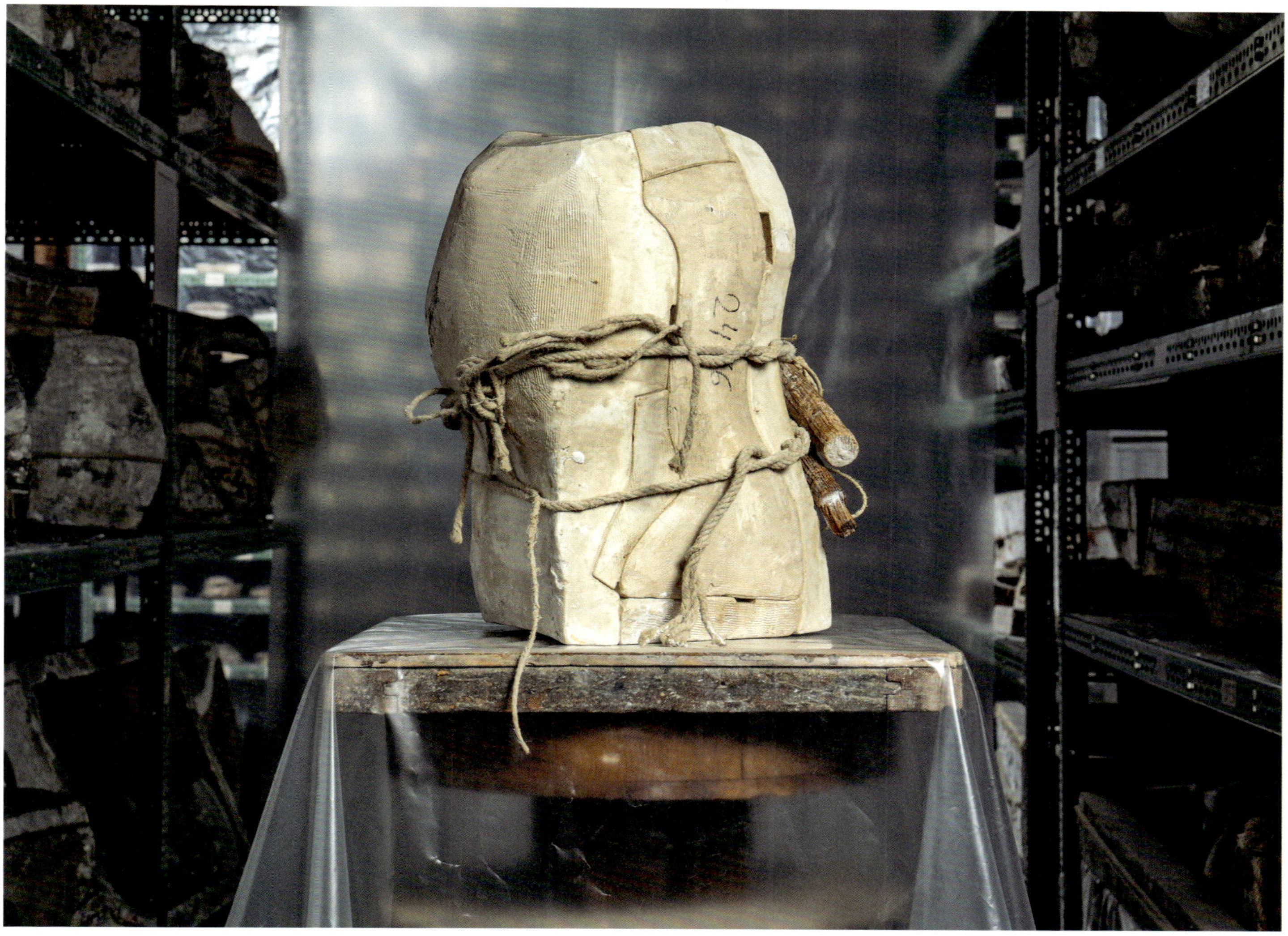

After Desiderio da Settignano
Niccolò da Uzzano
Master model and plaster
piece mould, 1914
Staatliche Museen zu Berlin,
Gipsformerei

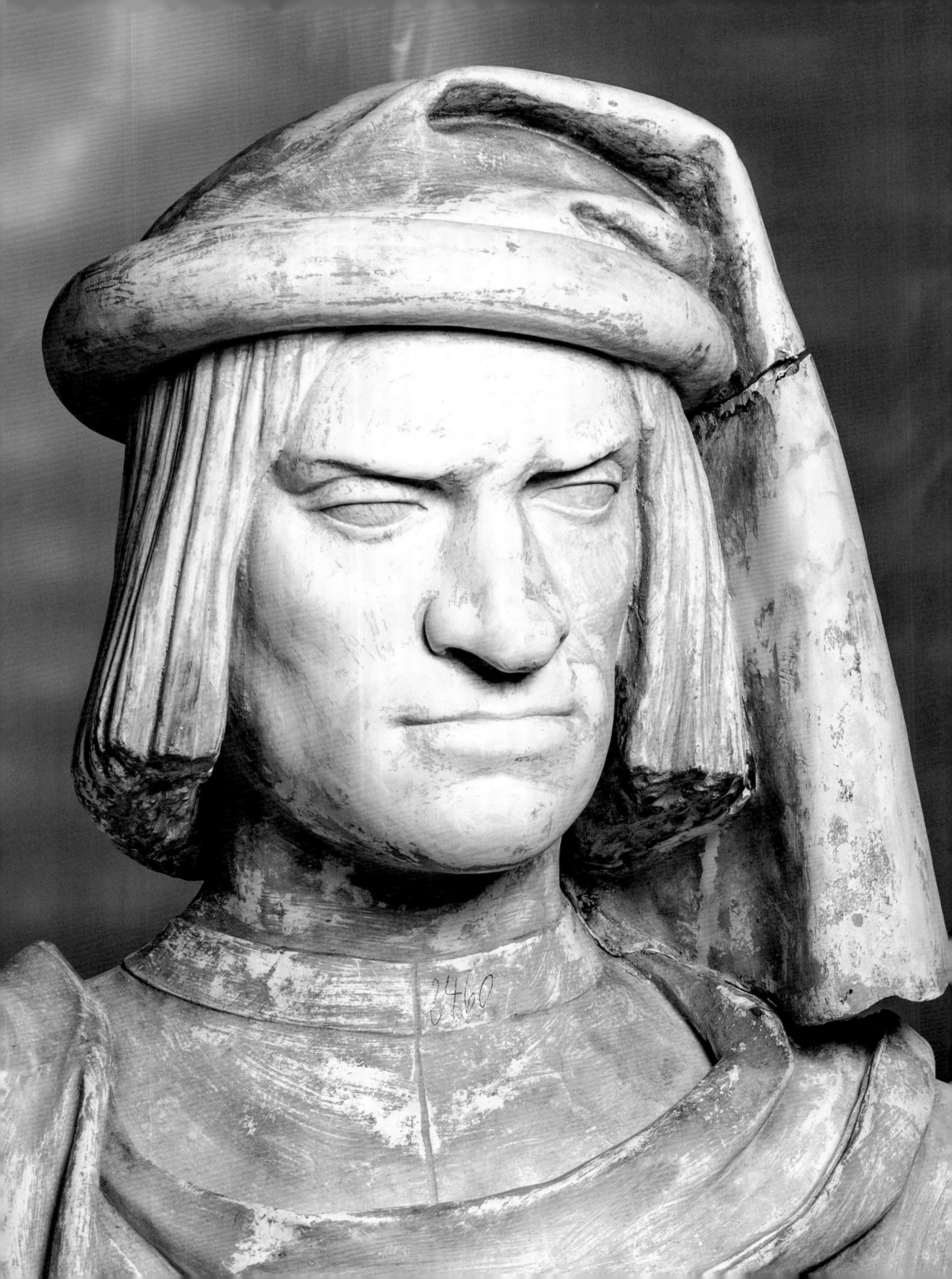
2460

Can That Still Be Called Art? Death Masks as Tools for Sculptors

Moritz Siebert

The portrait bust of Niccolò da Uzzano at the Museo Nazionale del Bargello in Florence is an impressive physiognomic study (ill. p. 130). The tired eyes are set deep in their sockets, the cheekbones are clearly discernible beneath the skin and the raised eyebrows slightly furrow the forehead. Modelled on civic portraits from antiquity, the gaze is directed upwards and to one side, conveying pensiveness and virtue.

No less impressive than the bust itself is the history of research surrounding it. For a long time this work was a point of controversy: neither the ascription to Donatello proved tenable, nor the identification of the portrait as that of the Florentine gonfalonier Uzzano — whether the bust was a work of art was another issue that exercised art historians. The debate that attracted the most attention, however, turned on the question of how the artist had managed to achieve such convincing realism. During the bust's restoration in the mid-1980s experts subjected it to close examination.[1] Seams were discovered at the neck and on the skull underneath the original colouring. The sculptor had apparently resorted to a sleight of hand to render the face so faithfully: he had taken a plaster cast of Uzzano's face and integrated it into the bust.

Facial masks, both from life and death masks, were part of the stock-in-trade in sculptors' workshops, and were used as models for portraits executed in marble or integrated into terracotta busts. They are mentioned as early as the first century CE by Pliny the Elder.[2] During the Renaissance the technique was especially widespread in and around Florence, pushed by the growing demand for sculpted portraits. In subsequent centuries, the practice seems to have receded. But in the late eighteenth century it enjoyed a revival — albeit in a new context. While there is evidence from all over Europe that facial casts were commonly used in sculpture workshops at this time, they were also beginning to play a role in anthropology as objects of research. The death mask, in particular, was more often made for its own sake, rendered as a private memento. This change of emphasis is marked by the death mask taken from Gotthold Ephraim Lessing, the first commoner in Germany on whom the honour of a death mask was bestowed (ill. p. 112). His mask unleashed a torrent of death masks taken from scholars and artists (ill. pp. 113–15). And while Lessing's death mask served a practical purpose as a model for a bust, it was also appreciated by the writer's admirers as a memorial object.

It is unknown whether neoclassicist sculptors of nineteenth century actually had models from the Renaissance in their mind's eye as they worked on facial casts, but it seems obvious that the only time when this practice was anywhere near as widespread was in the Renaissance. A great number of objects attest to the use of the technique during the quattrocento and the first decades of the sixteenth century: death masks, sepulchral figures and busts galore. Yet in relation to the wealth of artworks, written documents are few and far between. No more than two texts remain from the period which deal with the technique at some length. On the cusp of the fifteenth century Cennino Cennini writes about casts taken from animals, plants and human beings in his *Il Libro dell'Arte* (Treatise on Painting, see pp. 56–59).[3] Writing in the mid-sixteenth century, Giorgio Vasari retrospectively

Previous page

After an unknown artist
Lorenzo de' Medici
Master model, 1910
Staatliche Museen zu Berlin, Gipsformerei

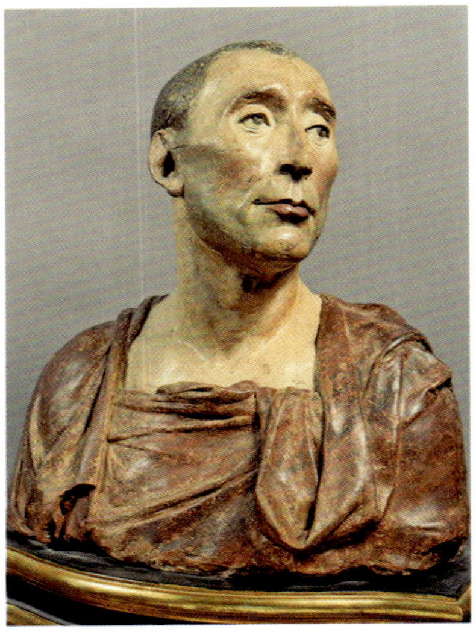

Desiderio da Settignano
Niccolò da Uzzano
Terracotta, painted
46 × 44 cm
Museo Nazionale del Bargello, Florence, 179

describes the facial cast as a tool of the sculptor's workshop in the quattrocento.[4] However, the one hundred and fifty years between Cennini's and Vasari's activities are marked by a scarcity of information on this prevalent practice.

The question arises then as to whether artists were in fact reticent about their use of this technique, because they did not want to jeopardise the reputation of their discipline. After all, there is a glaring contradiction between this practice and the aesthetic programme laid out by contemporary art theory: A cast head made of clay, formed exclusively by mechanical means without *disegno* or creativity, can that still be called art? It is certainly far from the artistic ideal of the time.

It has to be said, however, that practical realities sometimes run counter to art's ideals. Some Renaissance portraits were simply unrealisable without facial casts. Busts of saints, whose use as substitutes for holy relics was widespread, quite deliberately displayed traces reminiscent of death masks. In the *imagines maiorum*, a type of effigy of key importance in classical Rome, unmodified death masks were mounted on shields, while votive figures depended on casts to ensure their authenticity. And for the production of sepulchral statues, masks were simply the only way to preserve facial features at the moment of death.

An inventory list shows that artist Andrea del Verrocchio kept twenty 'maschere ritratte al naturale' (masks taken from nature) in his workshop.[5] This sheds some light on work practices in the Renaissance: artists stored masks in a kind of facial archive that was on hand at all times and even when the subjects had long passed. This is a decisive point about casts, which relates to an art context: they are a storage medium that reliably and durably preserves the visage of a person, placing them on a totally different level to that of generic images. They are seen to be truthful images.

The terracotta bust of Lorenzo de' Medici in the National Gallery of Art in Washington (ill right), presumably made by one of Verrocchio's disciples or followers, likewise used a death mask as model. Compared to the Uzzano bust, where it took five centuries to reveal the secrets of its origins, the Medici portraitist expended less effort in 'breathing life' into the face of his subject: it is not the traces of the work process that reveal the use of a death mask, but the bust's physiognomic characteristics — the wrinkles between the eyebrows, the vacant gaze and the lifeless mouth, all point to the model that was used (ill. right). Many versions of the bust were produced, some weaker in quality than others, but all are derived from the same death mask (ill. p. 128). The facial casts may also have served as a reference for later portraits. But what they quite clearly establish is that casting ensured an efficient workflow and reasonable likeness, without necessarily requiring talent.

Most likely the Lorenzo busts, rather than being exhibited in the Medici's ancestral portrait gallery, were produced for the art market, which underwent a significant change during this period. Indeed, facial casts could be produced fairly cheaply according to Vasari. In Florence, busts were found in almost every home at this time.[6] Terracotta and the technique of making casts opened the market to a less well-heeled clientele.

In the Renaissance, the facial cast was a multifaceted object — was there anything devious about it? It is unlikely that artists asked themselves this question. In their daily working life, the technique was simply a given. The mask may have guaranteed biological accuracy, but a high-quality portrait was a different matter altogether. The quality of a portrait depended on what the artist chose to make of it.

1 Andreina Andreoni, 'Scheda di restauro', in: *Donatello: Niccolò da Uzzano*, ed. Paola Barocchi, Giovanna Gaeta Bertela, Florence 1986, pp. 14–20.
2 Pliny the Elder, *Natural History*. ed. and trans. H. Rackham, 10 vols., London and Cambridge, MA 1961, vol. 9, pp. 373–75.
3 Cennino Cennini, *Il libro dell'arte. O trattato della pittura*, Milan 1984, p. 130–32.
4 See *Vasari's Lives of the Painters*, ed. and trans. A. B. Hinds, 4 vols., London and Toronto 1927, vol. 2, pp. 100–01.
5 Cornelio de Fabriczy, 'Andrea del Verrocchio ai servizi de' Medici', *Archivio storico dell'arte* 2, no. 1 (1895), p. 167.
6 *Vasari's Lives of the Painters*, pp. 100–01.

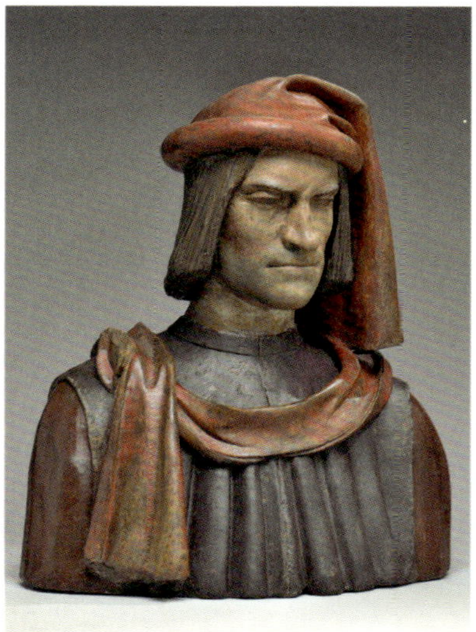

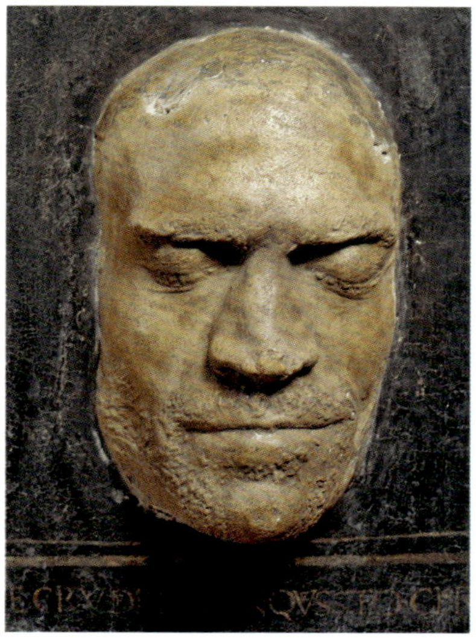

Workshop of Antonio Benintendis (attributed)
Lorenzo de' Medici, 1478/1521
Terracotta, painted
65.8 × 59.1 × 32.7 cm
National Gallery of Art, Washington, Samuel H. Kress Collection, 1934.4.92

Death Mask of Lorenzo de' Medici, 1492
Plaster on wood
58 × 44.5 cm
Museo Mediceo e Palazzo Medici Riccardi, Florence

The recumbent figure of the Sienese jurist Mariano Sozzini (1482–1556) is considered to be the first full-body cast in bronze of modern times that was at least partially moulded from nature. The painter, sculptor and goldsmith Lorenzo di Pietro (1410–1480), commonly known as Vecchietta, cast the face, hands and feet of the deceased jurist, thus creating a memorial sculpture of great physical immediacy. The corpse is of slender build and mostly covered in a jurist's robe, but its vein-crossed hands and feet lend it lifelikeness and a sense of power. The horizontal seam visible at the waist in the master model goes back to the original cast, which is today kept at the Museo Nazionale del Bargello in Florence. It shows that what we have here is a two-part cast, whose upper and lower components could only be joined together in the end at the cost of some reduction to the form — a technical difficulty which also appears with multi-piece plaster casts. In addition to this cast of the recumbent bronze, the Gipsformerei boasts two more funerary monuments from the quattrocento, whose reclining figures are based on moulds taken from the deceased: the tomb of Cardinal Jacob de Portugal (1461–1466) by Antonio Rossellino and the tomb of Bishop Benozzo Federighi (1455–1456) by Luca della Robbia.

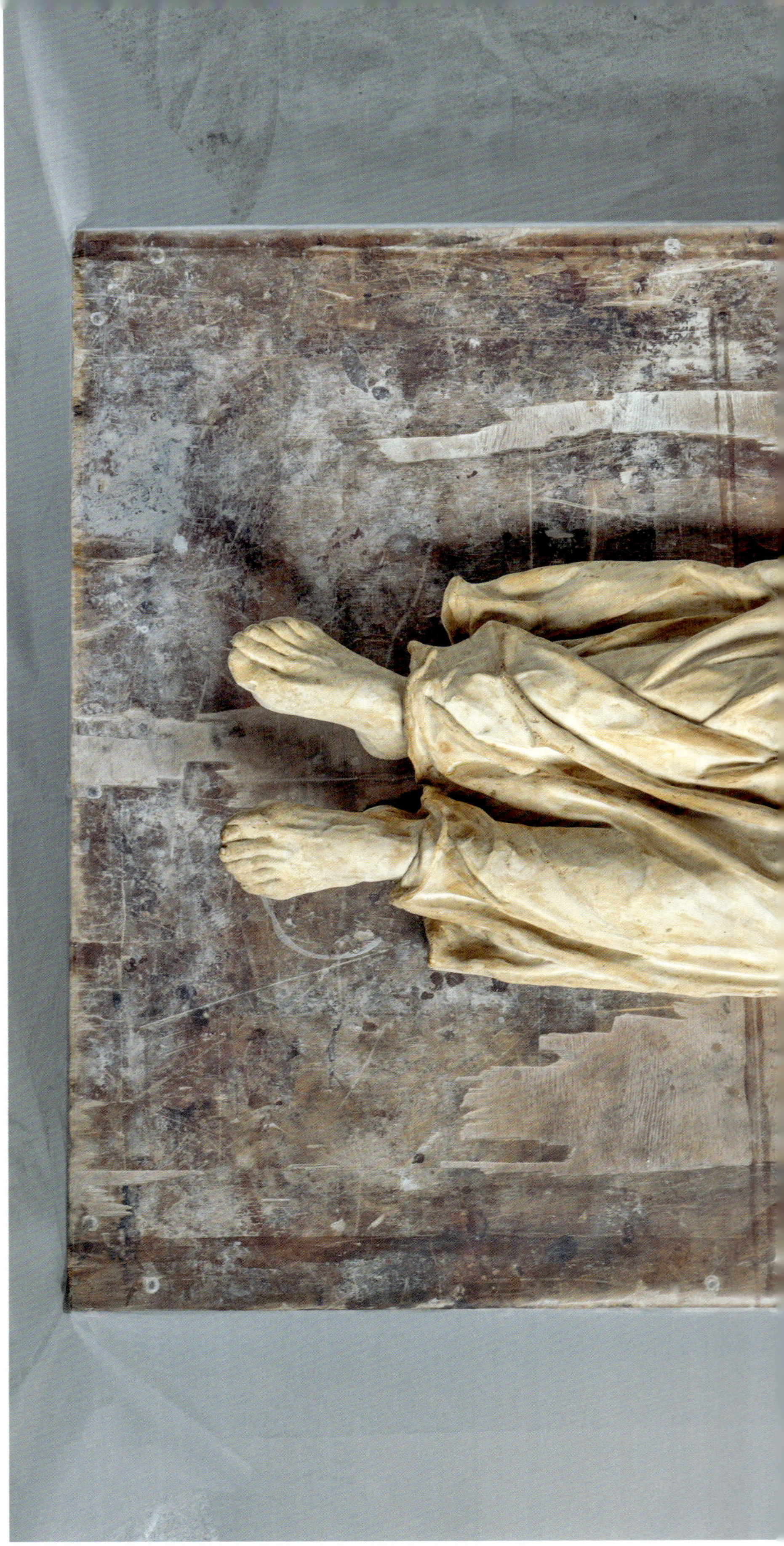

After Lorenzo di Pietro (Il Vecchietta)
Tomb Figure of Mariano Sozzini
Master model, 1882
Staatliche Museen zu Berlin,
Gipsformerei

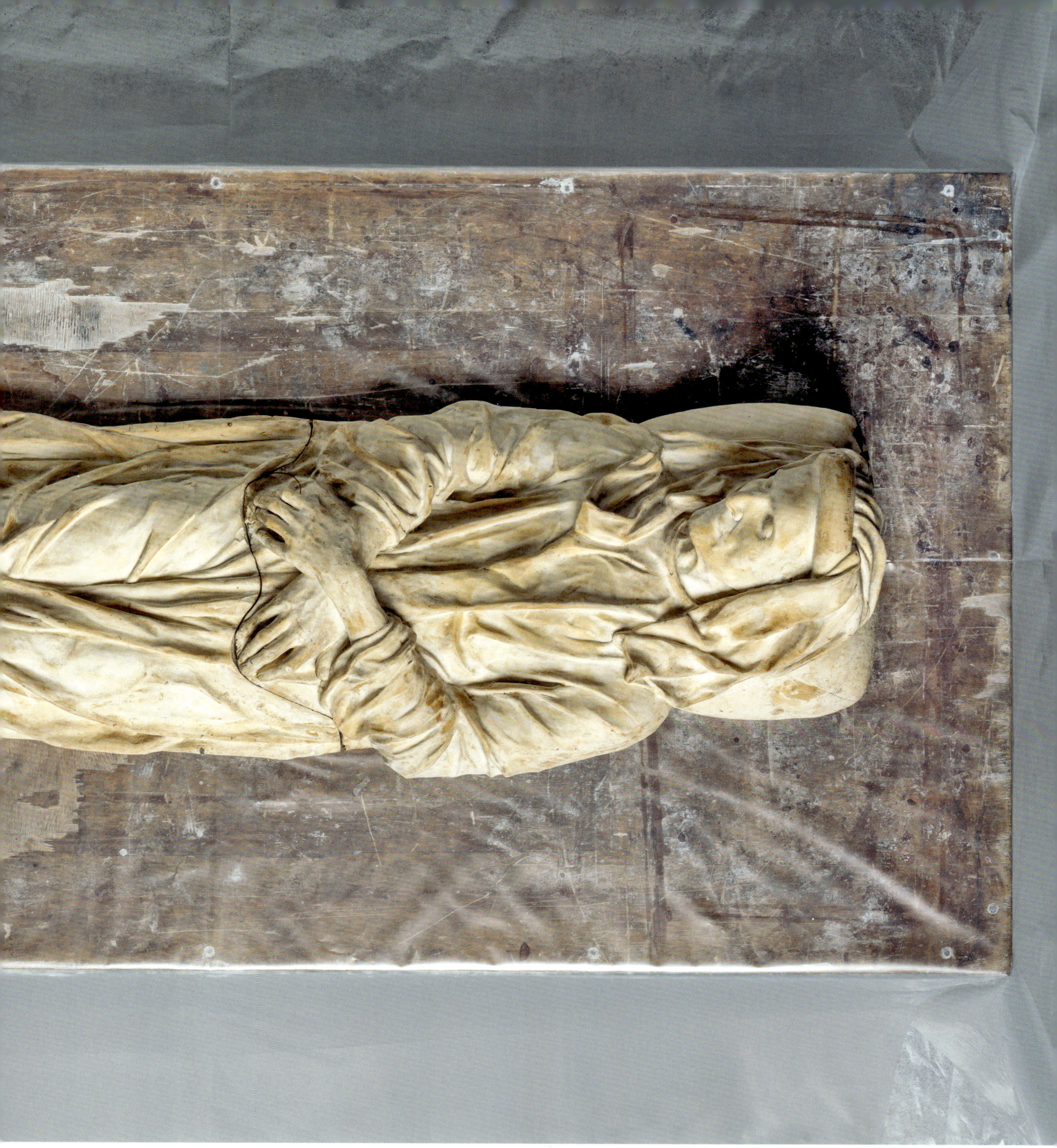

Teresa Margolles (b. 1963) studied Communication Science and Forensic Medicine. Starting her artistic career in the early 1990s, her work has repeatedly sparked controversy. A form of social critique, her work integrates traces of the victims of violence and crime in Mexico City. *Catafalco* (1997) is a sculpture comprised of two upright plaster negatives taken of autopsied corpses; they give the impression of being death masks expanded to the entire body. Standing to a height that puts the viewer in direct confrontation with anonymous death emerging from a sarcophagus-like plaster shell, the empty inside chillingly evokes the absent person. Organic relics such as hair, skin particles as well as fingerprints left in the plaster surface represent highly personal attributes, which starkly contrast with the anonymity of the portrayed. *Catafalco* is the product of the artist's collaboration with the group SEMEFO, active in the 1990s. Its name is an acronym of the Servicio Médico Forense in Mexico City. In a state system riddled with corruption, this collective of artists moved in the grey area of the law to create this work.

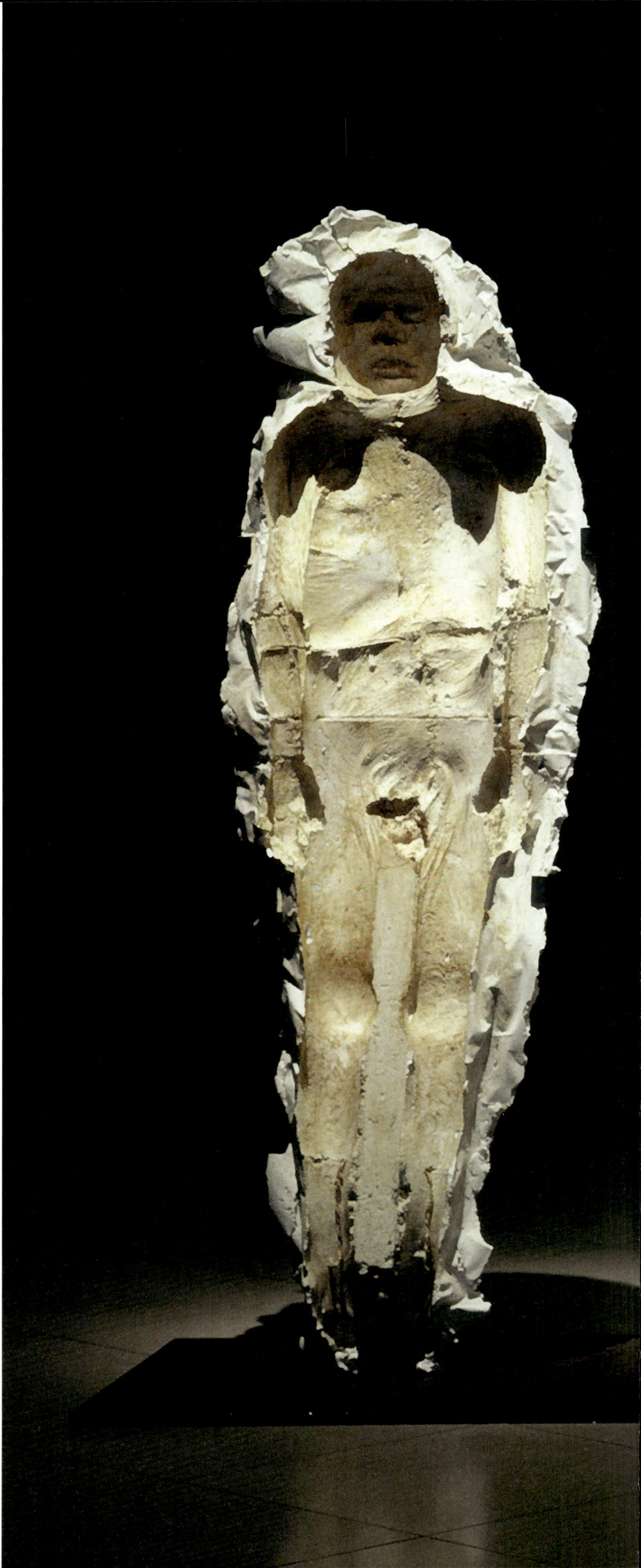

Teresa Margolles
Catafalco, 1997
Casts of the bodies of two murder victims
Realised in collaboration with the artist group SEMEFO
Museum für Moderne Kunst, Frankfurt am Main, on permanent loan from the artist, 2004

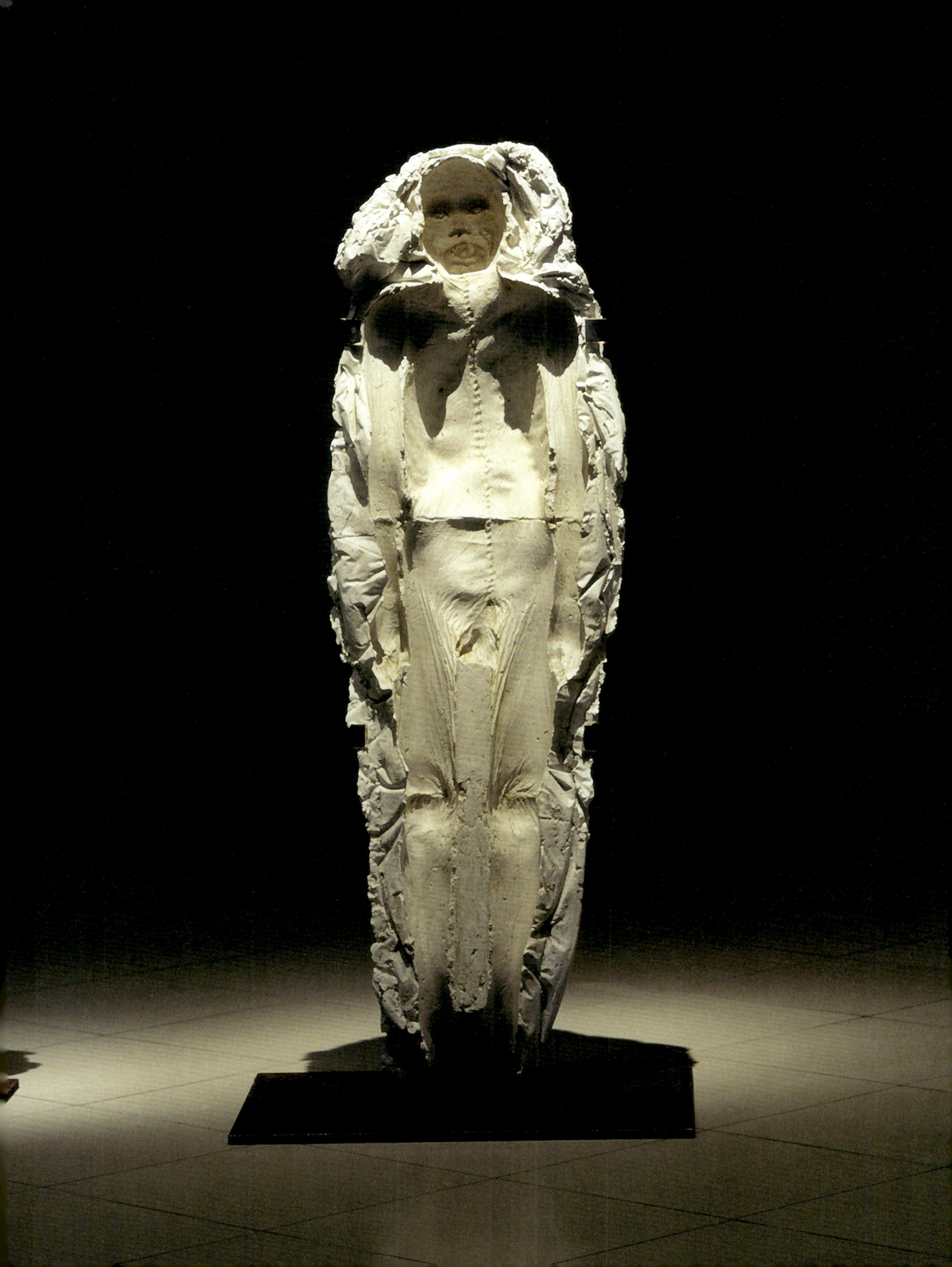

When Mount Vesuvius erupted in 79 CE, the Roman city of Pompeii was buried under several metres of volcanic ash and lava — all life was extinguished. Pompeii was only rediscovered in the mid-eighteenth century; the vestiges of ancient culture preserved in pumice stone are now among the most impressive remnants of that age. We owe the famous plaster casts of Pompeii's dead to the archaeologist Giuseppe Fiorelli, who lead the excavations in 1863. He had the cavities left in the hardened ash — not only by dead people and animals, but also by architectural elements and pieces of furniture — carefully filled with liquid plaster. Some of these cavities still contain human and animal skeletons. The attempts to secure finds in this way have continued to this day. In May 2018, similar methods were used to retrieve the cast of a horse in Pompeii. The casts of the nameless dead movingly document the moment of dying. Struggle and pain as well as what looks to be resignation and peaceful slumber are reflected in these effigies of human beings, conserved (almost) for eternity, first by lava, then by plaster.

Plaster Cast of a Recumbent Man, Who Lost His Life in the Eruption of Mount Vesuvius in 79 CE,
Pompeii, Terme Stabiane, 1868
Soprintendenza Archeologica di Pompei, Italy

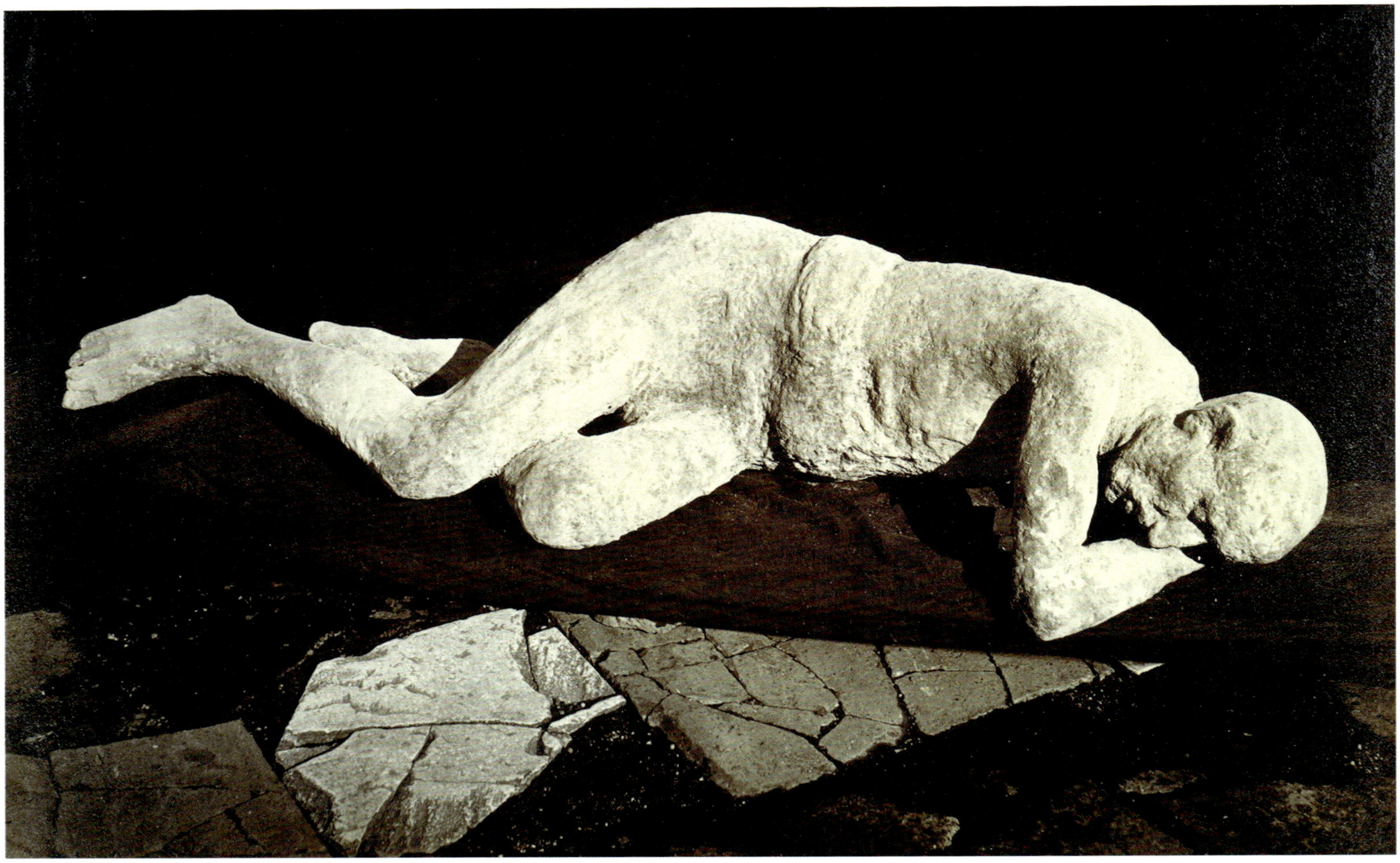

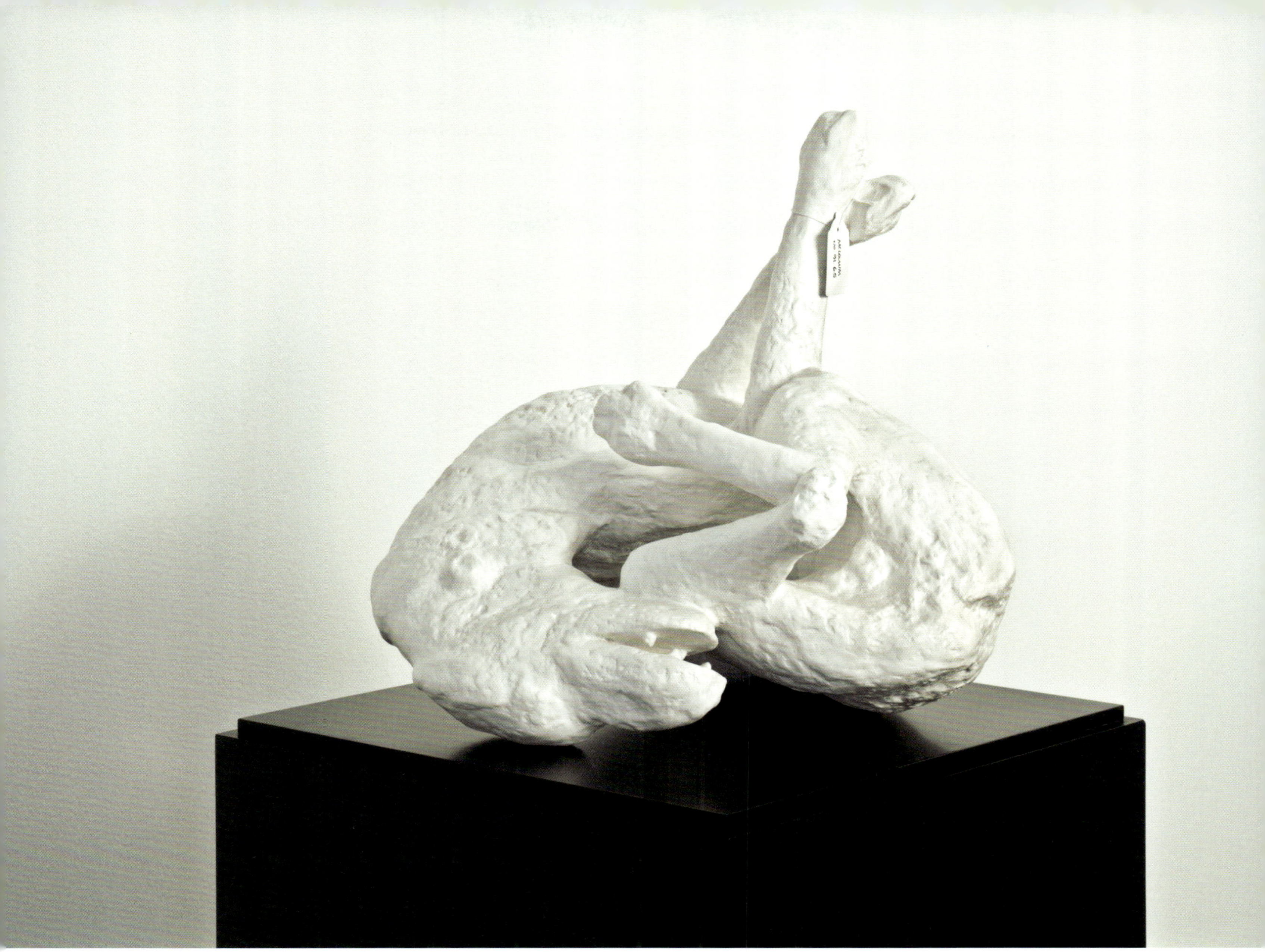

Allan McCollum
The Dog from Pompeii, 1991
Galerie Thomas Schulte, Berlin

Next page

Asta Gröting
Mausoleum, 2016
From the series *Berlin Fassaden*
Israel Museum, Jerusalem

'We live in a world filled with substitutions for things that are absent', US-American artist Allan McCollum (b. 1944) told Thomas Lawson in an interview in 1992. '[E]very copy, in a certain sense, only exists because the original is gone. So copies are always about something that's absent, and in that sense they carry a sense of mourning, death, or loss.' McCollum sees the plaster casts from Pompeii as copies made by nature, an interpretation that inspired him to make the cast of a chained watchdog the starting point for a conceptual work in the early 1990s. As he was unable to access the 'original', he obtained from Museo Vesuviano a piece mould based on the second-generation cast of the dog that enabled him to cast 'his' dog. He (re)produced a series of such casts and presented them in changing constellations of up to several hundred dogs. The man-made and serial copy of the cast is turned into an artwork by this creative act, even though its outward appearance differs only marginally from the exhibition copy of the dog from Pompeii, which is also shown in *Near Life*.

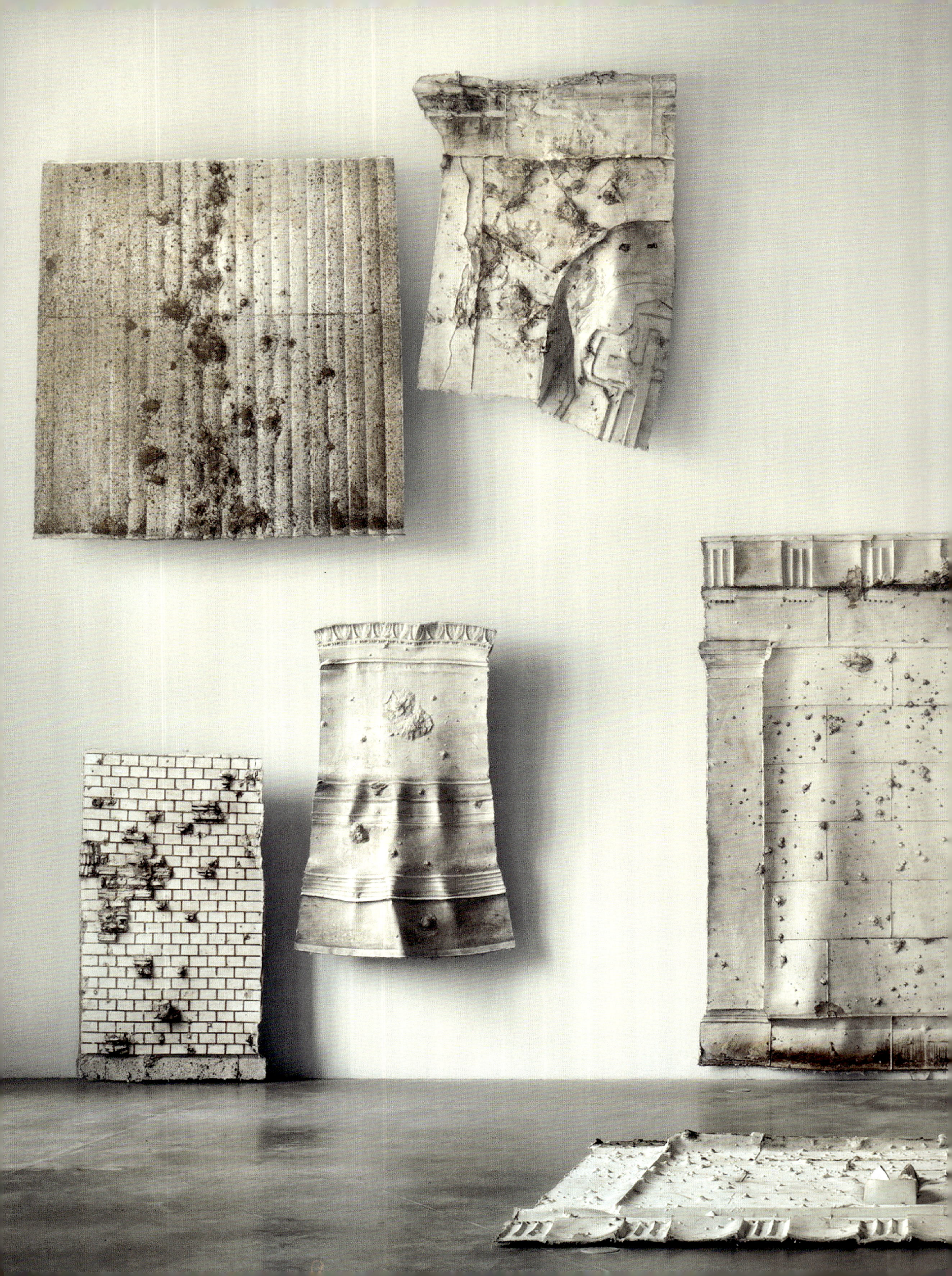

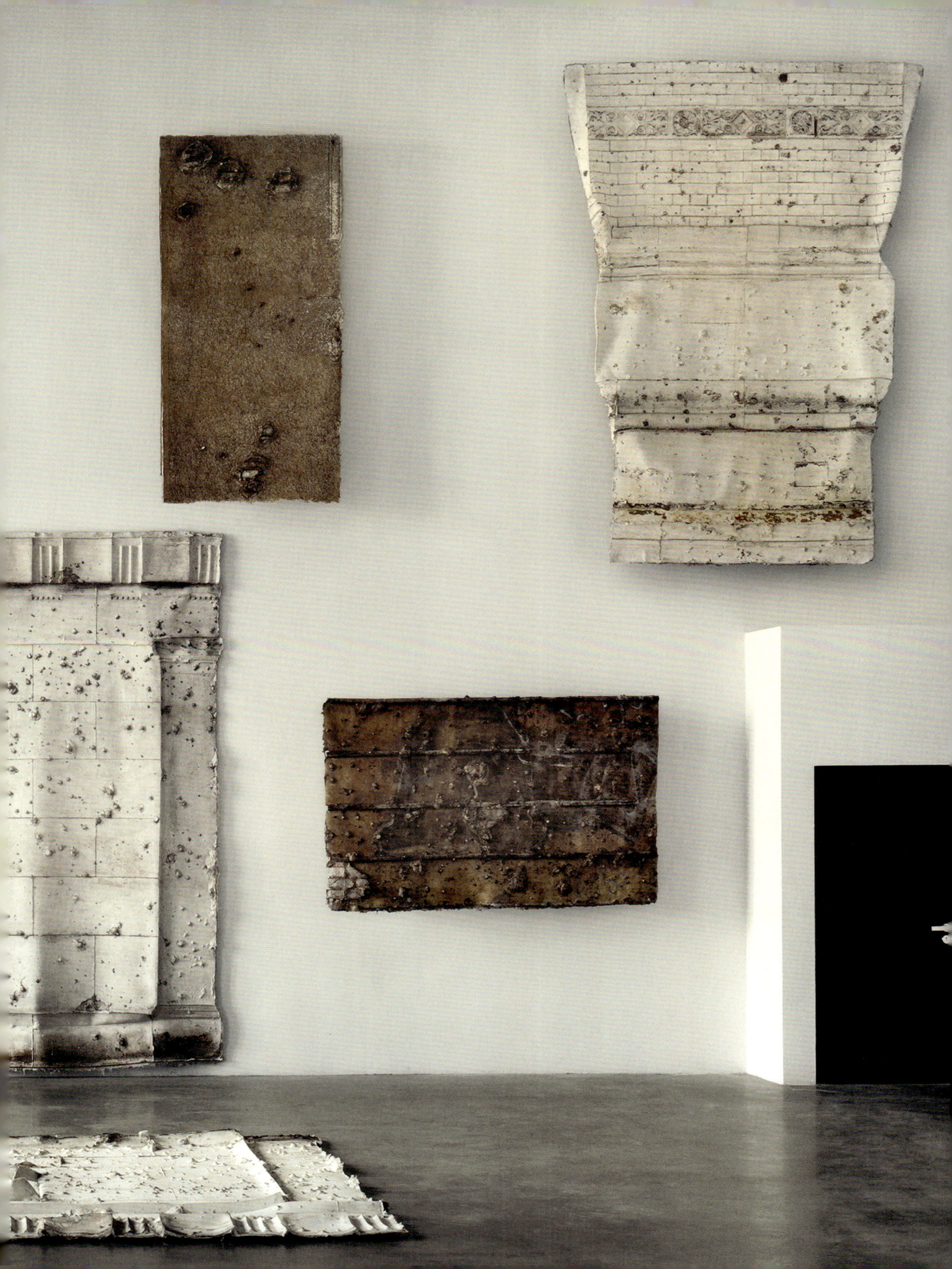

Excursus: Galvanoplastics A Recipe for Artificial Creation and Eternal Life?

Jörg Völlnagel

When Henry Cole (1808–1882), the director of London's Museum of Oriental Art and of the South Kensington Museum (today's Victoria and Albert Museum), published in 1867 his famous 'Convention for Promoting Universally Reproductions of Works of Art for the Benefit of Museums of All Countries', which bore the signatures of eleven European leaders, he explicitly mentioned three reproduction technologies in the document: casting, electrotyping and photography (ill. right). These technologies were to be used for the ambitious project of storing humanity's cultural legacy and helping to distribute faithful replicas in line with the ideal of a universal cultural memory. How topical this idea is today — even given a new lease of life in the times of 'Shared Heritage' — is shown by the newly enlarged edition of the declaration as part of the initiative Reproduction of Art and Cultural Heritage (ReACH), launched by the Victoria and Albert Museum in 2017 on the occasion of the 150th anniversary of Cole's published manifesto. The goals of the initiative do not differ substantially from Cole's, even though the digital age has other technologies and participative challenges at its core, which are duly taken into account by the updated version of the 'Convention'.

Apart from any technological promise of exact reproduction in different media and materials, there is another highly significant aspect that these three technologies have in common: they lend themselves to capturing life in the most direct and immediate manner; it is life itself that is supposedly preserved and stored thanks to the art of replication!

As for the technique of casting with plaster (and casting in general), which seems to have been in use since antiquity, its ability to approximate life, particularly evident in the casts after nature, features as one of the basic tenets of the exhibition *Near Life*, for which this publication serves as companion. In photography, too, we may note this proximity in the capture of an individual moment taken from life itself. And we are, of course, aware of civilisations marked by scepticism towards technology, where there is a strong aversion by some to having their picture taken, in the belief that the camera will deprive them of their soul. Photography not only prints likeness on film, it transfixes the soul of the person photographed — a horrifying and thoroughly devastating process in the view of those concerned. In the case of electrotyping, a procedure used since the early nineteenth century for producing metal casts of all kinds of objects, the link between technology and life is not immediately evident. Or what connection is there between perfect casts of gold cups, Celtic chariots, bronze cathedral doors or dental implants with life itself? Where is there such a link?

Let us *cast* a brief glance back to the beginnings of the galvanoplastic process. First, all three reproduction technologies share the fact that they are contact or indexical processes. This means that the 'indexical', the sign, is physically connected to the original object through casting it in plaster or some other suitable material, or as in the case of photography developed by photosensitive salts on paper or some other substrate, or using the method of electrotyping. The latter relates to the historical belief that electricity is an elixir coursing through the body and its muscles, imbuing them with life; there was also speculation that

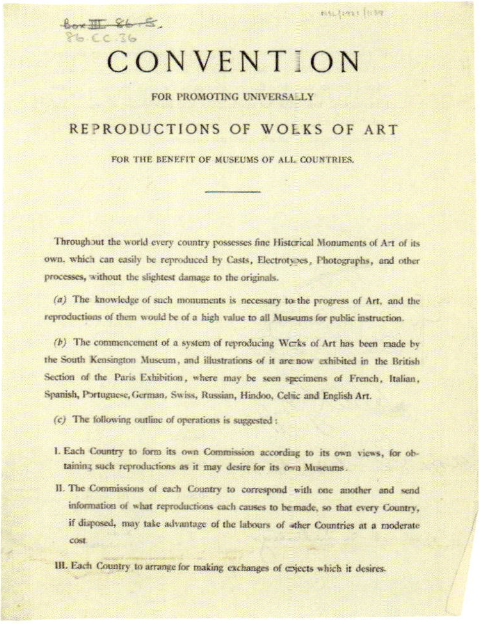

CONVENTION

FOR PROMOTING UNIVERSALLY

REPRODUCTIONS OF WOEKS OF ART

FOR THE BENEFIT OF MUSEUMS OF ALL COUNTRIES.

Throughout the world every country possesses fine Historical Monuments of Art of its own, which can easily be reproduced by Casts, Electrotypes, Photographs, and other processes, without the slightest damage to the originals.

(a) The knowledge of such monuments is necessary to the progress of Art, and the reproductions of them would be of a high value to all Museums for public instruction.

(b) The commencement of a system of reproducing Works of Art has been made by the South Kensington Museum, and illustrations of it are now exhibited in the British Section of the Paris Exhibition, where may be seen specimens of French, Italian, Spanish, Portuguese, German, Swiss, Russian, Hindoo, Celtic and English Art.

(c) The following outline of operations is suggested:

I. Each Country to form its own Commission according to its own views, for obtaining such reproductions as it may desire for its own Museums.

II. The Commissions of each Country to correspond with one another and send information of what reproductions each causes to be made, so that every Country, if disposed, may take advantage of the labours of other Countries at a moderate cost.

III. Each Country to arrange for making exchanges of objects which it desires.

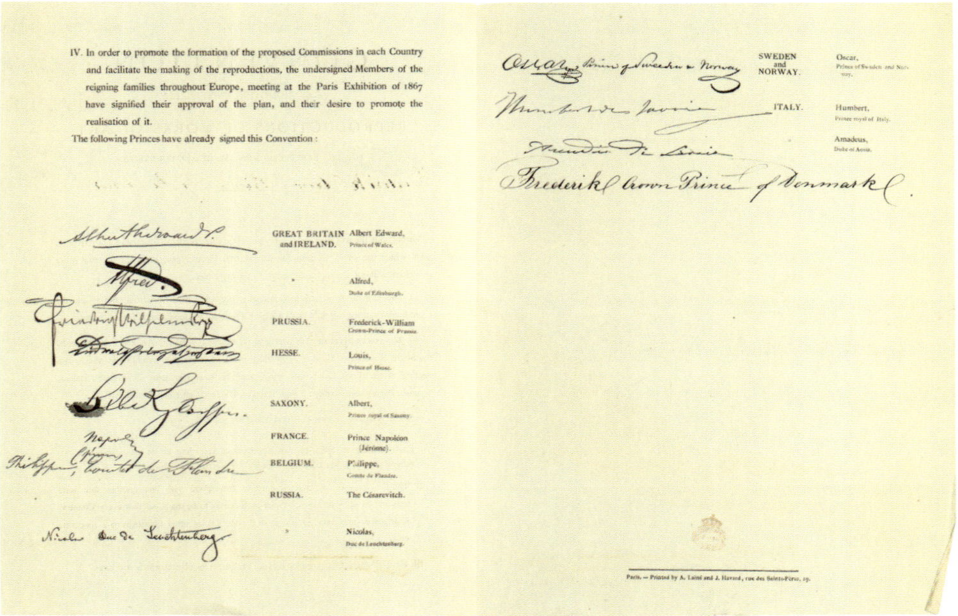

IV. In order to promote the formation of the proposed Commissions in each Country and facilitate the making of the reproductions, the undersigned Members of the reigning families throughout Europe, meeting at the Paris Exhibition of 1867 have signified their approval of the plan, and their desire to promote the realisation of it.

The following Princes have already signed this Convention:

GREAT BRITAIN and IRELAND.	Albert Edward, Prince of Wales.
»	Alfred, Duke of Edinburgh.
PRUSSIA.	Frederick-William Crown-Prince of Prussia.
HESSE.	Louis, Prince of Hesse.
SAXONY.	Albert, Prince royal of Saxony.
FRANCE.	Prince Napoléon (Jérôme).
BELGIUM.	Philippe, Comte de Flandre.
RUSSIA.	The Césarevitch.
»	Nicolas, Duc de Leuchtenberg.
SWEDEN and NORWAY.	Oscar, Prince of Sweden and Norway.
ITALY.	Humbert, Prince royal of Italy.
»	Amadeus, Duke of Aosta.

Paris. — Printed by A. Lainé and J. Havard, rue des Saints-Pères, 19.

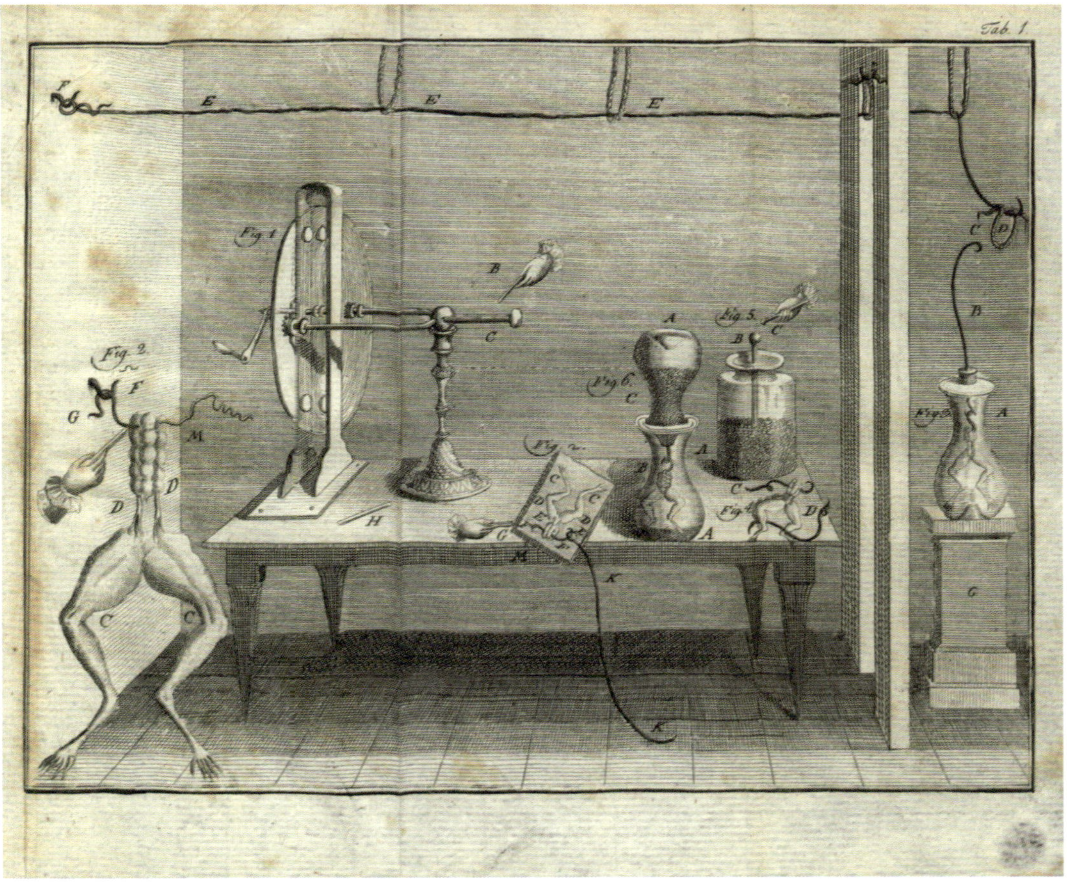

Convention for Promoting Universally Reproductions of Works of Art for the Benefit of Museums of All Countries, 1867
Victoria and Albert Museum, London, MSL/1921/1159

Luigi Galvani, *Aloysi Galvani Abhandlung über die Kräfte der thierischen Elektrizität auf die Bewegung der Muskeln*
Prague 1793, plate I
Staatsbibliothek zu Berlin – Preußischer Kulturbesitz, Abteilung Historische Drucke, Bibl. Diez oct 7519

it could bring dead organic matter back to life. This fascinating notion, which is closely linked to the genesis of galvanisation, was forgotten over time — like in plaster casting, it receded into the background, overshadowed by the power of the original artwork that lends the cast its shape.

Here is the place to briefly summarise the history of galvanisation, then: The story begins with anatomist and naturalist Luigi Galvani (1737–1798), who, in the 1780s, conducted pioneering experiments with what he called 'animal electricity'. During the course of these experiments he discovered, almost by chance, a process that was subsequently named after him: galvanisation. He described its function in his seminal work *De viribus electricitatis in motu musculari* (1791). The experiments involved studying frog legs. He noticed that the frog's muscles seemed to come alive when they were connected to a circuit involving copper and iron (ill. p. 141). Galvani put this down to the hypothetical existence of animal electricity — a false, but nevertheless momentous proposition. It motivated Italian physicist Alessandro Volta (1745–1827) to undertake his own experiments. Volta had realised that the muscle movements in the frog legs were caused by touch voltage, or, as he put it, 'contact electricity'. This insight led him to develop the voltaic pile and the trailblazing invention of the battery (ca. 1800). Galvani's nephew Giovanni Aldini (1762–1834), like Volta a physicist, but unlike him a 'Galvanist' in the mould of his uncle, not only conducted galvanic experiments before an audience, he extended them to include corpses, whose 'remaining vital forces' he proposed to release by applying an electrical circuit. It is hardly an exaggeration to consider these public performances as gruesome spectacles. Particularly famous are Aldini's experiments with the corpse of the newly executed double murderer George Foster, which he performed at the Royal College of Surgeons in January 1803 (ill. below). This event was a key source of inspiration for Mary Wollstonecraft Shelley's novel *Frankenstein or The Modern Prometheus* (1818) and for the birth of the Frankenstein myth. In its black-and-white adaptation to the big screen, *Frankenstein* (1931), directed by James Whale, quickly became a horror film classic in cinematic history. A quick reminder of the plot: in pursuit of his grand ambition to give life to dead matter, Faustian alchemist and naturalist Victor (Henry, in the movie) loses control of an experiment and brings the corpse of a criminal back to life, thereby creating a monster (ill. right).

But to return to science: The experiments by the three Italian naturalists and physicists on the origin and movement of electricity, along with the seminal research by Englishman Michael Faraday (1791–1867) on electrochemistry and electrolysis, paved the way for the development of electroplating as a

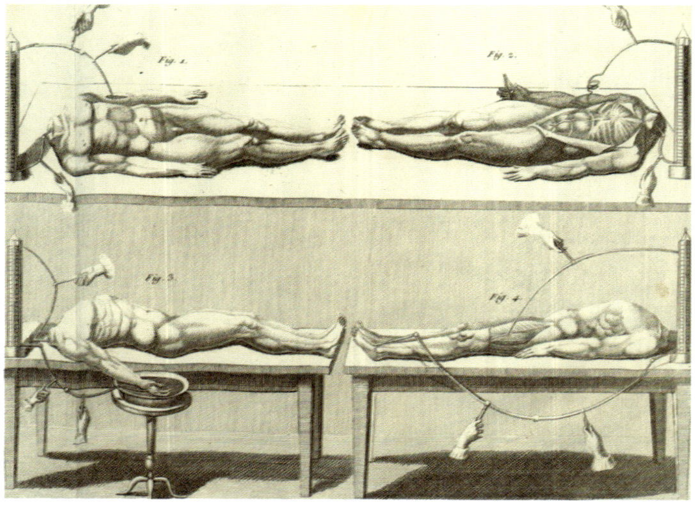

Giovanni Aldini
Essai Théorique Et Expérimental Sur Le Galvanisme
Paris 1804, plate III
Staatsbibliothek zu Berlin – Preußischer Kulturbesitz, Abteilung Historische Drucke, 4" My 9482

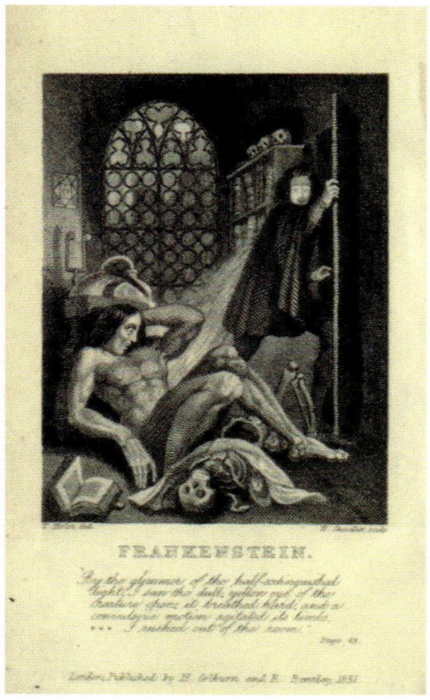

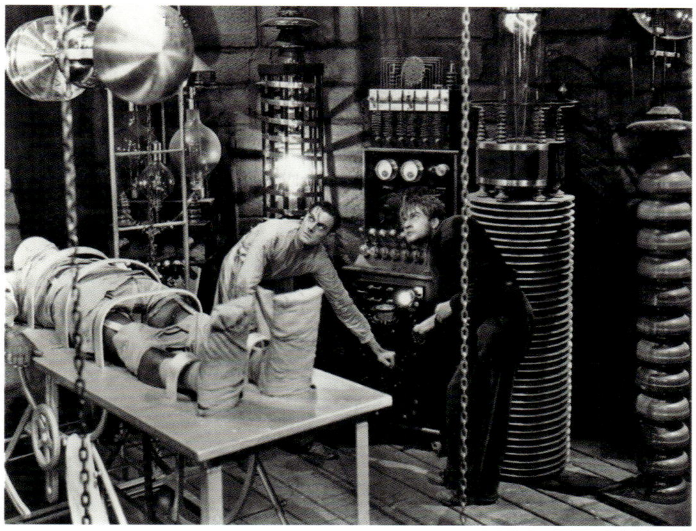

Mary Wollstonecraft Shelley
Frankenstein or The Modern Prometheus
London 1831, frontispiece,
British Library, London, 1153.a.9.(1.)

Film still from: *Frankenstein*, 1931
Directed by James Whale

reproduction technology in the early nineteenth century. In this process, electricity flows through a wire suspended in an electrolyte solution. From anode to cathode, the transporting atoms of the coating material (say, gold) attached to the positive pole are deposited as a thin layer on the model (which might be made of bronze, for example) attached to the negative pole. What this technology does, then, is to disassemble matter in one place and reassemble it elsewhere, in whatever shape is desired — a truly artificial, yet demiurgic achievement! Or to put it less poetically, electrotyping is a chemical method to manufacture metal objects or to coat objects made of base metals with gold or other precious metals. It is capable of producing perfect replicas, such as copies of three-dimensional works of art. This made it an indispensable method for the public collections and the museums of arts and crafts built in Europe in the late nineteenth century. It was this development that Cole, director of the first museum of decorative arts in the world, effectively brought attention to by writing his 1867 'Convention'. In the early twentieth century, replicas that owed their existence to developments in technology increasingly fell into disrepute. Now seen as cheap copies, they were (with very few exceptions) removed from museums and respectable collections. The overwhelming success early on tends to overshadow the most exciting aspect of its beginnings, seen now in retrospect: that the great artistic replication technologies were inspired by the spirit of the Enlightenment and the fascination of their protagonists with demiurgic creation and, finally, with the artificial reproduction of life itself.

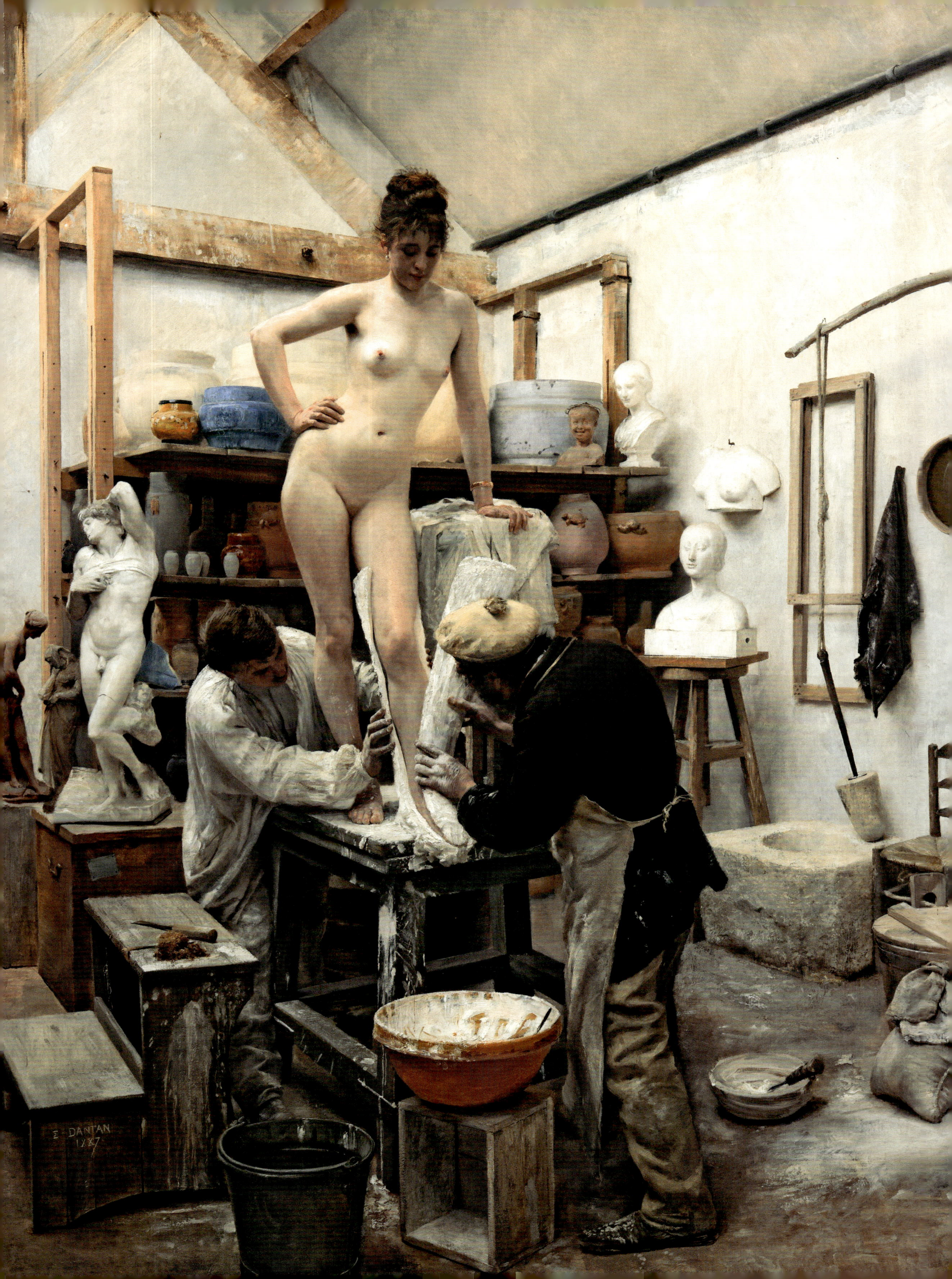
E. DANTAN
1887

In the Artist's Studio

In the workshop practice of sculptors, casts have always played an important role. From antiquity to the present, they have served as models that contribute to the conceptual aspect of the final artwork, as well as artistic tools which make them part of the work's material origins. In what might be be seen as paradigmatic, Édouard Dantan's painting *Un moulage sur nature* (1887) illustrates this double role. This painting of a studio vividly foregrounds the practice of life-casting, while in the background iconic sculptures, such as a reduced cast of Michelangelo's *Dying Slave* (1513–16) and the cast of a female bust, stand guard over the work process, maybe even inspire it. Does Dantan allude here to the oppositions between art and technology, free modelling and mechanical replication, creation and imitation? Or is he making a productive connection between these aspects, which are often difficult to tell apart?

In addition to Dantan's painting, there are other such scenes set in academies and studios that show both the workshops of sculptors furnished with exemplary casts and the casting process itself; they form the starting point of this chapter. The core, however, is informed by those casts of human body parts and of faces that — like the casts taken from animals in *Still Lifes and Nature morte* — once belonged to the collection of teaching aids in use at the Unterrichtsanstalt des Kunstgewerbemuseums in Berlin. They were integrated into the collection of the Gipsformerei in the late nineteenth century. These holdings comprise plaster effigies of stunning lifelikeness, which shed light on the blind spots in the histories of the two institutions. *Near Life* presents these works to the public for the very first time.

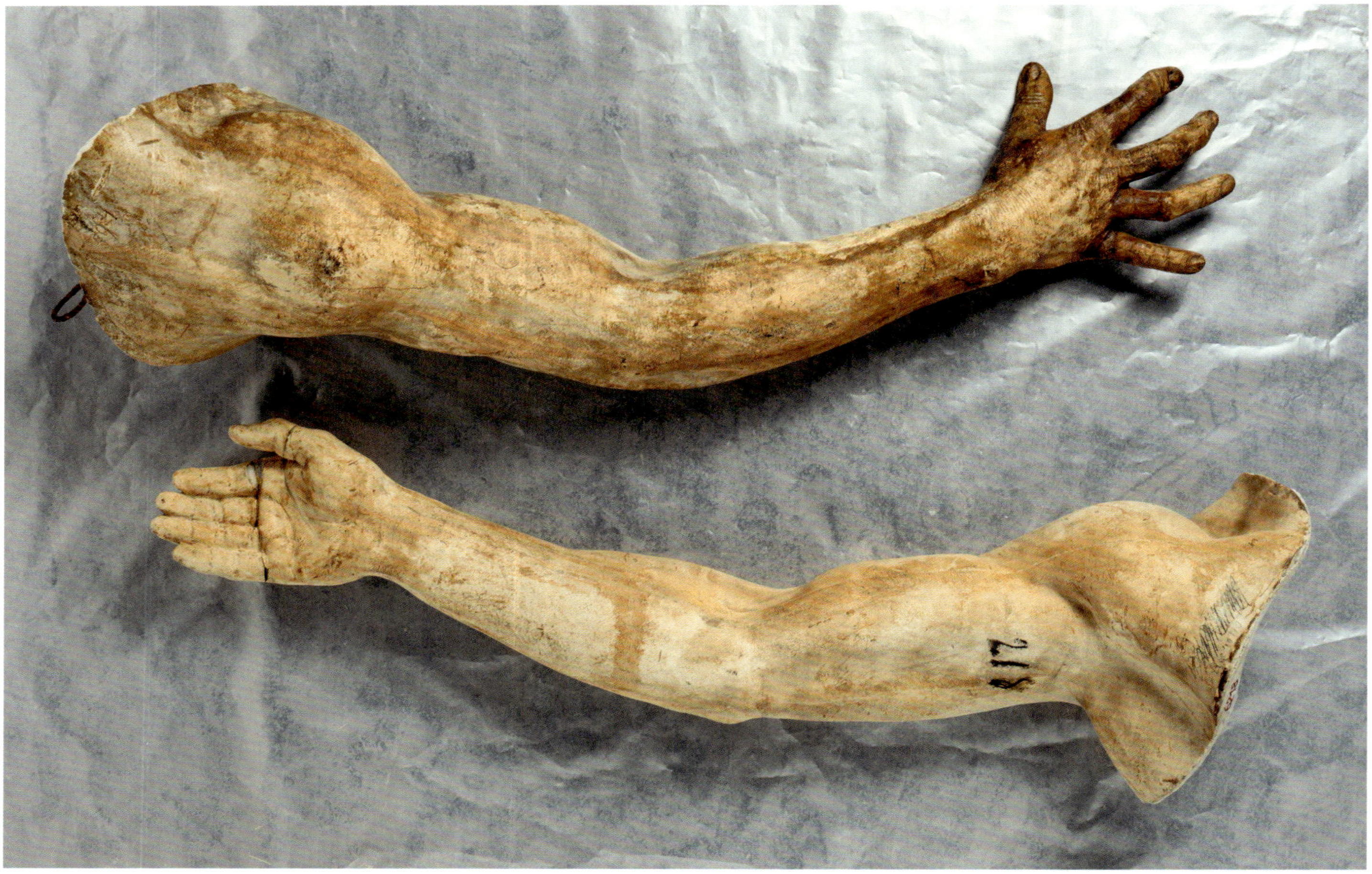

Writing in the magazine *Deutsches Kunstblatt* in early 1854, German art historian Friedrich Eggers (1819–1872) describes the studio of his painter friend Adolph Menzel (1815–1905). He mentions the artist's 'collection of plaster casts taken from human extremities and heads', which included 'only a few forms of ancient statuary that have stood the test of time. […] By far the most space is taken up by casts taken from nature, above all, by a number of the most diverse death masks; out of the two teachers of art, antiquity and nature, Menzel has accorded pride of place to the latter.' Eggers here points to a paradigm shift in the artistic practice of the nineteenth century: the study of antiquity was gradually replaced with that of nature. While plaster casts of ancient statuary were studied by artists from the Renaissance onwards, their interest moved more and more towards living nature during the nineteenth century. 'The classes of drawing from ancient statuary that used to be obligatory in the first phase of any art course had ceased to exist.' This is how the former art student Hermann Ebers, in a text titled *Aus meiner Studienzeit* (From My Student Days, ca. 1954), describes the years around the turn of the twentieth century at the Akademie der Bildenden Künste in Munich. 'The naturalistic tendencies prevalent at the time had put an end to these drawing classes, and the plaster casts of the antique masterpieces, which in the past had served as models for the drawings of beginners, now got bored stiff standing in the endless corridors of the academy building.' This development resulted in a growing number of natural casts in the collections of plaster casts of academies and training institutions. Casts taken 'from' or 'after' nature, which were used as teaching aids and study objects and were seen as representing bare life as opposed to idealised antiquity, are also to be found in the collection of the Gipsformerei. They are an invitation to extend to the observation of nature further speculations regarding the representative function that plaster casts perform for their 'originals'. Can impressions taken from the face (or any other part of the human body for that matter) serve as substitutes for human beings? Can the study of casts replace the communion with living nature?

Right Arm of a Man with Shoulder Tip and Splayed Finger

Right Arm of a Man with Shoulder Tip and Hand Open

Master models, 1871
Staatliche Museen zu Berlin, Gipsformerei

Adolph Menzel
Atelierwand, 1852
Staatliche Museen zu Berlin, Alte Nationalgalerie

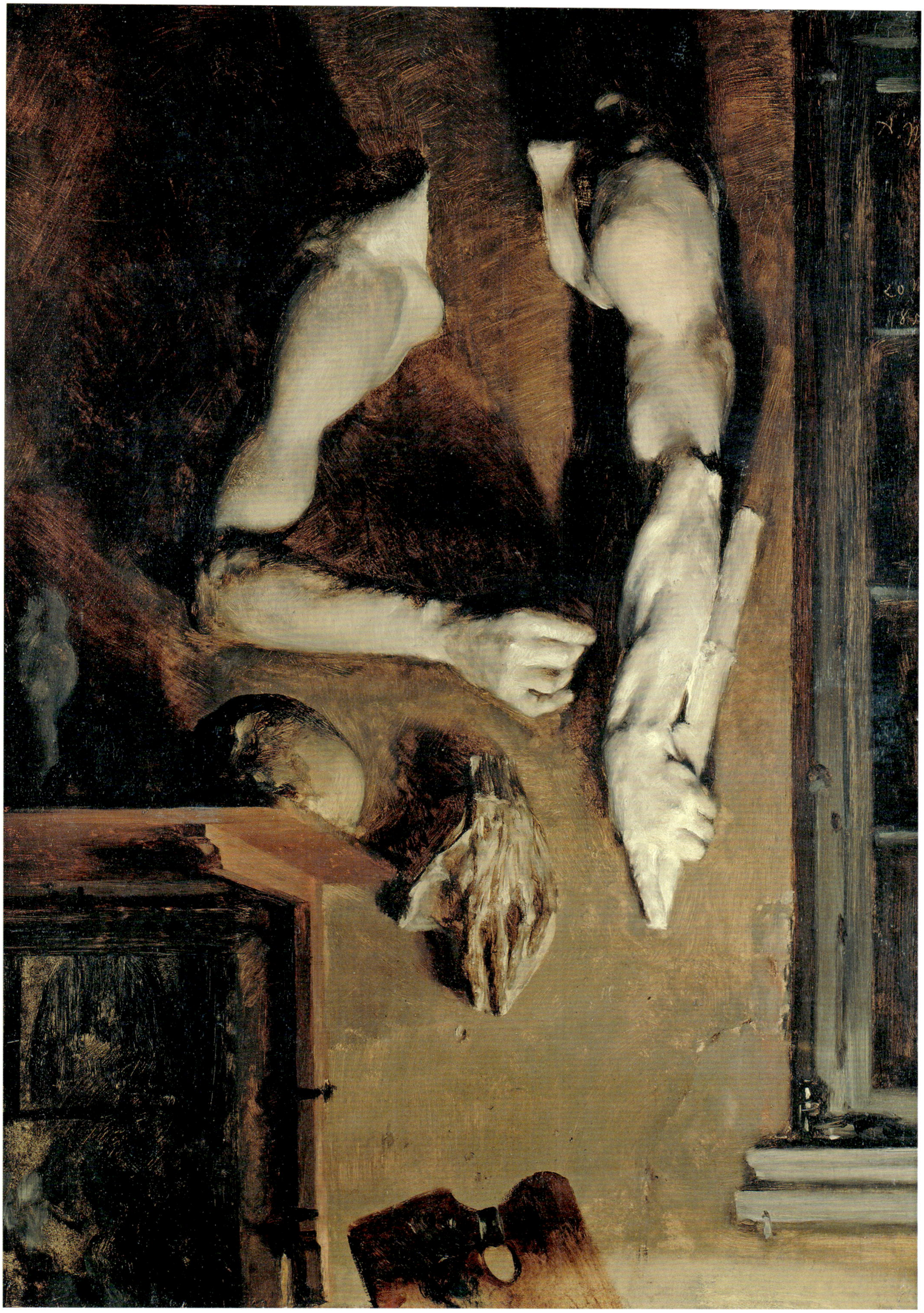

The wall of Adolph Menzel's studio replete with plaster casts, as described by art historian Friedrich Eggers, is at the centre of two famous paintings by the artist, both titled *Atelierwand* (Studio Wall). With its wall-based torsos (Venus de Milo and Laocoön), the later of the two works, dating from 1872, invokes the imitation of antiquity as a challenge to any artist in modern times — even though this challenge is immediately revoked by the death masks depicted on either side of the canvas. The 1852 study, now in the collection of the Alte Nationalgalerie, confines itself to the natural casts of two male arms and an anatomical model of a hand detailing its muscles. These casts are also to be found (in the same or a very similar form) in the collection of the Gipsformerei. A death mask and a cropped painter's palette complement the picture's inventory of this painting. Menzel's two versions of his *Atelierwand* are emblematic of the binaries such as tradition and modernity, wholeness and fragmentation, life and death, painting and sculpture, whose antagonism oscillated throughout the nineteenth century; this opposition between antiquity and nature relates to classicism struggling with romanticism, realism and modernity. The body parts made of plaster that Menzel had raised to the status of motifs worthy of depiction as early as the 1850s evoke, as though a vision, the disabled, shattered bodies so remote from ideal beauty that were to haunt modern art after the ordeal of the World Wars. Menzel's consummate control of the lighting creates painted impressions vibrant with life; seemingly contradicting the prejudice that there is invariably something rigid and lifeless about plaster casts. Lit from below, the casts look as if they are about to quietly detach themselves from the wall. Such light sources granting lifelikeness to dead matter are a reminder of the nocturnal tours of plaster cast collections popular in the eighteenth century, where the guide's lamp literally caused an impression of animation. Comparable is the practice of studying sculptures in flickering candlelight during the Enlightenment, which gave the surface of the sculptures an appearance of coming to life. Furthermore, the presence of the painter's palette at the lower edge of the Berlin *Atelierwand* brings into play the fiercely contested *paragone* between painting and sculpture. In the end — if this is indeed a plausible interpretation of what Menzel wanted to convey with this detail — it is only painting that is capable of rendering its subjects lifelike, while three-dimensional works are in danger of degenerating into cheap copies of death.

Adolph Menzel
Atelierwand, 1872
Oil on canvas
111 × 79.3 cm
Hamburger Kunsthalle, 1266

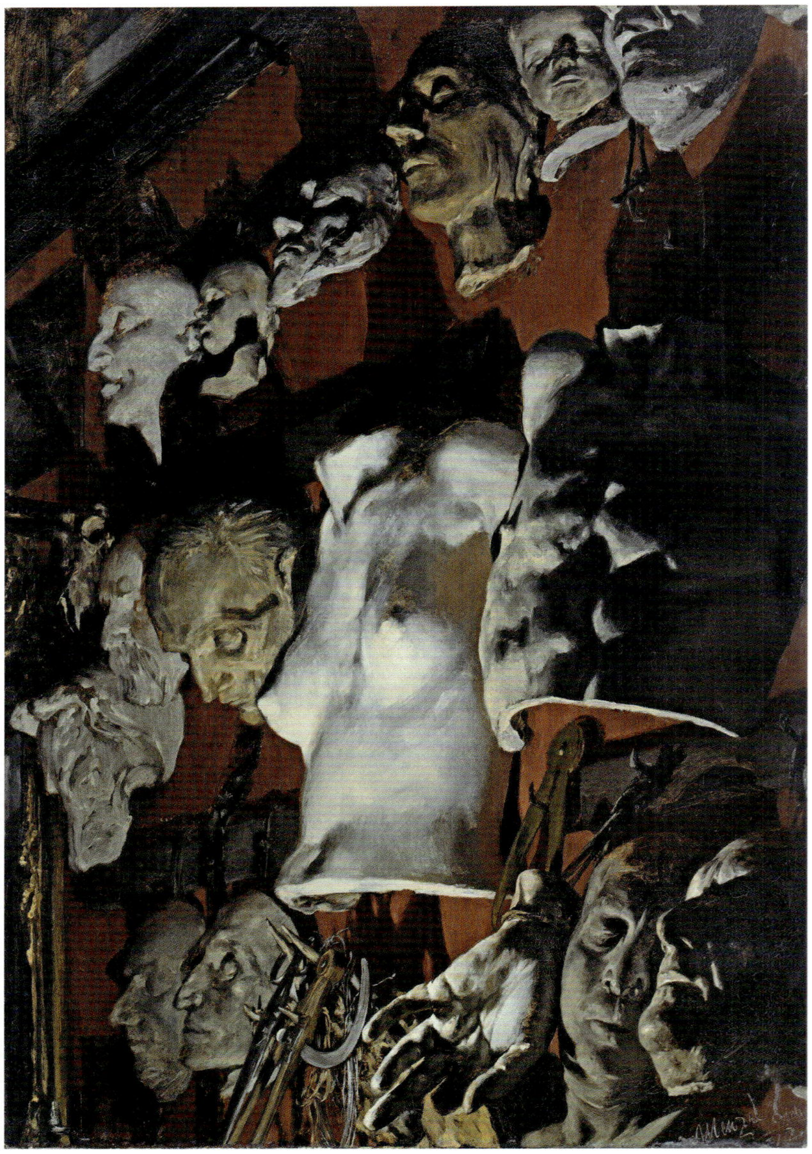

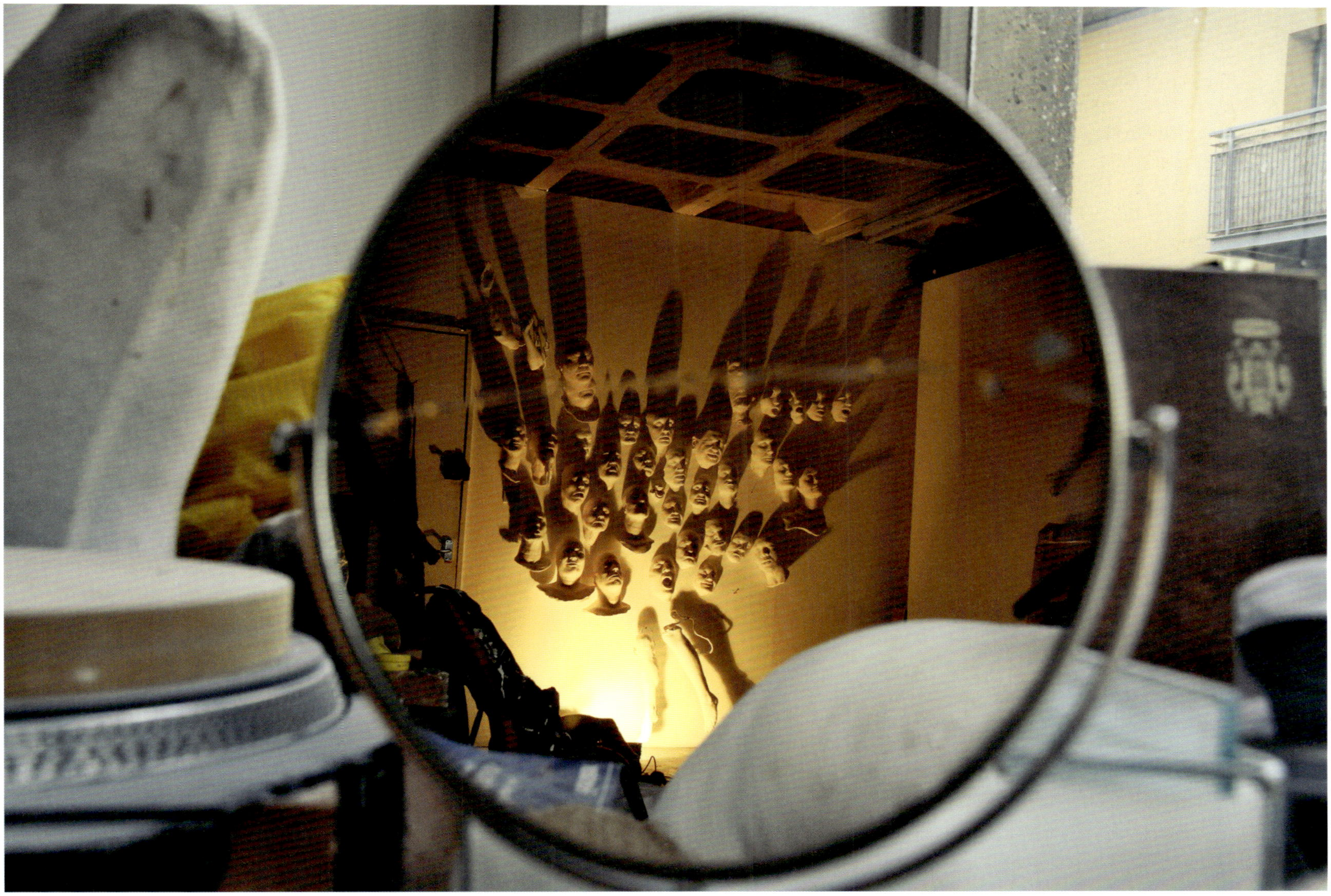

Liane Lang
Studio Spectres Cremer Street/ Hackney, 2012–19
Courtesy of the artist

Body parts made of plaster in the artist's studio, the fragmentation of the human body and the animation of allegedly lifeless matter are concerns of artist Liane Lang (b. 1973). In her video *Studio Spectres Cremer Street/Hackney* (2012–19), she picks up from where Menzel left off: not only elevating plaster casts to signifiers in their own right, they become protagonists in her spatio-temporal narrative. In the studio situation realised by Lang, the casts come to life along with brush and scissors, work clothes and tools. Face masks take to rocking to and fro on the wall; one of their wide open mouths throws up a pair of cotton work gloves and plaster leftovers on the floor amuse themselves. This poetic, humorous animation film seems to play havoc with the specific properties of living and lifeless matter, allowing a 'what if …' mental experiment to unfold and turning the empty studio into an arena for the revolt of things.

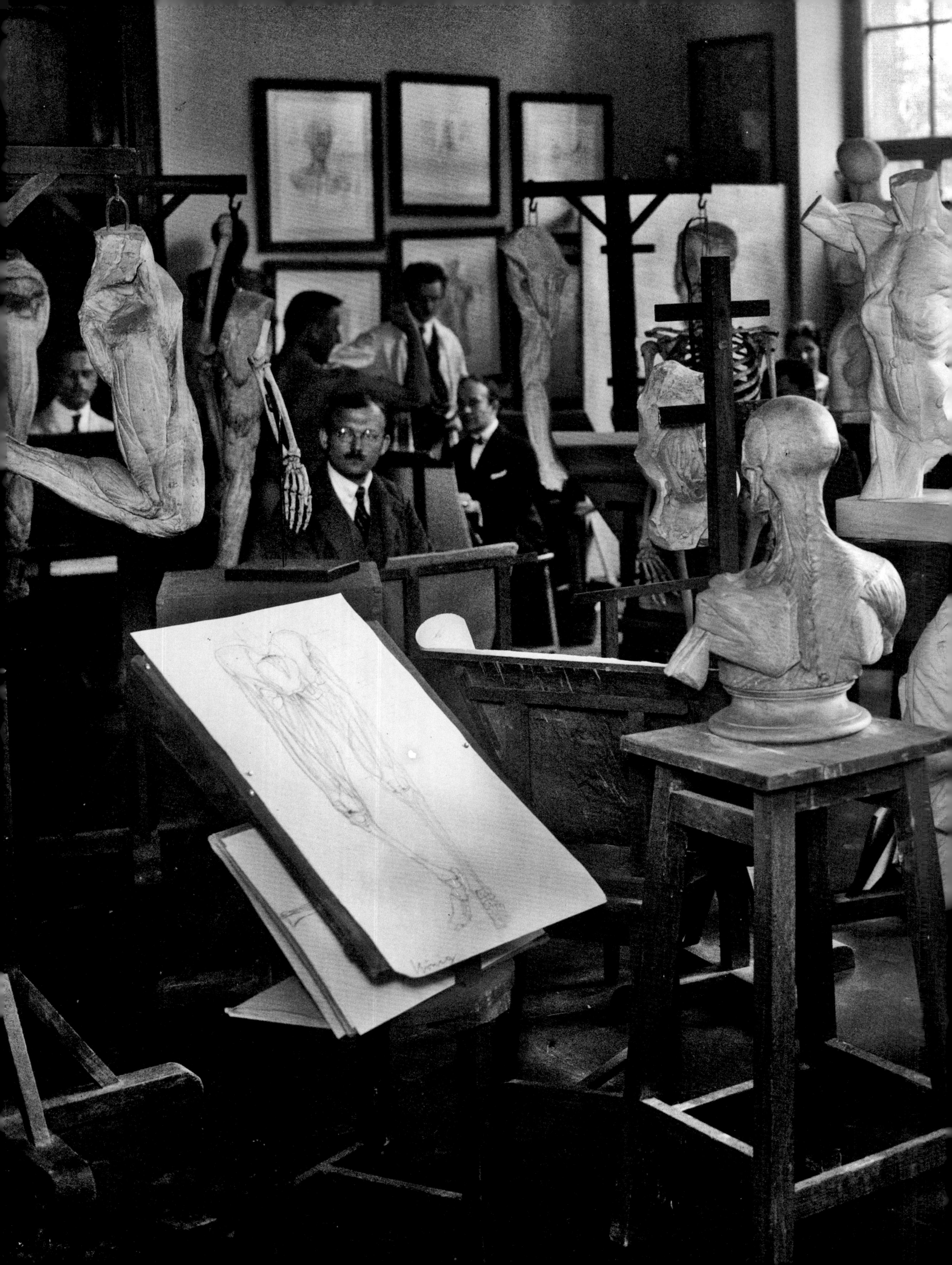

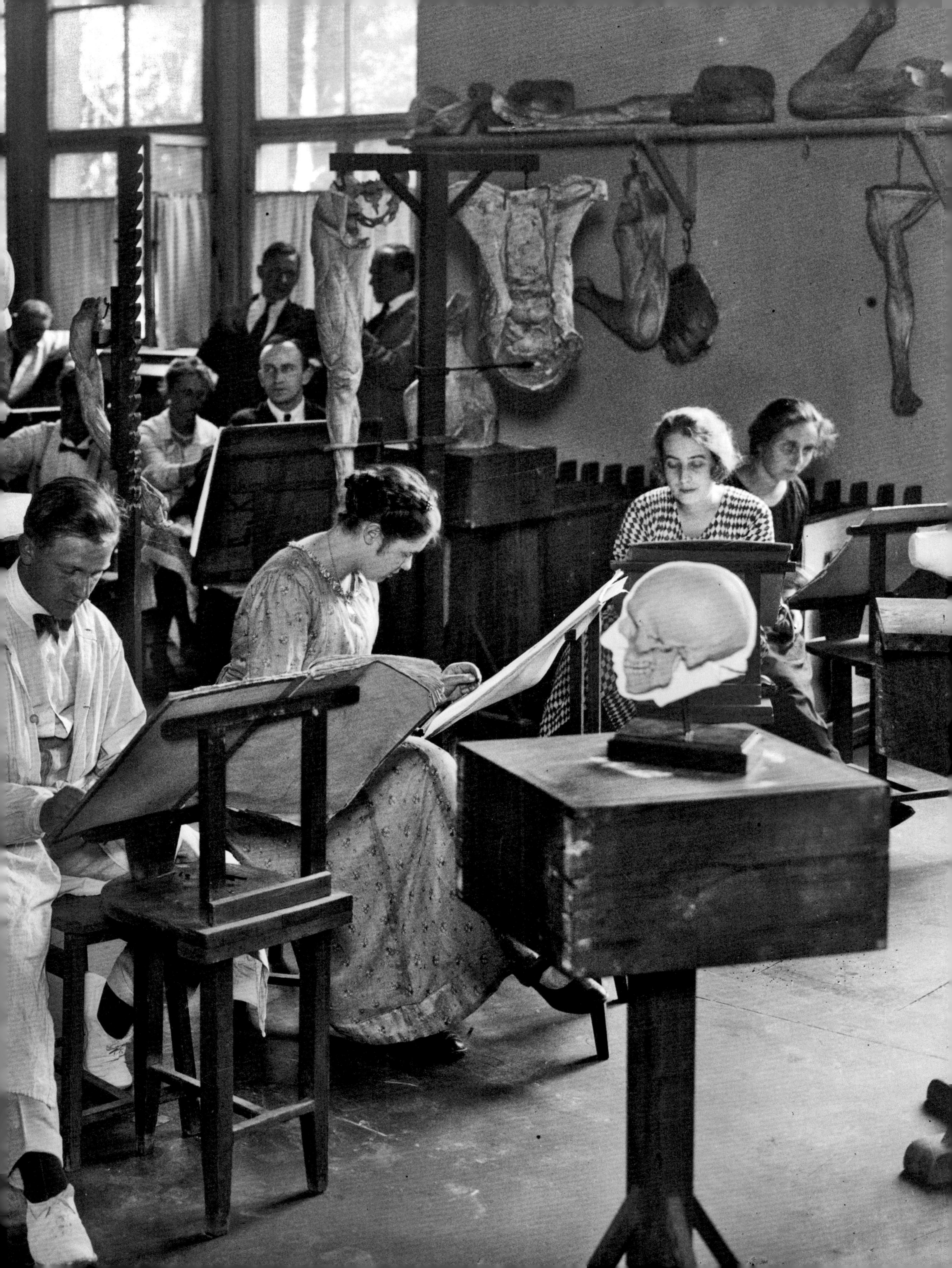

The use of antique sculptures for tuition and study purposes in modern times is attested by the many depictions of academies from the seventeenth to nineteenth centuries, including the drawing *Aktsaal der Kunst-Academie zu Berlin* (Life Drawing Hall at the Art Academy in Berlin, 1696) by Dutch baroque painter Augustin Terwesten (1649–1711). The Akademie der Künste in Berlin was founded in the same year as the drawing by Prussia's future king Friedrich I, similarly to the academies of Paris and Rome. Located on the upper floor of the Royal Stables on Unter den Linden, the Akademie was both an artists' society and training institution. Plaster casts, mostly procured from Rome, helped to introduce young artists and scholars to the study of antiquity.

As the collection of plaster casts was destroyed almost completely in a fire at the stables in 1743, the inventory of sculptures can only be reconstructed tentatively. Preserved fully in the form of graphic reproductions, Terwesten's drawing is one of the few sources we can draw on today. It proves that students at the Akademie had casts of the *Farnese Hercules*, the *Laocoön Group*, the *Medici Venus*, the *Farnese Hermes* and the *Satyr with Cymbals and Kroupezion* at their disposal to train eye and hand. The plaster cast collection of the Akademie der Künste was the foundation of the collection, which was prominently placed on display between 1855 and 1911 on the first floor of the Neues Museum and continuously supplied with new pieces made at the Gipsformerei.

Previous page

Willy Römer
Teaching Institute of the Kunstgewerbemuseum, Berlin (In the Art Room for Anatomical Drawing), 1920s
Staatliche Museen zu Berlin, Kunstbibliothek – Museum für Fotografie

Right

Willy Römer
Teaching Institute of the Kunstgewerbemuseum, Berlin (Anatomy Class and *Sculptors' Workshop)*, 1920s
Staatliche Museen zu Berlin, Kunstbibliothek – Museum für Fotografie

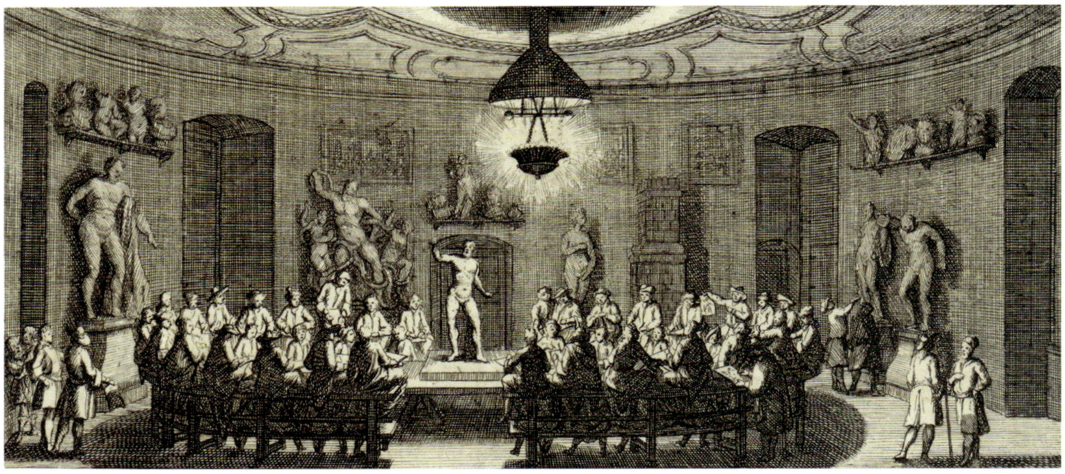

Constantin Friedrich Blesendorf (attributed) after a drawing by Augustin Terwesten
Der Aktsaal der Berliner Akademie der Künste, ca. 1700
Staatliche Museen zu Berlin, Kunstbibliothek

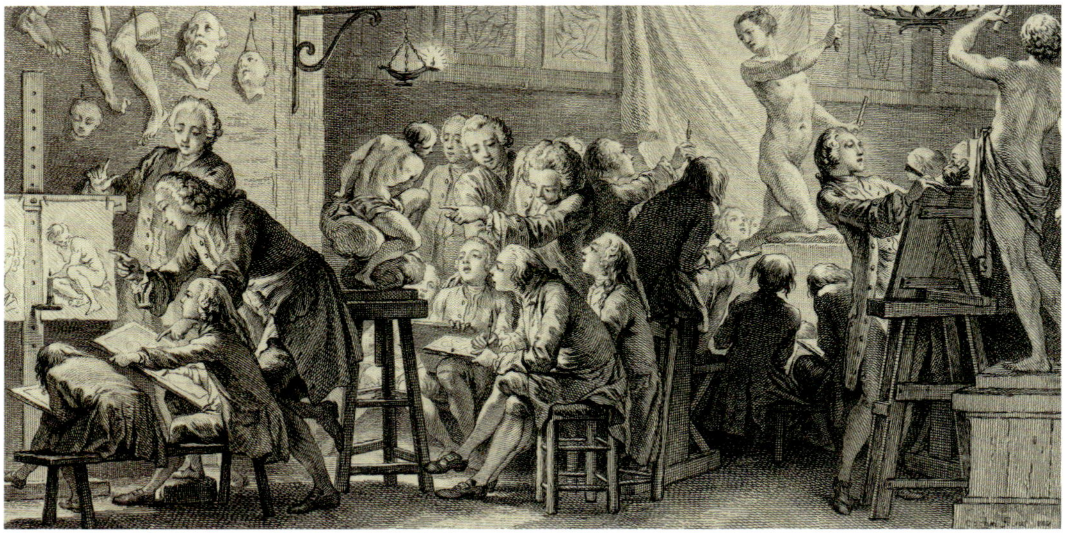

Charles-Nicolas Cochin (the Younger), Benoît Louis Prévost (engraver)
Zeichenkurs in der Akademie, nach einer Vorzeichnung für die Illustration in Diderots und d'Alemberts Encyclopédie, 1763
Staatliche Museen zu Berlin, Kupferstichkabinett

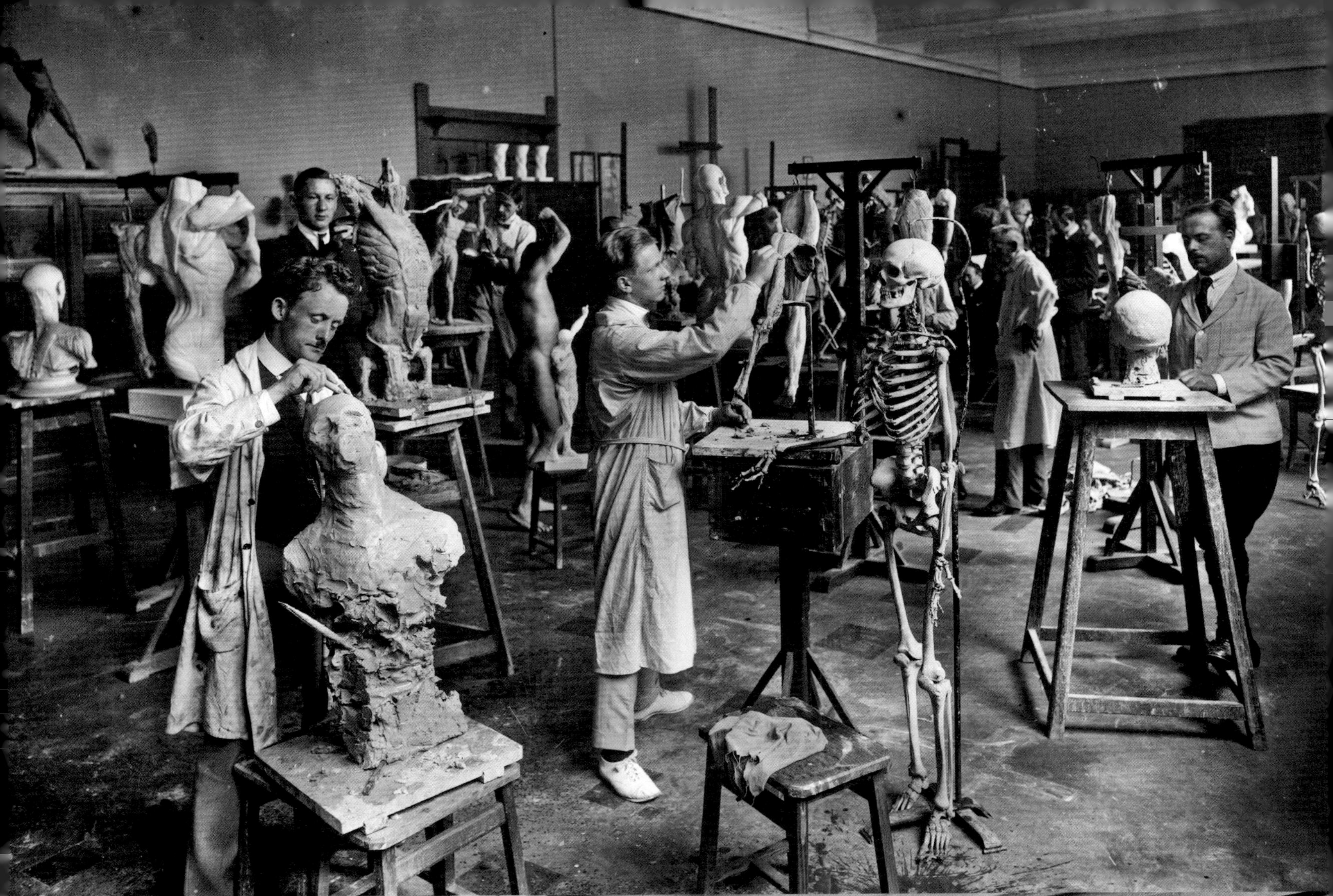

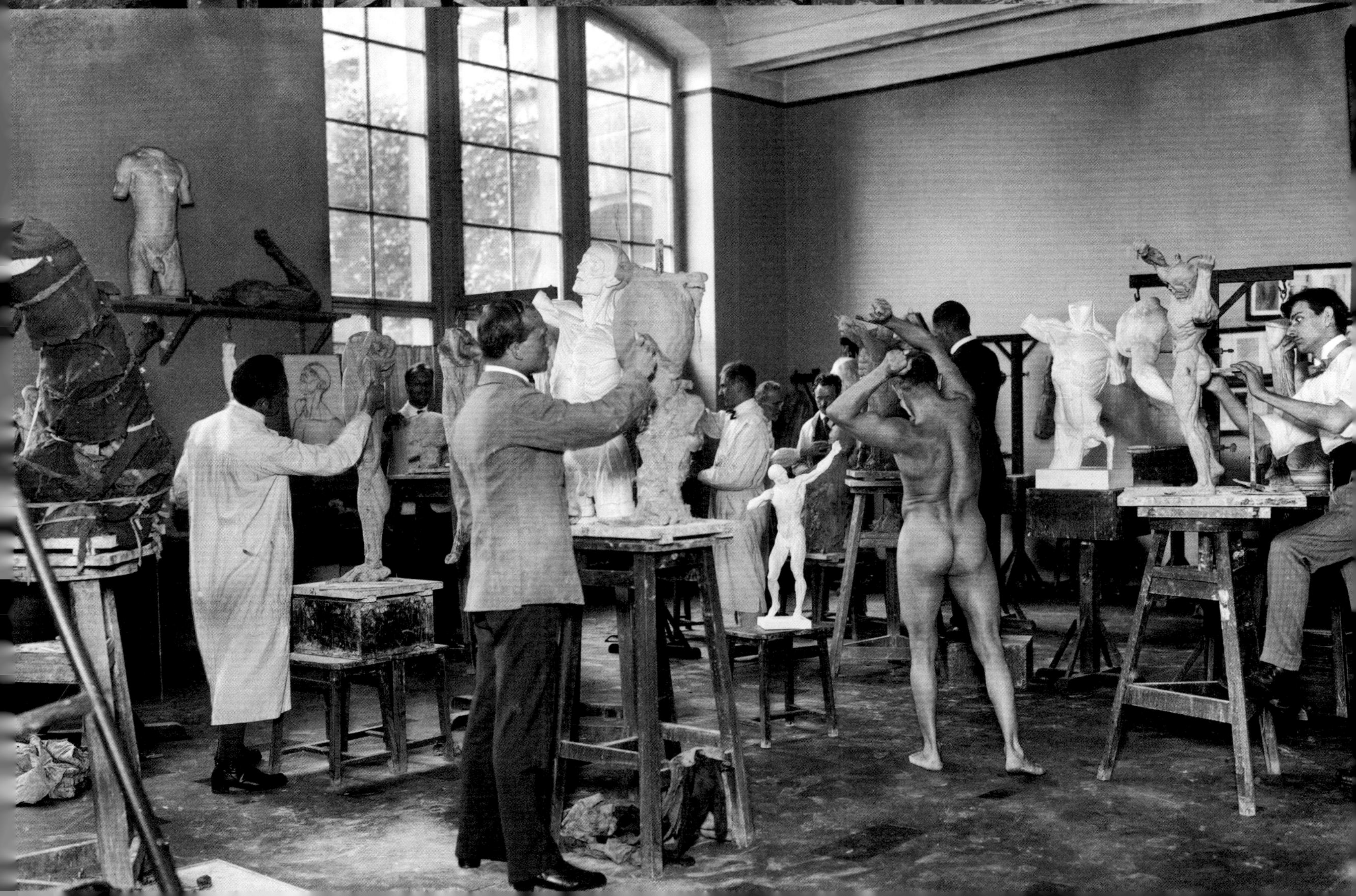

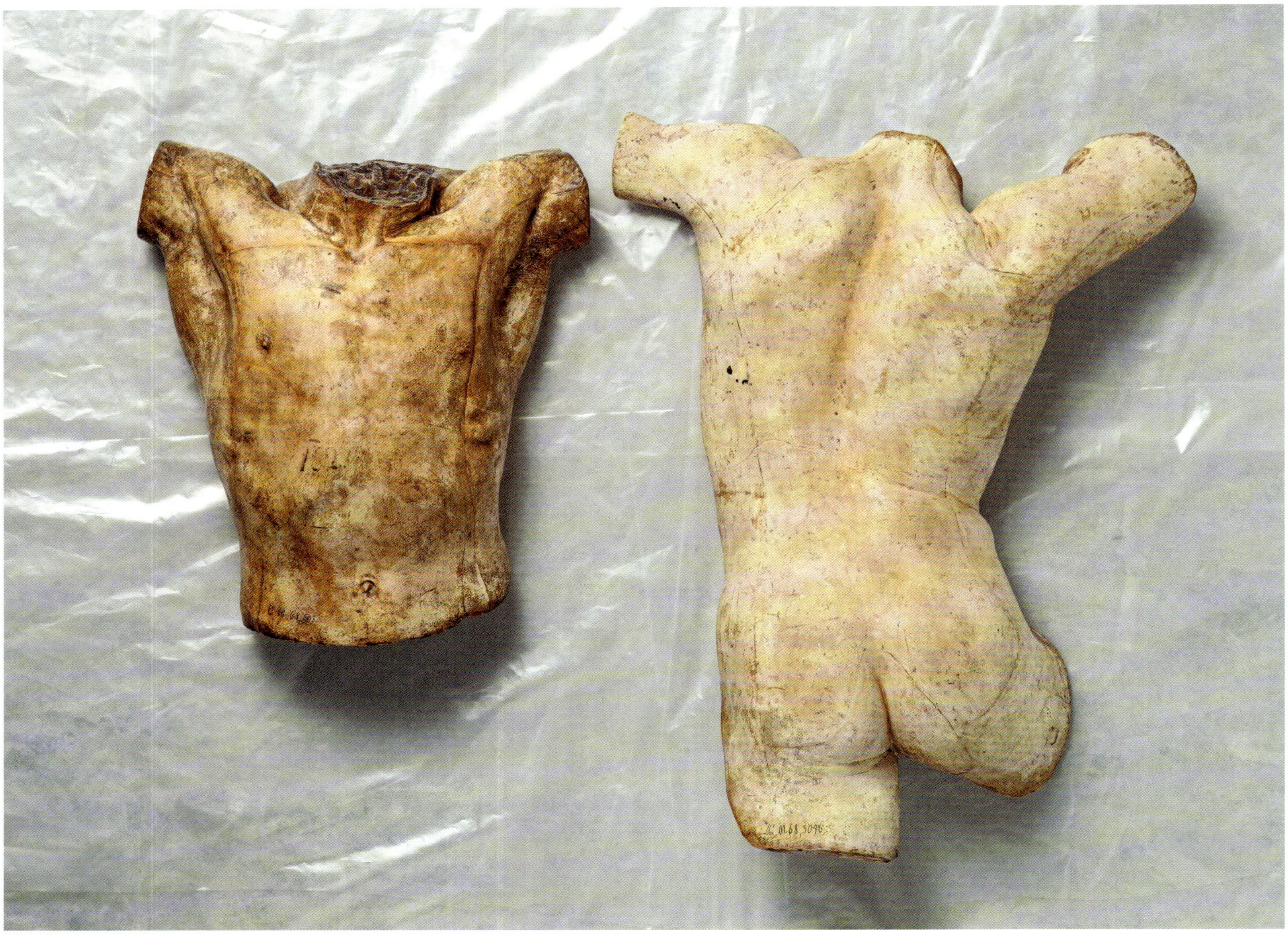

Male Torso (Front)

Male Torso (Back), former inv. no. 32

Master models, 1908 and 1870
Staatliche Museen zu Berlin,
Gipsformerei

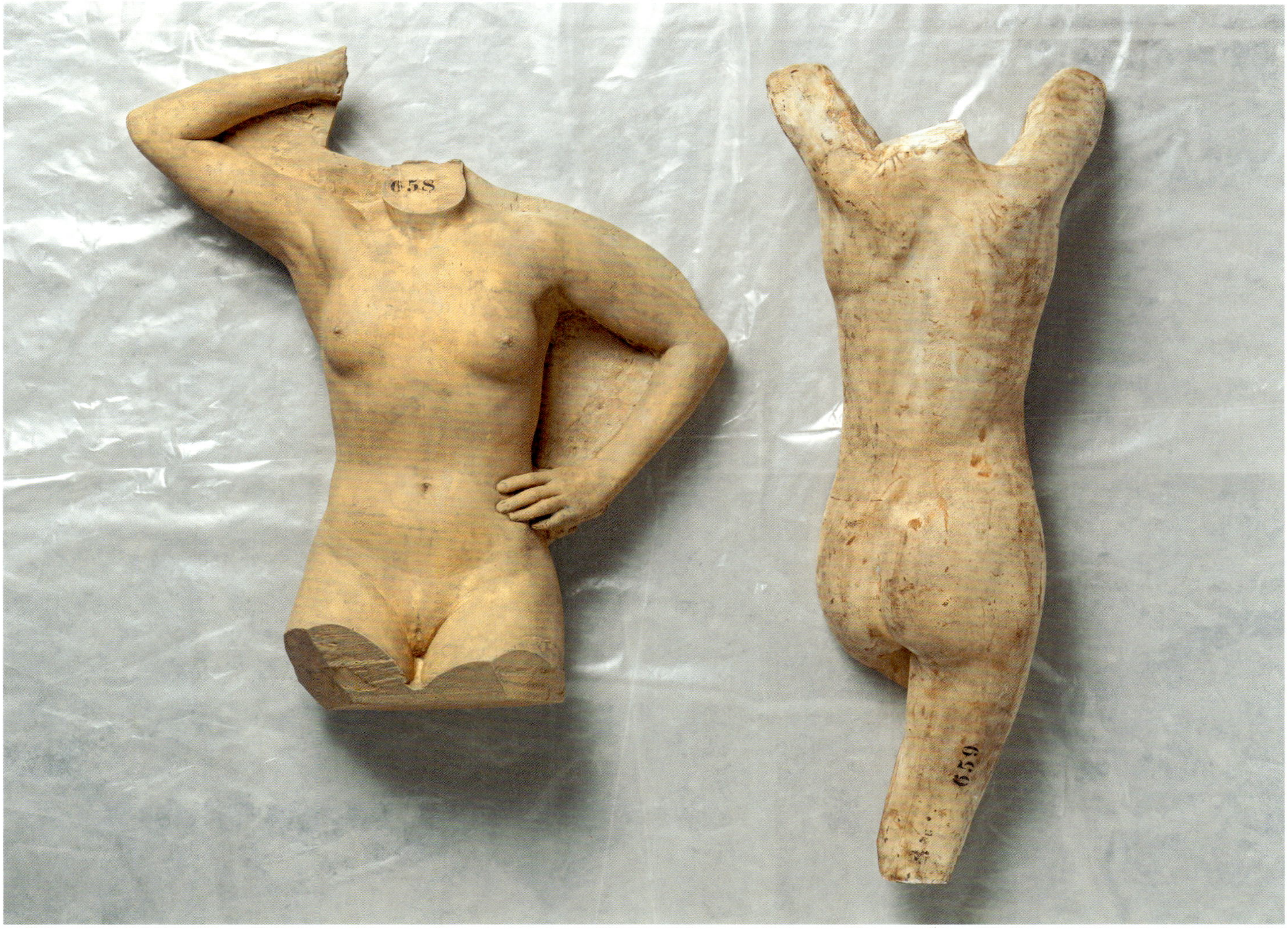

Female Torso (Front)

Female Torso (Back)

Master models, 1894
Staatliche Museen zu Berlin,
Gipsformerei

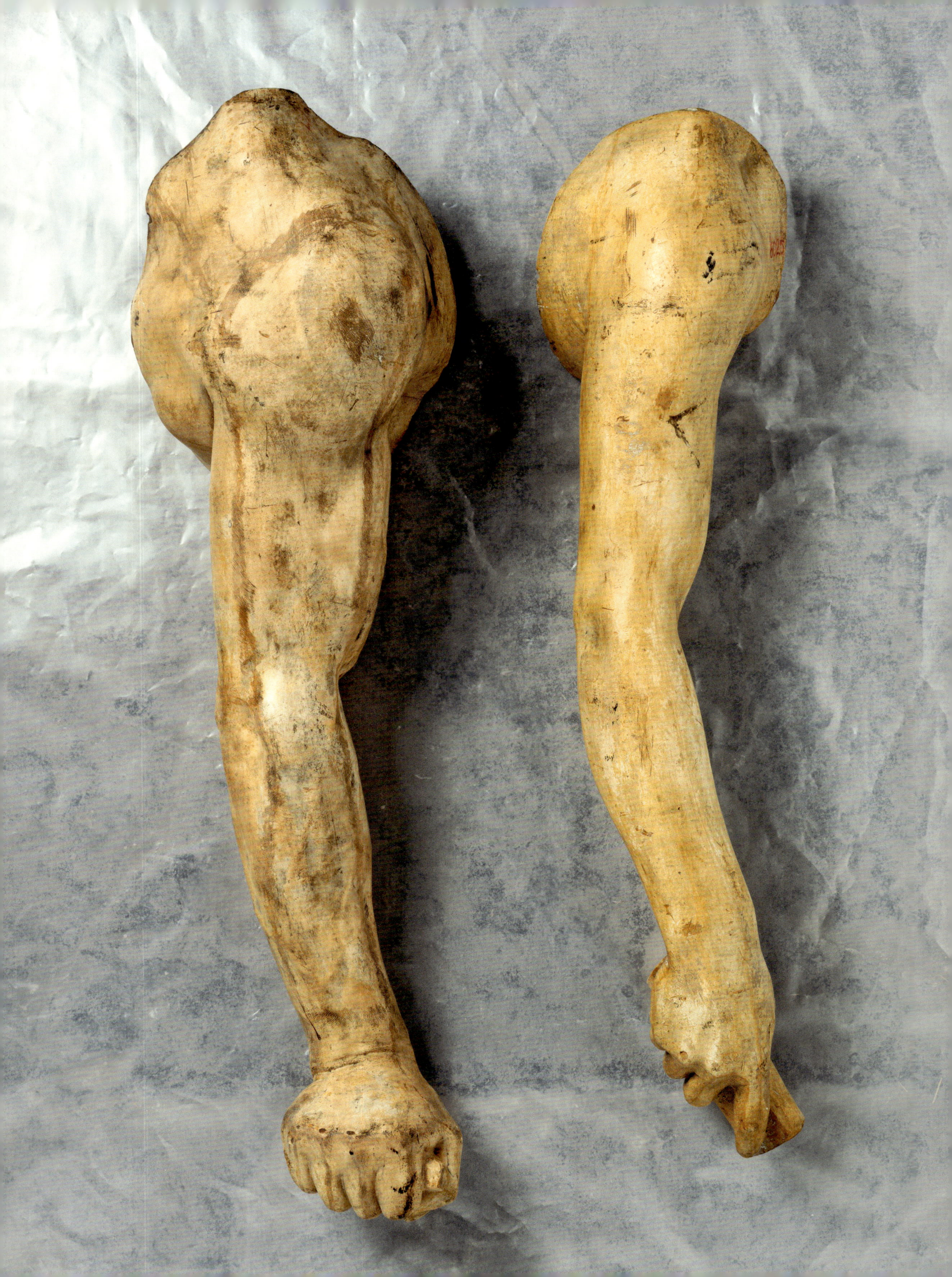

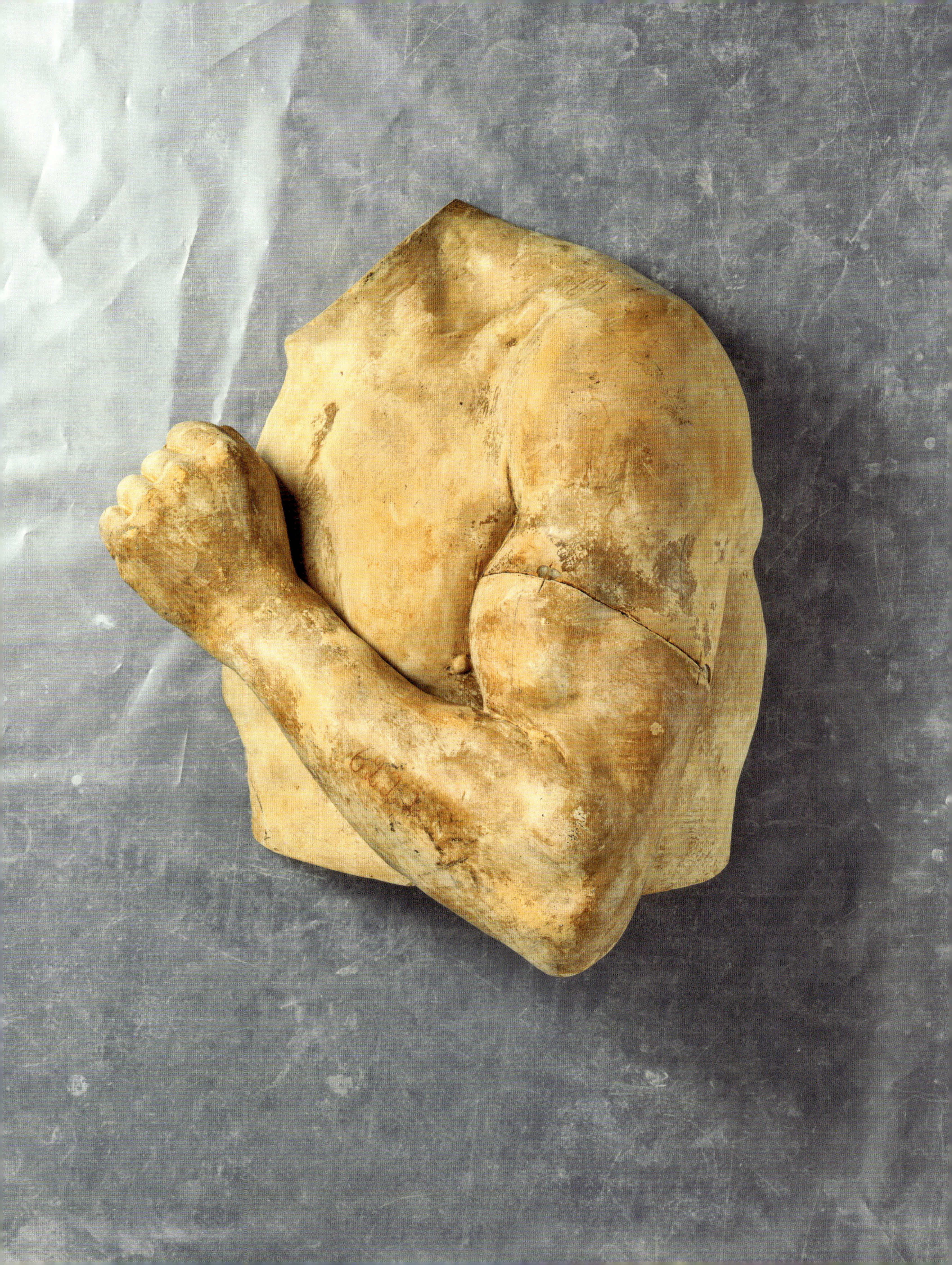

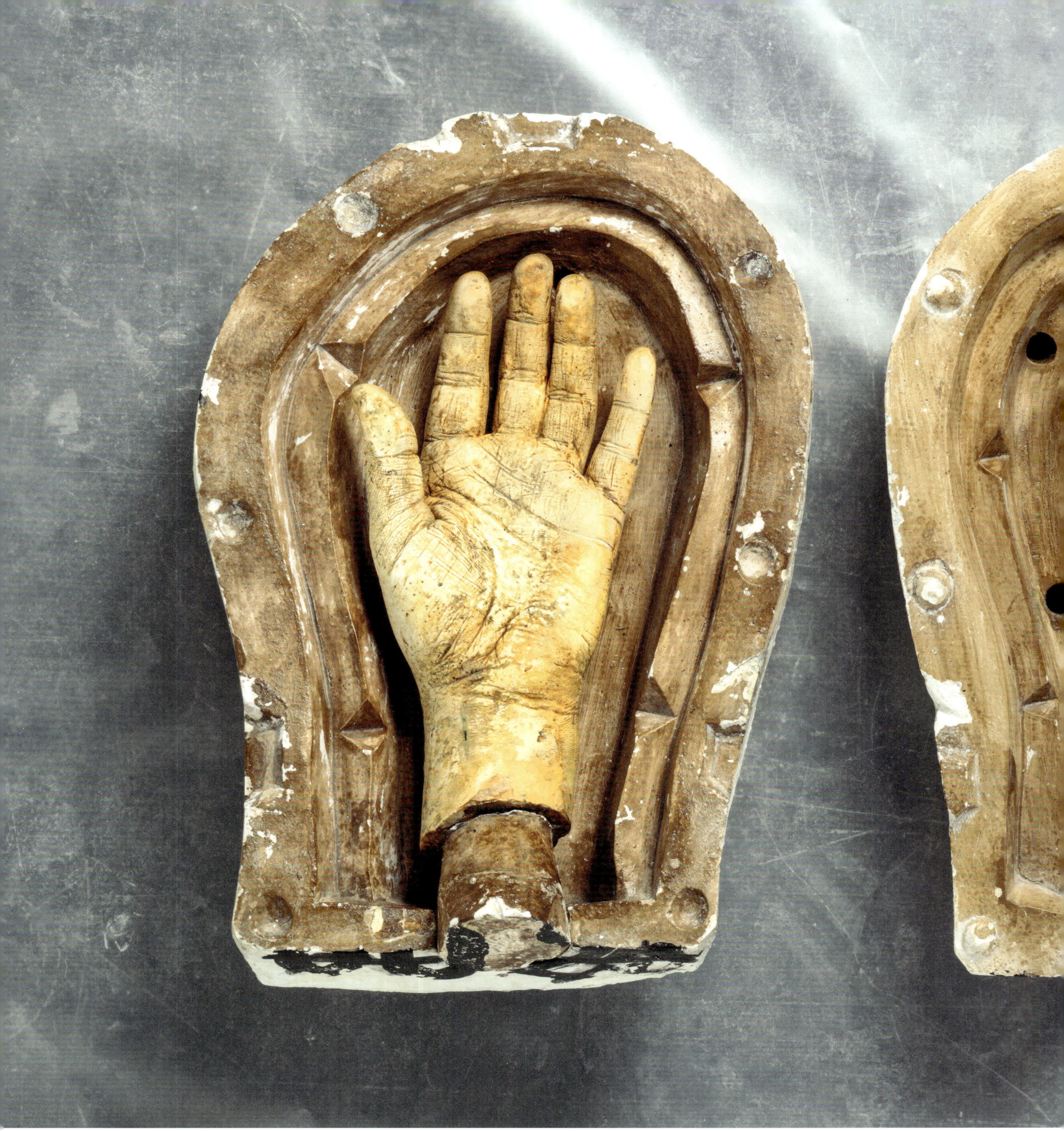

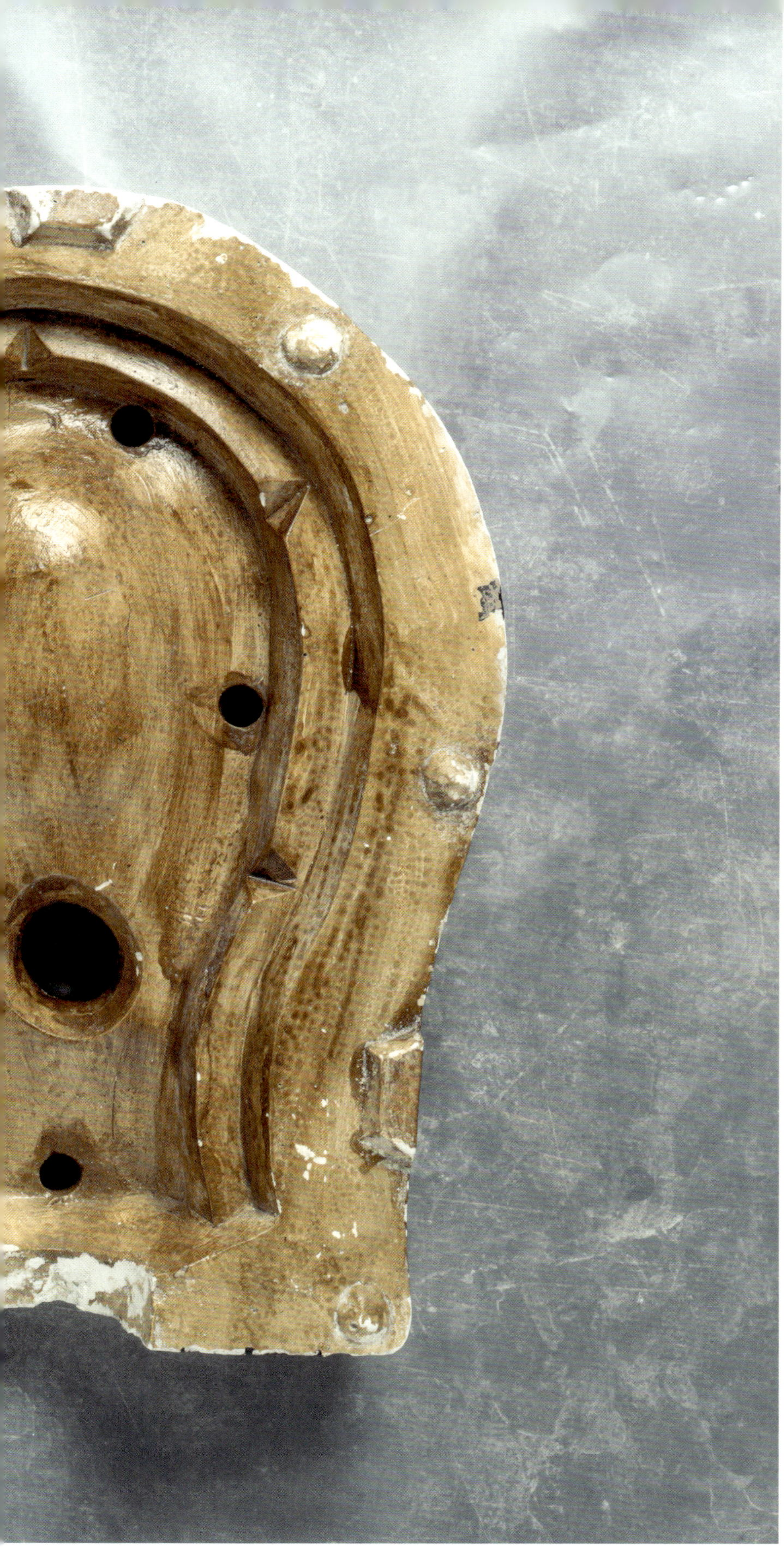

Previous page

Right Arm of a Man with Shoulder Tip and Clenched Fist

Right Arm of a Man with Shoulder Tip, the Hand Holding an Object, former inv. no. 39

Left Arm of a Man, Bent with Clenched Fist and Chest

Master models, 1871 and 1868
Staatliche Museen zu Berlin, Gipsformerei

Left

Left Hand of a Woman
Master model in mother mould, ca. 1900
Staatliche Museen zu Berlin, Gipsformerei

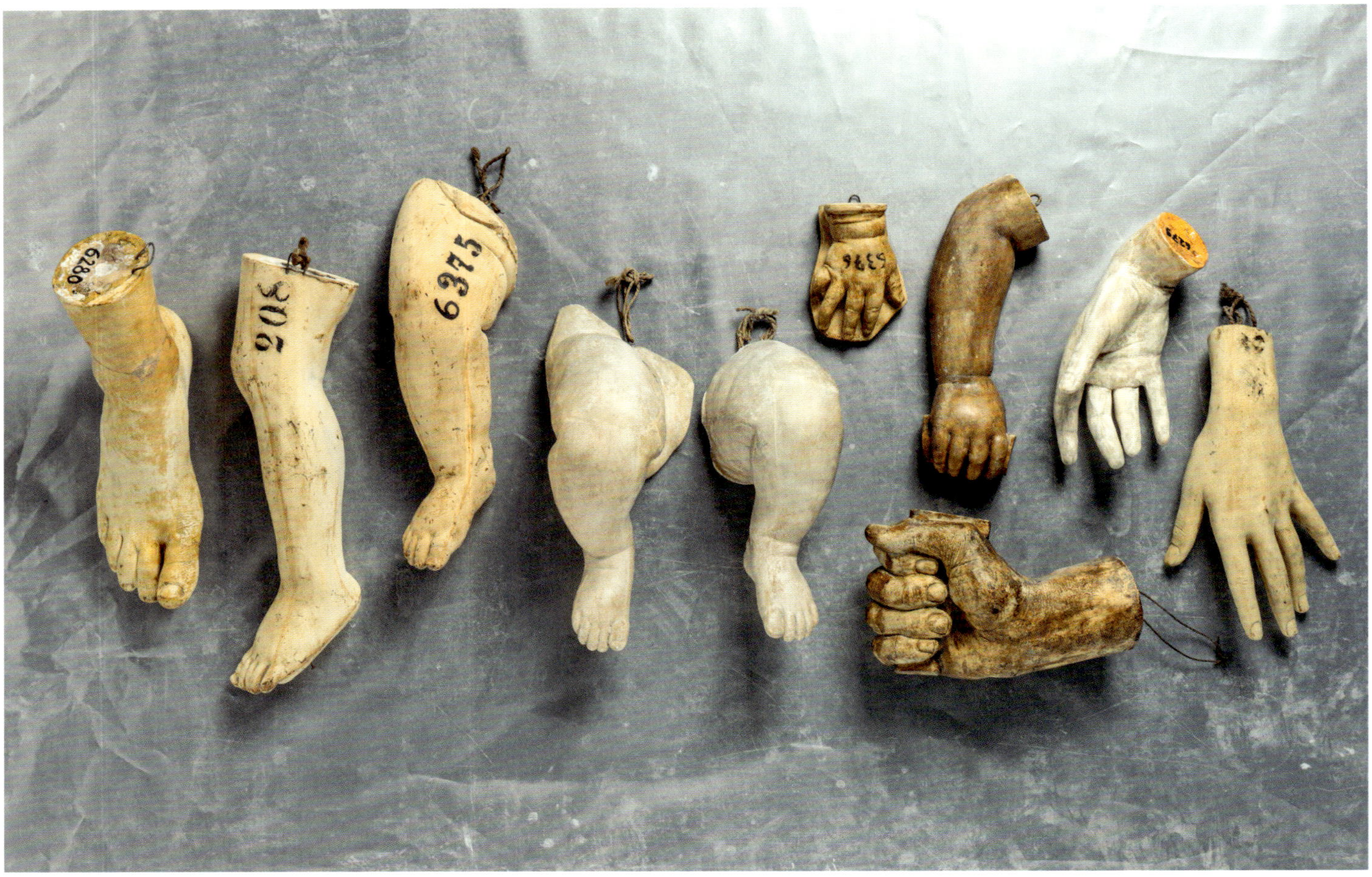

Right Foot of a Woman, Stretched

Left Leg of a Child

Right Leg of a Child

Right Leg of a Child, Bent

Left Leg of a Child, Bent

Right Hand of a Child on a Panel

Right Arm of a Child

Right Hand of a Man, Clenched, former inv. no. 14

Right Hand of a Woman with Fingers Bent

Left Hand of a Woman with Outstretched Fingers

Master models, 1871–86
Staatliche Museen zu Berlin, Gipsformerei

Pars pro toto: The Kunstgewerbemuseum Casts of Body Parts in the Collection of the Gipsformerei

Veronika Tocha

When the Kunstgewerbemuseum in Berlin relocated in 1881 from the Gropius'sches Diorama in Mitte to a new building on what was then Prinz-Albrecht Straße (today's Martin-Gropius-Bau), a 'plaster cast museum' was established in the basement, which from today's point of view is quite remarkable. The institution included a teaching collection, a manufacturer's warehouse and a sales gallery. Comprised of approximately three thousand items, the museum's collection of plaster casts was presented there in chronological order, ranging from antiquity to the baroque, across four rooms with a total floor space of 457 square metres.[1] All kinds of exemplary sculptural works were on display, on exhibition walls, in cabinets and display cases, wall-hung or freestanding. The exhibits were not only used for study purposes by students of the teaching institute linked to the museum, but also comprised the casts that were produced and offered for sale by the plaster casting workshop of the Kunstgewerbemuseum. There are three aspects of particular interest: first, the direct link between the manufacturing of the casts and the museum which put them on display; second, the intermittent coexistence of two casting workshops under the one roof of the Königliche Museen, including the Kunstgewerbemuseum from 1885 onwards; and, third, the nature and structure of the museum's plaster cast collection, which comprised not only arts and crafts and art-historical artefacts, but also 112 lifecasts of human and animal parts now integrated into the Gipsformerei collection. What implicit mission statement does the latter collection of casts owe its existence to? How did it come into being? And when precisely was it amalgamated with the collection of the Königliche Gipsformerei?

As the collection of plaster casts was housed in the basement of the newly built museum, it quite literally was a sub-museum. The casts and galvanoplastic replicas of artworks and objets d'art, which 'lend themselves to being made into a kind of facsimile of the original [...] through the use of colour or gold and silver plating' were integrated into the presentation of the collection on the ground and first floor, while those casts that 'retain the natural colour of plaster or have only been lightly tinted by being given a protective coating' were assembled 'primarily on account of their colour in a special section, the collection of plaster casts'.[2] The presentation and the understanding of these plaster casts differed significantly from the idea that was pursued in the mid-nineteenth century for the collection of casts presented in the Neues Museum, which at the time was declared to be 'the heart of all collections'.[3] What underpinned the exhibition at the Kunstgewerbemuseum, however, was its function as a teaching collection rather than the lack of appreciation of the actual plaster casts. So, in addition to their character as museum exhibits, they served a practical purpose, a fact that was further underlined by the way the items were marked: tags with numbers inscribed in red were attached to the plaster casts for sale. In terms of volume, this applied to roughly one tenth of the entire collection. Relevant prices and conditions of sale were to be gleaned from a catalogue which could be consulted courtesy of one of the guards or purchased at the museum 'bureau'[4] — a practice we are familiar with from today's art galleries and the like.

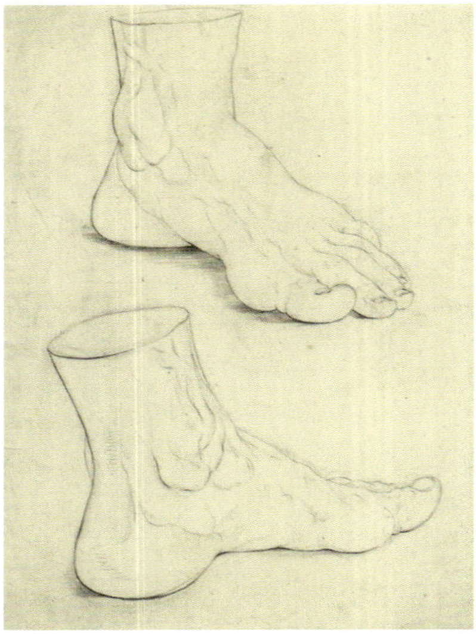

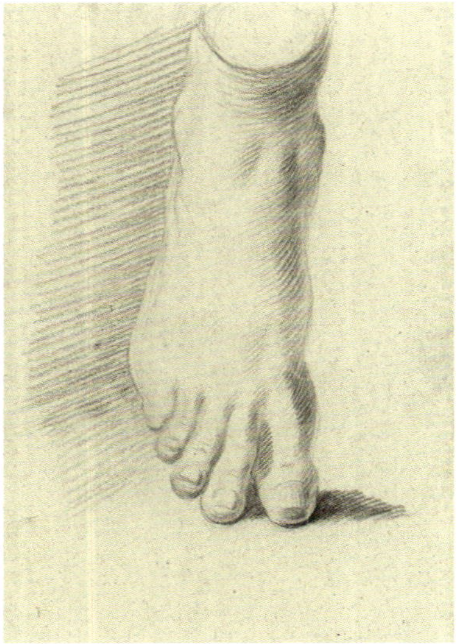

Philipp Otto Runge
Two Foot Studies (after Plaster Casts),
n. d.
Staatliche Museen zu Berlin,
Kupferstichkabinett

Johann Heinrich Ramberg
Right Foot of a Man, Seen from the Front, after Plaster Cast, n. d.
Staatliche Museen zu Berlin,
Kupferstichkabinett

Right Foot of a Woman, Stretched
Master model, 1878
Staatliche Museen zu Berlin,
Gipsformerei

On view for visitors to the collection of plaster casts at the Kunstgewerbemuseum were architectural elements such as freezes and capitals, arts and crafts objects (vases, candelabra, ornaments and such) and a small number of figurative sculptures and reliefs. To these objects we must add the school models dedicated to training purposes, including the casts after nature, and additional select art models of the kind mentioned above. The exhibition was therefore a mix of casts taken from works of art and casts taken from nature.[5] The regularly updated museum guidebook *Führer durch das Kunstgewerbemuseum* allows us to follow the spatial staging of the plaster casts on exhibition in detail. The 1885 museum guidebook lists, for instance, in an exhibition room dedicated to ancient art under the title 'Teaching Materials', the entry 'Wand 508 und 521: Abgüsse über Natur von menschlichen und Tier-Körpern — Anatomiefiguren — Verkleinerungen antiker Statuen — Büsten' (Wall 508 and 521: Casts Taken from Human Bodies and the Bodies of Animals — Anatomical Figures — Reduced-Scale Ancient Statues — Busts).[6] Such didactic groupings represented curated ensembles, where art objects dating from different periods were correlated with their potential sources in nature. This inevitably makes one think of Adolph Menzel's studio walls (ill. pp. 147 and 148).

The Kunstgewerbemuseum opened in 1867. Its founding statute announced a 'representative collection of artisanal objects and models in addition to a technical, artistic teaching institute and a library'.[7] Following the cue of the European Arts and Crafts Movement, teaching and training at the institute took equally into consideration 'the education of the public and of artisans', in other words, the refinement of taste of both 'consumers' and 'manufacturers'.[8] Even though by the 1870s the museum had attained the status of an outstanding art-historical collecting institution, its original remit was indeed that of education.

Established along with the museum in 1867, the teaching institute of the Kunstgewerbemuseum offered a curriculum of drawing and modelling that began with drawing from two-dimensional models, then developed to using plaster casts, and finally advanced students worked with nudes and nature (ill. pp. 150–51 and 153). The 'lack of models' which hampered the institute in its first few years, consequentially included a 'lack of three-dimensional models'.[9] By then the Königliche Gipsformerei could look back on a fifty-year history, during which it had accumulated a collection of more than a thousand objects. However, casts primarily taken from ancient statues had in most cases made their way into the Neues Museum or the private collections of the likes of Johann Wolfgang von Goethe and Wilhelm von Humboldt, 'having for the better part been selected for other reasons [...] than for their character as models to be used in drawing and modelling

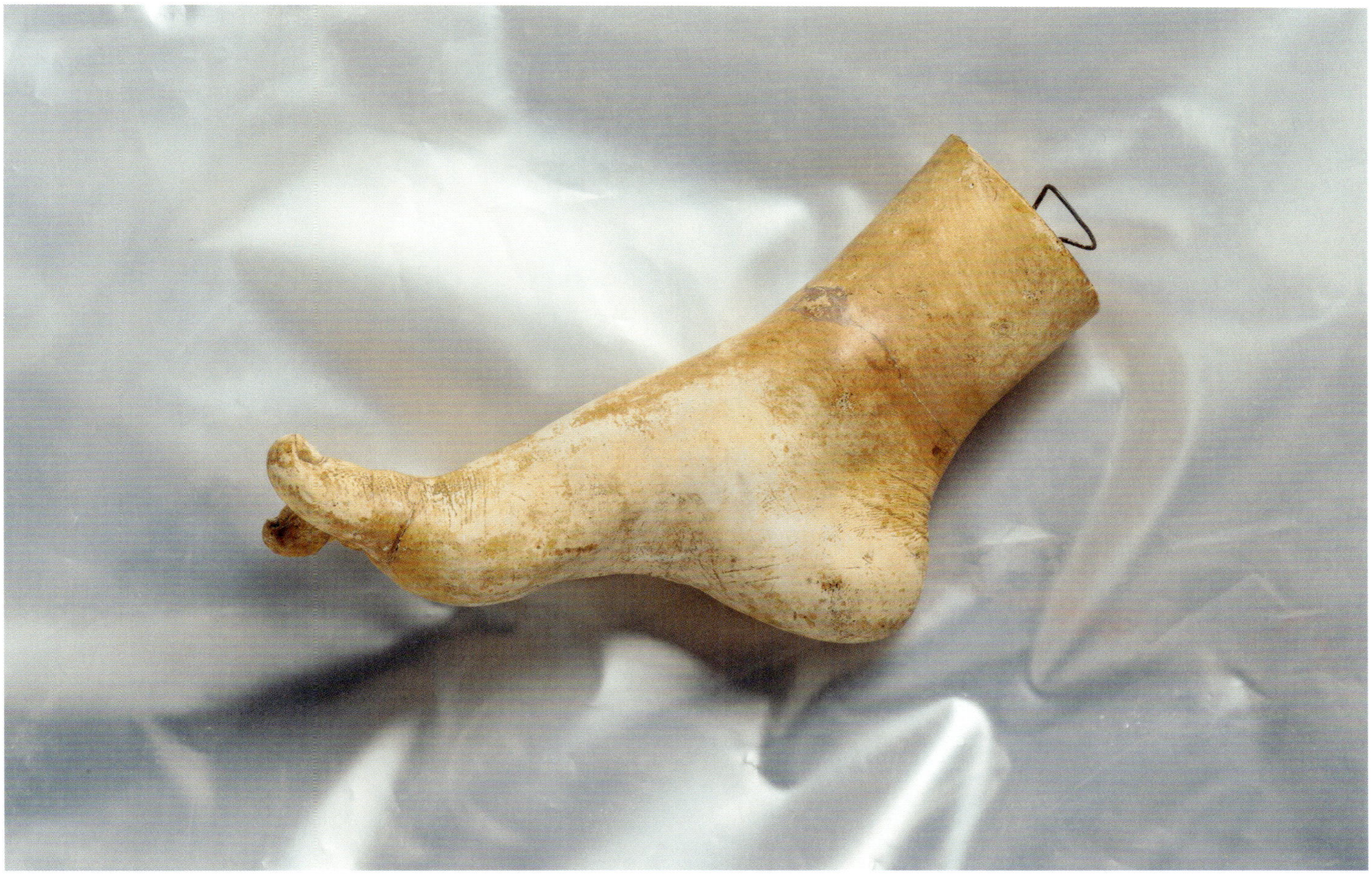

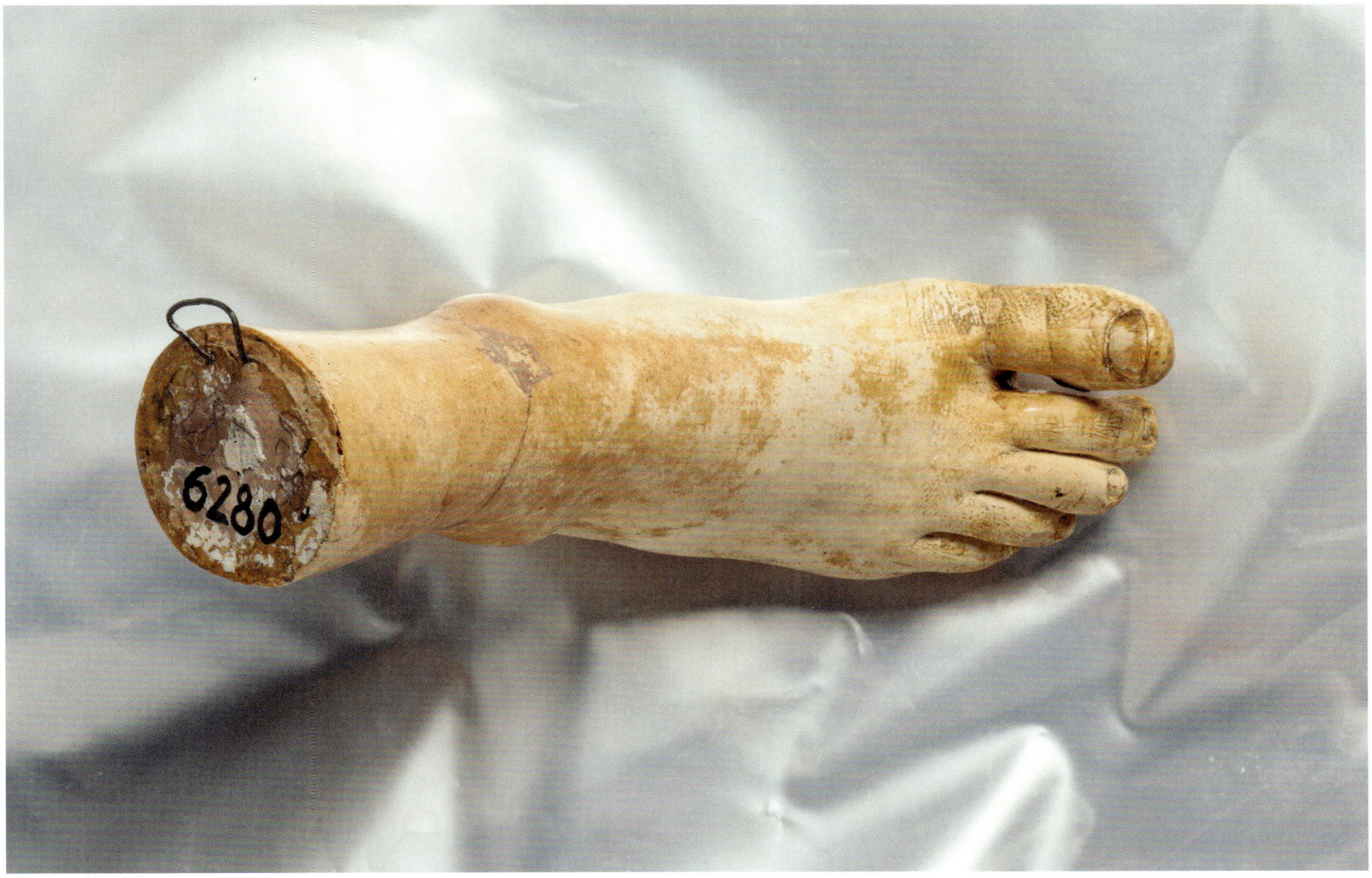
6280

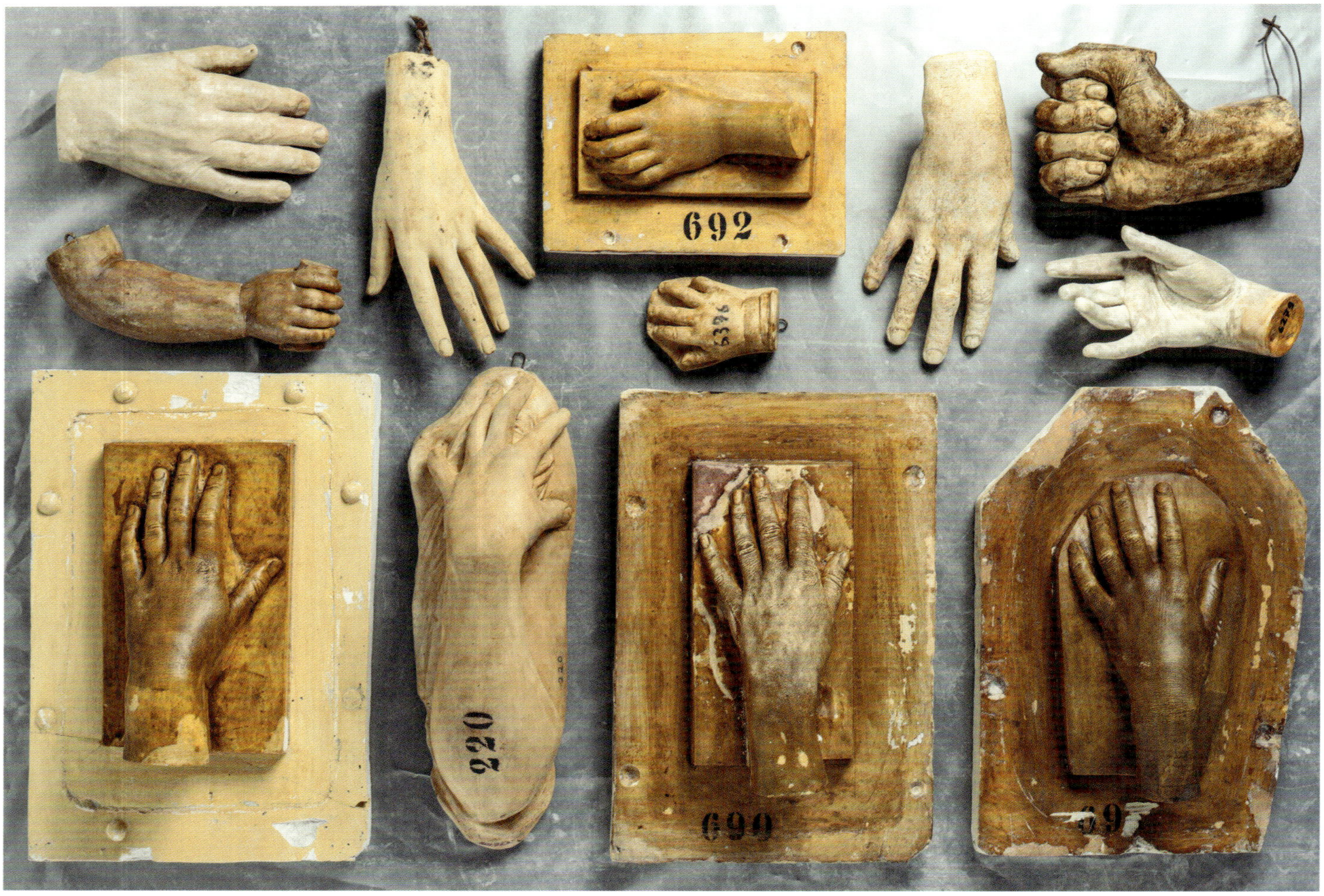

Right Hand of Johann Wolfgang von Goethe
Master model, 1820

Right Arm of a Child
Master model, 1868

Left Hand of a Woman with Outstretched Fingers
Master model, 1878

Left Hand of a Child on a Panel
Master model, 1894

Right Hand of a Child on a Panel
Master model, 1886

Right Hand of Franz Liszt, Playing
Master model, 1953

Right Hand of a Man, Clenched
Master model, 1868

Right Hand of a Woman with Fingers Bent
Master model, 1878

Left Hand of a Woman on a Panel
Master model, 1894

Left Arm of a Woman, Bent with Shoulder Tip, Partially Clothed
Master model, 1871

Left Hand of a Woman on a Panel
Master model, 1894

Left Hand of a Woman on a Panel
Master model, 1894

Staatliche Museen zu Berlin, Gipsformerei

classes'.[10] It was obvious that the teaching institute had to strike out in a new direction if it was to obtain the teaching aids it needed. It therefore established its own foundry, where casts were made to suit the institute's own requirements and for selling to other training institutions. Before the museum's relocation this workshop was housed privately: the sculptor Louis Sussmann-Hellborn (1828–1908), a member of the museum's founding committee, had 'ceded for many years several rooms in his house to the moulding shop and the foundry of the museum without receiving any financial compensation and had himself supervised and directed in person the entire operation of the foundry'.[11]

Even in these early years new sales catalogues were published every few years. Reviewed today, they not only document the incremental growth of the Kunstgewerbemuseum collection of plaster casts for sale, but allow us to approximately date existing objects, as done for *Near Life* and the work list in this book. The first price list from 1868 comprises seventy-five entries. Ten pieces have been identified as having been cast from nature. These include inventory no. 14 ('Male fist, cast from nature', ill. left), no. 32 ('Male back, cast from nature', ill. p. 154) and no. 39 ('Large male hand holding a staff, cast from nature', ill. p. 156).[12] In 1878, shortly before the museum's relocation, the collection already comprised three hundred plaster casts, thirty-five of which had been cast from nature. Dating from 1900, the last sales catalogue lists 789 entries, including 112 extant casts after nature. It must be kept in mind that new additions were not necessarily original or first casts; they might just as well have been reproductions of already existing casts from other collections. The production and the sale of plaster teaching aids were nothing out of the ordinary at that time. Other institutions had also decided to specialise in this area, such as the Gipsgießerei Gebrüder Micheli in Berlin, whose holdings went in the 1930s into the collection of the Gipsformerei, or the Modellir-Anstalt der Königlich-Württembergischen Centralstelle für Gewerbe & Handel in Stuttgart. The illustrated price list of these companies show that comparable or even identical models of body parts were on offer (ill. p. 167).

The sales catalogues also attest to the transfer of teaching aids to the collection of the Gipsformerei. The 1892 and 1895 editions open with the announcement that orders for plaster casts can be 'placed both with the Kgl. Kunstgewerbe-Museum (Berlin SW 11, Prinz-Albrecht-Straße) and the moulding workshop of the Kgl. Museen (Sophie-Charlotten-Straße 17/18)'. This seems to point to a transitional arrangement. A supplement to the catalogue from 1900 notes that orders may be forwarded 'from now on to the General Administration of the Royal Museums, Berlin C., Lustgarten'. Probably the relocation took years to complete, if not an entire decade. Plans for a merger must have been in the pipeline already around 1890, as the floor plans of the new building in Charlottenburg which the Königliche Gipsformerei moved to in 1891 show two areas on the second floor of the building's north wing marked 'Kunstgewerbe-Museum'.[13] The merger of the collections and the relocation of the production and sales departments of the arts and crafts objects were likely to have been effected in 1902 (at the latest). This can be inferred from a series of rather ambitious sales catalogues with photographic illustrations which appeared from the 1890s onwards: the 1893 and 1895 catalogues titled *Abbildungen der käuflichen Gipsabgüsse des Kunstgewerbe-Museums* (An Illustrated Catalogue of the Plaster Casts of the Kunstgewerbe-Museum for Sale) and the 1902 *Abbildungen der in der Formerei der königlichen Museen käuflichen Gipsabgüsse (Schulmodelle des Kunstgewerbemuseums)* (An Illustrated Catalogue of the Plaster Casts on Sale at the Formerei of the Royal Museums [Teaching Aids of the Kunstgewerbemuseum]) (ill. pp. 167 and 168–69). Compared with the 1895 edition, the 1902 catalogue with its thirty-two plates and almost nine hundred entries included a further six plates; increasing the number of objects on offer to almost one hundred — the Königliche Gipsformerei added pieces from its own collection which it deemed most suitable for teaching purposes. With the structures in place at the Gipsformerei, the marketing of the teaching aids acquired a totally new quality.

In the collection of the Gipsformerei, which is primarily comprised of cast works of art and in addition nineteenth-century European death masks and anthropological lifecasts from colonial times, a special role is given to the casts after nature from the collection of the Kunstgewerbemuseum and especially the human lifecasts. There is good reason to call the twenty-nine facial casts of women, men and children, the most interesting pieces in this group (ill. pp. 171–73). It is the excellent state of preservation of these master models, the technical perfection and the stunning lifelikeness of the effigies along with their status as historical 'snapshots', which sets this subgroup apart as something indeed very special. Wrinkled lips, forehead furrows, pores and skin irregularities, as well as eyebrows, eyelashes and hair, sometimes slightly matted but always thrown into relief by a layer of an agent such as grease applied for the moulding procedure, all are marks of an almost excessive realism. The same holds true for some cases of cast textiles, such as headwear or parts of garments. Despite the feature of closed eyes, these casts vibrate with life — just about the last thing one would associate with them is the death mask. At the same time these facial casts have a curiously anachronistic effect: the realistically rendered persons that confront us here are all in fact nineteenth-century Berliners who had their face moulded at the plaster casting workshop of the Kunstgewerbemuseum (or perhaps already at the Königliche Gipsformerei), roughly one hundred and twenty years ago.

Who were these people? Were they students of the Unterrichtsanstalt des Kunstgewerbemuseums, or others associated with it? Or were they professional models, as was common practice in the growing number of life drawing classes? Who, furthermore, were the children? How was it possible to subject them to the stressful procedure of moulding unharmed? How was the relaxed expression on these faces achieved? Were these faces really weighed down with liquid plaster for an estimated fifteen to twenty minutes? Could the answer be found in the use of other materials, other moulding techniques? Questions such as these cannot be definitively answered for the time being.

A single factual clue has survived that points to the author involved here. It might even prove helpful in trying to ascertain the identities of the moulded persons and the exact circumstances under which these casts were made: in the 1894 sales catalogue, numbers 658 to 692, later grouped together on Plate 17 of the illustrated catalogue (ill. pp. 168–69), were listed under the heading 'Körperteile und Köpfe, von Dr. Greeff über Natur geformt' (Casts of Body Parts and Heads Taken from Nature by Dr. Greeff). This seems to provide a clue as to who made the original moulds: we know at least the surname of the man. His first name, however, cannot be established beyond doubt. One trail leads to Professor Richard Greeff (1862–1938), at one point the director of the eye clinic at the Charité and an expert on medical wax casts of exterior diseases of the eye. He commissioned Fritz Kolbow (1873–1946), *mouleur* and freelance teaching aid manufacturer, to create the eye casts — only to sign them with his own name. The proximity between medical casts and plaster casts after nature and the coincidence in time and geography would make a connection between 'Dr. Greeff' and the famous ophthalmologist plausible. What undermines this thesis, however, at least partially, is the fact that a certain Dr. Greeff is also mentioned in the context of anthropological lifecasting as having demonstrated expertise in producing particularly demanding casts (ill. pp. 86–87). It appears that this 'Dr. Greeff' was given diverse moulding commissions by the Königliche Museen. Arguably, this expert and the creator of the teaching aids were one and the same person. Since this probably eliminates Richard Greeff, the search for the creator of these plaster casts must start again from scratch. Future research will need to focus on the reconstruction of other key data. This is particularly urgent for the human lifecasts, since ethical considerations — to emphasise this point once more — are involved.

1 *Das Kunstgewerbe-Museum zu Berlin: Festschrift zur Eröffnung des Museumsgebäudes*, Berlin 1881, p. 40.
2 Ibid., p. 38. Unless otherwise stated, translation by Otmar Binder.
3 Gertrud Platz-Horster, '"... der eigentliche Mittelpunkt aller Sammlungen ...": Die Gipssammlung im Neuen Museum 1855–1916', in: *Museale Spezialisierung und Nationalisierung ab 1830: Das Neue Museum in Berlin im internationalen Kontext*, ed. Ellinoor Bergvelt et al., Berlin 2011, pp. 191–207.
4 References to the types of labelling and the modalities of sales of the available casts can be found in guidebooks of the collection of the Kunstgewerbemuseum, see for example footnote 6.
5 See *Das Kunstgewerbe-Museum zu Berlin: Festschrift*, p. 39.
6 *Führer durch die Sammlung des Kunstgewerbe-Museums*, ed. Generalverwaltung der Königlichen Museen, 6th ed., Berlin 1885, p. 8.
7 *Deutsches Gewerbe-Museum zu Berlin: Führer und Satzungen*, ed. Carl Grunow, Berlin 1867, p. 5.
8 Ibid.
9 *Das Kunstgewerbe-Museum zu Berlin: Festschrift*, p. 53.
10 Ibid. See also Barbara Mundt, *Die deutschen Kunstgewerbemuseen im 19. Jahrhundert*, Studien zur Kunst des neunzehnten Jahrhunderts, 22, Munich 1974, pp. 165–66.
11 *Das Kunstgewerbe-Museum zu Berlin: Festschrift*, p. 54.
12 See *Deutsches Gewerbe-Museum zu Berlin*, Berlin 1867.
13 *Gipsformerei der Königlichen Museen in Charlottenburg*, floor plan no. 2, upper floor, colour lithograph on cardboard, 53.6 × 71.2 cm, Architekturmuseum, TU Berlin, inv. 29215. See also Thomas Schelper, 'Die Gipsformerei in Berlin-Charlottenburg: Von 1891 bis heute', in: *... von gestern bis morgen ... Zur Geschichte der Berliner Gipsabguss-Sammlung(en)*, ed. Nele Schröder and Lorenz Winkler-Horaček, exh. cat. Abguss-Sammlung Antiker Plastik Berlin, Winckelmann-Institut der Humboldt-Universität zu Berlin, Antikensammlung der Staatlichen Museen zu Berlin, Gipsformerei der Staatlichen Museen zu Berlin 13. October 2012–26 May 2013, Rahden 2012, pp. 105–12.

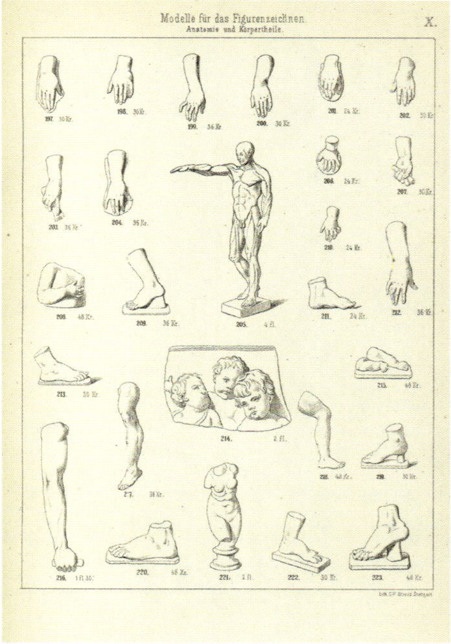

'Modelle für das Figurenzeichnen: Anatomie und Körpertheile' (Models for Figure Drawing: Anatomy and Body Parts)
In: *Illustrirte Preisliste der Gypsmodelle für den Unterricht im Freihandzeichnen, Projectionszeichnen & Modelliren [...]*, 1876, plate X
Staatliche Museen zu Berlin, Kunstbibliothek

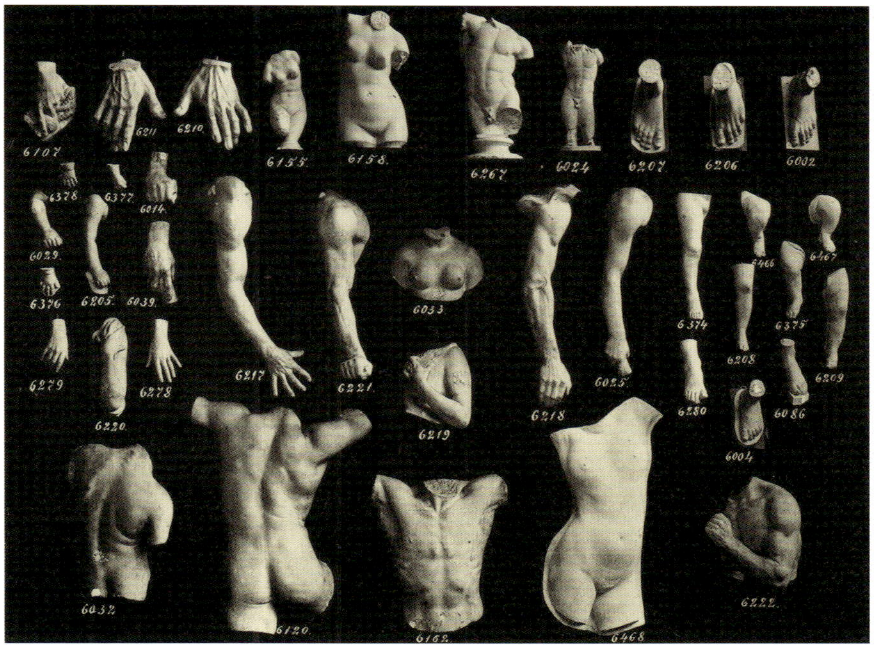

'Körperteile aus der Sammlung der Schulmodelle' (Body Parts from the Collection of Teaching Aids)
In: *Verzeichnis der käuflichen Gipsabgüsse des Kunstgewerbe-Museum (Nachtrag)*, 1893, plate 16
Staatliche Museen zu Berlin, Kunstbibliothek

Tafel 17.

No.		Preis M.	Preis Pf.	No.		Preis M.	Preis Pf.
6658	Weiblicher Rumpf	9	—	6676	Weiblicher Kopf	4	—
6659	Weiblicher Rücken	8	—	6677	desgl.	4	—
6660	Männlicher Kopf	4	—	6678	desgl.	4	—
6661	desgl.	4	50	6679	desgl.	4	—
6662	desgl.	4	—	6680	Knabenkopf	5	—
6663	desgl.	4	—	6681	desgl.	4	—
6664	desgl.	4	—	6682	Mädchenkopf	4	—
6665	desgl.	4	—	6683	desgl.	3	50
6666	desgl.	4	—	6684	Knabenkopf	3	50
6667	desgl.	4	—	6685	Mädchenkopf	3	50
6668	desgl.	4	50	6686	desgl.	3	50
6669	desgl.	4	—	6687	desgl.	3	50
6670	desgl.	4	50	6688	Kinderkopf	3	50
6671	desgl.	4	—	6689	Frauenhand	1	50
6672	Weiblicher Kopf	4	—	6690	desgl.	1	50
6673	desgl.	4	—	6691	desgl.	1	50
6674	desgl.	4	50	6692	Kinderhand	1	50
6675	desgl.	4	—				

'Heads and Body Parts from the Collection of Teaching Aids'
In: *Verzeichnis der in der Formerei der Königlichen Museen käuflichen Gipsabgüsse (Schulmodelle des Kunstgewerbe-Museums)*, 1893, plate 17
Staatliche Museen zu Berlin, Kunstbibliothek

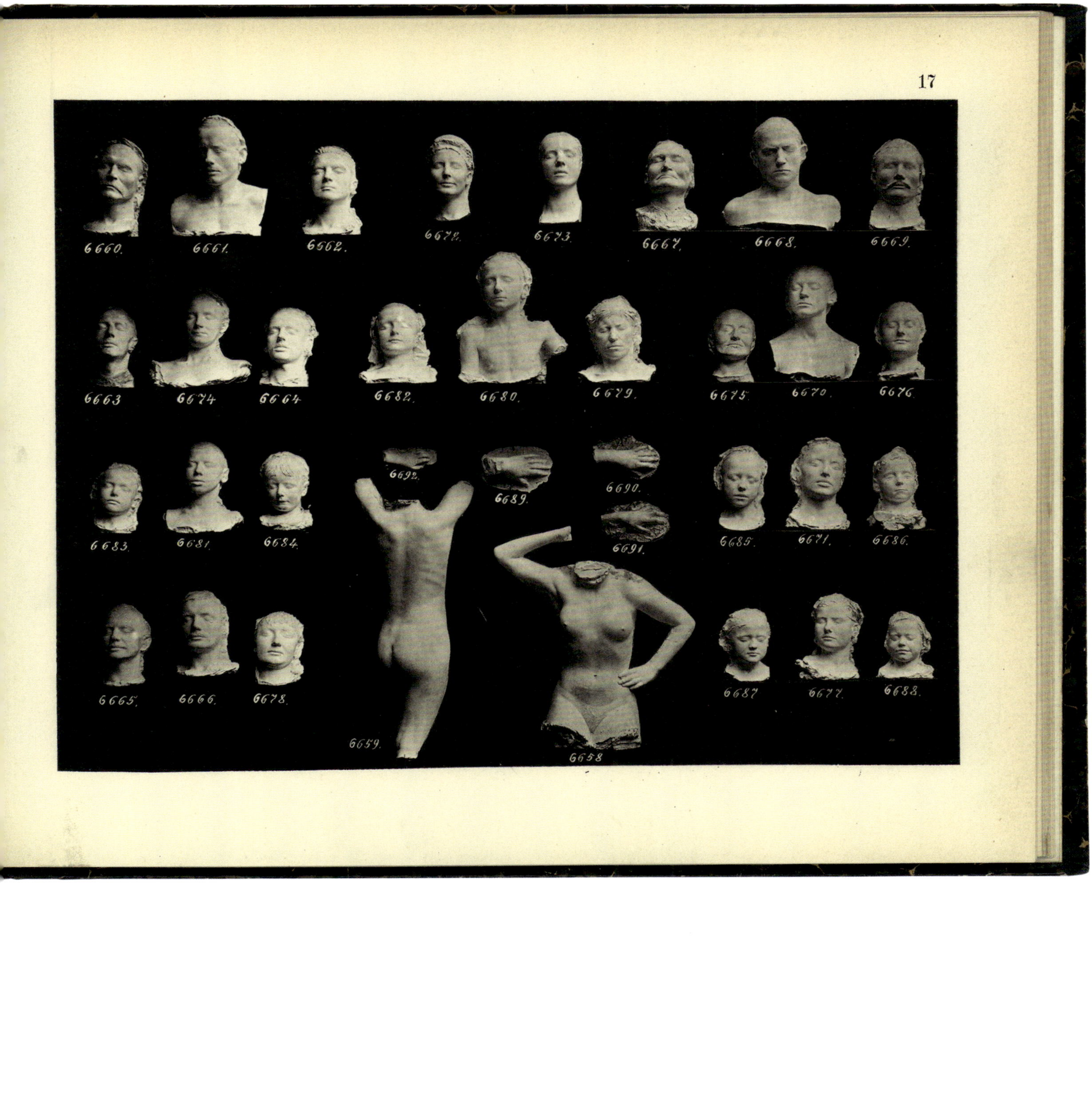

17
6660.
6661.
6562.
6672.
6673.
6667.
6668.
6669.
6663
6674
6664
6682.
6680.
6679.
6675.
6670.
6676.
6683.
6681.
6684.
6692.
6689.
6690.
6691.
6685.
6671.
6686.
6665.
6666.
6678.
6659.
6658
6687
6677.
6688.

Head of a Woman
Master model, 1894
Staatliche Museen zu Berlin, Gipsformerei

» These masks are absolutely extraordinary. The times when the persons who were moulded for these casts were alive are now in the distant past, but face-to-face with the casts you feel surprisingly close to them. There is nothing about the face masks to suggest that these people belonged to the nineteenth century, that they breathed an entirely different air from what we breathe today, and saw and heard entirely different things. Only few clues actually date these masks, such as traces of a lace shirt that was likely fashionable around the turn of last century. The casts are remarkably exact. Presumably they are original casts, which would mean that they are positives derived from the lost moulds of the face. Such casts are distinguished by an especially high degree of authenticity and closeness to the original. For the purposes of reproduction they were transformed into gelatine models, that is, they were worked on a plate and a mother mould was added, which covers the face like a lid. Sprue holes allow the gelatine to be poured in. The result is a negative mould which is used in turn to create new casts. However, the last time these model were used at the Gipsformerei was several decades ago.

Timo Klöppel, artistic plasterer

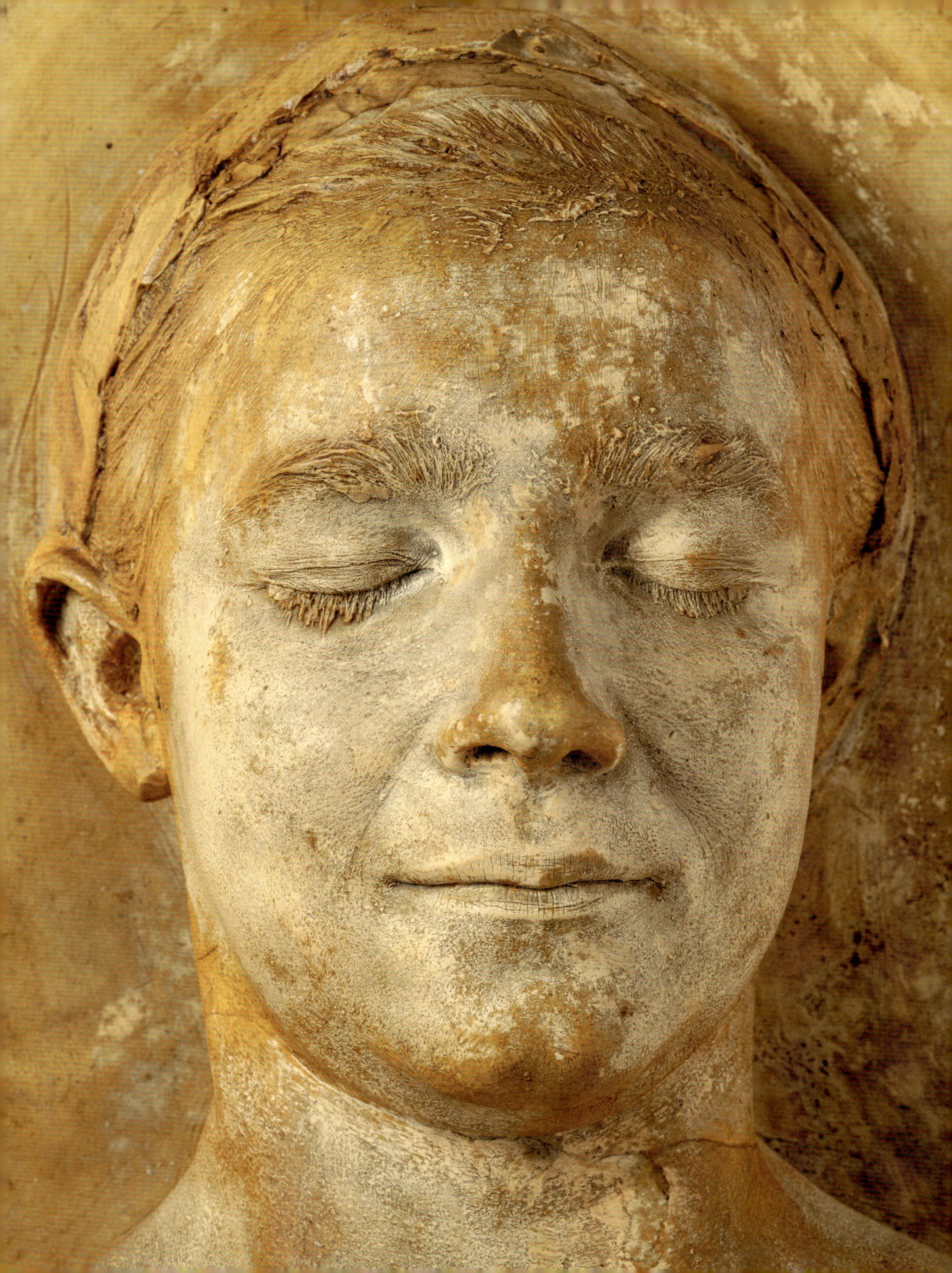

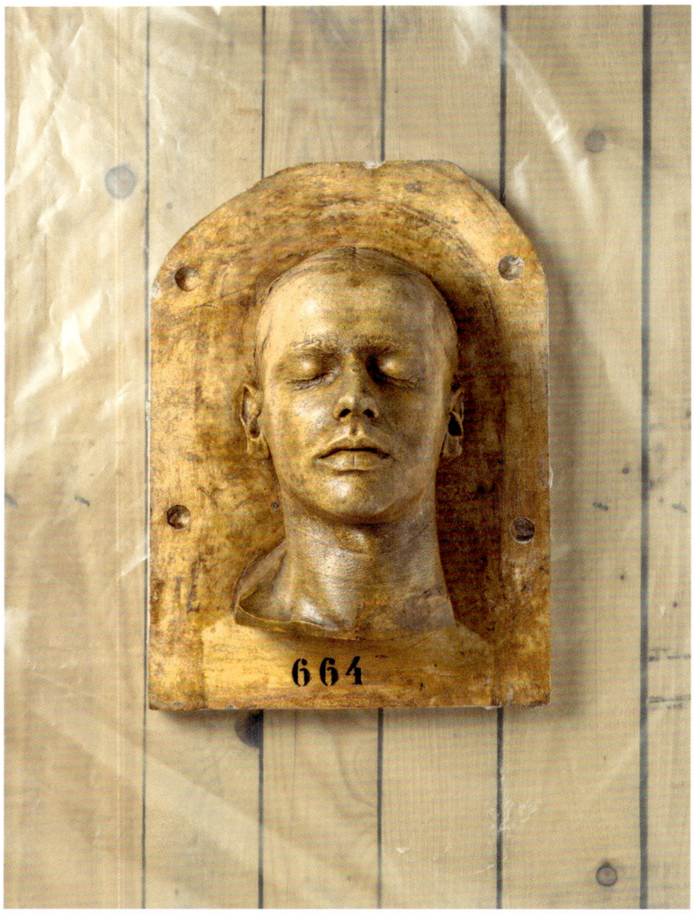

Head of a Man
Master model, 1894
Staatliche Museen zu Berlin,
Gipsformerei

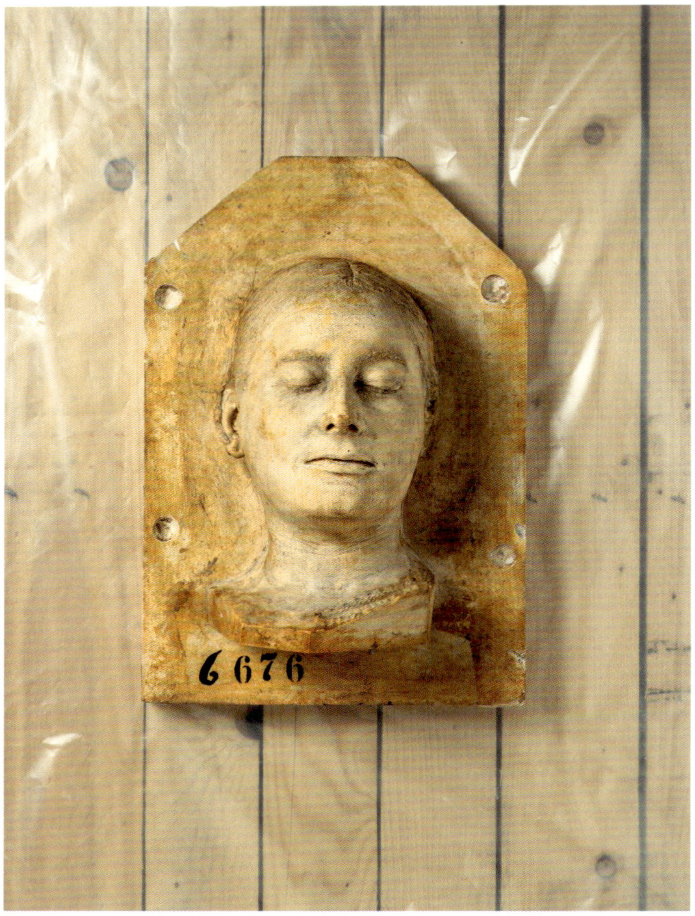

Head of a Woman
Master model, 1894
Staatliche Museen zu Berlin,
Gipsformerei

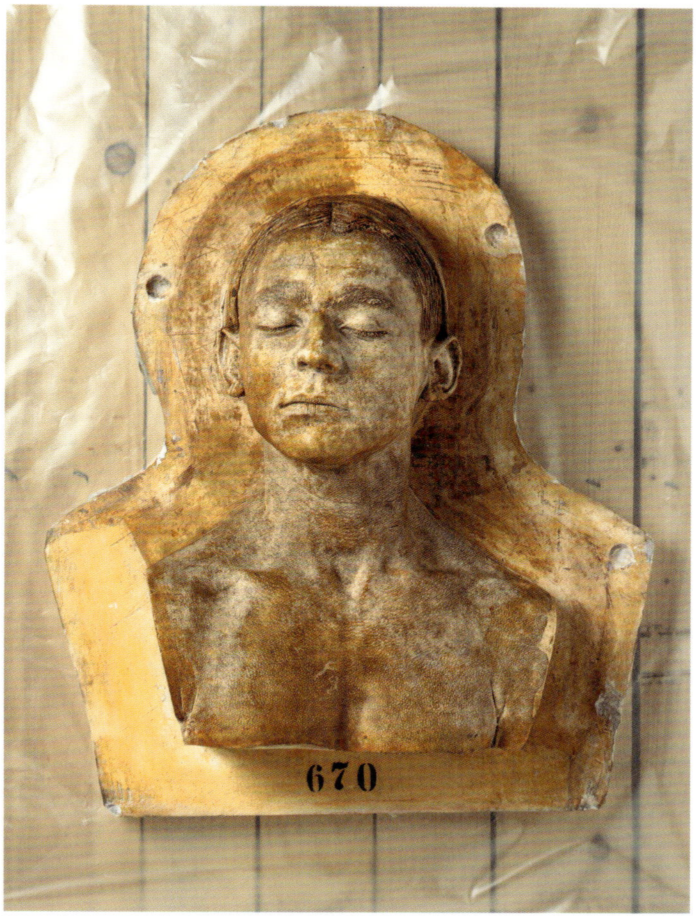

Head of a Man
Master model, 1894
Staatliche Museen zu Berlin,
Gipsformerei

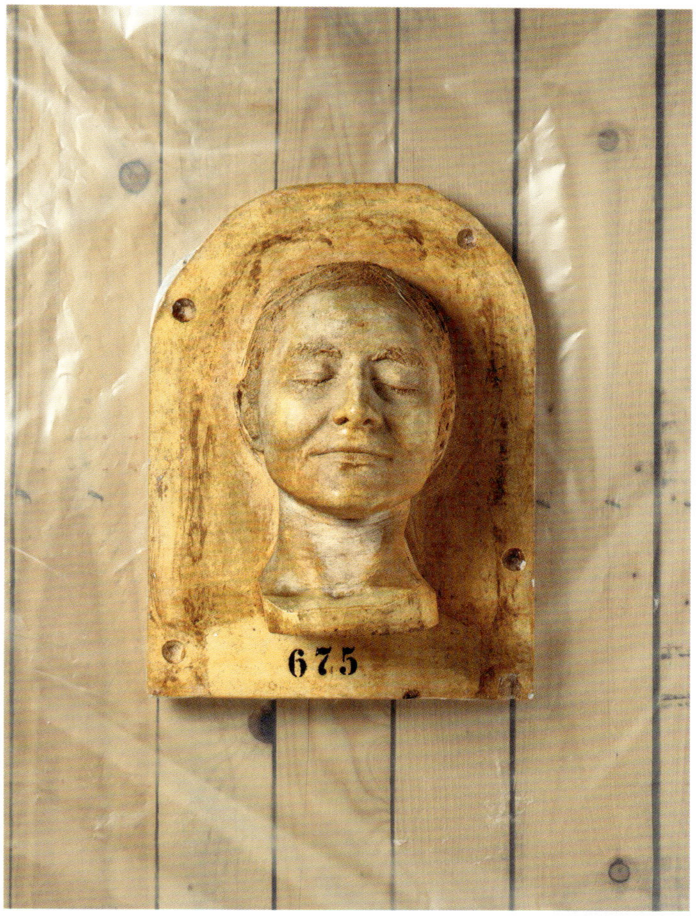

Head of a Woman
Master model, 1894
Staatliche Museen zu Berlin,
Gipsformerei

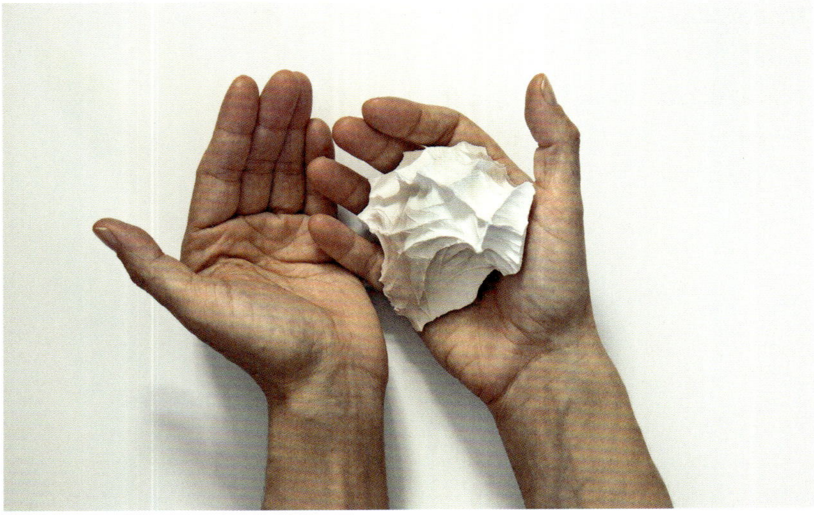

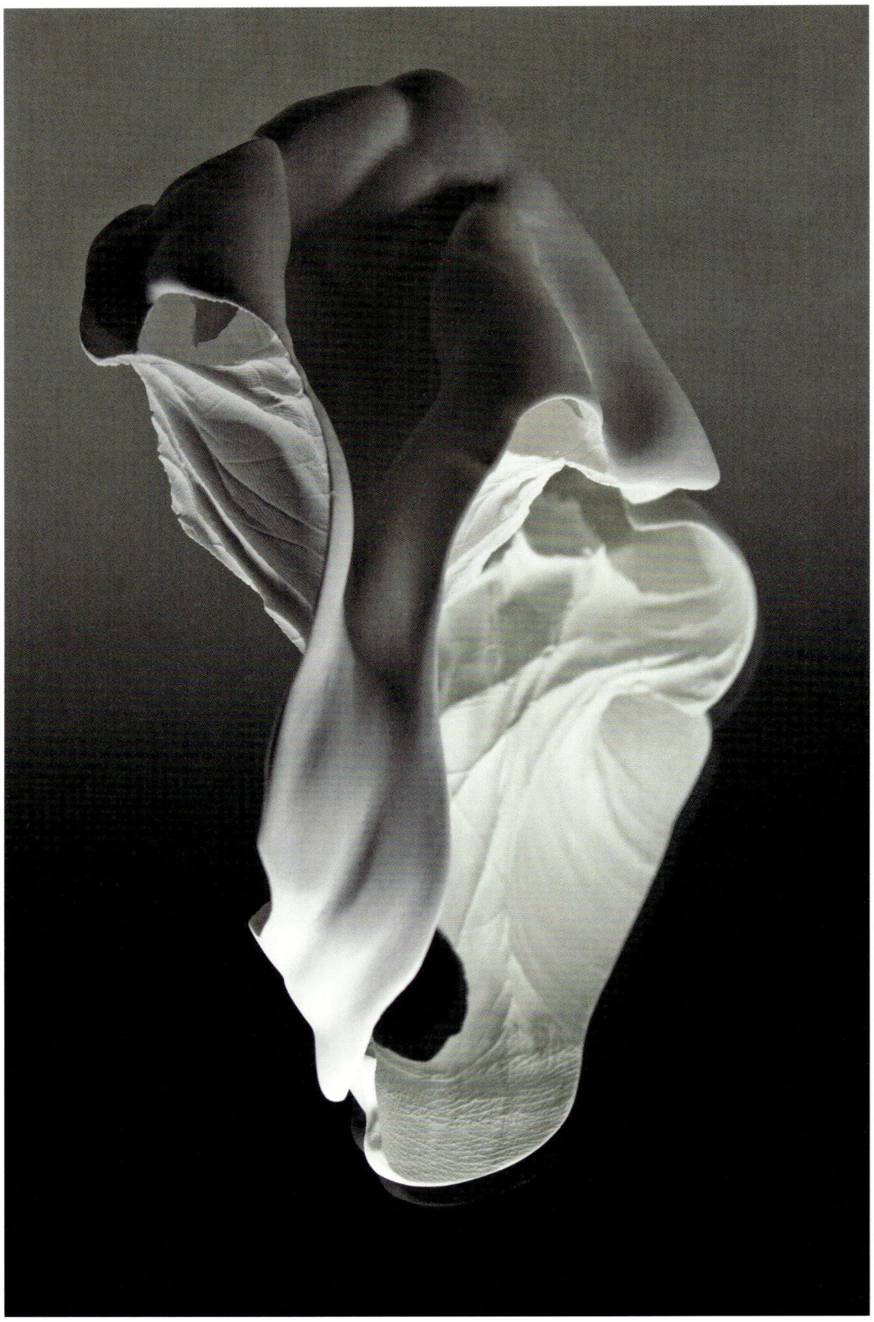

Pauline M'barek
Artefacts, 2014
Courtesy of the artist and Galerie
Thomas Rehbein, Cologne

»   A liquid jet of shiny white plaster pours into the cupped hands, which together constitute the mould. Once filled completely, it exceeds the capacity of the hands, runs and spreads over the tabletop underneath. The hands must now be kept absolutely still while the plaster turns firstly thick, then porous and matt. In the end, it heats up rapidly and solidifies. Then, eventually, first attempts are made to be released from the plaster. Shallow breathing is now required, as any sudden movement may result in spalling, fine hairline cracks or even a rough breakage. Minimal yet relieving movements of the fingers help to prise the skin loose, which increasingly clings to the plaster. Now each individual finger — yellowish-white from being encased in the literally skintight form — slowly extracts itself by pulling, pushing and pressing from the material that has solidified around the hands. In a stroke of luck, only the intact shell of hardened plaster remains. Thus, the plaster cast becomes a highly fragile membrane between a perceptible outside and a perceiving inside. Each downpour of plaster into the open hand is different: a delicate balance between control and chance. It is only by constant repetition that the movements of the body and the movements of matter become synchronised. Plaster as a fluid, amorphous material adapts to the object and the space surrounding it, penetrates into its smallest cavities, and creates a variety of different shapes from the protrusions and indentations, the wrinkles, furrows and grooves of the hand. Some moulds are reminiscent of a glove, while others appear shell-shaped and jagged, requiring translation by the intellect. The invisible volume of space (which, according to Georges Didi-Huberman, comes about blindly, 'in the inaccessible interior of touch', materialises in ever newer two-faced forms.

Pauline M'barek, artist

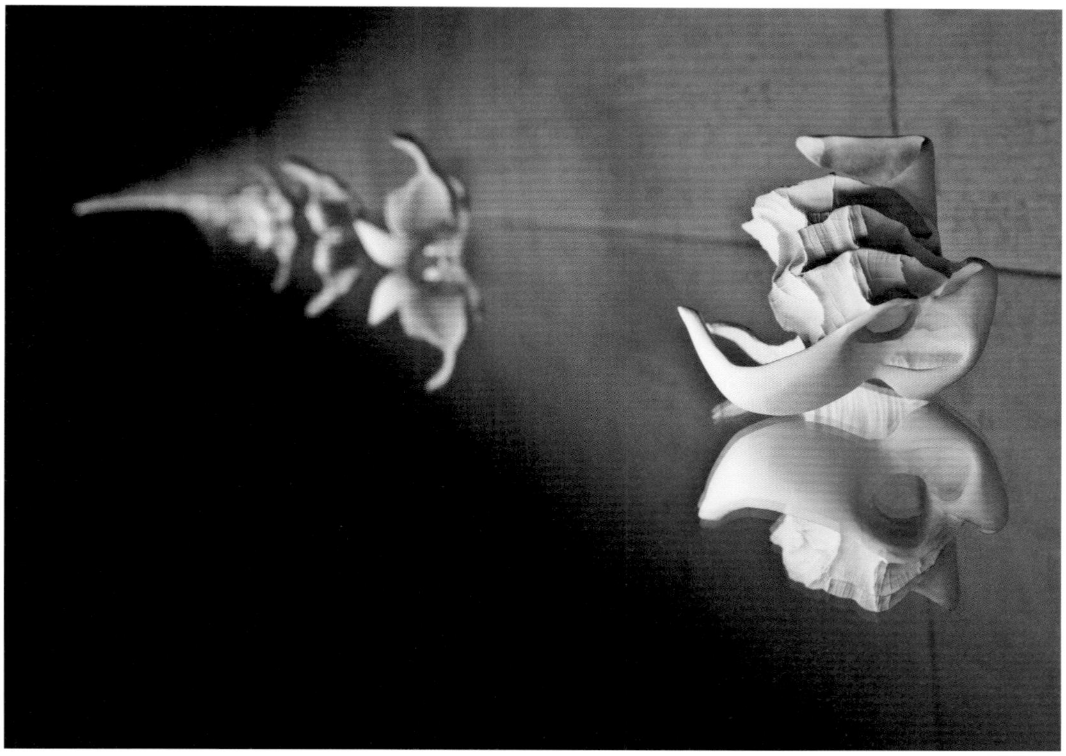

Meeting at the Workshop of Thutmose: Two Casts from Tell el-Amarna

Friederike Seyfried and Nadine Thieme

These two plaster casts (ÄM 21228 and ÄM 21356, ill. p. 180), half relief and in the round, are part of an extraordinary group of casts found in what has become known as the 'Workshop of Thutmose' in Tell el-Amarna. The twenty-three casts (and a few additional fragments) can be dated to 1351–34 BCE; they were found in the same place as the world-famous, painted bust of Queen Nefertiti (ÄM 21300).

The two casts depict the face of a common male person as opposed to the nine other casts of royal effigies in the group, some of which are sculpted in the round. While these are clearly idealised images, presumably moulded on existing stone sculptures, the fourteen face studies of private persons bear all the marks of highly individualised and lifelike renderings. Ludwig Borchardt (1863–1938), who excavated the Thutmose workshop, was the first to realise that these plaster casts necessitated rethinking ancient Egyptian art history. It is not surprising then that a great number of scientific papers and articles have focused on these works since. The most groundbreaking insights, however, have come from the latest research findings of a joint project by the Ägyptisches Museum, Staatliche Museen zu Berlin and the Imaging Science Institute (ISI), a cooperation of Charité — Universitätsmedizin, Berlin and Siemens Healthcare. This project in 2014 involved generating high-resolution computed tomographic data sets of the 'Workshop of Thutmose' plaster casts. The tomograms provide information on the internal structure of the stucco objects, which enables making hypotheses about the production process and assessments for restoration. The data also provided the possibility of producing three-dimensional measurements and analysis. The reduction of the surface differences of colour and shadows, the capability to virtually rotate the object in all directions and the possibility of virtual post-editing are great advantages for viewing, documenting and analysing the facial characteristics of the casts. All this is exemplarily shown in the objects ÄM 21228 and ÄM 21356, as the analysis has proven that these two casts were taken from the same person.

The above image on page 177 shows the perfect match in the facial profiles of the two objects. It also reveals what facial characteristics have been left out in ÄM 21356: the hairline, jaw angle, ears and the base of the neck are only rendered in object ÄM 21228.

As can be seen in the image on page 177, the facial traits are rendered in identical form, right down to the smallest detail in both casts. These details include: prominent mouth with deep mentolabial fold, sagging left corner of the mouth, asymmetrical nose with depressed left nostril, forehead furrows, laterally inclined eyebrows and asymmetrical cheeks. Both casts not only render the same person, but they also show that they are part of the same casting process. One question, however, is whether these are two casts of the same original yet differ in quality, or if the two objects were produced one after another and therefore represent different stages of the casting process.

The enlarged details on page 178 (top) show quite clearly that the two objects differ in the top regions of the face and to a lesser degree in other parts of object ÄM 21356 which display wave lines of crests and troughs: the lower left eyelid and less distinctly

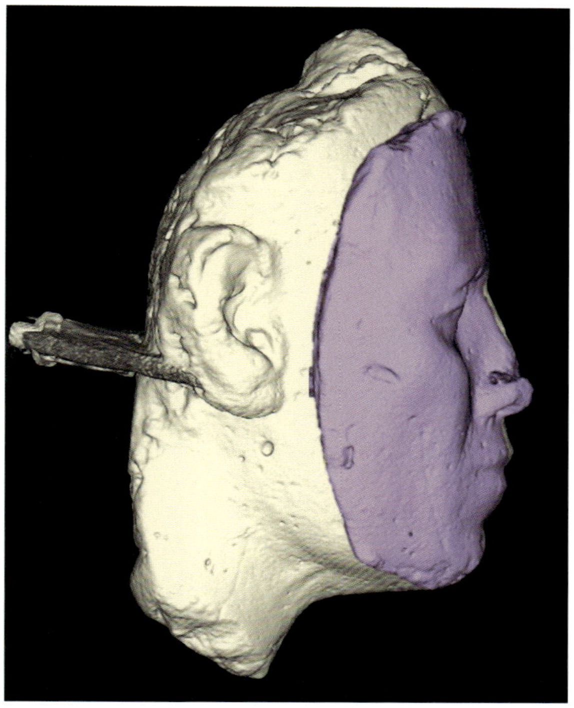

Lateral superimposition of the volume-rendering reconstruction of the object profiles: ÄM 21228 (white) and ÄM 21356 (purple)

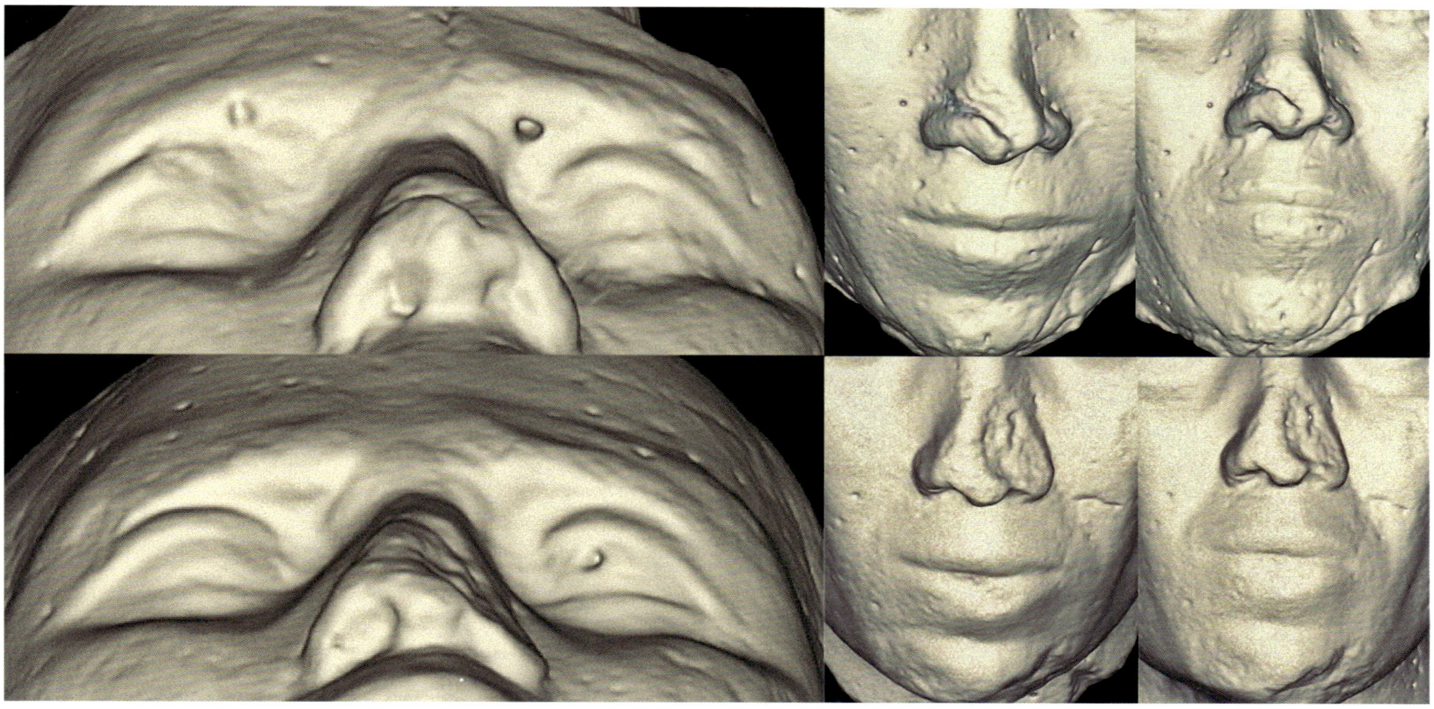

Rendering of details, top: ÄM 21356; bottom: ÄM 21228. Left: Enlarged details of the eye area with nose and forehead wrinkles seen from slightly below. Centre and right: Details of the mouth and nose area and nasolabial fold seen from slightly above and directly in front.

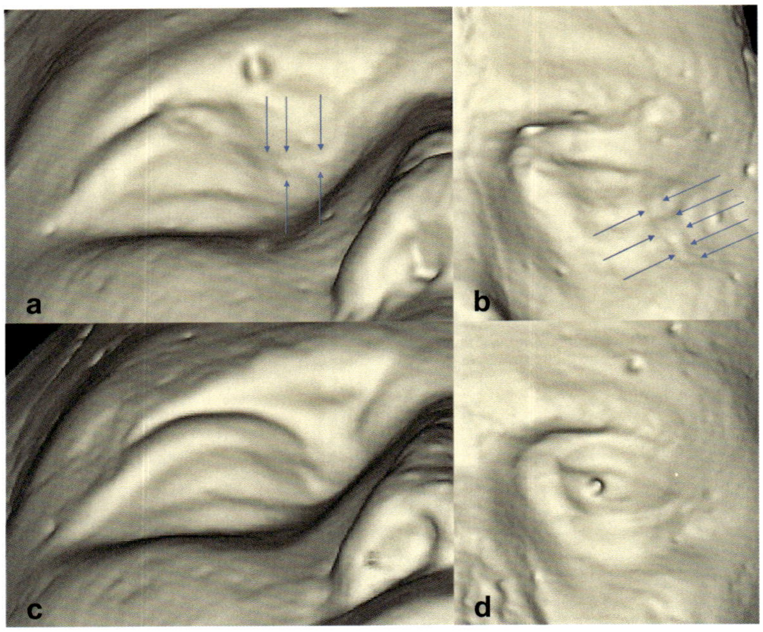

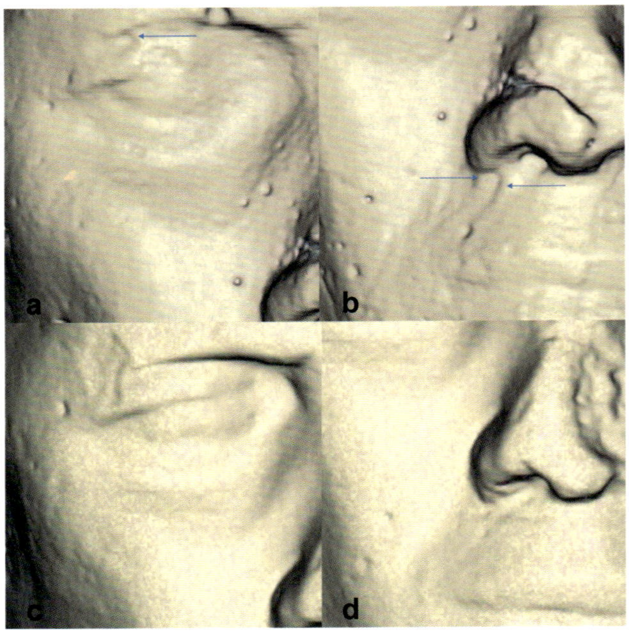

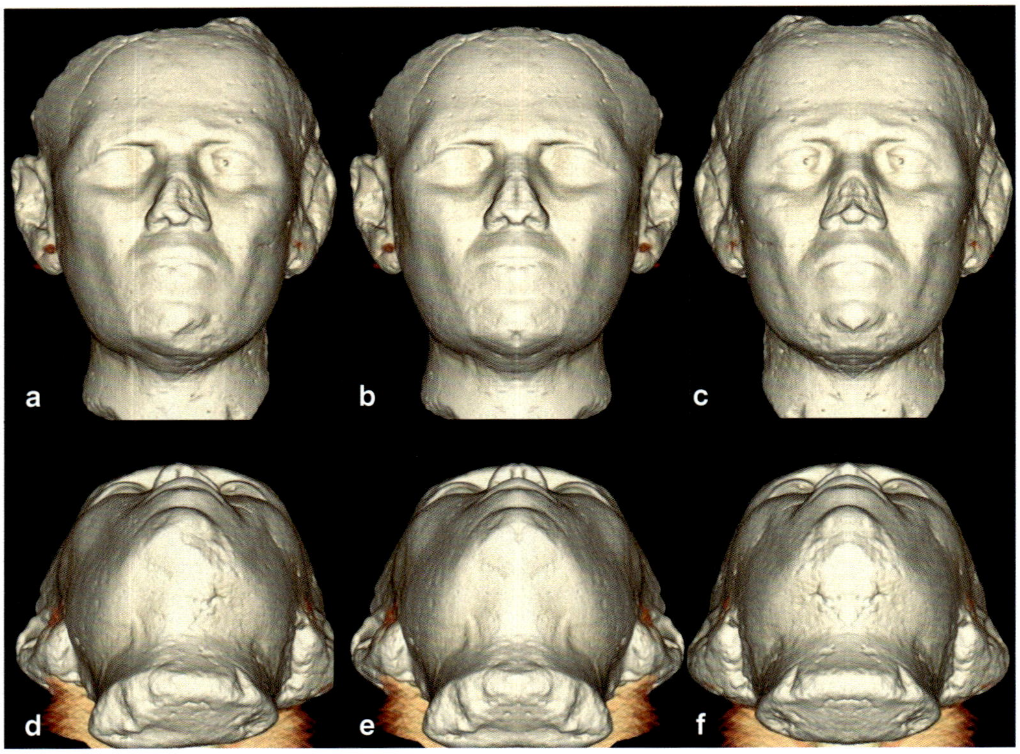

Enlarged details of the eye area
Top (a, b): ÄM 21356
Bottom (c, d): ÄM 21228

Enlarged details of the eyebrow area
and the area below the right nostril
Top (a, b): ÄM 21356
Bottom (c, d): ÄM 21228

ÄM 21228
Top: a) frontal view; b) mirror image of the right half of the face; c) mirror image of the left half of the face of the reconstruction
Bottom: d) view from below; e) mirror image of the right; f) left half of the face

the closed upper right eyelid as well as the regions above the right eyebrow and below the base of the right nostril. These markings are reminiscent of a separating piece of cloth spread on top of the original to be moulded. This leads to the tentative conclusion that ÄM 21356 was the result of a mould taken from ÄM 21228.

Facial asymmetry is not only a highly recognised characteristic, it is also an interesting phenomenon from a medical point of view. Apart from the congenital physiological asymmetry common to all faces — no face displays perfect axial symmetry — this face could point to minor nerve damage on the left side, a so-called central facial palsy. A further symptom of this weakness of the buccal branch of the facial nerve, over and above the slightly sagging corner of the mouth, could be how the labionasal fold flattens or deviates on the affected side towards the middle of the face. This is opposed to a peripheral facial nerve palsy, which would affect the muscles of the eye and flatten the furrows on the forehead.

The findings presented here do not allow for definitive conclusions to be made about the production process of the plaster casts as their examination and analysis are still a work in progress. The same is true of the attribution of the two plaster casts to a person already known from statues or sculptures. This is not yet possible, but is part of our current focus of research.

As regards to the production process of ancient plaster casts, which sculptors at the time needed for producing sculptural portraits of high-ranking dignitaries executed in stone (such as funerary statues made from the stone of the tombs themselves), two possible theories are currently under consideration: shaping clay or wax to produce a rough draft of the effigy, which the person in question would have had to model for, or taking a mould in the form of a life mask. The latter method would have required several intermediate interventions, since life masks necessitate having closed eyes, whereas all the el-Amarna plaster casts boast 'open eyes'. It is hoped that the ongoing research will yield definitive results in the near future, which will further our understanding of the production process of these unique plaster casts as well as shed new light on this remarkable group of finds.

Further reading:

Ludwig Borchardt and Herbert Ricke, *Die Wohnhäuser in Tell el-Amarna*, Wissenschaftliche Veröffentlichungen der Deutschen Orient-Gesellschaft 91, Berlin 1980.

Florian Reither, 'Die Stuckbildnisse aus Tell el-Amarna und ihr "Realismus"' (unpublished MA thesis, Göttingen 1995).

Günther Roeder, 'Lebensgroße Tonmodelle aus einer altägyptischen Bildhauerwerkstatt', *Jahrbuch der Preußischen Kunstsammlungen* 62 (1941), pp. 145–70.

Friederike Seyfried, 'The Workshop Complex of Thutmosis', in: *In the Light of Amarna. 100 Years of the Nefertiti Discovery*, ed. Seyfried, exh. cat. Ägyptisches Museum und Papyrussammlung, Staatliche Museen zu Berlin – Preußischer Kulturbesitz 7 December 2012–4 August 2013, Petersberg 2012, pp. 170–86.

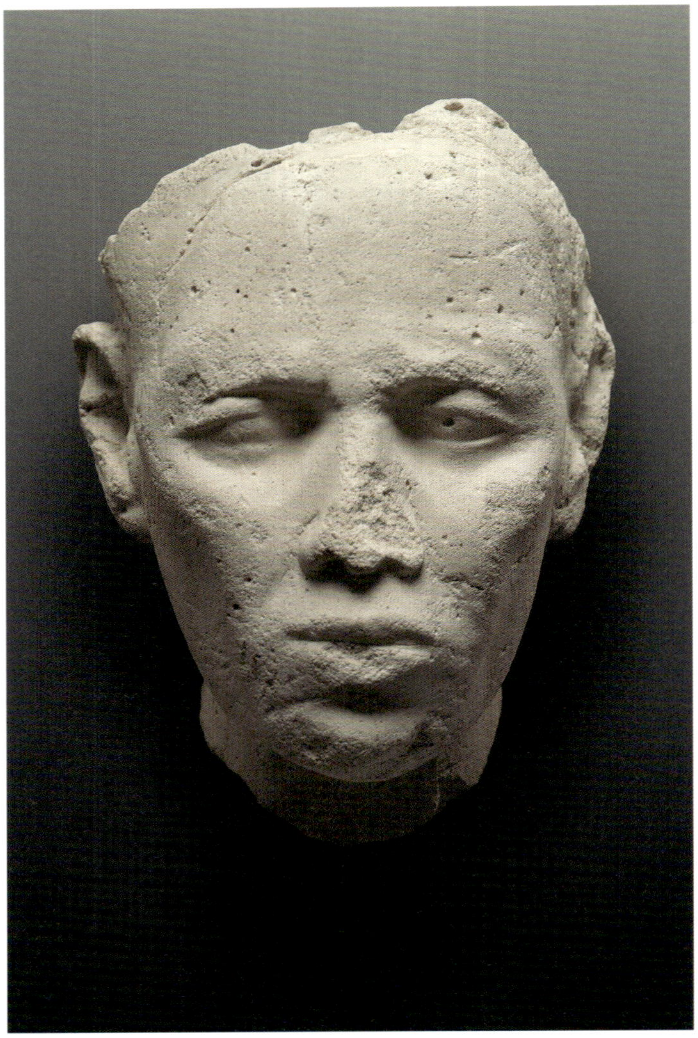

Plaster Model of Head of a Man,
New Kingdom, 18th Dynasty,
ca. 1340 BCE
Gypsum stucco
Staatliche Museen zu Berlin,
Ägyptisches Museum und
Papyrussammlung, ÄM 21228

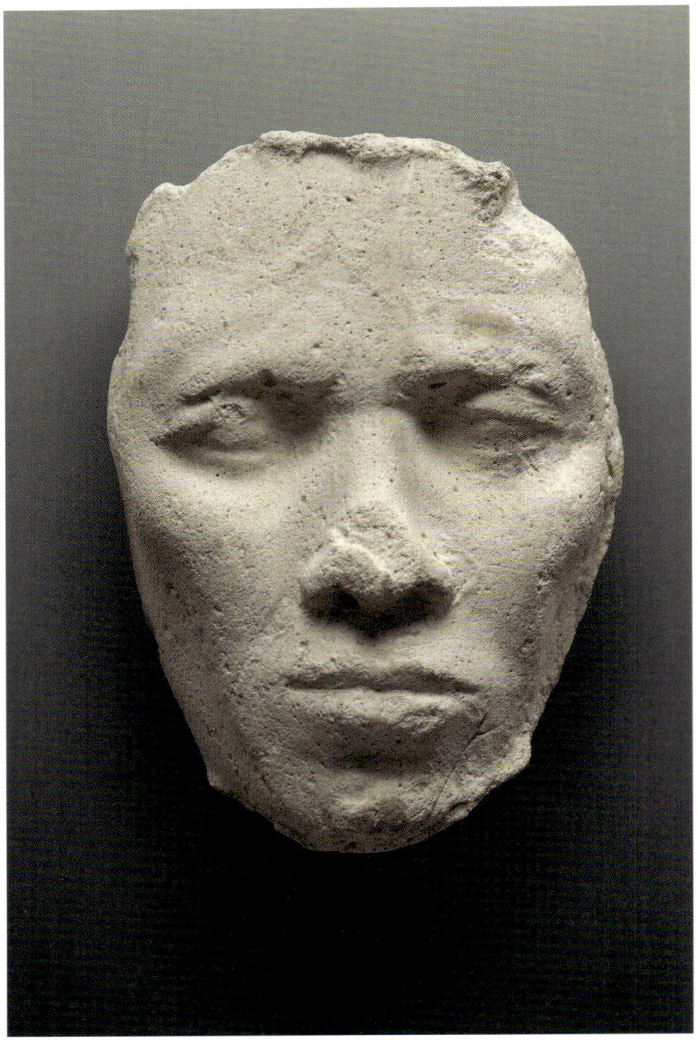

Plaster Model of Head of a Man,
New Kingdom, 18th Dynasty,
ca. 1340 BCE
Gypsum stucco
Staatliche Museen zu Berlin,
Ägyptisches Museum und
Papyrussammlung, ÄM 21356

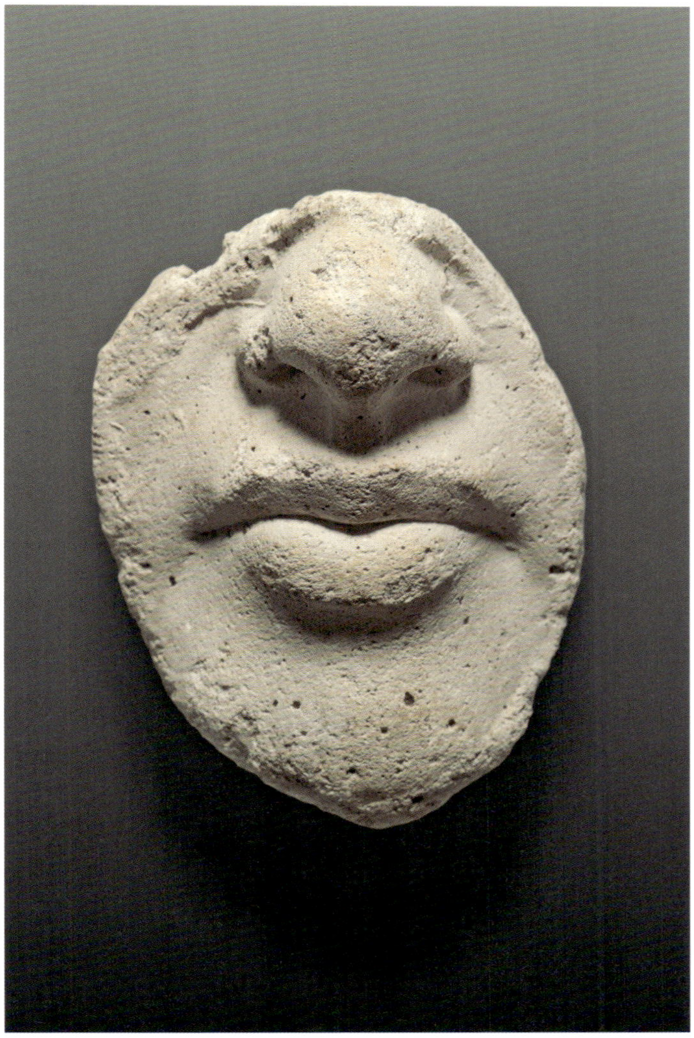

Cast of the Lower Half of a Face, Detail,
New Kingdom, 18th Dynasty,
ca. 1340 BCE
Staatliche Museen zu Berlin,
Ägyptisches Museum und
Papyrussammlung, ÄM 21235

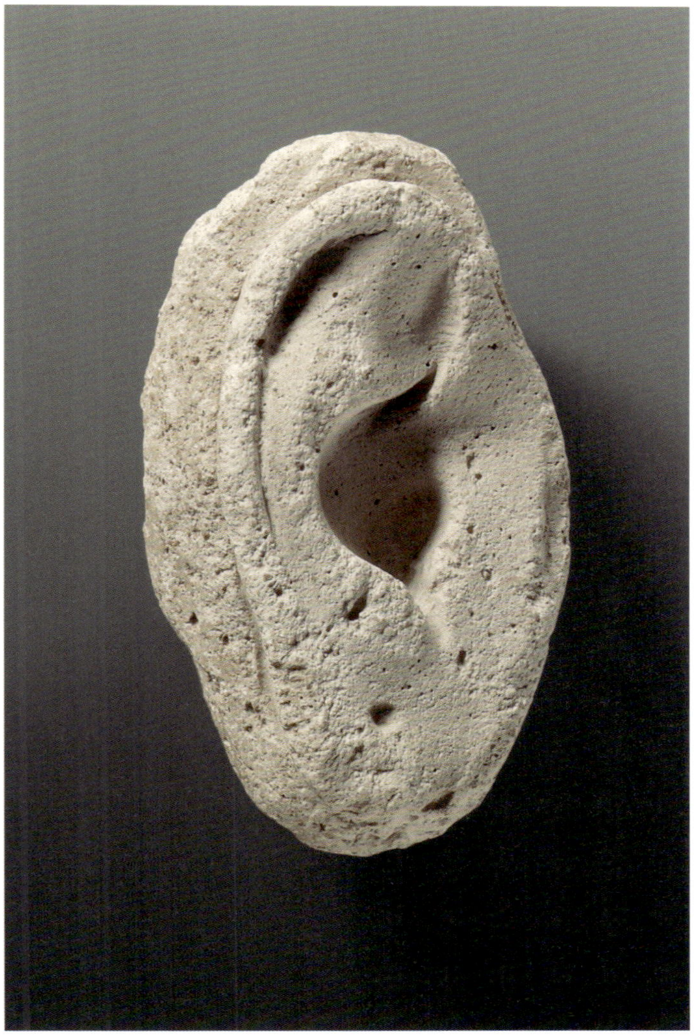

Plaster Model of a Right Human Ear,
New Kingdom, 18th Dynasty,
ca. 1340 BCE
Staatliche Museen zu Berlin,
Ägyptisches Museum und
Papyrussammlung, ÄM 21234

Terra incognita: Lifecasts in Antiquity

Manuel Flecker

'The first person who modelled a likeness in plaster of a human being from the living face itself, and established the method of pouring wax into this plaster mould and then making final corrections on the wax cast, was Lysistratus of Sicyon, the brother of Lysippus, of whom we have spoken. Indeed he introduced the practice of giving likenesses, the object aimed at previously having been to make as handsome a face as possible. The same artist also invented taking casts from statues, and this method advanced to such an extent that no figures or statues were made without a clay model.'[1] These are the words of Pliny the Elder, written in a section of his *Natural History* devoted to clay sculpture and referring to the brother of the famous late classical sculptor Lysippus, Lysistratus, of whom little else is known. While the passage is not without its issues,[2] the point Pliny makes is quite clear. He marks the transition from freely created clay sculptures to those made with moulds.[3] Lysistratus is said to have pioneered the process of plaster casting (*formam gypsi*), both of the human face and of statues. Regardless of the impact this 'invention' may have had on the development of Greek portraiture,[4] it is the casts taken from the human body that are underlined here. It also confirms that mould making during Pliny's time was widely practised or at least well-known, for his statement about this procedure is without a hint of anything unusual or far-fetched. It is all the more surprising, then, that the passage quoted above is — at least to my knowledge — the only record from antiquity which explicitly mentions the practice of taking moulds from the human body. This is odd, to say the least, in light of the well-documented, enormous scale on which technical reproduction was practised in antiquity.[5] Especially making clay and plaster casts of a wide variety of objects had been a common practice from the classical period onward. Writing in the late fourth century BCE, Theophrastus lists the sites where plaster is found, describes the substance's properties and identifies the moulding of objects as its main utilisation: 'It seems to be far superior to other earths for taking impressions, and it is generally used for this purpose, especially in Greece.'[6]

The plaster casts were used in a wide range of contexts for many different purposes well into late antiquity. Their most common use was in the production of sculptures, as it made the widespread distribution of copies possible. What is more difficult to determine is the extent to which plaster casts played an additional role as autonomous 'works of art'.[7] In the Roman era especially, there are many recorded cases where plaster casts were applied to the artisanal reproduction of monuments of all sizes. Today, it is enough to point to the finds made at Baiae, on north-west shore of the Gulf of Naples, and Begram, Afghanistan. In the ancient site of Baiae, more than four hundred fragments of plaster casts of famous statues dating from the classical and Hellenistic periods were discovered;[8] and a hoard of casts of ancient craftwork (mostly metal tableware decorated with reliefs) was found in Begram.[9]

The search for ancient moulds taken directly from the human body results only in the death mask. The pattern of archaeological finds suggests that the tradition of taking death masks — at least in Roman times — was common in various parts of the Mediterranean region. Most of the best known examples have been

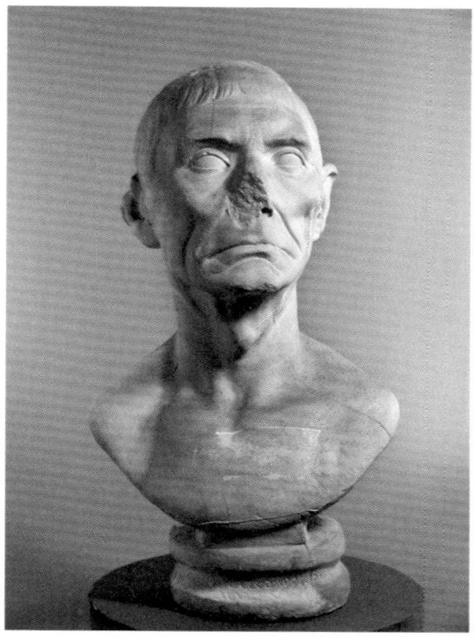

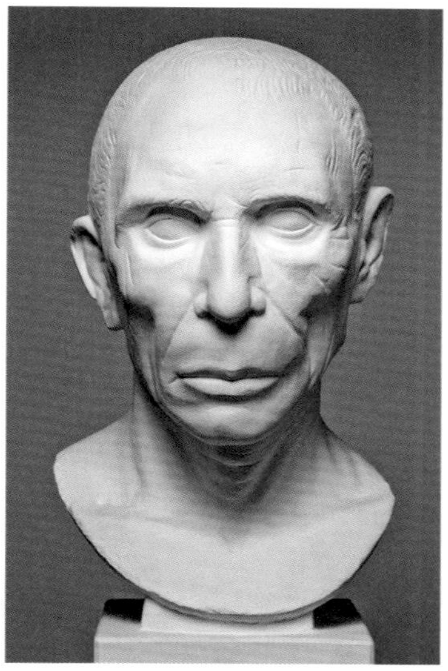

Plaster Cast after the Portrait Bust of Marcus Vilonius Varro, plaster, height 47 cm
(Original: Roman, ca. 98–117 BCE, Ny Carlsberg Glyptotek, Copenhagen)
Antikenmuseum der Universität Leipzig, Abgusssammlung, A 1253/G 231

Plaster Cast of the so-called Old Man from Dresden, 1990, plaster, height 34.5 cm
(Original: Augustan, Dresden, Skulpturensammlung)
Archäologisches Institut der Universität Göttingen, A 1600

found in tombs from the second and third centuries CE.[10] The tomb offered these fragile plaster objects protection and ensured their preservation. There is no easy answer to the question of whether death masks were in use throughout antiquity. Their prevalence in the middle of the Roman Empire is arguably due to a change in burial customs and votive rites rather than to chronological distribution. References to death masks can also be found in literary sources, such as Quintilian's *Institutio Oratoria* from the first century CE. It states: 'Another advocate, defending a woman, thought it a good idea to display a portrait of her husband; this repeatedly raised a laugh [...] and when it was finally put on display it proved so hideous (it was the old man's death mask) that it ruined also the effect of the preceding speech.'[11] Even though this is still a matter of controversy in archaeological research, a mere glance at Roman portraiture suffices in showing that death masks were repeatedly used as the basis for posthumous portraits. Especially in the late Republic and the early Imperial period of the Roman Empire, face casts taken from living persons seem to have been used in a number of cases to create portrait busts.[12]

Facial moulds taken from individuals, both living and dead, have been linked to the Roman *imagines maiorum*, the ancestral wax masks of Rome's leading families to which ancient sources ascribed exceptional faithfulness.[13] Suggestive as it is, this link has, however, not been established beyond doubt by the written sources. It was not least owing to the use of wax that let the imagines achieve their stunning lifelikeness. This is convincingly shown by the only wax effigy (though not an ancestral portrait) left from antiquity. It was found in a tomb in Cumae, a town located north-west of Naples, and is dated to around 300 CE. Complete with hair and glass eyes, it is remarkably alluring.[14] The lucid wax and the sophisticated use of materials contribute to its extraordinary lifelikeness. Whether the mask is based on a facial mould remains uncertain in spite of its marked individuality.

While it has been possible in the case of individual portraits to prove the use of facial moulds, the situation is much less conclusive with regard to ancient statuary. This is due to a lack of sustained study, for which two reasons can be cited. First, we lack direct evidence of the lifecasts and, secondly, the art discourse as it has developed since the Renaissance has contributed to discrediting mechanical reproduction. Extending from the Renaissance to the twentieth century, this dismissal of the cast as a tool for artistic production is still — even if only implicitly — the basis for evaluating ancient sculptures.[15]

It is highly significant, then, that the first real attempt to establish a link between the cast after nature and

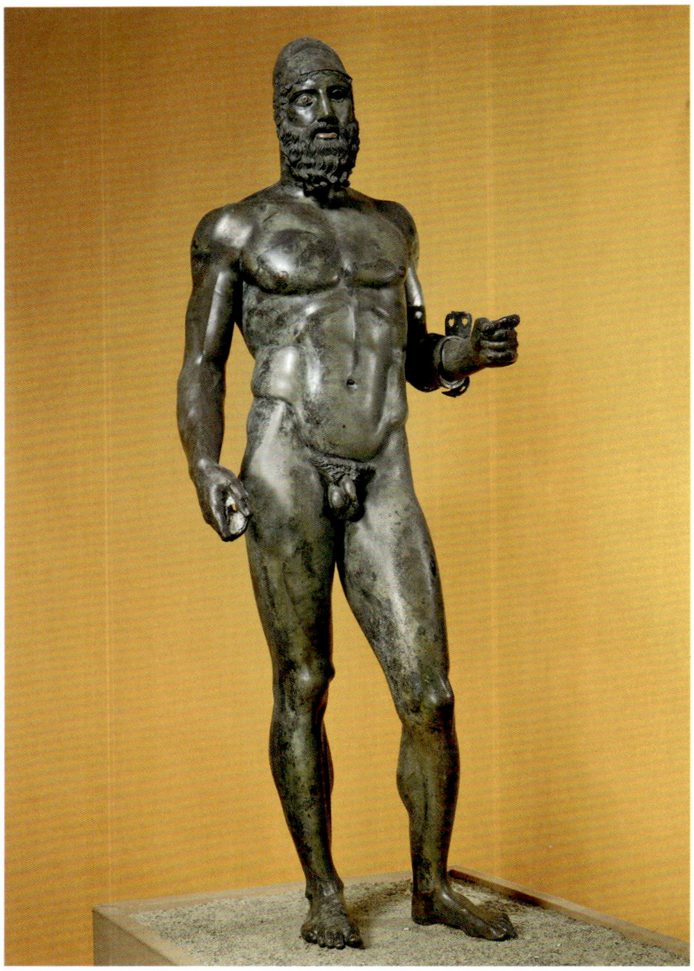
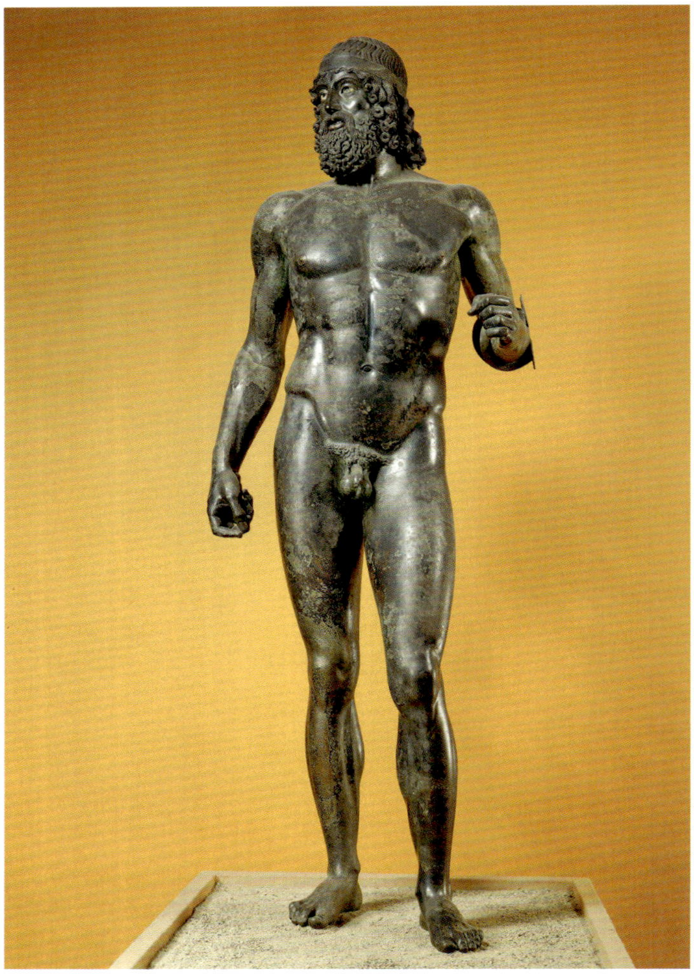

Riace Bronzes, 460–450 BCE
Bronze, height: 197 and 198 cm
Museo Nazionale della
Magna Grecia in Reggio Calabria,
12801 and 12802

the work of sculpture was recently made by the English sculptor Nigel Konstam.[16] He claims that both the torso and the extremities of the two early classical bronze Riace warriors discovered near Reggio Calabria, southern Italy, in 1972 were based on lifecasts (ill. left). His speculations come from an examination of the feet of the two bronze statues, which are decidedly elaborate. This sets the statues apart from the vast majority of comparable works of art. In addition to the naturalistic rendering of the toes, the feet have been modelled in a way that suggests they bear unequal weight. Even though this mere observation is insufficient to warrant the conclusion that the entire statues were based on lifecasts, let alone to confirm that the use of moulds was widespread at this time, Konstam's approach seems to point in the right direction: close-up autopsy and the identification of telltale details will be needed to supply proof of the use of lifecasts.

Yet, Konstam's theory has to date been met with little reception or evaluation. Only Rune Frederiksen has referred to it recently, calling the use of casts as early as the fifth century BCE as 'hardly surprising'.[17] In view of the large-scale technical reproduction assumed in antiquity and the broad range of objects manufactured by casting, it can hardly be justified to categorically dismiss the use of moulds taken from the human body. The period to which the Riace warriors are dated, Greece's early Classical age, that Guy Métraux suggests was a time of growing awareness of human life and health and a thriving exchange between sculptors, physicians and philosophers, would be a suitable place to start examining this phenomenon in greater detail.[18]

1 Pliny the Elder, *Natural History*, trans. H. Rackham, 10 vols., London and Cambridge, MA 1961, vol. 9, pp. 373–75.
2 See *ibid.*
3 Matthias Grawehr, *Petra ez Zantur: Ergebnisse der Schweizerisch-Liechtensteinischen Ausgrabungen. Terra Archaeologica* VI, *'Eine Bronzewerkstatt des 1. Jhs. n. Chr. von ez Zantur in Petra/Jordanien'*, Mainz 2010, pp. 117–19.
4 Ralf von den Hoff, 'Naturalism and Classicism: Style and Perception of Early Hellenistic Portraits', in: *Early Hellenistic Portraiture: Image, Style, Context*, ed. Hoff and Peter Schultz, Cambridge 2007, pp. 49–62, here pp. 53–54.
5 Andreas Grüner, 'Antike Reproduktionsmedien: Münze, Siegel und Stempel zwischen Serialität und Authentizität', in: *Multiples in Pre-Modern Art*, ed. Walter Cupperi, Zurich 2014, pp. 59–93.
6 *Theophrastus on Stones*, trans. Earle R. Caley and John F. C. Richards, Columbus, OH 1956, p. 60. See also Grawehr, *Petra ez Zantur*, p. 115–17.
7 Rune Frederiksen, 'Plaster Casts in Antiquity', in: *Plaster Casts: Making, Collecting and Displaying from Classical Antiquity to the Present*, ed. Frederiksen and Eckart Marchand, Berlin 2010, pp. 11–34.
8 See Christa Landwehr, *Die antiken Gipsabgüsse aus Baiae: Griechische Bronzestatuen in Abgüssen römischer Zeit, Archäologische Forschungen* 14, Berlin 1985; and Landwehr, 'The Baiae Casts and the Uniqueness of Roman Copies', in: Frederiksen, *Plaster Casts*, pp. 35–46.
9 See Michael Menninger, *Untersuchungen zu den Gläsern und Gipsabgüssen aus dem Fund von Begram (Afghanistan)*, Würzburg 1996.
10 Heinrich Drerup, 'Totenmaske und Ahnenbild bei den Römern', *Mitteilungen des Deutschen Archäologischen Instituts*, Römische Abteilung 87 (1980), pp. 81–129; and Patrick R. Crowley, 'Roman Death Masks and the Metaphorics of the Negative', *Grey Room* 64 (Summer 2016), pp. 64–103.
11 Quintilian, *The Orator's Education*, ed. and trans. Donald A. Russell, 5 vols., Cambridge, MA 2001, vol. 3, p. 37.
12 Manuel Flecker, 'Bedeutsame Banalität(en): Aspekte des römischen Porträts zwischen dem Ausgang der Republik und der Kaiserzeit', in: *Auf der Suche nach der Wirklichkeit: Realismen in der griechischen Plastik*, ed. Christiane Nowak and Lorenz Winkler-Horaček, exh. cat., Abguss-Sammlung Antiker Plastik des Instituts für Klassische Archäologie der Freien Universität Berlin, 22 February–8 July 2018, Rahden 2018, pp. 125–47.
13 See Harriet I. Flower, *Ancestor Masks and Aristocratic Power in Roman Culture*, Oxford 1996; and Manuel Flecker, 'Ahnenbild und Totenmaske: Die *imagines maiorum* und die Erforschung des römischen Porträts', *Antike Welt* 2 (2017), pp. 72–78.
14 Drerup, 'Totenmaske und Ahnenbild bei den Römern', pp. 93–94.
15 Jeanette Kohl, 'Gesichter machen: Büste und Maske im Florentiner Quattrocento', *Marburger Jahrbuch für Kunstwissenschaft* 34 (2007), pp. 77–99; and Flecker, 'Bedeutsame Banalität(en)', pp. 137–39.
16 Nigel Konstam and Herbert Hoffmann, 'Casting the Riace Bronzes 2: A Sculptor's Discovery', *Oxford Journal of Archaeology* 23 (2004), pp. 397–402.
17 Frederiksen, 'Plaster Casts in Antiquity', p. 21; see also Pablo Jiménez Salinas, *Die Rolle des Bronzegusses der griechischen Skulptur im klassischen Aufbruch*, BA thesis, Institut für Klassische Archäologie – Humboldt-Universität zu Berlin, accessed 3 February 2019, https://www.academia.edu/5145342/Die_Rolle_des_Bronzegusses_der_griechischen_Skulptur_im_klassischen_Aufbruch_BA-Arbeit.
18 See Guy P. R. Métraux, *Sculptors and Physicians in Fifth-Century Greece: A Preliminary Study*, Montreal 1995.

From 1984 to 2000 Donald Lokuta (b. 1946) shot roughly fifteen thousand photographs to document the activities of arguably the most famous twentieth-century artist working in plaster, George Segal (1924–2000). Lokuta began his collaboration with Segal as an art photographer, then became the sculptor's assistant and colleague before forming a lasting friendship with the artist. Lokuta's silver gelatin prints provide insights into Segal's distinctive working method and the trajectory of his sculptural production, from concept to full realisation. The photographs open the door to Segal's studio, a repurposed chicken coop in New Jersey, and reveal the private moments and humorous situations between the artist and the models he immortalised in plaster. As Segal's long-time companion, Lokuta was not only involved in creating countless plaster casts, he was also a model himself, as seen in the sculpture *The Homeless* (1989, ill. p. 189). Sensitively observed, the constellations and interactions taking place between Segal and the persons he cast in plaster and the nascent or completed casts themselves find expression in the medium of photography, which is as important for the interpretation of Segal's work as it is for examining the entanglement of art and technology as well as art and life which lie at the centre of *Near Life*.

Donald Lokuta

Studio Detail, Body Parts, 2000

George Segal Examining Castings for 'Street Crossing', 1992

Pages 188–89

Figure for 'The Graffiti Wall', 1990

George Segal with Model for 'Blue Woman on Black Bed', 1996

Figure for 'The Homeless' in Progress, 1989

Casting George Segal for 'George Segal, Self-portrait', 1990

Pages 190–91

'Woman on Park Bench' in Progress, 1998

From the series *George Segal: An Intimate Portrait*
Courtesy of the artist

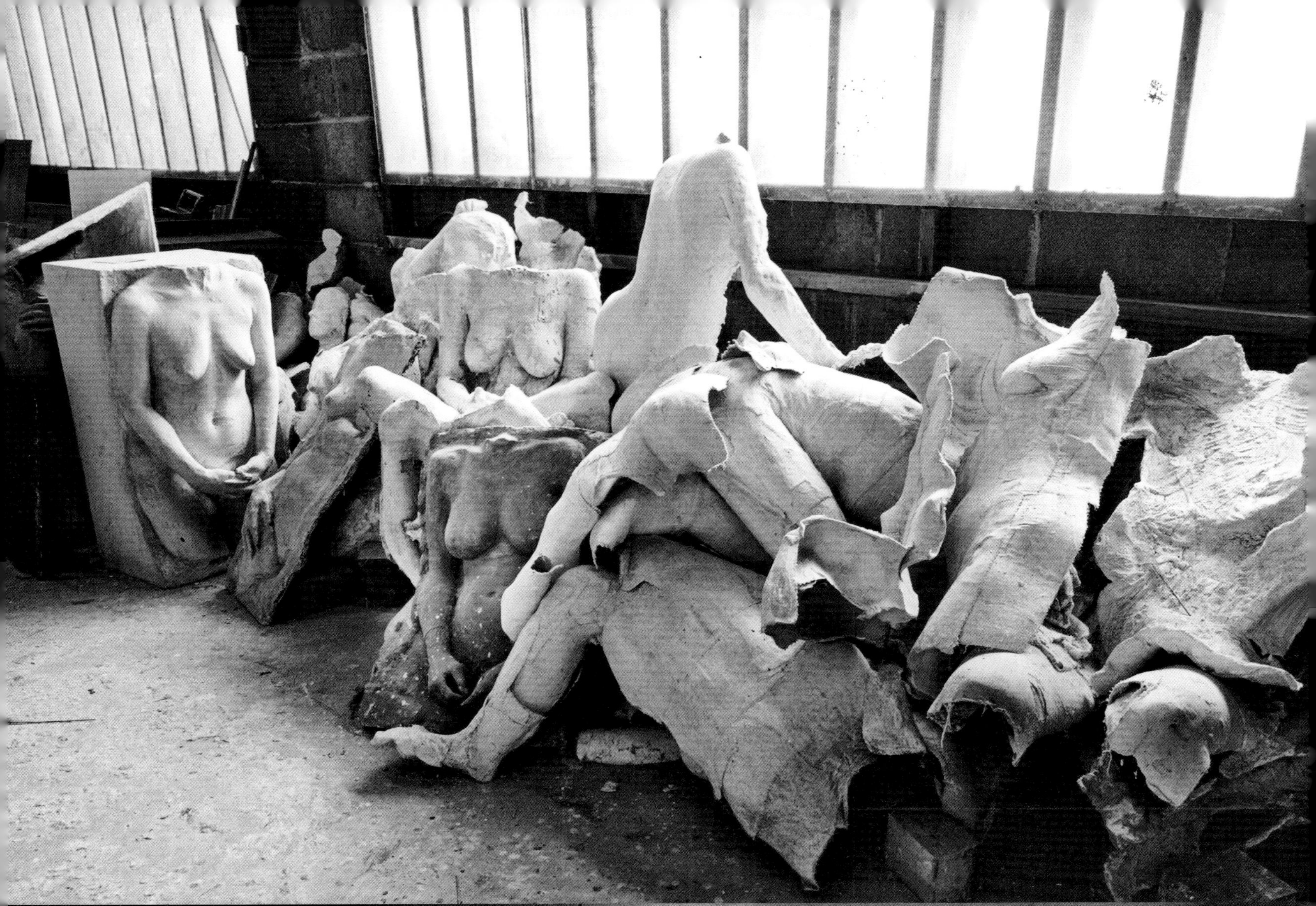
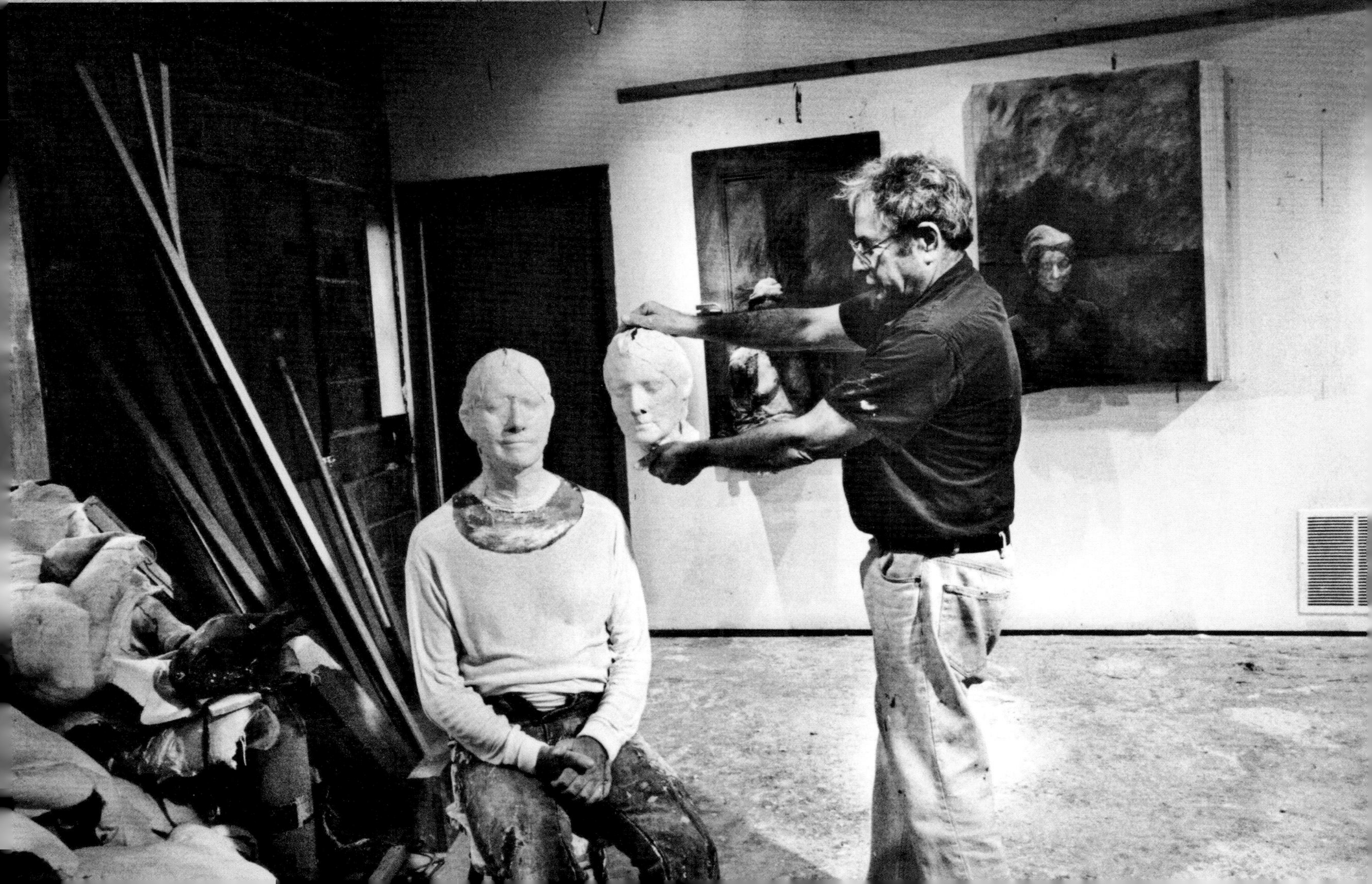

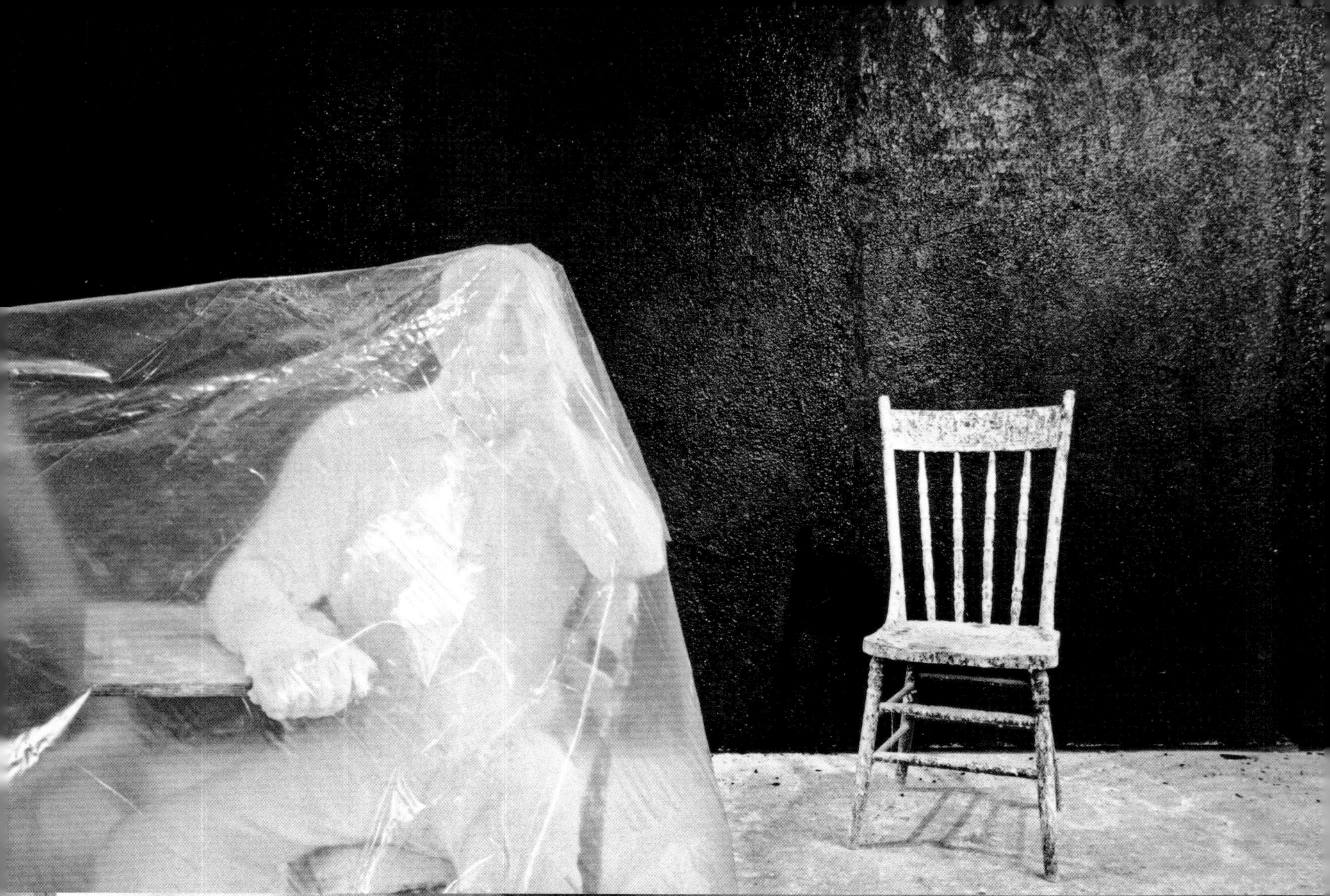

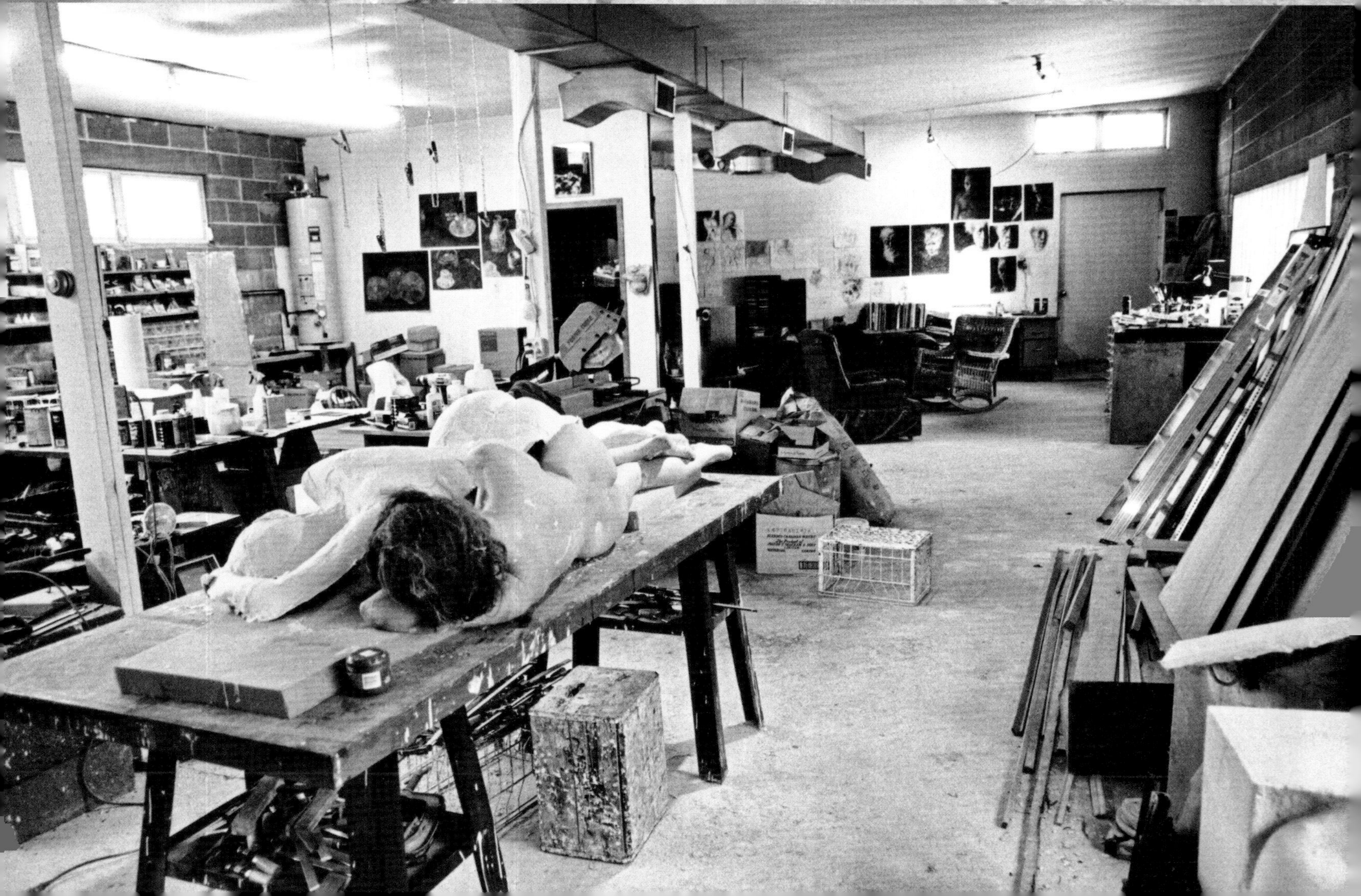

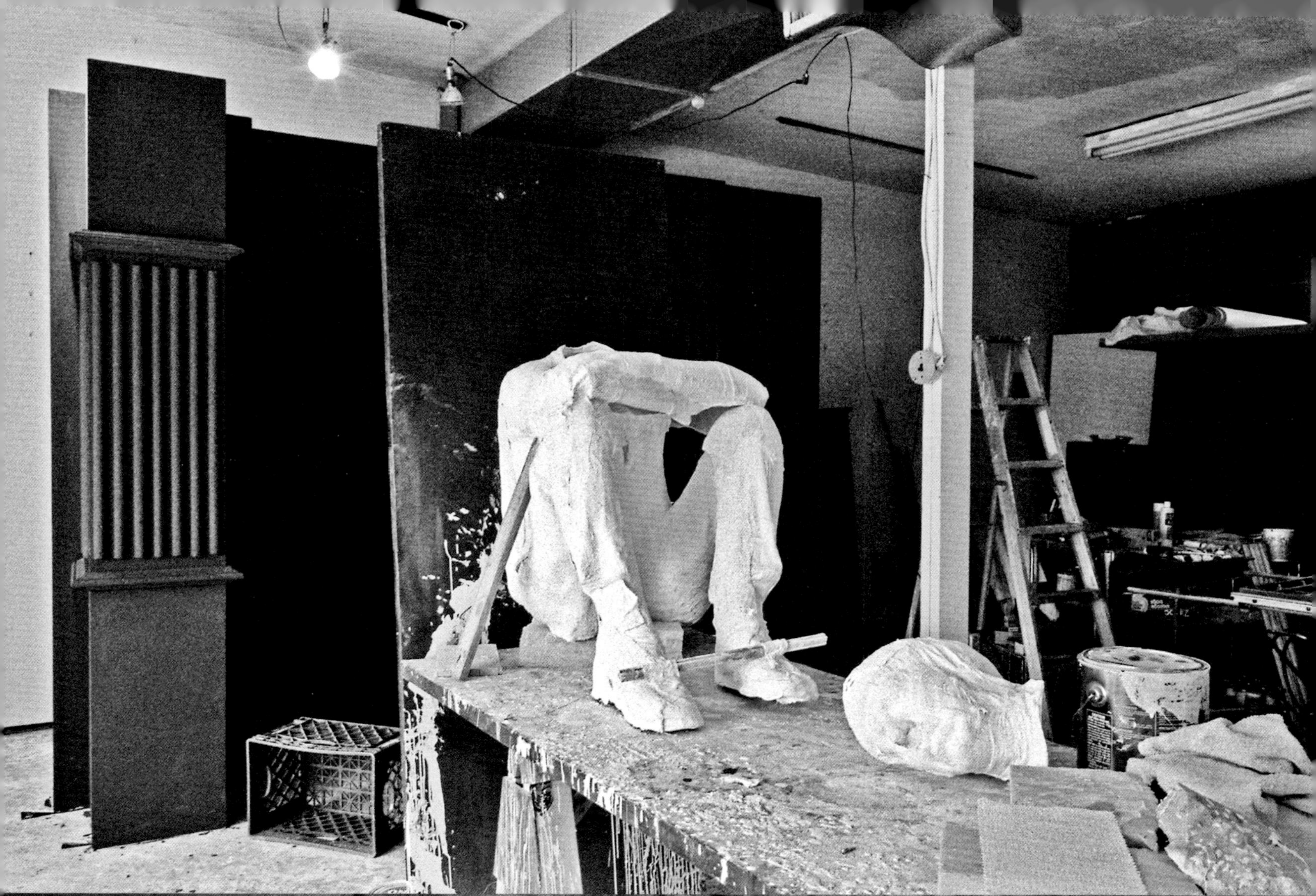

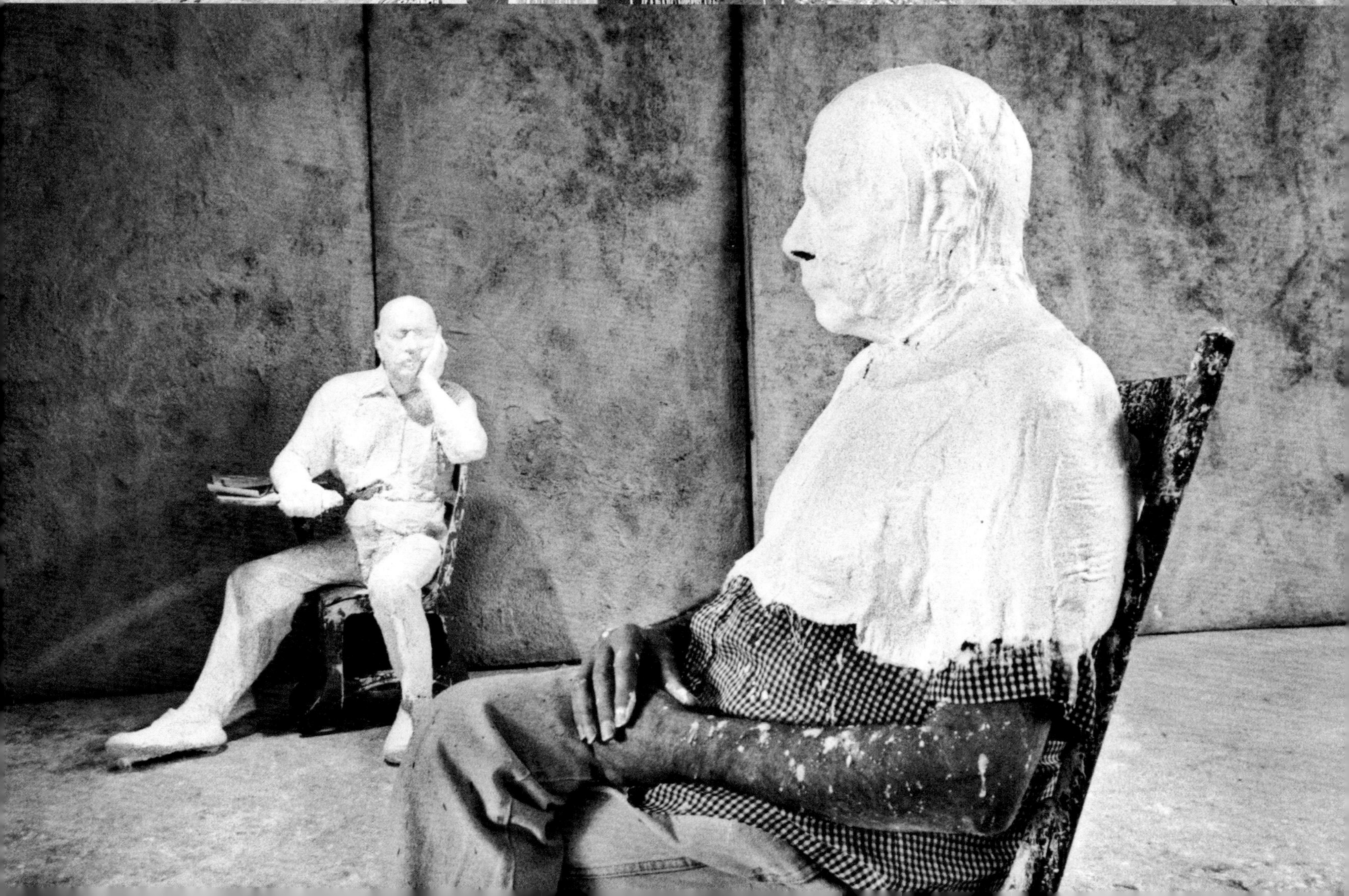

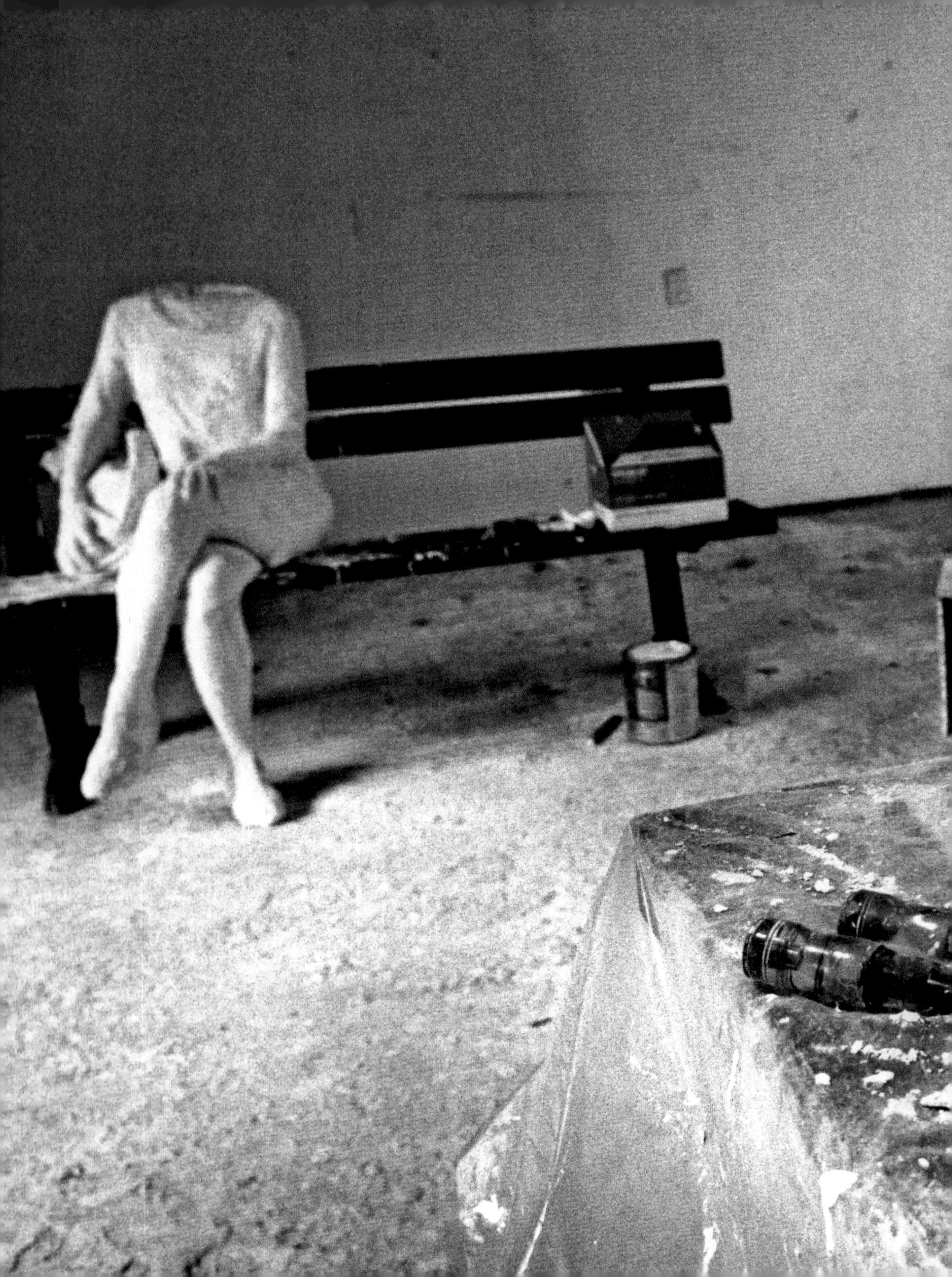

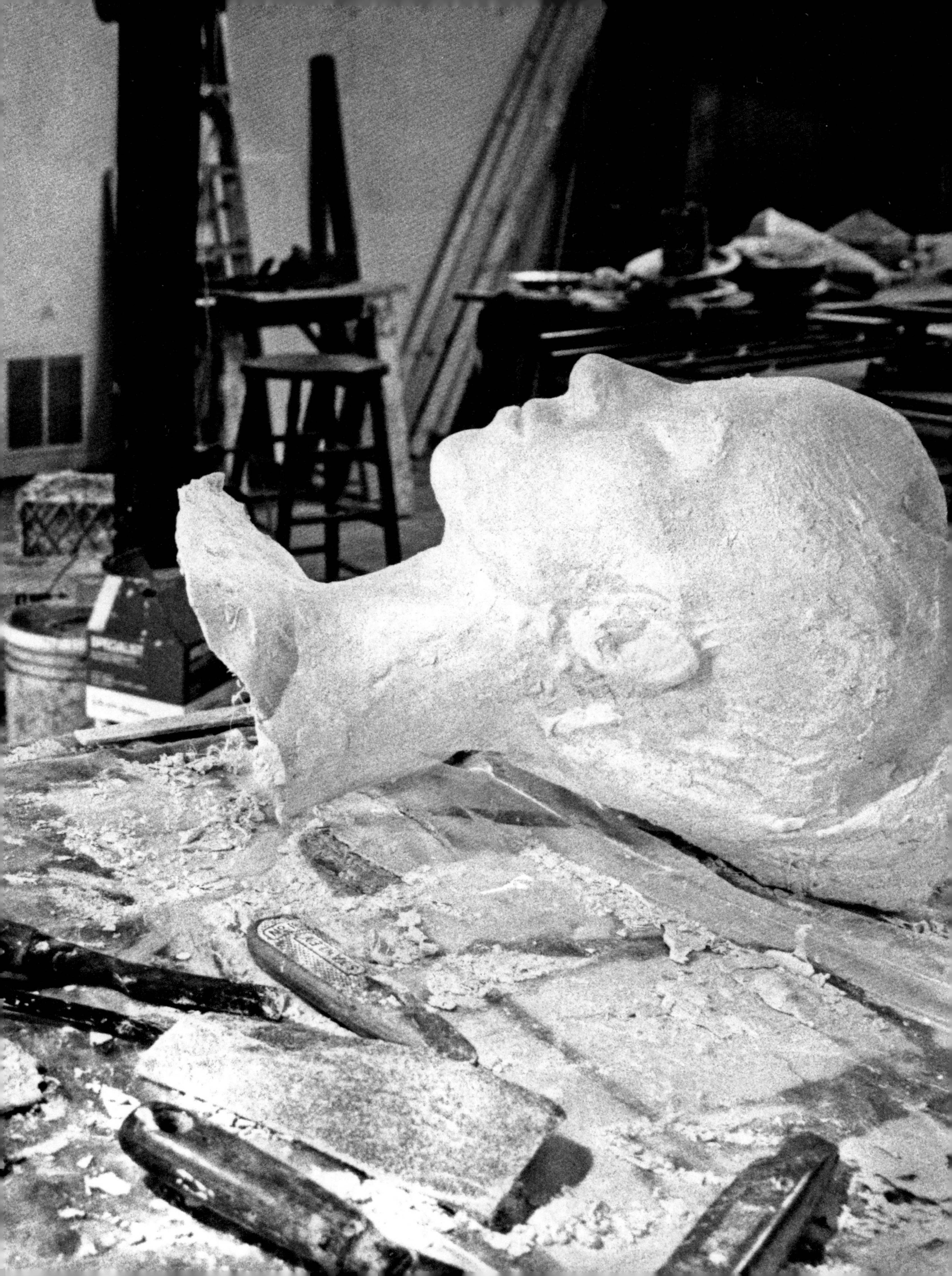

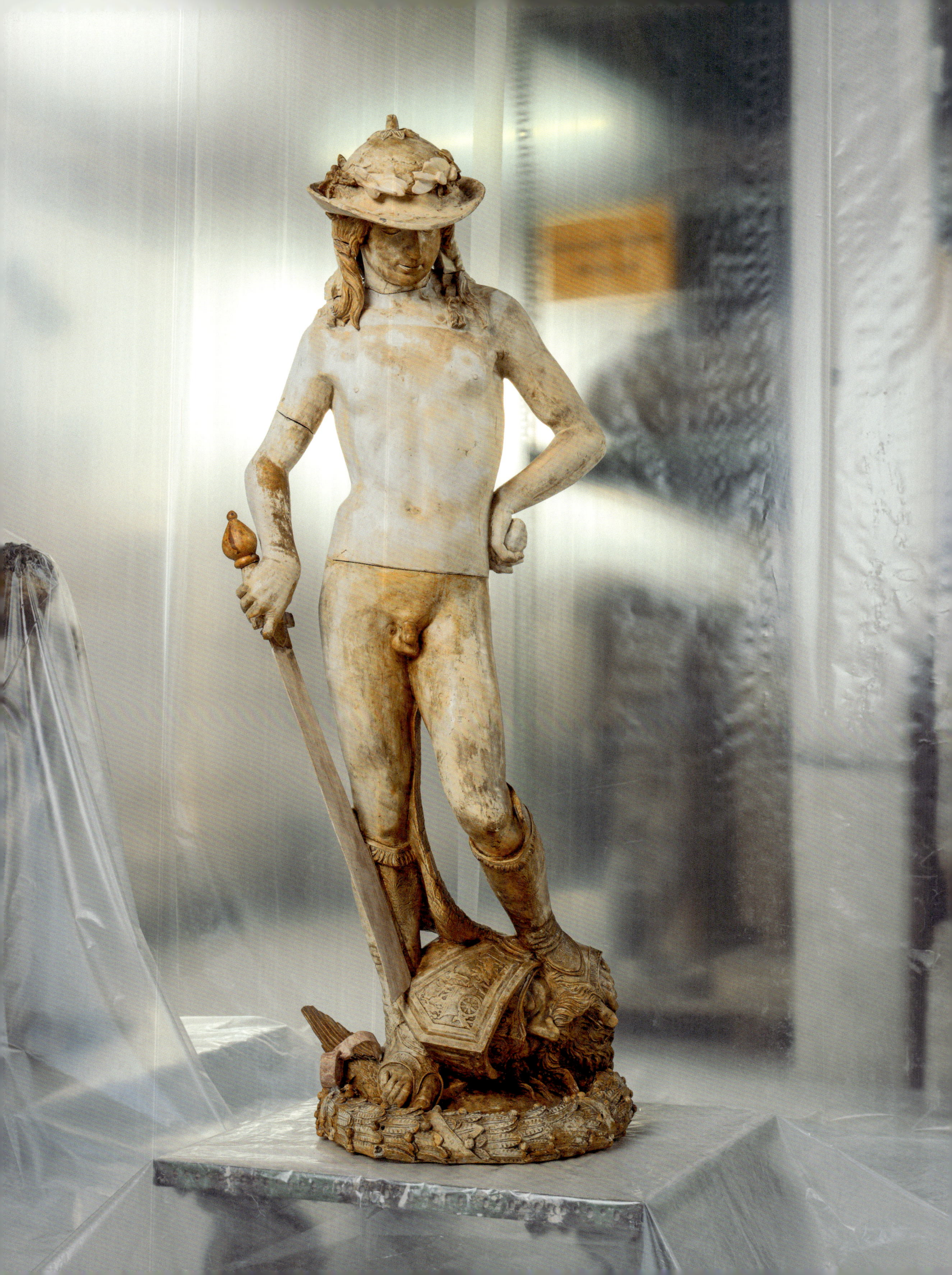

The Case against Casts

If in the past sculpture was seen to be especially lifelike and convincing, its creators sometimes found themselves accused of having used lifecasting techniques: that is, it was alleged, rightly or wrongly, that the work in question was based on a mould taken directly from the body of a model, rather than being the result of free modelling. Five masterpieces drawn from the history of sculpture will be discussed in this chapter to illustrate how doubts concerning the status of casts as genuine works of art sometimes ignited heated debate.

'In the courtyard of the Palace of the said Signori there is a life-size David, nude and in bronze. Having cut off the head of Goliath, he is raising one foot and placing it on him, holding a sword in his right hand. This figure is so natural in its vivacity and its softness, that it is almost impossible for craftsmen to believe that it was not moulded on the living form.' This is how Giorgio Vasari in *The Lives of the Most Excellent Painters, Sculptors, and Architects* (1550) describes Donatello's *David* (ca. 1440), considered to be the first free-standing male nude since antiquity and one of the most outstanding sculptures of the Italian Renaissance. Donatello, according to Georges Didi-Huberman, was the 'most important renewer of the moulding process' in the quattrocento, an age when this process 'was reviled as many times [...] as it was used'. He experimented with techniques and methods in a manner that is strikingly modern, and also made use of casts in other works as well, such as *Judith and Holofernes* (ca. 1454), where he moulded the legs of Holofernes and Judith's veil from nature. Vasari's praise of Donatello seems to suggest that *David* had come under suspicion as a cast within contemporary artists' circles. For Vasari, whose negative opinion on casting as an art form was to influence the historiography of art, the technique serves as proof of quality *ex negativo*: the graceful youth is in his eyes as lifelike and as close to nature *as* a cast, but in the end it is a great work of art precisely because it is not the product of a cast.

While there is no documentary evidence to support the thesis that artist Antonio Canova (1757–1822) used casts after nature, the suspicion that he did so in some of his sculptures has been expressed time and time again by art historians. Most recently, Maurizio Bernardelli Curuz has made such claim with regard to the famous *Paolina Borghese as Venus Victrix* (1808), whose wax-like surface seems to breathe with life. Curuz has shown that the plaster cast of Paolina's breast — now in the collection of Museo Napoleonico in Rome — was used for the execution of the sculpture's revealing recumbent figure to lend the marble 'lo stupefacente fremito della vita' (the breathtaking frisson of life). He has identified the subtle deformation of the nipple caused by the weight of plaster (both in the body cast and in the sculpture) as a twofold scandal, given that such a lifecast would not only imply an intimacy between sculptor and model deemed unacceptable at the time, but artistic trickery as well. The recumbent Paolina is shown here as an 'original plaster', that is, as the sculptural form that served as the basis for the figure's later realisation in marble. Canova commissioned the *formatori* (artistic plasterers) to make the form from his clay model. The surface of the plaster is covered with points attesting to the artisanal procedure. Original plaster casts are hybrids: they are technical aids, tools and models strictly designed to serve a purpose; in-process forms on the way to becoming the ostensibly superior, final version; and they are the first realisation of an artistic idea, the direct result of the creative act, and therefore the true original. Canova's work is located between the use of casting techniques, both ubiquitous in the studios and condemned by art critics in the Renaissance, and the modern emancipation and elevation of casts as works of art in their own right. According to his own testimony, the classicist sculptor harboured an aversion to the use of plaster. At the same time he has gone down in art history as a revivalist and moderniser of precisely this type of work. Canova exemplifies the contradictions of his age in regard to the reception of the cast.

Antonio Canova
Paolina Borghese Bonaparte as Venus Vitrix, 1807
Gypsoteca Canova Possagno

Antonio Canova
Plaster Cast of a breast of Paolina Bonaparte, ca. 1804–08
Plaster, 20 × 16 × 10 cm
Rom, Museo Napoleonico, MN 496

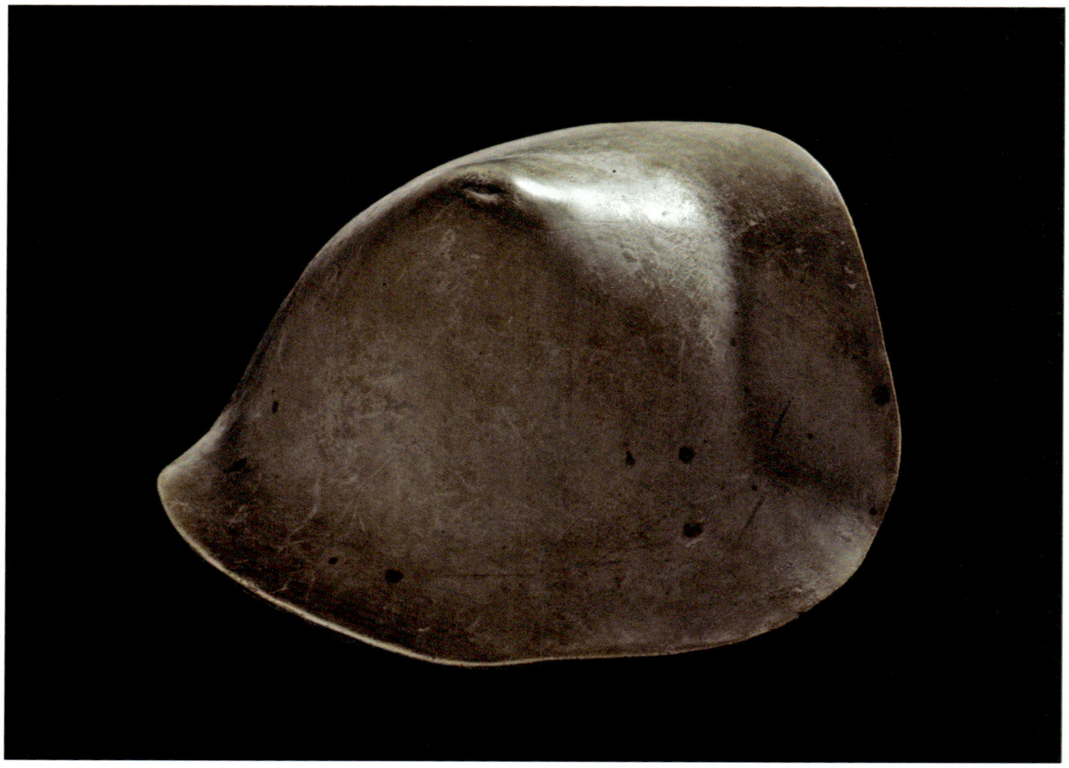

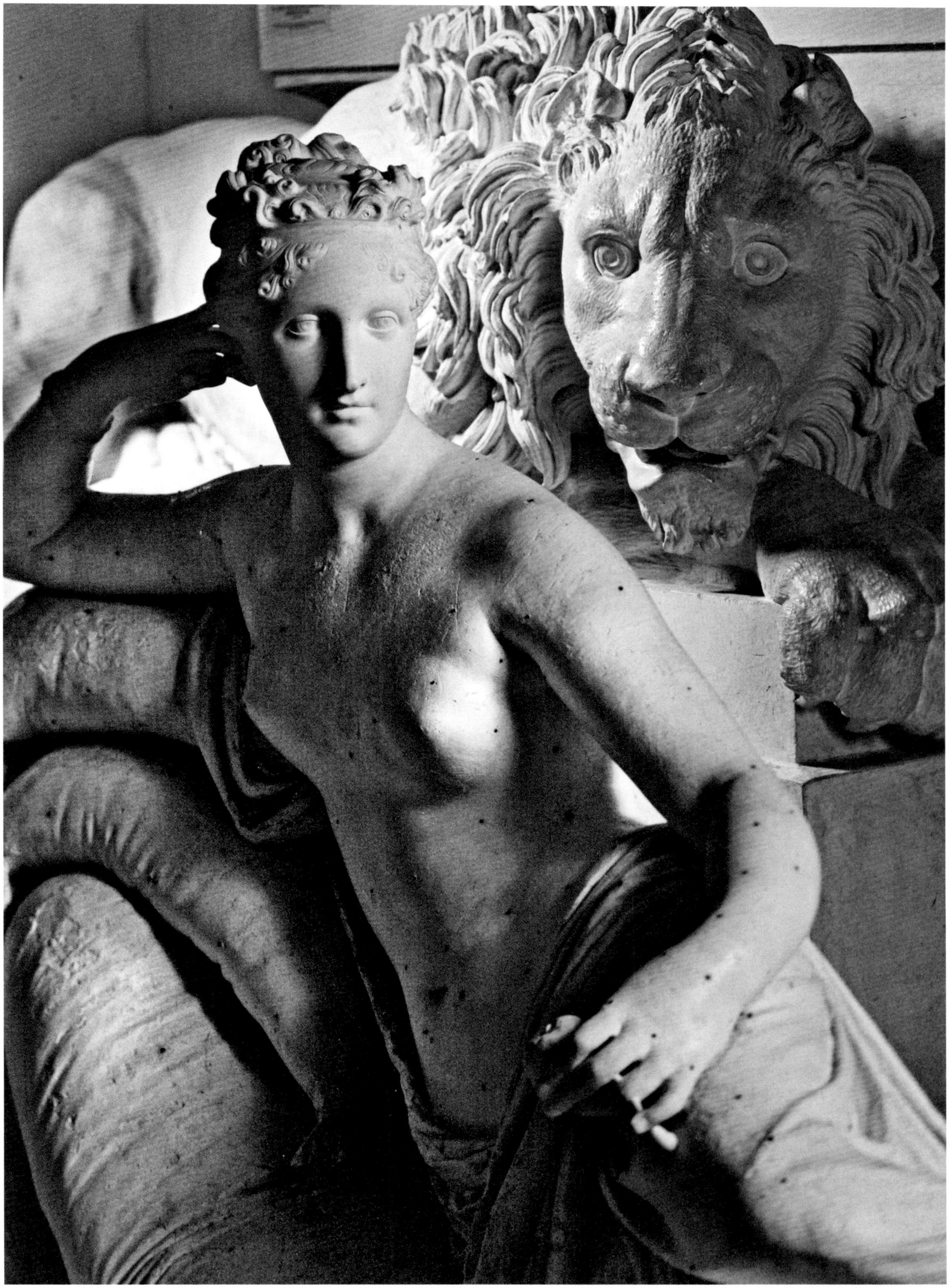

Modèle de l'age d'airain
Aug Neyt

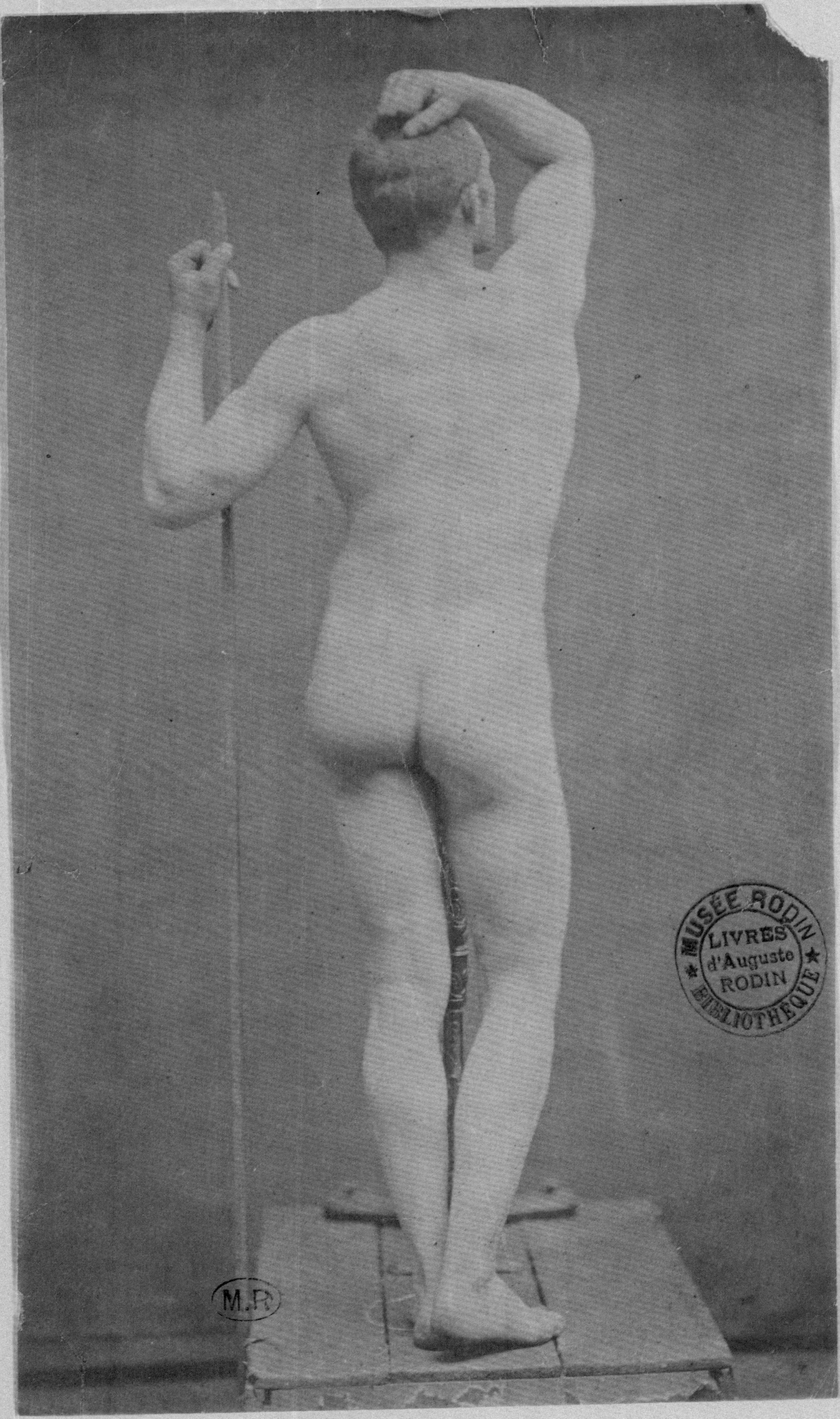

Gaudenzio Marconi
Rear view of Auguste Neyt, 1877
Albumin Print, 25.3 × 15 cm
Musée Rodin, Paris, PH 272

Auguste Rodin
The Age of Bronze, 1875–76
Staatliche Kunstsammlungen
Dresden, Skulpturensammlung

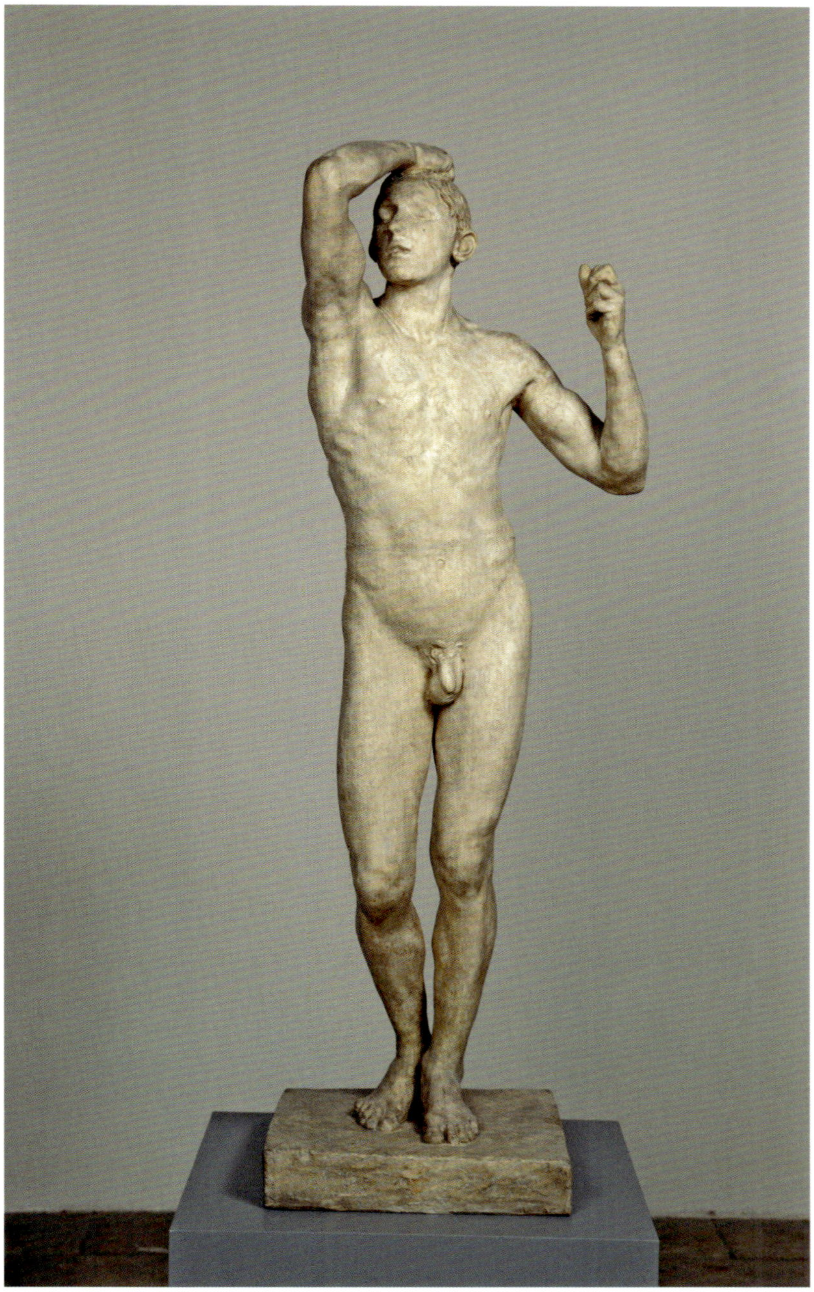

Arguably the most notorious case of a sculpture falling under the suspicion of being cast from life dates to the late 1870s. For eighteen months Auguste Rodin (1840–1917) had been at work on his powerfully modelled male nude, *The Age of Bronze*. In 1877, he presented it to the public in the Salons of Brussels and Paris. At a time when the tendency towards realism and the mimetic rendering of reality was omnipresent — much to the chagrin of the adherents of academism — attacks from the critics were not long in coming. The sculpture was taken as a lifecast. Rodin passionately defended himself against the charge, a charge amounting to fraud, levelled in the same way against fellow artists such as Jean-Baptiste Auguste Clésinger and Alexandre Falguière. He invited his critics to his studio and showed them photographs of his model, Auguste Neyt, pointing out the differences between the somewhat sturdier build of the soldier and his own figure. However, still in 1880 a commission of inquiry adjudged: 'Even if this figure may not be a cast in the literal sense, the role played by a lifecast is so prominent that one can no longer speak of a work of art.' Only by means of an expert report, compiled by several fellow sculptors, Rodin was fully exculpated in the end. Rodin's oeuvre is of seminal importance for the history of using plaster in art. Not only did he utilise original plaster casts in the preparatory stages of his sculptures before realising them in bronze or marble like other sculptors, he also created experimental plaster sculptures that had no practical purpose, whose fragmentary character gave them the appearance of avant-garde artworks. In this way, he made a significant contribution to the acceptance of plaster as a highly suitable material for the production of art in the twentieth century. *The Age of Bronze* is one of Rodin's most well-known sculptures: one hundred and fifty or so copies in bronze or plaster authorised by the artist are to be found today in collections and museums all over the world. The version on display in our exhibition *Near Life* is an early plaster cast from Dresden. According to curator Astrid Nielsen, the white cast was given a shellac coating and was recast in the 1950s or 1960s. Shellac traces are still clearly visible, despite the restoration to the cast in 2005. They are a reminder that even plaster casts made by artists themselves are in danger of being misunderstood as inferior reproductions.

From the nineteenth-century misgivings about the cast which discredited its use in sculpture, because of the supposedly simplistic, purely technical, styleless and un-artistic process of production, it is only a small step to the readymade as practised by Marcel Duchamp (1887–1968) from the 1910s onwards. The work *Female Fig Leaf* (1950–51) belongs to the conceptual tendencies of that art form, even though the small galvanised plaster sculpture is not itself a readymade. Duchamp made two casts of this object. He gave one of them as a gift to his artist friend Man Ray, authorising him to produce an edition of ten copies of the work. Given its title, *Female Fig Leaf*, the work was commonly interpreted by art critics as the cast of a vulva. In a pointed subversion of artistic convention, Duchamp's fig leaf is concerned less with veiling than with revealing the body and exposing it to the gaze. After doubts were raised as to whether this work was really a cast after nature, the New York-based Art Science Research Laboratory (ASRL) carried out a series of practical experiments in 2000. The interdisciplinary team, who conducted their research in a way Duchamp would probably have approved of, came to the surprising conclusion that *Female Fig Leaf* is unspecified in terms of gender. It depicts the perineum, an anatomical feature common to both human sexes. Whichever side of the debate you decide to align yourself with, the sculpture is certainly an inversion of the misgivings about casts, while the artist has succeeded in playing a trick on classic art history in more than one way.

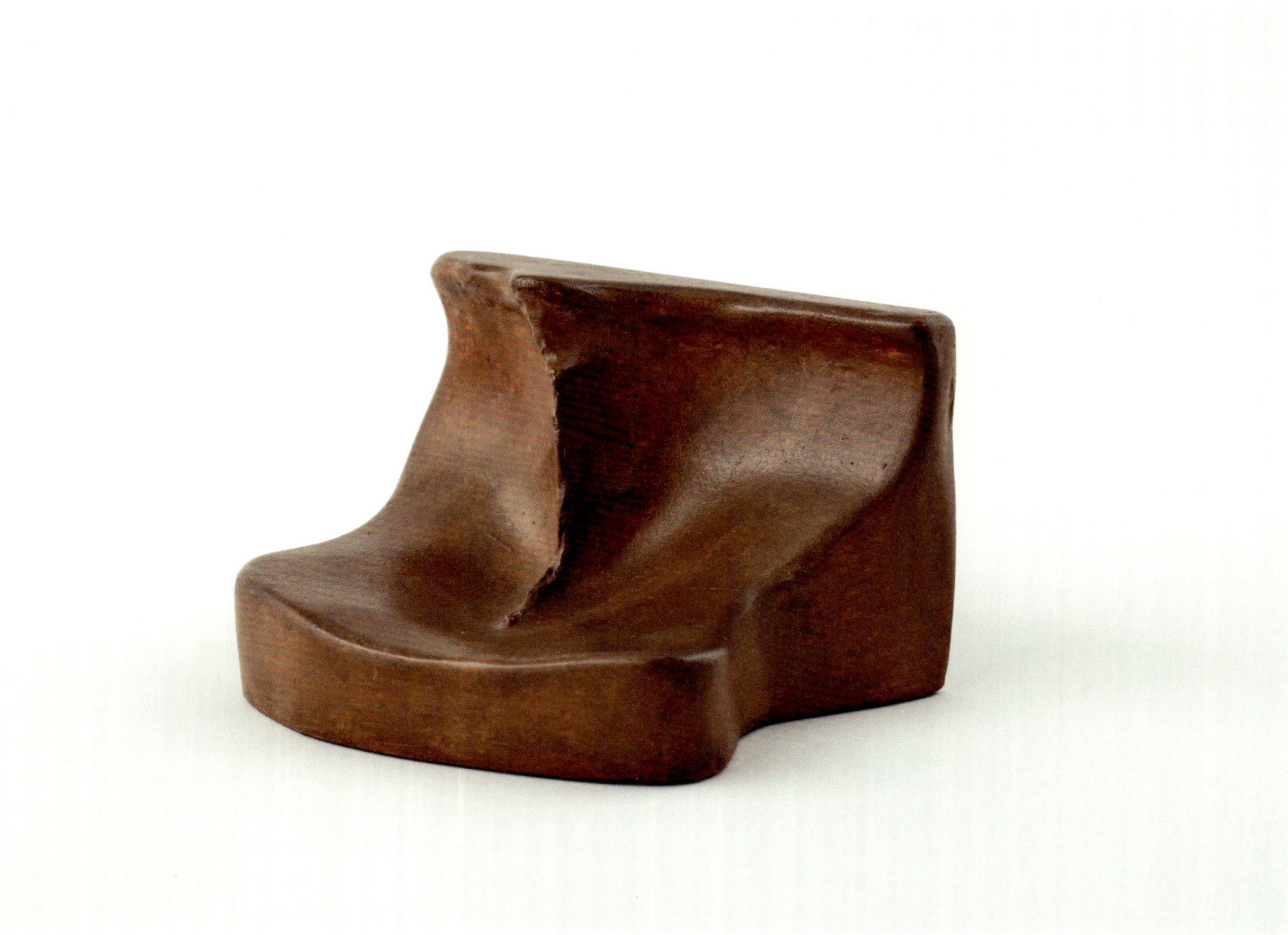

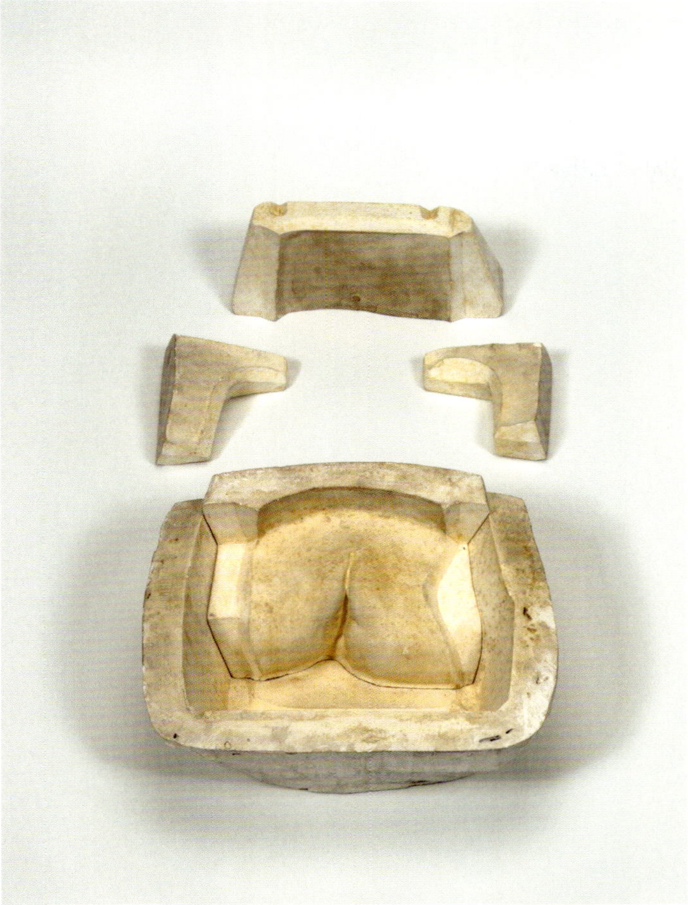

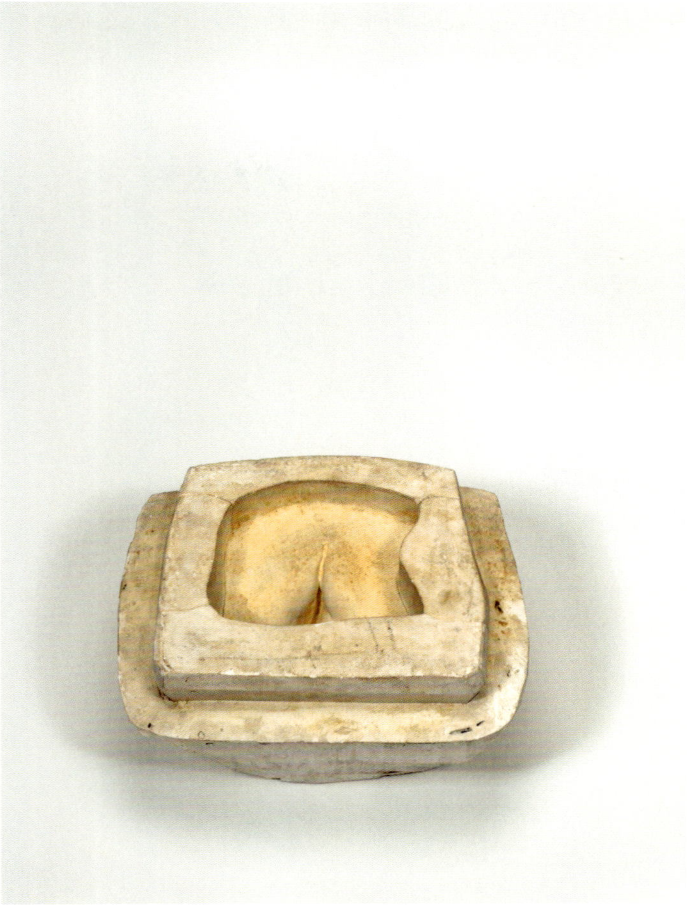

Marcel Duchamp
Feuille de vigne femelle (Female Fig Leaf), 1950–51
Staatliche Schlösser, Gärten und Kunstsammlungen Mecklenburg-Vorpommern, Schwerin

Marcel Duchamp
Plaster Piece Mould for Feuille de vigne femelle (Female Fig Leaf), 1950–51
Plaster, 13.5 × 27 × 23.5 cm
Centre Pompidou,
Paris, AM1990-104(2)

George Segal's *Woman on Park Bench* (1998/2009) gives the impression of being the plaster cast of a seated female, when in fact it is a whitened bronze. Segal (1924–2000) began 'double casting' his sculptures in the late 1960s. He used the plaster casts moulded with bandages soaked in liquid plaster — a method he became famous for — as matrices for a second cast. By the 1980s he was applying this technique to his bronzes. In the case of the whitened bronze casts, the historical misgivings about the cast transform into a discourse on materiality. Segal stands the hierarchical order on its head: allegedly inferior and subservient plaster is now ranked above bronze with its traditional prestige, suitability to art and durability. Furthermore, he reminds us of the frequently misunderstood yet crucial importance of plaster in the history of sculpture.

George Segal
Woman on Park Bench, 1998
Cast, 2009
Galerie Thomas Modern, Munich

» As to my casting, I can tell you that a mystery takes place that I never expected, and it's different each time. The simple act of somebody taking a position and putting pieces of cloth saturated in plaster on them, and having that person sit until sections harden has had a very unexpected side result. I think that's why I continue casting; otherwise I'd have been bored to tears and gone to something else long ago. First of all the wetness shows the muscles and bones underneath the clothing. It saturates the clothes to the point where you can see bone structure underneath. The discomfort to the person is of such a nature that they can't pretend with me; they have to relax, and they're just stoic and brave, or screaming and hysterical as they really are. It's very hard to be a fake with that kind of wet discomfort over such a long period of time. Maybe I'm a sadist, I don't know. But then I've also done the same person over six or seven times, and I've been absolutely amazed to find that even slight differences in state of mind come through that I can't control in the finished sculpture.

George Segal, 1972

Excerpt from 'The Sense of "Why Not?": George Segal on His Art', *Studio International* 174, no. 893, October 1967, pp. 146–49, here p. 149.

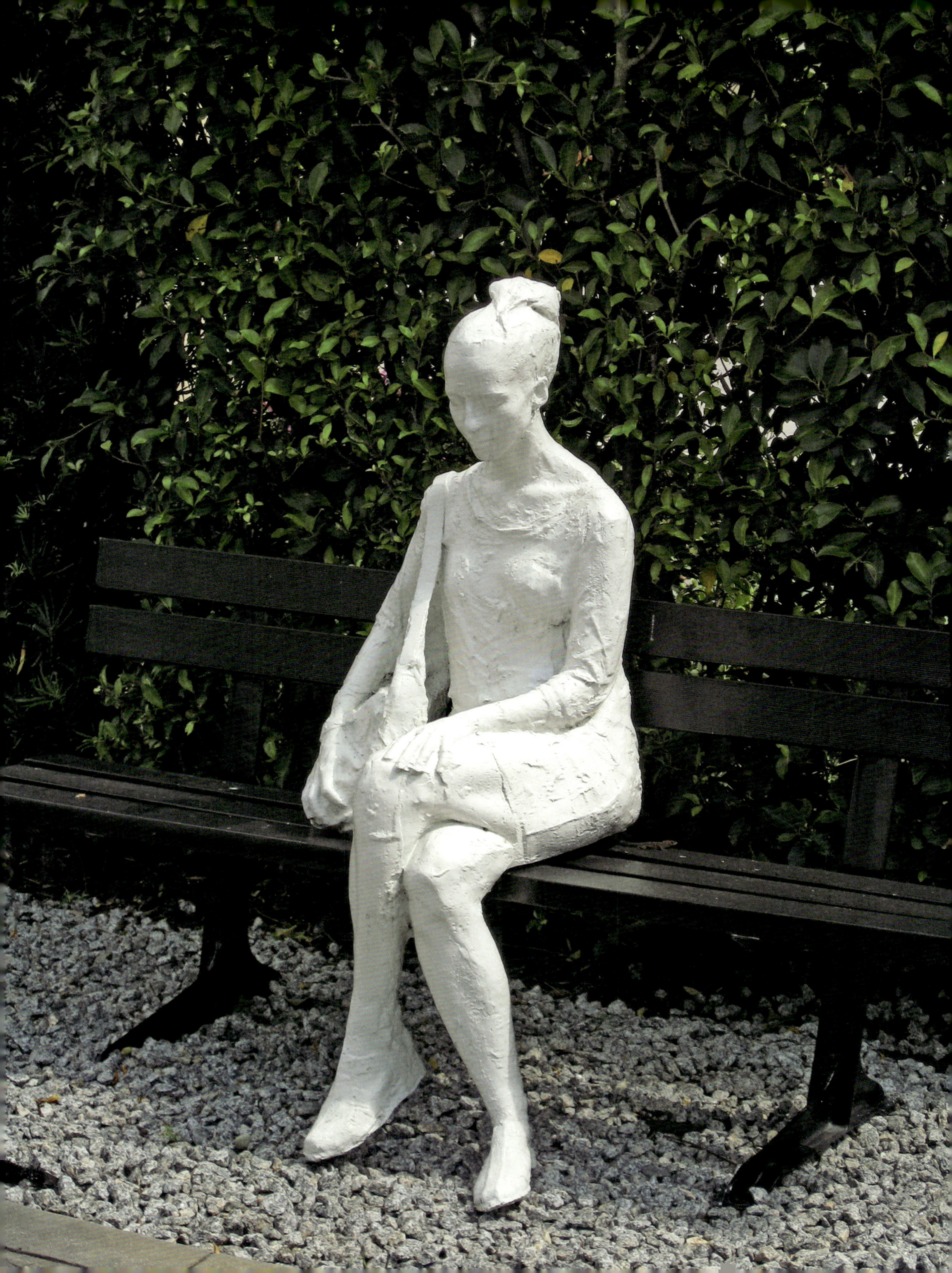

Casting as Art

A Conversation with Asta Gröting

Veronika Tocha: Asta Gröting, why do you work with casting techniques?

Asta Gröting: The first stage of my training as a sculptor was devoted to moulding and making casts. Modelling material on material was my conceptual choice from the word go, but it has taken me years and years to become fully aware of the conceptual and emotional possibilities inherent in this technique. What is conveyed by an impression, by the direct action of matter on matter, has great intensity. Touching takes place, comparable to the imprint a shoe leaves in snow or the classic positive-negative forming process. I connect existing forms and structures with the proof that contact had been made.

Veronika Tocha: Much of your work is to do with negatives, but *Acker* (Soil, 2012, ill. p. 26) is a positive.

Asta Gröting: That's right. We emptied twenty sacks of plaster on to a field. Once the plaster had set, we divided the whole thing into four parts and transported these to the studio, where the heavy plaster negatives were deposited on the floor. At first I was nonplussed — I had actually thought this was going to be it. But the negatives did not work, it was impossible to recognise them as part of a ploughed field. The furrows that in reality are deep incisions in the soil had become steep ridges in the negative. If things appear different to what we are used to, this causes a sense of surprise, producing positive feelings in the brain, in the frontal lobes of the cerebrum. But this only works when you recognise things for what they are and when you are able to form associations.

Veronika Tocha: And this is why you had to transform the negative into a positive, so that it is possible to understand what one is confronted with?

Asta Gröting: Exactly. *Acker* exists as a positive in several versions. I experimented with it. At first I made an earthy coloured *Acker*, then I painted it with phosphorus so that it emits light in the dark like the moon; the last few iterations are coated in various gold alloys. Moulding gives you the possibility of introducing variations from one cast to the next.

Veronika Tocha: In the exhibition, the gilded version is placed on display. Does gilding reflect a desire on your part to express an appreciation of agriculture?

Asta Gröting: Yes, I wanted to show how precious soil is. Up until only a few decades ago the majority of the population were farmers, working the land all day long. The harvest generated in this way fed kings, queens, civil servants, artists and thinkers. A tilled field allows you to see how all of human society is interconnected. Any kind of foodstuff contains the labour of farmers, immigrants, farmworkers, lorry drivers and depends in turn on the global climate and on centuries-old experiments with cultivation methods. It is the tilled field that ensures we are mutually connected with other people. Gold is a synonym both for material and spiritual abundance. It embodies what is precious, faithful, desirable and coveted. Gold's glow conveys warmth and brilliance, like light and the sun.

Veronika Tocha: Working with plaster plays an important role in your work. In the end, however, you usually end up working with other materials such as silicone. It is important in this context to remember that silicone

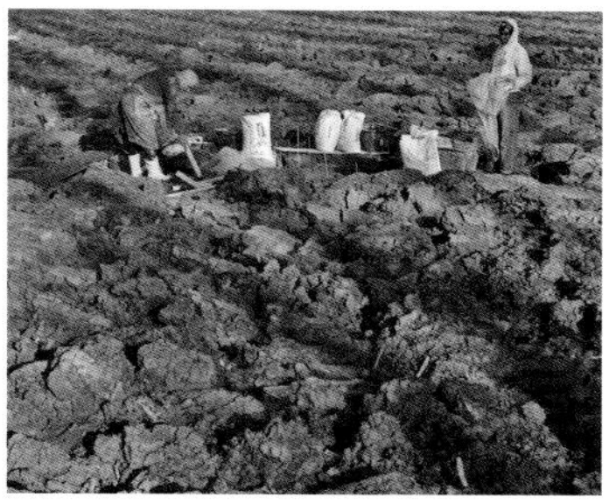 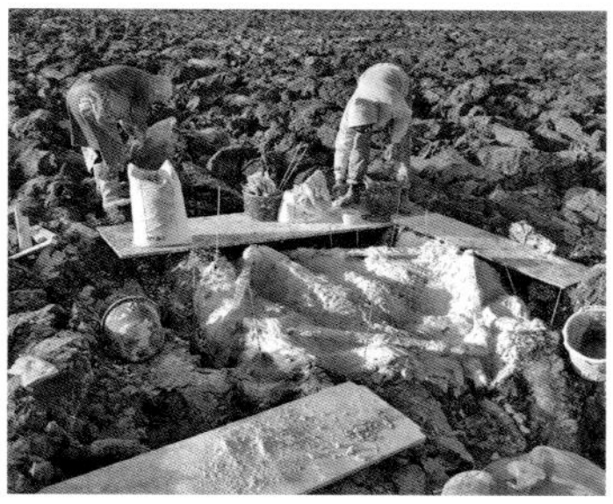 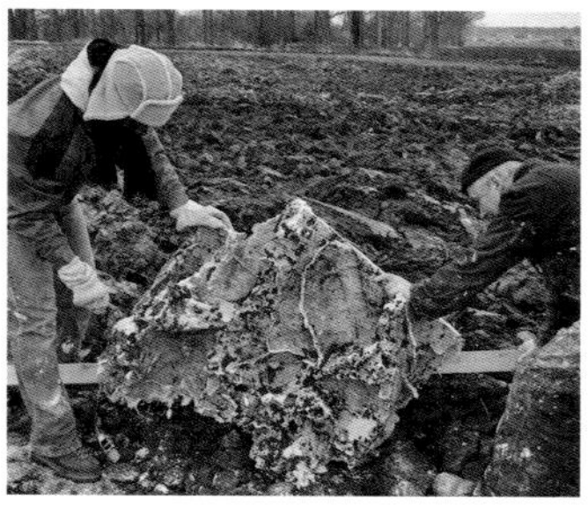 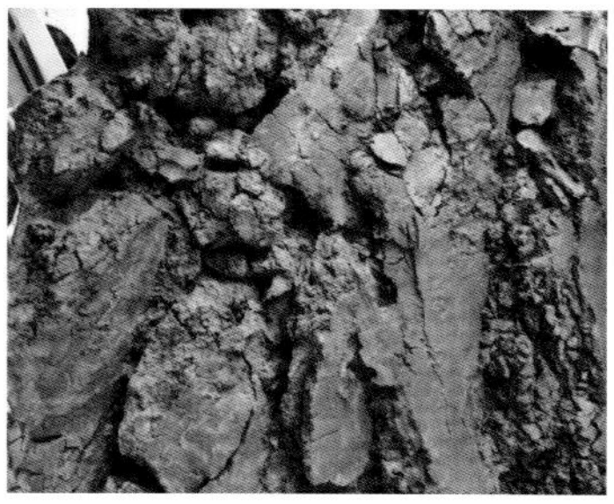

has now largely usurped the role of gelatine as the moulding material of choice in plaster casting.

Asta Gröting: Silicone is stable, durable and easily lends itself to tasks of all kinds. Moulding the four-metre-wide facade in individual plaster or gelatine elements, sixteen metres above the ground, would have been extremely challenging. You only do that if you are concerned with the upkeep of a tradition, as is the case with the Gipsformerei. There are those large-format plaster negatives taken from the Pergamon Altar, which have to be assembled like a 3D puzzle from hundreds of pieces. *Space between Lovers* (2008 and 2009/15, ill. p. 205). could not have been realised in plaster. Since this involved a couple having sex, we only had a few minutes for the moulding; this meant we had to use a material which required a minimum setting time. The material properties of silicone added an entirely new aspect. Removing the silicone from the bodies generated a form I could not possibly have thought of in advance. It had been my plan to conceptually turn the space between the couple inside out. Since the negative impression was a soft silicone skin, the form unfolded from there. This was not as I had planned. I had not even thought that far ahead as I was only keen on seeing what kind of form would emerge. Given silicone's material properties, the initial idea had been to make way for new possibilities: the first impression of a couple engrossed in a performance of intimacy was realised in a series of changeable forms and materials — in rose silicone and in crystal clear or silvery polyurethane.

Veronika Tocha: The sculpture of the lovers shows the most intimate moment imaginable between two people. Did you make use of the moulding technique to depict this moment as lifelike as possible?

Asta Gröting: No, what I wanted to see was something that cannot normally be seen: the space, the air, between a couple making love. This is actually a protected space; it comprises everything that one cannot say or does not want to say. This is generally true of human relationships. It concerns two people and what happens between them, with everything that belongs in that space, with what is concealed and what is unutterable and unnamable. Of all this I made an impression, based on physical touch through applying material to skin. As this was made visible, the question of touching became prominent and remained physically present as the negative. Furthermore, if the skin has access to an individual's physical and mental condition, it can in turn bring to the surface all kinds of feelings — historical and personal — which become visible in marks and traces. Conceptually and emotionally, all this is about togetherness, and the same is true of *Acker* and the facades (ill. pp. 138–39), in which internal space is brought to the surface by sculptural exploration.

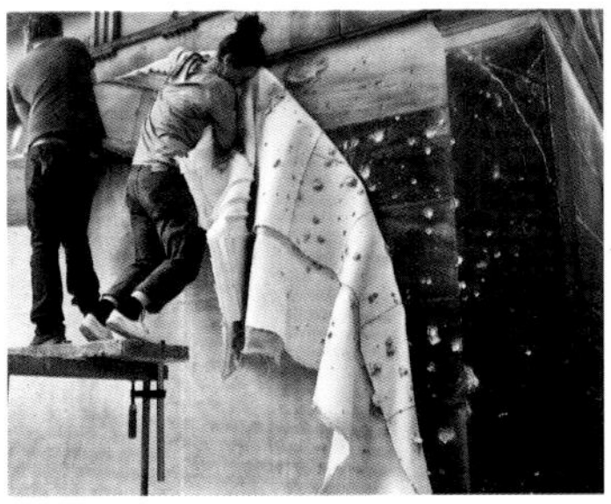
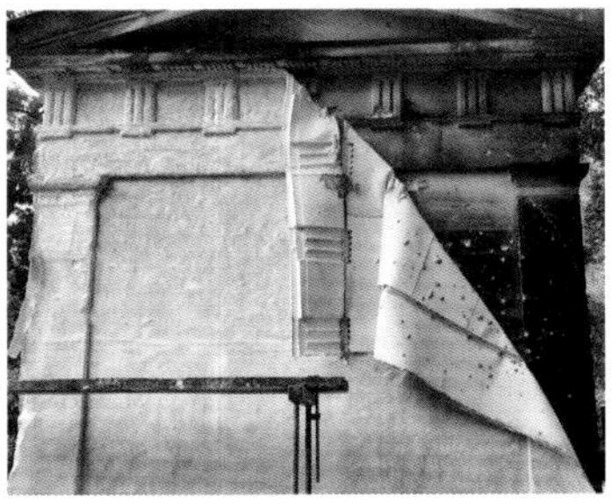
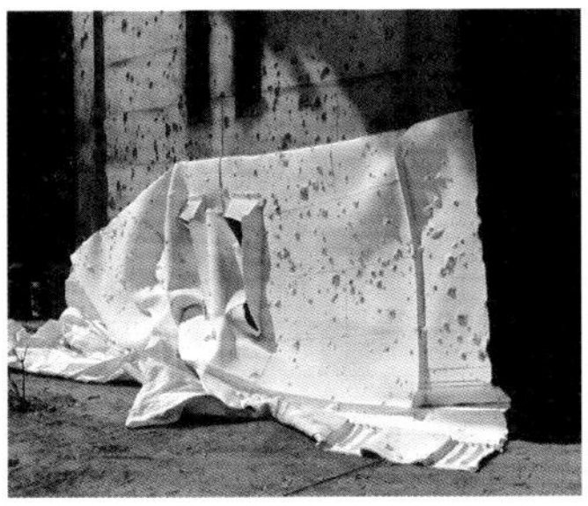
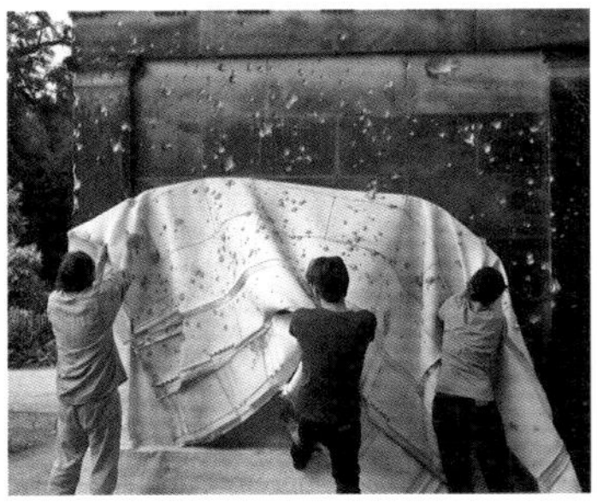

Veronika Tocha: What are we to make of the content of the facades?

Asta Gröting: During the clean-up of Berlin a great (and still growing) number of damaged house facades disappeared. It is part of the strategy of cities to create new, smooth facades and erase those that show wear and tear. I wanted to document Berlin's last surviving, war-damaged, bullet-pocked facades. The facade is a building's face. The terms 'facade' and 'face' obviously have a good deal in common. 'Facade' is derived from Latin *facies*, face. There are crumbling facades, and behind a facade a lot may remain hidden. A source of immediate fascination when one looks at a face are its scars and injuries. Facades, like faces, have scars and injuries. Evidence of damage, traces of destruction, cracks that leave open gaps exposing the past are experienced as more moving than the smooth and unruffled. The facades we moulded were damaged in the street fights between the Red Army and the Wehrmacht during the last two weeks of the war in April 1945. What interests me is what is suppressed: the wounds, the mental scars, the trauma which has perhaps been passed on to the next generation. It can be brought to the surface to be examined and experienced at close quarters.

Veronika Tocha: Conservation and documentation of a state of affairs that will likely cease to exist at some point in the future obviously play a significant role here.

Asta Gröting: Yes. But that is only one side of the coin. The flip side is again the desire to see. I happen to think this dilapidated state has great beauty. In my view, some of these facades should be left as they are rather than being vamped up — this should be done with no didactic hype at all. Visionary and utopian facades have every right to be smooth, but mediocre smooth facades are an eyesore for me. The facade negatives function like a photographic time exposure, spanning the interval between the grenade hit to the time when the mould was taken. The silicone impression preserves the surface in all its details: the graffiti, the dirt, the dust, the render. This is why for *Berlin Fassaden* (2017) I used gooey, supple silicone, which depicts everything faithfully, right down to the smallest details as well as bringing the bullet holes up to the surface.

Veronika Tocha: Making the negative visible is especially important in this case. No less crucial, though, is for the viewer to be aware that what they are dealing with here is a negative. The bullet holes, for instance, originally hollow spaces, now appear as regular cones jutting out to meet you.

Asta Gröting: Once you see the negative you get to see more than you would if you were looking at the positive. After all, you hardly ever stand in front of a facade and really inspect the wall up-close. When you catch sight of the negative, a sort of positive astonishment sets in, fostered by seeing something that is unusual, or even outrageous, comical too, and this astonishment may trigger a productive thought process. If you make things with your hands, you gain a totally different awareness of matter. Working with impressions means seeing things differently. It is one of the specific characteristics of the negative that it forces you to adopt a different perspective: you are looking outward from inside. Standing in front of the negative impressions of the facades, your gaze is directed from inside the wall to the outside, to the world. This perfectly corresponds to my working method of linking the conceptual with the emotional.

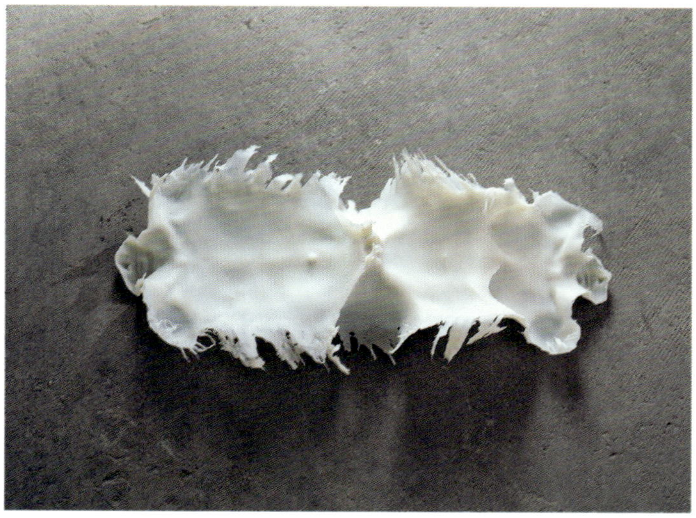

Asta Gröting
Space between Lovers, Unfolded, 2008
Silicon
25 × 55 × 147 cm
Galerie carlier | gebauer, Berlin, AG/2008/scu/9365

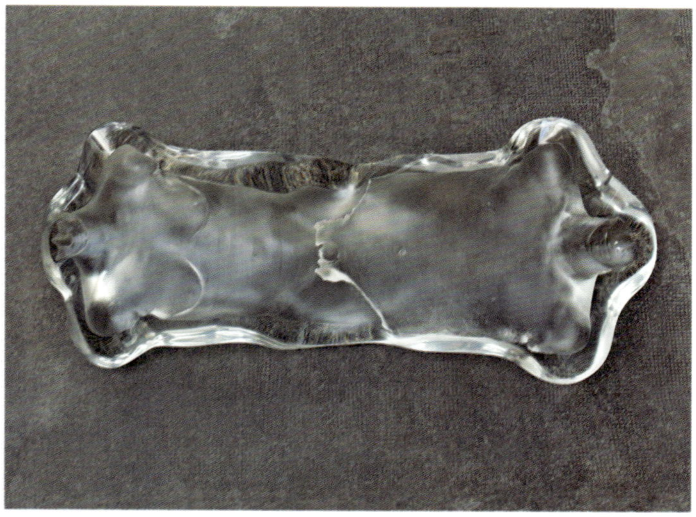

Asta Gröting
Space between Lovers, Unfolded and Clear, 2009/2015
Polyurethane
40 × 64 × 162 cm
Galerie carlier | gebauer, Berlin, AG/2015/scu/16024

After Polykleitos
Doryphoros
Master model, 1871
Staatliche Museen zu Berlin,
Gipsformerei

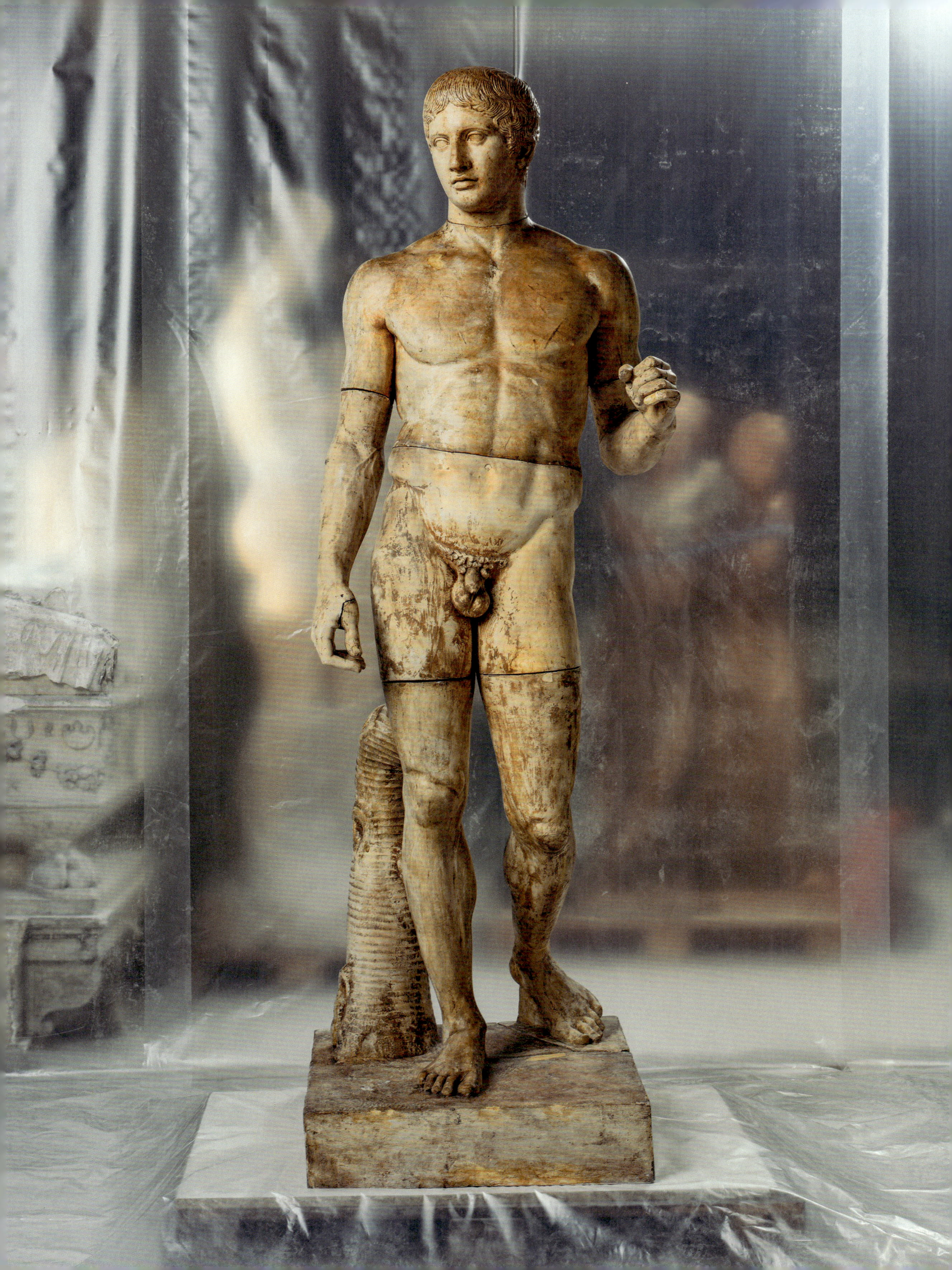

After Michelangelo Buonarroti
Slave for the Tomb of Pope Julius II
Master model, 1933
Staatliche Museen zu Berlin,
Gipsformerei

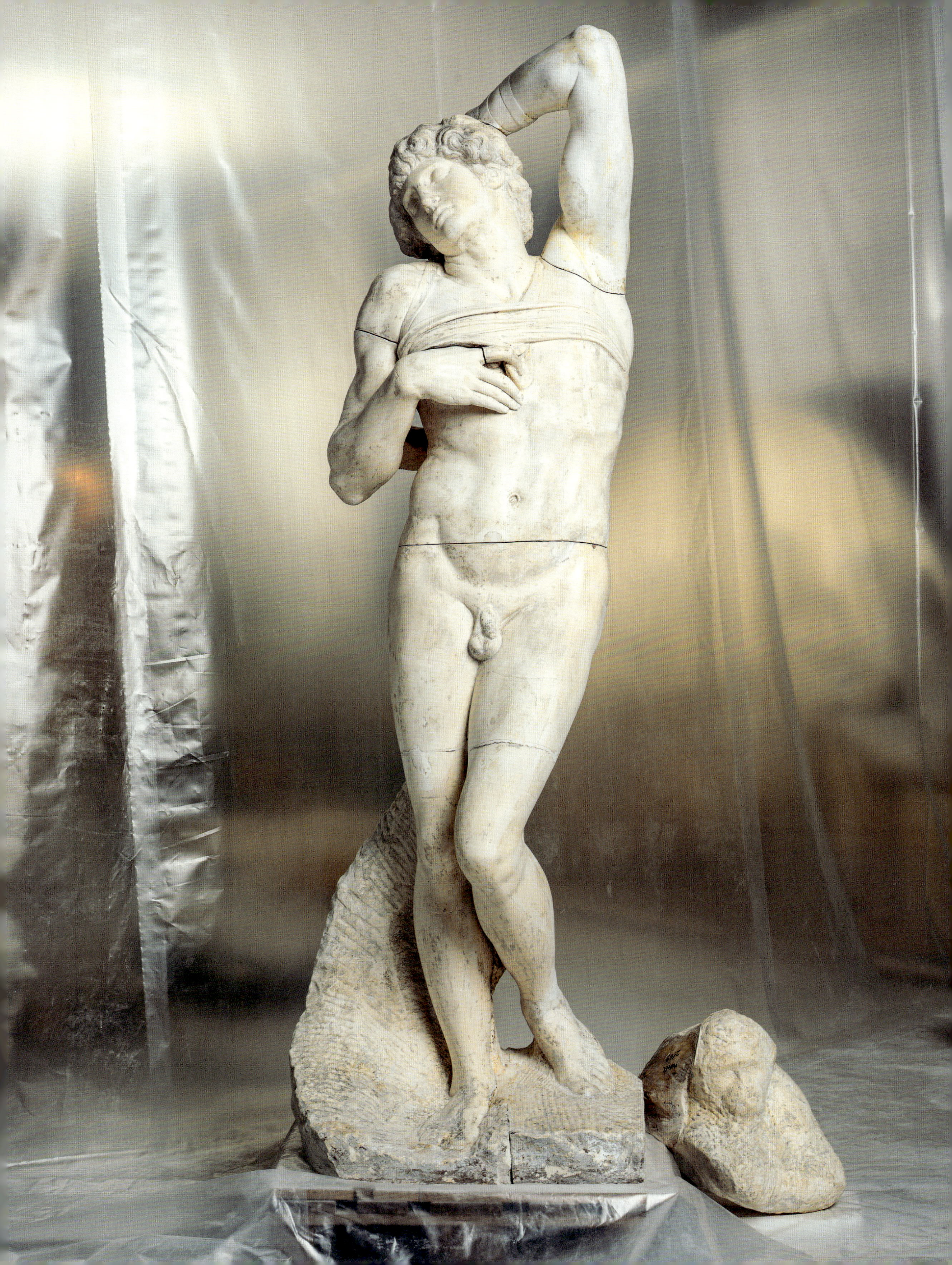

After the Naumburg master
Countess Uta of Naumburg
Painting model, 1937
Staatliche Museen zu Berlin,
Gipsformerei

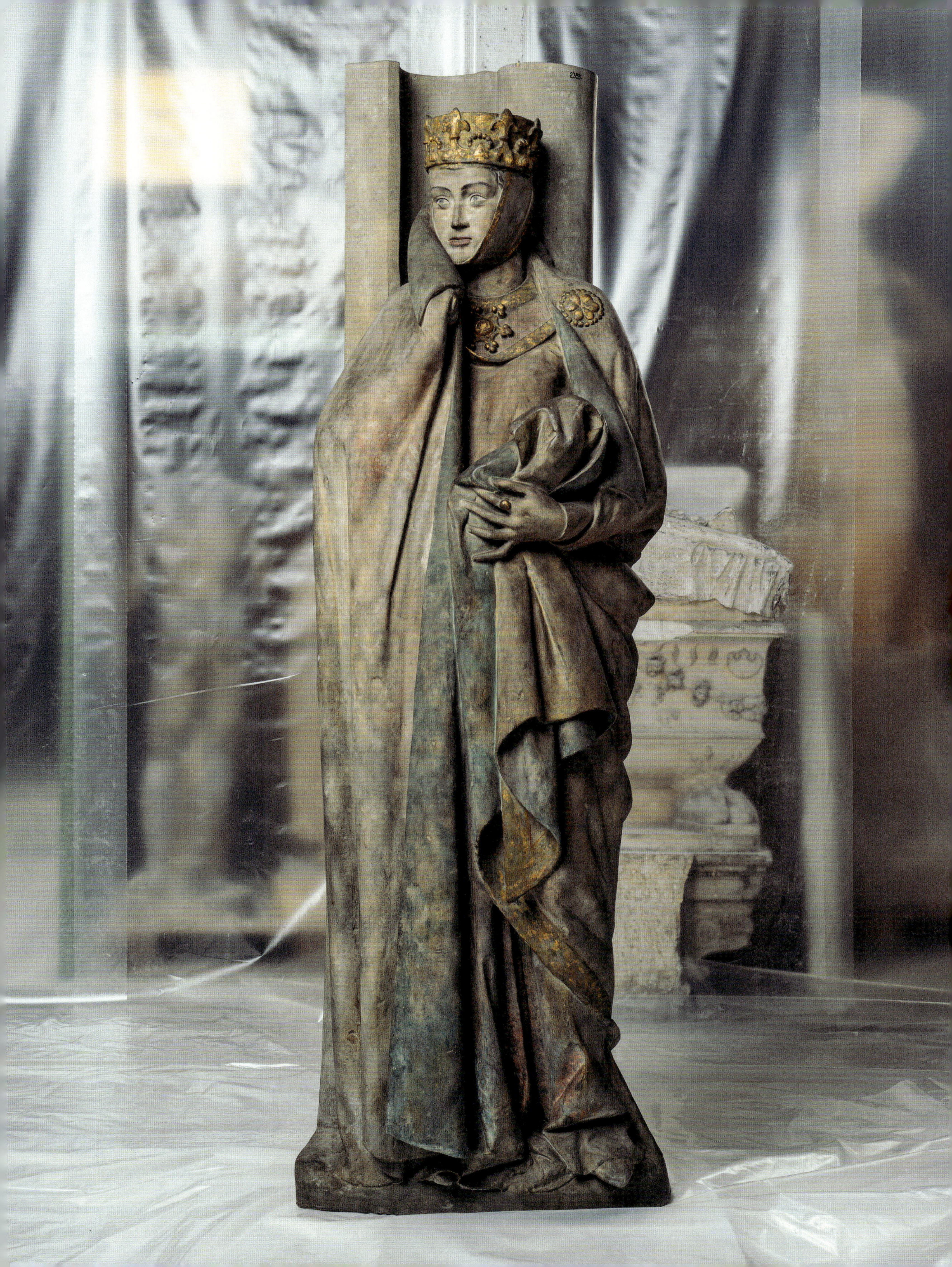

After Johann Gottfried Schadow
Crown Princess Luise of Prussia
and Princess Friederike
Master model with dismantled arms, 1926
Staatliche Museen zu Berlin, Gipsformerei

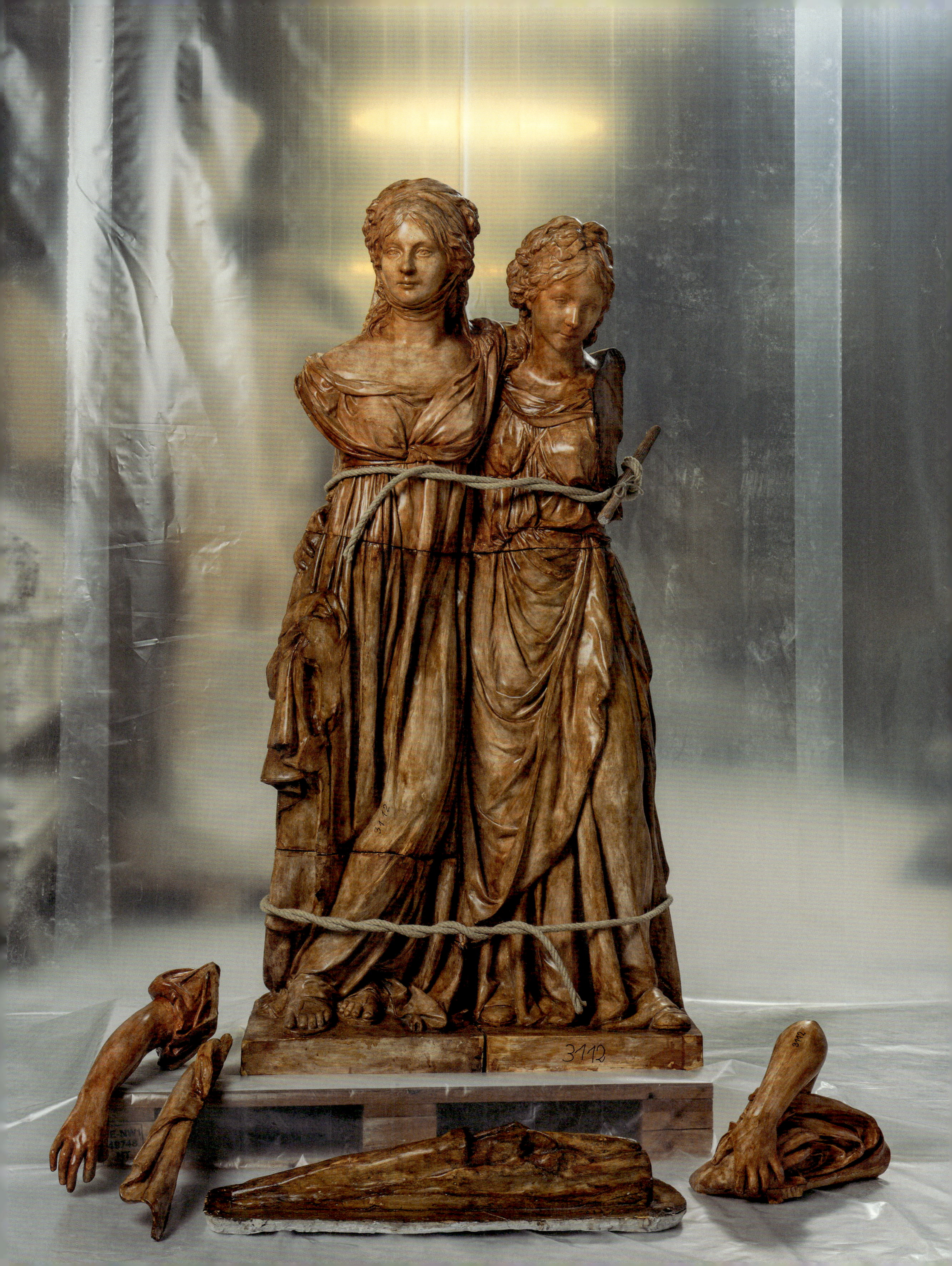
3112

Laocoön Group
Master model, 1844
Staatliche Museen zu Berlin,
Gipsformerei

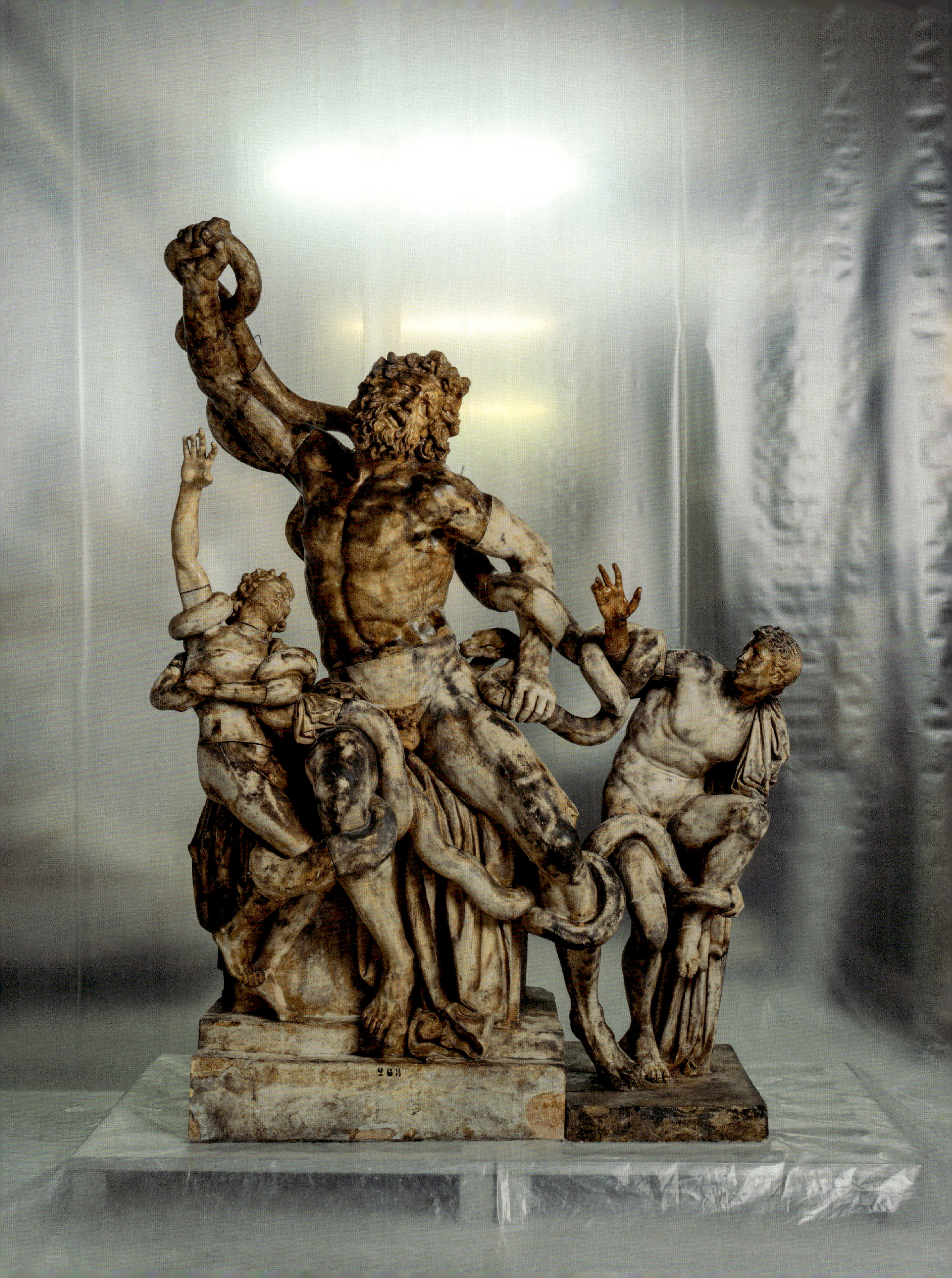

'Berlin Supplies the World with Gods':[1] The History of the Gipsformerei, Staatliche Museen zu Berlin, 1819–2019

Hans Georg Hiller von Gaertringen

Ich bin ganz anders, ganz speziell,
Ich bin ein Serienmodell.
(I'm totally different, very special,
I'm a production model.)
Haiyti, *Serienmodell*, 2018

The foundation of Berlin's Gipsformerei in 1819 was one of the initiatives of the Prussian state after the victory over Napoleon and part of its reform to reinvigorate art, science and industry.[2] The model for this reform, however, was the former enemy: France, a country in many respects more progressive than Prussia. Not only did the Louvre serve as a template for the first museum in Berlin, the Altes Museum, which opened in 1830, the Gipsformerei, too, was based on the Parisian museum's department *L'Atelier de moulage*, founded in 1794.[3] Following the example set by the Louvre, the Altes Museum was to have a plaster casting workshop installed alongside, and, as in Paris, the workshop in fact became operational a few years before the museum.

This integral aspect of the foundation of the Königliche Museen (Royal Museums) becomes clear from the memorandum Karl Friedrich Schinkel composed together with Aloys Hirt in 1825 for Friedrich Wilhelm III. In the document, they outline the concept for Berlin's first museum buildings, whose construction had by then just got underway. Schinkel and Hirt distinguished (both in terms of exhibition idea and use of space) between originals and casts, but they accorded pride of place to the casts of 'the principal works of antiquity'. In their planning, parts of the main floor and even the rotunda were to be set aside for 'the Aigina pediments, the beautiful remnants of the Parthenon, and from Phigalia, the Niobe group, etc.'[4]

The first proposal for the establishment of the Gipsformerei is said to have been put forward in 1815 by the writer Philipp Joseph Rehfues, who at the time was Prussia's military attaché in Paris; a position he held briefly.[5] Art historian Sibylle Einholz sums up his argument as follows: 'The especially favourable and amicable constellation that existed at that time among Europe's governments, united by a deep sense of relief after shaking free of the Napoleonic yoke, ensured that requests for the permission to take mouldings of outstanding sculptures would be acceded to in a spirit of goodwill. Replication of these works of art would contribute to a refinement of taste and to the establishment of an assuredly lucrative art industry. The balance sheet of the Parisian institution provided sufficient evidence for the demand of products from such an industry.[6] Given that plaster casts had to be purchased in Italy at high cost and the neoclassical period had pushed the demand for ancient works of art, such an enterprise seemed viable enough.

The search was now on for someone to lead the planned institution, someone equally proficient as a sculptor and as an expert on casting. Prussian Minister of the Interior Friedrich von Schuckmann chose the sculptor Christian Daniel Rauch. As the procurement of moulds was the most pressing concern, Rauch was commissioned on 1 February 1816 to travel to Italy with the task of uncovering what ancient works of art suitable for moulding could be found and in which museums.[7] The question of costs held high priority for the Ministry of the Interior. Rauch decided then to remain in Italy for two years to work on several projects to compensate. It was another year after his return in 1818 before the Ministry's aim of contributing 'to disseminating a proper understanding of art and a refined taste'[8] through the public access to collections of casts was within reach. To achieve this aim, a plaster casting workshop in Berlin was a necessity. On 8 December 1819 the *Abguss-Anstalt* (Plaster Casting Workshop) was formally established by a Royal cabinet directive. A catalyst for this development was presumably the arrival of the first worker: the Italian artistic plaster caster Domenico Bianconi, a citizen of Carrara, whose expertise was required for the foundation of the workshop, had arrived in Berlin after undertaking a journey over thirty-seven days by foot. (He worked twenty-eight years for Rauch and the Gipsformerei.)[9] Rauch had succeeded 'in transplanting a centuries-old tradition of Italian handcraft to the Prussian capital'.[10]

In the first decades of its existence, the Gipsformerei was part of Rauch's workshop rather than an autonomous outfit. The production of the casts occurred there at the so-called old Lagerhaus on Klosterstraße 76, which was also his place of residence from May 1818 (ill. below).[11] Rauch left the execution of the casts to his workmen. First and foremost among them was the Berlin stucco plasterer G. Carl Seeger (resident at Gipsstraße 15), who had been trained by Bianconi to be in charge of the casting outfit from 1824 onwards.[12] There were two apprentices: Seeger's son Christian, who succeeded his father's position after his untimely death,[13] and Friedrich Müller, one of Rauch's students, whose name appears as head of the workshop in 1843.[14] Procurement of moulds from Italy was the domain of another enterprising student, Emil Wolff, who took up residence in Rome in 1822.[15]

A particularly rich resource regarding the development of what was on offer at the Gipsformerei in this period are its historical price lists and sales catalogues. The oldest of such lists that still exist, dated to 1824 (ill. p. 218), 1828 and ca. 1843, each remain as single copies. In keeping with the spirit of neoclassicism, the 149 items on the first list were either classical works or

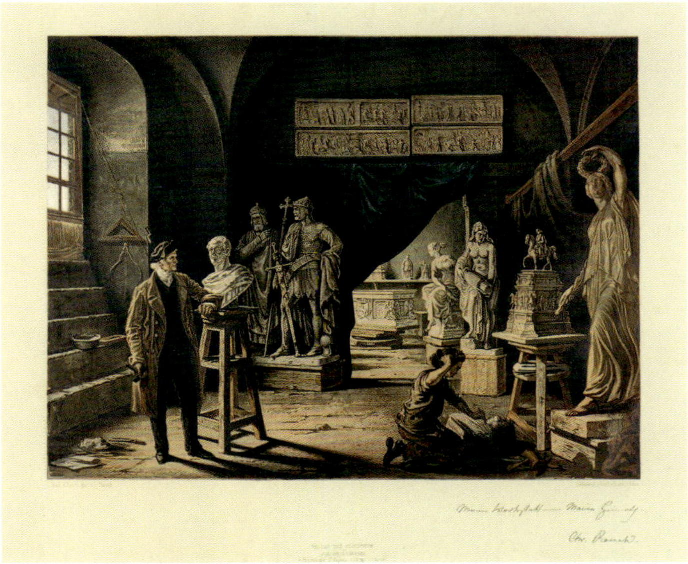

Storch and Kramer (Berlin) after
a drawing by Ludwig Pietsch
Christian Daniel Rauchs Werkstatt im Königlichen Lagerhaus, 1856
Colour lithograph
Museum Bad Arolsen

PREIS-COURANT

nachstehender, durch den Stuccateur *Carl Seeger* zu Berlin, im Königlichen Lagerhause, Kloster-Strafse No. 76. verkäuflicher Gips-Abgüsse antiker und moderner Sculpturen.

A. antike Sculpturen.

I. Statuen.

No.		Gröfse Rheinländ. Fufs	Zoll	Preis Thlr.	Gr.
1	Apollo von Belvedere (aus dem Museo vaticano)	7	2	47	—
2	Ganymed (sich anlehnend) aus dem Museo Chiaramonti im vatican	4	2	15	—
3	Amor (den Bogen spannend) aus dem Museo capitolino	4	2	15	—
4	Vestalin (colossal.) . . . im Augusteum zu Dresden	6	6	31	—
5	Ariadne oder Parze (sitzend (colossal.) . . ebendaselbst	5	6	52	12
6	Minerva (colossal.) ohne Arme . . . ebendaselbst	7	4	31	—
7	Vestalin, (lebensgrofs) . . . ebendaselbst	5	6	25	5
8	Minerva . . . ebendaselbst	4	—	18	14
9	Minerva, lebensgrofs in altgriechischem Styl ebendaselbst	4	9	12	9
10	Faun, lebensgrofs . . . ebendaselbst	5	—	15	22
11	Thetis oder Venus veluta . . . ebendaselbst	4	1	15	11
12	Bachus . . . ebendaselbst	5	8	7	17
13	Achilles, bekleidet mit Mantel und Tuni[illegible] [illegible] Antiken Tempel zu Potsdam	5	4	25	—
14	Ulysses, desgl. . . . ebendaselbst	6	—	25	—
15	Muse, mit dem eingehüllten auf einem Fels aufstützenden rechten Arm ebendaselbst	4	9	25	—
16	Muse, anlehnend . . . ebendaselbst	4	9	20	—
17	Muse, geradestehend . . . ebendaselbst	4	9	20	—
18	Muse, mit einer Gemme in der Hand, . . . ebendaselbst	4	9	20	—
19	Muse, mit einem Spiegel in der Hand, . . . ebendaselbst	4	9	17	—
20	Nymphe, Anchyrrhoé (Eigenthum Sr. Excellenz des St. M. v. Humbold zu Tegel.	5	10	15	—

II. antike Büsten und Köpfe.

No.		Gröfse Rheinländ. Fufs	Zoll	Preis Thlr.	Gr.
1	Juno ludovisi (colossal.)	4	10	25	—
2	Apollo Belvedere (im Museo vaticano)	2	6	6	—
3	Diana von Versailles (im Pariser Museum	2	4	5	—
4	Minerva mit der Aegis mit Greiffen am Helm, (in England befindlich	2	7	6	—
5	Apollo justiniani (Eigenthum des Grafen Pourtales zu Paris	2	7	5	—
6	Jason, (kleiner als die Natur)	1	10	2	—
7	Minerva, (colossal.) . . . im Antiken-Tempel zu Potsdam	2	9	5	12
8	Jupiter, . . . ebendaselbst			2	—
9	Heros, . . . ebendaselbst			1	12
10	Juno, . . . ebendaselbst			1	12
11	Faun, des Praxiteles . . . ebendaselbst			1	8
12	Vitellius, . . . ebendaselbst			1	18
13	Julius Caesar, . . . ebendaselbst			2	—

No.		Gröfse Rheinländ. Fufs	Zoll	Preis Thlr.	Gr.
14	Weibliche Büste mit antiken Fufs und Innschrift ebendaselbst	2		2	8
15	Bildnifs eines Sarmaten . . . ebendaselbst			1	8
16	Weiblicher Kopf mit der Mauerkrone, im Augusteum zu Dresden	1	9	1	13
17	Antinous, in aegyptischen Styl . . . ebendaselbst	1	9	1	13
18	Männliches Bildnifs . . . ebendaselbst	1	5	2	7

III. antike Basreliefs.

No.			Gröfse Rheinländ. Fufs	Zoll	Preis Thlr.	Gr.
1	Parzen, die drei, E. S. Ex. des St. M. von Humbold zu Tegel	lang / hoch	5 / 2	4 / 5	6	—
2	Latona, Diana, Apollo und Hebe, altgriechischen Styls in der Königlichen Kunst-Kammer zu Berlin	lang / hoch	5 / 2	5 / 2	6	—
3	Jupiter, Museo Rondanini, Eigenthum S. E. des St. M. v. Humbold zu Tegel	hoch / breit	2 / 1	2 / 6	2	—
4	Vulcan, Museo Rondanini . . . desgleichen	hoch / breit	2 / 1	2 / 6	2	—
5	Hierodule Museo Chiaramonti im Vatican	hoch / breit	2 / 1	2 / 6	2	—
6	Hierophant . . . ebendaselbst	hoch / breit	2 / 1	2 / 6	2	—
7	Busto, Kopf in runder Niesche mit 2 Victorien und 2 Adlern umgeben		1	5	2	7
8	Candelabre Fufs dreieckig, altgriechischen Styls mit basreliefs verziert, von seltener Schönheit, im Augusteum zu Dresden		4	3	27	21
9	Indische Gottheit, Indischer Sculptur Königliche Kunstkammer	hoch / breit	2 / 1	5 / 5	6	—
10	Hercules und Juno, des Florentiner Museums		—	7	—	12
11	Weibliches Bildnifs wahrscheinlich von Leonardo da Vinci im Augusteum zu Dresden		1	6	1	14

IV. Fragmente.

No.		Gröfse Rheinländ. Fufs	Zoll	Preis Thlr.	Gr.
1	Venus, Körper mit dem Kopf, im Augusteum zu Dresden	3	6	6	4
2	Nymphe, bekleidetes Untertheil, . . ebendaselbst	3	6	10	20
3	Grazien, Torso, in Athen gefunden, E. S. C. des St. M. v. Humbold zu Tegel	3	7	7	—
4	Amor, Torso (in schreitender Stellung) . . . desgleichen	2	—	3	—
5	Genius des Todes, in England befindlich	1	—	—	20
6	Füfse des Antinous, im Pallast Braschi zu Rom			2	—
7	Käuzchen auf einem Sculptur-Trümmer sitzend über Bronze geformt, im Museo zu Braunschweig	—	10	1	—
8	Ein Sarkophag-Fufs mit einem Greiff-Kopf E. S. E. des St. M. v. Humbold zu Tegel	1	8	2	—
9	Venus Torso in sehr bewegter Stellung	1	5	1	16
10	Apollo von Belvedere, beide Beine			4	—

B. Moderne Sculpturen.

I.

No.			Gröfse Rheinländ. Fufs	Zoll	Preis Rthl.	Gr.
1	Pferdekopf beinah Lebensgröfse				6	—
2	Löwe, schreitend	hoch / breit	3 / 1	10 / 4	5	—
3	Adler freistehend, mit ausgebreiteten Flügeln	hoch	1	8	27	—
4	Greiff, stehend				2	12
5	Greiff, springend	hoch	1	—	2	—
6	Blücher Statue für Breslau (Copie)		2	—	7	—
7	Sphynx, kleine Copie	lang	1	6	2	—
8, 9	Zwei kleine Adler, stehend, pro Stück 2 Rthlr.	Stück hoch		6	4	—
10	Adler lebensgrofs, auf dem Blitz stehend		2	3	9	—
11, 12	Zwei Schlangen über die Natur geformt, das Stück				1	—
13	Adlerkopf, über Marmor geformt		1	2	2	—
14	Parze, sitzend, von Asmus Karstens		1	6	2	—

II. Moderne Basreliefs.

No.			Gröfse Rheinländ. Fufs	Zoll	Preis Rthl.	Gr.
1	Jünglinge, zwei, vom Denkmahle Scharnhorsts, 4 Rthlr. 12 gr. jedes	hoch / breit	2 / 3	10 / 8	9	—
2	Victorie auf dem Adler, vom Denkmahl Bülows	hoch / breit	3 / 3	10 / 8	12	—
3	Adler, von demselben Denkmahl				12	—
4	Preufsischer Wappen-Adler		—	8	—	12
5	Adler mit einem Helm spielend		—	8	—	12
6	Adler in einem Lorbeerkranz sitzend, rund		1	1	1	12
7	Engels-Gestalt kniend ein Täfelchen haltend		1	10	2	—
8	Weibliche Figur desgleichen auf eine Tafel schreibend		1	10	2	12
9	Weiblicher Genius, etrurischer		1	10	2	—
10	Barberinische Löwe, kleine Copie		1 / —	2 / 8	1	12
11	Der heilige Hieronimus, (aus der Königlichen Kunst-Kammer) von Donatello		1	8	3	12

III. Moderne Bildnisse in Büsten.

No.		Gröfse Rheinländ. Fufs	Zoll	Preis Rthl.	Gr.
1	Sr. Majestät des Königs mit Uniform und Mantel (früher)	2	4	10	—
2	dieselbe . . . (die neueste)	2	4	10	—
3	dieselbe ohne Bekleidung	2	—	7	—
4	der höchstseligen Königinn Majestät mit dem Schleier	2	—	7	—
5	Sr. K. H. des Kronprinzen	2	—	7	—
6	dieselbe mit dem Mantel	2	4	10	—
7	I. K. H. der Frau Grofsfürstin Alexandra von Rufsland	1	10	7	—
8	dieselbe mit Bekleidung	2	—	10	—
9	Sr. K. H. des Grofsfürsten Nicolas	2	1	7	—
10	I. K. H. der Frau Frb-Grofs-Herzoginn von Meklenburg-Schwerin	2	—	7	—
11	dieselbe mit Bekleidung	2	4	8	—
12	Sr. K. H. des Prinzen Wilhelm, Bruder Sr. M. des Königs	2	—	7	—
13	I. K. H. der Prinzefsin Wilhelm	2	—	7	—
14	Sr. M. des Kaiser Alexander von Rufsland	2	—	6	—
15	Ihro Durchlaucht der regierenden Frau Herzoginn von Anhalt-Dessau	2	—	6	—
16	I. D. der regierenden Frau Herzoginn von Anhalt-Köthen	2	—	6	—
17	S. D. des Feld-Marschalls Fürsten Blücher von Wahlstatt			6	—
18	desgleichen Colossaler Köpf, der Statue desselben zu Breslau	3	—	12	—
19	der General-Major Graf von Brandenburg	2	2	6	—
20	S. Ex. des Feld-Marschalls Graf Kleist von Nollendorf	2	—	7	—
21	S. Ex. des Feld-Marschalls Graf York von Wartenburg			6	—
22	S. Ex. des General Grafen Bülow von Dennewitz			6	—
23	S. Ex. des General Grafen von Gneisenau	2	—	6	—
24	S. Ex. des Geheimen Staats-Minister von Kircheisen	2	5	10	—
25	S. Ex. des Geheimen Staats-Minister von Humboldt	1	8	6	—
26	S. D. des Staats-Kanzlers Fürst von Hardenberg	2	—	6	—
27	dieselbe mit dem Mantel	2	5	9	—
28	Goethe	1	9	5	—
29	Berzelius Physikus	2	—	6	—
30	Alexander von Humboldt	2	—	6	—
31	Heim Dr. Medicinae	2	—	6	—
32	Thorwaldsen Bildhauer	2	3	7	—
33	Zacharias Werner Dichter	1	10	6	—
34	Schinkel Architect	2	1	6	—
35	Wolff Philolog	2	—	6	—
36	Schadow Bildhauer	1	10	6	—
37	Rauch Bildhauer	2	1	6	—
38	Tieck Dichter	2	—	6	—
39	Jacobi Philosoph	1	9	6	—
40	Lorenzo Medicis magnifico (Maske)	1	3	1	4
41	Dante dessen Todten Maske	1	—	—	16

Vermerk. Bei sammtlichen vorangeführten Büsten ist die Abnahme der Gufs-Nahte mit inbegriffen, ohne Abnahme derselben sind die gröfseren 20 u. die kleineren 16 Gr. billiger.

IV. Verzierungen Alter und Neuer Sculptur.

No.		Gröfse Rheinländ. Fufs	Zoll	Preis Rthl.	Gr.
1	Consol (antiker) im Museo Vaticano	1	1	3	8
2 bis 22	mehrere Verzierungen verschiedener Arten und Gröfse, zusammen			15	20
23	Vase, antike Form, ganz einfach	1	3	1	—
24	Löwenkopf, männlicher, über die Natur geformt			2	16

Bemerkungen.

a. *Die Versendungen nach aufserhalb würden zweckmäfsiger durch Wasser- oder Land-Transport, als durch die Post zu bewirken sein.*

b. *Für die Verpackung welche der Stuccateur Carl Seeger zu übernehmen bereit ist, wird eine billige Vergütigung besonders in Rechnung gestellt.*

Price list of the *Abguss-Anstalt*, n.d. [1824]
Goethe- und Schiller-Archiv, Weimar

Friedrich Tieck
Christian Daniel Rauch
Master model, 1818
52.5 × 40 × 26 cm
Staatliche Museen zu Berlin, Alte Nationalgalerie, BII 164

Christian Daniel Rauch
Goethe im Hausrock
Original model, 1829
41 × 13 × 12 cm
Staatliche Museen zu Berlin, Alte Nationalgalerie, RM 26a

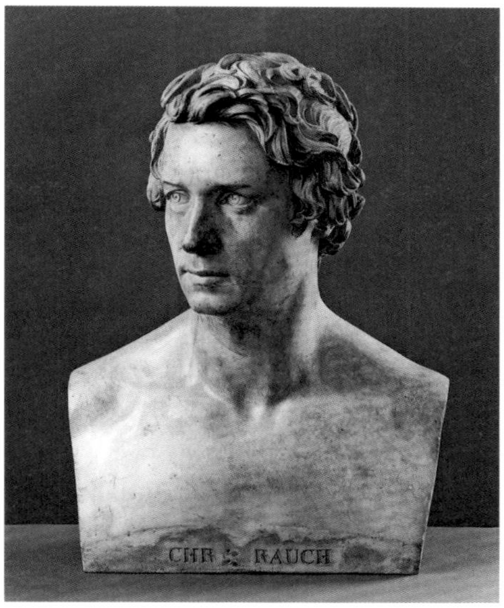

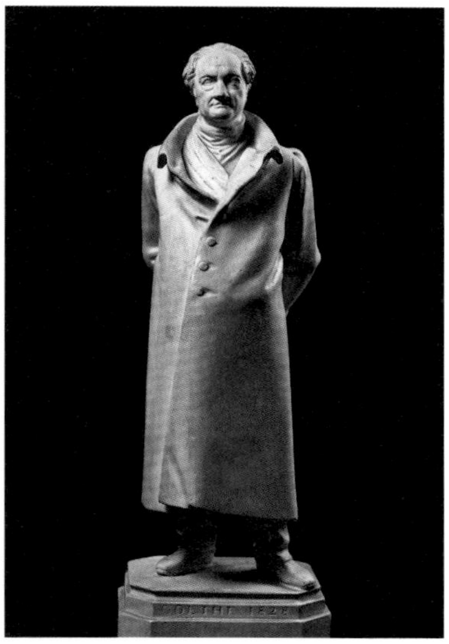

catering to the studies of the classicist.[16] The most prominent (and the most expensive) item was the *Apollo Belvedere* (ca. 120–140 CE), now installed at the Vatican, priced at 47 *Reichstaler*. The great majority of the fifty-seven casts of ancient sculptures had been moulded from statues close to hand, such as those in the Antikentempel in Potsdam and Dresden's Antikensammlung, which is referred to as the 'Augusteum' in the list.[17] How closely linked the Gipsformerei was at the time to the workshop of Rauch can be gathered from the sixty-six casts of 'modern sculptures' on offer, which with only a few exceptions were all works by the master. Rauch's own portrait bust was on sale as well. It was created in 1818 by Friedrich Tieck, who remained unnamed in the sales catalogue as did all the other artistic plasterers (ill. above).[18]

The second extant price list from 1828 shows that attempts were underway to replicate statuary in plaster with a creative twist. A Minerva from the collection in Dresden was now on offer not only as a cast of the fragmentary original for 12 *Reichstaler*, but also in a 'restored' edition by Rauch — only in this version did the figure present itself in flawless completeness. All telltale signs of the additional pieces used to connect the fragments were removed. No wonder then that this newly found perfection came at a price, 22 *Reichstaler* to be exact. At the same time the Gipsformerei struck out by marketing individual parts of statues at bargain prices. Anyone who found the *Apollo Belvedere* beyond their reach was free to purchase the statue's 'Eye and Mouth' for a mere 15 *Silbergroschen*. It seems that only a few years later the first experiments were made with lifecasts: tradition has it that Müller moulded a live dog in 1832.[19] The cast of a crocodile was added later to the sales catalogue (ill. p. 29).[20]

The price list of 1824 was rediscovered in the study of Johann Wolfgang von Goethe in Weimar.[21] In the later years of his life, the poet had befriended Rauch and shown a keen interest in his work — notably where his own person was concerned. The workshop gave Goethe his own bust (1820) by Rauch, model of a Goethe monument for Frankfurt (1823) and the statuette *Goethe im Hausrock* (1828, ill. above) as a gift. The statuette was also on sale for an interested public at the Gipsformerei for 4 *Reichstaler*. Goethe in plaster was a big seller with the Berliners, Carl Friedrich Zelter reported to Weimar in 1830: 'Your bust, Schiller's bust and that of our King are to be found in all shapes and sizes on the dressers and console tables of even the most humble dwelling.'[22] It seems that casts proved to be an ideal medium to encapsulate the nineteenth-century worship of genius. Furthermore, the orders Goethe placed with the Gipsformerei attest to how works of art around 1800 had become 'mobile', accessible and replicable. Ancient statues and busts which had either been dug up relatively recently or had stood for centuries in the same Italian palace were now placed on display in museums, which only added to their reputation and status as objects of desire. 'In Rome, where one is surrounded by such statues day after day, one becomes covetous and wishes to make them part of one's permanent surroundings, and the

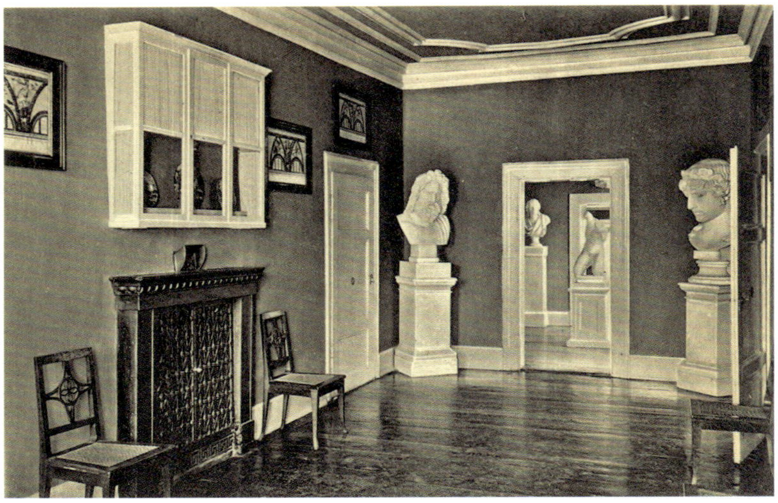

'Gelber Salon' (Yellow Lounge) at Goethe's house in Weimar, with Bust of Antinous (right)
Private collection postcard, ca. 1900

best way to do this is to acquire good plaster casts.'[23] Almost forty years after his first encounter with the ancient bust of Antinous at the Villa Mondragone near Frascati, Goethe still held it in his mind's eye. The work had been moved to the Louvre meantime, and so the Weimar prince of poets commissioned Rauch to produce a plaster cast. After some delay the sculptor was in a position to tell Goethe in 1828, that at last, 'I hope the colossus will be ready by spring to move in with you'[24] (ill. above).

The success story of plaster casts of ancient artworks in the nineteenth century doubles with the democratisation of art ownership. The once inaccessible cult statue framed by sacred space was transformed into a museum exhibit to be studied at close proximity and under optimal lighting conditions. This was soon followed by the phenomenon of the replica, which the public was free to buy to adorn their homes.

The mission statement of the Abguss-Anstalt included supplying Prussia's museums with casts of famous artworks whose originals were impossible to acquire. Upending Hirt's and Schinkel's 1825 planning, Wilhelm von Humboldt, head of the commission for the establishment of the Altes Museum, decreed in 1830: 'It goes without saying that plaster casts of statues will be excluded, without exception, from the Royal Museum.'[25] The museum for which he was co-responsible instead was to be exclusively the preserve of originals. Plaster casts only made their way into museums when the public's interest shifted from aesthetics to art-historical concerns. In 1841, a decision was made with regard to the second museum building, the Neues Museum, to reserve the prestigious main floor for the presentation of casts and so to create a universal museum of sculpture comprising an impressive array of masterpieces. Soon after the museum's opening the exhibition *Sammlung der Abgüsse* (Collection of Casts) displayed 'more than one thousand works' (ill. right).[26] The main supplier was Rauch's Abguss-Anstalt, which thus became the Museen-Formerei (Plaster Casting Workshop of the Royal Museums).[27] The production of the casts was moved from Rauch's workshop to Museumsinsel to facilitate transport of the objects to the Neues Museum.[28] This workshop was located in the museum's basement. Initially, the workshop was allocated one room, while the other rooms were rented out to a wholesale wine merchant, who then moved out in 1842, citing the 'general shift in temperature'.[29] However, the space was still insufficient and just one year later the Gipsformerei moved into the foundry on Münzstraße 10, where the new rooms were 'inaugurated by casting the Colossi of Monte Cavallo'.[30] This just goes to show that the technical developments for realising different formats of casts were steadily on the increase during the nineteenth century, as seen by the two colossal ancient statues of the 'Horse Tamers' (sixth–fifth century BCE), from Rome's Quirinal Hill that adorn the middle landing of the Neues Museum.

The Gipsformerei had become an institution of crucial importance to the museums of Berlin. However, it

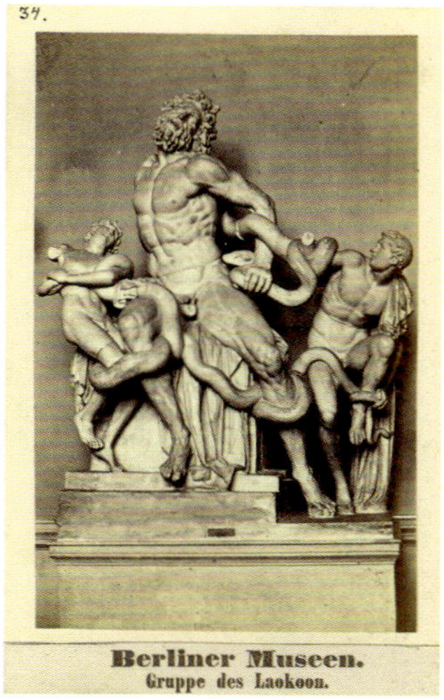

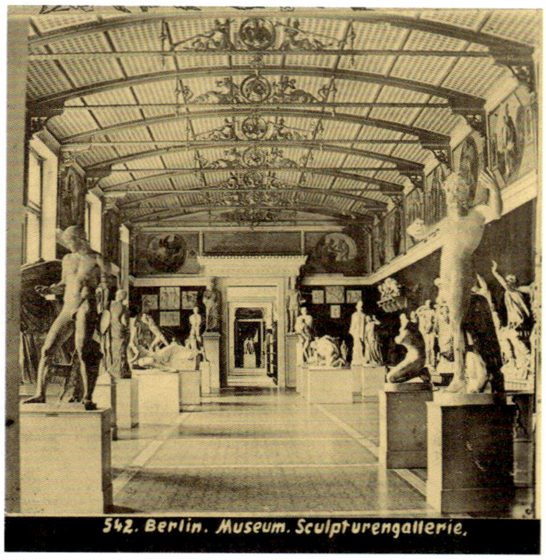

Stereoscopisches Institut Moser senior Berlin, Neues Museum, Berlin, *Laocoön Group* (plaster cast of the sculpture as shown at the museum), 1867–68
Collection Norbert Franken

Unknown photographer
'Berlin. Museum. Sculpturengallerie' (Hall of the Niobids, Neues Museum, Berlin, with plaster casts of works from Greco-Roman antiquity), before 1868
Collection Norbert Franken

did not restrict its production to their needs only, but continued to produce both for the market and archaeological collections as well as museums outside of Berlin. This is seen in the regularly updated sales catalogues, which list the Horse Tamers as the most expensive item: it was for sale in 1871 for 1,200 *Reichstaler*, an exorbitant sum by any standard.[31] Alongside the Gipsformerei, other smaller casting outfits in Berlin, such as Vicent and Thora (both mentioned as early as 1820),[32] Micheli (operational from 1824) and the foundry of Georg Eichler (ca. 1840),[33] served the growing commercial market.

The significance of the Museen-Formerei and the demands put forward by the newly founded museums of Berlin kept broadening the scope of works on offer. Each new collection area adopted by the Prussian art collections was reflected sooner or later in the sales catalogue of the Gipsformerei. The 1858 list, for instance, featured thirty works from Egypt for the first time: the Neues Museum with its Egyptian collection had opened three years previously. The 1824 sales catalogue had featured one ethnological object: an Indian deity from the art cabinet of the Schloss, which was on offer for five *Reichstaler*. However, the influence of non-European cultures only began to leave a noticeable mark after the opening of Berlin's Ethnologisches Museum in 1886. In 1882, only three works were included in the sales catalogue; twenty years later the inventory stood at two hundred eighty works. The countries of origin reflected the prevailing interest in particular cultures at the time: almost half the ethnological objects originated from the Aztecs of Mexico; Africa was represented by only one isolated exhibit of ornaments from Jumbe graves in East Africa. After 1945, the ethnological collection was expanded to become one of the largest subsections with almost 1,500 items, evident of the growing interest in non-European art and the expansion of the museum of non-European art and culture in Dahlem. The 'anthropological material', as it is called,[34] listed in the sales catalogue of 1893 leaves trace of the colonial era in the history of the Gipsformerei. This was the last collection area to be developed. Ethnological moulding campaigns conducted by German anthropologists resulted in the faces and bodies of Indigenous peoples being cast in plaster, which in turn expanded the scope of what was on offer at the Gipsformerei.[35]

In keeping with all the new collection areas, the main classical antiquity section continued to grow apace as well. A spectacular growth spurt occurred after 1874, the year marking the start of German excavation work in Olympia under new rules: all finds had to remain in place. The museums of Berlin reacted to this by despatching the sculptor Richard Grüttner to Greece. Grüttner and his team were commissioned with moulding all significant finds. One hundred and fifty such objects appeared in the sales catalogue of 1882 for the first time and have been marketed exclusively by the Gipsformerei ever since.[36]

Artworks dating from the periods between the Middle Ages and the baroque hardly featured at all in the

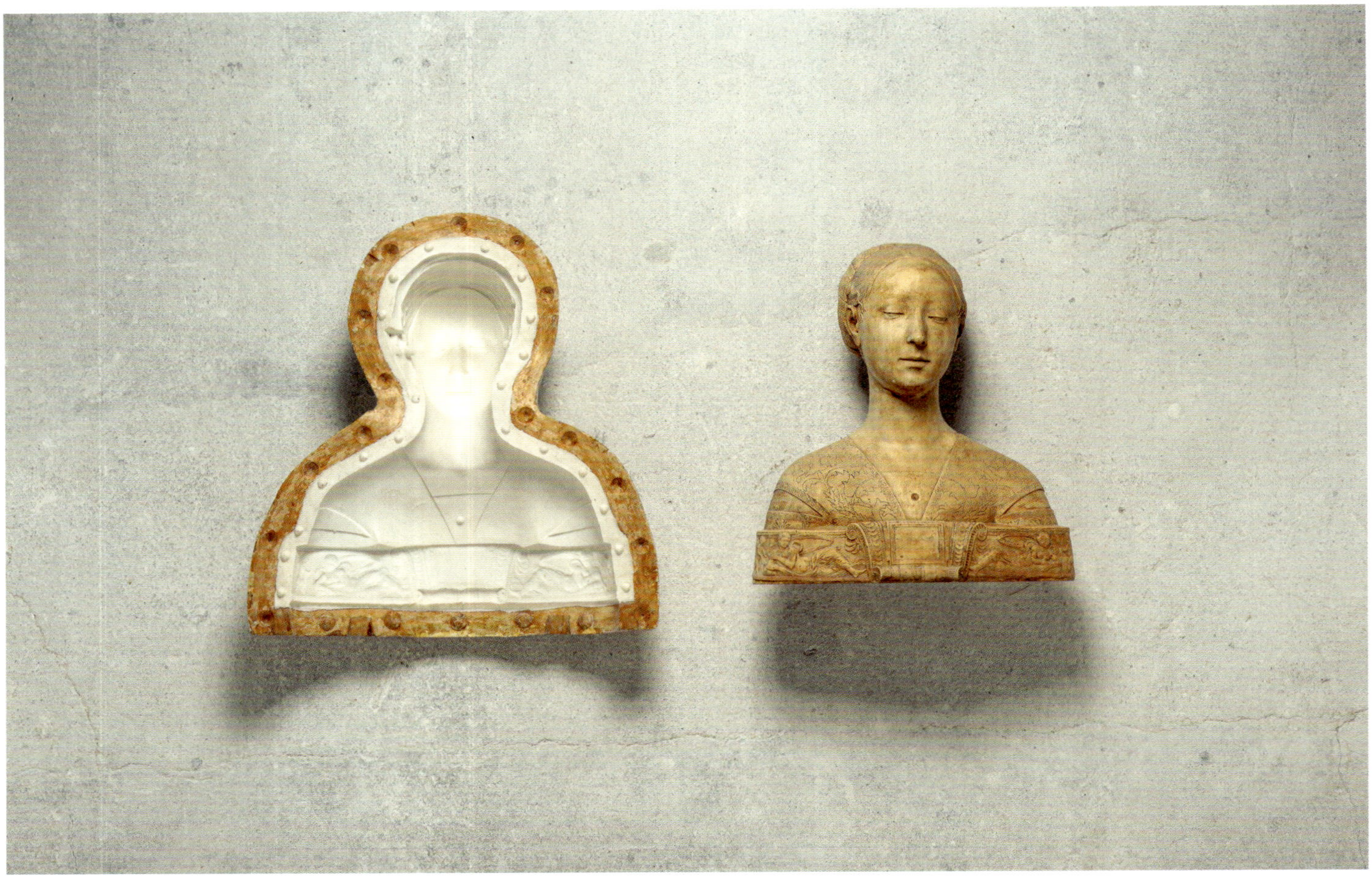

first sales catalogues. It was only after the cast collections were installed in the Neues Museum in 1855 that artworks from these eras were increasingly regarded as collectable objects. Expansion was most marked around 1900, when Wilhelm von Bode held the post of general director. Works from the Italian Renaissance were held in high esteem at this time, and so it is no wonder that many Italian masterpieces were added to the collection of the Gipsformerei, such as the *Portrait of a Neapolitan Princess* (ca. 1470) by Francesco Laurana. This bust was badly damaged in World War II and is today split into two pieces shared between the Bode Museum (head) and Moscow's Pushkin State Museum of Fine Arts (shoulders). The cast at the Gipsformerei has survived to give us an idea of what the original looked like (ill. above).

Around 1900, curators of Prussia's art collections, such as Bode, were still lavishly adding casts to their museums to document stylistic developments even when the originals were located in other places.[37] This allowed the Gipsformerei to gain prominent new acquisitions, such as the moulds of the *Bamberg Horseman* (early thirteenth century), who made his first appearance in the sales catalogue of 1893, or the complete set of the benefactors of Naumburg Cathedral in the following catalogue from 1906, including the famous *Uta von Naumburg* (mid-thirteenth century, ill. p. 211). One of the other collection areas was eclipsed at least temporarily: the subsection of architectural ornaments, numbering 215 items by 1871, was presumably integrated not long thereafter into the collection of the independent casting workshop of the newly established Kunstgewerbemuseum.[38]

The collection of works of neoclassicism and from the beginnings of the Gipsformerei under Rauch had only a small number of additions over time: in the ninety years between 1824 and 1914, its collection grew from 66 works to 126. This was due, above all, to the fact that after Rauch the collection concentrated on historical works to the complete exclusion of contemporary productions. It was only after 1945 that art from the early nineteenth century — having become historical

After Francesco Laurana
Portrait of a Neapolitan Princess
Silicone mould in mother mould, 2017, and master model, ca. 1924
(Original second half 15th century, Staatliche Museen zu Berlin, Skulpturensammlung and Museum für Byzantinische Kunst [head], Puschkin Museum Moscow [shoulder fragment])
Staatliche Museen zu Berlin, Gipsformerei

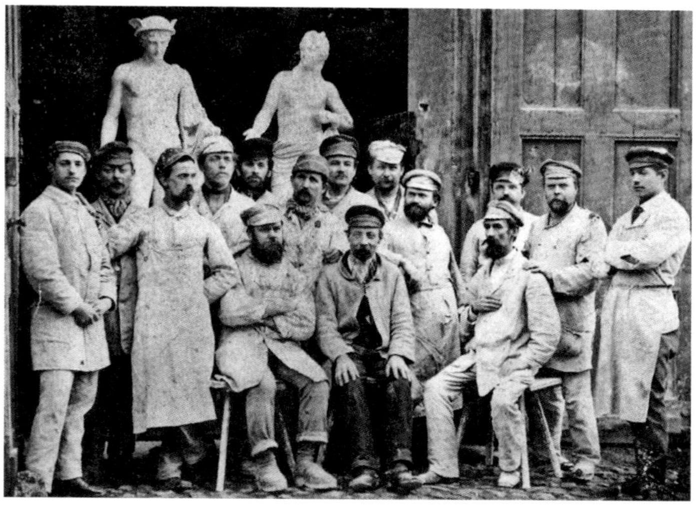

Unknown photographer
Staff of the Gipsformerei in Berlin-Charlottenburg, ca. 1900
Staatliche Museen zu Berlin, Gipsformerei

meantime — was considered worthy of collecting. The number of moulds has grown to today's total of 565 items. Iconic works were acquired, such as Johann Gottfried Schadow's *Prinzessinnengruppe* (Princesses Monument, 1795–97, ill. p. 213) and the portrait bust of Rauch's granddaughter, *Eugenie d'Alton* (1849). Modernism has never been a collection area of the Gipsformerei and the same is true of all subsequent art movements — *Rodin's Thinker* (1880–82) is one of the few exceptions from more recent art history.

In 1891, the Gipsformerei moved to the purpose-built establishment in Charlottenburg which it still occupies today (ill. above). Its relocation was partly due to its steadily growing collection, which numbered 1,500 moulds at the time, and in part to the tendency of museums to request ever larger objects — for works such as the northern entrance of the Liebfrauenkirche in Trier, the *Farnese Bull* (second century BCE–third century CE), or the *Bamberg Horseman*, the direct railway connection was undoubtedly a great advantage. There is also another reason why the relocation turned out to be most fortunate: the largely unique and irreplaceable moulds and casts would certainly not have survived World War II in the city centre with as little damage.

Today's repertoire of the Gipsformerei is much broader and all the more balanced in terms of the origins of its works of art and the eras they represent than it was in the nineteenth century. While it was relatively easy then to draw conclusions regarding the taste of the museum curators and private buyers from the sales catalogues, the Gipsformerei has become much more multilayered in the twentieth century. From Byzantine to nineteenth-century art, European art history is represented by the largest group of works, comprising roughly 2,000 objects. It is followed by works from non-European cultures, approximately 1,500 items. The former main collecting area of the Gipsformerei, Greco-Roman antiquity, with around 1,350 objects, has slipped to third place. The impressive expansion of the collection in the twentieth century is due in part to the development of collaborations, both national and international. Among its relatively recent acquisitions are a reliquary of the early thirteenth century from Quedlinburg Cathedral, the bust of the famous *Equestrian Statue of Bartolomeo Colleoni* (1480–88) by Andrea del Verrocchio in Venice, and Michelangelo's *Tondo Pitti* (1503–04) from Museo nazionale del Bargello in Florence. Far from being confined to works held by the museums in Berlin, the Gipsformerei has artworks in store from all over the world.

1 The title 'Berlin schickt Götter in die Welt' (Berlin Supplies the World with Gods) is borrowed from a feature article by Wolfgang Koeppen on the Gipsformerei in Berlin, first published in the *Berliner Börsen-Courier* on 14 May 1933. See 'Berlin schickt Götter in die Welt', in: *Gesammelte Werke*, vol. 5, *Berichte und Skizzen* 2, Frankfurt am Main 1990, pp. 66–68, here p. 66.
2 On the history of the Gipsformerei in Berlin, see Hans Georg Hiller von Gaertringen, *Meisterwerke der Gipsformerei: Kunstmanufaktur der Staatlichen Museen zu Berlin seit 1819*, Munich 2012. Prior groundbreaking research by Sibylle Einholz on the history of the Gipsformerei is included in Einholz, *'Feiner, weißer ... Gips!': Zur Bedeutung eines umstrittenen Materials*, exh. cat., Heimatmuseum Charlottenburg, 1 July–4 August 1991, Berlin 1991; Einholz, 'Enzyklopädie in Gips: Zur Sammlungsgeschichte der Berliner Museen', *Der Bär von Berlin* 41 (1992), pp. 75–96; Einholz, 'Die Jagd nach schönen Händen: Abformungen über Natur', *Museumsjournal* 1 (1994), pp. 56–59; and Einholz, 'Orte der Kontemplation und Erziehung: Zur Geschichte der Gipsabgusssammlungen in Berlin', in: *Meisterwerke mittelalterlicher Skulptur*, ed. Hartmut Krohm, Berlin 1996, pp. 11–39.
3 See Florence Rionnet, *L'Atelier de moulage du musée du Louvre (1794–1928)*, Paris 1996.
4 'J. Schinkel's und Hirt's Bericht an den König vom 31. October 1825', cited in Alfred von Wolzogen, *Aus Schinkels Nachlass: Reisetagebücher, Briefe und Aphorismen; Mitgetheilt und mit einem Verzeichniß sämmtlicher Werke Schinkels versehen*, Berlin 1862, p. 258. Unless otherwise stated, all translation by Otmar Binder.
5 Einholz, 'Orte der Kontemplation und Erziehung', p. 14; the later Prussian Minister of Culture Karl vom Stein zum Altenstein was the driving force of establishing the Gipsformerei. In 1815, he also initiated the foundation of the Bonn collection of casts, see Johannes Bauer and Wilfred Geominy (eds.), *Gips nicht mehr: Abgüsse als letzte Zeugen antiker Kunst*, exh. cat., Friedrich-Wilhelms-Universität Bonn and Akademisches Kunstmuseum, Antikensammlung der Universität Bonn, 14 December 2000–25 March 2001, Bonn 2000, p. 16. Rauch's biographer Friedrich Eggers, on the other hand, believes Prussian Minister of the Interior Friedrich von Schuckmann was the initiator of the museum; he is on record for having commissioned Rauch in February 1816 with building a collection of moulds. See Friedrich Eggers and Karl Eggers, *Christian Daniel Rauch*, 5 vols., Berlin 1873–87; especially Friedrich Eggers, vol. 1, Berlin 1873, pp. 156–57.
6 Einholz, 'Orte der Kontemplation und Erziehung', p. 14.
7 This plan did not find favour with all sculptors. Christian Friedrich Tieck, whose works were later integrated into the inventory of the Gipsformerei, fearing perhaps the competition of a soon to be commercially available antiquity, warned Christian Daniel Rauch in March 1816: 'There is a wish to make casts and to make a profit from the enterprise. A great deal of money is needed to make the requisite number of mouldings, and transporting the forms is expensive and involves toil and danger.' Bernhard Maaz, 'Zwischen Künstlermuseen und staatlicher Kunstpolitik: Gipssammlungen des 19. Jahrhunderts', in: *Berliner Gypse des 19. Jahrhunderts: Von der Idee zum Gipsabguss*, ed. Klaus Stemmer and Maaz, exh. cat., Abguss-Sammlung Antiker Plastik, Berlin, 15 July–17 October 1993, Berlin 1993, p. 15.
8 Eggers, vol. 1, p. 157.
9 Ibid., p. 260; also see Jutta von Simson, *Christian Daniel Rauch: Oeuvre-Katalog*, Berlin 1996, p. 22.
10 Gerhard Rupp, 'Gips, Zink und Bronze – Berliner Vervielfältigungsfirmen im 19. Jahrhundert', in: *Ethos und Pathos: Die Berliner Bildhauerschule 1786–1914*, exh. cat., Hamburger Bahnhof – Museum für Gegenwart – Berlin, 19 May–29 July 1990, Berlin 1990, pp. 337–51, here p. 337.
11 Eggers, vol. 1, p. 237.
12 See *Preis-Courant nachstehender, durch den Stuccateur Carl Seeger zu Berlin, im Königlichen Lagerhause, Kloster-Straße No. 76 verkäuflicher Gips-Abgüsse antiker und moderner Skulpturen* (1824), Goethe- und Schiller-Archiv, Weimar. On the question of dating, see fn. 16.
13 See *Preis-Courant nachstehender, durch den Stuccateur Christian Seeger zu Berlin, im Königlichen Lagerhause, Kloster-Straße No. 76 verkäuflicher Gips-Abgüsse antiker und moderner Skulpturen* (1828), Goethe- und Schiller-Archiv, Weimar, GSA 33/1184. Carl Seeger died of consumption apparently in 1829 at the age of thirty-four. See register of deaths, Berlin 1829, p. 143. Online: ancestry.de, accessed 16 February 2019.
14 See *Preis-Courant, nachstehender Gips-Abgüsse antiker und moderner Skulpturen, welche durch den Bildhauer Müller in Berlin, im Königlichen Lagerhause, Klosterstraße No. 76, im Flügel nach der Friedrichstraße, verkauft werden* (ca. 1843), Zentralarchiv SMB, Berlin, IV-NL Rauch VIII. 7.
15 Dietmar Vogel, 'Der Künstler als Agent: Der Deutsch-Römer Emil Wolff und sein Wirken für die Berliner Abgusssammlung', in: *Berliner Gypse des 19. Jahrhunderts*, pp. 17–27.
16 Johann Heinrich Meyer mentions the price list of 1824 in his short text 'Gypsabgüsse'. Originally intended for inclusion in vol. 3 of the journal *Über Kunst und Alterthum*, jointly edited by Meyer and Johann Wolfgang von Goethe, it was passed over for editorial reasons. It did not find its way into print until 1887, when it was erroneously attributed to Goethe in the *Weimarer Ausgabe* 49, no. 2, 1895. See Goethe, *Sämtliche Werke, 1: Abteilung*, vol. 22, Frankfurt am Main 1999, pp. 656, 659–60, 1405. The statement on p. 1405 that the 'aforementioned catalogue' (the 1824 price list) is 'no longer extant' does not correspond to the facts. A copy was discovered in Goethe's study. Like the second price list of 1828, it is now kept at the Goethe- und Schiller-Archiv in Weimar. Special thanks go to Dr. Ulrike Müller-Harang, Goethe- und Schiller-Archiv, Weimar.
17 This rather unusual name of the collection, which was housed at that time in the Japanisches Palais in Dresden, is likely the result of misguided research on the part of the compilers of the inventory, see Wilhelm Gottlieb Becker, *Augusteum: Dresden's antike Denkmäler enthaltend*, Leipzig 1804.
18 The catalogue states 'No. 37, the bust of sculptor Rauch, price: 6 Reichsthaler'.
19 Einholz, 'Orte der Kontemplation und Erziehung', p. 25; Gipsformerei no. 6700.
20 Ibid.; Gipsformerei no. 6580.
21 See fn. 16. See the price list as reprinted in the (Prussian) *Amtsblatt der Königlichen Regierung zu Breslau*, 28 July 1824, with the following postscript on p. 278: 'We believe it is our duty to direct the attention of all grammar schools, of all schools of drawing and building, and of all friends and supporters of the visual arts to this catalogue and to the opportunity it affords of multiplying at a low cost the tools that are needed to refine taste and hone artistic sensitivity.'
22 Johann Wolfgang von Goethe cited in Friedrich Wilhelm Riemer (ed.), *Briefwechsel zwischen Goethe und Zelter in den Jahren 1796 bis 1832*, vol. 6: *Die Jahre 1830 July bis 1832*, Berlin 1834, p. 62.
23 Johann Wolfgang von Goethe, *Italian Journey 1786–1788*, trans. H. W. Auden and Elizabeth Mayer, London 1970 [1962], p. 490. *Die italienische Reise* was first published in Leipzig in 1816.
24 Christian Daniel Rauch cited in Rolf H. Johannsen (ed.), *'Mit vieler Kunst und Anmuth': Goethes Briefwechsel mit dem Bildhauer Christian Daniel Rauch*, Göttingen 2011, p. 81.
25 Wilhelm von Humboldt cited in Einholz 'Orte der Kontemplation und Erziehung', p. 16.
26 See the *Verzeichnis der Abgüsse antiker Werke der Königlichen Museen*, Berlin 1872, which lists 1,350 objects on display at the Neues Museum.
27 Julius Dielitz, 'Die Gipsformerei der Königlichen Museen', in: *Zur Geschichte der Königlichen Museen in Berlin: Festschrift zur Feier ihres fünfzigjährigen Bestehens am 3. August 1880*, Berlin 1880, pp. 167–70, here p. 168.
28 Storage and sales remained for a long time at the Königliches Lagerhaus on Klosterstraße. It was noted as late as 1869 that the 'moulding and casting workshops of the Museum Administration' operated as 'a little known storeroom with casts for sale'. *Deutsche Bauzeitung*, no. 25, 1869, p. 297. The second outlet from 1846 onwards was the former production site of the Altes Museum. See Alexander Cosmar, *Neuester und vollständigster Wegweiser durch Berlin und Potsdam für Fremde und Einheimische*, Berlin 1851, p. 64.
29 Dielitz, 'Die Gipsformerei der Königlichen Museen', p. 168.
30 Ibid., p. 170.
31 See *Verzeichniss der im Königl. Museum zu Berlin käuflichen Gyps-Abgüsse* 11, Berlin 1871.
32 Vicent (Rosenthaler Straße 30) and Thora (An der Schleuse 12) cited in Heinrich Weber, *Der Vaterländische Gewerbsfreund*, Berlin and Leipzig 1820, p. 203; Rupp, 'Gips, Zink und Bronze', p. 337.
33 Friedrich Eggers, 'Die plastische Anstalt und Gypsgießerei von G. Eichler in Berlin', *Deutsches Kunstblatt* 7, no. 31 (1856), pp. 267–70.
34 See the chapter *Too near to Life* in this book, pp. 60–105.
35 The Neues Museum displayed such ethnographic lifecasts much earlier. Max Schasler, for instance, reported in 1861 on the exhibition of 'plaster casts of heads of Greenlandic natives'. Max Schasler, *Die Königlichen Museen von Berlin*, Berlin 1861, p. 123.
36 The same sales catalogue features the earliest finds from Pergamon.
37 Andreas Köstler, 'Simulacra: Die Abgusssammlung', in: *Einführung in die Kunstwissenschaft*, ed. Thomas Hensel and Andreas Köstler, Berlin 2004, pp. 61–72.
38 On the occasion of the relocation to the new building a *Formerei* (plaster casting workshop) is mentioned as part of the museum. *Das Kunstgewerbe-Museum zu Berlin: Festschrift zur Eröffnung des Museumsgebäudes*, Berlin 1881, p. 39. This plaster casting workshop had already existed in the 1870s at the Kunstgewerbemuseum. Sales figures for 1873 state 816 casts were sold from a total of 1,600 on offer. See *Berliner Städtisches Jahrbuch für Volkswirthschaft und Statistik*, Berlin 1874, p. 214. At least some of these forms were later passed on to the Gipsformerei. See Veronika Tocha's essay in this book, pp. 64–67.

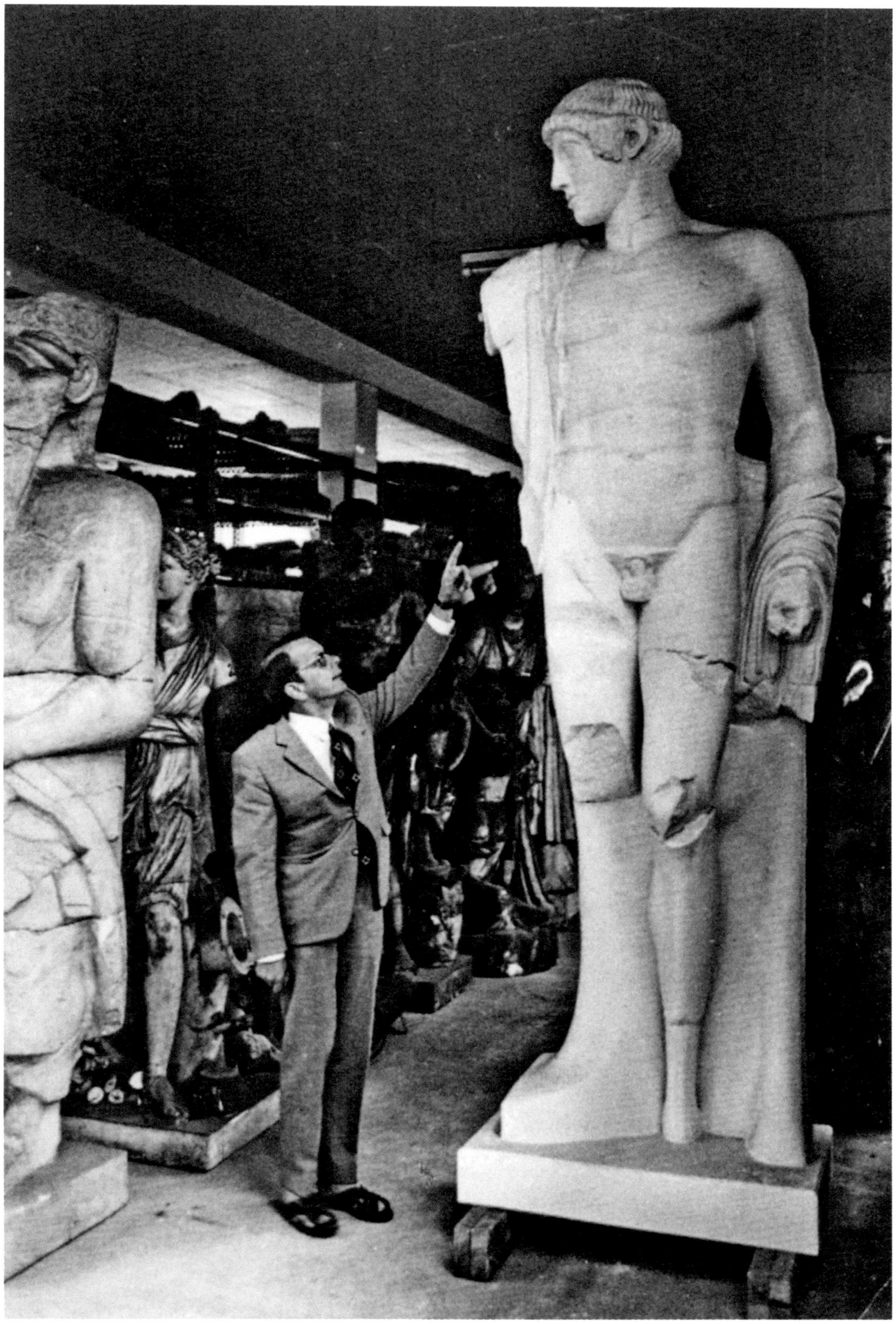

Unknown photographer
Ernst Kretschmann, then production manager at the Gipsformerei, with the Cast of Apollo from the West Pediment of the Temple of Zeus in Olympia, 1972
Staatliche Museen zu Berlin, Gipsformerei

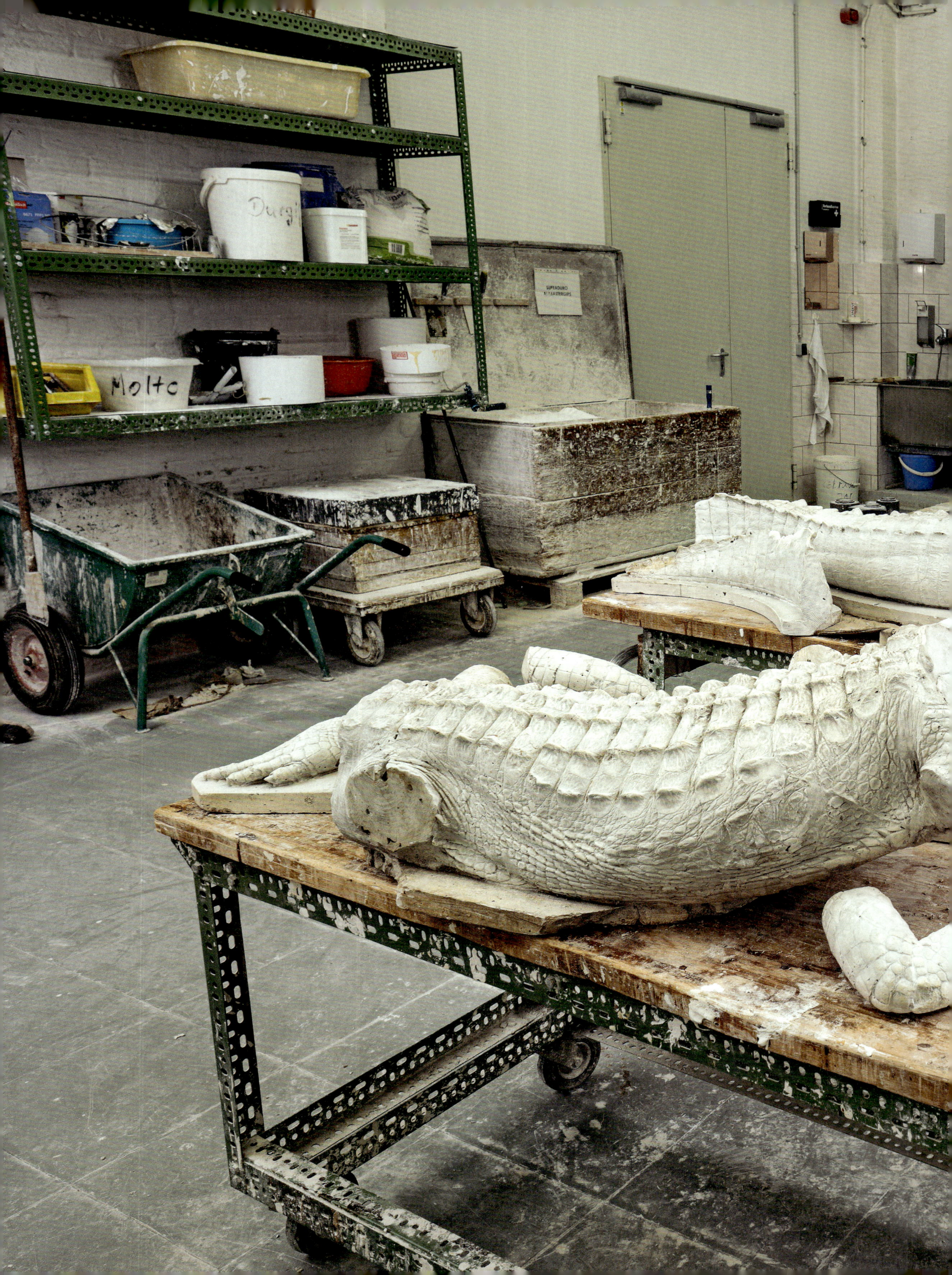

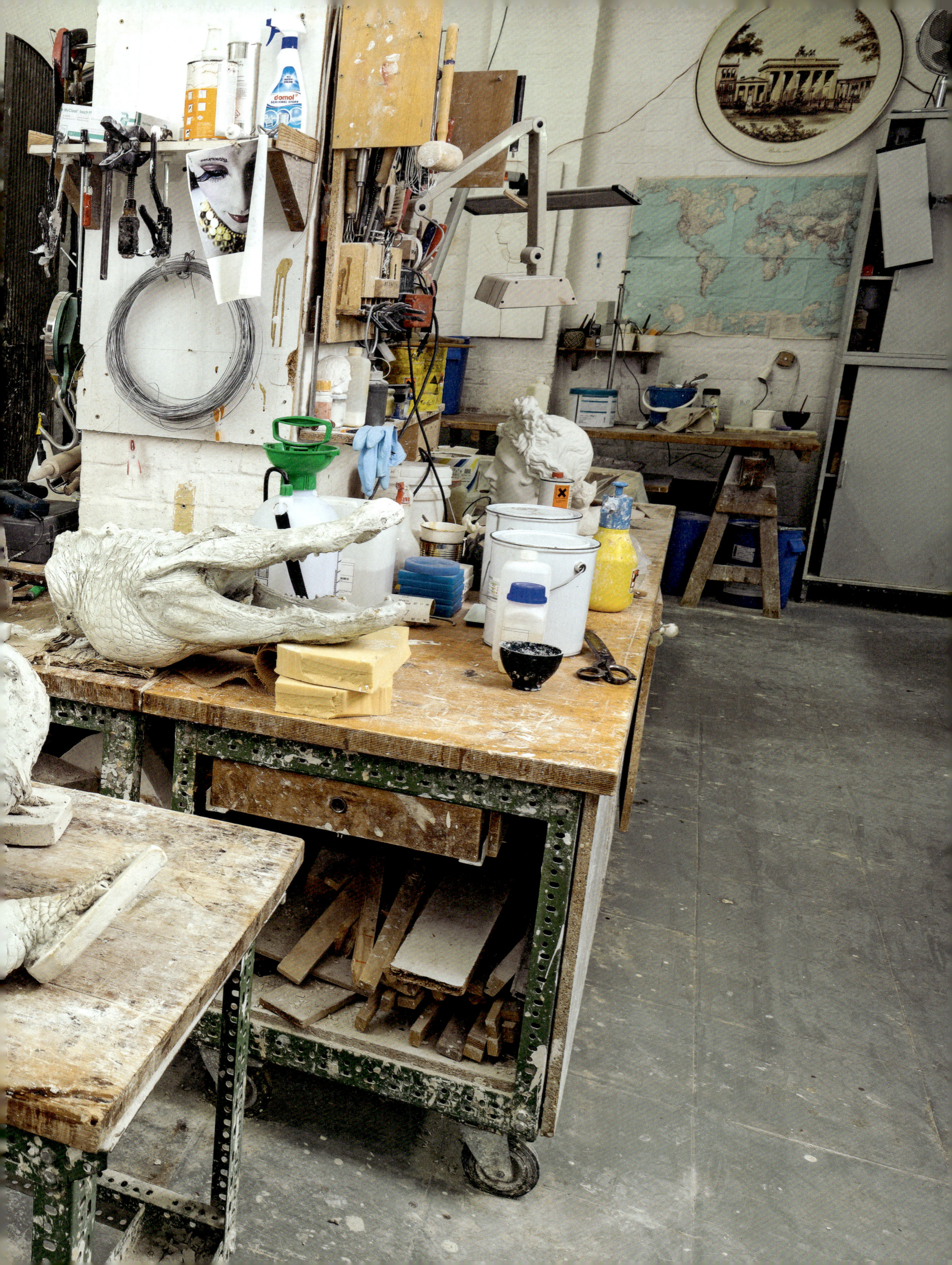
domol

Conservation and Restoration at the Gipsformerei: Mission, Challenges and Prospects

Aurelia Badde with Lothar Bogdanski, Jan Bürgel, Fabian Burg, Johanna Gassmann, Susanne Grimm, Cornelia Hoppe, Peter John-Schoubye, Timo Klöppel, Stefan Kramer, Daniel Meyer, Sandro di Michele, Marc Miniers, Rainer Palau, Thomas Schelper, Andreas Schipka, Robin Schulz and Hardy Zaubitzer

According to the statute of the Staatliche Museen zu Berlin, one of the core tasks of the Gipsformerei is to preserve and maintain its historical collection of models and moulds. The busy production of high-quality casts from the rich collection of original moulds has ensured that the traditional techniques and processes of plaster craftsmanship, notably the production and handling of gelatine and plaster piece moulds, have been preserved and passed-on for now two hundred years. The older the institution becomes, the clearer it is that not only the craft must be sustained, but also the collection has to be safeguarded according to professional standards. In the past, preventive care and maintenance concentrated primarily on the moulds and models of the casts, which were cleaned and restored in the course of processing orders. As in the case of the equestrian statue of the Great Elector by Andreas Schlüter (1700) that was ordered as a plaster cast by the Museo Internacional del Barroco in Puebla, Mexico, in 2016, the mould of which comprises around ten thousand plaster pieces.

The preparations for the special exhibition *Near Life* provided an opportunity to extend the care and preservation of the collection to models and moulds, which had predominantly been kept in storage for several decades or longer, and to systematically put the topics of conservation and restoration on the institution's agenda. To support this work, a specialist conservator-restorer was engaged. The jointly developed conservation concept provided for the presentability of the exhibits, while at the same time maintaining their tool-like character and usability. Between August 2018 and July 2019, conservation work was carried out on some two hundred models and moulds, which was recorded and photographically documented. The work primarily included cleaning, as the surface soiling was particularly pronounced on the old and less sought-after objects. Depending on the surface condition, the cleaning could be dry, with a vacuum cleaner and soft brushes, or damp with poultices, sponges and cotton wool. After cleaning, the surfaces of the models and moulds were often markedly patchy and disparate in appearance, due to their usage and long-term storage under partly suboptimal conditions. In order to preserve the functional value of the objects and to keep it identifiable, no unifying coating, in shellac for example, was applied here. On painting models, however, in addition to cleaning, the paint layers were consolidated, reintegrated and retouched. The consolidation of fractured or detached parts was as much a part of the interventions as the grouting of cracks, the conservation of reinforcement materials and the removal of overpaint. Fillings and reconstructions of minor losses were only carried out in a few cases: as mentioned above, the aim was to ensure the usability of the models and moulds as well as to maintain their traces of use.

The preservation of the collection also includes its reproduction: heavily used gelatine models and plaster piece moulds are continually replaced by new mouldings from the original model, so that the original accuracy of form and sharpness of detail are always guaranteed. Original models and their moulds are uniques, as are the painting models and plaster piece moulds; their restoration requires the exact knowledge and experience of the artistic plasterers who work with them. During the recent production of the replica plates of the large frieze of the Pergamon Altar ordered by the China Academy of Art in Hangzhou, for instance, it became apparent that many large moulds were in a critical state. Their necessary restoration includes, among other things, the crafting and fitting of missing or damaged plaster pieces and shell parts. With these particular plaster piece moulds as well as in general, it has proved to be advantageous to carry out the conservation work as simultaneously as possible with their use, so that the memory and experience gained with regard to the individual damage patterns and the resulting sources of error, are not lost during the next casting. The original models in the collection can be used as reference for the reconstruction work.

Preventive care and maintenance remains a topic of great relevance for the Gipsformerei. On the occasion of the *Near Life* exhibition and the two-hundredth anniversary of the institution, the need for a comprehensive survey of the objects and their concurrent cleaning and conservation has become clearer than ever. In view of the size of the total inventory with its approximately seven thousand objects, such a project represents a challenge. Due to the uniqueness of the collection, a systematic appraisal of the condition and relevance of the moulds and models is however necessary. The pending general renovation of the historic building of the Gipsformerei will involve an extensive relocation of the collection and offers a special opportunity to produce an expert inventory.

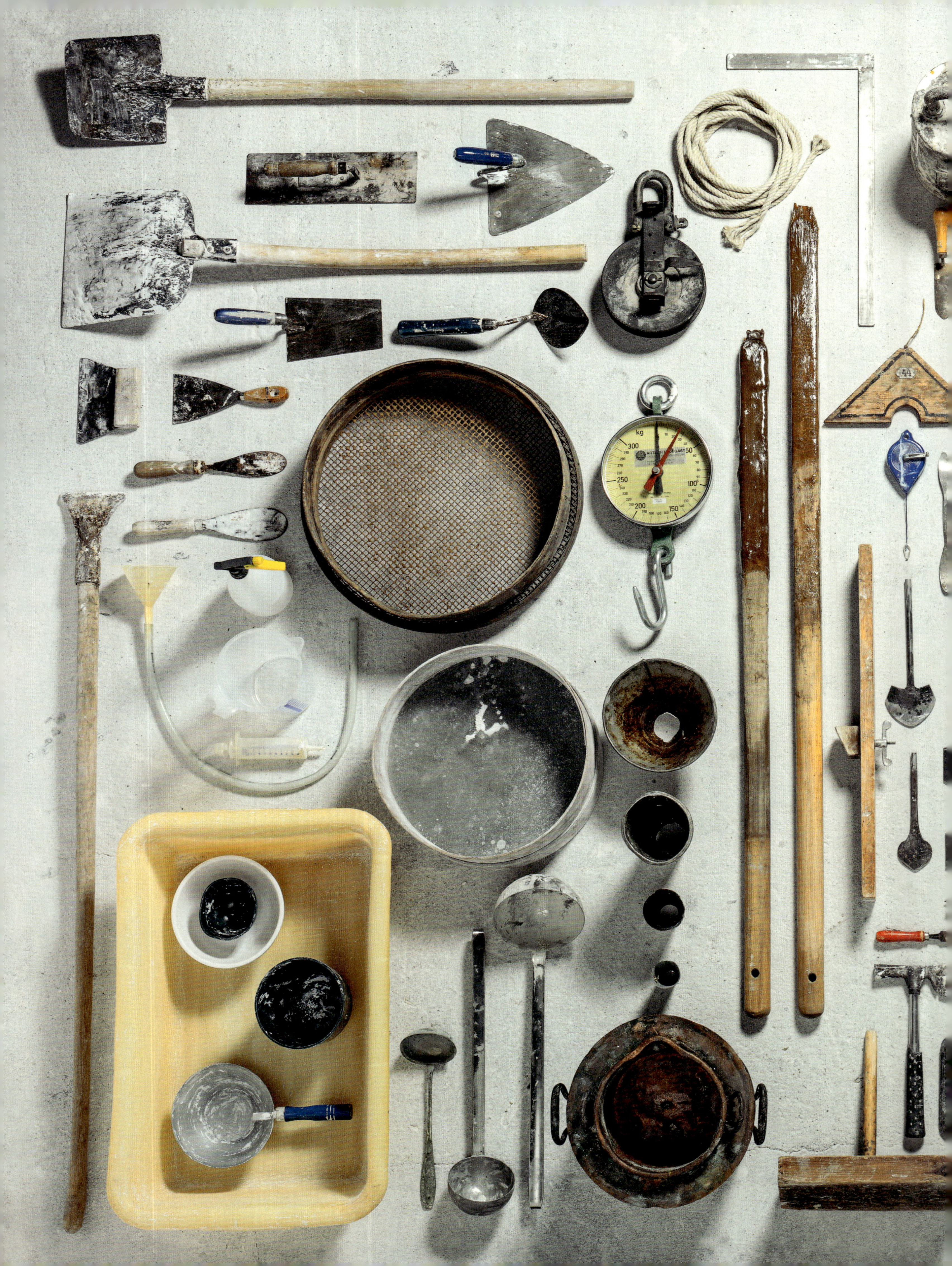
kg
300
250
200
150
100
50

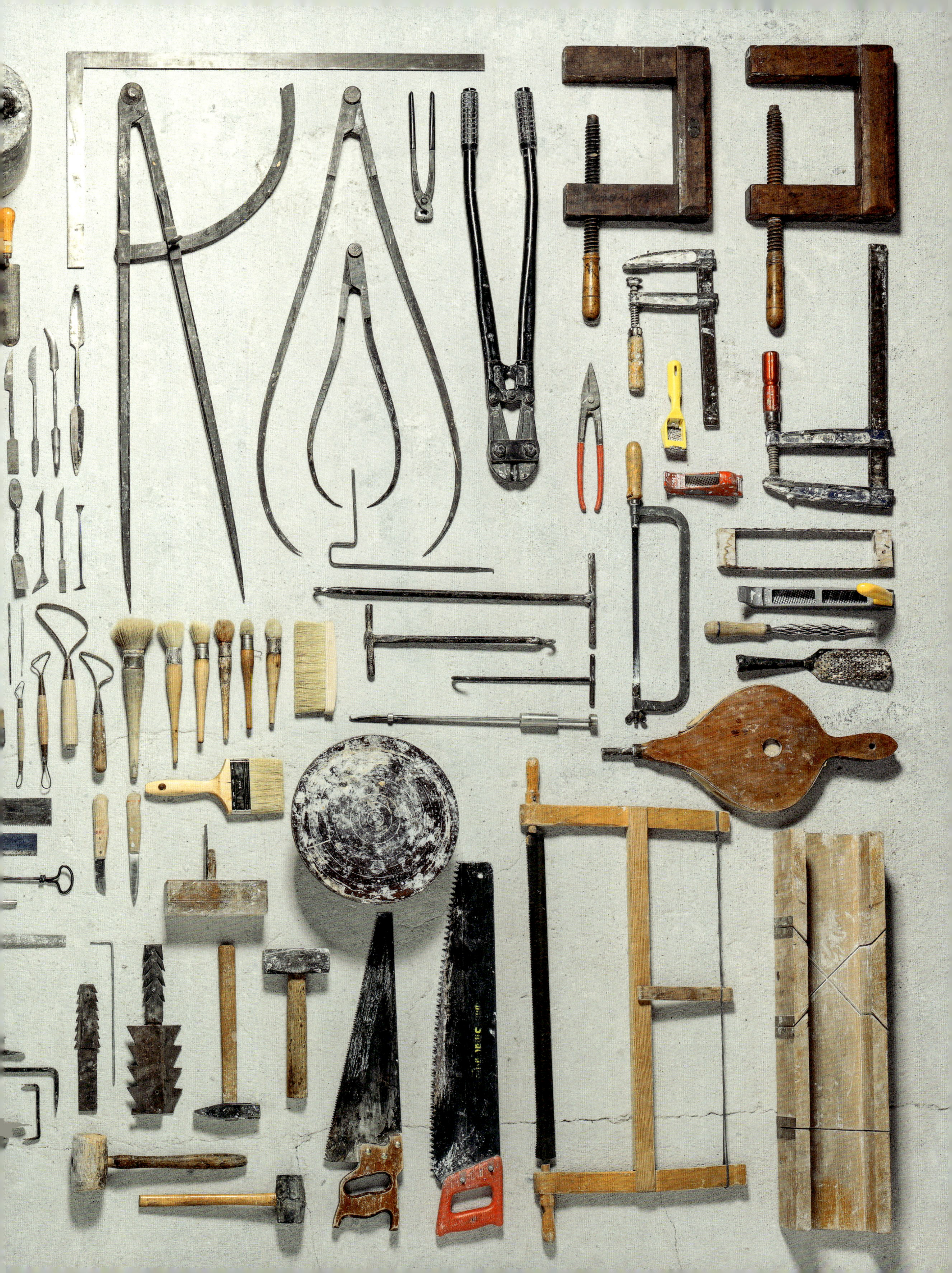

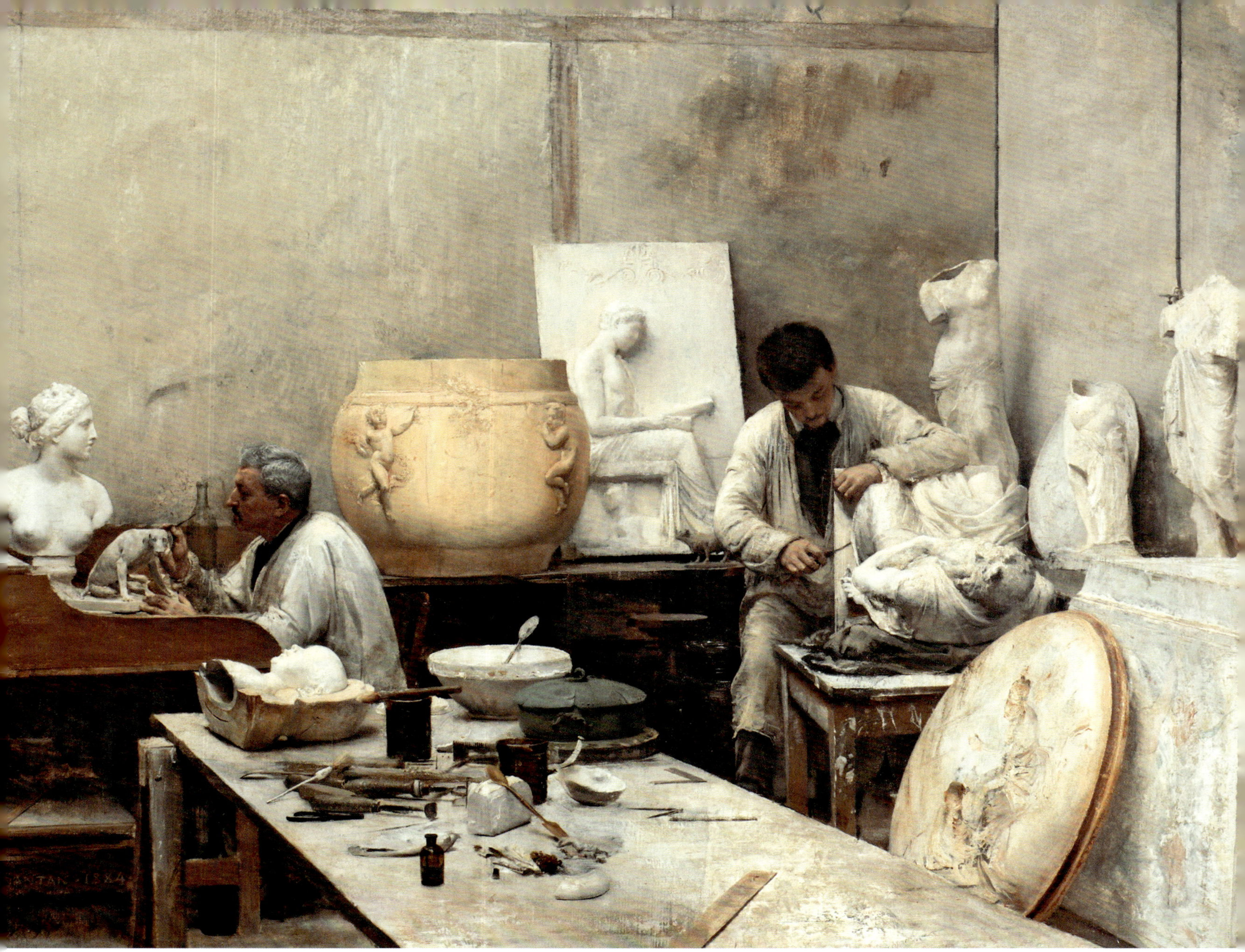

Édouard Joseph Dantan
Atelier de moulage, 1884
Centre national des arts plastiques, Paris
Long-term loan to the Musée des Beaux-Arts de Limoges since 1963, FNAC 609

Next page

Denis Diderot,
Jean Le Rond d'Alembert
Encylopédie: Sur les sciences, les arts libéraux, et les arts méchaniques; avec leur explication, sculpture, 1775, plates IV and II
Staatliche Museen zu Berlin, Kunstbibliothek

Glossary: Technology and Craftsmanship at the Gipsformerei

Fabian Burg, Timo Klöppel
and Thomas Schelper

Artistic Plasterers

The skills practised today by artistic plasterers at the Gipsformerei, Staatliche Museen zu Berlin were originally developed in the workshops of sculptors and stucco plasterers in eighteenth- and nineteenth-century Europe. It was in those workshops that plaster casters and moulders, decorative and stucco plasterers refined the historical moulding techniques that are still in use today. Most of these moulding professions, however, were hardly traceable in the first half of the twentieth century. Today, the Gipsformerei trains stucco plasterers and related practitioners over three years to become artistic plasterers (*Gipskunstformer*innen*). Elements of the training curriculum include: the crafting and use of various types of traditional moulds; moulding from the original; moulding and casting with plaster, polymer compounds and wax; retouching casts; and the preservation and conservation of the inventory. The Gipsformerei is one of the few places in the world where the craftsmanship and the traditional knowledge of the old moulding trades are still actively cultivated and passed on in the twenty-first century.

Cast

A cast is a cast replica of an object that is usually referred to as an original. The cast is obtained from a negative mould created by → **Moulding**. Depending on their size and shape, the casts are either solid or hollow. Plaster casts often consist of several cast segments and are reinforced by → **Reinforcements**, when required.

Casting after Nature / Lifecasting

A cast taken from nature is an → **Original Cast** in the broader sense. The term describes casts of human beings, animals (after life) or plants (after nature). The object is moulded (with a → **Lost Mould**), from which the positive cast is then obtained. The collection of the Gipsformerei comprises roughly five hundred lifecasts.

Gelatine Mould

From the end of the nineteenth century until the introduction of the → **Silicone Mould** in the 1960s, the gelatine mould, also known as the (animal) glue mould (ill. p. 237 top), was regularly used for the rapid → **Moulding** of objects and the production of casts. As a moulding material, gelatine enables flexible → **Moulding**, and thus large-scale moulding even of highly complex and undercut surfaces. Gelatine moulds are taken either directly from the original or from the model using the → **Mother Mould**. A model exclusively reserved for (animal) glue or gelatine moulds is often referred to as a gelatine or glue model. The gelatine is melted in a water bath and then poured over the object to be moulded. Once it has set, the image side of the gelatine mould is tanned with alum salt and treated with a → **Release Agent**. The resulting mould can only be used for some days before wearing out. However, the gelatine mass itself can be treated and reused. The technique of crafting and handling gelatine moulds is demanding and reserved for the experienced plasterer.

Keys and Locks

Keys are conical depressions (negative keys) and elevations (positive keys) in mould pieces, i.e. the parts that form the → **Mother Mould** or → **Plaster Piece Mould**. These keys interlock with great accuracy due to applying the key-lock principle, which prevents the pieces from becoming misaligned. They ensure that

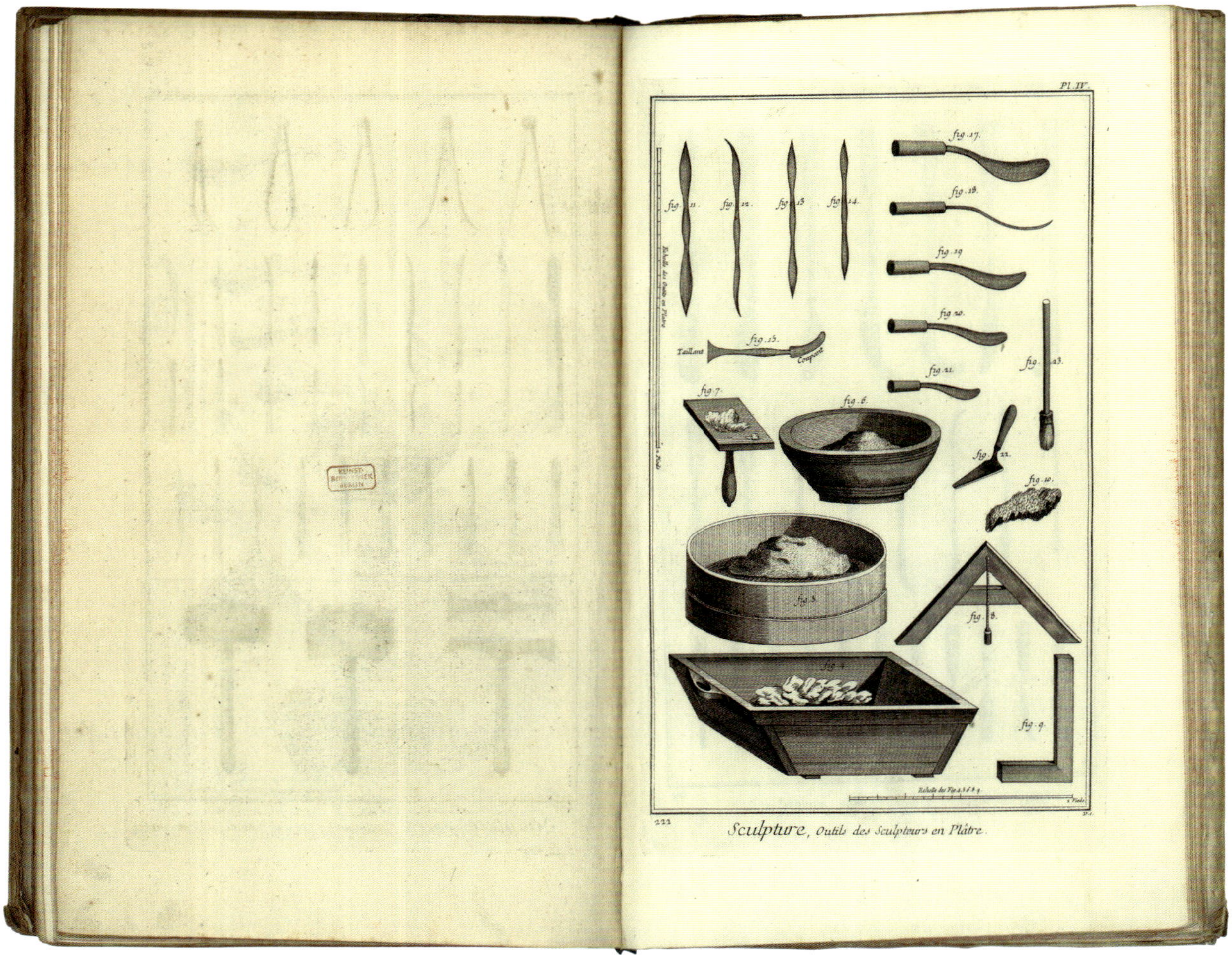
Pl. IV
Sculpture, Outils des Sculpteurs en Plâtre.

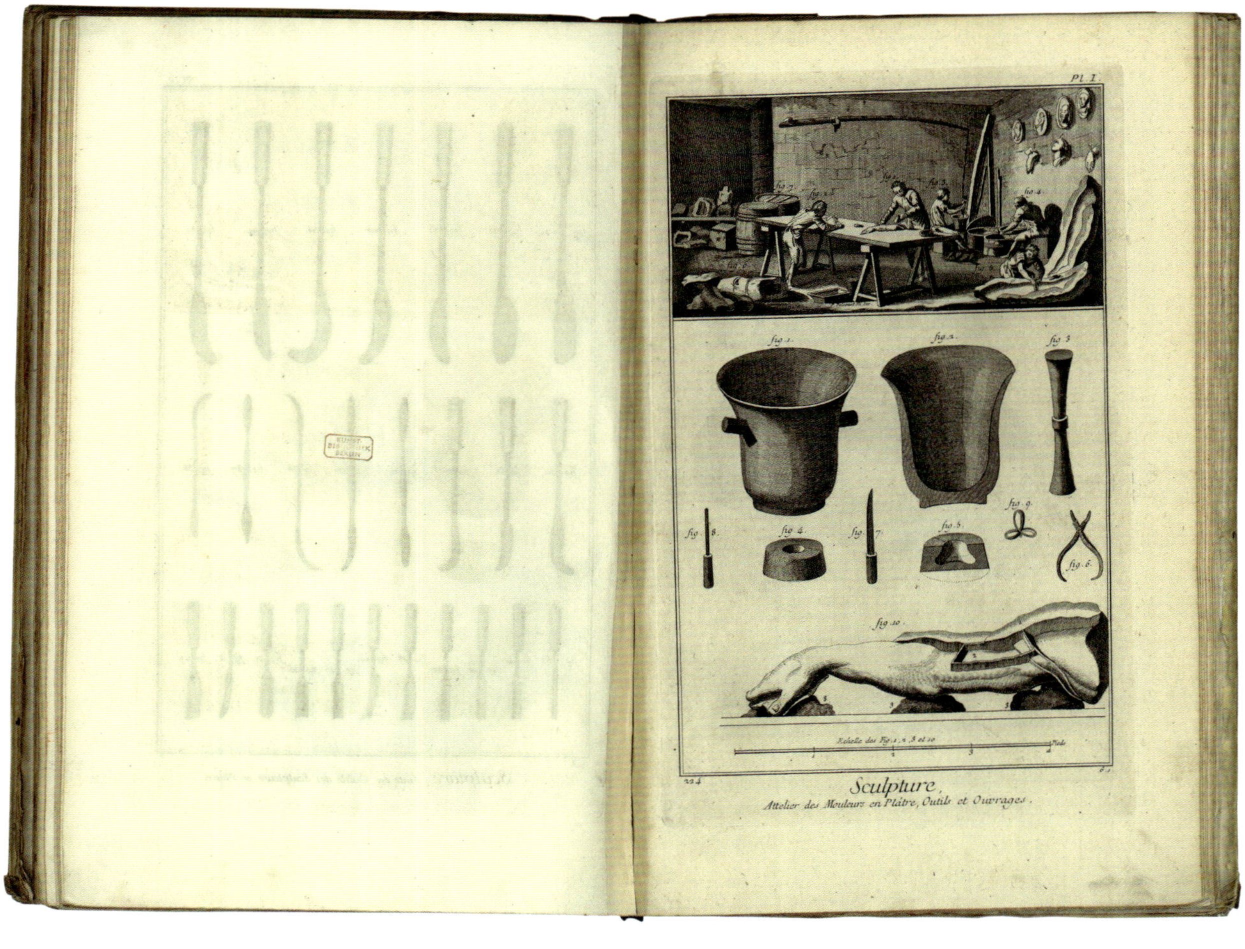
Pl. I
Sculpture,
Attelier des Mouleurs en Plâtre, Outils et Ouvrages.

the pieces which constitute the moulding fit next to each other exactly and form a closed mould. Keys are created successively in the mould crafting process, firstly by screwing negative keys into freshly set → **Plaster** using a screwdriver-like tool with a sharp diamond-shaped tip to form concave depressions. The positive counterpart results from the application of fresh plaster to these negative keys during the fabrication of an adjoining piece of the → **Mould**. A pair of negative and positive keys is called a lock.

Lost Mould

A lost mould is a casting mould which can only be used once and is destroyed after casting in order to (demould) the → **Cast**. This technique is applied when the original is pliable, as is the case with human skin or when modelled with moist clay. A first layer of liquid → **Plaster** is spread over the object. Once this layer has cured, a second layer is added to increase stability. The aim is to create a mould that, after curing, can be removed from the object without breaking. The mould can be divided in a controlled manner with the aid of a separating thread. The thread is placed directly on the first plaster layer and pulled through the still soft but already setting plaster. Once the plaster has completely set, the mould is carefully detached from the object, treated with a → **Release Agent**, assembled and then fixed in the → **Mother Mould**. The mould is then filled with plaster. After the plaster has set, the plaster mould is removed from the cast by carefully knocking it off, whereby it becomes lost.

Model

A model (also referred to as a master model) is ideally the first cast made from a mould taken directly from the original object (→ **Original Casts**). Thus, the model shows the maximum achievable proximity to the original. All other casts are derived from this model. It serves as a reference in mould making (→ **Gelatine Mould, Plaster Piece Mould, Silicon Mould)** and in the final → **Retouching** of the casts. The majority of the moulds in the Gipsformerei have corresponding models. Both the models and the moulds form the collection of the Gipsformerei.

Mother Mould / Outer Shell

The outermost layer of a mould that holds the individual moulded parts together and positions and stabilises the internal negative is known as the outer shell or mother mould. Thus, the mother mould offers the necessary structural support for both the mould elements made of elastic materials, such as → **Gelatine Mould** and → **Silicone Mould**, and the individual rigid plaster pieces of a → **Plaster Piece Mould**. The more complex a mould, i.e. the more perspectives an object offers, the more pieces of the mother mould is required. The individual pieces usually consist of several pieces of centimetres-thick → **Plaster**; in most cases these are then reinforced with iron rods and jute (→ **Reinforcements**). Modern materials, such as fibreglass reinforced epoxy resin, occasionally substitute the heavy yet fragile plaster. Their wall thickness is less, while they are more stable and lighter than the conventional mother moulds.

Mould

Mould (also called casting mould, negative mould or matrix) is a generic term for the three types of moulds used at the Gipsformerei (→ **Gelatine Mould**, → **Plaster Piece Mould** and → **Silicone Mould**). Approximately seven thousand moulds can be found in the Gipsformerei's inventory. Together with the → **Models** they form its collection.

Moulding

Moulding is a sculptural process in which the surfaces of an object are converted into a negative mould from which the positive can then be cast. This is achieved by creating → **Plaster Piece**, → **Gelatine**, → **Silicone** or → **Lost Moulds** and applying the respective casting material directly onto the object. See also → **Original Cast** and → **Casting after Nature**.

Original Cast

The term original cast is used for casts of artworks and artefacts; casts of human beings, animals and plants are referred to as lifecasts (→ **Casting after Nature**). In the past, casts of the original were made with → **Plaster Piece Moulds** and → **Gelatine Moulds**. Today, → **Silicone Moulds**, which can be adjusted to be both soft and tear resistant, are widely used. Depending on the original's materiality, a reversible application of a protective lacquer, tinfoil or a suitable → **Release Agent** is applied. The first cast that is made in an original mould is often referred to as the original model.

Painting Model

A painting model is a cast that is painted as an exact reproduction of the materiality and colour of the original. Materials such as marble, sandstone, wood, rose granite, precious metals or bronze are mimicked as accurately as possible, and ideally in direct comparison with the original. The painting model is usually indistinguishable from the original. It serves as a model for future coloured versions and remains in the collection, while the finished and painted casts leave the house. The collection of the Gipsformerei comprises approximately three thousand painting models. They are considered to be particularly valuable. The Gipsformerei did not produce painting models before the late nineteenth century.

Plaster (Gypsum)

Plaster is a natural crystalline mineral that has been mined since antiquity in both surface and underground mines. The extracted dihydrate, the gypsum, is a water-containing calcium sulphate. In the firing process, 15 per cent of the crystal water in the gypsum is extracted, which causes the gypsum crystals to decompose. After firing, the gypsum is finely ground to powder. This process is reversed when gypsum is scattered in water: new crystals are formed, which hardens the plaster and within a few minutes sets with an increase in volume of about one per cent. Plaster's extremely fine-grained structure and short processing time makes it an ideal material for → **Moulding** and producing → **Cast**. The gypsum used at the Gipsformerei has been sourced from Germany's Harz region for many decades. It is characterised by its purity, white colour, good workability and capability to render high levels of detail. Its purity is comparable to that of alabaster gypsum, although it is a little harder. Polymer or plastic-bonded gypsum and artificial stone masses are also processed at the Gipsformerei. Not only can they precisely imitate the material of the original, such as marble or bronze, but their resistance to weathering permits outdoor installation.

Plaster Piece Mould

Plaster piece moulds (also referred to as piece moulds, ill. right bottom) have been used since antiquity. Due to their precision and durability, and despite their high manufacturing and maintenance requirements, piece moulds were the most common moulding technique before World War II. After the founding of the Gipsformerei they were the most important type of moulds at the institution, and they held that status for a very long time. The inflexible piece moulds consist of numerous individual parts made of plaster, which are assembled as a three-dimensional puzzle and fixed in a rigid plaster shell (→ **Mother Mould**). The more complicated the original – with undercuts or free-standing elements such as arms and legs – the more complex and detailed the mould becomes. Some plaster piece moulds consist of several hundred parts and are assembled and maintained by experienced → **Artistic Plasterers**. They are usually made of either thick-walled plaster pieces dipped in wax, pieces of a plaster-wax-resin mixture and pieces of pure beeswax. Also referred to as wedges, all these pieces interlock seamlessly, fixed by → **Keys and Locks** and kept in place within the mother mould. The plaster pieces are hardened and sealed in a wax-resin bath using a special process. Gypsum-wax-resin pieces are used for problematic and fragile surface structures or carved areas such as hair with many fine burrs, depressions and vortices. The pure beeswax pieces are the ephemeral elements of a piece mould. They are cast hollow for each new cast from a custom-made mould. These very soft, flexible, disposable pieces are used for extreme undercuts and indents. An almost unlimited number of casts can be obtained from a plaster piece mould.

Reinforcements

Reinforcements are elements made of iron, jute or glass-fibre matting designed to stabilise the → **Cast**. Often wound steel structures (armouring) are fitted into casts – comparable to the skeleton of the human body. Due to its ability to absorb wet → **Plaster**, jute is ideally suited for integration into the interior of a cast. As sheathing for a steel construction and as flat overlapping inserts between plaster layers, jute ensures good cohesion of all elements and materials — comparable to the connective tissue of the human body. Casts made of polymer-bonded plaster or artificial stone are reinforced with fibreglass matting instead of jute.

Release Agent

In mould making, release agents are required to separate the mould pieces from the → **Models** or originals. The main components of today's commonly used agents are wax, grease, oil, soap and talcum. By adding solvents, release agents can be individually modified for use. For the traditional → **Plaster Piece Mould**, a special mixture of beeswax, oil and curd soap is used in the Gipsformerei.

Retouching

Retouching describes the process of adding the finishing touches to the → **Cast**. The surfaces of the cast are cleared of imperfections, casting seams are removed, exposed air bubbles are filled. If proximity to the original is to be demonstrated, the casting seams remain. This practice occurs, for example, when casts are used for scientific purposes, such as the comparison of objects in archaeology.

Shellac

Shellac is a natural product obtained from the excretions of a lac insect and is primarily used to seal → **Models**. All models at the Gipsformerei have a shellac coating, which distinguishes them from objects in academic or museum cast collections and characterises their property as tools. The dark (brown) shellac finish protects the → **Cast**, which is otherwise very susceptible to external influences and makes the models mouldable. Lighter (fair) shellac can serve as a binding agent in the application of paint to finished casts. Shellac is also used as a rust inhibitor: all steel elements inserted into a cast as → **Reinforcements** are treated with shellac. Originally shellac was produced mainly in India and South East Asia. The lac insect surrounds itself and its brood with a protective resinous liquid, which it extracts from the sap of the trees it colonises, mostly poplar figs. Branches infested with the lac insect are covered in a layer of resin up to one centimetre thick. After the lac insect brood has hatched, these lacquer branches are harvested and shredded. The obtained resin shreds are boiled, filtered and processed. Several hundred thousand insects are needed for one kilogram of shellac.

Silicone Mould

Since the 1960s and the invention of silicone rubber, originals have largely been moulded using this elastic material (ill. p. 239). There are two distinct silicone techniques: The first involves a silicone spread, which is prepared to a paste-like consistency and applied to the object to be moulded with a spoon spatula. This technique is used for on-site moulding of large immobile originals. For the second, which involves pouring silicone, the object must in most cases be placed in a horizontal position. This technique is therefore only applicable for small to medium-sized objects. In contrast to the two traditional types of moulds (→ **Plaster Piece Mould** and → **Gelatine Mould**), the crafting and handling of a silicone mould is relatively simple. It can be poured out very quickly, as it does not require extensive pre- and post-processing. In principle the silicone mould is similar to the → **Gelatine Mould**. Here, too, the elastic material is stabilised by the → **Mother Mould**. Difficult surfaces can be moulded over large areas. Casts from silicone moulds have hardly any seams, which simplifies → **Retouching**. One disadvantage of the silicone mould is its relatively short shelf life of several years; though the new addition curing silicones are much more durable than the older generation of

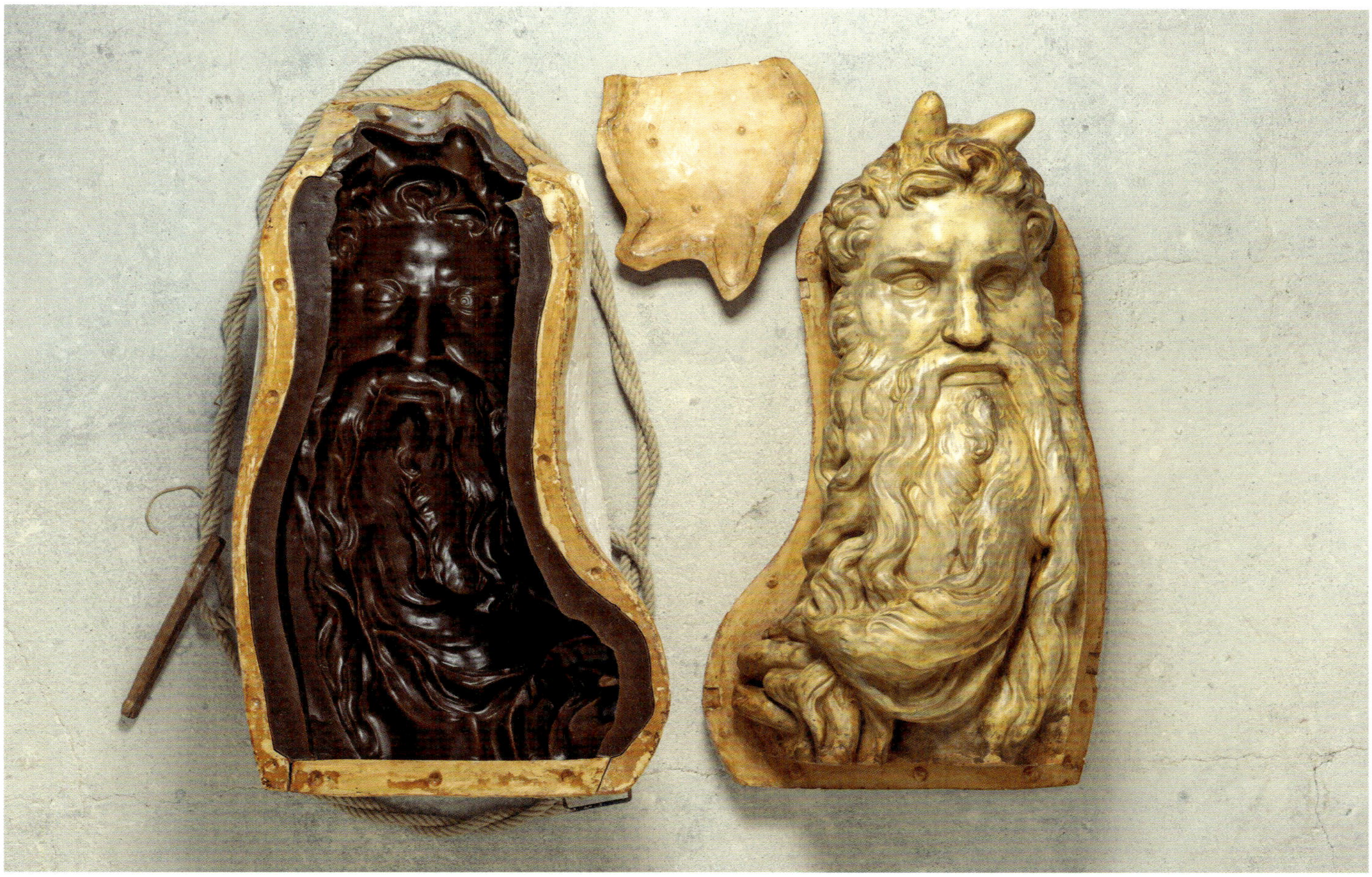

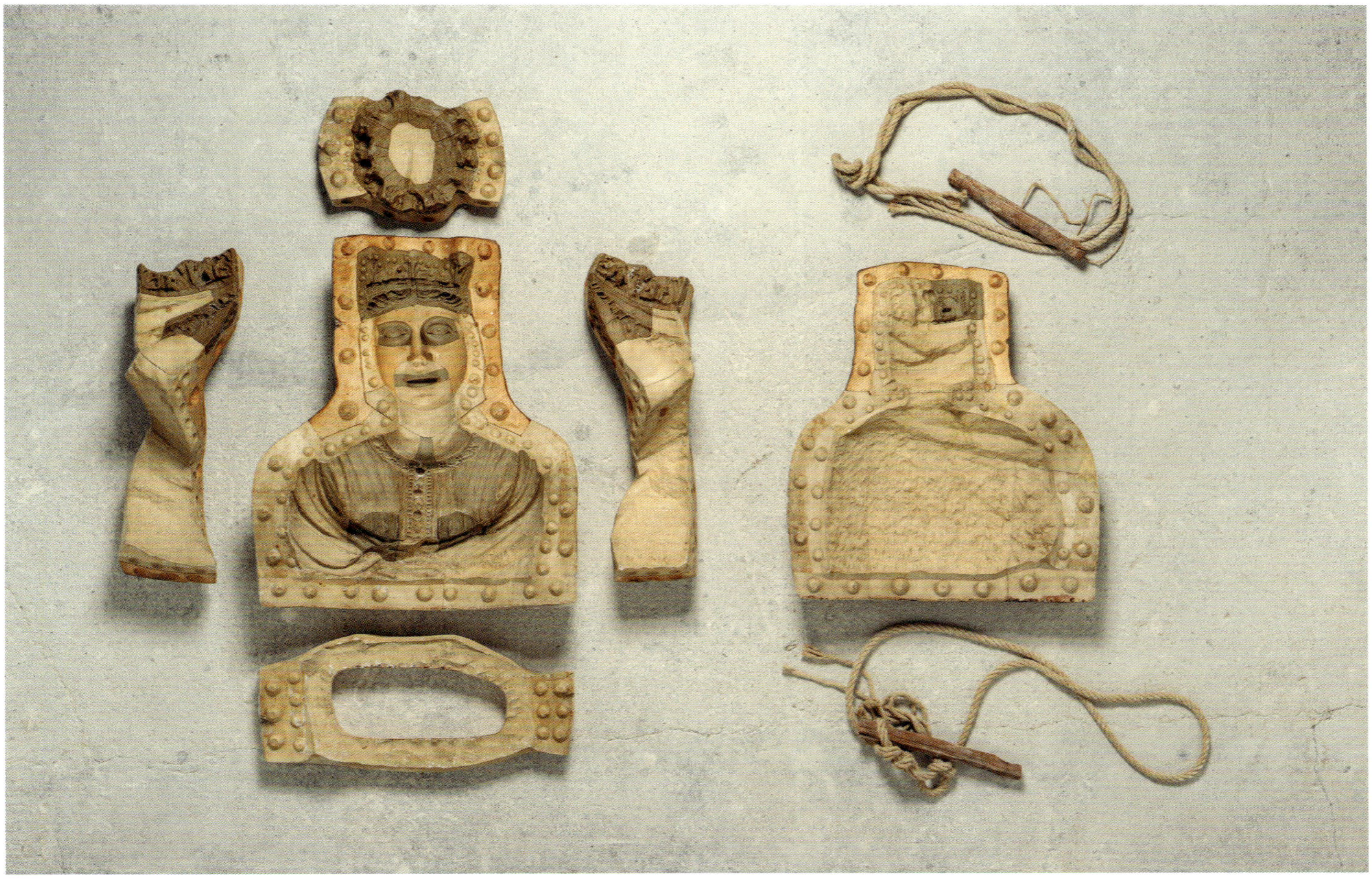

condensation curing silicones. The ease and speed associated with the handling of today's silicone moulds make them ideally suited for the serial production of casts.

Toggle

Wooden toggles are used in combination with hemp ropes and strings to tie and lash a closed → **Mould**. To that effect, a rope is loosely tied round an assembled → **Mother Mould**; a wooden crosspiece (the toggle) is then pushed between the mould and the rope and rotated successively, so that the rope wraps around the wood. As the rope tightens, the pieces of the mother mould are pulled closer together. When the mould is firmly aligned, the toggle is tied to the rope with a hemp string and the mould is ready for casting. In a similar way, plaster pieces that are not fixed into of a → **Plaster Piece Mould** with the technique of → **Keys and Locks** are fastened with a hemp string, which is threaded through a hole in the outer shell and firmly toggled to the mother mould.

3D Printing

3D printing virtualises an object by first scanning and carving it up into two-dimensional, vertically aligned thin layers (slices). The individual layers are then printed on a 3D printer, which renders the sequence of slice images as a three-dimensional object. There are powder-based printers that congeal a ceramic powder through dispensing a binding agent; others fuse filaments together; and a third type relies on a laser beam to sinter materials. Reproduction accuracy depends on the capabilities of the selected printer. On close inspection visible seams between individual layers of the finished product can clearly be seen; this is due to the relatively small build chambers of 3D printers currently in use. It is also the reason why life-size portrait busts still have to be printed in several parts and then glued together.

3D Scanning

3D scanning is used for the contactless digitisation of artworks in the realisation of → **3D Printing**. Structured light scanners have proven to be highly effective in digitally capturing sculptures. This optical measuring technique involves registering the exact position of individual measuring points on the object's detectable surfaces. A computer programme then transforms these 'point clouds' into virtual models, eliminating any flaws or missing pieces in the process. The first 3D-scanning project at the Gipsformerei was to produce a new model of the Nefertiti bust in 2009. The data was captured directly from the original in the Neues Museum using a structured light scanner.

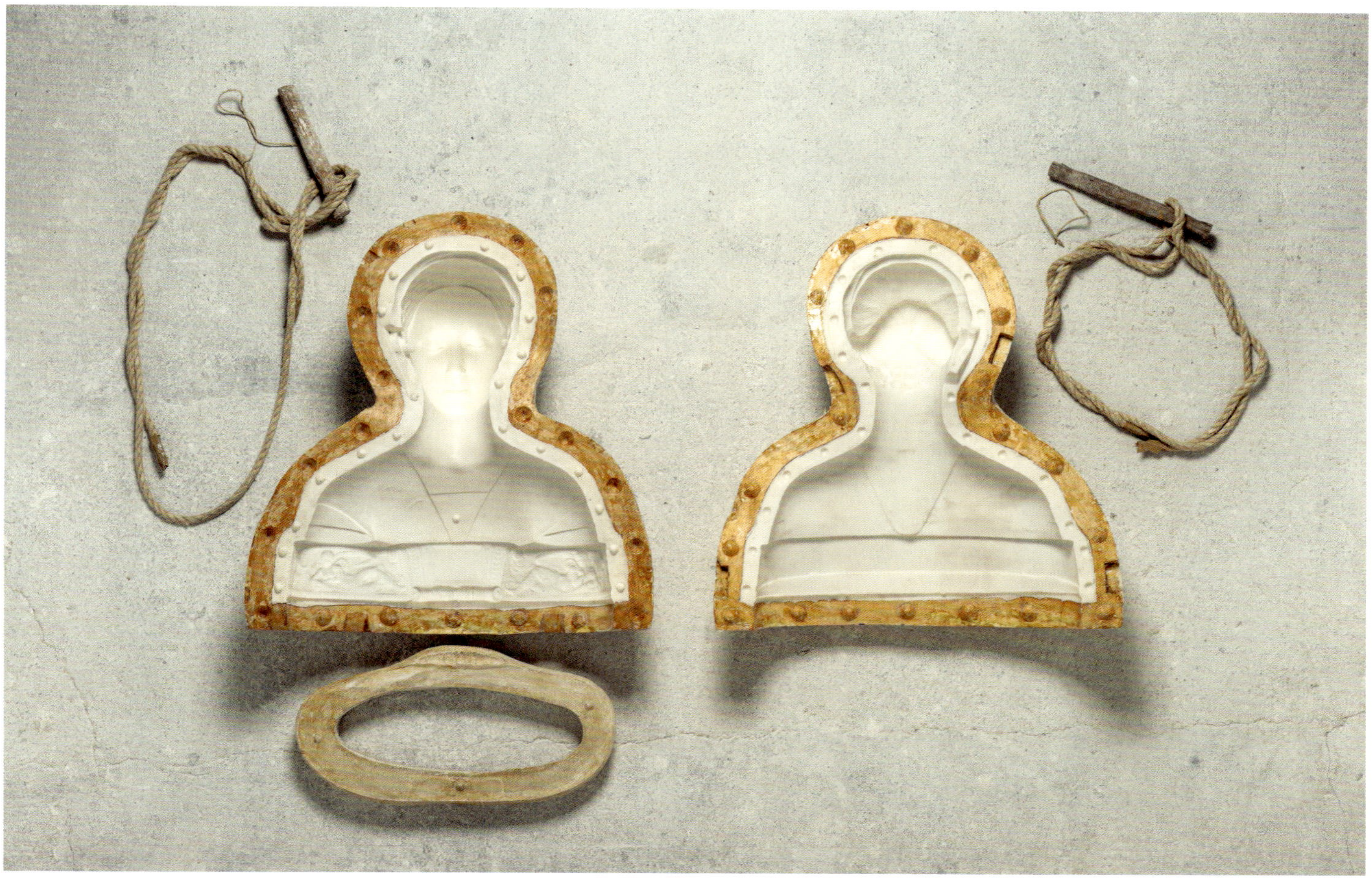

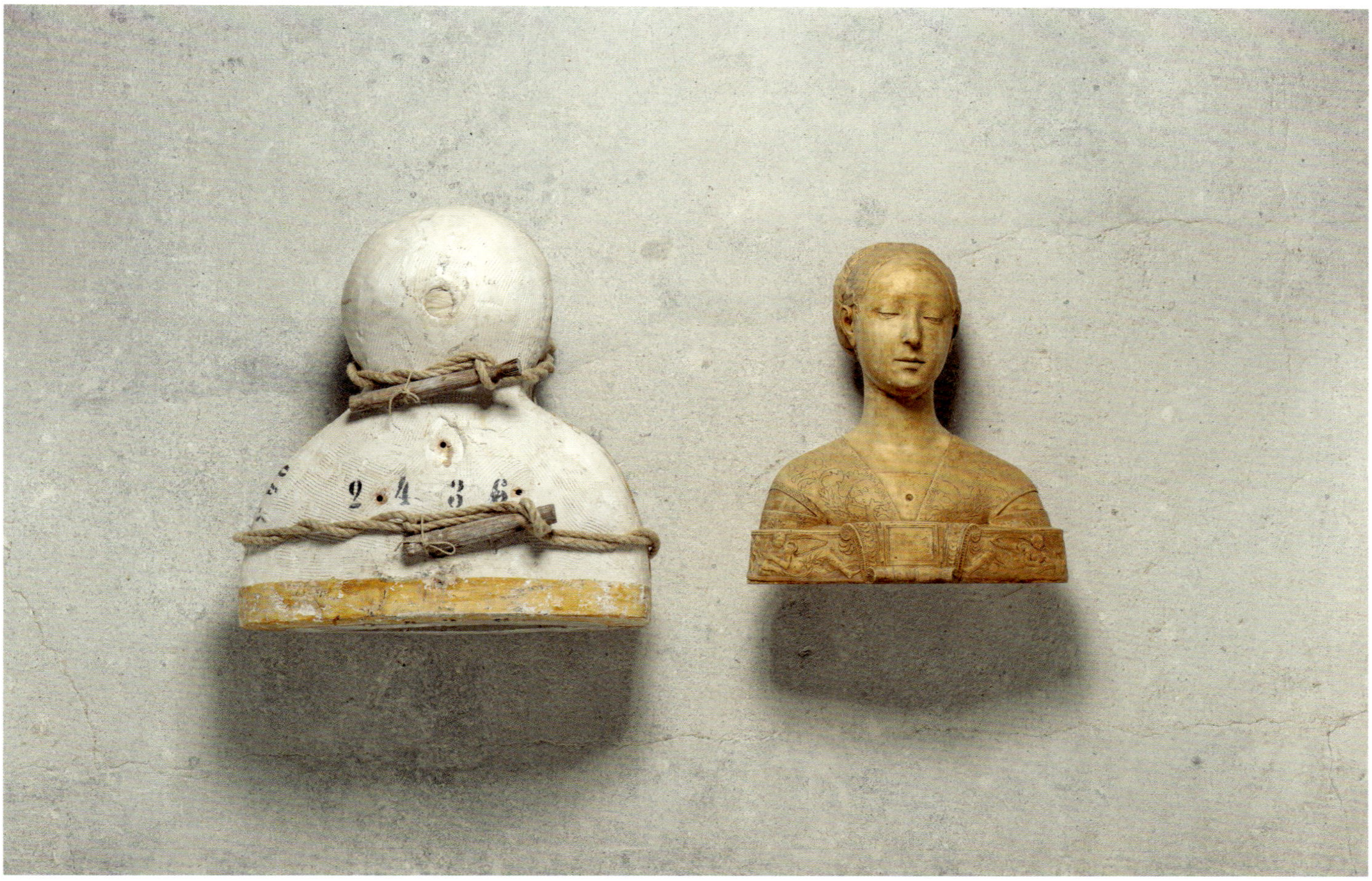
2 4 3 6

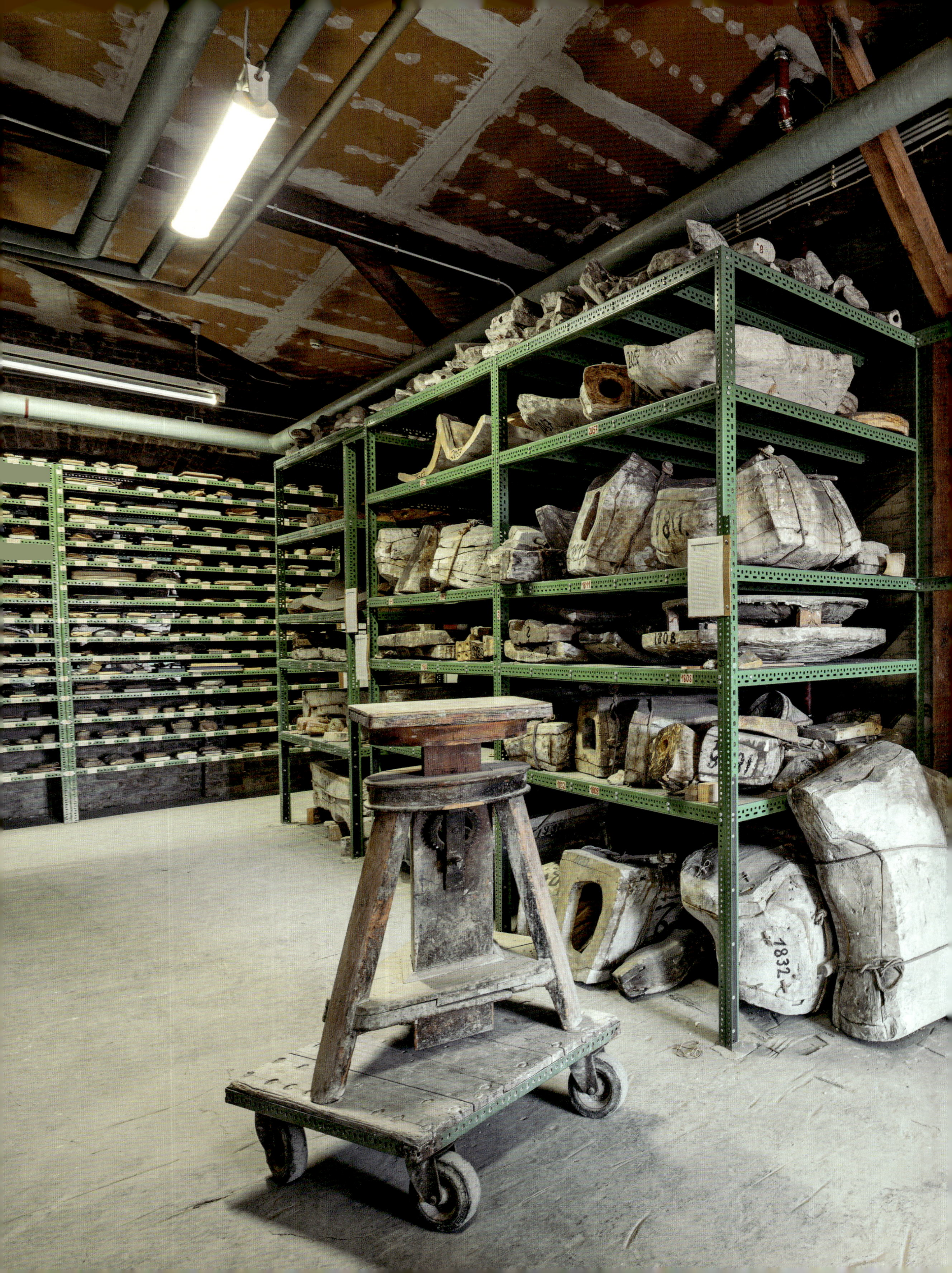
1811
1808
1832

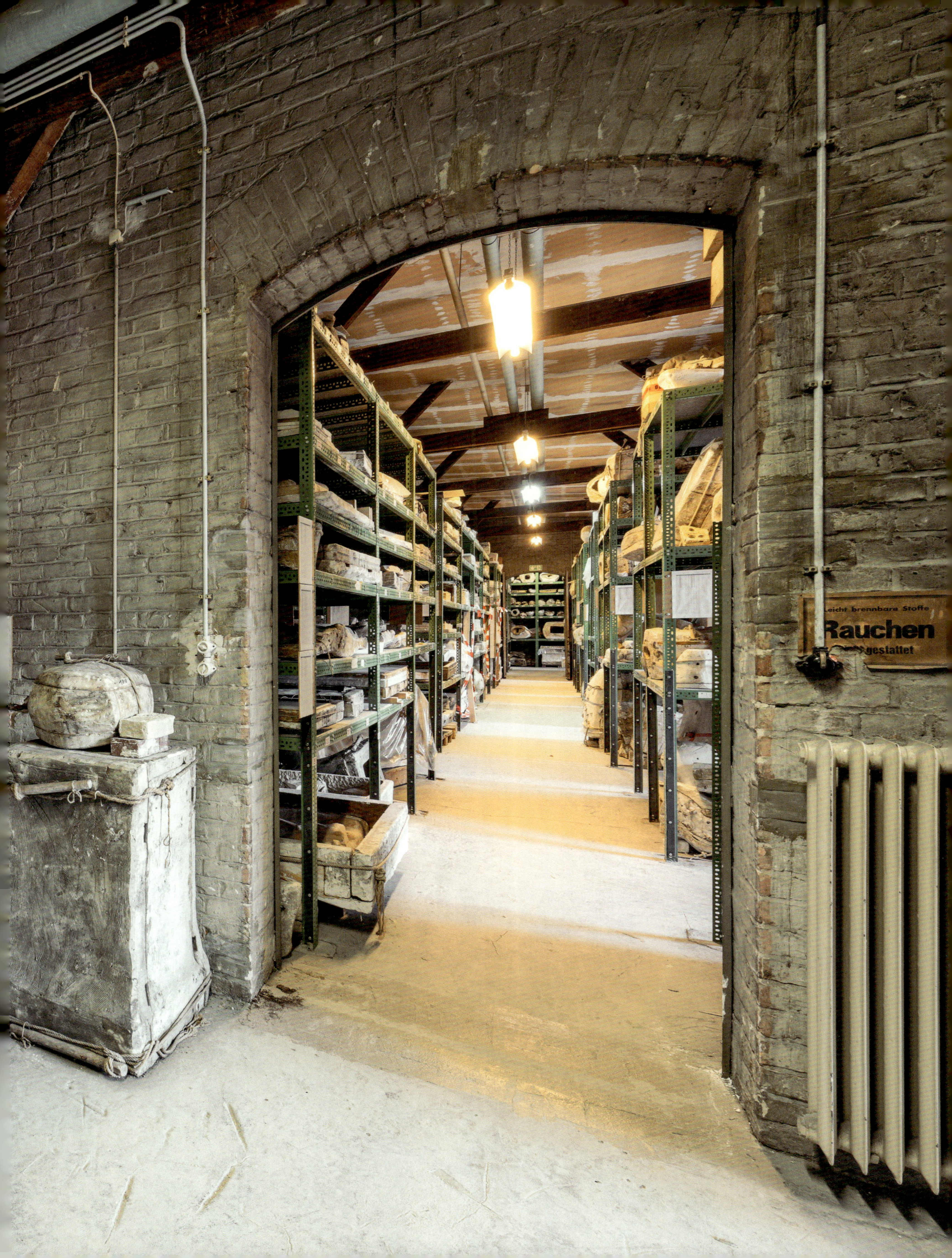
Leicht brennbare Stoffe
Rauchen
gestattet

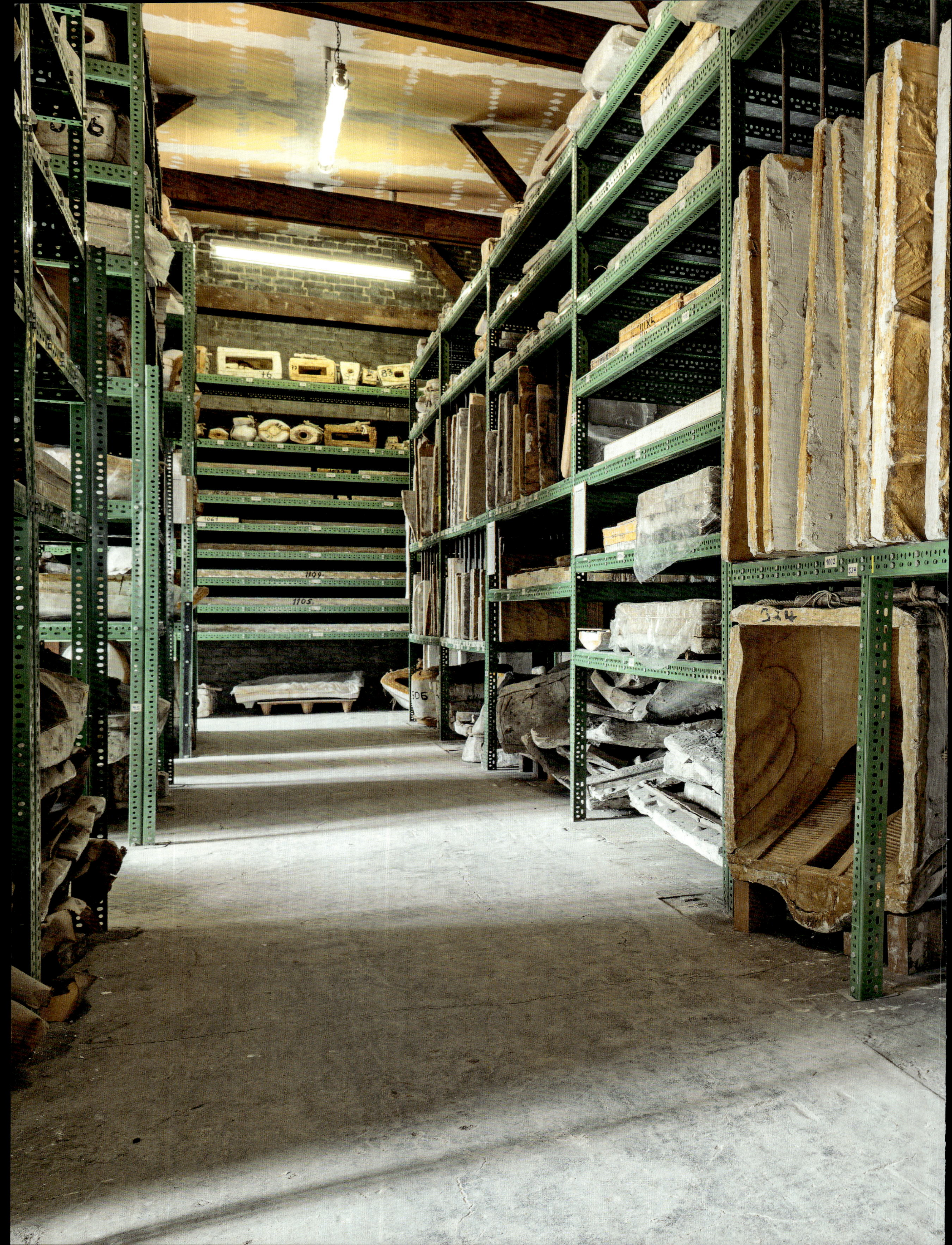
1109
1105

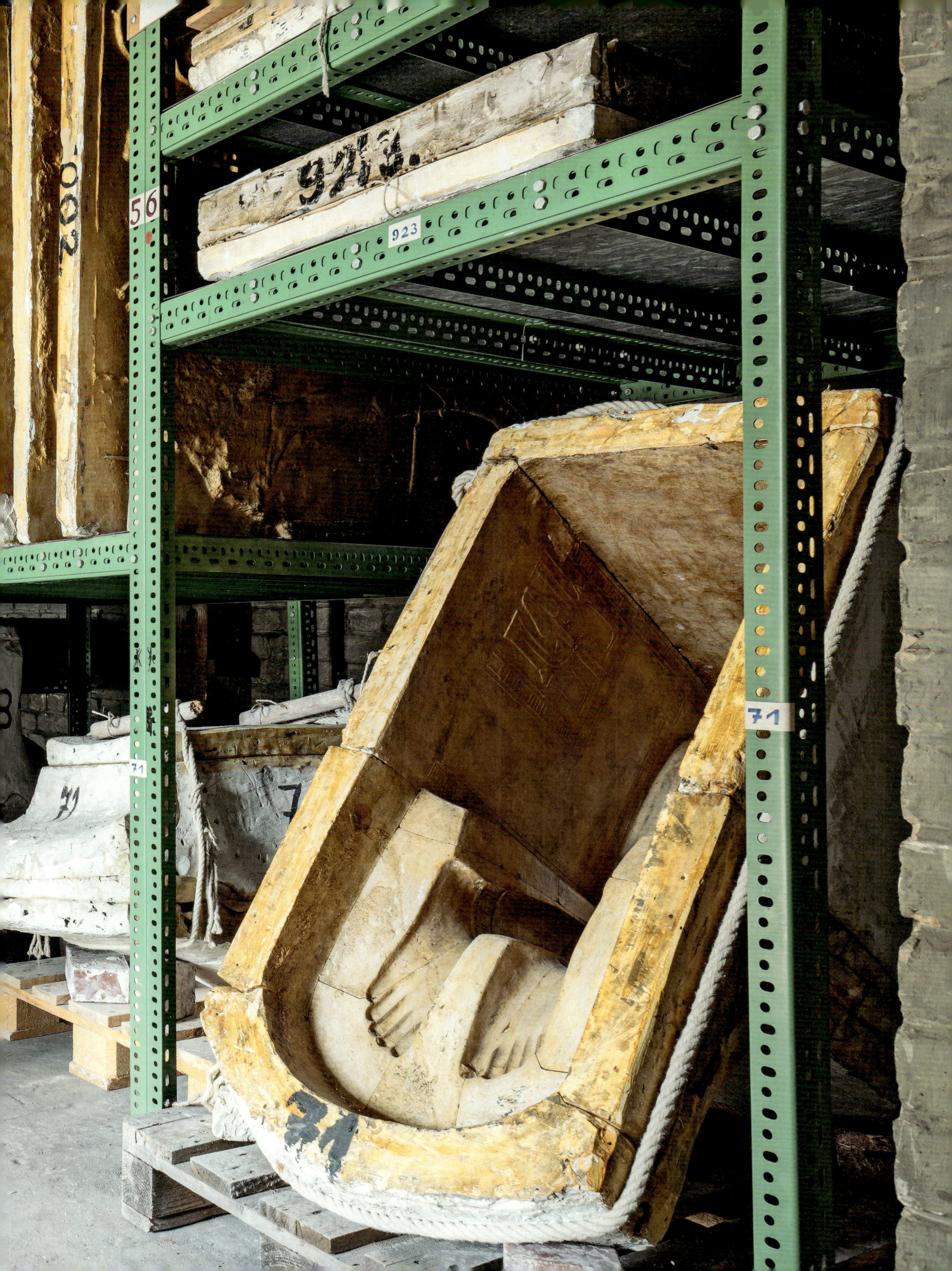
56
923
71

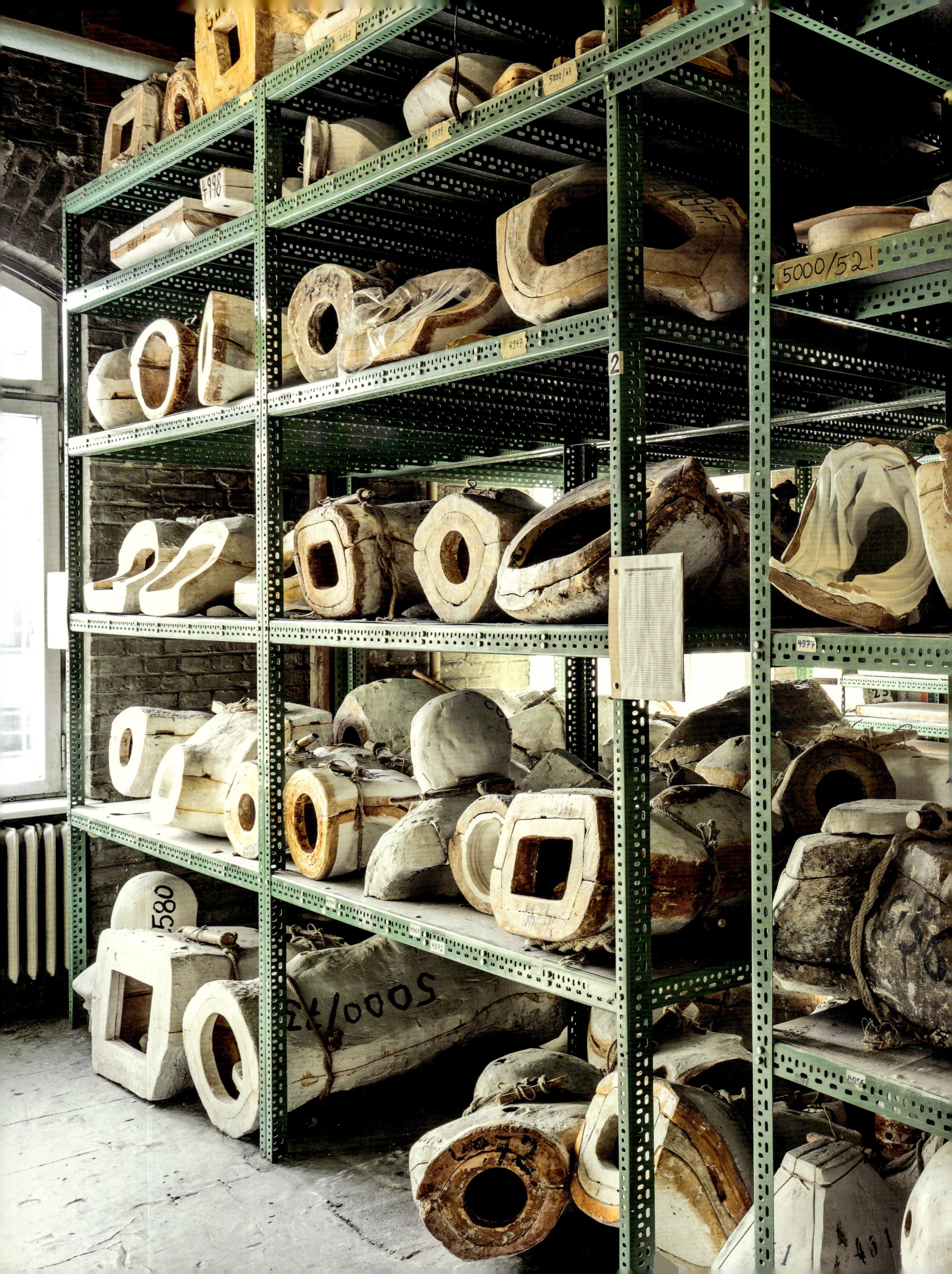
4998
5000/52
2
580

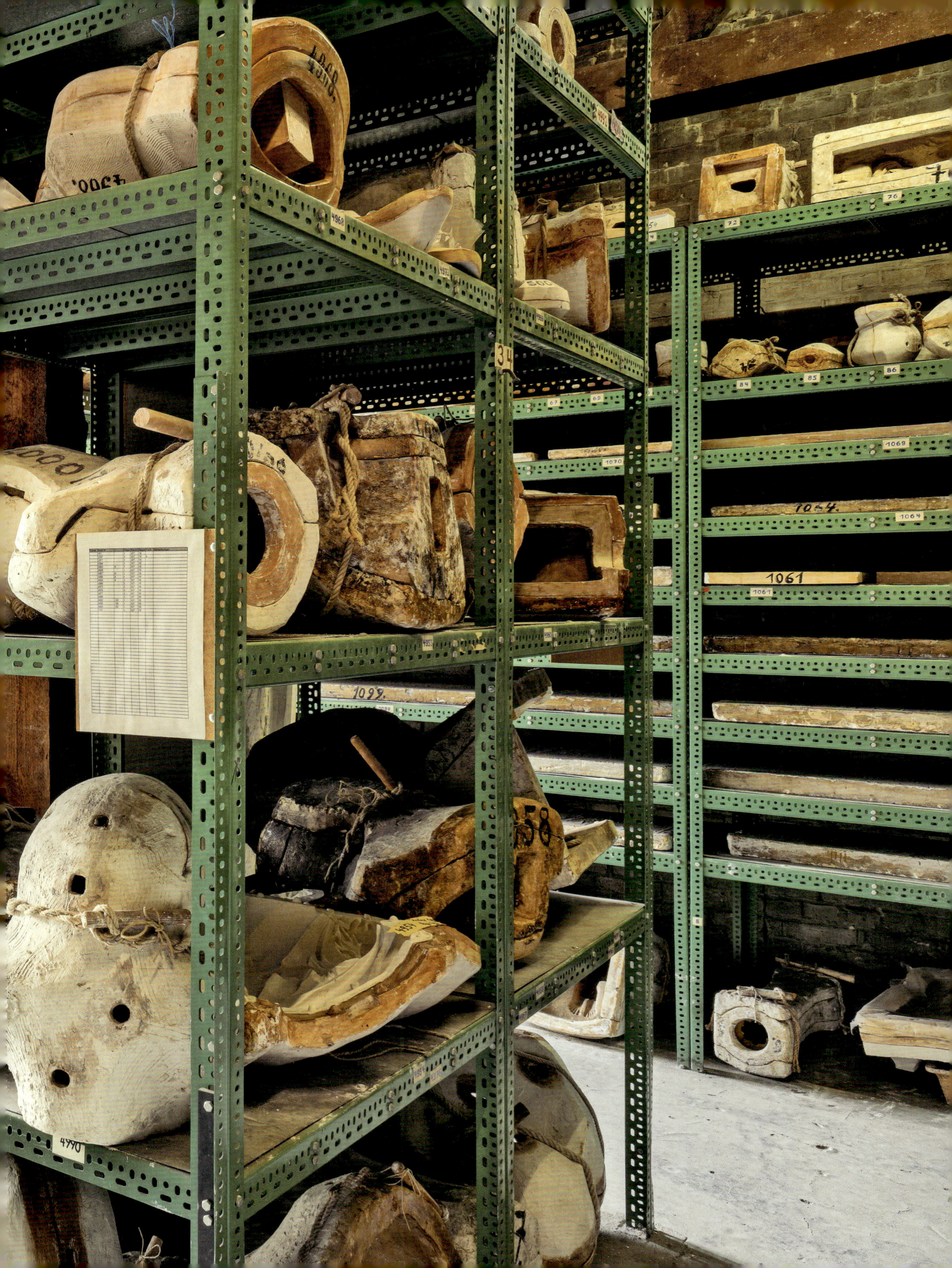

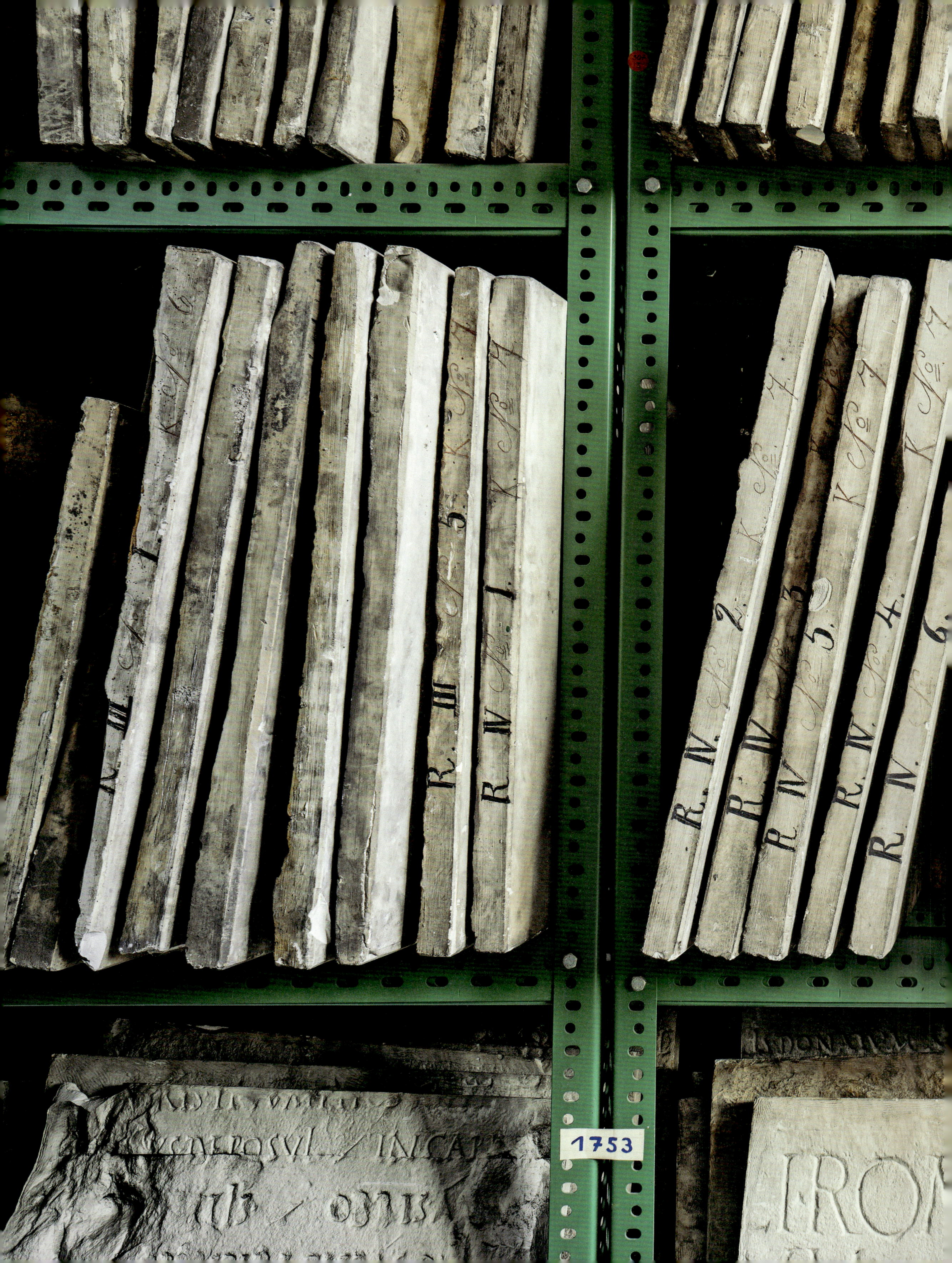
1753

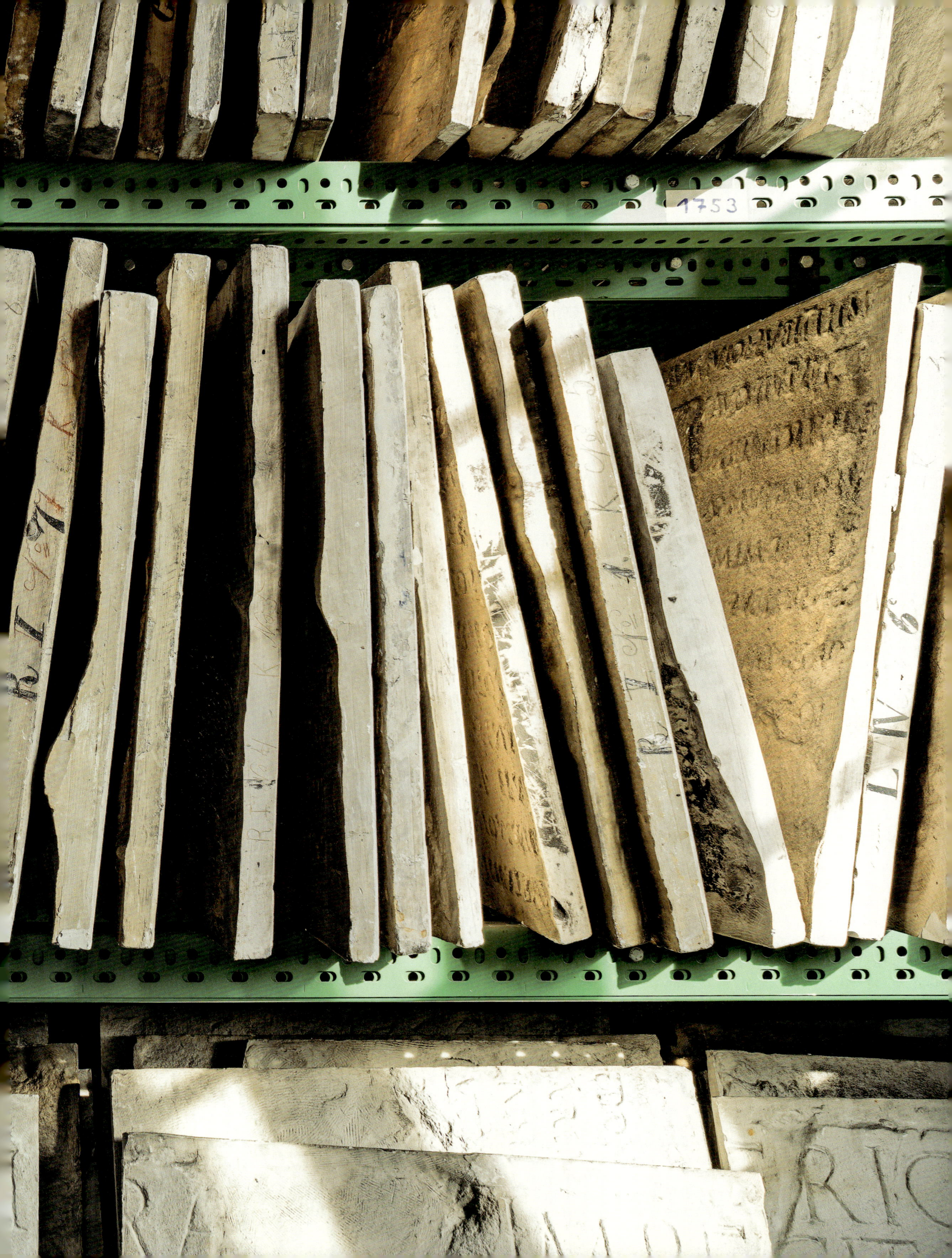
1753

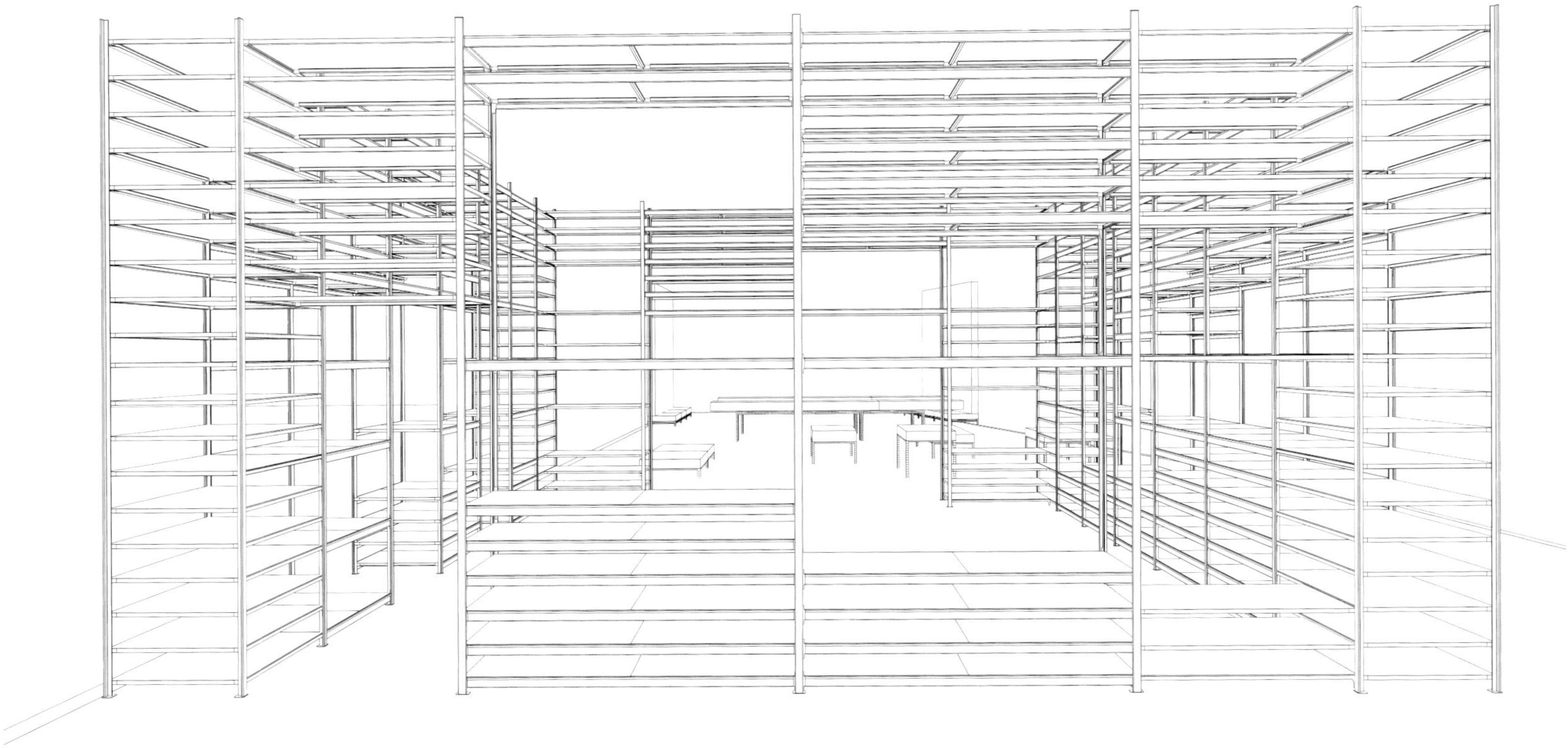

Schroeder Rauch
Heavy-load storage rack for
the *Prologue*, 2019

Transformation as a Concept: Notes on the Exhibition Architecture

Hanne König and Nicolas Rauch

The design of an exhibition results from an awareness that the interpretation and significance of each exhibited object are subject to change, depending on how, in what context and with what other exhibits that particular item is shown. The origins of the objects and how they were and are stored and exposed to view informs the exhibition design. Our concept for *Near Life: The Gipsformerei — 200 Years of Casting Plaster* encourages taking an intuitive approach to the exhibition to complement the more intellectual aspects. For this purpose, we have designed a scenography which is based on the principle of transformation. The reconfiguration of the display units serves the purpose of bringing about a continual change in the bodily movements of the visitors, thus enabling a physical and memorable experience of the exhibition.

On entering the exhibition hall visitors find themselves confronted with a series of large heavy-load storage racks which form a secluded space, the 'Prologue', where the history of the Gipsformerei, Staatliche Museen zu Berlin and different aspects of its workshop practice are first introduced. The racks reference the storage situation of the casting moulds and models at the Gipsformerei. This reconstruction shows the casts on display in their usual state and transports visitors to their customary storage place. It also presents the Gipsformerei as a collection, workshop and an institution with a long tradition.

On second glance, however, the exhibition set-up reveals ruptures that point to its essential staging. There are places where the functionality of the storage rack gives way to the elements of design and display: shelves are closely stacked, one on top of the other, acquiring the rhythmical structure reminiscent of stored commodities and shifting the apparent function of the racks as storage units to something on display for its own sake. Indeed, the rack transforms the space into a showroom, where visitors are free to either follow the exhibition narrative or allow their gaze to wander across whatever takes their fancy.

On either side of the Prologue's rack structure the exhibition's five thematic chapters unfold. The exhibition's layout extends to form an open constellation of display units. Two different methods of display have been developed: the rack system is used as a support structure that is open and exposed to view;

white cubes made of engineered wood are arranged on top of the rack structure. The cubes are somewhat like 'typical' plinths we associate with contemporary exhibition practice, which serve the purpose of giving the exhibited objects a more elevated position, of framing, situating and contextualising, while at the same time establishing a distance between objects. Here, the formal language aims at underlining the ambivalence inherent to the exhibits on display. After all, the moulds and models from the Gipsformerei oscillate in their function between tools and museum exhibits, between objects in daily use and as collection items.

In the configuration of the display units, each section is given its own design. The unit's dimensions and elevation from the ground (resting on worktables, counters and plinths) vary depending on the exhibition's thematic content. In turn, the bodily postures of the visitors adapt to this continuous change. In the first chapter, *Still Lifes and Nature morte*, casts from the world of animals and plants are placed on very low display structures — observation of nature sometimes involves taking in the view from above. *Too near to Life*, the second chapter, addresses highly sensitive holdings in the collection of the Gipsformerei, the anthropological casts and source materials and select exhibits. These are presented on archive tables to facilitate concentrated study and the review of historical evidence. A different approach is taken for the chapter *Ultimate Life*, where visitors are directly confronted with a slew of death masks — the visages of death are like mirrors for us to behold our own image. They also underline the mimetic qualities of the casts and their closeness to life. *In the Artist's Studio*, the chapter of the exhibition dedicated to studio practices since antiquity, presents a great number of fragmentary body casts. Here, the exhibited objects are displayed on an outsize worktable to emphasise the significance of casts for the sculptural process. *The Case against Casts* presents a small selection of sculptures whose origins are allegedly connected to an illicit use of the casts. Sculptures which usually stand on the floor or on a plinth are placed on low pedestals to emphasise. The *Epilogue*, marking the end of the exhibition, presents the casts of famous sculptures assembled on relatively high pedestals to create what seems to be a climactic moment, a pantheon of sorts of all-time greats. This moment, however, is immediately undercut by the recognition that what is in fact on display are 'mere' replicas, which in any case parade their nature as workshop models quite openly.

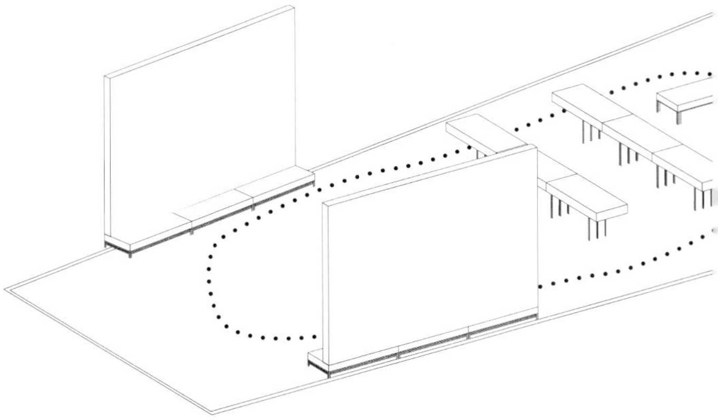

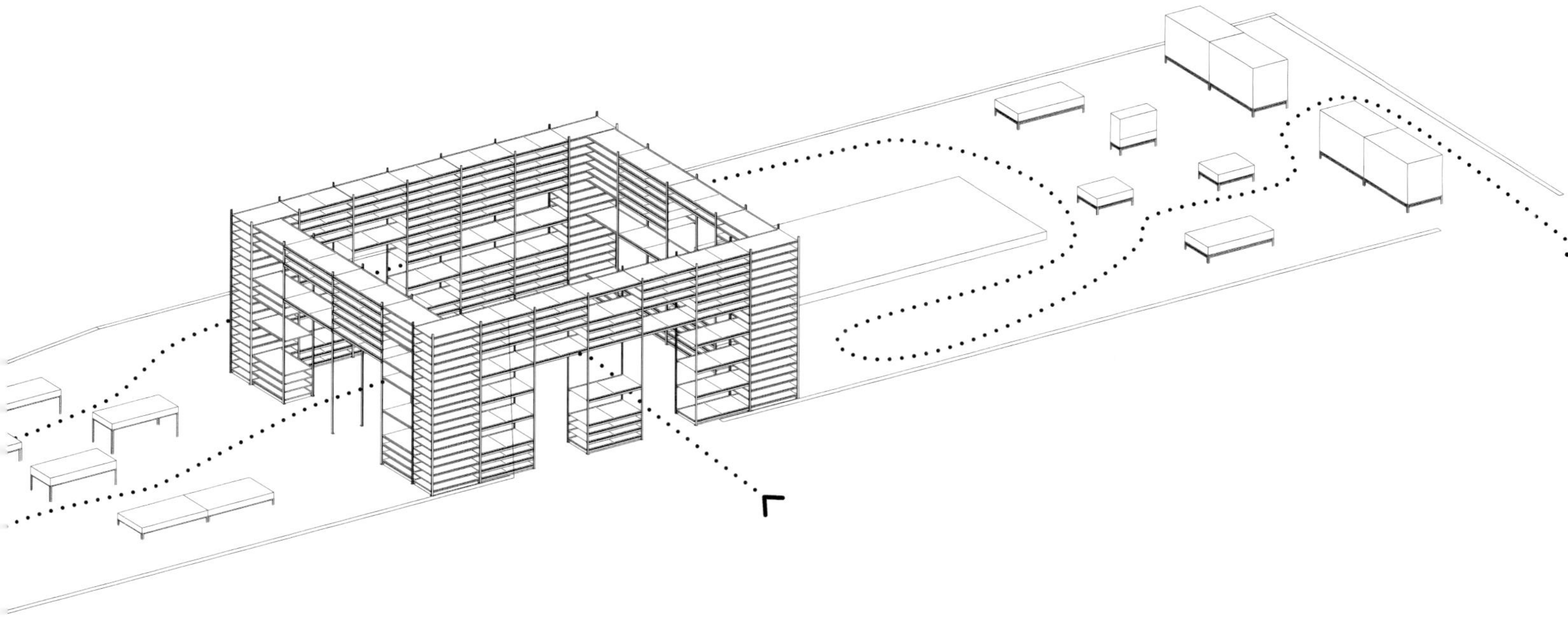

Schroeder Rauch
Overview and exhibition
layout, 2019

Still Lifes and Nature morte

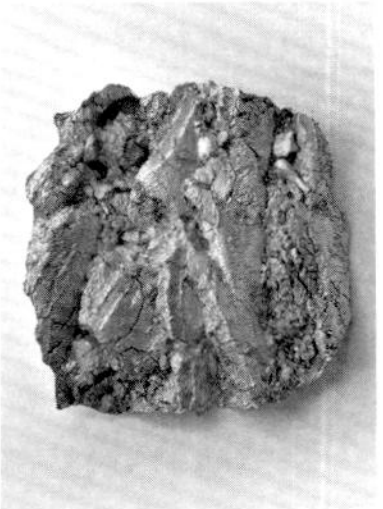

Asta Gröting (b. 1961)
Acker (Soil), 2012
Epoxy resin, 24-carat gold
187 × 184 × 8 cm
Galerie carlier | gebauer, Berlin, AG/scu/10563

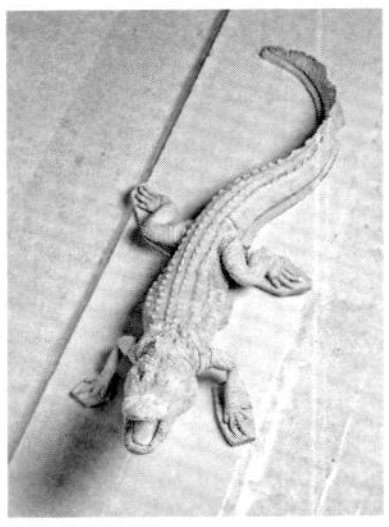

Crocodile
Master model, 1892
Plaster, shellacked
290 × 95 × 32 cm
Staatliche Museen zu Berlin, Gipsformerei, 6580

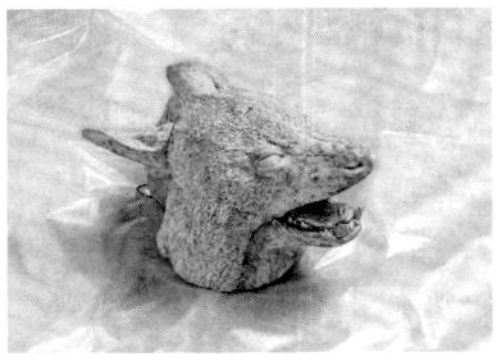

Head of a Wolf
Master model, 1892
Plaster, shellacked
23 × 23 × 36 cm
Staatliche Museen zu Berlin, Gipsformerei, 6496

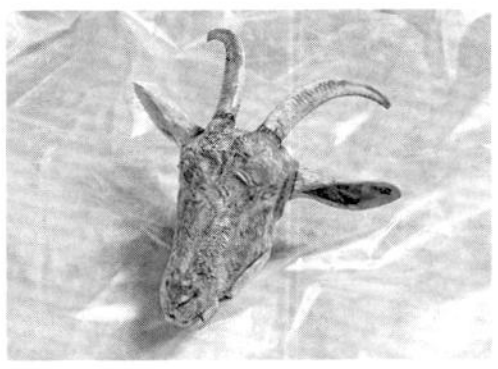

Head of a Goat with Short Horns
Master model, 1870
Plaster, shellacked
40 × 35 × 24 cm
Staatliche Museen zu Berlin, Gipsformerei, 6132

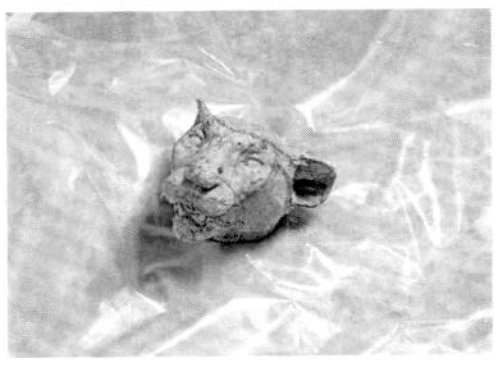

Head of a Panther
Master model, 1892
Plaster, shellacked
15.5 × 20 × 24.5 cm
Staatliche Museen zu Berlin, Gipsformerei, 6497

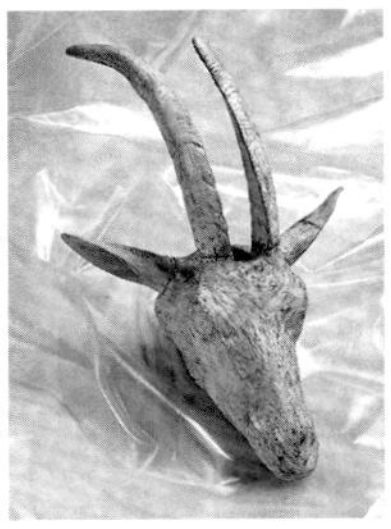

Head of a Goat with Long Horns
Master model, 1870
Plaster, shellacked
55 × 40 × 30 cm
Staatliche Museen zu Berlin, Gipsformerei, 6133

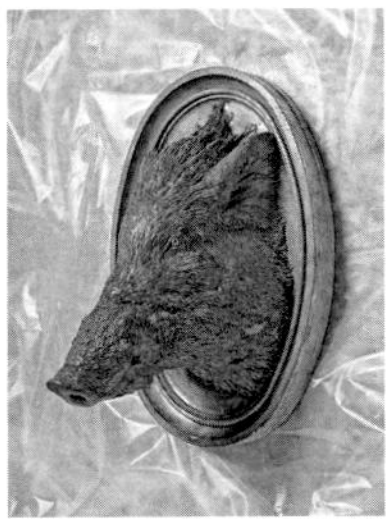

Head of a Boar
Master model, 1886
Plaster, shellacked
65 × 43 × 40 cm
Staatliche Museen zu Berlin, Gipsformerei, 6447

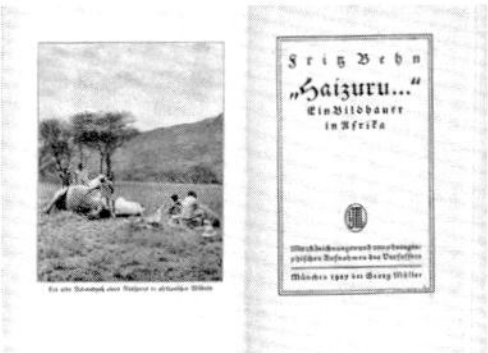

Fritz Behn (1878–1970)
'Haizuru …': Ein Bildhauer in Afrika
Munich 1917
Staatliche Museen zu Berlin, Ethnologisches Museum, Ao/Behn

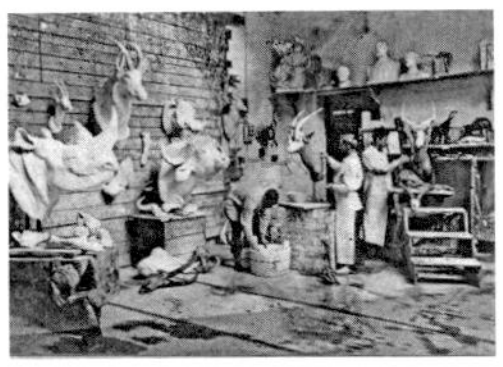

Unknown photographer
Studio of the Sculptor Fritz Behn in Munich, ca. 1910
Photograph (exhibition copy), 10 × 15 cm
Nuremberg, Germanisches Nationalmuseum, Deutsches Kunstarchiv, NL Behn, Fritz, AFS 3 (0002)

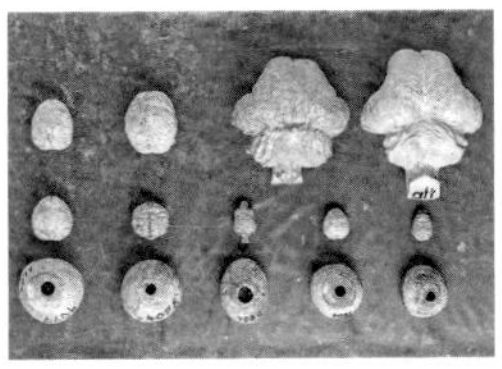

Braincase of a Gorilla
Master model, 1906
Plaster, shellacked
8 × 9 × 11.5 cm
Staatliche Museen zu Berlin, Gipsformerei, 4076

Braincase of a Human ('of the "Alpine" Race')
Master model, 1906
Plaster, shellacked
11 × 12 × 14 cm
Staatliche Museen zu Berlin, Gipsformerei, 4075

Braincase of an Elephant ('Young')
Master model, 1897
Plaster, shellacked
17 × 29 × 30 cm
Staatliche Museen zu Berlin, Gipsformerei, 4068

Braincase of an Elephant ('Old')
Master model, 1897
Plaster, shellacked
18.5 × 29 × 36 cm
Staatliche Museen zu Berlin, Gipsformerei, 4067

Braincase of an Orangutan
Master model, 1906
7 × 9 × 10.5 cm
Plaster, shellacked
Staatliche Museen zu Berlin, Gipsformerei, 4077

Braincase of a Seal
Master model, 1906
Plaster, shellacked
5.5 × 9 × 9 cm
Staatliche Museen zu Berlin, Gipsformerei, 4078

Braincase of a Dog
Master model, 1906
Plaster, shellacked
5 × 5 × 10.3 cm
Staatliche Museen zu Berlin, Gipsformerei, 4080

Braincase of a White-Handed Gibbon
Master model, 1906
Plaster, shellacked
4.5 × 5.5 × 7 cm
Staatliche Museen zu Berlin, Gipsformerei, 4081

Braincase of a Badger
Master model, 1906
Plaster, shellacked
4 × 5 × 7 cm
Staatliche Museen zu Berlin, Gipsformerei, 4079

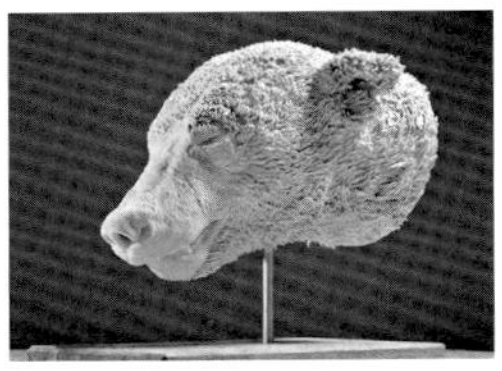

Head of Polar Bear Knut
3D print on the basis of a computer tomography, 2011
Polymer plaster, epoxy resin
42 × 57 × 64 cm
3D Labor am Institut für Mathematik
Leibniz-Institut für Zoo- und Wildtierforschung, Berlin

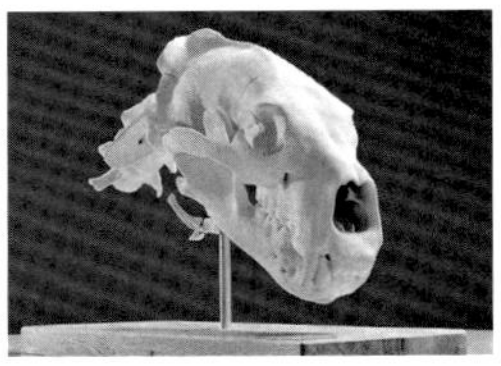

Skull of Polar Bear Knut
3D print on the basis of a computer tomography, 2011
Polymer plaster, epoxy resin
19 × 48 × 30 cm
3D Labor am Institut für Mathematik
Leibniz-Institut für Zoo- und Wildtierforschung, Berlin

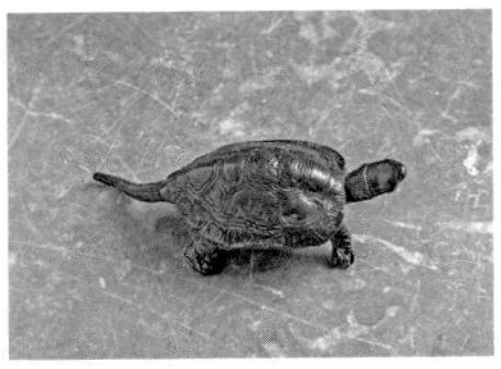

Andrea Briosco (Il Riccio) (1470–1532)
Tortoise, Padua, early 16th century
Bronze
2.5 × 4.5 × 9.2 cm
Staatliche Museen zu Berlin, Skulpturensammlung und Museum für Byzantinische Kunst, 2278

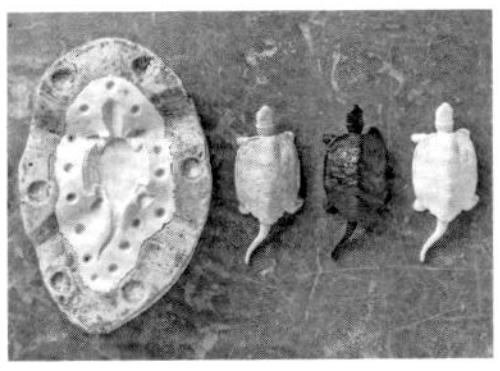

After Andrea Briosco (Il Riccio) (1470–1532)
Tortoise, Padua, early 16th century
Silicone mould in mother mould, ca. 2000
7.5 × 11 × 17 cm (external dimensions)
Master model, ca. 1920
Painting model, 1909
Raw cast, 2019
Each 2.3 × 3.5 × 9.2 cm
Staatliche Museen zu Berlin, Gipsformerei, 2199

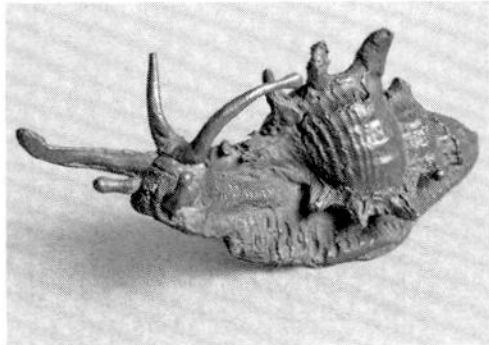

Unknown artist
Sea Snail, Padua, early 16th century
Bronze
7.9 × 3.5 × 3.5 cm
Kunsthistorisches Museum Wien, Kunstkammer, KK 5940

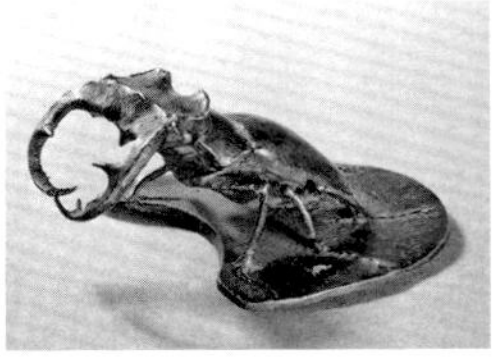

Andrea Briosco (Il Riccio) (1470–1532)
Stag Beetle, Padua, early 16th century
Bronze
3 × 5.4 × 7 cm

Staatliche Museen zu Berlin,
Skulpturensammlung und
Museum für Byzantinische
Kunst, 2102

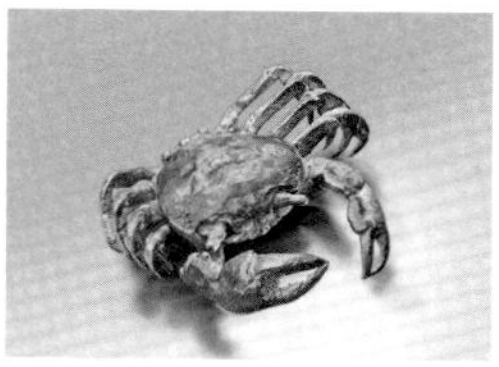

Andrea Briosco (Il Riccio)
(1470–1532)
Brown Crab, Padua,
early 16th century
Bronze
4.7 × 11.7 × 10.9 cm
Staatliche Museen zu Berlin,
Skulpturensammlung und
Museum für Byzantinische
Kunst, 2103

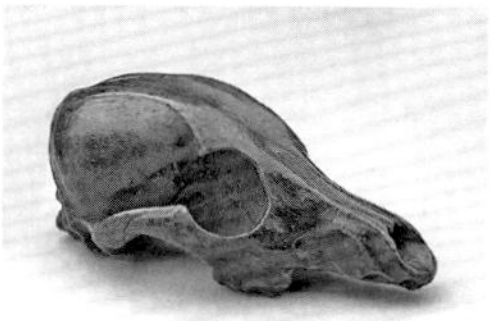

Unknown artist
Skull of a Foxhound,
Padua or Venice,
16th century
Bronze
11.3 × 5.8 × 4.7 cm
Staatliche Museen zu Berlin,
Skulpturensammlung und
Museum für Byzantinische
Kunst, 7219

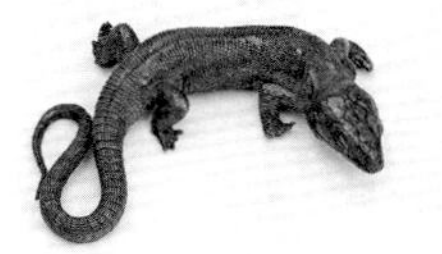

Wenzel Jamnitzer
(1508–1585)
Lizard, Nuremberg,
mid-16th century
Lead alloy
1.2 × 4.8 × 6.8 cm
Staatliche Museen zu Berlin,
Kunstgewerbemuseum,
K 5912

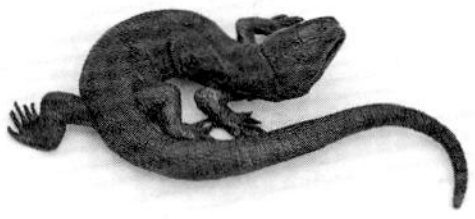

Wenzel Jamnitzer
(1508–1585)
Sand Lizard, Nuremberg,
mid-16th century
Copper alloy
1.4 × 3.8 × 9 cm
Staatliche Museen zu Berlin,
Kunstgewerbemuseum,
K 4399

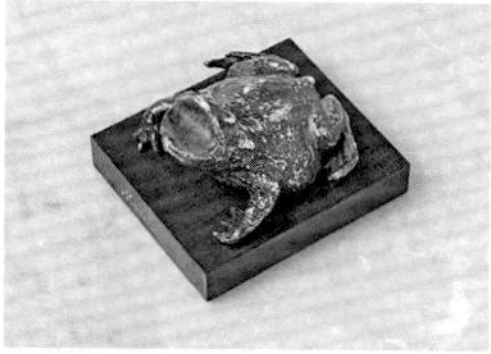

After Andrea Briosco
(Il Riccio) (1470–1532)
Toad
Painting model, 1933
Plaster, painted
7.2 × 11.3 × 10.5 cm
(Original: Padua,
early 16th century,
whereabouts unknown)
Staatliche Museen zu Berlin,
Gipsformerei, 2909

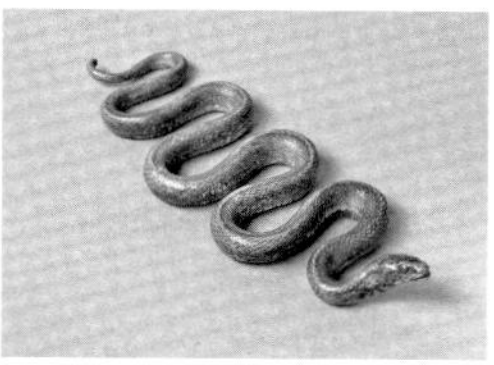

Unknown artist
Snake, Padua,
early 16th century
Lead-tin alloy,
partly painted
22 × 7 × 2.7 cm
Kunsthistorisches Museum
Wien, Kunstkammer,
KK 5907

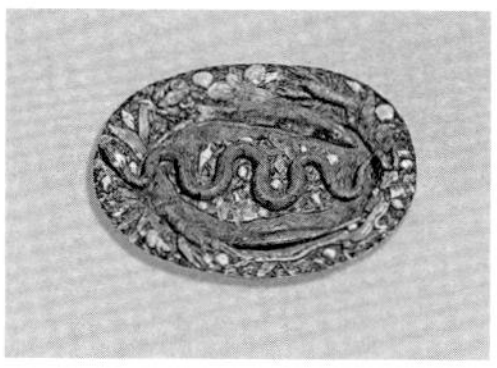

Bernard Palissy (1510–1590)
Bowl, late 16th century
Earthenware
6.5 × 47 × 36.5 cm
Museum für Kunst und
Gewerbe Hamburg,
1910.268

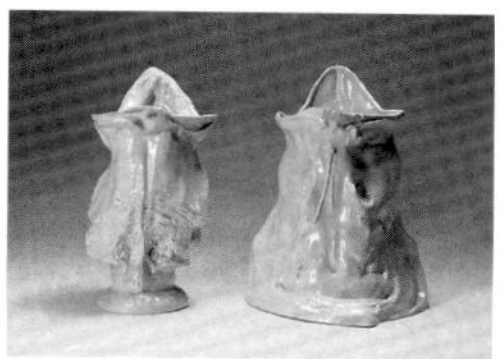

Maria Volokhova (b. 1980)
Pearlescence IN and
Pearlescence OUT, 2016
Porcelain, partly lustre
glazed
36 × 20 × 18 cm
and 40 × 27 × 32 cm
Courtesy of the artist

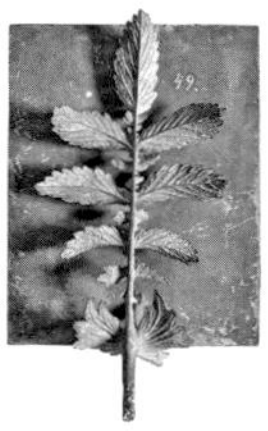

Giovanni Nisini for
Moritz Meurer (1839–1916)
Agrimony, Leaf, 1891–92
Bronze
13.8 × 10.9 × 4 cm
Universität der Künste Berlin,
Universitätsarchiv 321-49

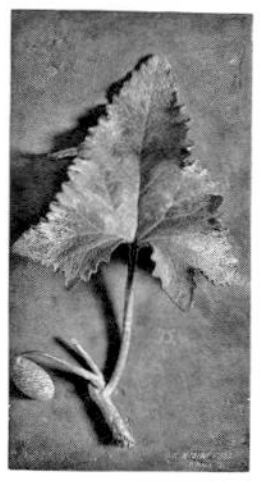

Giovanni Nisini for
Moritz Meurer (1839–1916)
Squirting Cucumber, Leaf,
1891–92
Bronze
24.5 × 12.8 × 7 cm
Universität der Künste Berlin,
Universitätsarchiv 321-45

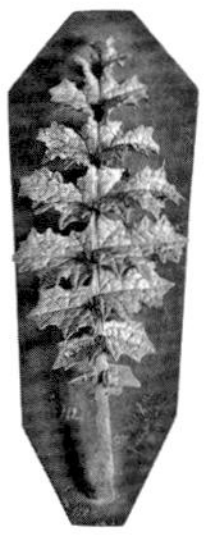

Giovanni Nisini for
Moritz Meurer (1839–1916)
Thistle, Leave, 1893–96
Bronze
20 × 7 × 3.5 cm
Universität der Künste Berlin,
Universitätsarchiv 321-104

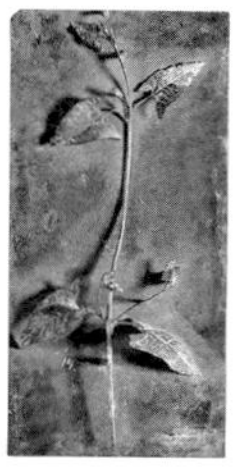

Giovanni Nisini for
Moritz Meurer (1839–1916)
Unspecified Plant,
Shoot with Young Leaves,
1891–92
Bronze
26 × 12.8 × 3.5 cm
Universität der Künste Berlin,
Universitätsarchiv
321-14

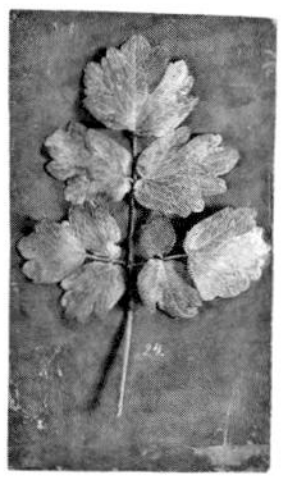

Giovanni Nisini for
Moritz Meurer (1839–1916)
Meadow Rue, Leaf,
1891–92
Bronze
22.2 × 12.7 × 2.5 cm
Universität der Künste Berlin,
Universitätsarchiv
321-24

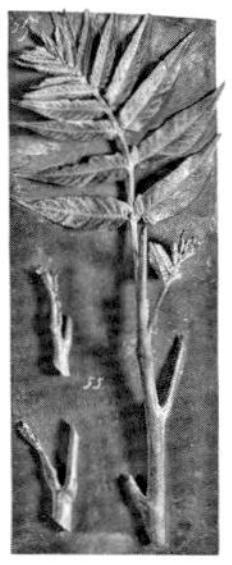

Giovanni Nisini for
Moritz Meurer (1839–1916)
Ailanthus, Leaf,
1891–92
Bronze
32.8 × 12.7 × 4.5 cm
Universität der Künste Berlin,
Universitätsarchiv
321-55

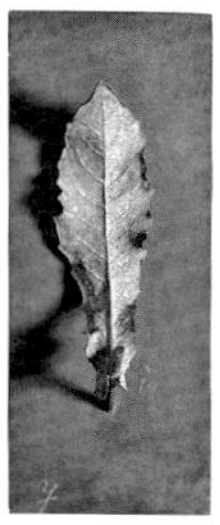

Giovanni Nisini for
Moritz Meurer (1839–1916)
Unspecified Plant, Leaf,
1891–92
Bronze
22 × 8.8 × 6.5 cm
Universität der Künste Berlin,
Universitätsarchiv
321-7

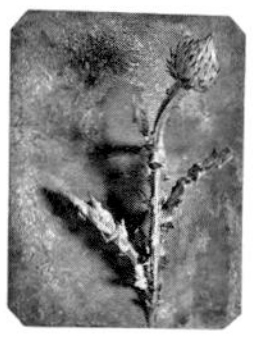

Giovanni Nisini for
Moritz Meurer (1839–1916)
Thistle, Terminal Bud,
1893–96
Bronze
15 × 11 × 5 cm
Universität der Künste Berlin,
Universitätsarchiv
321-104

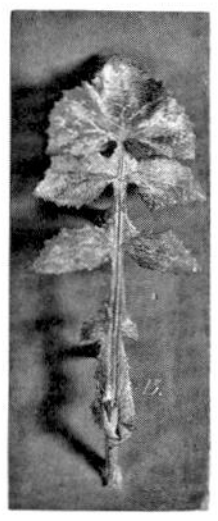

Giovanni Nisini for
Moritz Meurer (1839–1916)
Sow Thistle, Leaf, 1891–92
Bronze
21.7 × 8.8 × 4 cm
Universität der Künste Berlin,
Universitätsarchiv
321-15

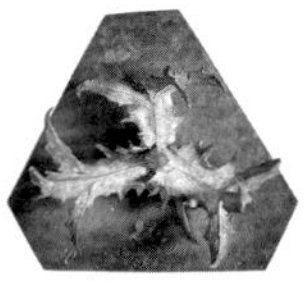

Giovanni Nisini for
Moritz Meurer (1839–1916)
Sea Holly, Stem with Leaves,
1891–92
Bronze
10 × 6.9 × 4 cm
Universität der Künste Berlin,
Universitätsarchiv
321-20

Too near to Life

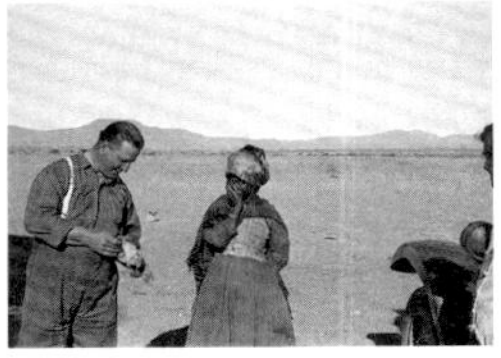

Hans Lichtenecker Showing the Face Mask of a Woman to a Woman called Lena,
South West Africa
(today's Namibia), 1931
Photograph
(exhibition copy)
Archive of Hans Lichtenecker
Private collection
Wolfgang Wiggers

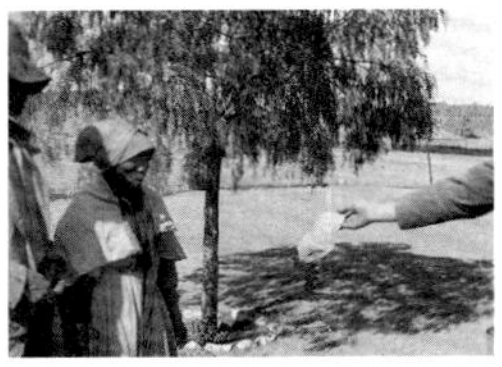

One of Hans Lichtenecker's Collaborators Showing a Face Mask to an Unidentified Woman,
South West Africa
(today's Namibia), 1931
Photograph
(exhibition copy)
Archive of Hans Lichtenecker
Private collection
Wolfgang Wiggers

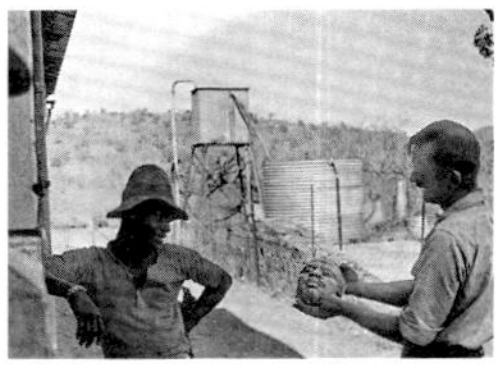

One of Hans Lichtenecker's Collaborators Showing a Face Mask to an Unidentified Man,
South West Africa
(today's Namibia), 1931
Photograph
(exhibition copy)
Archive of Hans Lichtenecker
Private collection
Wolfgang Wiggers

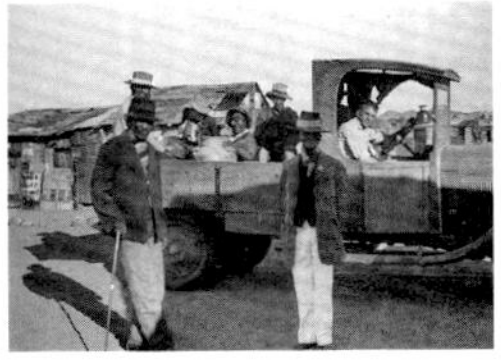

'A Cart Load of Models': People Are Taken to the Police Station at Keetmanshoop,
South West Africa
(today's Namibia), 1931
Photograph
(exhibition copy)
Archive of Hans Lichtenecker
Private collection
Wolfgang Wiggers

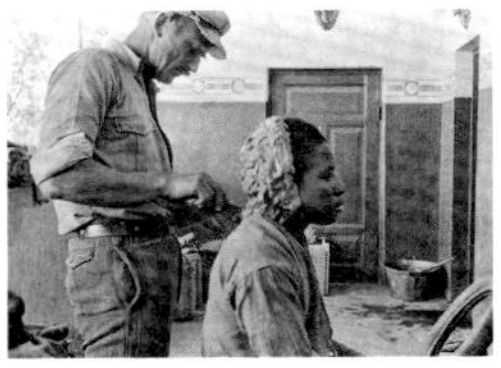

Casting an Unidentified Man,
South West Africa
(today's Namibia), 1931
Photograph
(exhibition copy)
Archive of Hans Lichtenecker
Private collection
Wolfgang Wiggers

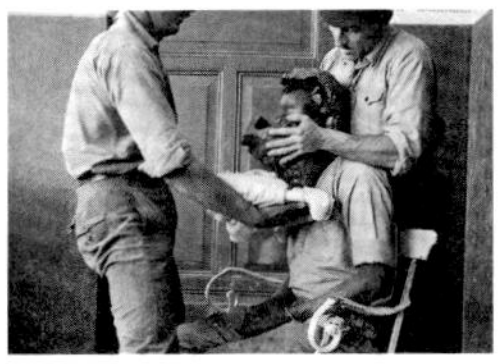

Casting Wilfred Tjiueza,
South West Africa
(today's Namibia), 1931
Photograph
(exhibition copy)
Archive of Hans Lichtenecker
Private collection
Wolfgang Wiggers

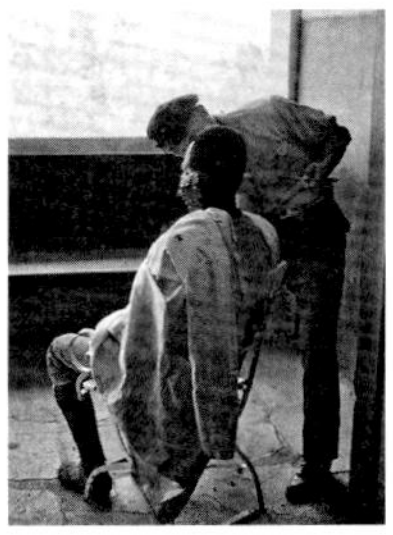

Casting Wilfred Tjiueza,
South West Africa
(today's Namibia), 1931
Photograph
(exhibition copy)
Archive of Hans Lichtenecker
Private collection
Wolfgang Wiggers

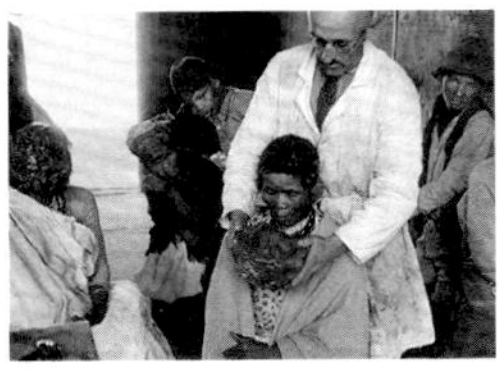

Casting an Unidentified Woman,
South West Africa
(today's Namibia), 1931
Photograph
(exhibition copy)
Archive of Hans Lichtenecker
Private collection
Wolfgang Wiggers

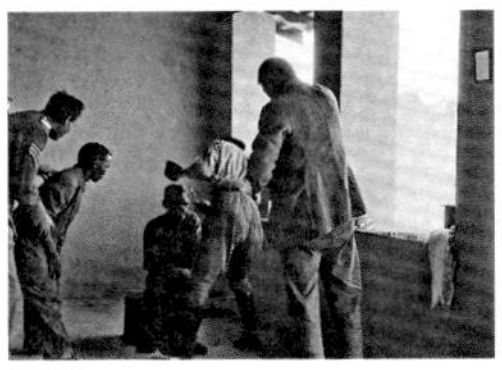

Casting an Unidentified Man,
South West Africa
(today's Namibia), 1931
Photograph
(exhibition copy)
Archive of Hans Lichtenecker
Private collection
Wolfgang Wiggers

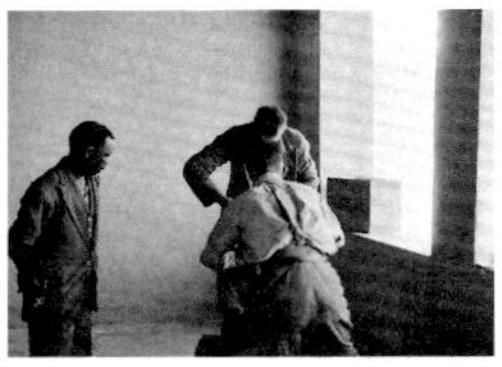

Casting an Unidentified Man,
South West Africa
(today's Namibia), 1931
Photograph (exhibition copy)
Archive of Hans Lichtenecker
Private collection
Wolfgang Wiggers

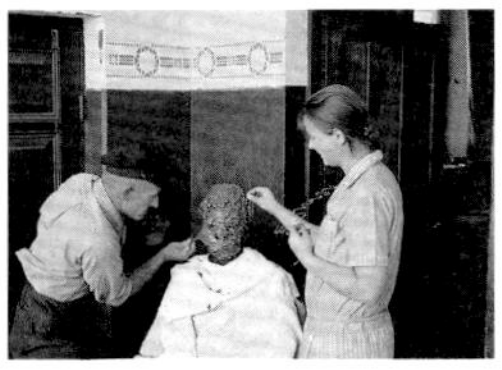

Casting Wilfred Tjiueza (?) by two of Hans Lichtenecker's Collaborators,
South West Africa
(today's Namibia), 1931
Photograph (exhibition copy)
Archive of Hans Lichtenecker
Private collection
Wolfgang Wiggers

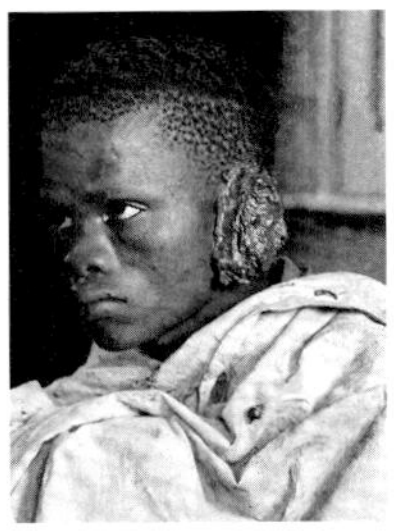

Casting the Ears of Thomas Goliath,
South West Africa
(today's Namibia), 1931
Photograph
(exhibition copy)
Archive of Hans Lichtenecker
Private collection
Wolfgang Wiggers

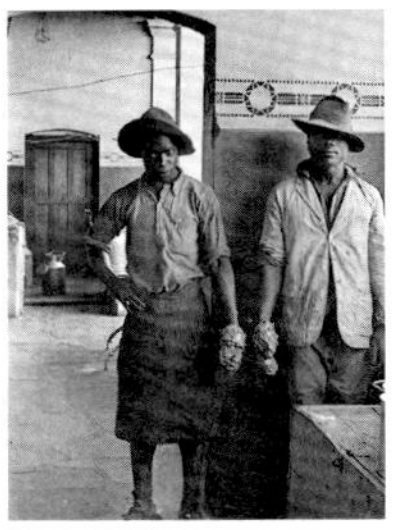

Hand Castings,
South West Africa
(today's Namibia), 1931
Photograph
(exhibition copy)
Archive of Hans Lichtenecker
Private collection
Wolfgang Wiggers

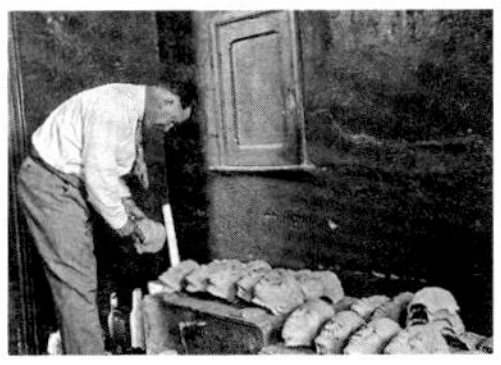

'Keetmanshooper Ausbeute' (Keetmanshoop Haul): Hans Lichtenecker with His Collection of Masks,
South West Africa
(today's Namibia), 1931
Photograph
(exhibition copy)
Archive of Hans Lichtenecker
Private collection
Wolfgang Wiggers

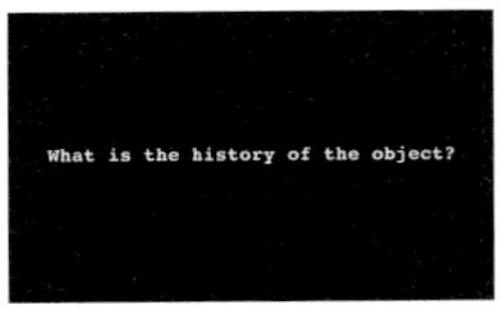

Pauline M'barek (b. 1979)
Object ID, 2012
HD video, b&w, 5' 5''
Courtesy of the artist and Galerie Thomas Rehbein, Cologne

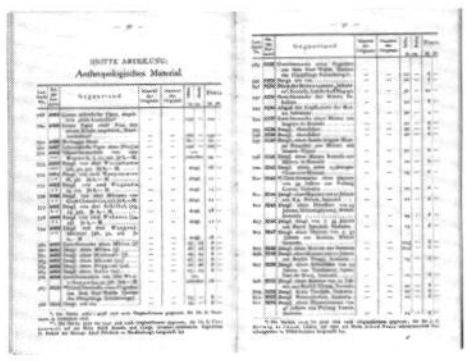

Verzeichnis der in der Formerei der Königlichen Museen käuflichen Gipsabgüsse (Prähistorische, ethnologische und anthropologische Gegenstände), Königliche Museen zu Berlin, General-Verwaltung (ed.), Berlin 1911
Staatliche Museen zu Berlin, Kunstbibliothek, GF 1/1911/1

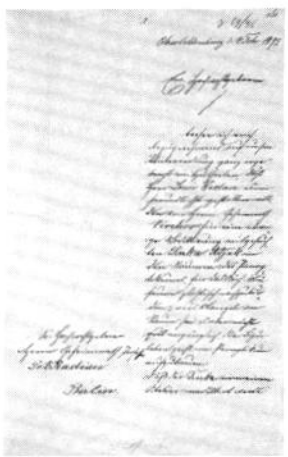

Handwritten letter from Ernst Bernardien to Adolf Bastian, 4 February 1895
Staatliche Museen zu Berlin, Ethnologisches Museum, E 69/1896 150A, 150B, 151C, I B 15 Afrika

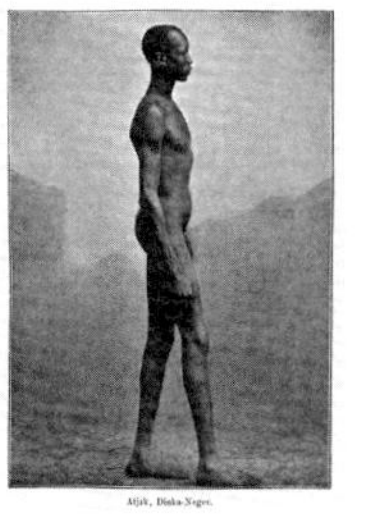

Zeitschrift für Ethnologie 27 (1895)
Staatliche Museen zu Berlin, Kunstbibliothek, Lipp Ad 41 kl-27.1895

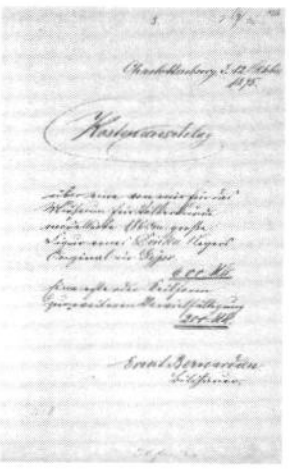

Handwritten estimate of Ernst Bernardien for casting the figure of Adjak in plaster, 12 October 1895
Staatliche Museen zu Berlin, Ethnologisches Museum, E 69/1896 153, I B 15 Afrika

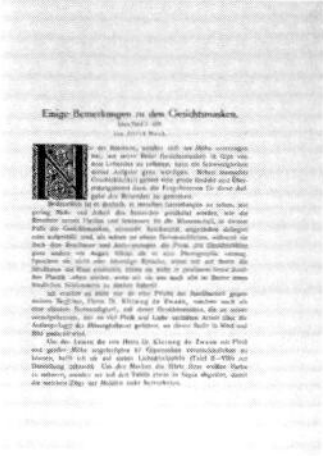

Alfred Maaß (1863–1946)
Durch Zentral-Sumatra, vol. 2, Berlin 1912,
Staatliche Museen zu Berlin, Ethnologisches Museum, Mw

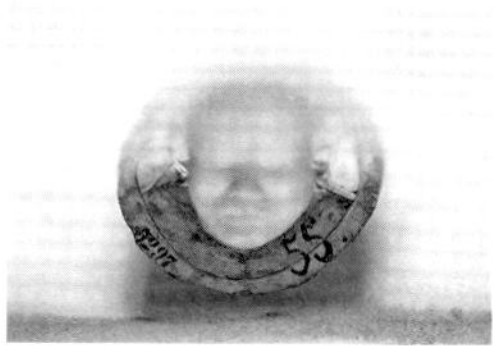

Plaster Piece Mould for the Face Mask of a Not Yet Identified Man ('[Face Mask] of a Twenty-Four-Year-Old Man from Moeara Lemboe, Sumatra'), moulded by Johannes Pieter Kleiweg de Zwaan, 1907
Plaster, shellacked
29.5 × 28 × 15.5 cm
Staatliche Museen zu Berlin, Gipsformerei, 5297

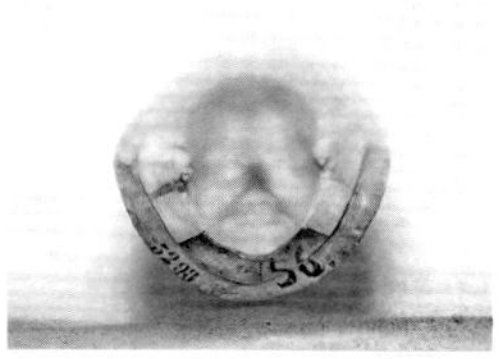

Plaster Piece Mould for the Face Mask of a Not Yet Identified Man ('[Face Mask] of a Thirty-Year-Old Man from the Same Place'), moulded by Johannes Pieter Kleiweg de Zwaan, 1907
Plaster, shellacked

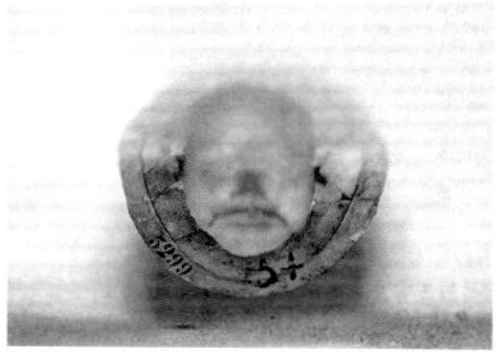

Plaster Piece Mould for the Face Mask of a Not Yet Identified Man ('Face Mask of a Thirty-Five-Year-Old Man from Goenoeng Silihan, Sumatra'), moulded by Johannes Pieter Kleiweg de Zwaan, 1907
Plaster, shellacked
29.6 × 28.5 × 15.9 cm
Staatliche Museen zu Berlin, Gipsformerei, 5299

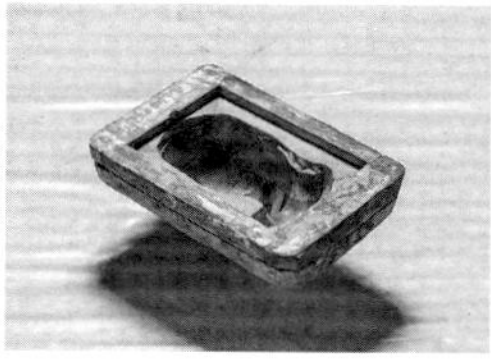

Plaster Piece Mould for Face Mask of a Man Called Gromosmito, moulded by Otto Finsch, remoulded by Louis and Gustave Castan, ca. 1883/87
Plaster, shellacked
Approx. 40 × 30 × 18 cm
Staatliche Museen zu Berlin, Gipsformerei, 5365

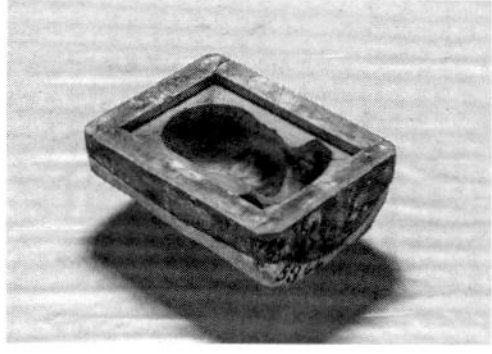

Plaster Piece Mould for Face Mask of a Man Called Pa Kasimín, moulded by Otto Finsch, remoulded by Louis and Gustave Castan, ca. 1883/87
Plaster, shellacked
Approx. 40 × 30 × 18 cm
Staatliche Museen zu Berlin, Gipsformerei, 5366

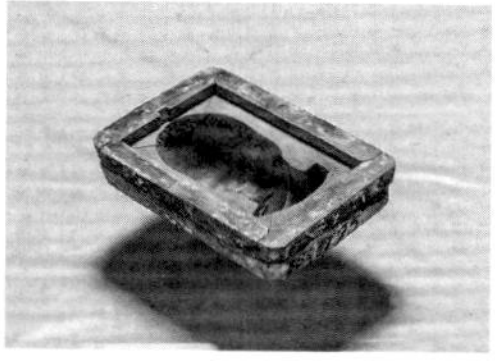

Plaster Piece Mould for Face Mask of a Man Called Liman, moulded by Otto Finsch, remoulded by Louis and Gustave Castan, ca. 1883/87
Plaster, shellacked
Approx. 40 × 30 × 18 cm
Staatliche Museen zu Berlin, Gipsformerei, 5368

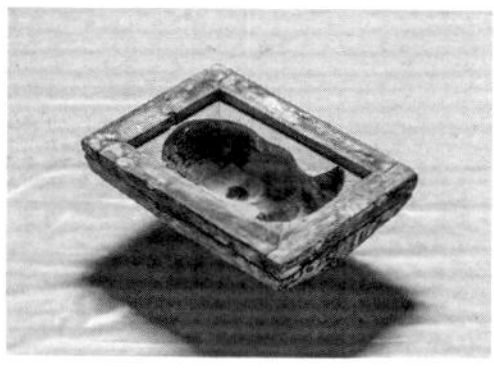

Plaster Piece Mould for Face Mask of a Man Called Tútur, moulded by Otto Finsch, remoulded by Louis and Gustave Castan, ca. 1883/87
Plaster, shellacked
Approx. 40 × 30 × 18 cm
Staatliche Museen zu Berlin, Gipsformerei, 5369

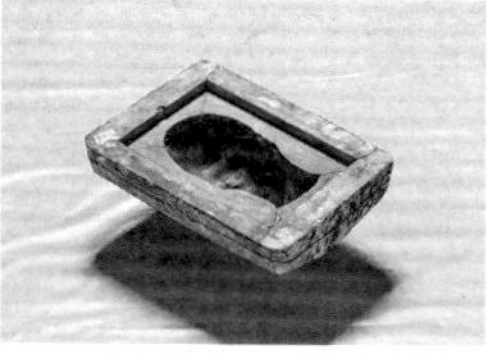

Plaster Piece Mould for Face Mask of a Man Called Mauk, moulded by Otto Finsch, remoulded by Louis and Gustave Castan, ca. 1883/87
Plaster, shellacked
Approx. 40 × 30 × 18 cm
Staatliche Museen zu Berlin, Gipsformerei, 5370

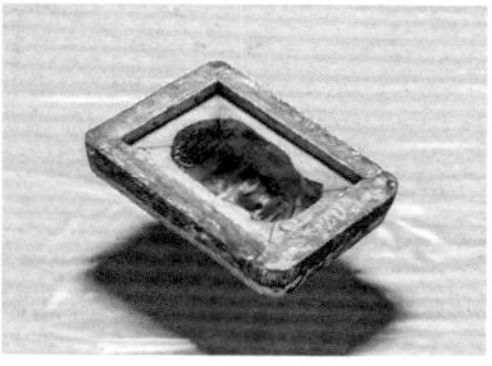

Plaster Piece Mould for Face Mask of a Man Called Bakálang, moulded by Otto Finsch, remoulded by Louis and Gustave Castan, ca. 1883/87
Plaster, shellacked
Approx. 40 × 30 × 20 cm
Staatliche Museen zu Berlin, Gipsformerei, 5371

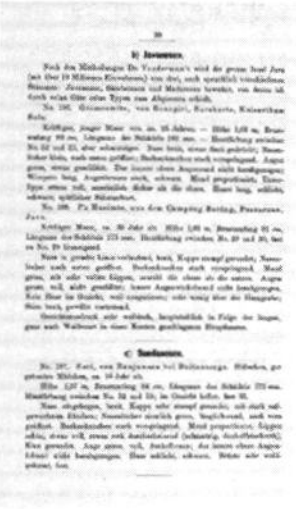

Otto Finsch (1839–1917)
Anthropologische Ergebnisse einer Reise in der Südsee und dem malayischen Archipel in den Jahren 1879–1882: Beschreibender Catalog der auf dieser Reise gesammelten Gesichtsmasken von Völkertypen, mit 60 Körpermessungen
In: *Zeitschrift für Ethnologie* 15 (1883), supplement
Staatliche Museen zu Berlin, Kunstbibliothek, Lipp Ad 41 kl-15.1883

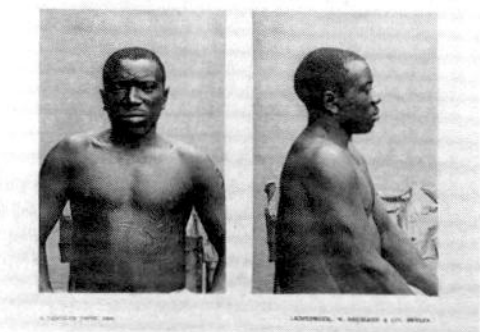

Deutschland und seine Kolonien; Amtlicher Bericht über die Erste Deutsche Kolonial-Ausstellung
ed. Hans Hermann Graf von Schweinitz, et. al., Berlin 1897
Staatliche Museen zu Berlin, Ethnologisches Museum, Gp/Deu

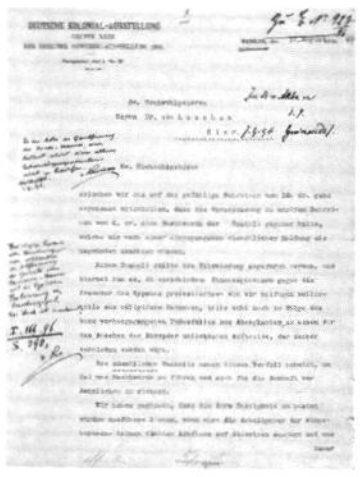

Typewritten letter of the Working Committee of the Deutsche Kolonial-Ausstellung to Felix von Luschan, 17 August 1896
Staatliche Museen zu Berlin, Ethnologisches Museum, E 927/1896 47, I B 16 Afrika

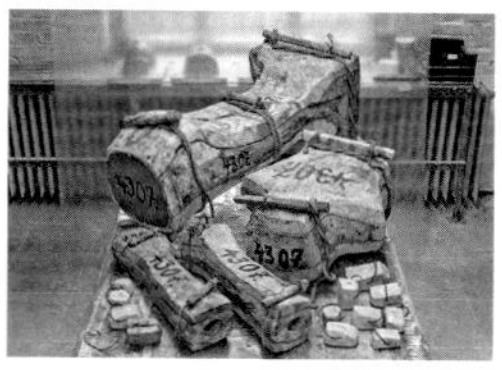

Plaster Piece Mould of the Lifecast of a Man called N'Kurui ('Luschan's Bushman'), 1906
Plaster, shellacked
Height of the figure: 147 cm
Staatliche Museen zu Berlin, Gipsformerei, 4307

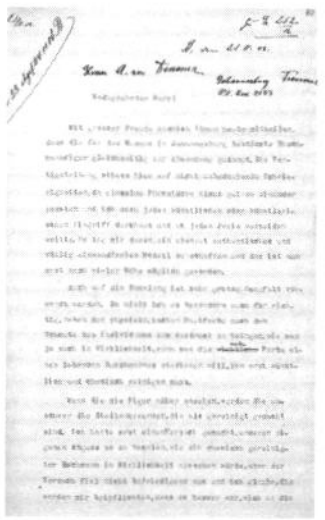

Typewritten letter of Felix von Luschan to A. von Dessauer, 23 November 1906
Staatliche Museen zu Berlin, Ethnologisches Museum, E 252/1906 40, I B 36 Afrika

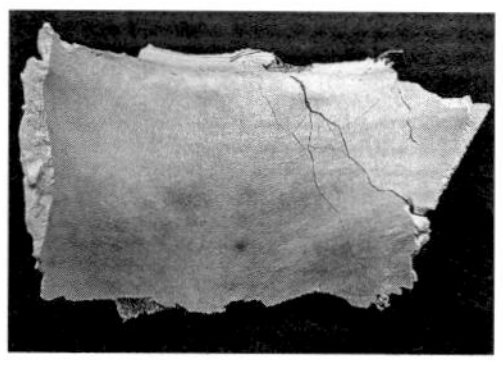

Margit Berner, Britta Lange, Thomas Schelper, Kerstin Stoll
Lost Mould, 2013
Fragment to match the lost mould of a full-body cast
Plaster, jute
14 × 35 × 20 cm
Private collection

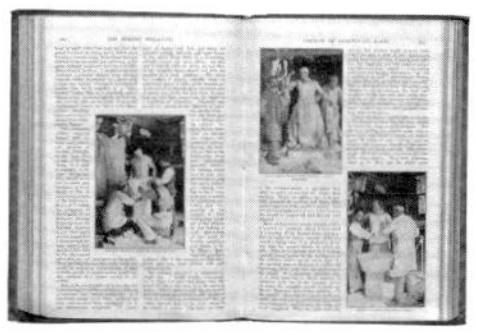

'Sandow in Plaster of Paris: A Unique Cast',
in: *The Strand Magazine* 22, no. 130 (October 1901),
Technische Universität, Universitätsbibliothek, 8 Zi 2184/22

Ultimate Life

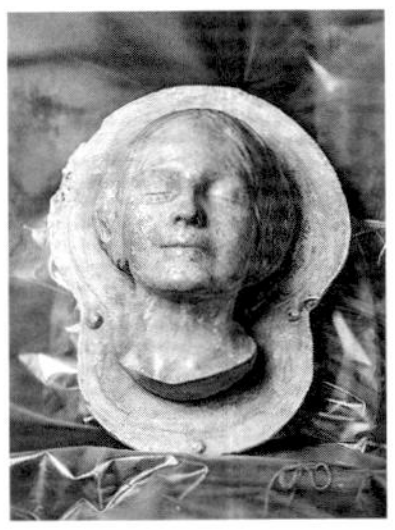

The Unknown Woman of the Seine ('L'Inconnue de la Seine')
Painting model, before 1950
Plaster, painted
42 × 32 × 19.2 cm (with panel)
(Original: ca. 1900, whereabouts unknown)
Staatliche Museen zu Berlin, Gipsformerei, 5572

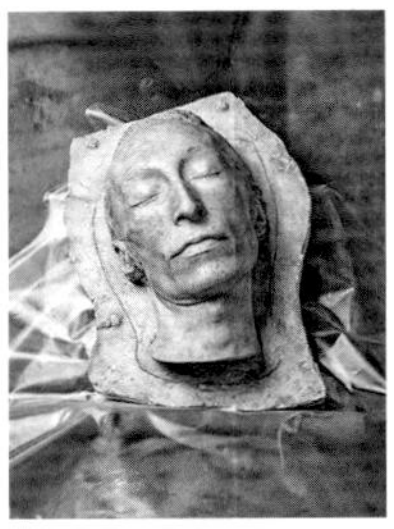

Death Mask Carl Maria von Weber (1780–1826)
Master model, before 1950
Plaster, shellacked
38.7 × 28 × 19 cm (with panel)
(Original: 1826, whereabouts unknown)
Staatliche Museen zu Berlin, Gipsformerei, 5567

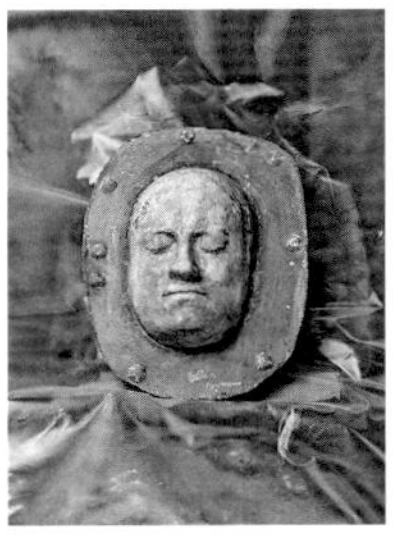

Death Mask of Charles XII, King of Sweden (1697–1718)
Master model, before 1950
Plaster, shellacked
33.5 × 23.5 × 16.5 cm (with panel)
(Original: 1718, Military Club of Stockholm)
Staatliche Museen zu Berlin, Gipsformerei, 554

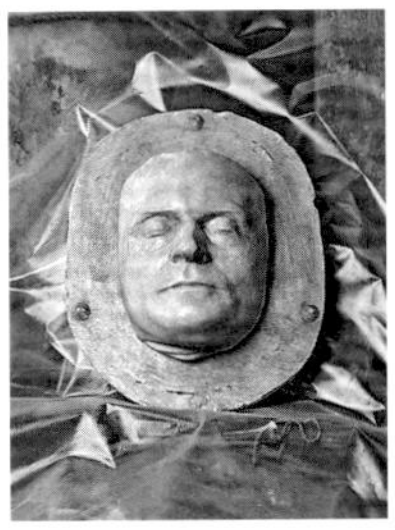

Death Mask of Gotthold Ephraim Lessing (1729–1781)
Master model, before 1950
Plaster, shellacked
33.5 × 28 × 13 cm (with panel)
(Original: 1782, Deutsches Literaturarchiv, Weimar)
Staatliche Museen zu Berlin, Gipsformerei, 5573

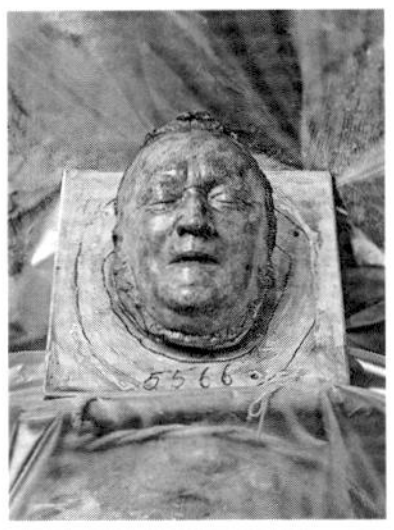

Death Mask of Richard Wagner (1813–1883)
Master model, before 1950
Plaster, shellacked
36.7 × 32.8 × 19 cm (with panel)
(Original: Augusto Benvenuti, 1883, Reuter-Wagner-Museum, Eisenach)
Staatliche Museen zu Berlin, Gipsformerei, 5566

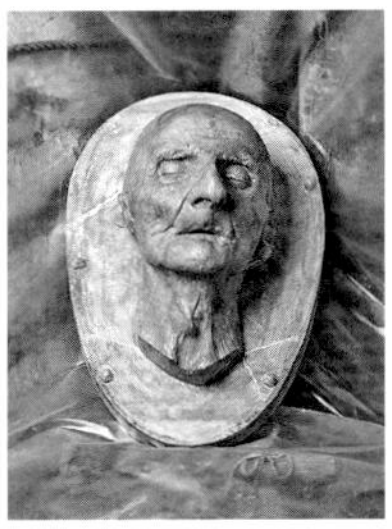

Death Mask of Anton Bruckner (1824–1896)
Master model, before 1950
Plaster, shellacked
31 × 16.5 × 16 cm
(Original: 1896, Staatsbibliothek zu Berlin – Preußischer Kulturbesitz)
Staatliche Museen zu Berlin, Gipsformerei, 5522

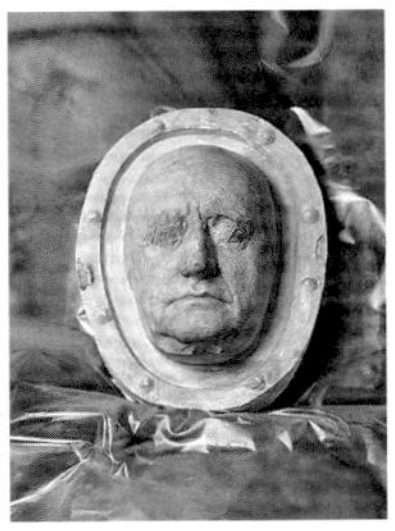

After Carl Gottlieb Weisser (1779–1815)
Life Mask of Johann Wolfgang von Goethe (1794–1832)
Master model, before 1950
Plaster, shellacked
36 × 28 × 17.3 cm (with panel)
(Original: 1807, Goethe-Nationalmuseum, Weimar)
Staatliche Museen zu Berlin, Gipsformerei, 3138

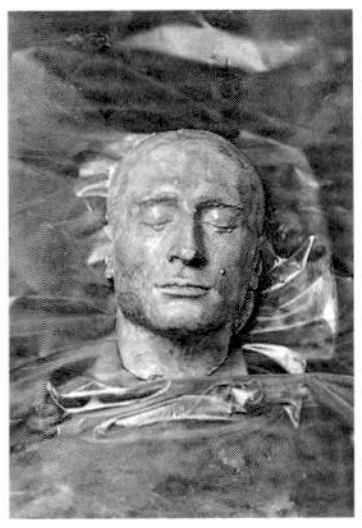

Life Mask Franz Liszt (1811–1886)
Master model, before 1950
Plaster, shellacked
16 × 15.5 × 27.5 cm
(Original: 1838, whereabouts unknown)
Staatliche Museen zu Berlin, Gipsformerei, 5544

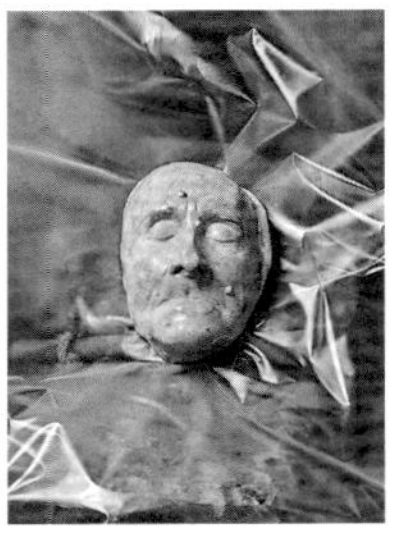

Death Mask Franz Liszt (1811–1886)
Master model, before 1950
Plaster, shellacked
12.5 × 16.5 × 25 cm
(Original: Johann Christian Weißbrodt, 1886, Herzogin Anna Amalia Bibliothek, Weimar)
Staatliche Museen zu Berlin, Gipsformerei, 5545

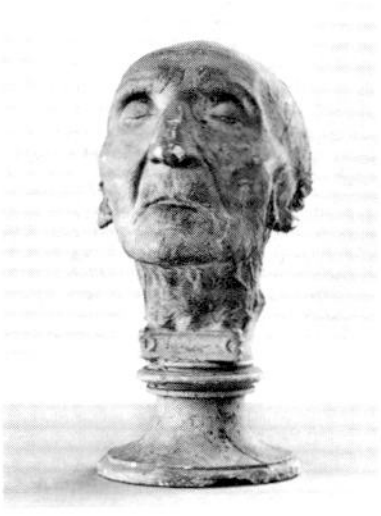

Unknown artist
Death Mask of Johann Gottfried Schadow (1764–1850), 1850
Plaster, 35.5 × 17 × 22 cm
Staatliche Museen zu Berlin, Alte Nationalgalerie, B II 369

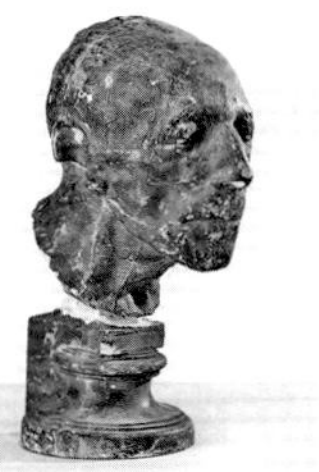

After Johannes Eckstein (1736–1817)
Death Mask of Frederick II of Prussia
Cast, 1786
Plaster, brownish coating
39 × 18 × 23 cm
Staatliche Museen zu Berlin, Alte Nationalgalerie, B II 362

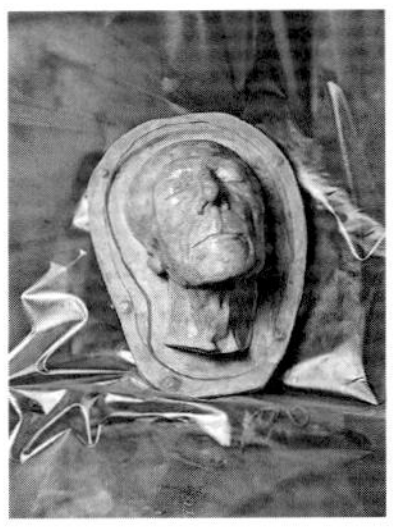

Death Mask of Frederick II of Prussia (1712–1786)
Master model, 1935
Plaster, shellacked
33.5 × 23.5 × 16.5 cm (with panel) (Original: Johannes Eckstein, 1786, former Hohenzollern Museum Schloss Monbijou, Berlin)
Staatliche Museen zu Berlin, Gipsformerei, 3135

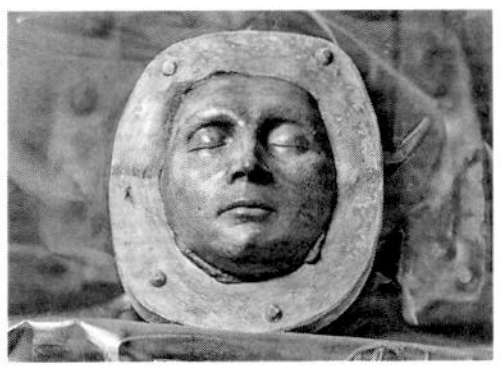

Death Mask of Louise Queen of Prussia (1776–1810)

Master model, before 1965
Plaster, shellacked
25 × 21 × 10.7 cm (with panel)
(Original: Christian Philipp Wolff, 1810, Berlin, Stiftung Preußische Schlösser und Gärten, Berlin-Brandenburg)
Staatliche Museen zu Berlin, Gipsformerei, 4978

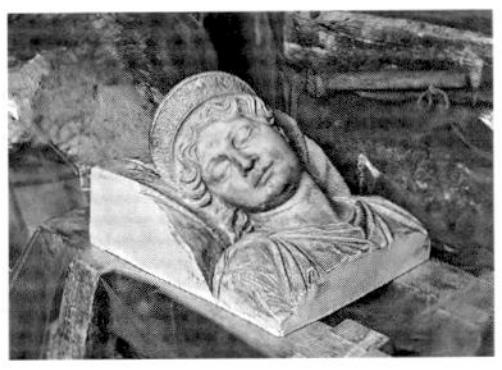

After Christian Daniel Rauch (1777–1857)
Recumbent Bust of Louise Queen of Prussia
Master model, before 1965
Plaster, shellacked
32 × 41 × 43 cm
(Original: Christian Daniel Rauch, second version of Louise's tomb figure, 1827, Stiftung Preußische Schlösser und Gärten, Berlin-Brandenburg)
Staatliche Museen zu Berlin, Gipsformerei, 5000-54

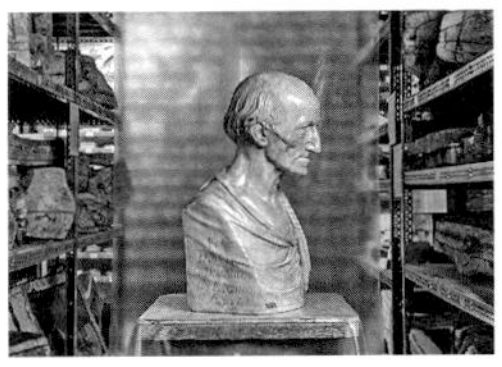

After Johann Gottfried Schadow (1764–1850)
Carl Friedrich Christian Fasch
Master model, 1986
Plaster, shellacked
54 × 30 × 28 cm
(Original: 1800, Staatliches Institut für Musikforschung – Stiftung Preußischer Kulturbesitz)
Staatliche Museen zu Berlin, Gipsformerei, 3021

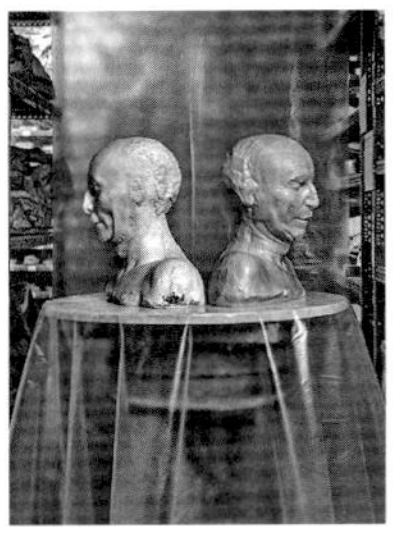

After an unknown artist
Death Mask of Filippo Brunelleschi Realised as a Bust

Master model, 1882
Plaster, shellacked
38 × 41.5 × 22.5 cm
(Original: 1446, Museo dell' Opera del Duomo, Florence)
Staatliche Museen zu Berlin, Gipsformerei, 2431

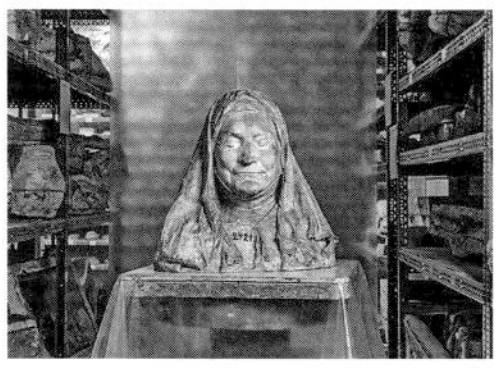

After an unknown artist
Death Mask of an Unknown Woman Realised as a Bust
Master model, 1882
Plaster, shellacked
39 × 42.5 × 25 cm
(Original: late 15th century, Museo Nazionale del Bargello, Florence)
Staatliche Museen zu Berlin, Gipsformerei, 2421

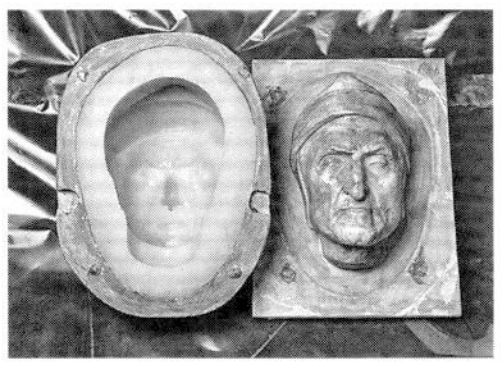

After an unknown artist
So-called Death Mask of Dante Alighieri (1265–1321)
Master model, before 1950
Plaster, shellacked
40 × 30.2 × 19 cm (with panel)
(Original: ca. 1500, Palazzo Vecchio, Florence)
Staatliche Museen zu Berlin, Gipsformerei, 5534

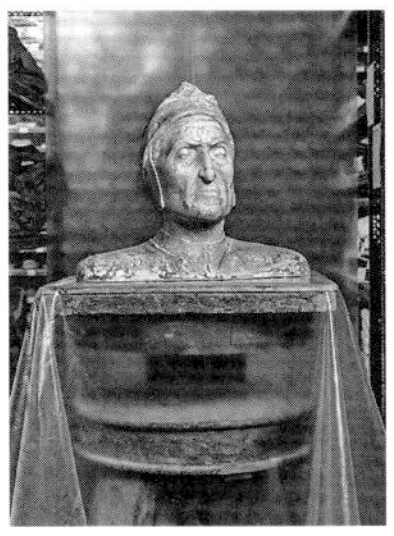

After an unknown artist
Death Mask of Dante Alighieri Realised as a Bust
Master model, 1995
Plaster, shellacked
33.5 × 43.5 × 21.5 cm
(Original: presumably 19th century, whereabouts unknown)
Staatliche Museen zu Berlin, Gipsformerei, 2550

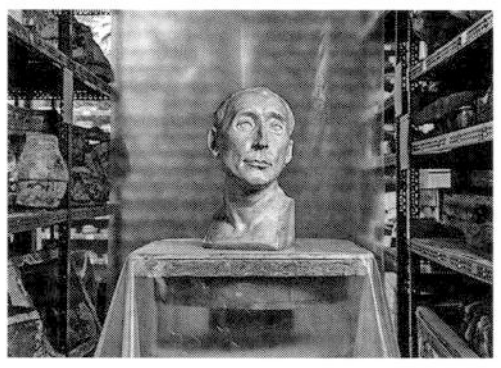

After Desiderio da Settignano (1430–1464)
Niccolò da Uzzano
Master model, 1914
Plaster, shellacked
34 × 20 × 22 cm
(Original: 1455–70, Museo Nazionale del Bargello, Florence)
Staatliche Museen zu Berlin, Gipsformerei, 2476

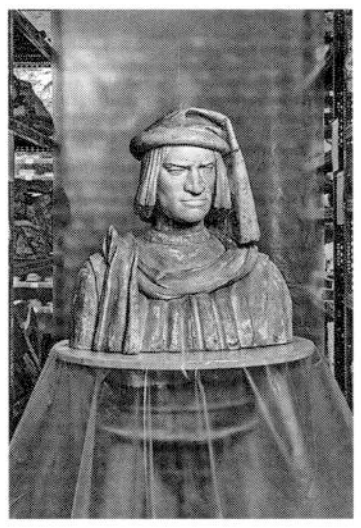

After an unknown artist
Lorenzo de' Medici
Master model, 1910
Plaster, shellacked
63 × 59 × 33 cm
(Original: 1530–50, Staatliche Museen zu Berlin, Skulpturensammlung und Museum für Byzantinische Kunst)
Staatliche Museen zu Berlin, Gipsformerei, 2460

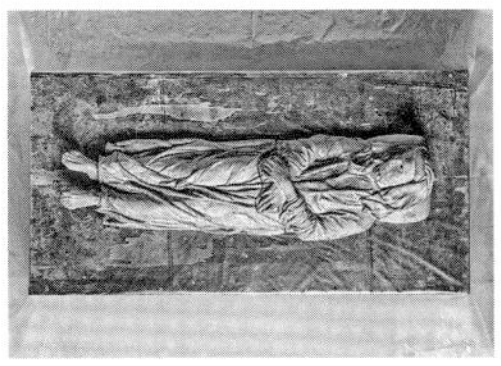

After Lorenzo di Pietro (Il Vecchietta) (1410–1480)
Tomb Figure of Mariano Sozzini
Master model, 1882
Plaster, shellacked
163 × 47 × 32 cm
(Original: ca. 1467, Museo Nazionale del Bargello, Florence)
Staatliche Museen zu Berlin, Gipsformerei, 2217

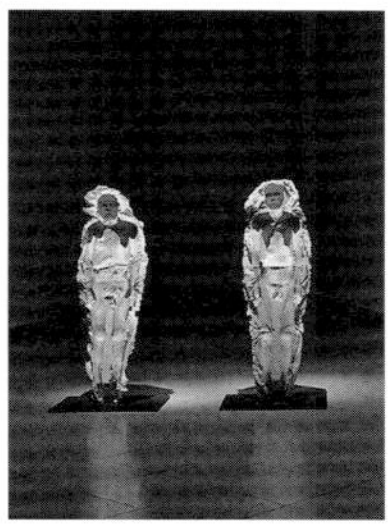

Teresa Margolles (b. 1963)
Catafalco, 1997
Plaster and organic material; casts of the bodies of two murder victims
169 × 54 × 16 cm and 167 × 54 × 18 cm
Realised in collaboration with the artist group SEMEFO
Museum für Moderne Kunst, Frankfurt am Main, on permanent loan from the artist, 2004 / 51.1-2L

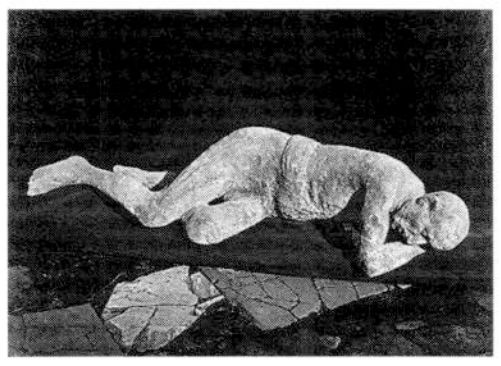

Plaster Cast of a Recumbent Man, Who Lost his Life in the Eruption of Mount Vesuvius in 79 CE, Pompeii, Terme Stabiane, 1868
(Exhibition copy)
Plaster
161 × 60 × 30 cm
Parco Archeologico di Pompei

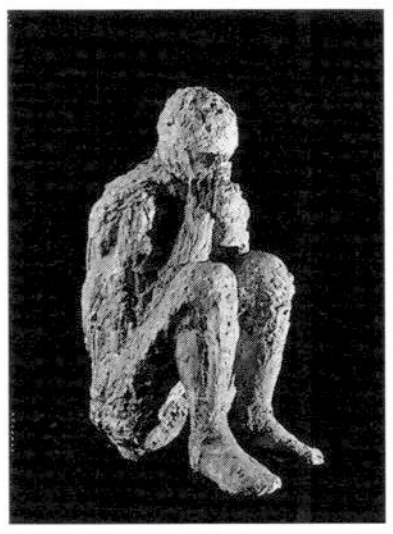

Plaster Cast of a Seated Man, Who Lost His Life in the Eruption of Mount Vesuvius in 79 CE, Pompeii, Palestra Grande, 1938
(Exhibition copy)
Plaster
90 × 50 × 60 cm
Parco Archeologico di Pompei

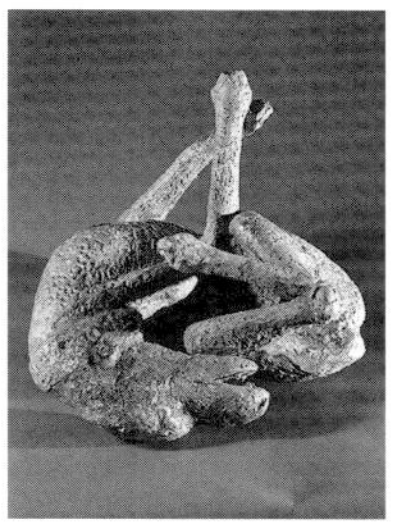

Plaster Cast of a Chained Dog, Which Lost its Life in the Eruption of Mount Vesuvius in 79 CE, Pompeii, Casa di Marcus Vesonius Primus, 1874
(Exhibition copy)
Plaster
Approx. 60 × 60 × 60 cm
Parco Archeologico di Pompei

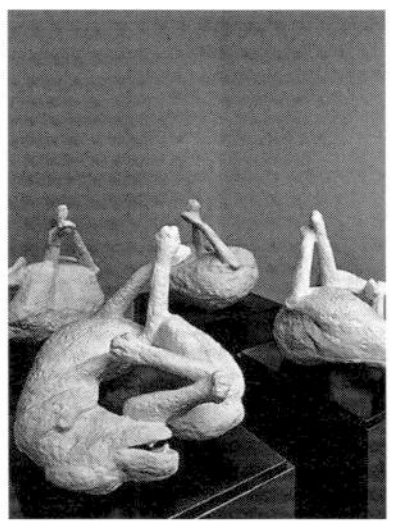

Allan McCollum (b. 1944)
The Dog from Pompeii, 1991
Polymer-modified hydrocal
Four dogs, each 53 × 53 × 53 cm
Galerie Thomas Schulte, Berlin

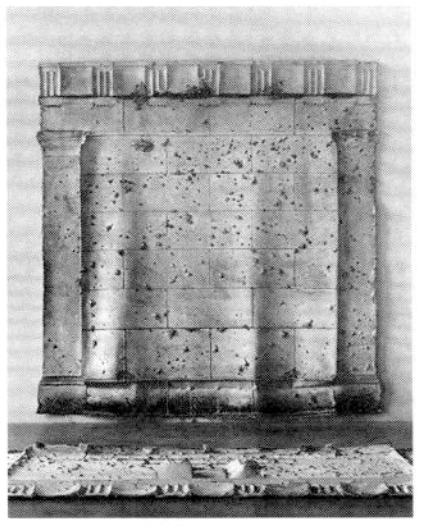

Asta Gröting (b. 1961)
Mausoleum, 2016
From the series *Berlin Fassaden*
Silicone and jute
373 × 373 × 10 cm
Israel Museum, Jerusalem

In the Artist's Studio

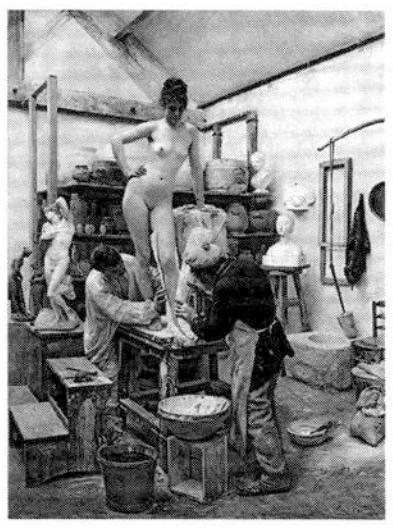

Édouard Joseph Dantan (1848–1897)
Un moulage sur nature, 1887
Oil on canvas
165 × 131.5 cm
Göteborgs konstmuseum, Sweden, F 21

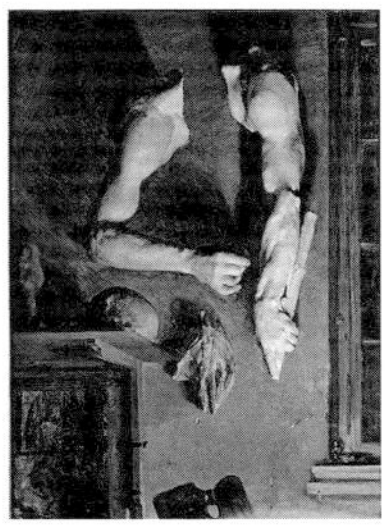

Adolph Menzel (1815–1905)
Atelierwand, 1852
Oil on paper, mounted on a wood panel
61 × 44 cm
Staatliche Museen zu Berlin, Alte Nationalgalerie, A I 904

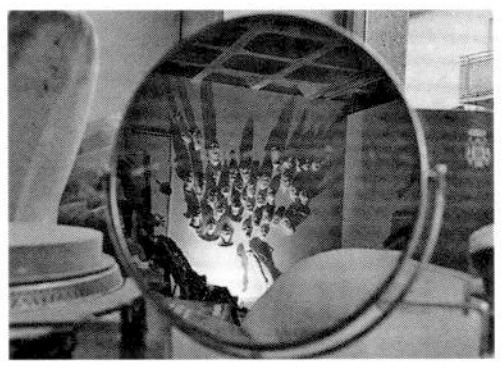

Liane Lang (b. 1973)
Studio Spectres, Cremer Street/Hackney, 2012–19
HD video, 5' (loop)
Courtesy of the artist

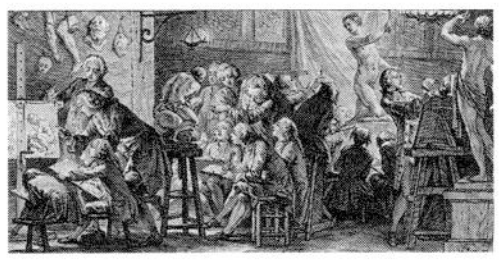

Charles-Nicolas Cochin, the Younger (1715–1790), Benoît Louis Prévost (1735–1804, engraver)
Zeichenkurs in der Akademie, nach einer Vorzeichnung für die Illustration in Diderots und

d'Alemberts Encyclopédie, 1763
Copper engraving
10.7 × 20.8 cm
Staatliche Museen zu Berlin, Kupferstichkabinett, 292-1927

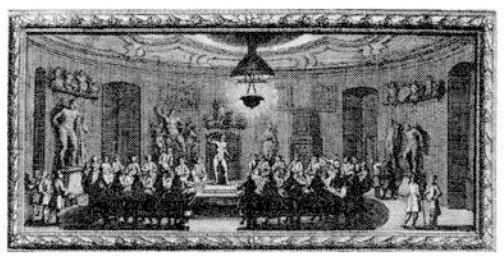

Constantin Friedrich Blesendorf (1674–1754) (attributed)
Der Aktsaal der Berliner Akademie der Künste, ca. 1700
Copper engraving, after a drawing by Augustin Terwesten (1649–1711)
39.8 × 55.3 cm
Staatliche Museen zu Berlin, Kunstbibliothek, OS 4261, 3mtl

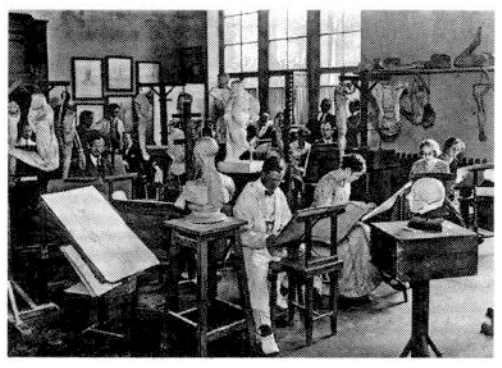

Willy Römer (1887–1979)
Teaching Institute of the Kunstgewerbemuseum, Berlin (In the Art Room for Anatomical Drawing), 1920s
Photograph
Approx. 10 × 15 cm
Staatliche Museen zu Berlin, Kunstbibliothek – Museum für Fotografie, WR_05598_01

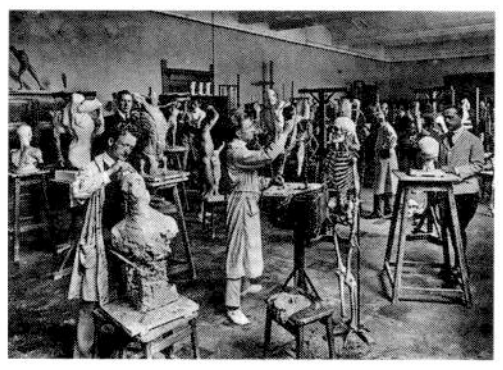

Willy Römer (1887–1979)
Teaching Institute of the Kunstgewerbemuseum, Berlin (Anatomy Class), 1920s
Photograph
Approx. 10 × 15 cm
Staatliche Museen zu Berlin, Kunstbibliothek – Museum für Fotografie, WR_05597_01

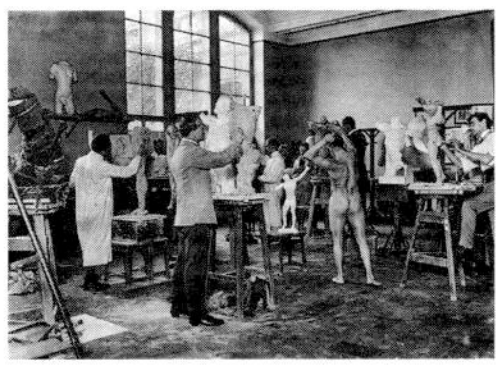

Willy Römer (1887–1979)
Teaching Institute of the Kunstgewerbemuseum, Berlin (Sculptors' Workshop), 1920s
Photograph
Approx. 10 × 15 cm
Staatliche Museen zu Berlin, Kunstbibliothek – Museum für Fotografie, WR_05600_01

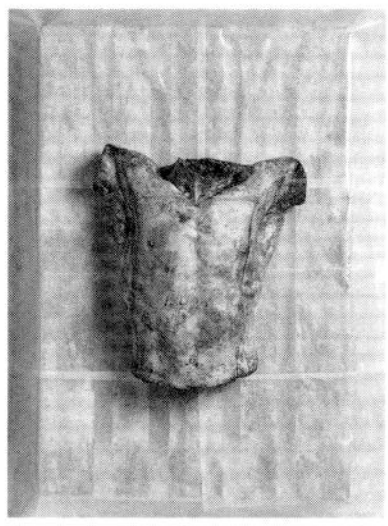

Male Torso (Front)
Master model, ca. 1908
Plaster, shellacked
20 × 55 × 58 cm
Staatliche Museen zu Berlin, Gipsformerei, 6162

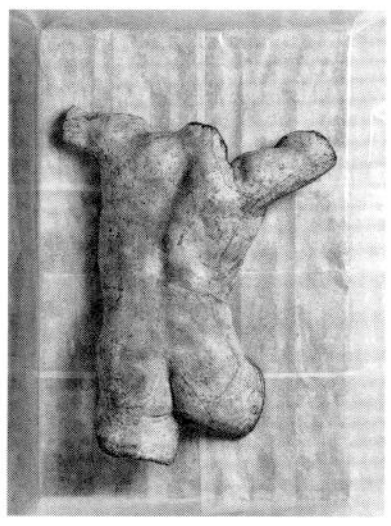

Male Torso (Back)
Master model, 1870
Plaster, shellacked
21 × 68.5 × 87 cm
Staatliche Museen zu Berlin, Gipsformerei, 6120

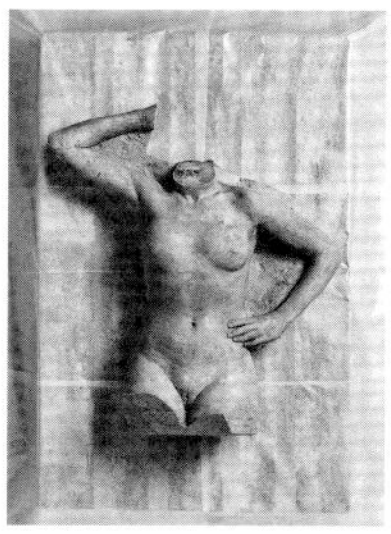

Female Torso (Front)
Master model, 1894
Plaster, shellacked
86 × 80 × 20 cm
Staatliche Museen zu Berlin, Gipsformerei, 6658

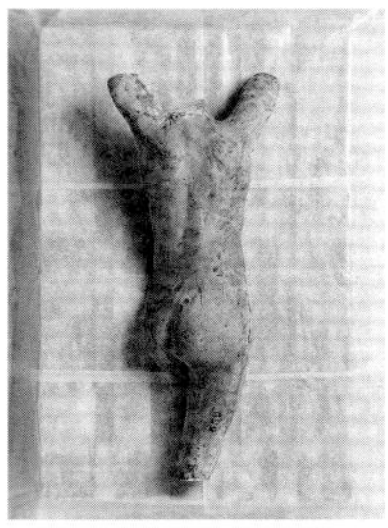

Female Torso (Back)
Master model, 1894
Plaster, shellacked
21 × 43.5 × 103 cm
Staatliche Museen zu Berlin, Gipsformerei, 6659

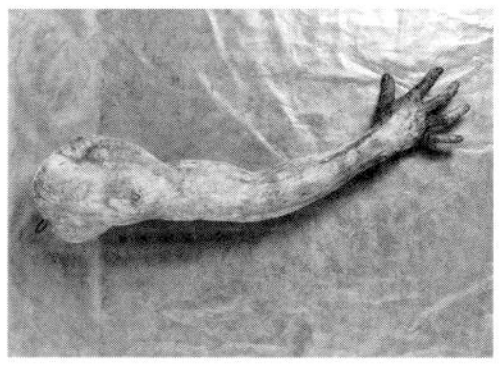

Right Arm of a Man with Shoulder Tip and Splayed Finger
Master model, 1871
Plaster, shellacked
18 × 23 × 91 cm
Staatliche Museen zu Berlin, Gipsformerei, 6217

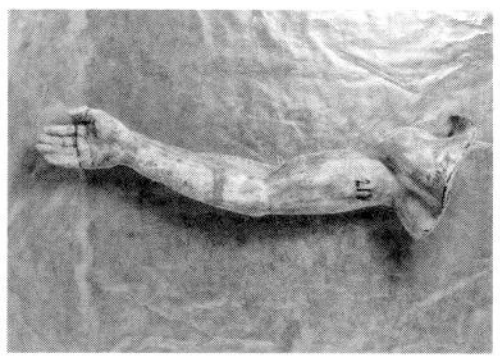

Right Arm of a Man with Shoulder Tip and Hand Open
Master model, 1871
Plaster, shellacked
23 × 27 × 87 cm
Staatliche Museen zu Berlin, Gipsformerei, 6218

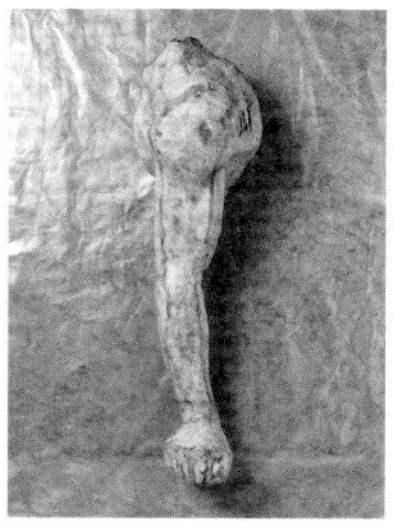

Right Arm of a Man with Shoulder Tip and Clenched Fist
Master model, 1871
Plaster, shellacked
19.5 × 80 × 23 × cm
Staatliche Museen zu Berlin, Gipsformerei, 6221

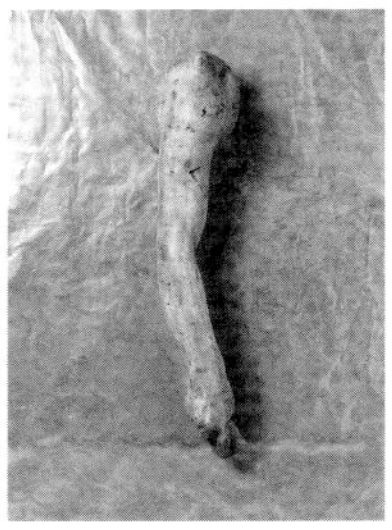

Right Arm of a Man with Shoulder Tip, the Hand Holding an Object
Master model, 1868
Plaster, shellacked
15 × 18 × 73 cm
Staatliche Museen zu Berlin, Gipsformerei, 6025

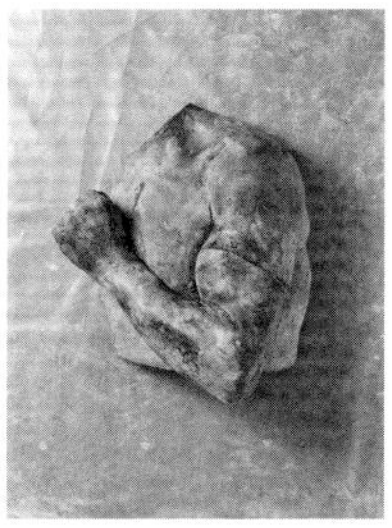

Left Arm of a Man, Bent with Clenched Fist and Chest
Master model, 1871
Plaster, shellacked
10.5 × 19.5 × 39 cm
Staatliche Museen zu Berlin, Gipsformerei, 6222

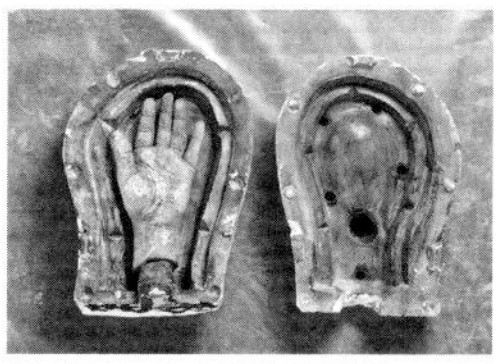

Left Hand of a Woman
Master model in mother mould, ca. 1900
Plaster, shellacked
5.5 × 10 × 21.5 cm (hand); 13 × 21.5 × 29.5 cm (mother mould)
Staatliche Museen zu Berlin, Gipsformerei

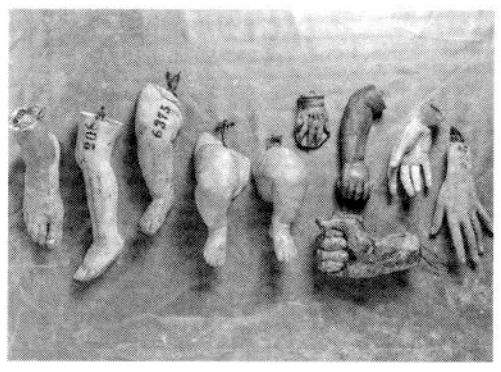

Right Foot of a Woman, Stretched
Master model, 1878
Plaster, shellacked
17 × 8.5 × 24 cm
Staatliche Museen zu Berlin, Gipsformerei, 6280

Left Leg of a Child
Master model, 1871
Plaster, shellacked
9 × 9 × 33 cm
Staatliche Museen zu Berlin, Gipsformerei, 6208

Right Leg of a Child
Master model, 1886
Plaster, shellacked
8.5 × 10 × 33 cm
Staatliche Museen zu Berlin, Gipsformerei, 6375

Right Leg of a Child, Bent
Master model, 1886
Plaster, shellacked
13.5 × 11.5 × 26 cm
Staatliche Museen zu Berlin, Gipsformerei, 6466

Left Leg of a Child, Bent
Master model, 1886
Plaster, shellacked
12.5 × 8.5 × 24 cm
Staatliche Museen zu Berlin, Gipsformerei, 6467

Right Hand of a Child on a Panel
Master model, 1886
Plaster, shellacked
6 × 13.5 × 25.7 cm
Staatliche Museen zu Berlin, Gipsformerei, 6376

Right Arm of a Child
Master model, 1868
Plaster, shellacked
24 × 7.5 × 6 cm
Staatliche Museen zu Berlin, Gipsformerei, 6029

Right Hand of a Man, Clenched
Master model, 1868
Plaster, shellacked
21 × 13 × 11 cm
Staatliche Museen zu Berlin, Gipsformerei, 6014

Right Hand of a Woman with Fingers Bent
Master model, 1878
Plaster, shellacked
7 × 10.5 × 20.5 cm
Staatliche Museen zu Berlin, Gipsformerei, 6279

Left Hand of a Woman with Outstretched Fingers
Master model, 1878
Plaster, shellacked
6 × 15 × 24 cm
Staatliche Museen zu Berlin, Gipsformerei, 6278

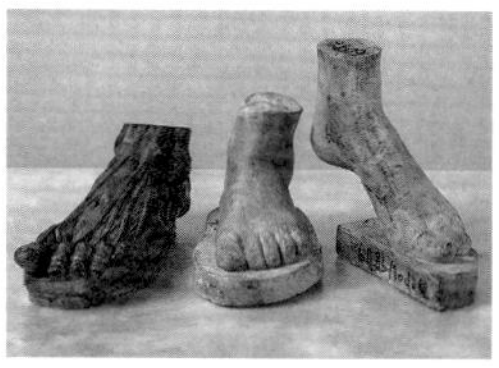

Left Foot of a Woman
Master model, 1868
Plaster, shellacked
12 × 10.5 × 28 cm
Staatliche Museen zu Berlin, Gipsformerei, 6040

Left Foot of a Boy
Master model, 1868
Plaster, shellacked
13.6 × 12 × 24 cm
Staatliche Museen zu Berlin, Gipsformerei, 6004

Left Foot, Anatomical
Master model, 1869
Plaster, shellacked
21 × 8 × 23 cm
Staatliche Museen zu Berlin, Gipsformerei, 6086

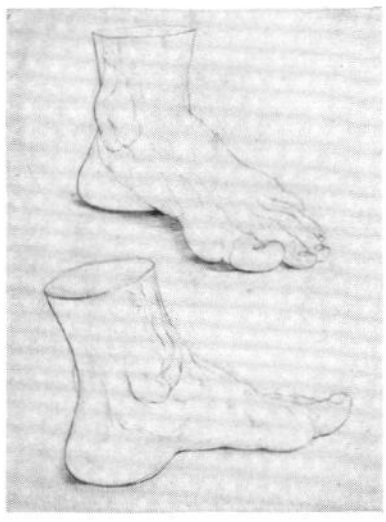

Philipp Otto Runge (1777–1810)
Two Foot Studies (after Plaster Casts), n. d.
Black chalk on paper
38.7 × 29.9 cm
Staatliche Museen zu Berlin, Kupferstichkabinett, SZ Runge 13

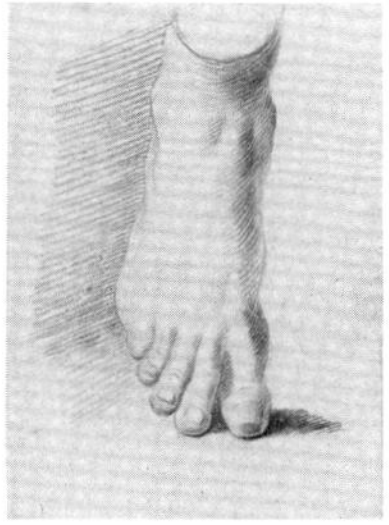

Johann Heinrich Ramberg (1763–1840)
Right Foot of a Man, Seen from the Front, after Plaster Cast, n. d.
Chalk on paper
34.5 × 24.8 cm
Staatliche Museen zu Berlin, Kupferstichkabinett, KdZ 3248

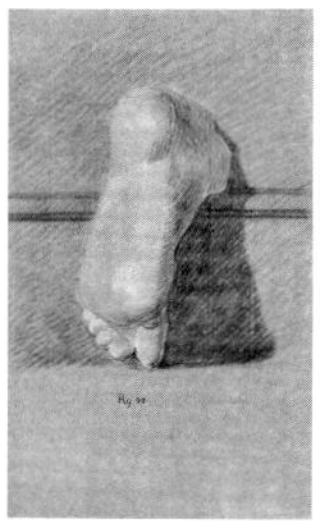

Johann Heinrich Ramberg (1763–1840)
Left Foot of a Man, Seen from the Sole, after Plaster Cast, n. d.
White and black chalk on paper
33 × 20.5 cm
Staatliche Museen zu Berlin, Kupferstichkabinett, KdZ 3250

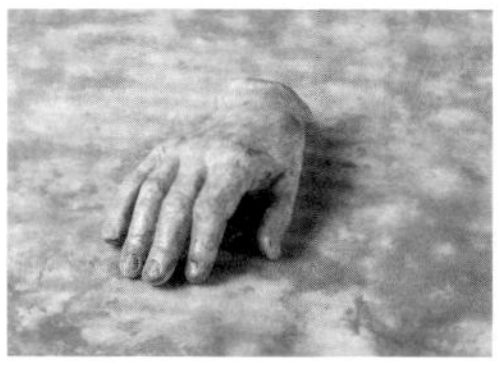

Right Hand of Johann Wolfgang von Goethe
Master model, 1820
22 × 13 × 8 cm
Plaster, shellacked
Staatliche Museen zu Berlin, Gipsformerei, 5580

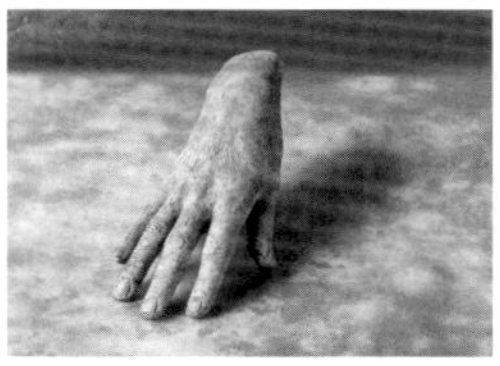

Right Hand of Franz Liszt, Playing
Master model, 1953
Plaster, shellacked
25 × 13 × 6 cm
Staatliche Museen zu Berlin, Gipsformerei, 5579

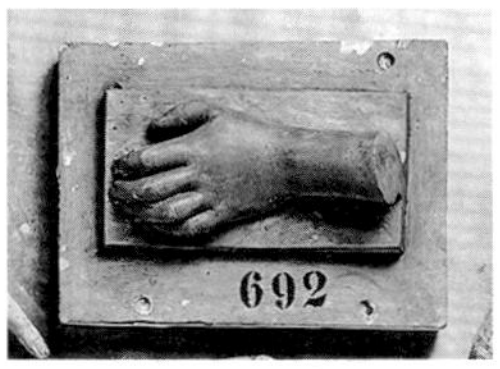

Left Hand of a Child on a Panel
Master model, 1894
Plaster, shellacked
17 × 8 × 4.8 cm
Staatliche Museen zu Berlin, Gipsformerei, 6692

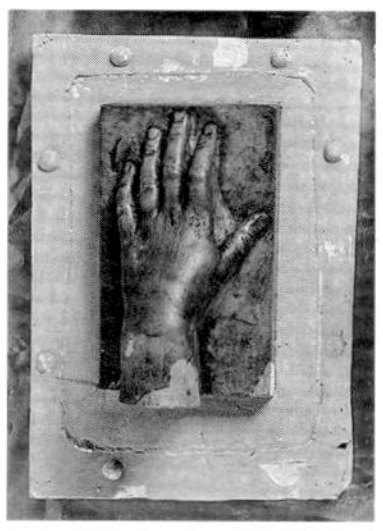

Left Hand of a Woman on a Panel
Master model, 1894
Plaster, shellacked
24 × 18 × 9 cm
Staatliche Museen zu Berlin, Gipsformerei, 6689

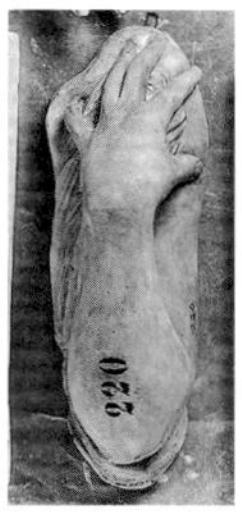

Left Arm of a Woman, Bent with Shoulder Tip, Partially Clothed
Master model, 1871
Plaster, shellacked
16.6 × 13 × 39 cm
Staatliche Museen zu Berlin, Gipsformerei, 6220

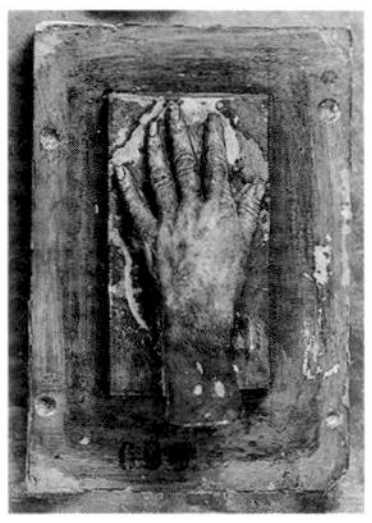

Left Hand of a Woman on a Panel
Master model, 1894
Plaster, shellacked
24 × 12 × 8.5 cm
Staatliche Museen zu Berlin, Gipsformerei, 6690

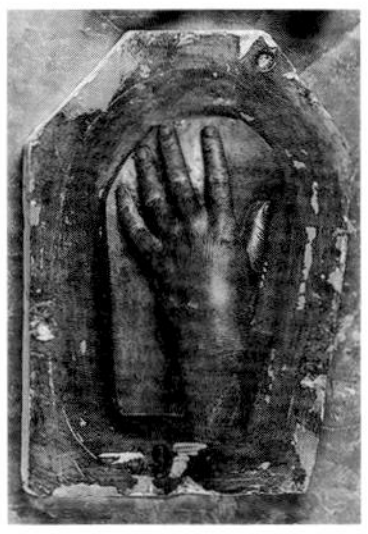

Left Hand of a Woman on a Panel
Master model, 1894
Plaster, shellacked
26 × 18 × 7 cm
Staatliche Museen zu Berlin, Gipsformerei, 6691

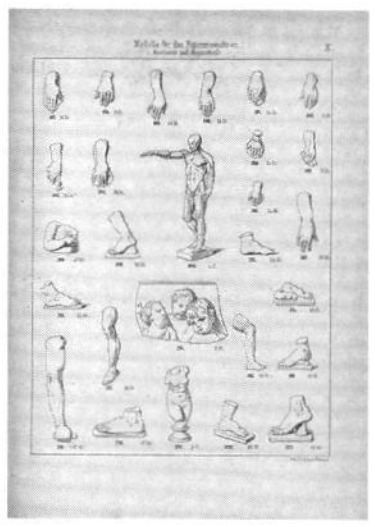

Illustrirte Preisliste der Gypsmodelle für den Unterricht im Freihandzeichnen, Projectionszeichnen & Modelliren [...], Stuttgart 1876
Staatliche Museen zu Berlin, Kunstbibliothek, F 2481 mtl

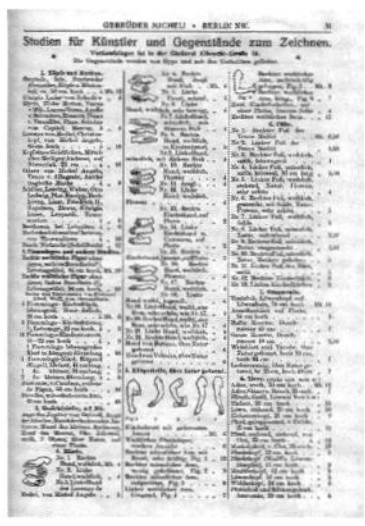

Preis-Verzeichnis plastischer Bildwerke, Gebrüder Micheli Bildhauer-Werkstätten, Berlin ca. 1900
Private collection

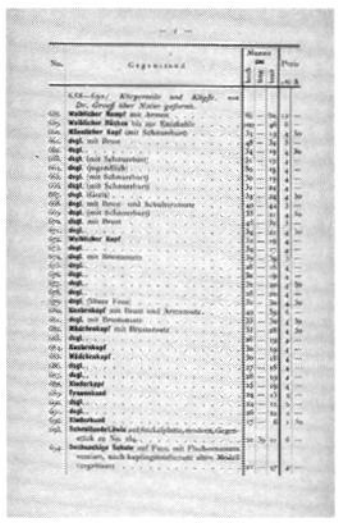

Verzeichnis der in der Formerei der käuflichen Gipsabgüsse des Kunstgewerbe-Museums, ed. Königliche Museen zu Berlin, General-Verwaltung, Berlin 1892, supplement 1894
Staatliche Museen zu Berlin, Kunstbibliothek, F 2449 kl-1892

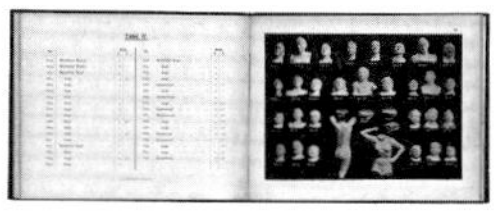

Verzeichnis der in der Formerei der Königlichen Museen käuflichen Gipsabgüsse (Schulmodelle des Kunstgewerbe-Museums), ed. Königliche Museen zu Berlin, General-Verwaltung, Berlin 1902
Staatliche Museen zu Berlin, Kunstbibliothek, F2462 kl

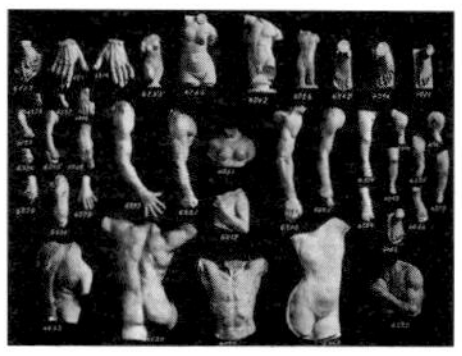

Abbildungen der käuflichen Gipsabgüsse des Kunstgewerbe-Museums, ed. Königliche Museen zu Berlin, General-Verwaltung, Berlin 1893
Staatliche Museen zu Berlin, Kunstbibliothek, F 2460 kl

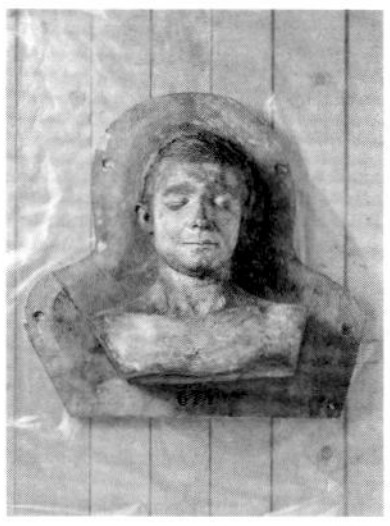

Head of a Woman
Master model, 1894
Plaster, shellacked
50 × 53 × 20 cm
Staatliche Museen zu Berlin, Gipsformerei, 6674

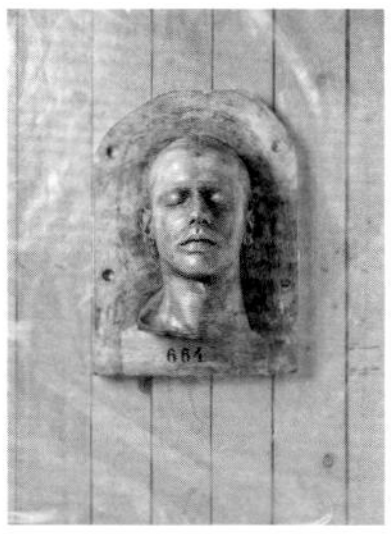

Head of a Man
Master model, 1894
Plaster, shellacked
43 × 32 × 21 cm
Staatliche Museen zu Berlin, Gipsformerei, 6664

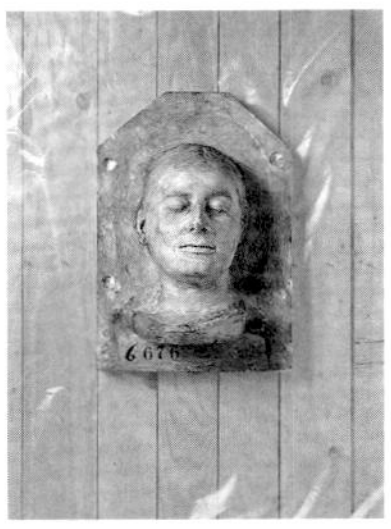

Head of a Woman
Master model, 1894
Plaster, shellacked
44 × 31 × 19 cm
Staatliche Museen zu Berlin,
Gipsformerei, 6676

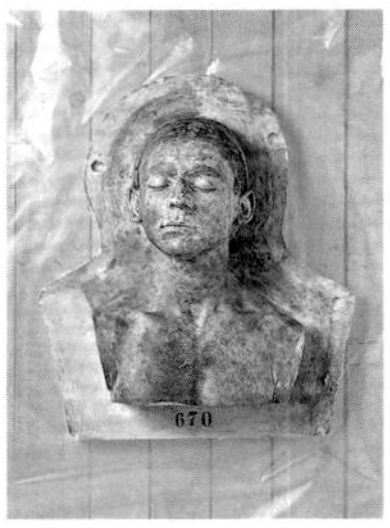

Head of a Man
Master model, 1894
Plaster, shellacked
59 × 47 × 22.5 cm
Staatliche Museen zu Berlin,
Gipsformerei, 6670

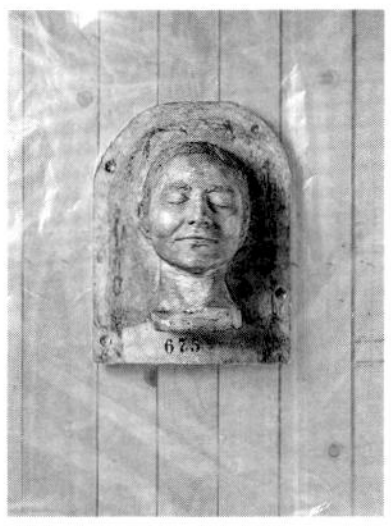

Head of a Woman
Master model, 1894
Plaster, shellacked
41 × 30 × 19 cm
Staatliche Museen zu Berlin,
Gipsformerei, 6675

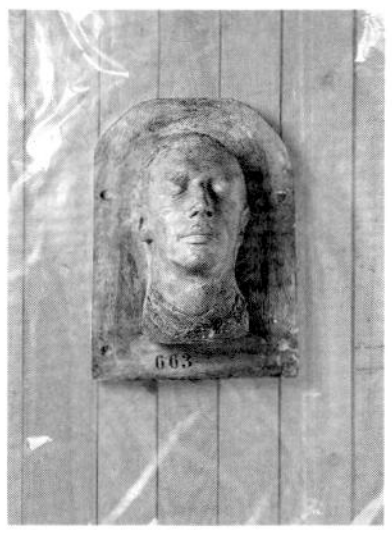

Head of a Man
Master model, 1894
Plaster, shellacked
43 × 32.5 × 21 cm
Staatliche Museen zu Berlin,
Gipsformerei, 6663

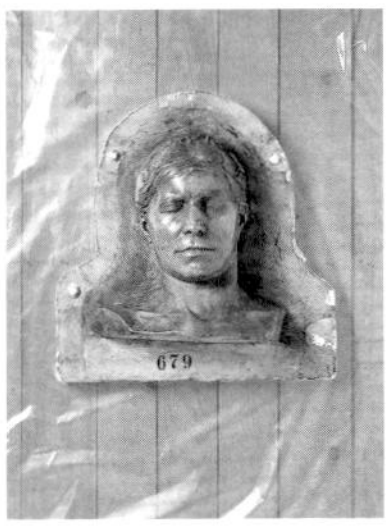

Head of a Woman
Master model, 1894
Plaster, shellacked
46 × 44 × 19 cm
Staatliche Museen zu Berlin,
Gipsformerei, 6679

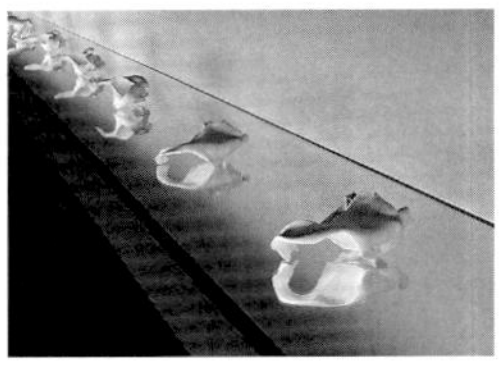

Pauline M'barek (b. 1979)
Artefacts, 2014
Plaster casts on
illuminated mirror board
Courtesy of the artist
and Galerie Thomas
Rehbein, Cologne

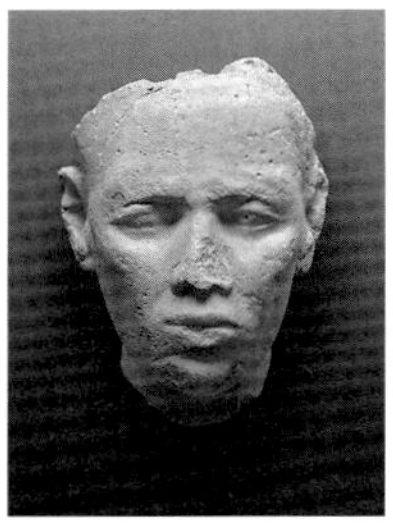

Plaster Model of Head of a Man, New Kingdom,
18th Dynasty,
ca. 1340 BCE
Gypsum stucco
24 × 18 × 14 cm
Staatliche Museen zu Berlin,
Ägyptisches Museum
und Papyrussammlung,
ÄM 21228

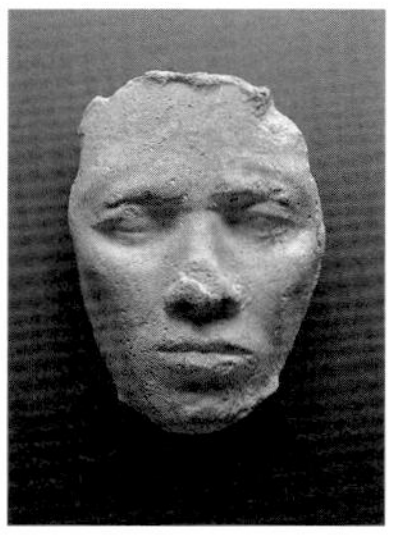

Plaster Model of Head of a Man, New Kingdom,
18th Dynasty,
ca. 1340 BCE
Gypsum stucco
18 × 13 × 7.8 cm
Staatliche Museen zu Berlin,
Ägyptisches Museum
und Papyrussammlung,
ÄM 21356

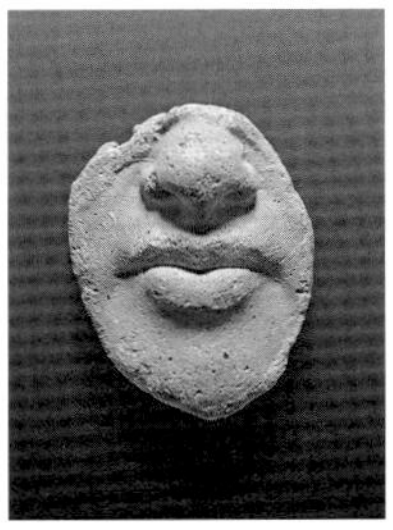

Cast of the Lower Half of a Face, Detail, New Kingdom,
18th Dynasty,
ca. 1340 BCE
Gypsum stucco
10 × 7.8 × 5.9 cm
Staatliche Museen zu Berlin,
Ägyptisches Museum
und Papyrussammlung,
ÄM 21234

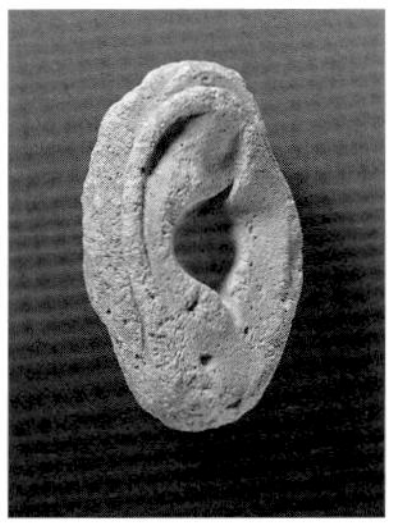

Plaster Model of a Right Human Ear, New Kingdom,
18th Dynasty,
ca. 1340 BCE
Gypsum stucco
9.8 × 4.8 × 3.7 cm
Staatliche Museen zu Berlin,
Ägyptisches Museum
und Papyrussammlung,
ÄM 21235

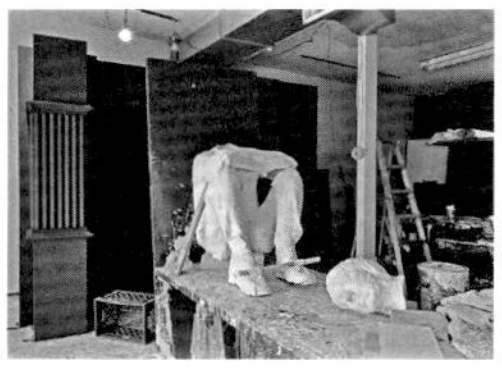

Donald Lokuta (b. 1946)
Figure for 'The Homeless' in Progress, 1989
From the series *George Segal: An Intimate Portrait*
Silver gelatin print
21.5 × 31.5 cm
Courtesy of the artist

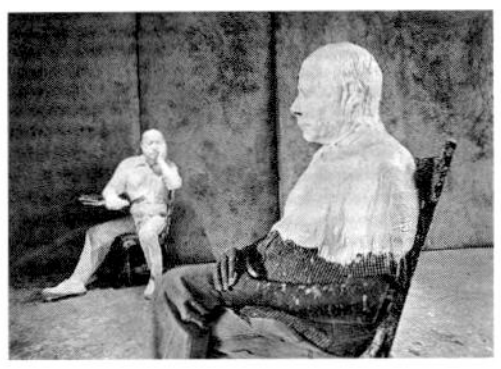

Donald Lokuta (b. 1946)
Casting George Segal for 'George Segal, Self-Portrait',
1990
From the series *George Segal: An Intimate Portrait*
Silver gelatin print
21.5 × 32 cm
Courtesy of the artist

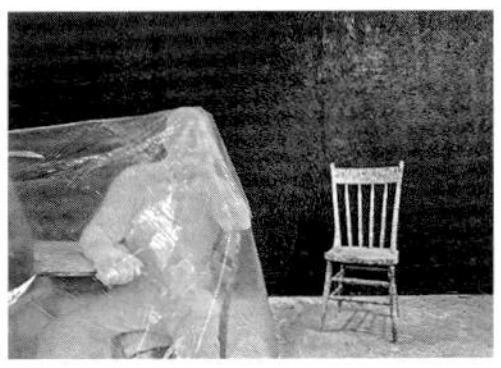

Donald Lokuta (b. 1946)
Figure for 'The Graffiti Wall',
1990
From the series *George Segal: An Intimate Portrait*
Silver gelatin print
21.5 × 32 cm
Courtesy of the artist

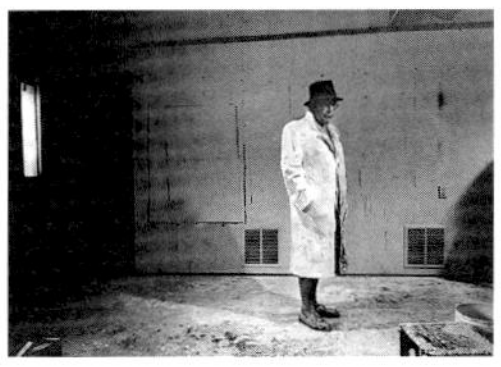

Donald Lokuta (b. 1946)
Casting George Segal for a Figure in 'Depression Bread Line', 1991
From the series *George Segal: An Intimate Portrait*
Silver gelatin print
22 × 32 cm
Courtesy of the artist

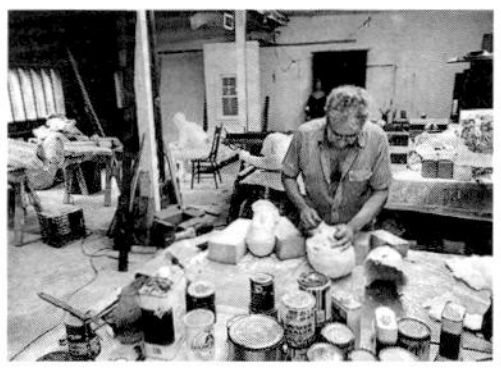

Donald Lokuta (b. 1946)
George Segal Sculpting the Heads for 'Appalachian Farm Couple', 1991
From the series *George Segal: An Intimate Portrait*
Silver gelatin print
22 × 31.7 cm
Courtesy of the artist

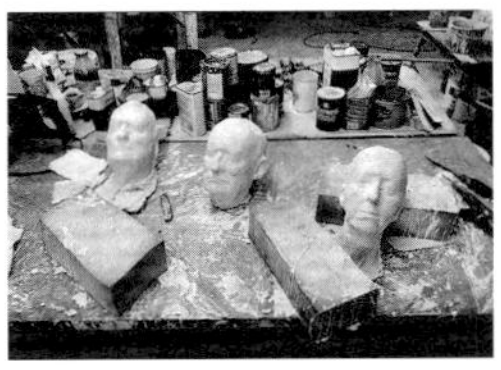

Donald Lokuta (b. 1946)
Heads for 'Appalachian Farm Couple', 1991
From the series *George Segal: An Intimate Portrait*
Silver gelatin print
21.8 × 32 cm
Courtesy of the artist

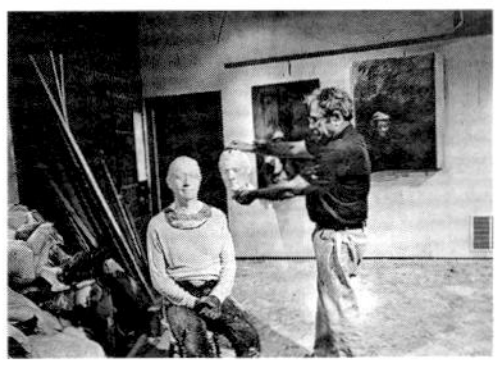

Donald Lokuta (b. 1946)
George Segal Examining Castings for 'Street Crossing', 1992
From the series *George Segal: An Intimate Portrait*
Silver gelatin print
22 × 32 cm
Courtesy of the artist

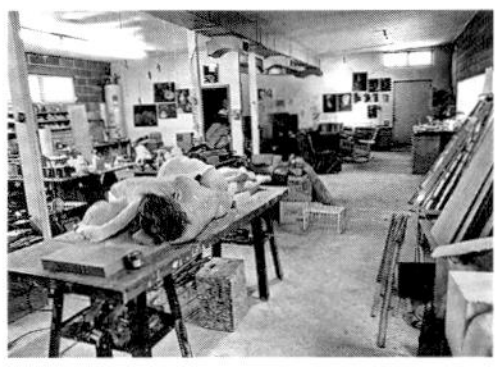

Donald Lokuta (b. 1946)
George Segal with Model for 'Blue Woman on Black Bed',
1996
From the series *George Segal: An Intimate Portrait*
Silver gelatin print
22 × 32.8 cm
Courtesy of the artist

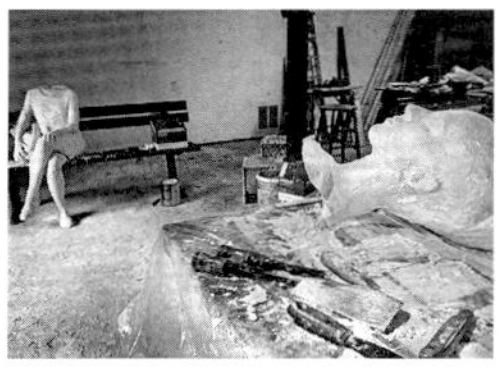

Donald Lokuta (b. 1946)
'Woman on Park Bench' in Progress, 1998
From the series *George Segal: An Intimate Portrait*
Silver gelatin print
22 × 32 cm
Courtesy of the artist

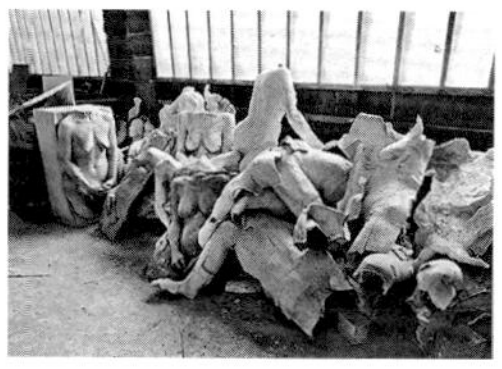

Donald Lokuta (b. 1946)
Studio Detail, Body Parts, 2000
From the series *George Segal: An Intimate Portrait*
Silver gelatin print
21.5 × 31.5 cm
Courtesy of the artist

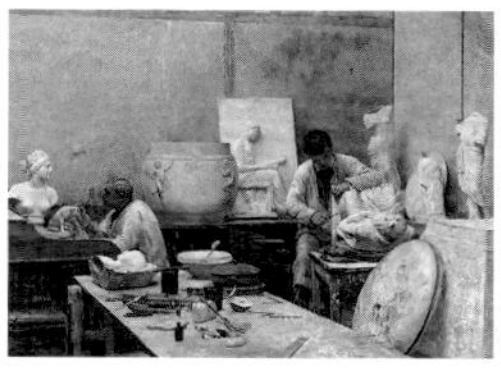

Edouard Joseph Dantan (1848–1897)
Atelier de moulage, 1884
Oil on canvas
97 × 130 cm
Centre national des arts plastiques, Paris
Long-term loan to the Musée des Beaux-Arts de Limoges since 1963,
FNAC 609

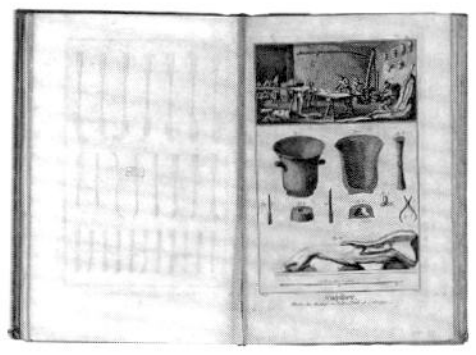

Denis Diderot (1713–1784), Jean-Baptiste le Rond d'Alembert (1717–1783)
Encylopédie: Sur les sciences, les arts libéraux, et les arts méchaniques; avec leur explication, sculpture,
Livorno 1775
Staatliche Museen zu Berlin, Kunstbibliothek,
RA X 320 mtl

The Case against Casts

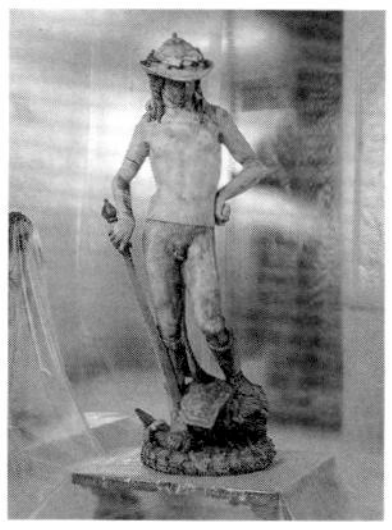

After Donatello (ca. 1386–1466)
David
Master model, 1882
Plaster, shellacked
160 × 53 × 53.5 cm
(Original: ca. 1440, Museo Nazionale del Bargello, Florence)
Staatliche Museen zu Berlin, Gipsformerei, 2204

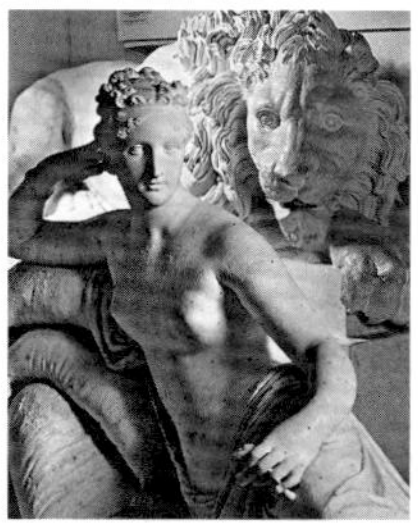

Antonio Canova
Paolina Borghese Bonaparte as Venus Vitrix, 1807
Plaster
87 × 185 × 65 cm
Gypsoteca Canova Possagno, 190

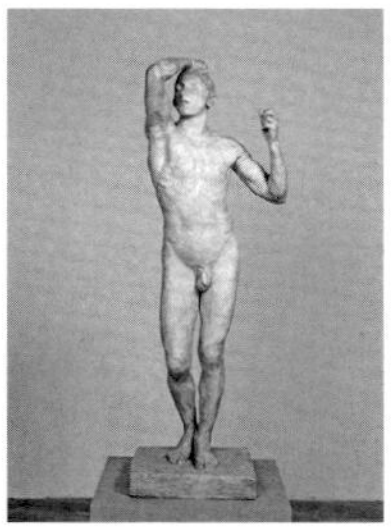

Auguste Rodin (1840–1917)
The Age of Bronze, 1875–76
Plaster cast
181 × 66 × 70 cm
Staatliche Kunstsammlungen Dresden, Skulpturensammlung, 1738,
Abg.-ZV 1885

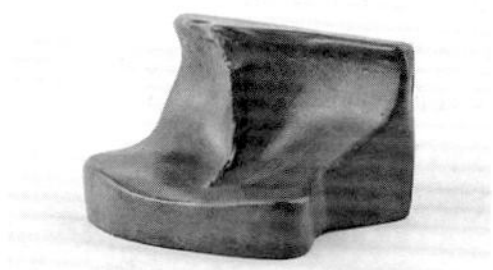

Marcel Duchamp (1887–1968)
Feuille de vigne femelle (Female Fig Leaf),
1950–51
Plaster cast, electroplated
9 × 14 × 12.5 cm
Staatliche Schlösser, Gärten und Kunstsammlungen Mecklenburg-Vorpommern, Schwerin,
Pl 617

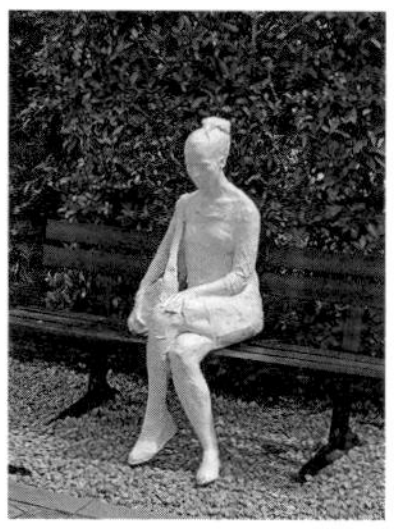

George Segal (1924–2000)
Woman on Park Bench, 1998
Cast, 2009
Bronze with white patina and aluminium
Edition 6 copies and 3 APs
134.6 × 182.8 × 91.4 cm
Galerie Thomas Modern, Munich

Epilogue

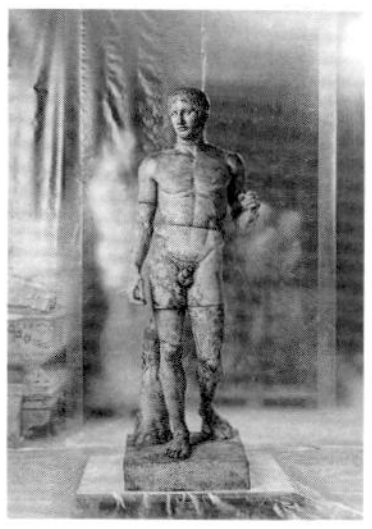

After Polykleitos (480–late 5th century BCE)
Doryphoros
Master model, 1871
Plaster, shellacked
212 × 58 × 52 cm
(Original: 5th century BCE, Roman copy at Museo Archeologico Nazionale di Napoli)
Staatliche Museen zu Berlin, Gipsformerei, 213

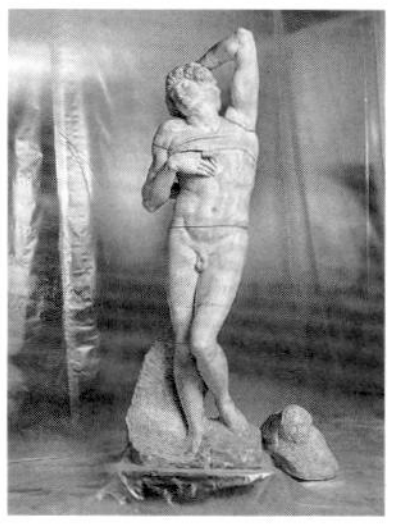

After Michelangelo Buonarroti (1475–1564)
Slave for the Tomb of Pope Julius II
Master model, 1933
Plaster, shellacked
215 × 72 × 52 cm
(Original: 1505–45, Musée du Louvre)
Staatliche Museen zu Berlin, Gipsformerei, 2169

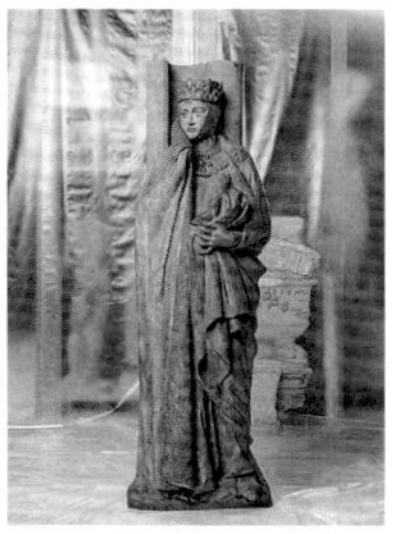

After the Naumburg master (13th century)
Countess Uta of Naumburg
Painting model, 1937
Plaster, painted
195 × 63.5 × 49.5 cm
(Original: ca. 1250, Naumburger Dom)

Staatliche Museen zu Berlin, Gipsformerei, 2355

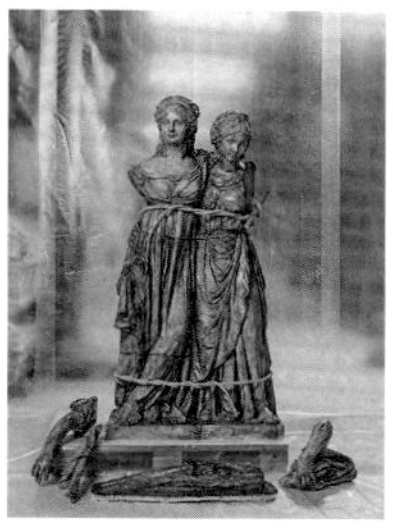

After Johann Gottfried Schadow (1764–1850)
Crown Princess Louise of Prussia and Princess Friederike
Work model, 1926
Plaster, shellacked
174 × 91 × 67 cm
(Original: 1795–97, Staatliche Museen zu Berlin, Alte Nationalgalerie)
Staatliche Museen zu Berlin, Gipsformerei, 3112

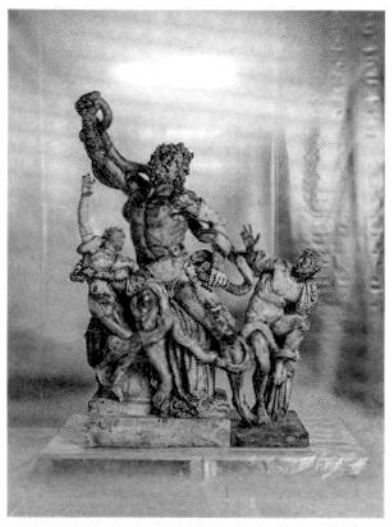

Laocoön Group
Master model, 1844
Plaster, shellacked
242 × 184 × 100 cm
(Original: ca. 1st century BCE, Roman copy at Vatican Museums, Rome)
Staatliche Museen zu Berlin, Gipsformerei, 263

Selected Bibliography

Benkard, Ernst. *Das ewige Antlitz: Eine Sammlung von Totenmasken*, foreword by Georg Kolbe, Berlin 1927.

Bernardelli Curuz, Maurizio. 'La scoperta: L'inconfessabile segreto di Canova', *StileArte*, no. 110 (July / August 2007), pp. 4–11.

Berner, Margit, Anette Hoffmann and Britta Lange. *Sensible Sammlungen: Aus dem anthropologischen Depot*, Hamburg 2011.

Didi-Huberman, Georges (ed.). *La Ressemblance par contact: Archéologie, anachronisme et modernité*, Paris 1997.

Einholz, Sibylle. 'Die Jagd nach schönen Händen: Abformungen über Natur', *Museumsjournal*, no. 1 (1994), pp. 56–59.

Einholz, Sibylle. 'Orte der Kontemplation und Erziehung: Zur Geschichte der Gipsabgusssammlung in Berlin', in: *Meisterwerke mittelalterlicher Skulptur: Die Berliner Gipsabgusssammlung*, ed. Hartmut Krohm, exh. cat., Skulpturensammlung der Staatlichen Museen zu Berlin – Stiftung Preußischer Kulturbesitz, Bode-Museum, Berlin, 29 June–3 November 1996, Berlin 1996, pp. 11–39.

Einholz, Sybille (ed.). *'Feiner, weißer ... Gips!': Zur Bedeutung eines umstrittenen Materials, 100 Jahre Gipsformerei der Staatlichen Museen in Charlottenburg*, exh. cat., Heimatmuseum Charlottenburg, Berlin, 1 July–4 August 1991, Berlin 1991.

Felfe, Robert. *Naturform und bildnerische Prozesse: Elemente einer Wissensgeschichte in der Kunst des 16. und 17. Jahrhunderts*, Berlin and Boston 2015.

Frederiksen, Rune and Eckart Marchand (eds.). *Plaster Casts: Making, Collecting and Displaying from Classical Antiquity to the Present*, Berlin and Boston 2010.

Friederici, Angelika. *Castan's Panoptikum: Ein Medium wird besichtigt* (journal series), esp. *Lebendmasken aus Papua-Neuguinea* (no. 6), *Völker der Welt auf Castans Bühnen* (no. 10), *Otto Finsch: Lebendmasken aus der Südsee* (no. 20), Berlin 2009, 2011 and 2014.

Gerchow, Jan (ed.). *Ebenbilder: Kopien von Körpern, Modelle des Menschen*, exh. cat., Ruhrlandmuseum, Essen, 26 March–30 June 2002, Ostfildern 2002.

Girst, Thomas. 'Von Ready-mades und Asstricks', in: *Marcel Duchamp: Die Schweriner Sammlung*, ed. Kornelia von Berswordt-Wallrabe, Schwerin 2003, pp. 30–36.

Goldenbaum, Laura. 'Der Zeugniswert des Körpers oder *anima forma corporis*: Der quattrocenteske Bronzegisant des Sieneser Rechtsgelehrten Mariano Sozzini', in: "Grabmal und Körper: Zwischen Repräsentation und Realpräsenz in der Frühen Neuzeit," ed. Philipp Zitzlsperger, conference proceedings, *kunsttexte.de: E-Journal für Kunst- und Bildgeschichte* (April 2010).

Gramaccini, Norberto. 'Das genaue Abbild der Natur: Riccios Tiere und die Theorie des Naturabgusses seit Cennino Cennini', in: *Natur und Antike in der Renaissance*, exh. cat., Liebighaus, Frankfurt am Main, 5 December 1985–2 March 1986, Frankfurt am Main 1985, pp. 198–225.

Haak, Christina and Miguel Helfrich (eds.). *Casting: Ein analoger Weg ins Zeitalter der Digitalisierung? Ein Symposium zur Gipsformerei der Staatlichen Museen zu Berlin*, Heidelberg 2016.

Hiller von Gaertringen, Hans Georg, and Miguel Helfrich (eds.). *Meisterwerke der Gipsformerei: Kunstmanufaktur der Staatlichen Museen zu Berlin seit 1819*, Munich 2012.

Höcherl, Heike. *Rodins Gipse: Ursprünge moderner Plastik*, Frankfurt am Main 2003.

Hoffmann, Anette (ed.). *What We See: Reconsidering an Anthropometrical Collection from Southern Africa; Images, Voices and Versioning*, Basel 2009.

Kammel, Frank M. 'Der Gipsabguss: Vom Medium der ästhetischen Norm zur toten Konserve der Kunstgeschichte', in: *Ästhetische Probleme der Plastik im 19. und 20. Jahrhundert*, ed. Andrea M. Kluxen, Nuremberg 2001, pp. 47–72.

Klier, Andrea. *Fixierte Natur: Naturabguss und Effigies im 16. Jahrhundert*, Berlin 2004.

Kris, Ernst. *Erstarrte Lebendigkeit: Zwei Untersuchungen*, Zurich 2012.

Lange, Britta. 'Prekäre Situationen: Anthropologisches Sammeln im Kolonialismus', in: Thomas Schnalke, Holger Stoecker, and Andreas Winkelmann (eds.), *Sammeln und Bewahren, Erforschen, Zurückgeben? Menschliche Gebeine aus der Kolonialzeit in akademischen und musealen Sammlungen*, ed. Thomas Schnalke, Holger Stoecker and Andreas Winkelmann, Berlin 2013, pp. 45–68.

Maaz, Bernhard and Klaus Stemmer. *Berliner Gypse des 19. Jahrhunderts: Von der Idee zum Gipsabguss*, exh. cat., Abguss-Sammlung Antiker Plastik, Berlin, 15 July–17 October 1993, Alfter 1993.

Maaz, Bernhard (ed.). *Nationalgalerie Berlin: Das XIX Jahrhundert, Bestandskatalog der Skulpturen*, vol. 1: A–P, vol. 2: R–Z, Leipzig 2006.

Nielsen, Astrid. *Auguste Rodin im Albertinum*, Dresden 2017.

Nikolai, Angela and Sabine Thümmler (eds.). *Form Follows Flower: Moritz Meurer, Karl Blossfeldt & Co.*, exh. cat., Kunstgewerbemuseum, Staatliche Museen zu Berlin, 20 October 2017–14 January 2018, Berlin and Munich 2017.

Normand-Romain, Antoinette Le, Laurent Busine and Isabelle Vassalo. *Vers l'âge d'airain: Rodin en Belgique*, exh. cat., Palais des Beaux-Arts Charleroi, 7 September–14 December 1997, Charleroi 1997.

Papet, Edouard. *A fleur de peau: Le moulage sur nature au XIXe siècle*, exh. cat., Musée d'Orsay, Paris, 29 October 2001–27 January 2002; Henry Moore Institute, Leeds, 16 February–12 May 2002; Hamburger Kunsthalle, Hamburg, 14 June–1 September 2002; Museo Vincenzo Vela, Ligornetto, 14 September–17 December 2002, Paris 2001.

Pliny the Elder. *Natural History*, 10 vols., trans. D. E. Eichholz, Cambridge, MA and London 1962.

Pohl, Joseph. *Die Verwendung des Naturabgusses in der italienischen Porträtplastik der Renaissance*, Würzburg 1938.

Roller, Stefan (ed). *Die große Illusion. Veristische Skulpturen und ihre Techniken*, exh. cat., Liebighaus, Frankfurt am Main, 1 October 2014–1 March 2015, Munich 2014.

von Schlosser, Julius. *Tote Blicke: Geschichte der Porträtbildnerei in Wachs, ein Versuch*, ed. Thomas Medicus, Berlin 1993.

Schröder, Nele and Lorenz Winkler-Horaček (eds.). *... von gestern bis morgen ... Zur Geschichte der Berliner Gipsabguss-Sammlung(en)*, exh. cat., Abguss-Sammlung Antiker Plastik, Berlin, Winckelmann-Institut der Humboldt-Universität zu Berlin, Antikensammlung der Staatlichen Museen zu Berlin, Gipsformerei der Staatlichen Museen zu Berlin, 13 October 2012–26 May 2013, Rahden 2012.

Siebert, Moritz. *Totenmaske und Portrait: Der Gesichtsabguss in der Kunst der Florentiner Renaissance*, Baden-Baden 2017.

Stamm, Lars. *Indexikalische Körperplastik: Der Naturabguss in der Kunst des 20. Jahrhunderts*, Göttingen 2013.

Sysling, Fenneke. *Racial Science and Human Diversity in Colonial Indonesia*, Singapore 2016.

Syson, Luke and Sheena Wagstaff, et al. *Like Life: Sculpture, Color, and the Body*, exh. cat., Metropolitan Museum of Art, New York, 21 March–22 July 2018, New York 2018.

Uppenkamp, Bettina. 'Potentiale der Bescheidenheit: Über kunstvolle und kunstlose Möglichkeiten in Gips', in: *Material in Kunst und Alltag*, ed. Monika Wagner and Dietmar Rübel, Berlin 2002, pp. 137–62.

Vasari, Giorgio. *Lives of the Painters, Sculptors, and Architects*, 2 vols, trans. Gaston du C. de Vere, London 1996.

We would like to express our gratitude to the artists and lenders who have enriched *Near Life: The Gipsformerei — 200 Years of Casting Plaster* with their works.

Artists

Asta Gröting
Liane Lang
Donald Lokuta
Teresa Margolles
Pauline M'barek
Allan McCollum
Maria Volokhova

Lenders

Galerie carlier | gebauer, Berlin
Galerie Thomas Modern, Munich
Galerie Thomas Rehbein, Cologne
Galerie Thomas Schulte, Berlin
Göteborgs Konstmuseum
Gypsoteca Antonio Canova, Possagno
Kunsthistorisches Museum Wien
Musée des Beaux-Arts Limoges / Centre national des arts plastiques Paris
Museum für Kunst und Gewerbe Hamburg
Museum für Moderne Kunst, Frankfurt am Main
Soprintendenza Archeologica di Pompei
Staatliche Kunstsammlungen Dresden
Staatliche Museen zu Berlin
– Ägyptisches Museum und Papyrussammlung
– Alte Nationalgalerie
– Antikensammlung
– Ethnologisches Museum
– Kunstbibliothek – Museum für Fotografie
– Kunstgewerbemuseum
– Kupferstichkabinett
– Skulpturensammlung und Museum für Byzantinische Kunst
Staatliche Schlösser, Gärten und Kunstsammlungen
Mecklenburg-Vorpommern, Schwerin
Technische Universität Berlin, Institut für Mathematik, 3D Labor
Technische Universität Berlin, Universitätsbibliothek
Universität der Künste Berlin, Universitätsarchiv
Wolfgang Wiggers

We would like to thank our colleagues at the Directorate General of the Staatliche Museen zu Berlin and the Central Administration of the Stiftung Preußischer Kulturbesitz who were involved in the realisation of this exhibition.

Directorate General

Construction Department
Education and Outreach
Information and Communications Technology
Inner Service
Museum Development Planning
Press, Communication, Sponsorship
Publications, Merchandising
Research, Exhibitions, Projects
Security
Technics

Central Administration

Central Procurement Services
Department of Organisation, Budget and Financial Services, and Internal Services
Human Resources Department
Media and Communications Department

Acknowledgements

Marion Ackermann, Susanne Anger, Zoltan Arendt, Katrin Bäsig, Rolf Basler, Katharina Baumecker, David von Becker, Margit Berner, Jutta Billig, Julia Binter, Dirk Blübaum, Jan Böttger, Wibke Bornkessel, Francis Brady, Joachim Brand, Brit Broberg, Stephanie Brodel, Matthias Bruske, Uwe Büttner, Julien Chapuis, Pauline Choulet, Jürgen Christof, Anna Civale, Francisca Cruz, Alexandra Czarnecki, Tina Dähn, Violaine Daniels, Wolfgang Davis, Christian Degler, Tahir Della, Ludger Derenthal, Yvette Deseyve, Florentine Dietrich, Martina Dlugaiczyk, Sabine Drexler, Beate Ebelt-Borchert, Frank Eberle, Maren Eichhorn-Johannsen, Heribert Eisenhardt, Michael Eissenhauer, Michael Falser, Angela Fischel, Manuela Fischer, Manuel Flecker, Ramona Föllmer, Martin Franken, Fabian Fröhlich, Yvonne Geister, Hanka Gerhold, Kerstin Gericke, Sandra Gerstl, Ralph Gleis, Barbara Gottschalk, Gerhard Graulich, Asta Gröting, Mario Guderzo, Carsten Güth, Sabine Haag, Sven Haase, Christina Hanus, Hans-Jürgen Harras, Konstanze Hausstätter, Nicola Hederich, Stefanie Heinlein, Erika Heller, Catalina Heroven, Uwe Heuer, Hans Georg Hiller von Gaertringen, Anja Hirche, Anette Hoffmann, Sophie Hoffmann, Sabine Holschneider, Ulrike Holzapfel, Samuel Jerichow, Katrin Käding, Dietmar Katz, Ingolf Kern, JiYoung Kim, Udo Kittelmann, Stefanie Klamm, Jürgen Klebs, Michael Klühs, Lars-Christian Koch, Hanne König, Paul Kopitzke, Dagmar Korbacher, Sabine Kowollik, Mario Kramer, Nora Krause, Mechtild Kronenberg, Heike Kropff, Sabine Kühne, Ilja Labischinski, Britta Lange, Tore Lærdal, Lothar Lambacher, Grit Lederer, Pia Lehmann, Ann Liénard, María López-Fanjul, Norbert Lünnemann, Marikka Männle, Martin Maischberger, Eckart Marchand, Luise Maul, Ralph Melcher, Kristina Mösl, Christian Morawe, Clara Nack, Patricia Nagel, Luigi Nerone, Sibylle Niekisch, Astrid Nielsen, Angela Nikolai, Ralf Nitschke, Michael Noack, Margot Notarius, Eva Nygårds, Regine Oelsner, Massimo Osanna, Johanna Osterrieter, Maren Otto, Hermann Parzinger, Antje Penz, Armin Peupelmann, Susanne Pfeffer, Miriam Plünnecke, Marlene Poeckh, Sabine Pöggel, Harald Pöhle, Annika Pohl-Ozawa, Patrick Presch, Annette Preuß, Paulus Rainer, Thomas Rehbein, Helen Reich, Martin Roßbacher, Neville Rowley, Dietmar Schenk, Sabine Schiewer, Andrea Schindelmeier, Joachim Schlüter, Vincent Schmidt, Thomas Schnalke, Sarah Schönewald, Andreas Scholl, Frank Scholze, Sabine Schulze, Hartmut Schwandt, Christian Seel, Claudia Seidel, Friederike Seyfried, Moritz Siebert, Carolin Stanneck, Christiane Steiger-Büchel, Volko Steinig, Julia Steinmetz, Sven Stienen, Kerstin Stoll, Frank Talke, Alexander Tastarczyk, Nadine Thieme, Sabine Thümmler, Cordula Treimer, Jörg Völlnagel, Dorothee Wagner, Hilke Wagner, Marion Warther, Manja Weinert, Joachim Weinhold, Navena Widulin, Tanja Wieczorek, Matthias Wiedebusch, Albrecht Wiedmann, Tina Willim, Petra Winter, Frank Wolf, Ute Wolf, Moritz Wullen, Pirko Zinnow

Colophon

This catalogue is published on the occasion of the exhibition
Near Life: The Gipsformerei — 200 Years of Casting Plaster
Staatliche Museen zu Berlin, James-Simon-Galerie
30 August 2019 to 1 March 2020

Exhibition

Deputy director-general and director Gipsformerei: Christina Haak
Curator and exhibition manager: Veronika Tocha
Project management: Andrea Müller
Curatorial assistant: Justine Tutmann
Gipsformerei: Miguel Helfrich (manager), Stefan Kramer (workshop manager), Lothar Bogdanski, Jan Bürgel, Fabian Burg, Johanna Gassmann, Susanne Grimm, Cornelia Hoppe, Peter John-Schoubye, Timo Klöppel, Wolfgang Kluge, Andreas Kroll, Dirk Kunc, Daniel Meyer, Sandro di Michele, Marc Miniers, Rainer Palau, Thomas Schelper, Andreas Schipka, Ulrich Schröder, Robin Schulz, Roland Wilhelm, Uwe Wraase, Marcel Zander, Hardy Zaubitzer
Conservation: Aurelia Badde
Exhibition architecture: Schroeder Rauch
Exhibition graphics: StudioKrimm
Visual communication: Agentur BOROS
Audio guide: Martin Baer (script and direction), Oliver Brood (sound design)
Exhibition construction: SCHULTE Lagertechnik Sundern and REMOS GmbH Interior | Design | Media Appenweier

Media Partners of the exhibition are *ARTE* and *Der Tagesspiegel*.

Publication

For the Staatliche Museen zu Berlin, edited by Christina Haak, Miguel Helfrich and Veronika Tocha
Concept and texts: Veronika Tocha
Photography: Philip Radowitz
Design and typsetting: StudioKrimm / Melanie Achilles, Barbara Krimm
Managing editor: Julia Stoff
Copy editors: Rea Triyandafilidis, Laura Preston
Translation: Otmar Binder
Proofreading: Mika Hayashi Ebbesen, Iris Ströbel, Rea Triyandafilidis

Publication management for the museums: Marika Mäder, Sigrid Wollmeiner
Image editors: Andrea Müller, Julia Stoff
Editorial direction Prestel: Nora Schröder
Production management Prestel: Corinna Pickart
Lithography: LVD
Printing and binding: Kösel GmbH & Co. KG, Altusried-Krugzell
Typeface: Academica Book, Union
Paper: Symbol Tatami white

FSC® www.fsc.org MIX Paper from responsible sources FSC® C013736

Verlagsgruppe Random House FSC® N001967

www.smb.museum, www.prestel.com
Bibliographical data of the Deutsche Nationalbibliothek: The Deutsche Nationalbibliothek lists this publication in the Deutsche Nationalbibliografie; detailed bibliographic information is available on the Internet at www.dnb.de.
A CIP catalogue record for this book is available from the British Library.

Prestel Publishing Ltd.
14–17 Wells Street
London W1T 3PD

Prestel Publishing
900 Broadway, Suite 603
New York, NY 10003

ISBN
978-3-7913-5940-3 (English trade edition)
978-3-88609-829-3 (English museum edition)

Printed in Germany

Image credits: Unless indicated otherwise: Staatliche Museen zu Berlin, Gipsformerei, photo: Philip Radowitz
p. 10 © Rheinisches Bildarchiv Köln, rba_c010394, p. 12 Sophie de Juvigny, *Éduard Dantan 1848–1897*, Paris 2002, photo: Dietmar Katz, p. 26 Asta Gröting / VG Bild-Kunst, Bonn 2019, photo: Nic Tenwiggenhorn, pp. 34–35 Staatliche Museen zu Berlin (SMB), Ethnologisches Museum (EM), photo: Dietmar Katz, p. 36 Nuremberg, Germanisches Nationalmuseum, Deutsches Kunstarchiv, NL Behn, Fritz, AFS 3 (0002), p. 37 SMB, EM, photos: Dietmar Katz, p. 41 © Ralf Günther / Leibniz-IZW, p. 44 Kunsthistorisches Museum Wien, Kunstkammer; SMB, Skulpturensammlung (SBM), photo: Walter Steinkopf; SMB, SBM, photo: Philip Radowitz; SMB, SBM, photo: Antje Voigt, p. 45 SMB, SBM, photos: Antje Voigt; SMB, Kunstgewerbemuseum, photo: Saturia Linke; SMB, Gipsformerei (GF), photo: Philip Radowitz, p. 46 Kunsthistorisches Museum Wien, Kunstkammer, p. 47 Museum für Kunst und Gewerbe Hamburg, photo: Maria Thrun, p. 48 © Maria Volokhova, photo: Falk Buchröder, p. 49 © Maria Volokhova, p. 51 photo: Die Kulturgutscanner – Viola Rosenau, Museum-Naturalienkabinett Waldenburg i. S.; Universität der Künste Berlin, Universitätsarchiv, inv. no. 321-153, pp. 53–55 © Die Photographische Sammlung / SK Stiftung Kultur, Köln, photos: Susanne Fern, Quelle: Universität der Künste Berlin, Universitätsarchiv, pp. 60, 62–63 photos: Wolfgang Wiggers, pp. 65, 67 stills: Pauline M'barek, pp. 68–69, 70 bottom SMB, Kunstbibliothek (KB), photos: Dietmar Katz, pp. 70–71 SMB, EM, photos: Martin Franken, pp. 72–73 SMB, KB, photos: Dietmar Katz, p. 74 SMB, EM, photos: Dietmar Katz, pp. 76–77, 78–79, 81, 82–83, 84–85, 86 SMB, KB, photos: Dietmar Katz, pp. 87, 89 SMB, EM, photos: Martin Franken, p. 93 © Margit Berner, Britta Lange, Thomas Schelper, Kerstin Stoll, pp. 108–09 photos: Bernt-Erik Rossavik / Lærdal Medical / Stockphoto, p. 115 SMB, Nationalgalerie (NG), photo: Klaus Göken, p. 117 SMB, NG, photo: Andres Kilger, p. 130 © bpk / Scala, p. 131 © National Gallery of Art, Washington (NGA Images); © bpk / Scala, pp. 134–35 Museum MMK für Moderne Kunst, Frankfurt am Main, on permanent loan from the artist © Teresa Margolles, realised in collaboration with the artist group SEMEFO, p. 136 © bpk / Giorgio Sommer, p. 137 © Allan McCollum, photo: Sergio Belinchon, pp. 138–39 exhibition KINDL – Zentrum für Zeitgenössische Kunst, Berlin / VG Bild-Kunst, Bonn 2019, photo: Jens Ziehe, p. 141 Victoria and Albert Museum, London; Staatsbibliothek zu Berlin – SPK, p. 142 Staatsbibliothek zu Berlin – SPK, p. 143 © Courtesy of Universal Studios Licensing LLC, p. 144 © Hossein Sehatlou – Göteborgs Konstmuseum, 2015, p. 147 © bpk / SMB, NG, photo: Jörg P. Anders, p. 148 © bpk / Hamburger Kunsthalle, photo: Elke Walford, p. 149 photo: Liane Lang Studio, pp. 150–51, 153 © bpk / SMB, KB, Photothek Willy Römer, photos: Willy Römer, p. 152 SMB, KB, photo: Dietmar Katz; © bpk / SMB, Kupferstichkabinett, photo: Dietmar Katz, p. 162 SMB, Kupferstichkabinett, photos: Dietmar Katz, pp. 167–69 SMB, KB, photos: Dietmar Katz, pp. 174–75 © photos: Pauline M'barek, 2016 and 2014, pp. 177–78 Nadine Thieme, pp. 180–81 SMB, Ägyptisches Museum und Papyrussammlung, photos: Sandra Steiß, p. 183 © Antikenmuseum der Universität Leipzig, Abgusssammlung, photo: Marion Wenzel; photo: Stephan Eckhardt, p. 184 © bpk / Scala, pp. 187–91 © The George and Helen Segal Foundation / VG Bild-Kunst, Bonn 2019, Donald Lokuta, p. 194 © Soprintendenza Capitolina ai Beni Culturali – Museo Napoleonico, p. 195 Gypsoteca Canova Possagno, photo: Giovanni Porcellato, p. 196 © Musée Rodin, Paris, p. 197 © bpk / Staatliche Kunstsammlungen Dresden, photo: Werner Lieberknecht, p. 198 © Association Marcel Duchamp / VG Bild-Kunst, Bonn 2019, p. 199 © bpk / CNAC-MNAM / Bertrand Prévost © Association Marcel Duchamp / VG Bild-Kunst, Bonn 2019, p. 201 © The George and Helen Segal Foundation / VG Bild-Kunst, Bonn 2019, pp. 203–04 photos: Asta Gröting, p. 205 © Asta Gröting / VG Bild-Kunst, Bonn 2019, photo: Nic Tenwiggenhorn; © Asta Gröting / VG Bild-Kunst, Bonn 2019, photo: Hans Georg Gaul, p. 217 Museum Bad Arolsen, p. 218 Goethe- und Schiller-Archiv, Weimar, photos: Dietmar Katz, p. 219 SMB, NG, photos: Andres Kilger, p. 220 private collection, photo: Georg Hiller von Gaertringen, p. 221 Fotosammlung Norbert Franken, pp. 223, 225 SMB, GF, p. 232 and back cover © Domaine public / Cnap, photo: Musée des Beaux-Arts de Limoges, Frédéric Magnoux, p. 234 © SMB, KB, photos: Dietmar Katz, pp. 248, 250–51 Schroeder Rauch.
Text credits: p. 34 Fritz Behn, *'Haizuru …': Ein Bildhauer in Afrika*, Munich 1917, pp. 233–235, trans. Otmar Binder, pp. 56–59 Cennino Cennini da Colle di Valdelsa, *A Treatise on Painting* (1437), trans. Mrs Merrifield, with an introductory preface, copious notes, and illustrations in outline from celebrated pictures, London 1844, pp. 100–05, p. 62 Kana Je's Recordings, trans. from Otjiherero by Rhyn Tjituka, in: Anette Hoffmann, Britta Lange, Regina Sarreiter (eds.), *What We See: Reconsidering an Anthropometrical Collection from Southern Africa; Images, Voices, Versioning*, Basel 2009, pp. 134–35, pp. 97–104 'Sandow in Plaster of Paris. A unique cast', in: *The Strand Magazine* 22, no. 130 (October 1901), pp. 461–68, p. 110 Georg Kolbe, 'Das Abnehmen von Totenmasken', in: Ernst Benkard, *Das ewige Antlitz. Eine Sammlung von Totenmasken*, mit einem Geleitwort von Georg Kolbe, Berlin 1927, pp. XLI–XLIII, here p. XLI, trans. Otmar Binder, p. 212 Johann Gottfried Schadow, 'Die Werkstätte des Bildhauers', in: Julius Friedlaender (ed.), Gottfried Schadow, *Aufsätze und Briefe, nebst einem Verzeichnis seiner Werke*, Düsseldorf 1864, pp. 51–64, here p. 60, trans. Otmar Binder, p. 200 George Segal, 'The Sense of "Why not?". George Segal on His Art', in: *Studio International* 174, no. 893, October 1967, pp. 146–49, here p. 149.